Ubuntu

12.04

Desktop

Applications

and

Administration

To my nephew,

Justin

Ubuntu 12.04 Desktop: Applications and Administration
Richard Petersen

Surfing Turtle Press

Alameda, CA

www.surfingturtlepress.com

Please send inquires to: editor@surfingturtlepress.com

ISBN 1-936280-43-4

ISBN-13 978-1-936280-43-8

E-ISBN-13 (ebook) 978-1-936280-44-5

E-ISBN (ebook) 1-936280-44-2

Library of Congress Control Number: 2012938460

Preface

This book covers the Ubuntu 12.04 (Precise Pangolin) release, focusing on applications and administrative tools. The emphasis here is on what users will face when using Ubuntu, covering topics like installation, applications, software management, the Ubuntu desktops (Unity, GNOME, and KDE), shell commands, network connections, and system administration tasks. Ubuntu 12.04 introduces several new features, as well as numerous smaller modifications. It is a long-term support release. The Ubuntu desktop with the Unity interface is examined in detail. Unity uses a Launcher and a Dash (dashboard) to manage access to applications and devices. Advanced components are also examined such as the GRUB 2 boot loader, PulseAudio sound configuration, and Disk Utility (Udisks) for storage device configuration and information (SMART).

Ubuntu 12.04 Desktop edition provides two desktop interfaces: the Ubuntu desktop interface and Ubuntu 2D, which does not require graphics acceleration. The Ubuntu desktop uses a Launcher and a Dash (dashboard) to manage access to applications and devices. In addition, Ubuntu 12.04 desktop is based on GNOME 3, with several new desktop configuration tools and the System Settings dialog. In addition, features of the messaging, user switcher, and desktop menus, as well as the Nautilus file manager, are covered. The Kubuntu desktop, which uses KDE, provides a very different interface using plasma containers to support the panel, menu, desktop, configuration tools, and plasmoid applets. Changes include enhancements of the Unity interface with launcher and dash, refinements to the Ubuntu Software Center, and Ubuntu One setup and configuration. Rhythmbox is the default music player and Thunderbird is the default mail client.

Part 1 focuses on getting started, covering Ubuntu information and resources, using Ubuntu Live CD/DVD/USB discs, installing and setting up Ubuntu, upgrading Ubuntu, basic use of the desktop interface, and connecting to wired and wireless networks. Repositories and their use are covered in detail, including the third-party Medibuntu repository that holds popular third party applications. The Ubuntu Software Center and Synaptic Package manager, which provides easy and effective software management, are both discussed.

Part 2 keys in on office, multimedia, mail, Internet, and social media applications such as the Evolution and Thunderbird email applications, the Totem media player, the Rhythmbox music player, the LibreOffice office suite, Gwibber, and Ubuntu One. The section includes coverage of the PulseAudio sound interface with its volume control support, Firefox and Rekonq Web browsers, the Empathy messenger client, and VoIP applications like Skype and Ekiga. Ubuntu Studio graphics and Mythbuntu multimedia editions are also referenced.

Part 3 covers the Ubuntu and Kubuntu desktops. Ubuntu Unity interface features a Launcher, Dash, and indicator menus. The Kubuntu desktop is examined which is based on the KDE desktop with features such as plasmoids, activities, panels, menus, KWin desktop effects, and the new Icon-Only Task Manager. The shell interface is also explored, with its command editing, directory navigation, and file operations.

Part 4 deals with administration topics, first discussing system tools like the GNOME system monitor, the Disk Usage Analyzer, and Disk Utility (Udisks). Then a detailed chapter on Ubuntu system administration tools is presented, covering tasks such as managing users and file systems, Bluetooth setup, network folder and file sharing, and GRUB 2 configuration. The network connections chapter covers a variety of network tasks, including manual configuration of wired and wireless connections, and firewalls (the Gufw and Firestarter). Printer administration and installation is discussed, including configuration for local and remote printers.

Overview

Part 3: Desktops

Part 4: Administration

Contents

Part 1: Getting Started

Part 2: Applications

5. Office Applications and Editors **167**

7. Mail (email) and News **223**

8. Internet Applications **239**

Part 3: Desktops

12. Shells 373

Part 4: Administration

13. System Tools 407

14. System Administration 421

16. Printing **489**

Table Listing **503**

Figure Listing **507**

Index **521**

Part 1: Getting Started

Introduction

Installation

Usage Basics

Managing Software

1. Ubuntu 12.04 Introduction

Ubuntu Releases

Ubuntu 12.04

Ubuntu Release

Ubuntu Editions

Ubuntu Live CD and USB

Ubuntu Software

Ubuntu Help and Documentation

Open Source Software

History of Linux and UNIX

Ubuntu Linux is currently one of the most popular end-user Linux distributions (**http://www.ubuntu.com**). Ubuntu Linux is managed by the Ubuntu foundation, which is sponsored by Canonical, Ltd (**http://www.canonical.com**), a commercial organization that supports and promotes open source projects. Ubuntu is based on Debian Linux, one of the oldest Linux distributions, which is dedicated to incorporating cutting-edge developments and features (**http://www.debian.org**). Mark Shuttleworth, a South African and Debian Linux developer, initiated the Ubuntu project. Debian Linux is primarily a Linux development project, trying out new features. Ubuntu provides a Debian based Linux distribution that is stable, reliable, and easy to use.

Ubuntu is designed as a Linux operating system that can be used easily by everyone. The name Ubuntu means "humanity to others." As the Ubuntu project describes it: "Ubuntu is an African word meaning 'Humanity to others", or "I am what I am because of who we all are." The Ubuntu distribution brings the spirit of Ubuntu to the software world."

The official Ubuntu philosophy lists the following principles.

1. Every computer user should have the freedom to download, run, copy, distribute study, share, change, and improve their software for any purpose, without paying licensing fees.

2. Every computer user should be able to use their software in the language of their choice.

3. Every computer user should be given every opportunity to use software, even if they work under a disability.

The emphasis on language reflects Ubuntu's international scope. It is meant to be a global distribution that does not focus on any single market. Language support has been integrated into Linux in general by its internationalization projects, denoted by the term i18n. You can find information about il8n at **http://www.openi18n.org**.

Making software available to all users involves both full accessibility supports for users with disabilities as well as seamless integration of software access using online repositories, making massive amounts of software available to all users at the touch of a button. Ubuntu also makes full use of Linux's automatic device detection ability, greatly simplifying installation as well as access to removable devices and attached storage.

Ubuntu aims to provide a fully supported and reliable, open source and free, easy to use and modify, Linux operating system. Ubuntu makes the following promises about its distribution.

Ubuntu will always be free of charge, including enterprise releases and security updates.

Ubuntu comes with full commercial support from Canonical and hundreds of companies around the world.

Ubuntu includes the very best translations and accessibility infrastructure that the free software community has to offer.

Ubuntu CDs contain only free software applications; we encourage you to use free and open source software, improve it and pass it on (Ubuntu repositories contain some proprietary software like vendor graphics drivers that is also free).

Ubuntu 12.04

Ubuntu 12.04 introduces several new features, as well as numerous smaller modifications. It is a long-term support release. Ubuntu 12.04 provides two desktop interfaces: the Ubuntu desktop interface and Ubuntu 2D (no hardware acceleration). Ubuntu is the default desktop, provided your system supports hardware graphics acceleration. Both use the new Ubuntu Unity desktop interface. Unity uses a Launcher and a Dash (dashboard) to manage access to applications and devices (see Figure 1-1). In addition, Ubuntu 12.04 provides improvements to the Software Center, Ubuntu One setup and configuration, and the Unity Launcher. Rhythmbox is the default music player, and Thunderbird is the default email client..

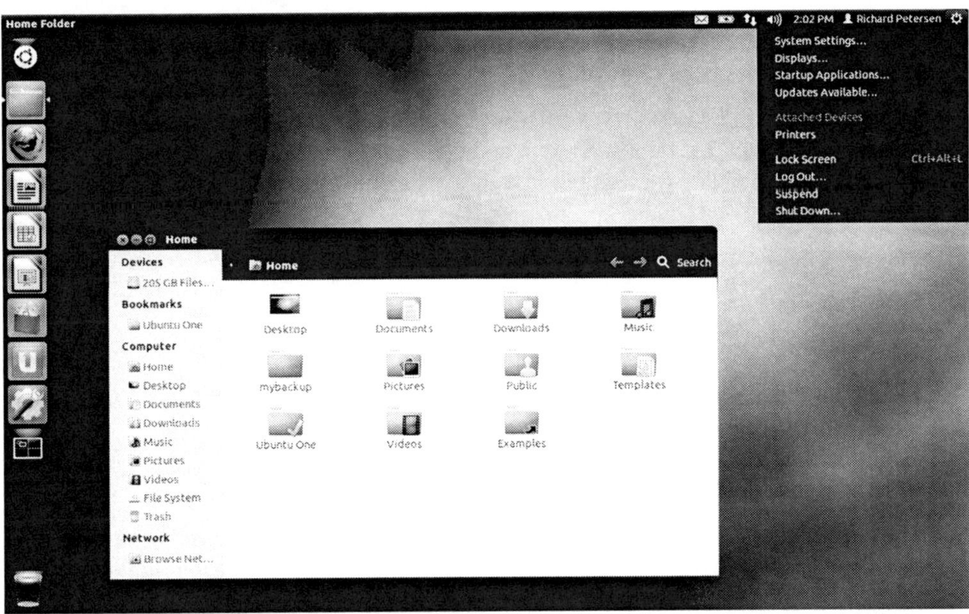

Figure 1-1: Ubuntu 12.04 Ubuntu (Unity) Desktop

For documentation check:

```
https://help.ubuntu.com/12.04/
```

Check the Ubuntu Release Notes for an explanation of changes.

```
https://wiki.ubuntu.com/PrecisePangolin/ReleaseNotes
```

Ubuntu 12.04 New Features

A list of Ubuntu features new with version 12.04, as well as key changes from the last long term release, 10.04, follows.

Desktop

The Ubuntu Desktop features the Unity user interface with a launcher, dash, and indicator menus. Referred to as simply the Ubuntu desktop, Unity is the default desktop.

Ubuntu Unity is based on GNOME 3.2.

Unity 2D provides a Unity desktop that does not require accelerated graphics. It is the default backup and is used if supporting acerbated drivers are not installed yet for Unity.

The indicator session menu (power icon) shows device and application entries for display configuration, Bluetooth devices, printers, attached devices, startup applications, and updates.

There is improved quicklist and progress bar support for applications on the launcher.

The User Switcher menu lets you switch to different users easily.

The Messaging menu provides quick access to instant messaging, broadcast, and email (The MeMenu has been removed).

Several GNOME 3 system tools such as Power, Users, and Appearance replace the previous GNOME 2 versions. System and configuration tools are now accessible from the System Settings dialog (accessible from the Session menu or from the System Settings icon on the Launcher).

Improved application switcher using Alt-tab keys.

Improved side bars.

New power icon for the Session menu.

For the Desktop menu, the Places menu in previous versions has been replaced by a Go menu, which access locations such as Network and Computer. The Nautilus file manager menu features a bookmarks menu, which you can use to access your bookmarked folders, including your default folders such as Documents and Pictures.

The new GNOME 3.2 desktop interface is available but not supported (Universe repository). The Ubuntu Classic desktop with GNOME 2.3 has been removed.

For ARM based netbooks and devices using OMAP, Ubuntu provides a unity-2d desktop image.

Unity Features

The nautilus quicklist provides easy access both default and custom bookmarks, along with an "Open in a new window" option. A quicklist is also provided for copy operations, letting you check or cancel copying.

The Dash home icon is now the first icon in the Launcher (it is no longer on the top panel).

You can access lenses from the list of buttons at the bottom of the dash. The new Music and Video search lenses are accessible from here.

Ubuntu Unity uses the Compiz window manager, using the Compiz Ubuntu Plugin to configure unity features. The Compiz support for Unity is very specific. Do not enable other Compiz features that may conflict with Unity such as the Desktop cube.

Ubuntu Unity supports window and Launcher animations such as pulsing Launcher items for Launcher application notifications and window expansion and reduction for maximizing and minimizing a window.

The Ubuntu Unity panel consists of indicator menus and an applications menu It cannot be modified by the user.

Ubuntu Unity indicator buttons display colors for a certain status (red for system actions, orange for system warnings, blue for new information, green for approved, and grey for no status)

Ubuntu Unity uses a global applications menu for the active window's menu bar (as used on Apple Macs). The menu bar is no longer displayed within windows. Move the mouse to the top panel to display the menu bar for the active window.

When clicking on the desktop background or if no windows are open, the desktop menu bar is displayed as the global applications menu, with Go menu for accessing the Computer and Network folders, the Help menu to open the Ubuntu Desktop Guide and the File, View, and Edit menus for folder and icon tasks.

The Unity dash provides a dynamic search, displaying matching results as you type in a search pattern. Results are organized into those frequently used, installed, and available for download. Clicking on an item in the "Apps available for download" section, opens the Ubuntu Software Center to that package, letting you download and install the package.

The Launcher has an auto-hide feature that hides the Launcher when a window is maximized or a window occupies the left side of the screen. Move the mouse to the left side to display the Launcher. This feature is turned off by default. To turn it on, use the System Settings Appearance tool's Behavior tab.

When an application opens, a Launcher item for it is added to the Launcher. Click on the Launcher item to minimize a displayed application window, or to display a minimized window.

Applications can be pinned and locked to the Launcher. Drag and application from the dash to the Launcher or, for open applications, right-click and choose "Lock to Launcher". When an application is installed, it is pinned to the launcher and locked there. You can manually unlock it, removing it from the Launcher.

From the Launcher, to open an additional instance of an application (such as a new home folder or browser), click on the Launcher item using the middle mouse button, or right-click on the Launcher item and choose "Open in a New Window."

If an application has several open windows, clicking on its Launcher item zooms out to display only the open windows for that application (windows spread). Click the one you want to make the active window.

Clicking the Launcher workspace switcher displays all workspaces on the full screen, letting you move open windows between them, and choosing one by clicking on it.

The number of workspaces can only be changed using the Gconf configuration editor or a **gconf2** command in a terminal window. There is no preferences dialog for changing the number of workspaces.

System tools

The hibernate shut down option has been dropped.

The GNOME 3 System Settings dialog is accessible from the Session menu or the Launcher. It provides access to older tools as well as new GNOME 3 configuration tools. The Users tool provides no configuration for groups.

System Settings features three categories: personal, hardware, and system.

The Appearance tool features two tabs: Look and Behavior. Look is used to configure your background, and Behavior configures the Launcher.

The Privacy tool provides options for restricting logging based on files and applications. You can also delete previous history logs, setting time limits.

LightDM replaces GDM as the login display manager.

GTK 3 library is used.

Ubuntu Software Center has an improved interface using a toolbar instead of a sidebar tree. It provides features such as sub-screens listing featured and new software, and user ratings and reviews. A top rated view has been added to category listings. Backport repository is enabled by default. Personalized recommendations are supported, based on installed software.

Kernel 3.2 with more driver support and bug fixes.

Synaptic software center is no longer installed by default.

Ubuntu One is managed using a new Control Panel with tabs for Account (user information and service level), Cloud Folders (sync control), and Devices (systems using Ubuntu One). Syncing for Evolution mail contacts is no longer supported.

If you want to use the older GNOME "User and Groups" and Shares tools, install the **gnome-system-tools** package.

Applications

The HUD (Heads-UP Display) provides an intelligent search of menu entries of the current application, and the indicator menus.

Rhythmbox replaces Banshee as the default music application.

Thunderbird replaces Evolution as the default mail client.

Deja Dup is the default backup application. Deja Dup front end for duplicity provides simple backups using rsync.

Gwibber has a new interface and improved functionality.

Computer Janitor has been dropped.

Libre Office replaces Open Office as the Office Suite. With its purchase of Sun, Oracle now controls Open Office. Libre Office is derived from Open Office, but is fully independent and open source.

Nautilus provides undo support.

The Messaging indicator menu notifies you of the messaging status for mail, IM, and broadcast services. You can also access the Ubuntu One control center. You can use the menu to set up your messaging applications.

Kubuntu 12.04

Kubuntu uses KDE 4.8:
https://wiki.ubuntu.com/PrecisePangolin/ReleaseNotes/Kubuntu,
http://www.kubuntu.org/news/12.04-release, and
http://www.kde.org/announcements/4.8/

The Muon Software Center replaces KPackageKit as the KDE package manager, and features a new interface with 12.04.

The icon tasks option for the Plasma panel shows panel objects as icons, similar to the Unity Launcher.

Calligra is the new version of the older KOffice suite, which is no longer available.

Activities management has a new user interface, making it easier to associate applications with activities.

Search on KDE has unified the KFind and Dolphin search into a simplified search bar.

Dolphin supports faceted browsing, a filter panel to perform searches using file meta data.

Samba file sharing for folders is supported from dolphin directly.

Phonom uses a Gstreamer backend, which provides standard multimedia codec support for both Kubuntu and Ubuntu (GNOME and Unity).

The **kubuntu-full** set of packages, provided with the Kubuntu DVD or downloadable as a meta package, provides an extensive set of KDE applications.

Kubuntu supports Own Cloud, the KDE remote file server. Own Cloud is part of the KDE Social Desktop. It provides services similar to Ubuntu One such as storing files, synchronizing with your computers, backups, versioning, and sharing. You can set up your own server, or use a hosted server.

The Kubuntu default Web browser is Rekonq, which is based on WebKit.

KDE Active is a new KDE interface for tablets.

Ubuntu Features

A list of Ubuntu features incorporated from Ubuntu 11.10 and earlier is listed here.

The installation program (Ubiquity) has been updated to provide better disk detection and formatting options.

The Sound Preferences dialog provides a sound testing capability.

The Ubuntu Font Family provides libre/open fonts (TTF) for Ubuntu,
http://font.ubuntu.com/.

Gwibber social broadcast messaging for accessing your broadcast accounts like Twitter.

Ubuntu provides two official themes, Ambiance and Radiance. Ambiance is the default and uses darker colors, whereas Radiance uses lighter colors.

Skype VoIP is supported by Ubuntu directly and is available from the Ubuntu partner repository.

Support for IPod and IPod Touch on GNOME.

GRUB2 boot loader replaces GRUB with configuration in **/etc/default/grub** and updating with **update-grub**.

Startup is managed by Upstart providing for much faster startup times.

Storage devices along with power management are handled by Udisks (udisks and upower). Other devices are handled by udev directly.

Network Manager configures all network connections, even manually. You can also use Network Manager to configure IPv6 connections and wireless networks.

PolicyKit authorization used polkit-1 to allow users limited controlled administrative access for some tools.

The UTouch multitouch and gesture capability for devices supporting gesture interfaces: **https://wiki.ubuntu.com/Multitouch**.

Ubuntu Releases

Ubuntu provides both long-term and short-term support releases. Long-term support releases (LTS), such as Ubuntu 12.04, are released every two years. Short-term releases, such as Ubuntu 11.10, are provided every six months between the LTS versions. They are designed to make available the latest applications and support for the newest hardware. Each has its own nickname, like Precise Pangolin for the 12.04 release. The long-term support releases are supported for three years for desktops and five years for servers, whereas short-term support releases are supported for 18 months. In addition, Canonical provides limited commercial support for companies that purchase it.

Installing Ubuntu is easy to do. A core set of applications are installed, and you can add to them as you wish. Following installation, additional software can be downloaded from online repositories. There are only a few install screens, which move quickly through default partitioning, user setup, and time settings. Hardware components such as graphics cards and network connections are configured and detected automatically. With the new Ubuntu Software Center (installed by default on all systems), you can find and install additional software with the click of a button.

The Ubuntu distribution of Linux is available online at numerous sites. Ubuntu maintains its own site for the desktop edition at **http://www.ubuntu.com/ubuntu/**. You can download the current release of Ubuntu Linux from **http://www.ubuntu.com/download/desktop**.

Ubuntu Editions

Ubuntu is released in several editions, each designed for a distinct group of users or functions. Editions install different collections of software such as the GNOME desktop, the KDE desktop, servers, educational software, and multimedia applications. Table 1-2 lists the edition Web sites where you can download ISO images for these editions. ISO images can be downloaded directly or by using a BitTorrent application like Transmission. Jigdo and Metalink downloads are also supported which make effective use of mirrors. If you have already downloaded a pre-release ISO image, like a beta version, you can use zsync to download just the final changes, greatly reducing download times.

The Ubuntu Desktop edition provides desktop functionality for end users. The Ubuntu Desktop release provides a Live CD using the GNOME desktop. Most users would install this edition. You can download the Desktop edition from the Download page, which you can access from the Ubuntu site (**http://www.ubuntu.com**) by clicking on the Download tab.. The page address is:

```
http://www.ubuntu.com/download/desktop
```

You can choose either the 32-bit or the 64-bit versions, though 32 bit is the default.

Those who want to run the Ubuntu desktop on their netbook use the same Ubuntu Desktop CD. Since Ubuntu 11.04, the Ubuntu Netbook Edition (UNE) has been merged into the Ubuntu Desktop CD. On this page, the Window Installer button lets you download Wubi, which runs Ubuntu as a file image on your Windows system (Download tab, Ubuntu tab, Windows Installer tab).

For Upgrade instructions, click on the link at the bottom of the page named Do you want to upgrade? **Follow our simple guide.**

```
http://www.ubuntu.com/download/desktop/upgrade
```

On the download desktop page, you can click on the link

Take a look at a full list of our previous versions and alternative downloads

to open the Alternative Download page.

```
http://www.ubuntu.com/download/desktop/alternative-downloads
```

The Alternative Downloads page provides information on the Alternative Ubuntu CD, BitTorrent files for downloading all the Ubuntu 12.04 CD editions including the desktop CD, alternate CD, and server CDs. A DVD download section lets you link to an Ubuntu mirror where you can locate the DVD download page with download files for BitTorrent, zsync, and metalink, as well as a direct download link. You can also access the page directly from the cdimages site at:

```
http://cdimages.ubuntu.com/releases/precise/release/
```

On the desktop download page, you can click on the link

Buy 12.04 Desktop CDs from the shop

to connect to the Ubuntu Shop on the shop canonical site where you can buy Ubuntu CDs at a low price. On the Ubuntu Shop page, click on the "CDs and DVDs" link at the left.

```
http://shop.canonical.com/
```

Those who want to run Ubuntu as a server, to provide an Internet service such as a Web site, would use the Ubuntu Server edition. The Server edition provides only a simple command line interface; it does not install the desktop. It is designed primarily to run servers. Keep in mind that you could install the desktop first, and later download server software from the Ubuntu repositories, running them from a system that also has a desktop, though there are overhead costs for a server running a desktop. You do not have to install the Server edition to install and run servers. You can download the Server edition from the Ubuntu Server download page, which you can access from the Ubuntu site (**http://www.ubuntu.com**) by clicking on the Download tab and then the Server sub-tab. The page address is:

```
http://www.ubuntu.com/download/server
```

Users who want more enhanced operating system features such as RAID arrays, LVM file systems, or file system encryption would use the Alternate edition. The Alternate edition, along with the Desktop and Server editions, can be downloaded directly from.

```
http://releases.ubuntu.com/precise/
http://releases.ubuntu.com/releases/12.04/
```

Ubuntu Editions	Description
Ubuntu Desktop	Live CD and Install with the Unity interface, **http://www.ubuntu.com/download/desktop**.
Server Install	Install server software (no desktop), **http://www.ubuntu.com/download/server**
Alternate Install	Install enhanced features, **http://releases.ubuntu.com/precise/**.
Kubuntu	Live CD and Install using the KDE desktop, instead of GNOME, **http://www.kubuntu.org**. Add to Ubuntu desktop with the **kubuntu-desktop** or **kubuntu-full** metapackages.
Business Desktop Remix	Ubuntu desktop with a collection of packages designed for business needs, **http://www.ubuntu.com/business/desktop/remix**.
Xubuntu	Uses the Xfce desktop instead of GNOME, **http://www.xubuntu.org**. Useful for laptops.
Edubuntu	Installs Educational software: Desktop, Server, and Server add-on CDs, **http://www.edubuntu.org**
Ubuntu Studio	Ubuntu desktop with multimedia and graphics production applications, **http://ubuntustudio.org**. Add to Ubuntu desktop with the **ubuntustudio-desktop** metapackage
Mythbuntu	Ubuntu desktop with MythTV multimedia and DVR applications, **http://www.mythbuntu.org**. Add to Ubuntu desktop with the **mythbuntu-desktop** metapackage
Lubuntu	Lightweight version of Ubuntu based on the LXDE desktop, **https://wiki.ubuntu.com/Lubuntu**

Table 1-1: Ubuntu Editions

The BitTorrent downloads can also be accessed from the "Alternative downloads" page.

```
http://www.ubuntu.com/download/desktop/alternative-downloads
```

Apple Mac compatible Ubuntu Desktop and Alternate CDs can also be downloaded from cdimages site:

```
http://cdimages.ubuntu.com/releases/precise/release/
```

For Open Multimedia Applications Platform (OMAP versions 3 and 4) netbooks and devices, check the OMAP page at:

```
https://wiki.ubuntu.com/ARM/OMAP
```

Users that want to run Ubuntu on an OMAP netbooks and devices can download and Ubuntu OMAP images from the cdimages site. The images provide a Unity-2D desktop for use on low powered non-accelerated hardware.

```
http://cdimages.ubuntu.com/releases/precise/release/
```

Other editions use either a different desktop or a specialized collection of software for certain groups of users. The Kubuntu edition uses the KDE desktop instead of GNOME. Xubuntu is a stripped down and highly efficient desktop (Xfce), ideal for low power use on laptops and smaller computer. The Edubuntu edition provides educational software that can be used with a specialized Edubuntu server, providing educational software on a school network. The Ubuntu Studio edition provides a collection of multimedia and image production software. The Mythbuntu edition is designed to install and run the MythTV software, letting Ubuntu operate like a Multimedia DVR and Video playback system. Lubuntu is a new version based on the LXDE desktop, providing a very lightweight version of Ubuntu. The Ubuntu Desktop Business remix provides a collection of software supported by Canonical for business applications.

You can download editions from the respective edition Web sites. Edubuntu and Kubuntu are available at **http://releases.ubuntu.com**. The others can be downloaded from **http://cdimages.ubuntu.com**.

http://www.edubuntu.org   Educational version

http://www.xubuntu.org   Xfce desktop version

http://www.kubuntu.org   KDE desktop version

Ubuntu supports the Ubuntu Server, Kubuntu, and Edubuntu editions officially. The Xubuntu, Mythbuntu, and Ubuntu Studio editions are not supported, but are officially recognized. These are all considered derivatives of the original Ubuntu Desktop. You can find out more about these derivatives at: **http://www.ubuntu.com/project/about-ubuntu/derivatives**, which you can access from the Ubuntu site (**http://www.ubuntu.com**). Click the Project tab, then the About Ubuntu tab, and then the Derivatives sub-tab. Links to their Web sites are provided on the Ubuntu derivatives page, where you can then download their live/install CDs. All these editions can be downloaded from their respective Web sites, as well as from:

```
http://cdimages.ubuntu.com/
```

The **http://releases.ubuntu.com** and **http://cdimages.ubuntu.com** sites hold both BitTorrent and full image files for the editions they provide. The **http://releases.ubuntu.com** site also provides jigdo and metalink downloads from multiple mirrors, and zsync files for synchronizing downloads. Table 1-2 lists Web sites where you can download ISO images for the various editions.

Keep in mind that most of these editions are released as Live CDs or Live DVD discs, for which there are two versions, a 32-bit x86 version and a 64-bit x86_64 version. Older computers and small netbooks may only support a 32-bit version, whereas most desktop computers will support the 64-bit versions. Check your computer hardware specifications to be sure. The 64-bit version should run faster, and most computer software is now available in stable 64-bit packages.

URL	Internet Site
http://www.ubuntu.com/download/ubuntu/download	Primary download site for Desktop CDs
http://releases.ubuntu.com/precise/	Download site for Desktop, Alternate, Server CDs, including alternate install methods like torrent, zsync, jigdo, and metalink.
http://cdimages.ubuntu.com/releases/precise/release/	Download site for Install/Live DVD. Also includes Apple Mac compatible Ubuntu Desktop and Alternate CDs, and Ubuntu images for OMAP devices.
http://cdimages.ubuntu.com/	Download site for all Ubuntu editions, including Kubuntu, Xubuntu, Edubuntu, Mythbuntu, and Ubuntu Studio. Check also their respective Web sites.

Table 1-2: Ubuntu CD ISO Image locations

Ubuntu Live CD/DVD/USB

The Ubuntu Desktop CD and the Install DVD can both operate as LiveCDs (the Server and Alternate editions do not), so you can run Ubuntu from any CD/DVD-ROM drive. You can also install the Ubuntu Desktop CD image to a USB drive. In effect, you can carry your operating system with you on a CD/DVD-ROM or a USB drive. New users can also use the Live-CD/USB to try out Ubuntu to see if they like it. The Ubuntu Desktop CD will run as a Live CD automatically using GNOME as the desktop. If you want to use the KDE desktop as your Live CD instead, you would use the Kubuntu CD. To create a Live USB, you install the Ubuntu Desktop CD image to a USB drive using the Ubuntu USB creator application, usb-creator, accessible from the Customization dash.

In addition to the standard Live CD/DVDs, Ubuntu also provides Live USB images for specialized small computers, both the Netbook PCs and handhelds using Intel Atom processors. These are available as IMG images that use a different tool to burn to a USB drive, USB ImageWriter.

Ubuntu Desktop Live CD

The Desktop Live CD provided by Ubuntu includes a basic collection of software packages. On the Ubuntu Desktop Live CD, you use Ubuntu 2D (the Unity 2D version). Other than this limitation, you will have a fully operational Ubuntu desktop (see Figure 1-2). You have the full set of administrative tools, with which you can add users, change configuration settings, and even add software, while the Live CD is running. When you shut down, the configuration information is lost, including any software you have added. Files and data can be written to removable devices like USB drives and CD/DVD write discs, letting you save your data during a Live CD session.

When you start up the Ubuntu Desktop CD/DVD/USB, the startup screen is displayed (Chapter 2, Figure 2-2), with the "Try Ubuntu without any change to your computer" option selected. This option starts up the Live CD, and will start automatically after a few seconds. The Live CD desktop is then displayed (see Figure 1-2) and you are logged in as the ubuntu user. The launcher on the left side displays dash home, an install Ubuntu icons, and home folder, followed by application icons for a Web browser (Firefox), Open Office applications, the Ubuntu Software Center, Ubuntu One, and System Settings. On the top panel to the right is a network connection icon for Network Manager, which you can configure for wireless access. At the right side of the top panel is a Session button for shutting down your system.

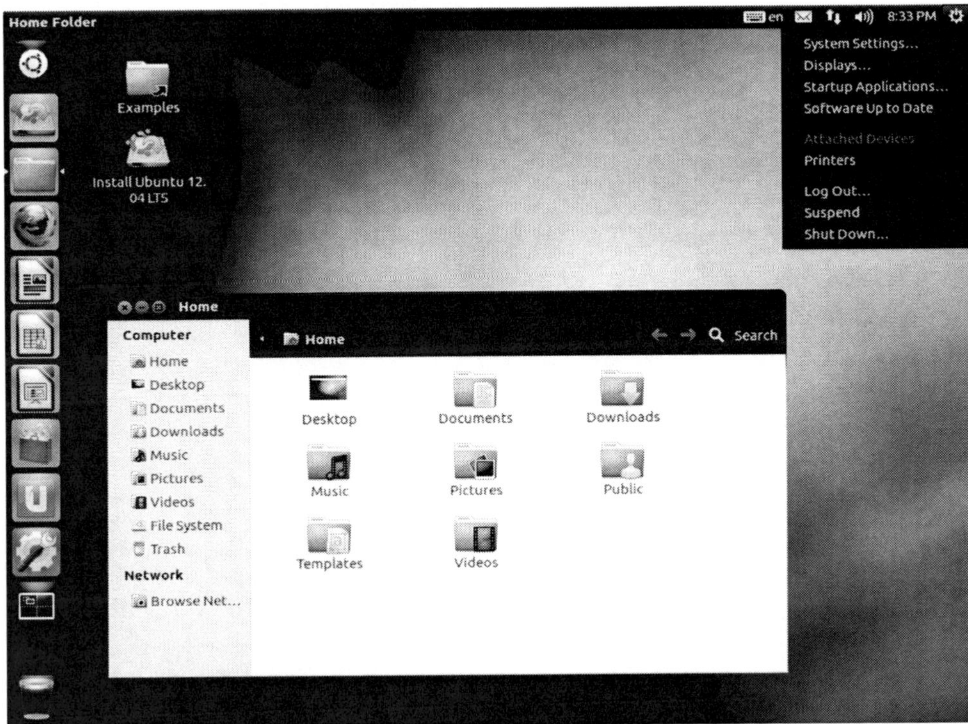

Figure 1-2: Ubuntu Live CD

On the desktop, an icon is displayed for an Examples directory. Here you will find example files for sound and video files.

You can save files to your home directory, but they are temporary and disappear at the end of the session. Copy them to a DVD, USB drive, or another removable device to save them.

All the Live CD/DVD/USBs also function as install discs for Ubuntu, providing a basic collection of software, and installing a full-fledged Ubuntu operating system that can be expanded and updated from Ubuntu online repositories. An Install icon lets you install Ubuntu on your computer, performing a standard installation to your hard drive. From the Live CD desktop, double-click the Install icon on the desktop or on the Launcher to start the installation.

Ubuntu Live USB drive

With the USB Startup Disk Creator utility, you can install any Ubuntu disc image on a USB drive. The USB Live/install drive is generated using the CD image that you first have to download. Click "Startup Disk Creator" icon on the Customization or System dash to open the Make Startup Disk window with an entry at the top to select an ISO image and an entry below to select the USB drive to use. Click the Other button to locate a specific disk image to use (see Figure 1-3). Then click the "Make Startup Disk" button to install the ISO on the USB drive.

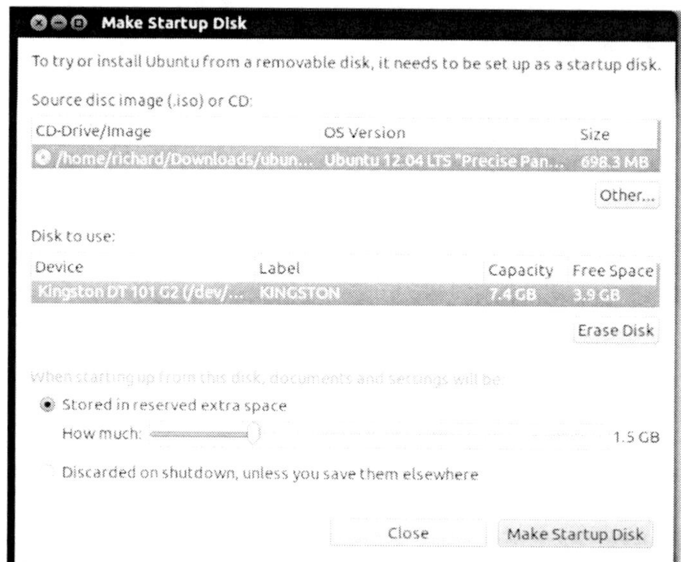

Figure 1-3: USB Startup Disk Creator

The "Make Startup Disk" operation will not erase any data already on your USB drive. You can still access it, even Windows data. The Ubuntu Live OS will coexist with your current data, occupying available free space.

To boot from the Live USB, be sure your computer (BIOS) is configured to boot from the USB drive. The Live USB drive will then start up just like the Live CD, displaying the install screen with options to try Ubuntu or directly install.

When you create the Live USB drive, you have the option to specify writable memory. This will allow you to save files to your USB drive as part of the Ubuntu Live operating system. You can save files to your Document or Pictures directory and then access them later. You can also create new users, and give those users administrative permission, just as you would on a normally installed OS. With the System Settings' User Accounts tool you could even have the new user be the automatic login, instead of the ubuntu user. In effect, the Ubuntu Live USB drive becomes a portable Ubuntu OS. Even with these changes, the Ubuntu Live USB remains the equivalent of a Live CD, just one that you can write to. There is no GRUB boot loader. You still use the install start up screen. In addition, you cannot update the kernel. One advantage of this approach is that your other data can coexist on the USB drive, accessible by other operating systems.

If you want a truly portable Ubuntu OS, just perform a standard installation to a USB drive, instead of to a hard drive. You will have to create a new clean partition on the USB drive to install to. You would either reduce the size of the current partition, preserving data or simply delete it, opening up the entire drive for use by the new Ubuntu OS.

Ubuntu Software

All Linux software for Ubuntu is currently available from online repositories. You can download applications for desktops, Internet servers, office suites, and programming packages, among others. Software packages are distributed primarily through the official Ubuntu repository. Downloads and updates are handled automatically by your desktop software manager and updater. Many popular applications are included in separate sections of the repository. During installation, your system is configured to access Ubuntu repositories. You can update to the latest software from the Ubuntu repository using the update manager.

A complete listing of software packages for the Ubuntu distribution, along with a search capability is located at:

```
http://packages.ubuntu.com
```

In addition, you could download from third-party sources software that is in the form of compressed archives or in DEB packages. DEB packages are archived using the Debian Package Manager and have the extension **.deb**. Compressed archives have an extension such as **.tar.gz**. You also can download the source version and compile it directly on your system. This has become a simple process, almost as simple as installing the compiled DEB versions.

Due to licensing restrictions, multimedia support for popular operations like MP3, DVD, and DivX are included with Ubuntu in a separate section of the repository called multiverse. Ubuntu includes on its restricted repository NVIDIA and ATI vendor graphics drivers. Ubuntu also provides as part of its standard installation, the generic X.org drivers that will enable your graphics cards to work.

All software packages in the Ubuntu repositories are accessible directly with the Ubuntu Software Center and the Synaptic Package Manager, which provide easy software installation, removal, and searching.

Due to further licensing issues, popular applications and codecs like Google Earth and DVD video support are provided by the Medibuntu.org repository (Adobe Acrobat Reader and Skype are part of the Ubuntu Partner repository). This is a third party repository which does not have repository support initially configured. You have to implement repository support manually before you can access the Medibuntu software packages with the Ubuntu Software Center or the Synaptic Package Manager. See Chapters 4 for details on how to configure the Medibuntu.org repository access for your system.

Ubuntu Help and Documentation

A great deal of help and documentation is available online for Ubuntu, ranging from detailed install procedures to beginner questions (see Table 1-3). The documentation for Ubuntu 12.04 is located at **https://help.ubuntu.com/12.04/**. The Firefox Web browser start page displays links for two major help sites: Ubuntu documentation at **http://help.ubuntu.com** and Ubuntu Community at **http://www.ubuntu.com/community**. For detailed online support, check the

Ubuntu forums at **http://ubuntuforums.org**. In addition, there are blog and news sites as well as the standard Linux documentation. Ubuntu Community features Ubuntu documentation, support, blogs, and news. A Contribute section links to sites where you can contribute in development, artwork, documentation, and support. The Ask Ubuntu site is a question and answer site based on community support, which provides answers to many common questions (**http://askubuntu.com**).

For mailing lists, check **https://lists.ubuntu.com**. There are lists for categories like Ubuntu announcements, community support for specific editions, and development for areas like the desktop, servers, or mobile implementation. For more specialized tasks like Samba support and LAMP server installation check **http://www.ubuntugeek.com**.

Site	Description
https://help.ubuntu.com/12.04	Help pages and documentation for 12.04
http://packages.ubuntu.com	Ubuntu software package list and search
http://ubuntuforums.org	Ubuntu forums
http://askubuntu.com	Ask Ubuntu Q&A site for users and developers (community based)
http://fridge.ubuntu.com	News and developments
http://planet.ubuntu.com	Member and developer blogs
http://blog.canonical.com	Latest Canonical news
http://www.tldp.org	Linux Documentation Project Web site
http://www.ubuntu.com/community	Links to Documentation, Support, News, and Blogs
https://lists.ubuntu.com	Ubuntu mailing lists
http://www.ubuntugeek.com	Tutorials and guides for specialized tasks

Table 1-3: Ubuntu help and documentation

help.ubuntu.com

Ubuntu-specific documentation is available at **https://help.ubuntu.com**. Here on listed links you can find specific documentation for different releases. Always check the release help page first for documentation, though it may be sparse and cover mainly changed areas. The Ubuntu LTS release usually includes desktop, installation, and server guides. For 12.04 the Documentation section provides the Ubuntu Desktop Guide (Ubuntu Desktop Help), the Ubuntu Server Guide, and Ubuntu installation using the Alternate CD. The Ubuntu Desktop Guide covers the Unity interfaces, and is the same guide installed with your desktop, accessible from the desktop help menu.

```
https://help.ubuntu.com/12.04/ubuntu-help/index.html
```

One of the more helpful pages is the Community Contributed Documentation page, **https://help.ubuntu.com/community**. Here you will find detailed documentation on installation of all Ubuntu releases, using the desktop, installing software, and configuring devices. Always check the page for your Ubuntu release first. The page includes these main sections:

Getting Started with Ubuntu: links FAQs and information on how to move from using other operating systems like Windows or Mac.

Installation: Link to Install page with sections on desktop, server, and alternate installations.

Getting to know and work with your system: Sections on managing software and hardware. Links to pages on drives and partitions, input devices, wireless configuration, printers, sound, video, and laptops.

Customizing and Maintaining Ubuntu: Links to system administration, security, and troubleshooting pages. System administration covers topics like adding users, configuring the GRUB boot loader, setting the time and date, and installing software. The Security page covers lower level issues like IPtables for firewalls and how GPG security works.

FAQs and See Also: Links to official documentation, man pages, and release notes.

ubuntuforums.org

Ubuntu forums provide detailed online support and discussion for users (**http://ubuntuforums.org**). An Absolute Beginner section provides an area where new users can obtain answers to questions. Sticky threads include both quick and complete guides to installation for the current Ubuntu release. You can use the search feature to find discussions on your topic of interest. The main support categories section covers specific support areas like networking, multimedia, laptops, security, and 64-bit support.

Other community discussions cover ongoing work such as virtualization, art and design, gaming, education and science, Wine, assistive technology, and the Ubuntu cloud. Here you will also find community announcements and news. Of particular interest are third-party projects that include projects like Mythbuntu (MythTV on Ubuntu) and Ubuntu Women.

The forum community discussion is where you talk about anything else. The **http://ubuntuforums.org/** site also provides a gallery page for posted screenshots as well as RSS feeds for specific forums.

Ubuntu news and blog sites

Several news and blog sites are accessible from the News page at **https://wiki.ubuntu.com/Home**.

http://fridge.ubuntu.com The Fridge site lists the latest news and developments for Ubuntu. It features the Weekly newsletter, latest announcements, and upcoming events.

http://planet.ubuntu.com Ubuntu blog for members and developers

http://blog.canonical.com and **http://www.canonical.com/about-canonical/news-and-events** Canonical news

Linux documentation

The Linux Documentation Project (LDP) has developed a complete set of Linux manuals. The documentation is available at the LDP home site at **http://www.tldp.org**. The Linux documentation for your installed software will be available at your **/usr/share/doc** directory.

Open Source Software

Linux is developed as a cooperative Open Source effort over the Internet, so no company or institution controls Linux. Software developed for Linux reflects this background. Development often takes place when Linux users decide to work together on a project. Most Linux software is developed as Open Source software. The source code for an application is freely distributed along with the application. Programmers over the Internet can make their own contributions to a software package's development, modifying and correcting the source code. As an open source operating system, the Linux source code is included in all its distributions and is freely available. Many major software development efforts are also open source projects, as are the KDE and GNOME desktops along with most of their applications. You can find more information about the Open Source movement at **http://www.opensource.org**.

Open source software is protected by public licenses that prevent commercial companies from taking control of open source software by adding modifications of their own, copyrighting those changes, and selling the software as their own product. The most popular public license is the GNU General Public License (GPL) provided by the Free Software Foundation. Linux is distributed under this license. The GNU General Public License retains the copyright, freely licensing the software with the requirement that the software and any modifications made to it are always freely available. Other public licenses have been created to support the demands of different kinds of open source projects. The GNU Lesser General Public License (LGPL) lets commercial applications use GNU licensed software libraries. The Qt Public License (QPL) lets open source developers use the Qt libraries essential to the KDE desktop. You can find a complete listing at **www.opensource.org**.

Linux is currently copyrighted under a GNU public license provided by the Free Software Foundation (see **http://www.gnu.org/**). GNU software is distributed free, provided it is freely distributed to others. GNU software has proved both reliable and effective. Many of the popular Linux utilities, such as C compilers, shells, and editors, are GNU software applications. In addition, many open source software projects are licensed under the GNU General Public License (GPL). Most of these applications are available on the Ubuntu software repositories. Chapter 4 describes in detail the process of accessing these repositories to download and install software applications from them on your system.

Under the terms of the GNU General Public License, the original author retains the copyright, although anyone can modify the software and redistribute it, provided the source code is included, made public, and provided free. In addition, no restriction exists on selling the software or giving it away free. One distributor could charge for the software, while another could provide it free of charge. Major software companies are also providing Linux versions of their most popular applications. (you can use the Wine, the Windows compatibility layer, to run many Microsoft applications on Linux, directly.)

Linux

Linux is an fast, stable, and open source operating system for PCs and workstations that features professional-level Internet services, extensive development tools, fully functional graphical user interfaces (GUIs), and a massive number of applications ranging from office suites to multimedia applications. Linux was developed in the early 1990s by Linus Torvalds, along with other programmers around the world. As an operating system, Linux performs many of the same functions as UNIX, Macintosh, and Windows. However, Linux is distinguished by its power and flexibility, along with being freely available. Most PC operating systems, such as Windows, began their development within the confines of small, restricted personal computers, which have become more versatile and powerful machines. Such operating systems are constantly being upgraded to keep up with the ever-changing capabilities of PC hardware. Linux, on the other hand, was developed in a different context. Linux is a PC version of the UNIX operating system that has been used for decades on mainframes and is currently the system of choice for network servers and workstations.

Technically, Linux consists of the operating system program, referred to as the kernel, which is the part originally developed by Linus Torvalds. However, it has always been distributed with a large number of software applications, ranging from network servers and security programs to office applications and development tools. Linux has evolved as part of the open source software movement, in which independent programmers joined to provide free quality software to any user. Linux has become the premier platform for open source software, much of it developed by the Free Software Foundation's GNU project. Most of these applications are also available on the Ubuntu repository, providing packages that are Debian compliant.

Linux operating system capabilities include powerful networking features, including support for Internet, intranets, and Windows networking. As a norm, Linux distributions include fast, efficient, and stable Internet servers, such as the Web, FTP, and DNS servers, along with proxy, news, and mail servers. In other words, Linux has everything you need to set up, support, and maintain a fully functional network.

Linux is distributed freely under a GNU General Public License (GPL) as specified by the Free Software Foundation, making it available to anyone who wants to use it. GNU (which stands for "GNU's Not Unix") is a project initiated and managed by the Free Software Foundation to provide free software to users, programmers, and developers. Linux is copyrighted, not public domain. The GNU General Public License is designed to ensure that Linux remains free and, at the same time, standardized. Linux is technically the operating system kernel—the core operations—and only one official Linux kernel exists. Its power and stability have made Linux an operating system of choice as a network server.

Originally designed specifically for Intel-based personal computers, Linux started out as a personal project of computer science student Linus Torvalds at the University of Helsinki. At that time, students were making use of a program called Minix, which highlighted different UNIX features. Minix was created by Professor Andrew Tanenbaum and widely distributed over the Internet to students around the world. Torvalds's intention was to create an effective PC version of UNIX for Minix users. It was named Linux, and in 1991, Torvalds released version 0.11. Linux was widely distributed over the Internet, and in the following years, other programmers refined and added to it, incorporating most of the applications and features now found in standard UNIX systems. All the major window managers have been ported to Linux. Linux has all the networking tools, such as FTP file transfer support, Web browsers, and the whole range of network services such as e-mail, the domain name service, and dynamic host configuration, along with FTP, Web, and print servers. It also has a full set of program development utilities, such as C++ compilers and debuggers. Given all its features, the Linux operating system remains small, stable, and fast.

Linux development is overseen by The Linux Foundation (**http://www.linuxfoundation.org**), which is a merger of The Free Standards Group and Open

Source Development Labs (OSDL). This is the group with which Linux Torvalds works to develop new Linux versions. Linux kernels are released at **http://kernel.org/**.

ubuntu

2. Installing Ubuntu

Install CD and DVDs

Installation Overview

Installation with the Ubuntu Desktop CD

Alternate and DVD Installation

Recovery

Re-Installing the Boot Loader

Wubi: Windows-based installer

Installing Ubuntu Linux is a very simple procedure using just a few screens with default entries for easy installation. A pre-selected collection of software is installed. Most of your devices, like your display and network connection, are detected automatically. The most difficult part would be a manual partitioning of the hard drive, but you can use automatic partitioning for fresh installs, as is usually the case. As an alternative, you can also install Ubuntu on a virtual hard disk on your Windows system.

Install CD and DVDs

In most cases, installation is performed using an Ubuntu Desktop CD that will install the Ubuntu desktop along with a pre-selected set of software packages for multimedia players, office applications, and games. The Ubuntu Desktop CD is also designed to run from the CD disc, while providing the option to install Ubuntu on your hard drive. This is the disc image you will download from the Ubuntu download site. The Ubuntu Desktop CD has both 32 and 64-bit versions. If you want to use the 64-bit version, be sure you have a CPU that is 64-bit compatible (as are most current CPUs). The 64-bit version is faster.

```
http://www.ubuntu.com/download/desktop
```

You can also download the Ubuntu Desktop CD ISO image directly from:

```
http://releases.ubuntu.com/precise
```

The Ubuntu DVD ISO image is at a different location:

```
http://cdimages.ubuntu.com/releases/precise/release/
```

Installation choices

Ubuntu tailors its installs by providing different CD/DVD install disc for different releases and versions (see Table 2-1). The Desktop CD is not the only Ubuntu installation available. Ubuntu provides two other CDs, the Server CD designed for servers and the Alternate CD, which provides specialized features like LVM and RAID. The Alternate CD also supports small installations, automated installations, customized OEM systems, and the upgrading of older releases that have no network access. The Ubuntu DVD, though also a Live DVD, also includes the same install options as the Alternate CD, as well as the server software included on the Server CD. The Wubi installation option will install a fully functional Ubuntu system on a virtual hard disk on a Windows system.

Desktop CD Run as a Live CD or install Ubuntu Linux with the Ubuntu desktop and a standard set of applications.

Desktop USB Run as Live USB or install Ubuntu Linux with the Ubuntu desktop and a standard set of applications, uses the Ubuntu Desktop CD image installed on USB drive.

Server install CD   Install Ubuntu with a standard set of servers, uses the command line interface (no desktop).

Alternate CD Installs specialized features like LVM, RAID, encrypted file systems, small systems, and OEM configurations.

Wubi Install to a virtual hard disk in Windows.

Install/Live DVD Install Ubuntu Linux with the Ubuntu desktop and a more extensive set of applications. The Text Mode Install also allows you install servers as well as just a command line system without the desktop. You can also set up LVM and RAID arrays during the installation.

Ubuntu releases	Description
Ubuntu Desktop Live/Install CD/USB	Primary Ubuntu release, Ubuntu desktop, can be burned to either CD disc or USB drive.
Ubuntu Desktop CD/Wubi	Insert Ubuntu Desktop CD in Windows system, and you can perform a Wubi installation.
Ubuntu Alternate CD	Support for specialized features like LVM, RAID, encrypted file systems, OEM distributions, and small memory.
Ubuntu Server CD	Server only installation, no desktop, command line interface
Ubuntu Install/Live DVD	Ubuntu DVD, primarily for installs, large software collection on disc, can operate as a Live DVD; Text mode install has same options as the Alternate CD.
Ubuntu Editions	
Kubuntu	Installs the KDE desktop and software instead of GNOME, **http://www.kubuntu.org**.
Edubuntu	Installs Educational software: Desktop, Server, and Server add-on CDs, **http://www.edubuntu.org**
Xubuntu	Installs Xfce desktop, **http://www.xubuntu.org**
Ubuntu Studio	Install Ubuntu multimedia and graphics applications, **http://www.ubuntustudio.org**.
Mythbuntu	MythTV multimedia software collection for Ubuntu, **http://www.mythbuntu.org**

Table 2-1: Ubuntu releases and versions

The Desktop CD, Alternate CD, and Server CD are available at:

```
http://releases.ubuntu.com/precise
```

The Install/Live DVD is available at:

```
http://cdimages.ubuntu.com/releases/precise/release/
```

The Install/Live DVD is meant to install primarily Ubuntu, and provides a large selection of software, though it can also serve as a Live DVD. It has the advantage of providing a large collection of installable software without needing network access to a repository. It also includes all the servers, all those also found on the Server CD. All releases have 32 and 64-bit versions.

Other Ubuntu editions include Kubuntu and Edubuntu (see Table 2-1). The Kubuntu CD installs KDE as the desktop instead of GNOME (Ubuntu desktop), along with KDE software. You could also install Kubuntu later on an Ubuntu desktop install by selecting the **kubuntu-desktop** meta-package for software installation (Ubuntu Software Center). Kubuntu can then become an option in your login window sessions menu. You should download these editions from their Web sites directly. They are also available from the Ubuntu download sites. For Kubuntu you can use:

```
http://cdimages.ubuntu.com/kubuntu/releases/precise/release/
```

Edubuntu is installs a collection of educational software, instead of the standard GNOME office and multimedia applications. The Edubuntu version provides three CDs, a desktop, server, and server add-on. The server add-on provides additional educational applications.

```
http://cdimages.ubuntu.com/edubuntu/releases/12.04/release/
```

The Mythbuntu, Xubuntu, and Ubuntu Studio are all available, along with all the other editions and Ubuntu releases, on the cdimage server at:

```
http://cdimages.ubuntu.com/
```

Using BitTorrent: Transmission

Most current Linux and Windows systems support BitTorrent for downloading. BitTorrent provides an efficient, safe, and fast method for downloading large files. Various BitTorrent clients are available, including one from the original BitTorrent developer. Transmission is the preferred BitTorrent client for Ubuntu 12.04. When downloading a new release, just when it comes out, BitTorrent is often the only practical solution. In addition, it is the preferred download method for the DVD. One exception is if you have a slow Internet connection. BitTorrent relies on making multiple connections that can use up bandwidth quickly. For slow connections, especially just for the Desktop CD, you may want to download directly from the Ubuntu site.

The BitTorrent files for all versions (Desktop, DVD, Alternate, and Server) can be found at the primary download sites, along with direct downloads:

```
http://releases.ubuntu.com/releases/12.04
http://cdimages.ubuntu.com/releases/precise/release/
```

Jigdo (Jigsaw Download)

Jigdo (Jigsaw Download) combines the best of both direct downloads and BitTorrent, while maximizing use of the download data for constructing various editions. In effect, Jigdo sets up a BitTorrent download operation using just the Ubuntu mirror sites (no uploading). Jigdo automatically detects the mirror sites that currently provide the fastest download speeds and downloads your image file from them. Mirror sites accessed are switched as download speeds change. If you previously downloaded directly from mirrors, with Jigdo you no longer have to go searching for a fast download mirror site. Jigdo finds them for you.

See the Jigdo Download HowTo page at **http://help.ubuntu.com** for more details.

```
https://help.ubuntu.com/community/JigdoDownloadHowto
```

Jigdo is available for the server and alternate CD/DVDs. It is not used for the desktop versions (32 or 64 bit).

Jigdo downloads make use of **.jigdo** and **.template** files, which you can find at **http://releases.ubuntu.com**. The jigdo file for an i386 Alternate CD is:

```
ubuntu-12.04-alternate-i386.jigdo
```

Its full URL would be:

```
http://releases.ubuntu.com/releases/12.04/ubuntu-12.04-alternate-i386.jigdo
```

To run Jigdo you can use either the **jigit** or **jigdo-lite** commands. For **jigit**, first install the **jigit** package. The **jigit** command uses a **.jigit.conf** configuration file to specify the **.jigdo** and template files to use. Create your own **.jigit.conf** file and specify the URL for the jigdo and template files (be sure to use the preceding period when creating the **.jigit.conf** file name).

```
JIGDO=http://releases.ubuntu.com/precise/ubuntu-12.04-alternate-i386.jigdo
TEMPLATE=http://releases.ubuntu.com/precise/ubuntu-12.04-alternate-i386.template
```

Then run the **jigit** command in a terminal window with the disc image name. At the

Jigdo organizes the download into central repository that can be combined into different spins. If you download the Ubuntu desktop CD, and then later the server CD, the data already downloaded for the desktop CD can be used to build the server CD, reducing the actual downloaded data significantly. You will be prompted to provide the location of any mounted CD or CD image.

As an alternative, you can install the **jigdo-file** package and run the **jigdo-lite** command. You will be prompted for a **.jigdo** file. You can provide the URL for the **.jigdo** file for the ISO image you want, or download the **.jigdo** file first and provide its path name.

Metalinks

Metalinks are XML files that work like mirror lists, allowing download clients to easily choose a fast mirror and perform a more controlled download. You would use a download client that supports metalinks, like KGet, **gget**, or **aria2**. For more information about using metalink with Ubuntu see:

```
https://wiki.ubuntu.com/MetalinkIsoDownloads
```

For general information see.

```
http://en.wikipedia.org/wiki/Metalink
```

A metalink file will have the extension **.metalink**. The metalink file for the Alternate 64-bit CD is:

```
ubuntu-12.04-alternate-amd64.metalink
```

Metalink files for the Ubuntu editions are available at:

```
http://releases.ubuntu.com/releases/12.04/
```

Zsync

Ubuntu also provides zsync download for its Ubuntu ISO images. The **zsync** program operates like **rsync**, but with very little overhead. It is designed for distributing a single file to many locations. In effect, you are synchronizing your copy to the original. The zsync program is designed to download just those parts of the original that the downloaded copy needs. It uses a **.zsync** file that has the name of the ISO image you want to download. You can download **.zsync** files for Ubuntu ISO images from the **http://releases.ubuntu.com/precise/** download page.

The **zsync** program is very useful for users you have already download a pre-release version of an Ubuntu ISO image, such as the beta version. You would then rename the beta image file to that of the new release, and then perform a zsync operation on it using the appropriate **.zsync** file provided by the Ubuntu download page. Only those parts of the final version that differ from the beta version would be downloaded, greatly reducing the actual amount of data downloaded.

You can install **zsync** using the Synaptic Package Manager. For more information, see the zsync Man page and the Zsync site: **http://zsync.moria.org.uk/**. For information on how to use zsync with Ubuntu see:

```
http://ubuntu-tutorials.com/2009/10/29/use-zsync-to-update-existing-iso-images/
```

Installing Multiple-Boot Systems

The GRUB boot loader already supports multiple booting. Should you have both Ubuntu and Windows systems installed on your hard disks; GRUB will let you choose to boot either the Ubuntu system or a Windows system. During installation, GRUB will automatically detect any other operating systems installed on your computer and configure your boot loader menu to let you access them. You do not have to perform any configuration yourself.

If you want a Windows system installed on your computer, you should install it first if it is not already installed. Windows would overwrite the boot loader installed by a previous Ubuntu system, cutting off access to the Linux system. If you installed Windows after having installed Ubuntu, you will need to re-install the Ubuntu GRUB boot loader. See the section at the end of this Chapter on re-installing the boot loader. There are several ways you can do it, most very simple.

If you have already installed Windows on your hard drive and configured it to take up the entire hard drive, you can select the "Install alongside" option during installation to free up space and set up Ubuntu partitions.

Tip: You can also use the Ubuntu Live CD to start up Ubuntu and perform the necessary hard disk partitioning using GParted.

Hardware Requirements

Most hardware today meets the requirements for running Ubuntu. Ubuntu can be installed on a wide variety of systems, ranging from the very weak to the very powerful. The install procedure will detect most of your hardware automatically. You will only need to specify your keyboard, though a default is automatically detected for you. Ubuntu netbook support is intenerated into the Ubuntu Desktop CD.

Listed here are the minimum hardware requirements for installing a standard installation of the Ubuntu system on an Intel-based PC:

A 32-bit or 64-bit Intel- or AMD-based computer.

An Intel or compatible (AMD) microprocessor is required. For the Ubuntu Desktop a 1 GZ MHz processor or more is recommended

For 64-bit systems, be sure to use the 64-bit version of Ubuntu, which includes a supporting kernel.

A CD-ROM, DVD-ROM, or USB drive. Should you need to create a bootable DVD/CD-ROM, you will need a DVD/CD-RW drive. For a USB Live drive at least a 1GB drive.

Normally you will need at least 1GB RAM minimum, with 2 or more recommended.

8 GB of hard disk space

See the Ubuntu System Requirements page at **http://help.ubuntu.com** for details:

```
http://help.ubuntu.com/community/Installation/SystemRequirements
```

Installation Overview

Installing Ubuntu involves several processes, beginning with creating Linux partitions, and then loading the Ubuntu software, selecting a time zone, and creating new user accounts. The installation program used for Ubuntu is a screen-based program that takes you through all these processes, step-by-step, as one continuous procedure. You can use either your mouse or the keyboard to make selections. When you finish with a screen, click the Continue button at the bottom to move to the next screen. If you need to move back to the previous screen, click Back. You can also press TAB, the arrow keys, SPACEBAR, and ENTER to make selections.

Installation is a straightforward process. A graphical installation is easy to use, providing full mouse support.

Most systems today already meet hardware requirements and have automatic connections to the Internet.

They also support booting a DVD-ROM or CD-ROM disc, though this support may have to be explicitly configured in the system BIOS.

If you are installing on a blank hard drive or on a drive with free space, or if you are performing a simple update that uses the same partitions, installing Ubuntu is a simple process. Ubuntu also features an automatic partitioning function that will perform the partitioning for you.

A preconfigured set of packages are installed, so you will not even have to select packages.

For a quick installation, you can simply start up the installation process by placing your DVD or CD disc in the CD/DVD drive and starting up your system. Graphical installation is a simple matter of following the instructions in each window as you progress. Installation follows a few easy stages:

1. **Welcome**   A default language is chosen for you, like English, so you can usually just click Continue.

2. **Preparing to install**   On the "Preparing to install" screen your system is checked and you can opt to install updates during installation and certain third party software such as the Fluendo MP3 codec.

3. **Installation type**   For automatic partitioning you have different options depending on what other operating systems may have been installed on your hard drive. For drives that have other operating systems installed, you can install alongside them, or, if Ubuntu 11.10 is installed, choose to upgrade, or choose to erase the entire disk. In all cases you can also

choose to partition your disk manually instead. As soon as you click the "Install Now' button, formatting and installation begins.

4. **Installation type: partitioner**   Used for manual partitioning only, in which you set up partitions yourself. Otherwise this is skipped.

5. **Where are you?, Time Zone**   Use the map to choose your time zone or select your city from the drop-down menu.

6. **Keyboard Layout**   A default is chosen for you; you can usually just click Continue.

7. **Who are you?**   Set up a username and host name for your computer, as well as a password for that user. You can also choose to login automatically, as well as encrypt your home folder.

After the installation, the CD disc ejects and you will be asked to remove it and press ENTER. This will reboot your system.

Installation with the Ubuntu Desktop CD

The Ubuntu Desktop CD is designed for running Ubuntu from the CD (Live CD) and installing Ubuntu. Most users will use the Ubuntu Desktop CD to install Ubuntu. You can first start up Ubuntu, and then initiate an installation, or install directly. Just place the CD disc in the CD/DVD-ROM drive before you start your computer. After you turn on or restart your computer, the installation program starts up.

Tip: Most computers are already set up to boot first from the CD/DVD-ROM drive. If your computer cannot boot the CD/DVD disc, then the boot sequence may be set up in the wrong order. You may first have to change the boot sequence setting in your computer's BIOS so that the computer will try to boot first from the CD/DVD-ROM. This requires some technical ability and knowledge of how to set your motherboard's BIOS configuration.

On most screens, a Continue button is displayed on the lower-right corner of an installation dialog. Once finished with a screen, you click Continue to move on. In some cases, you will be able to click a Back button to return to a previous screen. As each screen appears in the installation, default entries will be selected, usually by the auto probing capability of the installation program. If these entries are correct, you can click Continue to accept them and go on to the next screen.

A menu bar at the top of the screen holds menu buttons for network, sound, power, and accessibility menus. The sound menu lets you adjust the sound or mute it. For more options, choose Sound Settings to open the Sound configuration dialog, which lets you set the output volume, choose a sound device should there be more than one, and adjust the alert volume.

Figure 2-1: Install CD network menu and Edit Connections dialog

Figure 2-2: Install CD Power menu and System Settings dialog

The network menu lets you configure network access, letting you choose a connection. For more complex connections, choose Edit Connection to configure wired, wireless, vpn, and dsl connections (see Figure 2-1). You can also disable networking, performing an offline install.

The session menu lets you restart, lock, or shut down your system. From the session menu you can also choose System Settings to open the System Settings dialog (see Figure 2-2). You can use System Settings to configure your hardware if necessary.

To configure your display settings choose Displays from the session menu, which opens a display dialog where you can set the screen resolution.

Welcome, Language, and Preparing to install

When the Ubuntu Desktop CD first boots, it displays a Welcome screen (see Figure 2-3) with buttons for two options as shown here.

```
Try Ubuntu
Install Ubuntu
```

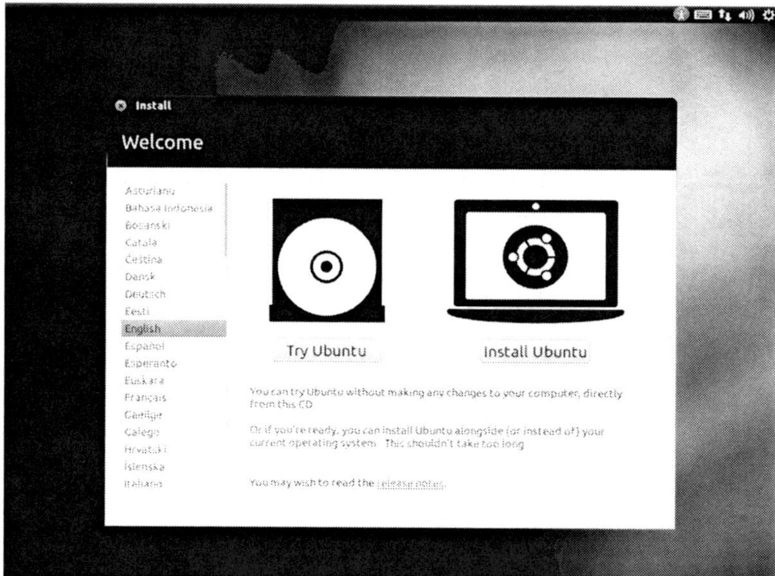

Figure 2-3: Install Welcome screen for Ubuntu Desktop CD

On the Welcome screen, select the language you want from the list on the left. A default language will already be selected, usually English. A link at the bottom of the right pane will display the Ubuntu release notes.

Click the "Install Ubuntu" button to start up the installation.

The "Try Ubuntu" button will start Ubuntu as a Live CD. However, even if you just opt to try Ubuntu, you can still perform an installation from the Live CD. To install, click the Install icon on the desktop (see Figure 2-4). The Install window opens to the Welcome screen for choosing your language, but without the button for choosing to try Ubuntu. Click the Continue button to start the installation.

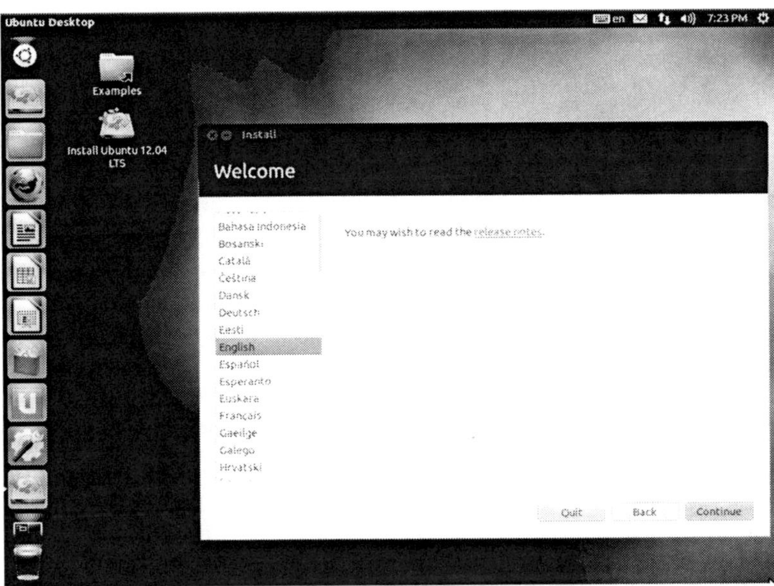

Figure 2-4: Live CD (Desktop) with Install icon.

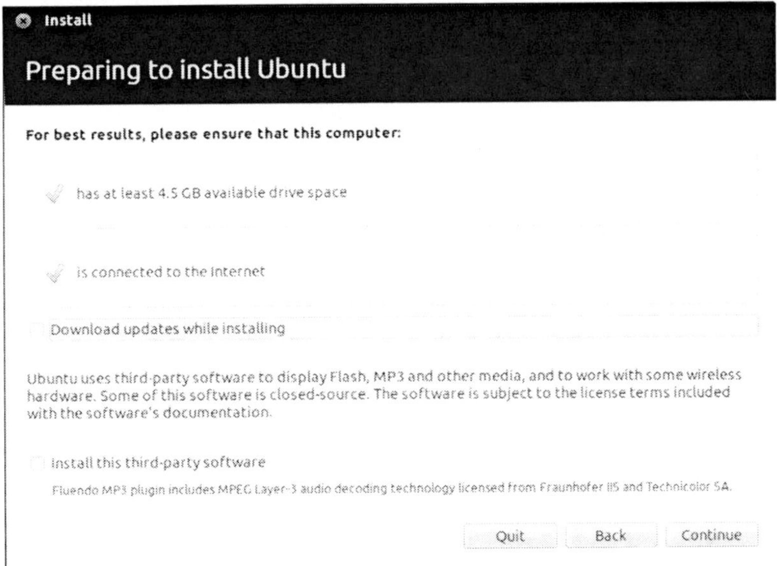

Figure 2-5: Preparing to install Ubuntu

The "Preparing to install Ubuntu" dialog appears that checks the recommended storage and connection requirements (see Figure 2-5): 4.5 GB of disk space, an Internet connection, and, if you are installing on a laptop, a plugged in power source (battery power is not recommended). The dialog also lets you choose to install the third party (non-open source) licensed Fluendo MP3 playback codec. You can also choose to download current updates while installing, using the latest packages and avoiding an extensive update after the install. This can take longer though. Click the Continue button to continue.

Your system detects your hardware, providing any configuration specifications that may be required.

Installation type

You are then asked to designate the Linux partitions and hard disk configurations you want to use on your hard drives. Ubuntu provides automatic partitioning that cover most situations, like using a blank or new hard drive and overwriting old partitions on a hard drive. Ubuntu can even re-partition a system with an operating system that uses all of the hard drive, but with unused space within it. In this case, the install procedure reduces the space used by the original operating system, and installs Ubuntu on the new free space. A default partition layout sets up a swap partition and a root partition of type **ext4** (Linux native) for the kernel and applications.

Warning: Like Ubuntu 11.10 and 11.04, Ubuntu 12.04 has changed the point at which changes are made to the hard disk and installation begins. Instead of presenting a "Ready to Install" screen after providing configuration information, formatting and installation begins right after the "Installation type" screen, as soon as you click the Install Now button.

Alternatively, you can configure your hard disk manually (the "Something else" option). Ubuntu provides a very simple partitioning scheme you can use to set up Linux partitions. Unless you are using the Alternate CD to install, LVM, RAID, and encrypted file systems are not supported during the install process.

With Ubuntu 12.04, for multiple boot systems using Windows, Ubuntu automatically detects a Windows system.

No partitions will be changed or formatted until you click the "Install Now" button. You can opt out of the installation until then, and your original partitions will remain untouched.

Warning: The "Erase disk and install Ubuntu" option will wipe out any existing partitions on the selected hard drive. If you want to preserve any partitions on that drive, like Windows or other Linux partitions, always choose a different option such as "Install Ubuntu alongside ..." or "Something else".

You are given choices, depending on the state of the hard disk you choose. A hard disk could be blank, have an older Ubuntu operating system on it, or have a different operating system such as Windows already installed. If an operating system is already installed, it may take up the entire disk or may only use part of the disk with the remainder available for the Ubuntu installation.

Tip: Some existing Linux systems may use several Linux partitions. Some of these may be used for just the system software, such as the boot and root partitions. These can be formatted. Others may have extensive user files, such as a **/home** partition that normally holds user home directories and all the files they have created. You should *not* format such partitions.

No detected operating systems

If no operating systems are detected on the hard drive, which is the case with a drive with only data files or a blank hard drive, you are given two choices: to use the entire disk or to specify partitions manually (see Figure 2-6). The message displayed on the Installation type dialog is:

"This computer currently has no detected operating systems. What would you like to do?"

You are given two choices.

```
Erase disk and install Ubuntu
Something else
```

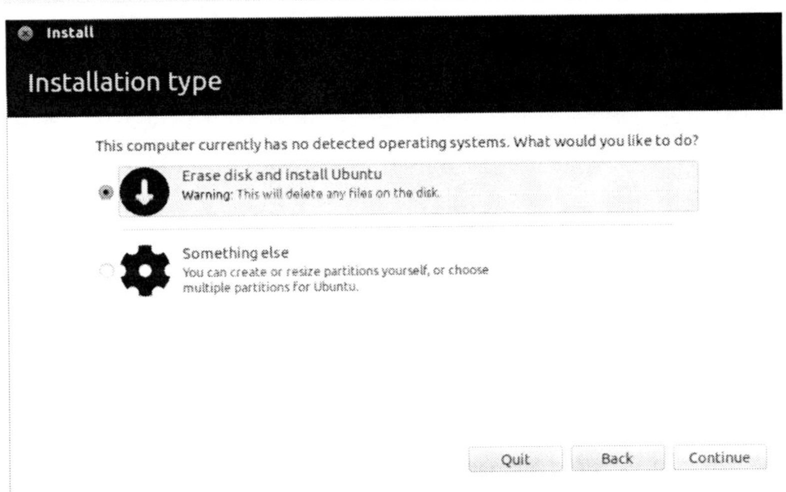

Figure 2-6: No detected operating systems

Erase disk and install Ubuntu

The "Erase disk and install Ubuntu" option is used usually on blank hard drives, though you can also use it on disks with file systems you no longer want. It will destroy any existing partitions if there are any, creating new partitions. Your hard drive will then have only your new Ubuntu system on it.

When you select this option, the install dialog displays the drive to be formatted from the Select drive drop-down menu and the device name and size of the disk to be formatted (see Figure 2-7).

Your hard drive is automatically partitioned creating two partitions, a primary partition for your entire file system (a root file system, /), and a swap partition. The swap partition is set up as a logical partition within an extended partition.

If you already have partitions on your disk, a warning message is displayed below the hard disk information listing the number of partition that will be deleted and providing a link to the "advanced partitioning tool" (manual partitioning).

3 partitions will be deleted, use the advanced partitioning tool for more control

Figure 2-7: Erase and use the entire disk

To erase the disk, click the Install Now button to perform formatting and continue with installation and configuration.

Automatic partitioning creates a small swap partition that is smaller than the size of your RAM memory. Normally a swap partition is the same size as RAM memory. A computer with 4 GB of memory should have a swap partition of the same size.

Detected Ubuntu operating system

If you have another Ubuntu operating system on your disk, you will have an option to erase the Ubuntu system and replace it with Ubuntu 12.04. If the installed Ubuntu system is version 11.10, then you are also given the option to upgrade your system, preserving your personal files and installed software (see Figure 2-8). You are also given the option to erase the installed operating system, and install the new system (Erase Ubuntu 11.10 and reinstall).

If there current system has enough unused space, you are also given an install alongside option, resizing the disk to free up space and installing 12.04 in added partitions on the free space. This will keep your original Linux system, as well as install the new one.

The message displayed on the Installation type dialog is something like this:

"This computer currently has Ubuntu 11.10 on it. What would you like to do?"

You are given three choices. The Upgrade Ubuntu option is selected by default.

```
Upgrade Ubuntu 11.10 to 12.04
Erase Ubuntu 11.10 and reinstall
Something else
```

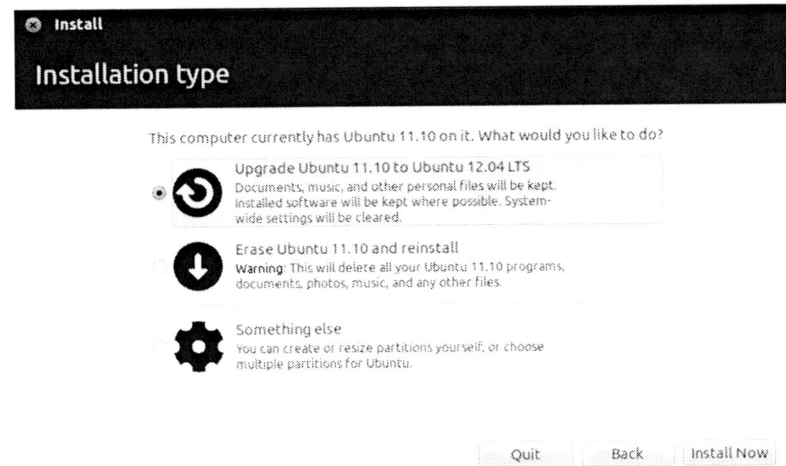

Figure 2-8: Install on disk with Ubuntu system

On systems that also have Windows installed alongside Ubuntu, you are given the same options, but with an added option to erase everything including your Windows system (see figure 2-9). You are warned that both Windows and Ubuntu are installed on your system. Should you choose to erase Ubuntu 11.10 and reinstall (the first entry), your Windows system will be preserved.

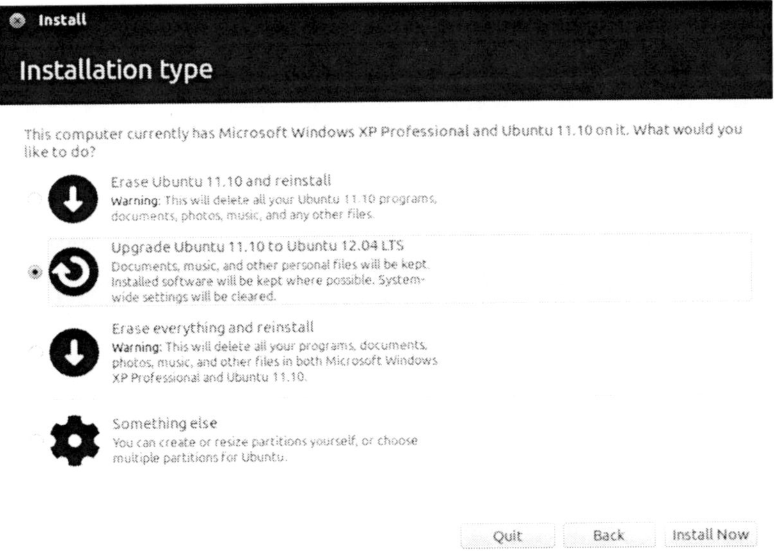

Figure 2-9: Install on disk with Ubuntu and Windows systems

You are given four choices. The Upgrade Ubuntu option is selected by default.

```
Erase Ubuntu 11.10 and reinstall
Upgrade Ubuntu 11.10 to 12.04
Erase everything and reinstall
Something else
```

Detected other operating systems with free space

If you have another operating system on your disk that has been allocated use of part of the disk, you will have an option beginning with "Install Ubuntu alongside" with the name of the installed operating system listed. A system with Windows XP already installed will have the option "Install Ubuntu alongside Microsoft Windows XP Professional" (see Figure 2-10). This option is selected initially.

The message displayed on the Installation type dialog is:

"This computer currently has Microsoft Windows XP Professional on it. What would you like to do?"

You are given three choices.

```
Install alongside other operating systems
Replace Microsoft Windows XP Professional with Ubuntu
Something else
```

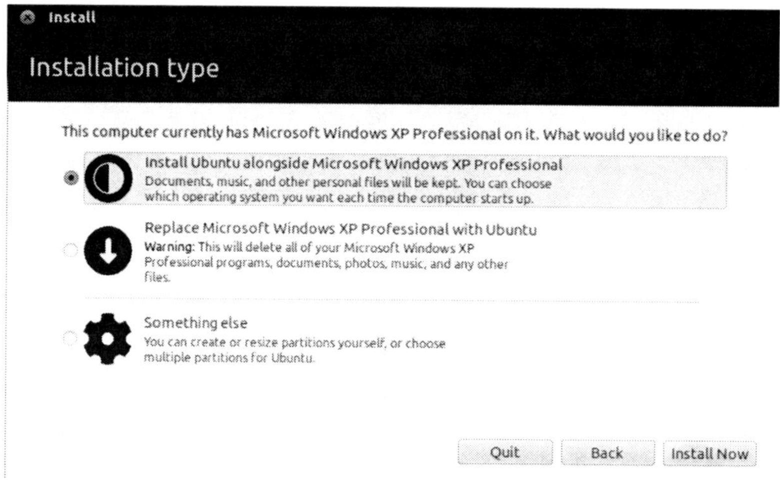

Figure 2-10: Install Ubuntu alongside

Detected other operating system using entire disk (resize)

If you have another operating system on your disk that has been allocated use of the entire disk, you will have an option beginning with "Install Ubuntu alongside" with the name of the installed operating system listed. A system with Windows XP already installed will have the option "Install Ubuntu alongside Microsoft Windows XP Professional" (see Figure 2-11). This option is selected initially.

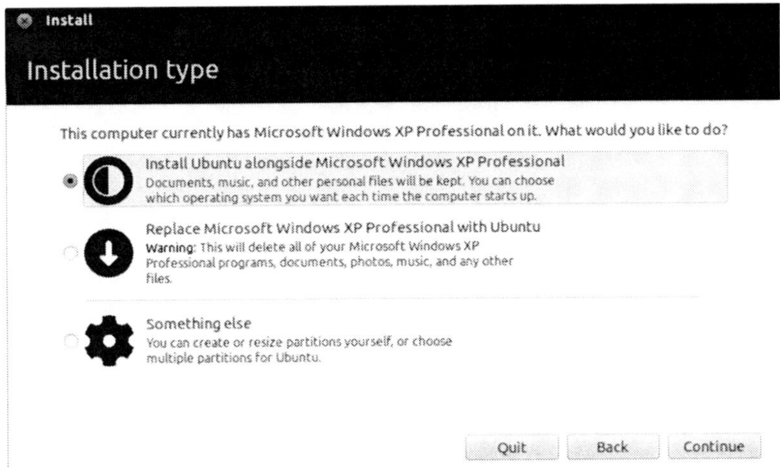

Figure 2-11: Install alongside other operating systems (freeing space on a full hard disk, resize)

This option is designed for use on hard disks with no unallocated free space but with a large amount of unused space on an existing partition. This is the case for a system where a partition has already been allocated the entire disk. This option will perform a resize of the existing partition, reducing that partition, and then creating an Ubuntu partition on that free space. Be warned that this could be a very time consuming operation. If the original operating system was used heavily, the disk could be fragmented, with files stored all over the hard disk. In this case, the files have to be moved to one area of the hard disk, freeing up continuous space on the remaining area. If the original operating system was used very lightly, then there may be unused continuous space already on the hard drive. In this case, re-partitioning would be quick.

On the "Install alongside" dialog two partition are displayed, the original showing the new size it will have after the resize, and the new partition for Ubuntu 12.04 formed from the unused space (see Figure 2-12). The size is automatically determined. You can adjust the size if you want by clicking on the space between the partitions to display a space icon, which you can drag left, or right to change the proportional sizes of the partitions.

Upon clicking the Install Now button, a dialog will prompt you with the warning that the resize cannot be undone and it may take a long time (see Figure 2-13). Click Continue to perform the resize, or click Go Back to return to the "Installation type" screen. The time it will take depends on the amount of fragmentation on the disk. If the unused space is mostly continuous (never been used), then the partitioning could happen very fast. On a more heavily used hard disk that is fragmented, partitioning could take longer. The disk would first be de-fragmented with files in the space to be freed up moved next to the used space.

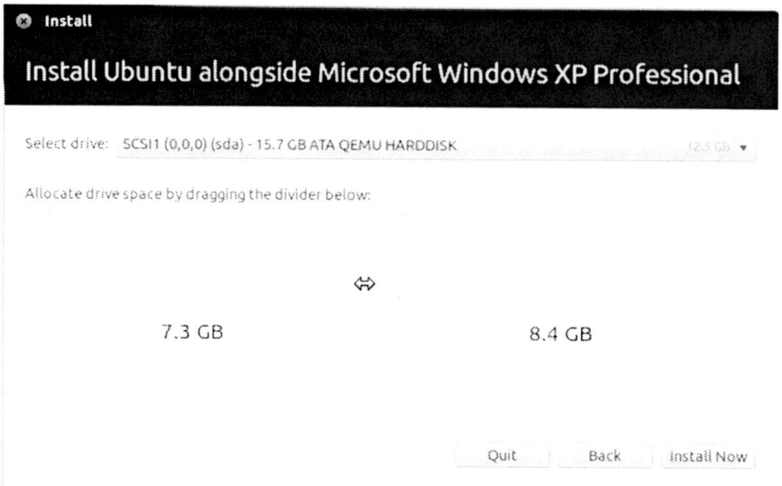

Figure 2-12: Install alongside partition resize

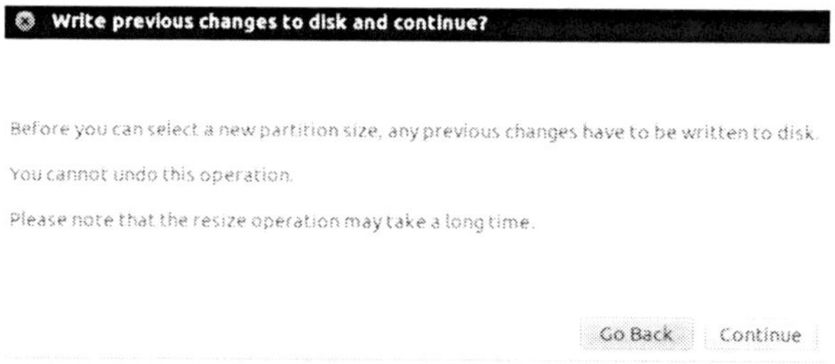

Figure 2-13: Resize warning

Something else

All install situations will include a "Something else" option to let you partition the hard drive manually. The "Something else" option starts up the partitioner, which will let you create, edit, and delete partitions. You can set your own size and type for your partitions. Use this option to preserve or reuse any existing partitions. When you have finished making your changes, click the Install Now button to continue. At this point, your partitions are changed and software installed, while you continue with the remaining install configuration for time zone and user login.

The partitioner screen displays the partitions on your current hard disk, and lists options for creating your Linux partitions. A graphical bar at the top shows the current state of your hard disk, showing any existing partitions, if any, along with their sizes and labels.

A Boot Loader section at the bottom of the screen provides a drop-down menu of hard drives where you can install the boot loader (see Figure 2-10). Your first hard drive is selected by default. If you have several hard drives on your system, you can choose the one on which to install the boot loader. Systems with only one hard drive such as laptops have only one hard drive entry.

Creating new partitions on a blank hard drive manually

To create partitions on a blank hard drive manually, choose "Something else". The partitioner interface starts up with the "Installation type" screen, listing any existing partitions (see Figure 2-14). A graphical bar at the top will show the partition on your selected hard drive. For a blank hard drive, this will be empty. Your current hard disks and their partitions are listed in the main scrollable pane, with headings for Device, Type, Mount point, Format, Size, and Used space for each partition. For a blank hard drive, the hard drive is listed with a free space entry for the entire drive. At the bottom of the screen are actions you can perform on partitions and free space: New partition table, Add, Change, Delete, and Revert.

For a new blank hard drive, you first create the partition table by clicking the New Partition Table button. This displays a warning that it will erase any data on the drive. Click Continue. The warning dialog is there in case you accidentally click the New Partition Table button on a drive that has partitions you want to preserve. In this case, you can click Go Back and no new partition table is created (see Figure 2-15).

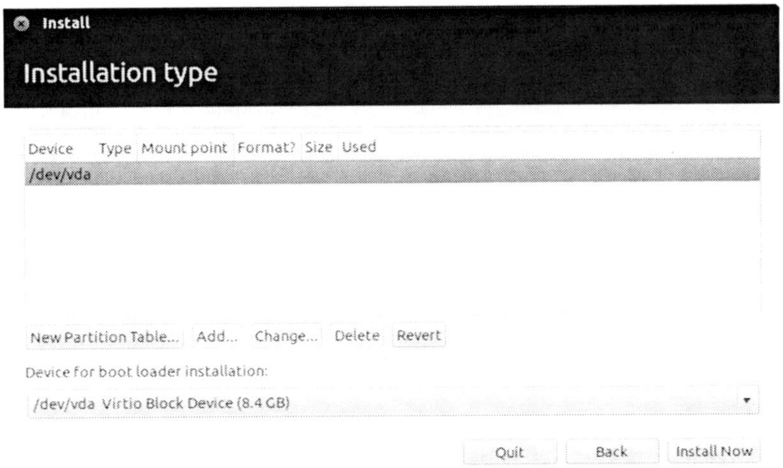

Figure 2-14: Manually partitioning a new hard drive

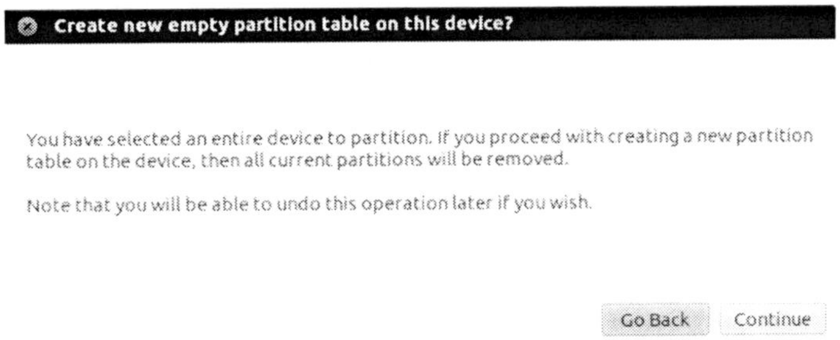

Figure 2-15: Create a new partition table on a blank hard drive

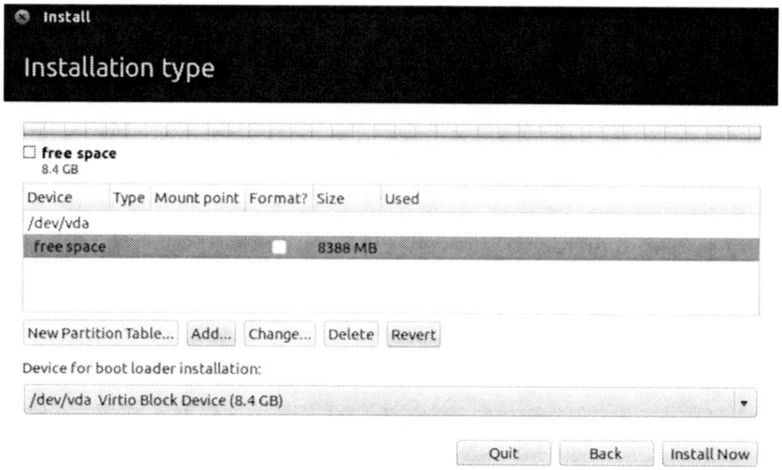

Figure 2-16: Select free space on a blank hard drive

You will have to create at least two partitions, one swap and the other a Linux partition where your system will be installed.

To create a new partition, select the free space entry for the hard disk (see Figure 2-16) and click the Add button. This opens a Create Partition dialog where you can choose the file system type (Use as) and the size of your partition (see Figure 2-17). Do this for each partition.

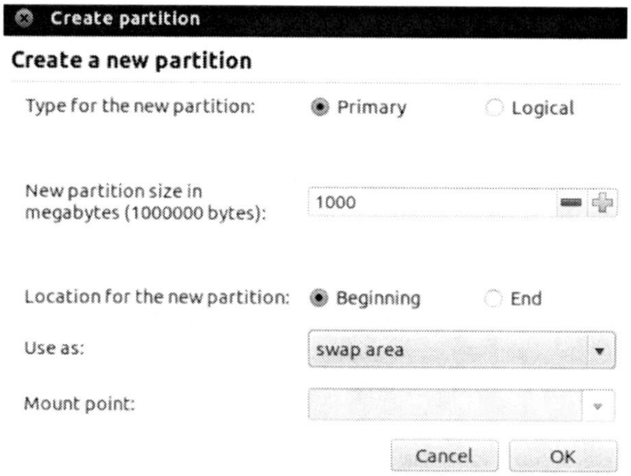

Figure 2-17: Create a new root partition

The Create Partition dialog displays entries for the partition type (Primary or Logical), the size in megabytes, the location (beginning or end), the file system type (Use as), and the Mount point. For the partition type, the "Do not use" partition entry is initially selected. Choose a partition type from the drop-down menu. Select "Ext4 journaling file system" for the root partition and choose Swap for the swap partition.

The swap partition will have no mount point. You only set the size, normally to the amount of your computer's RAM memory (see Figure 2-18).

For the root partition, from the Mount point drop down menu choose the mount point /, which is the root directory (see Figure 2-18). This is where your system will be installed. The size of the partition is specified in megabytes. It will be set to the remaining space. If you have not already set up the swap partition, reduce the size to allow space for the swap partition.

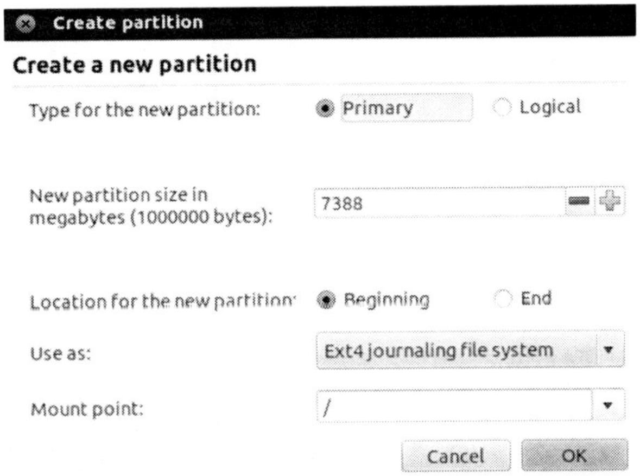

Figure 2-18: Create a new swap a partition

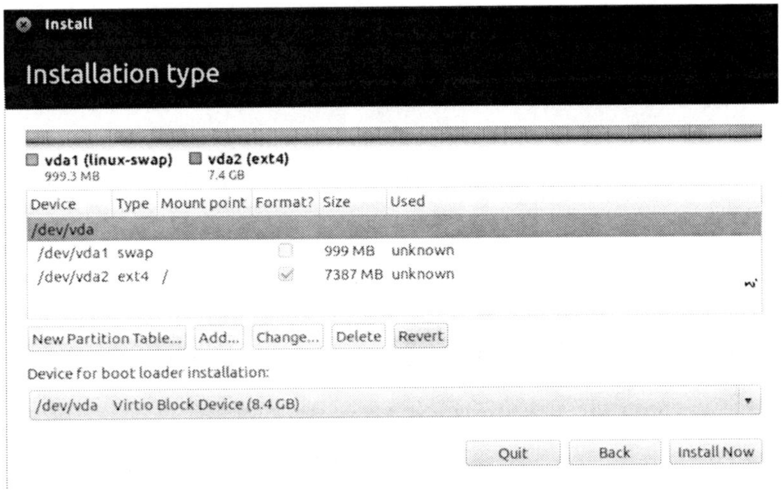

Figure 2-19 Manual partitions

If you make a mistake, you can edit a partition by selecting it and clicking the Change button. This opens an Edit partitions window where you can make changes. You can also delete a partition, returning its space to free space, and then create a new one. Select the partition and click the Delete button. The partition is not actually deleted at this point. No changes are made at all until you start installing Ubuntu. The "Revert" button is always available to undo all the changes you specified so far, and start over from the original state of the hard disk.

When you have finished setting up your partitions, you will see entries for them displayed. The graphical bar at the top will show their size and location (see Figure 2-19). Click the Install Now button to perform the partitioning, formatting, and installation.

Reuse existing Linux partitions on a hard drive

If you already have a hard drive with Linux partitions that you want to reuse, you choose the "Something else" option on the "Installation type" screen (see Figure 2-6). In this case, you have a hard disk you are using for Linux, with partitions already set up on the hard drive for your Ubuntu systems. However, you do not want to keep any of the data on those partitions. This situation occurs if you are using a previous Ubuntu version, but want a fresh install instead of an upgrade, and you do not want to perform any partitioning, keeping the current partition configuration. You can just overwrite the existing Ubuntu root partition. In effect, you just want to reuse those partitions for the new release, creating an entirely new install, but with the old partitions. With this action, all current data on those partitions will be destroyed. This procedure avoids having to change the partition table on the hard drive. You just keep the partitions you already have. In this case, you wish to overwrite existing partitions, erasing all the data on them.

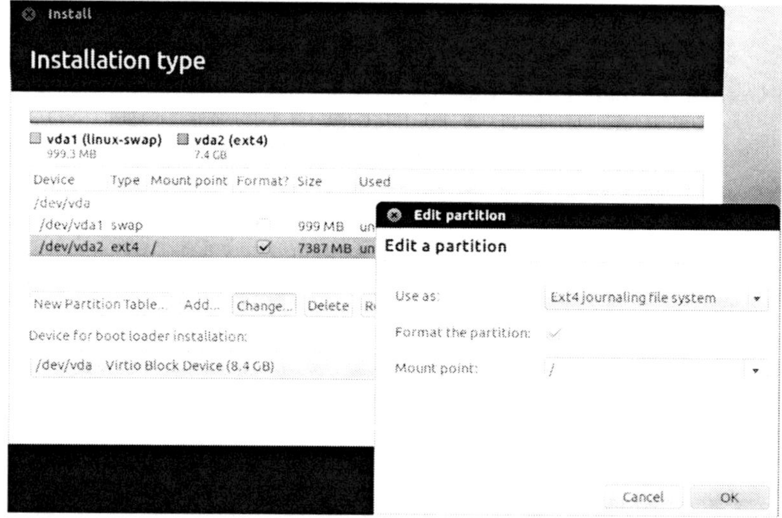

Figure 2-20: Reuse existing partitions on a hard drive

This procedure is used often for users that have already backed up their data, and just want to create a fresh install on their hard disk with the new release. Also, a Linux system could be configured to save data on a partition separate from the root partition, like a separate partition for the **/home** directories. In this case, you would only need to overwrite the root partition, leaving the other Linux partitions alone.

The partitioner interface lists any existing partitions. The graphical bar at the top will show the partition on your selected hard drive. The depiction changes as you add, delete, or edit your partitions (see Figure 2-18). Each partition device name and label will be displayed. Unused space will be labeled as free space.

Each hard disk is labeled by its device name, such as **sda** for the first Serial ATA device. Underneath the hard disk graphics bar are labels for the partitions and free space available, along with the partition type and size. The partitions are identified by their colors. At the bottom of the screen are actions you can perform on partitions and free space: New Partition Table, Add, Change, Delete, and Revert.

Note: The New partition table becomes active whenever the top-level hard drive device name is selected instead of a particular partition. This will be initially selected when your Prepare partition screen if first displayed, activating the New partition table button. Do NOT click it. It will wipe out any existing partitions.

To edit an existing partition, click on its entry and click the Change button. A dialog opens with entries for the partition type (Use as), a format checkbox, and the mount point (see Figure 2-18).

To re-use partitions, all you have to do is edit your existing root partition. You will see your partitions listed. You can leave the swap partition alone.

You will have to know which partition is your root partition. It will have the type **ext4**. Once selected, the Change button will become active, which you click to open an Edit window. Select the type, which for Ubuntu 12.04 would be "Ext4 journaling file system", the **ext4** file system type. Then select the mount point, which, for the root partition, is /. The size remains the same (see Figure 2-17). Once finished, you will see your Windows partition (**ntfs**) if there is one, as well as the swap and Linux root partition (**ext4**).

Once you have edited the root partition, you can click the "Install Now" button to continue on.

Where Are You?

On the "Where are you?" screen, you can set the time zone by using a map to specify your location (see Figure 2-21). The Time Zone tool uses a map feature that displays the entire earth, with sections for each time zone. Click on your general location, and the entire time zone for your part of the world will be highlighted in green. The major city closest to your location will be labeled with its current time. The selected city will appear in the text box located below the map. You can also select your time zone entering the city in the text box below. As you type in the city name, a pop-up menu appears showing progressively limited choices. The corresponding time zone will be highlighted on the map, along with the city time.

Click the Continue button to continue.

At the same time as the "Where are you?" dialog appears, Ubuntu begins to format your partitions, copy files to your hard drive, and install the software. A progress bar at the bottom of the dialog shows the progression of the copy process. You can click an expansion arrow next to the progress bar to open a small terminal section that displays the install operations as they occur.

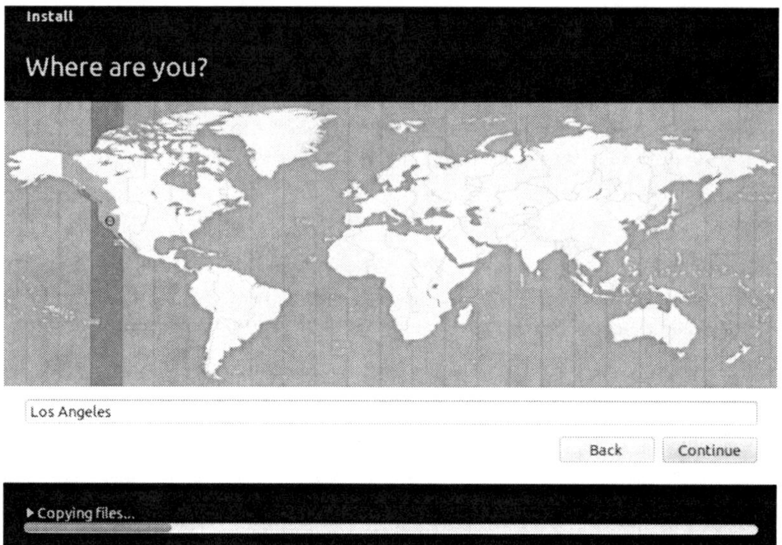

Figure 2-21: Where Are You, Time zone

Keyboard Layout

You are then asked to select a keyboard layout, "Choose your keyboard layout." Keyboard entries are selected first by location in the left scroll box, and then by type on the right scroll box. A default is already selected, such as USA (see Figure 2-22). If the selection is not correct, you can choose another keyboard, first by location in the left scroll box, and then by type on the right scroll box.

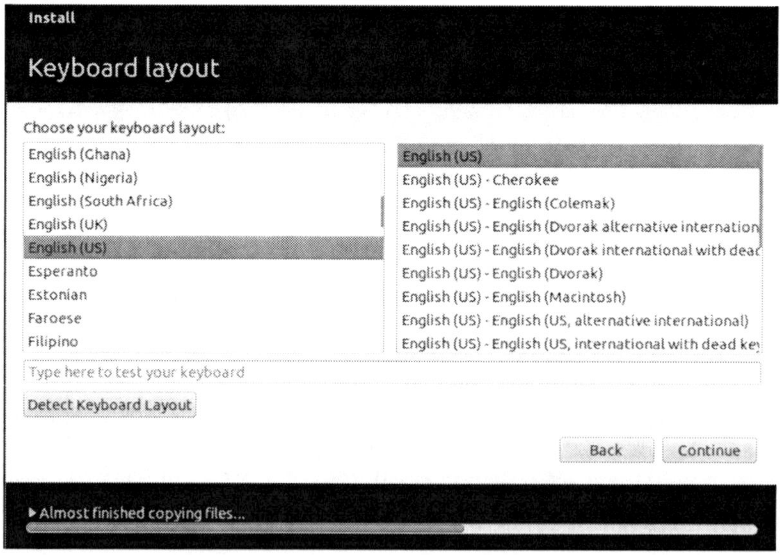

Figure 2-22: Keyboard Layout

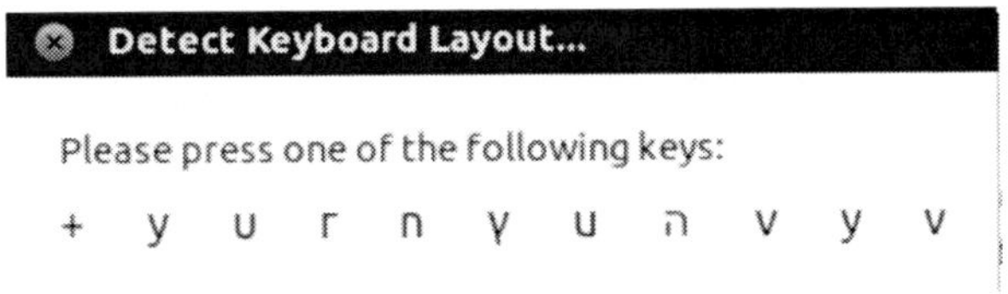

Figure 2-23: Keyboard Layout Guess option

To test your keyboard, click on the text box at the bottom of the screen and press keys, "Type here to test your keyboard."

The "Figure out keyboard layout" button tries to detect the keyboard using your input (see Figure 2-23). A series of dialogs opens prompting you to press keys and asking you if certain keys are present on your keyboard. When the dialogs finish, the detected keyboard is then selected in the "Choose your keyboard layout" scroll boxes.

Click the Continue button to continue.

Who Are You?

On the Who are you? screen you enter your name, your user log in name, and password (see Figure 2-24). When you enter your name, a user name will be generated for you using your first name, and a computer name will be entered using your first name and your computer's make and model name. You can change these names if you want. The name for the computer is the computer's network host name. The user you are creating will have administrative access, allowing you to change your system configuration, add new users and printers, and install new software. When you enter your password a Strength notice is displayed indicating whether it is too short, weak, fair, or good. For a good password include numbers and uppercase characters.

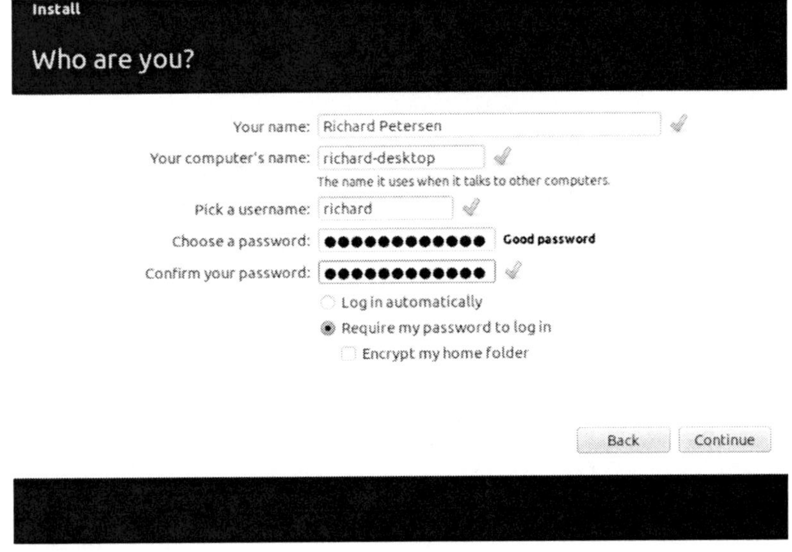

Figure 2-24: Who are you?

At the bottom of the screen, you have the options: "Log in automatically" and "Require my password to log in." The "Require my password to log in" option has an additional check box for "Encrypt my home folder." Choose the "Log in automatically" option to have your system login to your account when you start up, instead of stopping at the login screen. The "Require my password to log in" entry provides a standard login screen. If you choose "Encrypt my home folder" private directory encryption is set up for your home folder, encrypting all the home folder files and subdirectories.

Note: If your computer supports a camera, the next screen will prompt you to choose an image to use for the user. You can choose an icon or snap a picture of yourself.

Importing from Windows

If your hard disk has a Windows system on it, then you are prompted to import your personal files from your Windows system (see Figure 2-25).

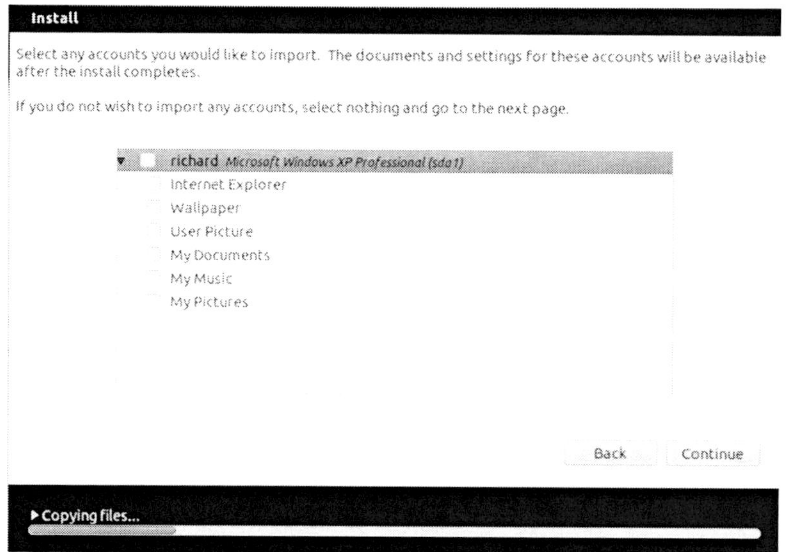

Figure 2-25: Importing personal files from Windows system

Install Progress

Your installation continues with a slide show of Ubuntu 12.04 features such as Web browsers, social services, the Ubuntu music store, the Ubuntu Software Center, Shotwell photo editing, and Ubuntu One synching, You can click on the arrow tabs at either end to move through the slide show manually (see Figure 2-24).

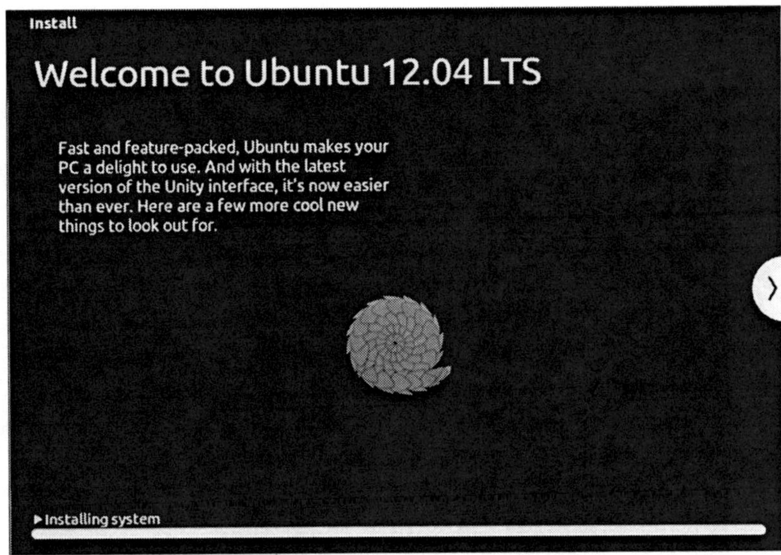

Figure 2-26: Install progress slide show

Once finished, the Installation Complete dialog appears (see Figure 2-26). Click the Restart Now button to restart and reboot to the new installation. Your CD disc is ejected, and a screen will appear prompting you to remove the disc, and then press ENTER. If you installed from the LiveCD session, you are also given the option to return to the LiveCD session.

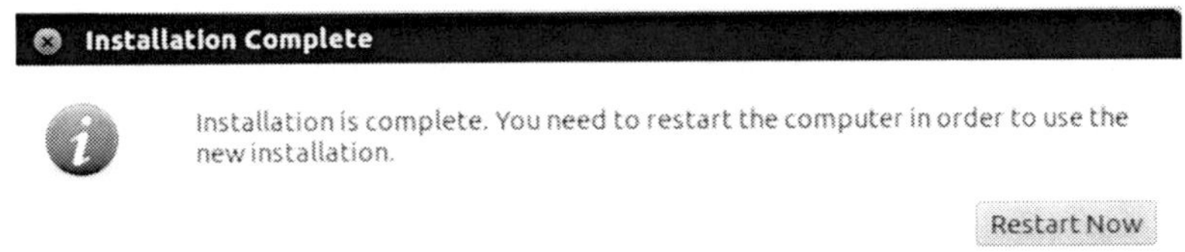

Figure 2-27: Installation completed

Installation Startup for the Ubuntu Alternate CD and Install/live DVD

The Ubuntu Alternate CD and Install/Live DVD use the original installation start up screen used in previous releases. A simple cursor-based menu is displayed whose items you can choose using your keyboard arrow keys and the ENTER key. Function keys allow you to choose install options.

Ubuntu Install/Live DVD

The Install/Live DVD is designed for users who intend to perform an installation, though it also serves as a Live DVD. It is a full DVD with about 2GB of software on the disc. As with the CD, you will have the option to just try Ubuntu or go directly to the Install procedure. The Install option will install the Ubuntu desktop. The Install DVD install screen (see Figure 2-28) displays the following options:

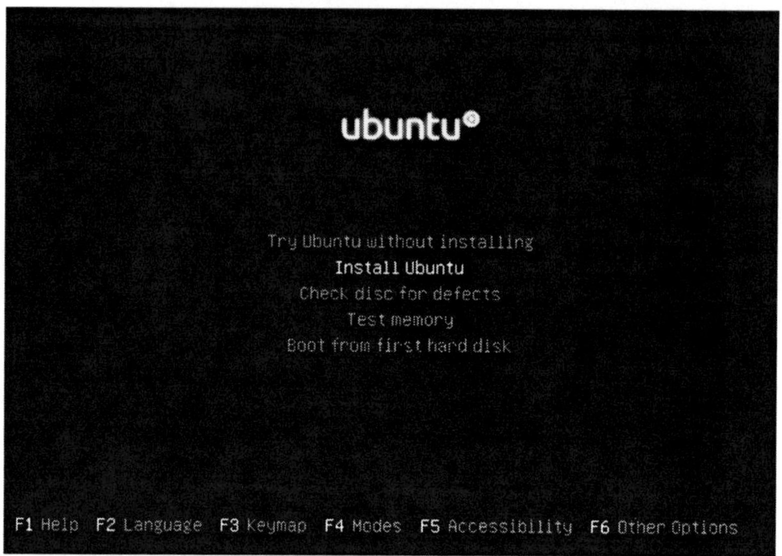

Figure 2-28: Install DVD Install screen

```
Try Ubuntu without installing
Install Ubuntu
Check CD for defects
Test Memory
Boot from first hard disk
```

You can also use the DVD to boot from the first hard disk, should there be an Ubuntu system already installed there, "Boot from first hard disk." This can be helpful if you have problems booting to your system. You can use the DVD to boot to the installed system and then try to configure a solution.

Alternate CD

The Ubuntu Alternate CD displays a cursor-based install screen (see Figure 2-29). The Alternate CD supports specialized features like LVM, RAID, and encrypted file systems. For very detailed key installation topics from obtaining the CD to starting up the system for the first time, as well as appendices on partitioning and automatic installs, check the "Installing Ubuntu 12.04 from the Alternate CD" at:

```
https://help.ubuntu.com/12.04/installation-guide/index.html
```

The Alternate CD uses a text-based installation interface. You use the TAB key to move between entries, and the arrow and spacebar keys to select and choose items in a menu. Installation tasks are similar to those of the Ubuntu DVD.

The Alternate CD provides options for to setting up LVM partitions (see Figure 2-30). A default LVM partition will create a separate boot partition and then an LVM Group partitions with volumes for the swap and root partitions.

You are informed of the changes in partitions that will be formatted. You then create a new user, and the software is installed.

If an installed system fails for some reason, you can use the Ubuntu Alternate CD to try to fix it. Choose "Rescue a broken system" to start up the system in the command line, mounting it to a directory from which you can access the broken system. You can then try to change configuration settings to fix the problem. You will be able to choose from the same menu described later in the "Rescue a broken system" section.

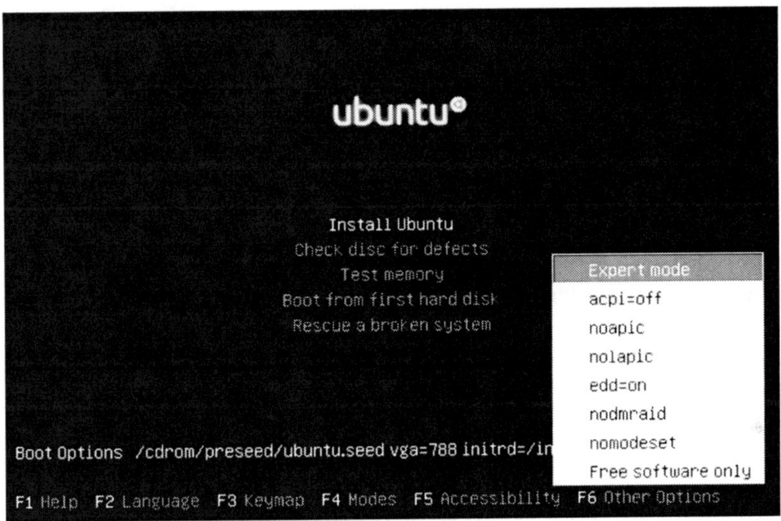

Figure 2-29: Alternate CD Install screen

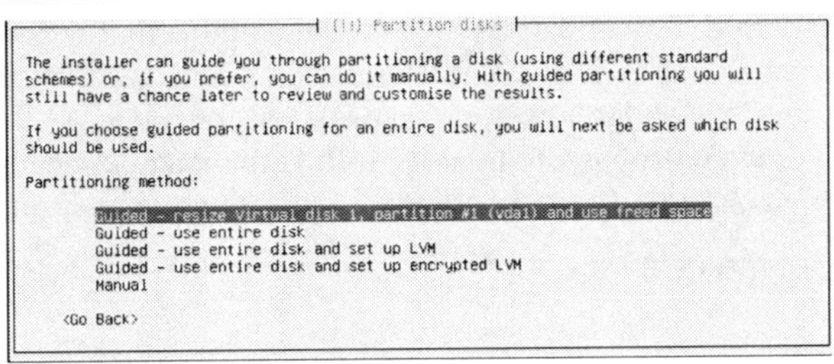

Figure 2-30: Alternate partition choices

Ubuntu Install Options for Alternate CD and Live/Install DVD

The Alternate CD and Live/Install DVD have the same initial install screen where you can choose options (see Figures 2-28 and 2-27). Along the bottom of the screen are options you can set for the installation process. These are accessible with the function keys, 1 through 6. Press ESC to close a menu without making a selection.

```
F1 Help F2 Language F3 Keymap F4 Modes F5 Accessibility F6 Other Options
```

A description of these options is listed here:

F1 Help Boot parameters and install prerequisites

F2 Languages   List of languages, pop-up menu

F3 Keymap   Languages for keyboard, pop-up menu

F4 Modes List of possible install modes: For the Ubuntu Alternate CD there are four modes: Normal, OEM install, Install a command-line system, and Install an LTSP server. The OEM install is a special kind of installation that allows an administrator to configure the installation before turning over access. The command line only install allows you to perform a command line only installation (like the Server CD). For the Ubuntu DVD you have two modes for the standard installation: OEM and use of a driver CD. Install with driver update CD is used for a CD with more current driver updates, particularly for newer hardware. The driver CD allows you to use a CD with special drivers for your system.

F5 Accessibility   None, High Contrast (Contrast setting), Magnifier, Screen Reader, Braille Terminal (Braille support), Keyboard Modifiers, and On-Screen Keyboard.

F6 Other options, Opens an editable text line labeled Boot Options that lists the options of the currently selected menu choice. You can add other options here, or modify or remove existing ones. As you move down the list of menu choices, you will see the listed options change, showing the boot options for that choice. The Other Option menu lists several specialized options like acpi=off, noapic, nolapic, edd=on, nodmraid (hardware RAID), and Free Software only.

Use the arrow keys to move from one menu entry to the next, and press ENTER to select the entry. Should you need to add options press the TAB key. A command line is displayed where you can enter the options. Current options will already be listed. Use the backspace key to delete and arrow keys to move through the line. Press the ESC key to return to the menu.

The OEM install mode (Modes) is used for organizations that will be installing Ubuntu on several machines, but want to add their own applications and configurations to the install. The OEM install will set up an OEM default user with a password provided by the installer. When the installer is ready to turn over control to a regular user, then the installer can run the **oem-prepare** command that will set up a normal user and password, removing the OEM user.

Tip: Pressing ESC from the graphics menu places you at the boot prompt, boot, for text mode install.

Upgrading

You can upgrade a current Ubuntu system to the next release using the APT package manager or an Alternate CD. Upgrading is a simple matter of updating software to the new release versions, along with updating your GRUB configuration. Check the following site for upgrade details:

```
https://help.ubuntu.com/community/PreciseUpgrades
```

You can only upgrade to Ubuntu 12.04 from Ubuntu 11.10 or from Ubuntu 10.04. Be sure you have first performed any needed updates for your Ubuntu 11.10 system. It must be completely up to date before you perform an upgrade to Ubuntu 12.04.

You cannot upgrade from Ubuntu 10.10, 11.04, or earlier to 12.04 directly. To upgrade from an earlier release other than 10.04, first upgrade sequentially up to 11.10. For example, to upgrade from 11.04, you would first upgrade to 11.10, and then you can upgrade from 11.10 to 12.04. To upgrade from 10.04 check the release notes. Be sure to start the update manager with the **update-manager -d** command in a terminal or command window (Atl-F2).

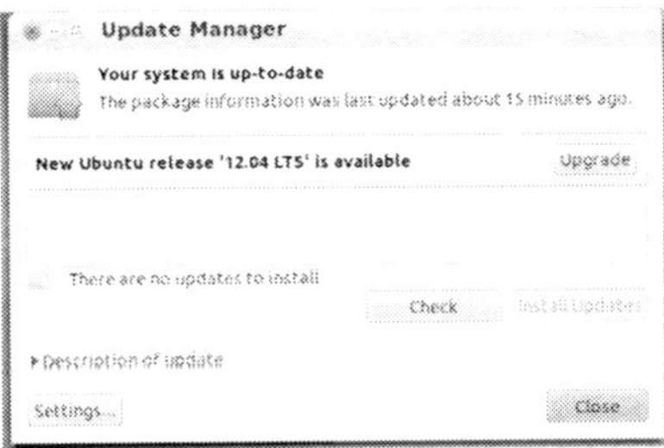

Figure 2-31: Upgrade message

Upgrade over a network from Ubuntu 11.10

To upgrade your system using your Internet connection, you can use the Update Manager. The upgrade will be performed by downloading the latest package versions from the Ubuntu repository, directly. When a new release becomes available, Update Manager will display a message notifying you of the new release (provided it is configured to do so). An Upgrade button will be displayed next to the message should you decide to upgrade your system to that release (see Figure 2-31). If you want to stay with the Ubuntu 11.10 release for now, you just ignore the message. Should you want to upgrade to the new release, in this case Ubuntu 12.04, you click the Upgrade button to start the upgrade. Be sure first to update all you current software. An upgrade should be performed from the most recent versions of your current release's software packages.

You can also start the update manager directly for the distribution upgrade by entering the following on a command line (the **-d** option performs a distribution upgrade). Use either a terminal window or press Alt-F2 to open a Run Application window.

```
gksu update-manager -d
```

A Distribution Upgrade dialog opens showing the progress of the upgrade (see Figure 2-32). The upgrade procedure will first prepare the upgrade, detecting the collection of software packages that have to be downloaded. A dialog will notify you of software packages for which support has ended (older deprecated software). Then a dialog will then open asking if you want to start the upgrade, displaying both a Cancel and Start Upgrade button (see Figure 2-33). You can still cancel the upgrade at this time and nothing will be changed on your system (click the Cancel button). To continue with the Upgrade, click the Start Upgrade button.

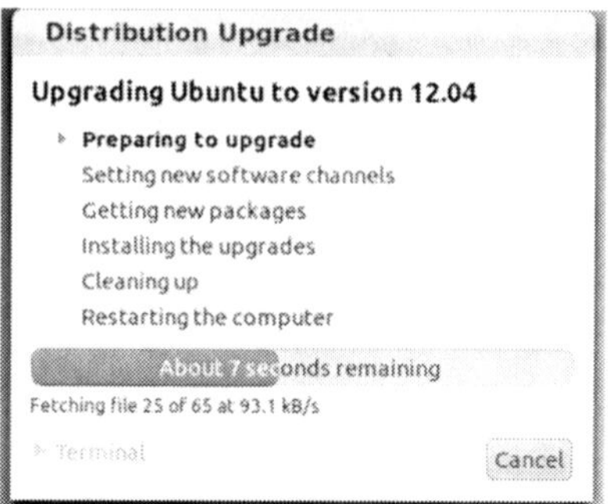

Figure 2-32: Distribution Upgrade dialog

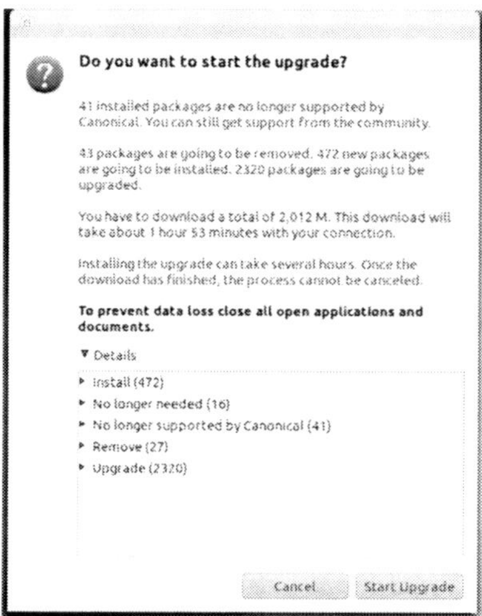

Figure 2-33: List of Upgrade packages with Cancel and Start Upgrade buttons

The Distribution Upgrade dialog is again displayed (see Figure 2-34). Packages are downloaded (Getting new packages), and then installed on your system (Installing the upgrades). The download process can take some time depending on the speed of your Internet connection.

If the download is taking too long, you can click the Cancel button and run the upgrade later. A dialog is displayed telling you that the download will continue later from where it left off.

To start the upgrade again, first start the Update Manager, click the Upgrade button, and proceed through the initial steps again, though this time will be much faster (Release notes, Preparing to upgrade, Setting new software channels). The Getting new packages stage will continue with next package.

Note: Depending on the packages you are upgrading, you may have to enter configuration information through the terminal interface. Click the terminal arrow to open the terminal interface and respond to any prompts that may occur.

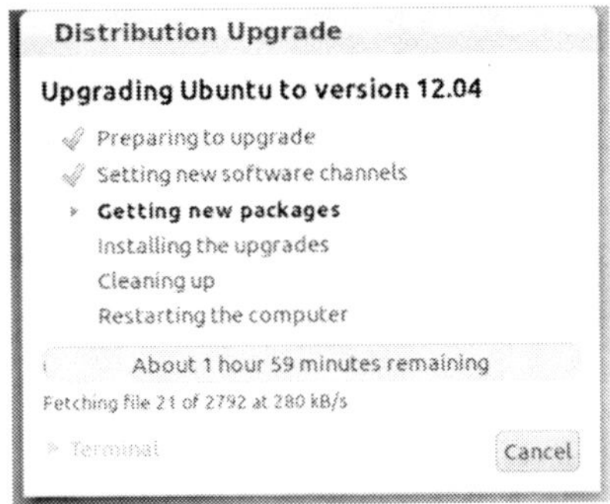

Figure 2-34: Distribution Upgrade dialog, downloading packages

If you modified your GRUB configuration file (**/etc/default/grub**), then during the install packages process for the upgrade, you will be prompted whether to keep your local modified version or the new version provided with the release. A dialog will open with the query "What do you want to do about modified configuration file grub". Several options are available from the drop down menu. The default is to keep your current grub file. However, this will use your old Ubuntu kernel from the previous release. To use the new kernel, select the first option, the "Install the package maintainer's version" entry.

You also have the option to examine the differences between your current grub configuration file and the new maintainer's version, as well as opening a shell to display the versions. Performing a three-way merger is something you would do if you had set up your own customized version entries.

Once the upgrade is completed, a completion message is displayed. Reboot to start your system with the new release and its kernel.

Upgrade using a CD (Alternate CD)

If the Ubuntu servers are busy or slow, you may find it easier and faster to upgrade using the Alternate CD. You can choose to install packages from the CD instead of from the Ubuntu repository, avoiding a lengthy download over a network.

Keep in mind that upgrading using packages on the CD only upgrades to the package versions in the official release, not the latest updated versions available on the Ubuntu repository. You would still have to perform an added update for the 12.04 packages from the Ubuntu repository, which could be time consuming, depending on the number of packages that have to be updated.

To upgrade from a CD, you use the Alternate CD, not the Ubuntu Desktop CD. Download the Alternate CD ISO image file from the **http://releases.ubuntu.com/precise** site.

```
http://releases.ubuntu.com/precise/
```

Then burn the ISO image file to a CD disc and insert it. You can also mount the CD ISO image file directly on your Ubuntu system using the following command, which uses a **mount** command with the **loop** option to mount the ISO image to the **/media/cdrom** device interface. First create the **/media/cdrom** folder if it does not already exist.

```
sudo mkdir -p /media/cdrom
sudo mount -o loop ~/Desktop/ubuntu-12.04-alternate-i386.iso /media/cdrom
```

Once inserted and mounted, the Alternate CD will display a dialog prompting you to upgrade using that CD.

If the dialog is not displayed you can manually start it with the following command to run the **cdromupgrade** command on the Alternate CD.

```
gksu "sh /cdrom/cdromupgrade"
```

The upgrade progresses much like the network upgrade. The Distribution Upgrade dialog is displayed with tasks listed for Preparing to upgrade, Setting new software channels (for downloading updated packages), and Getting new packages.

Upgrading to a new release with apt-get

You can also use the **apt-get** command in a terminal window or on a command line interface to upgrade your system. To upgrade to an entirely new release you use the **dist-upgrade** option. A **dist-upgrade** would install a new release, preserving your original configuration and data. This option will also remove obsolete software packages.

```
sudo apt-get update
sudo apt-get dist-upgrade
```

Recovery, rescue, and boot loader re-install

Ubuntu provides the means to start up systems that have failed for some reason. A system that may boot but fails to start up, can be started in a recovery mode, already set up for you as an entry on your boot loader menu. A system that you cannot even boot may require work that is more advanced. You can access such a broken system using the Alternate CD. If you just need to re-install the boot loader (required if you re-installed Windows on a dual boot system after your Ubuntu install), then you can use the Alternate CD with the "Rescue a broken system" option, and then choose to re-install the boot loader.

Recovery

If for some reason your system is not able to start up, it may be due to conflicting configurations, libraries, or applications. Select the recovery mode entry from the GRUB boot menu, the Ubuntu kernel entry with the (recovery mode) label attached to the end, as shown here.

```
Ubuntu, with Linux 3.2.0-23-generic-pae (recovery mode)
```

This will start up a menu where you can use the arrow and ENTER keys to select from several recovery options (see Figure 2-35). These include resume, clean, dpkg, grub, netroot, and root. Short descriptions for each item are displayed on the menu.

The root option will start up Ubuntu as the root user with a command line shell prompt. In this case, you can boot your Linux system in a recovery mode and then edit configuration files with a text editor such as Vi, remove the suspect libraries, or reinstall damaged software with **apt-get**.

The resume entry will start up Ubuntu normally, but into the command line mode.

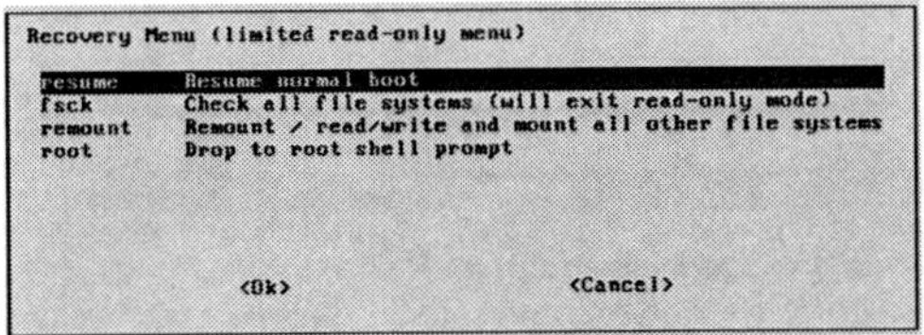

Figure 2-35: Recovery options

The **grub** entry will update the grub boot loader. With GRUB2, your hard drive is re-scanned, detecting your installed operating systems and Ubuntu kernels, and implementing any GRUB configuration changes you may have made without updating GRUB.

Rescue a broken system

If you are not able to start up your system from your hard disk install, you can boot up with either the Ubuntu DVD or the Alternate CD and choose "Rescue a broken system" from the Start up menu (see Figure 2-36).

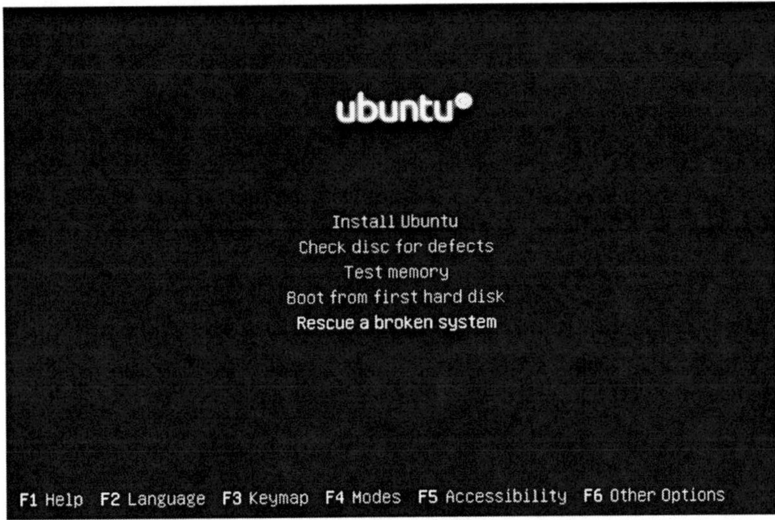

Figure 2-36: Alternate CD choices (Rescue a broken system)

Follow the prompts to start up your system, selecting the hard disk partition when requested. The "Enter rescue mode" screen appears which provides options to mount your system (see Figure 2-37). Your broken system will be mounted and made accessible with a command line interface. You can then use command line operations and editors to fix configuration files.

If you need to reinstall the boot loader, you can choose the "Reinstall GRUB boot loader" entry.

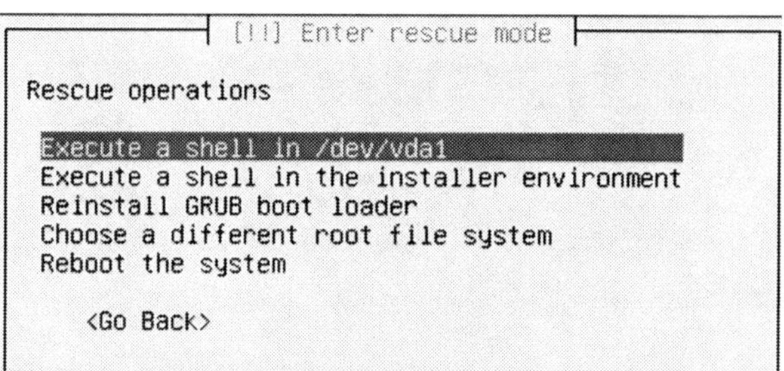

Figure 2-37: Alternate CD rescue mode choices

Re-Installing the Boot Loader

If you have a multiple-boot system, that runs both Windows and Linux on the same machine, you may run into a situation where you have to re-install your GRUB boot loader. This problem occurs if your Windows system completely crashes beyond repair and you have to install a new version of Windows, if you added Windows to your machine after having installed Linux, or if you upgraded to a new version of Windows. A Windows installation will automatically overwrite your boot loader (alternatively, you could install your boot loader on your Linux partition instead of the master boot record, MBR). You will no longer be able to access your Linux system.

There are several ways to reinstall the Grub boot loader. The easiest way is to use the Alternate CD or the Ubuntu DVD. Download and burn the Alternate CD or Ubuntu DVD, and then boot your system from the disc. Be sure you first know what device your Ubuntu system is installed on. When you boot up the Alternate CD or Ubuntu DVD, it displays as its last entry "Rescue a broken system", see Figure 2-34.

Follow the prompts to start up your system, selecting the hard disk partition when requested. When the "Enter rescue mode" screen appears, select "Reinstall GRUB boot loader" (see Figure 2-35). The following screen will prompt you to enter the partition on which to install the boot loader. The master boot record can be referenced with hd(0,0).

You also can reinstall your boot loader manually, using your Ubuntu Desktop CD. The procedure is more complicated as you have to mount your Ubuntu system. On the Ubuntu Desktop CD Live session, you can use GParted to find out what partition your Ubuntu system uses (System | Administration | Partition). In a terminal window (Applications | Accessories | Terminal), create a directory on which to mount the system.

```
sudo mkdir myubuntu
```

Then mount it, making sure you have the correct file system type and partition name (usually **/dev/sda5** on dual boot systems).

```
sudo mount -t ext4 /dev/sda5  myubuntu
```

Then use **grub-install** and the device name of your first partition to install the boot loader, with the **--root-directory** option to specify the directory where you mounted your Ubuntu file system. The **--root-directory** option requires a full path name, which for the Ubuntu Desktop CD would be **/home/ubuntu** for the home directory. Using the **myubuntu** directory for this example, the full path name of the Ubuntu file system would be **/home/ubuntu/myubuntu**. You would then enter the following **grub-install** command.

```
sudo grub-install --root-directory=/home/ubuntu/myubuntu /dev/sda
```

This will re-install your current GRUB boot loader. You can then reboot, and the GRUB boot loader will start up.

Wubi: Windows-based installer

Wubi is an Ubuntu installer that lets you install and run Ubuntu from Windows. It is a simple, safe, and painless way to install Linux for users who want to preserve their Windows system, without having to perform any potentially hazardous hard disk partition operations to free up space and create new hardware partitions for Ubuntu.

Wubi is already integrated into the Ubuntu 12.04 Desktop CD. Using Wubi, you do not have to create a separate partition for Ubuntu. A file created on your Window system functions as a virtual disk, and Ubuntu is installed on this virtual disk, which operates like a hard disk with a Linux file system installed on it. The Windows boot loader is modified to list a choice for Ubuntu. When Windows starts up, you have the choice to start Ubuntu instead.

The Wubi installation of Ubuntu is fully functional in every way. Though it uses a virtual hard disk, it is not a virtual system. When you start Ubuntu, you are only running Ubuntu. The only differences from a standard install is that the system is installed on a file, rather than an actual hard disk partition, and the original Windows boot loader is used instead of the GRUB boot loader. As far as usage is concerned, operations are the same, though with slightly slower disk access. You can find out more about Wubi at **http://www.wubi-installer.org**.

Check the Ubuntu Wubi Guide for detailed information about installation and management issues like boot problems, virtual disk creation, and details of the Wubi installation for Ubuntu.

```
http://wiki.ubuntu.com/WubiGuide
```

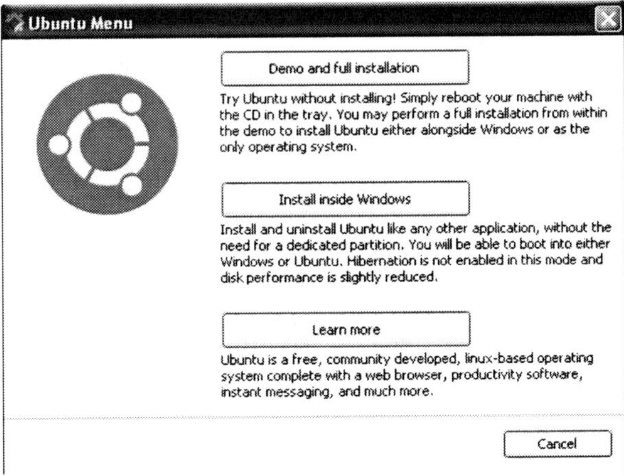

Figure 2-38: Ubuntu CD Menu on Windows

To install Ubuntu with Wubi, insert the Ubuntu Desktop CD into you CD/DVD drive when using Windows. The Ubuntu CD Menu automatically starts up, giving you the option to perform the standard install (restart and possibly partition your drive), or "Install inside Windows" (use a Wubi virtual hard disk file on Windows), see Figure 2-38. The "Learn more" option opens the Ubuntu Web site.

Figure 2-39: Ubuntu Setup window for Wubi

The Setup screen will prompt you for the drive on which to install the virtual disk file, the installation size is the size for the virtual disk file; the desktop environment (Ubuntu); the language to use; and a username and password. You then click the Install button to download and install Ubuntu (see Figure 2-39). Clicking the Accessibility button opens a dialog where you can specify accessibility install options like contrast, magnifier, Braille, and on-screen keyboard. Wubi then installs the Ubuntu desktop. Your language, keyboard, partitions, and user login have already been determined from the setup window. Wubi will first copy over files from the Desktop install disk, and then prompt you to reboot. When you reboot, your Windows boot menu is displayed with an entry for Ubuntu. Use the arrow keys to select the Ubuntu entry and press ENTER. Ubuntu will then start up. The first time it will complete the installation showing just a progress bar on the desktop, formatting, installing software, detecting hardware, and configuring your system. Once finished you reboot and select Ubuntu again. Ubuntu will start up. It is fully functional. You can configure your system, install hardware drivers, and set preferences just as you do for any Ubuntu system.

Wubi sets up an **ubuntu** directory on the hard drive partition on which you installed Ubuntu, usually the **c:** drive. Here you will find **boot** and **disks** subdirectories. In the **disks,** subdirectory is your virtual hard disk where Ubuntu is installed. You will also find another virtual hard disk file for your swap disk. Your Ubuntu virtual disk will be named, **root.disk**, as in **c:\ubuntu\disks\root.disk**. Keep in mind that Ubuntu is installed as a file on your Windows system. Be careful not to delete the ubuntu directory. Should you reformat your Windows partition for any reason, you would lose the Ubuntu system also.

You can uninstall a Wubi installed Ubuntu system using Window's Add/Remove Software.

3. Usage Basics: Login, Desktop, Network, and Help

Accessing your Ubuntu System

Display Manager

Ubuntu Unity

Network Connections: wired and wireless

System Settings

Help Resources (Ubuntu Desktop Guide)

Command Line Interface

Terminal Window

Using Ubuntu has become an intuitive process, with easy-to-use interfaces, including graphical logins and desktop interfaces, including the new Unity interface and Kubuntu (KDE). Even the standard Linux command line interface is user-friendly with editable commands, history lists, and cursor-based tools. To start using Ubuntu, you have to know how to access your system and, once you are on the system, how to execute commands and run applications. Access is supported through a graphical login. A simple screen appears with menus for selecting login options and your username. Once you access your system, you can interact with it using windows, menus, and icons.

Linux is noted for providing easy access to extensive help documentation. It is easy to obtain information quickly about any Linux command and utility while logged in to the system. You can access an online manual that describes each command or obtain help that provides explanations that are more detailed. All the desktops provide help systems with easy access to desktop, system, and application help files.

Accessing Your Ubuntu System

You access your Ubuntu system using the GRUB bootloader to first start Ubuntu, and then use the display manager to login to your account. Once logged in, you also can switch to other users using the Session menu. You can also login as a guest user, letting others quickly use your computer without access to your files. From the desktop Session menu (power button, top right) you can shut down, restart, or suspend your system. It is also possible to access Ubuntu using a command line interface only, bypassing the desktop interface and its required graphical support.

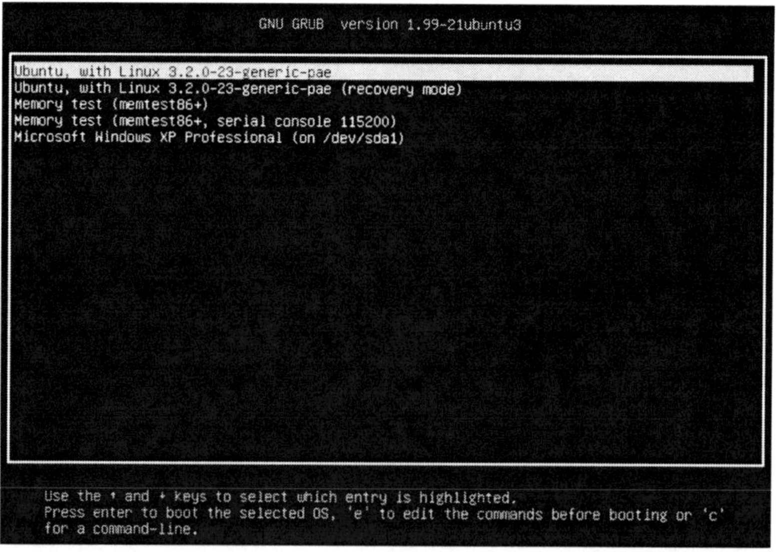

Figure 3-1: Ubuntu GRUB menu

GRUB Boot Loader

When your system restarts, the GRUB boot loader will quickly select your default operating system and start up its login screen. If you have just installed Ubuntu, the default operating system will be Ubuntu.

If you have installed more than one operating system, you can select one using the GRUB menu. The GRUB menu is displayed for several seconds at startup, before loading the default operating system automatically. Press any key to have the GRUB wait until you have made a selection. Your GRUB menu is displayed as shown in Figure 3-1.

The GRUB menu lists Ubuntu and other operating systems installed on your hard drive such as Windows. Use the arrow keys to move to the entry you want and press ENTER

For graphical installations, some displays may have difficulty running the graphical start up display. If you have this problem, you can edit your Linux GRUB entry and remove the **splash** term at the end of the **linux** line. Press the **e** key to edit a GRUB entry (see Figure 3-2).

To change a particular line, use the up/down arrow keys to move to the line. You can use the left/right arrow keys to move along the line. The Backspace key will delete characters and simply typing will insert characters. The editing changes are temporary. Permanent changes can only be made by directly editing the GRUB configuration **/etc/default/grub** file, and then running the following command.

```
sudo update-grub
```

When your Ubuntu operating system starts up, an Ubuntu logo appears during the startup. You can press the ESC key to see the start up messages instead. Ubuntu uses Plymouth with its kernel modesetting ability to display a startup animation. The Plymouth Ubuntu logo theme is installed by default.

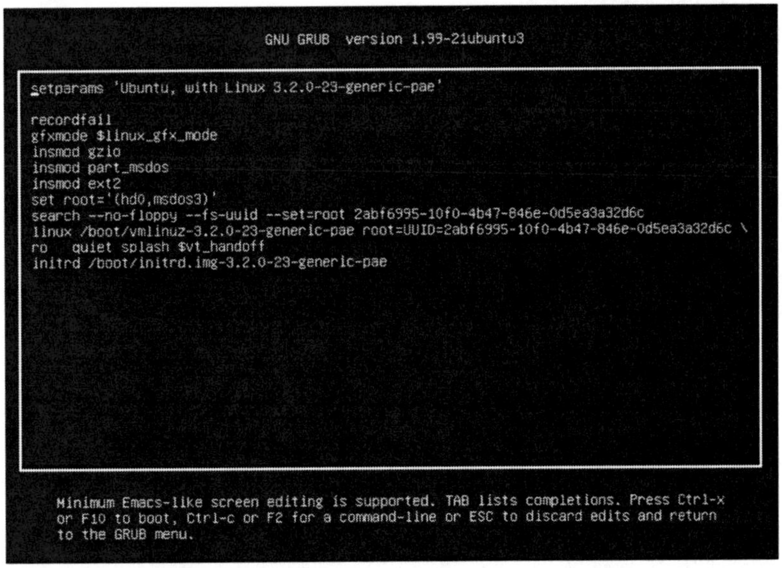

Figure 3-2: Editing a GRUB menu item

The Light Display Manager: LightDM

The graphical login interface displays a login window with a box listing a menu of usernames. The currently selected user name displays a text box where you then enter your password. Upon pressing ENTER, you login to the selected account and your desktop starts up.

Graphical logins are handled by the Light Display Manager (LightDM). The LightDM manages the login interface along with authenticating a user password and username, and then starting up a selected desktop. The CTRL-ALT-BACKSPACE keys for restarting the X server is disabled by default, use "Key sequence to kill X server" option in the Keyboard Layout Options dialog to enable it (Keyboard Layout on the Customization dash; then on the Keyboard Layout dialog click the Options button to open the Keyboard Layout Options dialog).

From the LightDM, you can shift to the command line interface with the CTRL-ALT-F1 keys, and then shift back to the LightDM with the CTRL-ALT-F7 keys. The keys F1 through F6 provide different command line terminals, as in CTRL-ALT-F3 for the third command line terminal.

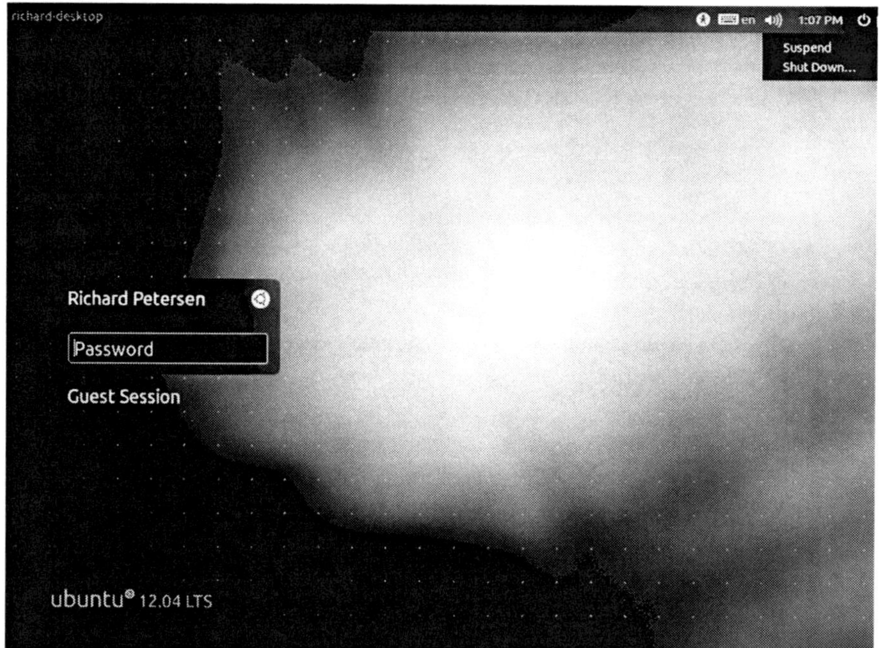

Figure 3-3: LightDM Login Screen with user list

When the LightDM starts up, it shows a listing of users (see Figure 3-3). A session (power icon) menu at the top right of the screen shows the entries Suspend and Shut Down. The time is displayed next to the Power icon. Passing the mouse over the time expands it to the calendar, showing the date. Next to the time, the sound menu lets you adjust or mute the sound. The keyboard menu lets you choose a keyboard. The accessibility menu can displays options such as the on-screen keyboard, high contrast, and the screen reader.

You can use the arrow keys to move through the list of users. For the selected user, you are prompted to enter the user's password (see Figure 3-4). Once entered, press ENTER. The desktop then starts up.

The Guest Session user has no password, just a simple Log In button.

The Ubuntu icon to the right of the user name displays a menu (see Figure 3-4) from which you can select the desktop interface you want to start up. The menu shows all installed possible desktop interfaces. Here you can select Ubuntu 2D instead of Ubuntu, or choose KDE to use the KDE Desktop. The KDE option is not shown unless you have already installed KDE. The interface you selected in your previous login is chosen automatically. Once you have made your choice, click the Back entry to return to the user listing with the password text box. Enter your password and press ENTER to start up Ubuntu with the chosen interface.

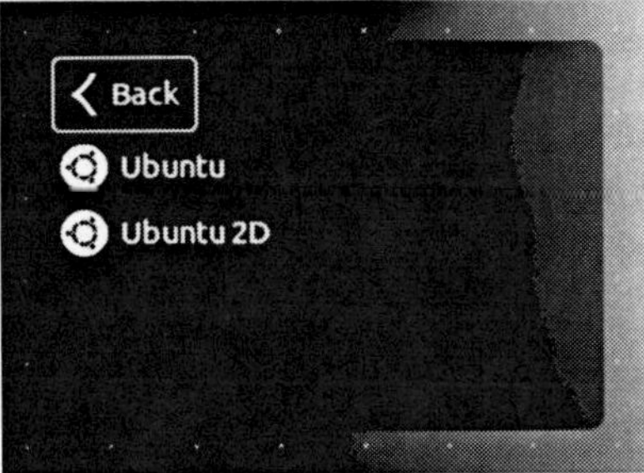

Figure 3-4: LightDM Login screen with desktop choices

If you log out from a user desktop, you will return to the LightDM login screen. To shut down your Ubuntu system, select the Shut Down entry in the session menu (power icon, top right). You can also shut down the system directly from the Ubuntu desktop by clicking the session icon on the top panel to the right. The desktop Session menu is displayed with entries for Lock Screen, Log Out, Suspend, and Shut Down. Restart is an option on the Shut Down dialog.

Tip: To restart the system from the login screen using the keyboard you first have to enter the command line interface. Press Ctrl-Alt-F1 to enter the command line interface, and then press Ctrl-Alt-Del to restart the system.

The Session menu and the User Switcher

The Ubuntu desktop displays a Session menu on the right side of the top panel as the sprocket power icon (see Figure 3-5). You likely will use the Session menu to logout or shut down your system. The last section of the menu shows entries for Log Out, Suspend, and Shutdown. The Log Out entry logs out of your session and returns to the Login screen. From the menu, you can also shut down or restart your system directly from the desktop. To restart, choose Shutdown, which displays a dialog with a Restart button. Use the Lock Screen entry to lock desktop access.

The Session menu also provides quick access to common configuration tools for displays, printers, Webcam, startup applications, the Update Manager, and attached devices. A System Settings entry opens the GNOME 3 System Settings dialog from which you can access desktop administrative tools such as those for users, mouse and touchpad, and Bluetooth.

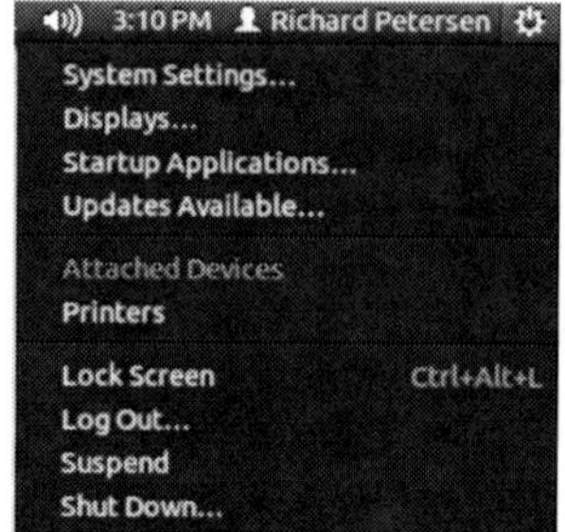

Figure 3-5: Desktop Session menu with logout and shutdown actions.

The Ubuntu desktop displays a User Switcher menu as the user's name on the right side of the top panel next to the sprocket power icon (see Figure 3-6). If you click the user name, the menu appears showing user switching entries and User Accounts access. The User Switcher menu lets you switch to another user, without having to log out or end your current user session. The user switching operations will keep you logged in while you login to another user. Your active programs will continue to run in the background.

On the User Switcher menu the "Switch User Account" entry lets you login from the login screen as a user not currently logged in (see Figure 3-6). Following the Switch User Account entry is a listing of users you can login as directly. Guest Session allows a guest login. Users logged in already will have a check mark next to their names. Selecting one of these entries suspends your current session and starts up the login screen with the user list positioned at that user.

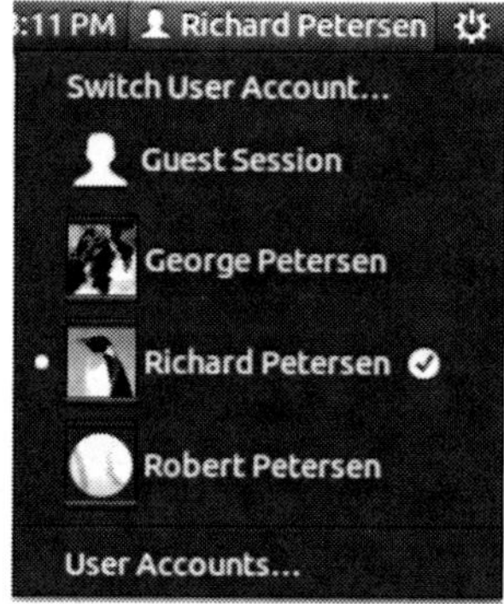

Figure 3-6: User Switcher menu

Selecting the "Switch User Account" entry suspends your current session and starts up the login screen, listing all the users you can choose to login as (see Figure 3-6). Users already logged in display a triangle to the left of the name. To switch a user, select the user from the user listing and then enter the user's password.

If you log out of a user you have switched to (Log Out entry), LightDM login screen start up letting you login as a different user. If you choose to switch to a user already logged in, then the login dialog for the lock screen will appear for that user. From the lock screen, you can login (Unlock) or choose to switch to another user (Switch User). A logged in user's original session will continue with the same open windows and applications running when the user switched off.

You can easily switch back and forth between logged-in users, with all users retaining their session from where they left off. When you switch off from a user, that user's running programs will continue in the background.

Guest login

Ubuntu supports a guest account, allowing you to let other users use your system, without having to give them a user account of their own or use someone else's. It is designed for situations like letting someone use your laptop to check a Web site quickly. The Guest login is accessible from the User Switcher menu as the Guest Session entry (see Figure 3-5). The guest user is immediately placed on their own desktop as the guest user, while your account remains locked. The guest user name will appear on the User Switcher menu icon on the top panel. Upon logging out from the guest account, the LightDM login screen is displayed, letting you login to your own account again. The guest user can also use the User Switcher menu to switch to another user, while the guest session remains logged in. This way the guest user's work is retained, while you access another user or your own account. You can then switch back to the guest user. The guest user's open windows and work will be restored.

Lock Screen

You can choose to lock your screen and suspend your system by choosing the Lock Screen entry in the Session menu. To start up again, press the spacebar and the Lock Screen dialog appears (see Figure 3-7). On the lock screen, click the Unlock button to start up your desktop session again.

From the lock screen, you also can switch to another user by clicking the Switch User button. The LightDM login screen starts up and you can login as another user.

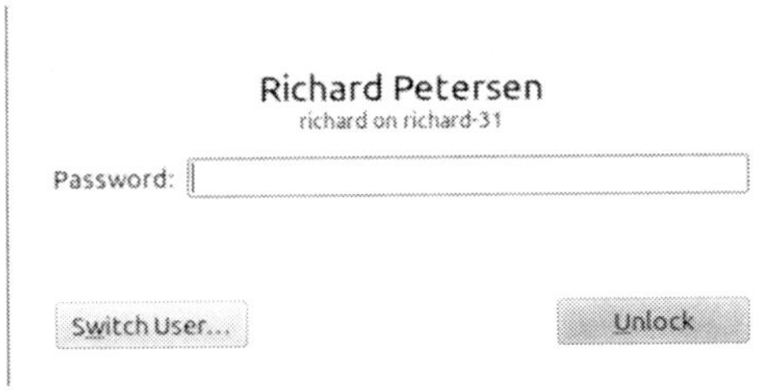

Figure 3-7: Lock Screen

Shut down and Logging out

To shut down from the Ubuntu desktop, click the session icon (power sprockets) on the right side of the top panel to open the Session menu. The Shut down options are displayed at the bottom of the menu: Log out, Suspend, and Shut down (see Figure 3-5). Restart is an option on the Shut Down dialog. To logout, you can use the Session menu Log Out entry, which returns you to the login screen where you login again as a different user.

There are several ways to shut down your system.

Session menu: select one of the shut down options (see Figure 3-2).

Press the power button on your computer. This opens a menu with shutdown options (see Figure 3-9).

Should your display freeze or become corrupted, one safe way to shut down and restart is to press a command line interface key (like CTRL-ALT-F1) to revert to the command line interface, and then press CTRL-ALT-DEL to restart. You can also login on the command line interface (terminal) and then enter the **sudo halt** command.

When you select the Shut Down or Log Out entry from the Session menu, the appropriate dialog is displayed (See Figure 3-8). From the Shut Down dialog, you can also choose to restart by clicking the Restart button.

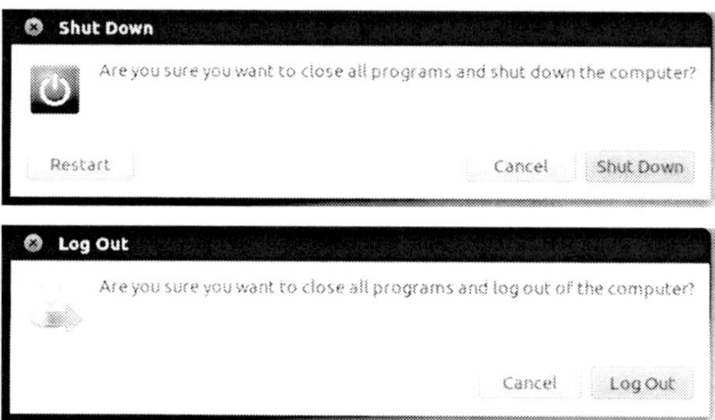

Figure 3-8: Shut Down and Log Out dialogs

You can also press your computer power button to shut down, restart, or suspend your system, which displays a shut down dialog with menu entries for Shut Down, Restart, and Suspend (see Figure 3-9). If you do not make a choice, the Shut Down entry is performed automatically in one minute. A countdown of the seconds remaining is shown on the dialog.

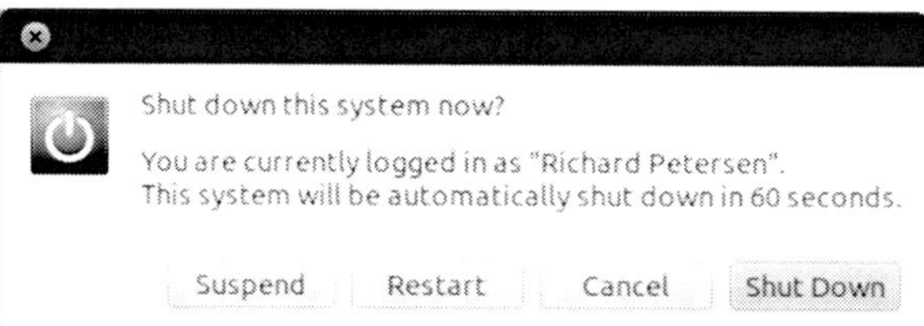

Figure 3-9: Shut down dialog

Use Suspend to stop your system temporarily, using little or no power. Press the space key to redisplay the locked login screen where you can access your account again and continue your session from where you left off.

Accessing Linux from the Command Line Interface

You can access the command-line interface by pressing CTRL-ALT-F1 at any time (CTRL-ALT-F7 returns to the graphics interface). For the command line interface, you are initially given a login prompt. The login prompt is preceded by the hostname you gave your system. In this example, the hostname is **richard-desktop**. When you finish using Linux, you log out with the **logout** command. Linux then displays the same login prompt, waiting for you or another user to log in again. This is the equivalent of the login window provided by the GDM. You can then log in to another account.

Once you log in as a user, you can enter and execute commands. To login enter your username and your password. If you make a mistake, you can erase characters with the BACKSPACE key. In the next example, the user enters the username **richard** and is then prompted to enter the password:

```
Ubuntu 12.04 richard-desktop tty1

turtle login: richard
Password:
```

When you type in your password, it does not appear on the screen. This is to protect your password from being seen by others. If you enter either the username or the password incorrectly, the system will respond with the error message "Login incorrect" and will ask for your username again, starting the login process over. You can then reenter your username and password.

Once you enter your username and password, you are logged in to the system and the command line prompt is displayed, waiting for you to enter a command. the command line prompt is a dollar sign (**$**). On Ubuntu, your prompt is preceded by the hostname and the directory you are in. The home directory is indicated by a tilde (~).

```
richlp@richard-desktop:~$
richlp@richard-desktop:~$ cd Pictures
richlp@richard-desktop:~/Pictures$
```

To end your session, issue the **logout** or **exit** command. This returns you to the login prompt, and Linux waits for another user to log in.

```
richlp@richard-desktop:~$ logout
```

To, instead, shut down your system from the command line, you enter the **halt** command. This command will log you out and shut down the system.

```
richlp@richard-desktop:~$ halt
```

The Ubuntu Desktop (Unity)

Ubuntu 12.04 supports two major different desktop interfaces: Ubuntu and Kubuntu. The Ubuntu Desktop CD installs as defaults both Ubuntu and Ubuntu 2D. The Ubuntu desktop uses the new Ubuntu Unity interface.

Ubuntu requires hardware acceleration support provided by the appropriate display driver. Ubuntu uses the Compiz window manager, designed to provide 3D desktop effects with an accelerated graphics driver. If your current graphics driver does not support hardware acceleration, you will be logged in using the Ubuntu 2D desktop. This is the Ubuntu desktop, but without the Compiz window manager, using the older Metacity window manager instead, which supports only a 2D graphics driver.

As an alternative, Ubuntu installs the Unity 2D desktop, which provides a simplified Unity interface that does not require hardware acceleration. It will work on the provided xorg graphics drivers. Choose Unity 2D from the LightDM Session menu to access it.

The Kubuntu CD installs the KDE desktop interface. You can also install KDE on an Ubuntu desktop system using the Ubuntu Software Center KDE meta-packages: **kubuntu-desktop** or **kubuntu-full**. Although the GNOME and KDE interfaces appear similar, they are very different desktop interfaces with separate tools for selecting preferences.

Key press	Action
SHIFT	Move a file or directory, default
CTRL	Copy a file or directory
CTRL-SHIFT	Create a link for a file or directory
F2	Rename selected file or directory
CTRL-ALT-Arrow (right, left, up, down)	Move to a different desktop
CTRL-w	Close current window
ALT-spacebar	Open window menu for window operations
ALT-F2	Open Run command box
ALT-F1	Open Applications menu
Ctrl-F	Find file

Table 3-1: Window and File Manager Keyboard shortcuts

Ubuntu uses the Ubuntu Ambiance theme for its interface with the Ubuntu screen background and menu icons as its default (see Figure 3-11). Another Ubuntu theme is available called Radiance. Ambience is a darker color theme, while Radiance uses lighter colors. The Ambiance theme is used in the examples in this book. You can change to the Radiance theme on the Appearance dialog's Look tab's Theme menu. The Appearance tool is accessible from the Customization dash and from System Settings.

The Ambience and Radiance themes place the window control buttons (close, maximize, and minimize buttons) on the left side of a window title bar, as shown here. There are three window buttons: an x for close, a dash (-) for minimize, and a square for maximize. The close button is highlighted in orange.

window buttons 

To move a window, click and drag its title bar. Each window supports Minimize, Maximize, and Close buttons located on the left side of the title bar. Double-clicking the title bar will maximize the window. Many keyboard operations are also similar as listed in Table 3-1.

Ubuntu Unity

Logging in to the Ubuntu desktop uses the Ubuntu Unity interface. Unity is designed to make the best use of screen space, placing a launcher on the left side to free up vertical space, making the window menu bar part of the top panel, along with indicator menus for Network Manager, and sound volume, messaging, time and date, the User Switcher, and the Session menu (see Figure 3-10).

Icon	Launcher item
	Dash home
	Home Folder
	Firefox Web browser
	Libre Office Writer
	Libre Office Calc
	Libre Office Impress
	Ubuntu Software Center
	Ubuntu One
	System Settings
	Workspace Switcher
	Trash

Table 3-2: Ubuntu Unity Launcher default items and icons

The Unity interface features a Launcher for applications and tasks, with icons for the dash home, the home folder, the Firefox browser, LibreOffice applications (Writer, Calc, and Impress), the Ubuntu Software Center, Ubuntu One, and System Settings. There are also icons for accessing workspaces and the trash. You can use the System Setting's Appearance tool to configure changes to your Unity interface such as Launcher hiding options and the size of the Launcher item icons.

Note: Compiz is window manager used by Unity, which makes use of the Ubuntu Unity Plugin to configure Compiz for Unity. The configuration of Compiz window manger to support Unity is very specific. You should not make any other changes to Compiz window manager, other than those on the Ubuntu Unity Plugin. You can access the Ubuntu Unity Plugin by first installing the CompizConfig Settings Manager, which you can then access from the Customization dash.

The dash home button at the top of the Launcher (Ubuntu logo) opens the dash, displaying a search box to let you search for applications. At the bottom of the dash are icons for different lenses: home, applications, files & folders, music, and videos. Click on an icon to open that lense. Clicking on the applications button (books) opens the Applications dash with a filter menu for accessing different application categories such as Internet, Multimedia, and System. Applications are organized into the most frequently used, those installed, and those available for download, which connects directly to the Ubuntu Software Center.

You can close the dash by clicking the dash close button (**x**) located at the top left side of the panel, or by pressing the ESC key. You can expand it to full screen by clicking the square button at the lower right corner of the dash.

With Unity, Icons have become much more important for identifying an application. Instead of names on menus, users focus more on the icon in the Launcher and on the Dash. Table 3-2 lists the default launcher item icons.

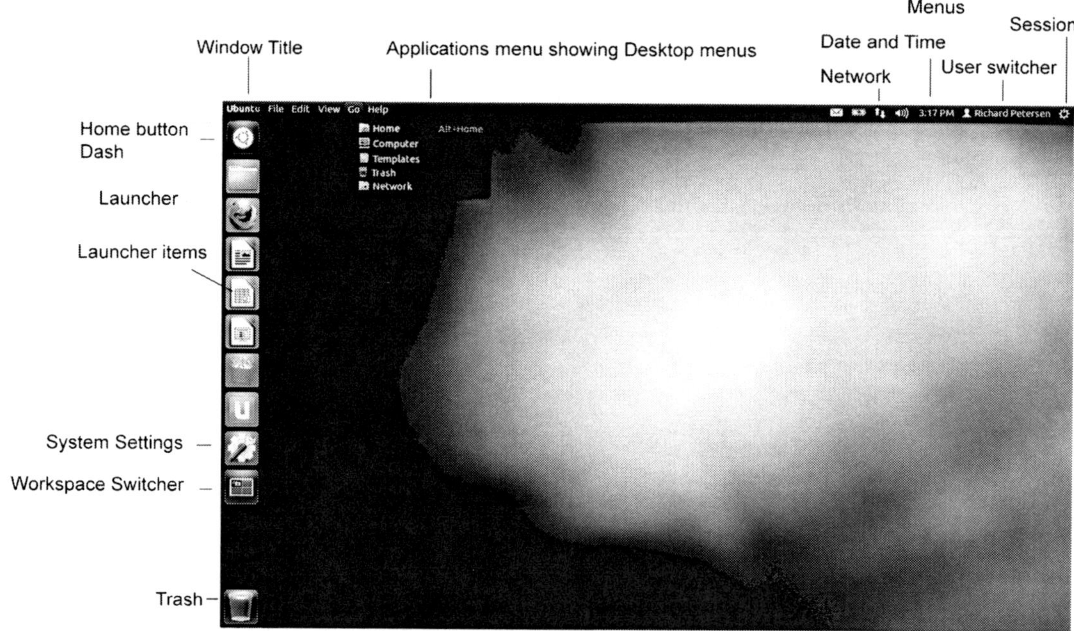

Figure 3-10: Ubuntu Unity interface

The top panel displays the applications menu and the indicator menus. The left side of the top panel is the application menu, showing the menu bar for the currently selected open window. When you click on the desktop background, the applications menu shows the desktop menus, including File, Edit, View, Go, and Help. The Go menu provides entries for the Computer and Network windows, as well as the Trash and Home Folder (see Figure 3-10).

The right side of the top panel holds indicator menus for the network manager, sound volume, messaging, Date and time, the User Switcher, and the Session menu (configuration tools and shut down options).

When you click on a window, its title is displayed on the top panel. When you move your mouse to the left side of the top panel, that window's menu bar is displayed in the applications menu (see Figure 3-11).

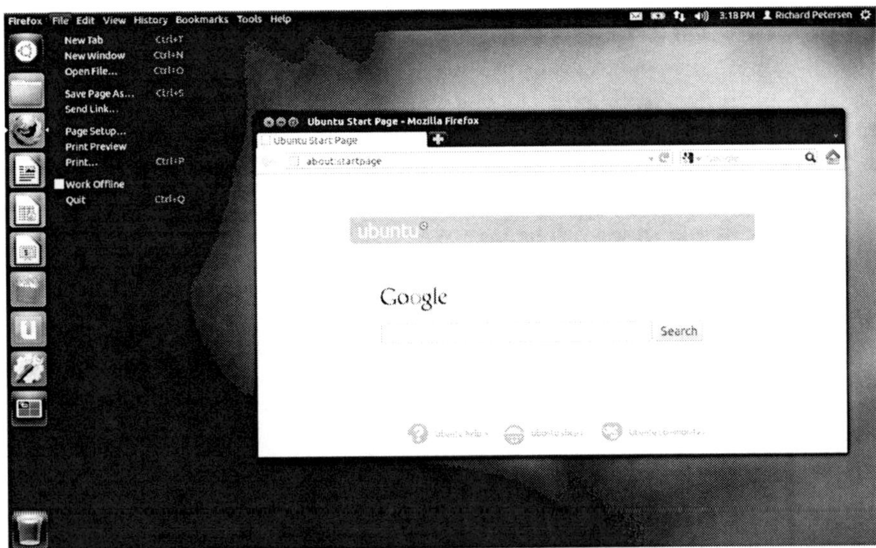

Figure 3-11: Ubuntu Unity interface with selected window and applications menu

Ubuntu 2D

The Ubuntu 2D screen, shown in Figure 3-12, displays a desktop very similar to the Ubuntu desktop, but does not require accelerated graphics support (3D). One key difference is that there is no Desktop menu. If you do not have an accelerated video driver installed, then Ubuntu 2D is your default. Ubuntu 2D uses the Metacity window manager instead of Compiz. Desktop enhancements available with Compiz are not presents on Ubuntu 2D, such as moving windows on the workspace switcher.

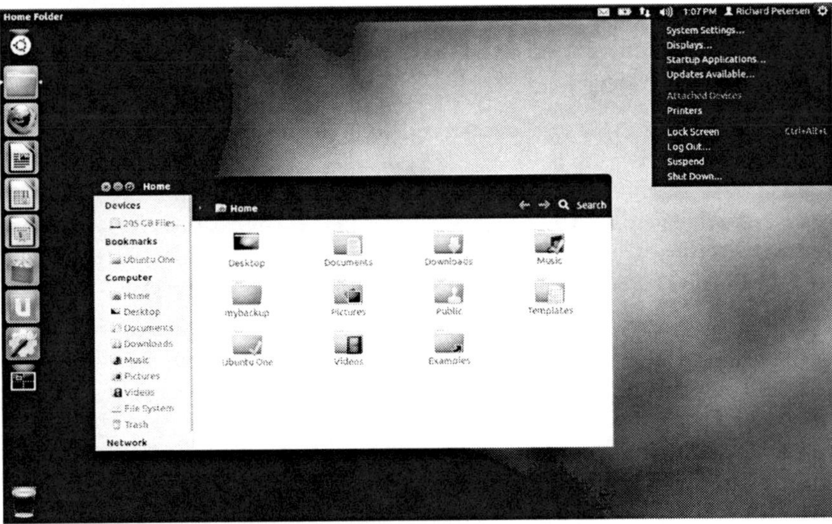

Figure 3-12: Ubuntu 2D

Gnome file manager (Nautilus)

Ubuntu (Unity) uses the Nautilus file manager. You can access your home folder from its entry in the Go menu, or by clicking the Home Folder item in the Launcher. A file manager window opens showing your home directory. Your home directory will already have default directories created for commonly used files. These include Pictures, Documents, Music, Videos, and Downloads.

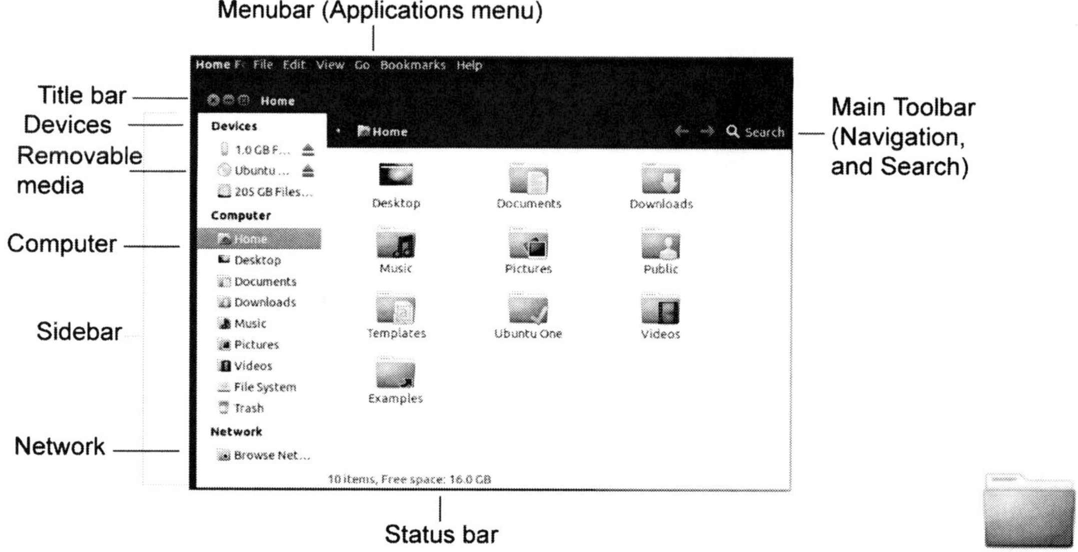

Figure 3-13: File manager for home folder

Your office applications will automatically save files to the Documents directory by default. Image and photo applications place image files in the Pictures directory. The Desktop folder will hold all files and directories saved to your desktop. When you download a file, it is placed in the Downloads directory.

The file manager window displays several components, including a browser toolbar, location bar, and a sidebar showing devices, file systems, and folders. On Ubuntu (Unity), the file menu is located in the applications menu on the top bar. When you open a new folder, the same window is used to display it, and you can use the forward and back arrows to move through previously opened directories. The location bar displays folder buttons showing your current folder and its parent folders. You can click on a parent folder to move to it. Figure 3-13 shows the file manager window.

The file manager also supports tabs. You can open up several folders in the same file manager window. To open a new tab, select New Tab from the File menu or press **Ctrl-t**. You can use the entries in the Tabs menu to move from one tab to another, or to rearrange tabs. You also can use the Ctrl-PageUp and Ctrl-PageDown keys to move from one tab to another. Use the Shift-Ctrl-PageUp and Shift-Ctrl-PageDown keys to rearrange the tabs.

touch actions	Effects
single tap	left click
double one finger tap	double click
double one finger press and drag	click and drag
two finger tap	right click
two finger swipe up/down	scroll up or down (if edge scrolling enabled)
two finger swipe right/left	scroll left or right (if horizontal scrolling enabled)
three finger pinch	maximize and restore windows
three finger press and drag	move windows
pinch	zoom a window
Ctrl - two finger swipe	zoom a window
three finger touch	resize or move a window showing grab handles, click and drag edges and corners to change the size, click and drag center control to move window.
three pinch	open all windows for an application
three pinch twice	open all windows
four finger tap	open the dash
four finger swipe left or right	open the Launcher

Table 3-3: Touchpad controls

The file manager supports full drag-and-drop capabilities using combinations of key presses and mouse clicks (see Table 3-1). You can drag folders, icons, and applications to the desktop or other file manager windows open to other folders. The move operation is the default drag operation (you can also press the SHIFT key while dragging). To copy files, press the CTRL key and then click-and-drag before releasing the mouse button. To create a link (short cut), hold down both the CTRL and SHIFT keys while dragging the icon to where you want the link to appear, such as the desktop.

Touchpad controls

Ubuntu provides the utouch touch controls for use with touch screen supported hardware (see Table 3-3). You can enable and configure your touchpad on the Mouse Preferences Touchpad tab, accessible from the Customization dash and from System Settings as Mouse. The Touchpad tab provides General and Scrolling options. You can disable the touchpad when typing and enable mouse clicks. For scrolling, you can enable edge or two finger scrolling, as well as horizontal scrolling.

Check the Ubuntu Multitouch site for more information
https://wiki.ubuntu.com/Multitouch. For applications that do not support touch controls, you can use the Ginn utility to configure basic touch support. Ginn stands for Gesture Injector: No-GEIS, No-Toolkits. See the Ginn site for more information: **https://wiki.ubuntu.com/Multitouch/Ginn**.

Laptop Power Management and Wireless Networks

For working on a laptop, you will need two important operations: power management and support for multiple network connection, including wireless and LAN. Both are configured automatically. For power management, Ubuntu uses the Power dialog accessible from System Settings dialog and from the Customization dash. On a Laptop, the battery icon displayed on the panel will show how much power you have left, as well as when the battery becomes critical. It will also indicate an AC connection, as well as when the battery is recharging.

For network connections, Ubuntu uses Network Manager. Network Manager will detect available network connections automatically. Click on the Network Manager icon in the upper panel to the right. This displays a pop-up menu showing all possible wireless networks, as well as any wired networks. You can then choose the one you want to use. The name and strength of each wireless connection will be listed. When you try to connect to an encrypted wireless network, you will be prompted for the security method and the password. Wireless networks that you successfully connect to will be added to your Network Manager configuration. You also have the option to connect to a hidden wireless network as well as create a connection of your own.

You can also use the GNOME 3 Network tool, accessible from System Settings as Network, to quickly turn your wireless connection on or off.

Network Connections

Network connections will be set up for you by Network Manager, which will detect your network connections automatically, both wired and wireless. Network Manager provides status information for your connection and allows you to switch easily from one configured connection to another as needed. For initial configuration, it detects as much information as possible about the new connection.

Wired connections will be started automatically. For wireless connections, when a user logs in, Network Manager selects the connection preferred by that user. The user can choose the wireless connection to use from a menu of detected wireless networks.

Figure 3-14: Network Manager wired, wireless, and disconnected icons.

The network menu displays a Network Manager icon on the top panel to the right. The Network Manager icon will vary according to the type of connection and your connection status. An Ethernet (wired) connection would display two arrows pointing in opposite directions. A wireless connection will display a staggered wave graph (see Figure 3-14). If no connection is active (wireless or wired), an empty wave graph is displayed. When Network Manager makes a wired or wireless connection, it displays a pulsing staggered wave graph. If you have both a wired and wireless connection, and the wired connection is active, the wired connection image (opposite arrows) will be used.

Network Manager wired connections

For computers connected to a wired network, like an Ethernet connection, Network Manager will automatically detect the network connection and establish a connection. Most networks use DHCP to provide network information like an IP address and network DNS server automatically. With this kind of connection, Network Manager can connect automatically to your network whenever you start your system. The network connection would be labeled something like Wired connection 1. When you connect, a connection established message is displayed, as shown here.

The Network Manager panel icon will display the arrows pointed in opposite directions, as shown here.

On KDE, the Network Manager icon for wired connections is shown here.

The Network Manager menu displays your wired connection, shown here as Wired connection 1.

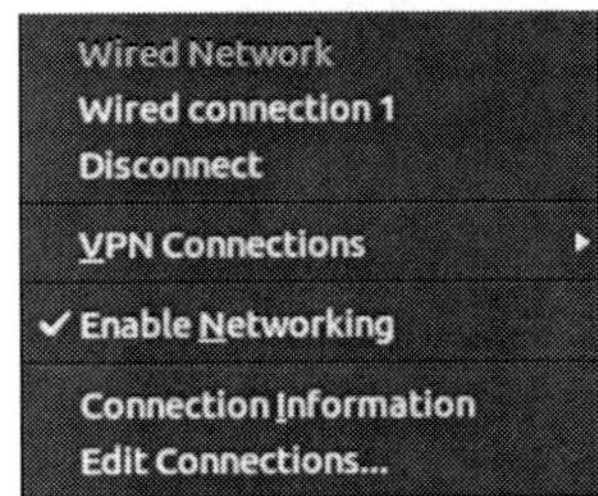

To disconnect your wired connection, you can choose the Disconnect entry on this menu. The menu will then show that your are disconnected. The wired connection will be displayed as a connection option. To reconnect later, choose an available wired connection, in this example Wired connection 1.

Network Manager wireless connections

With multiple wireless access points for Internet connections, a system could have several different network connections to choose from, instead of a single-line connection like DSL or cable. This is particularly true for notebook computers that could access different wireless connections at different locations. Instead of manually configuring a new connection each time one is encountered, the Network Manager tool can configure and select a connection to use automatically.

Network Manager will scan for wireless connections, checking for Extended Service Set Identifiers (ESSIDs). If an ESSID identifies a previously used connection, then it is selected. If several are found, then the recently used one is chosen. If only a new connection is available, then Network Manager waits for the user to choose one. A connection is selected only if the user is logged in.

Open the Network Manager emnu to see a list of all possible network connections, including all available wireless connections (see Figure 3-15). Wireless entries display the name of the wireless network and a wave graph showing the strength of its signal. Computers with both wired and wireless devices show entries for both Wired Network and Wireless Networks. Computers with only a wireless device only show entries for Wireless Networks. You can disable the display of wireless networks by selecting Enable Wireless from the menu. The check mark next to this entry is removed, and wireless detection is disabled. To re-activate your wireless connections, click the Enable Wireless entry again. A checkmark is displayed next to the entry and your wireless connections are now listed in the Network Manager menu.

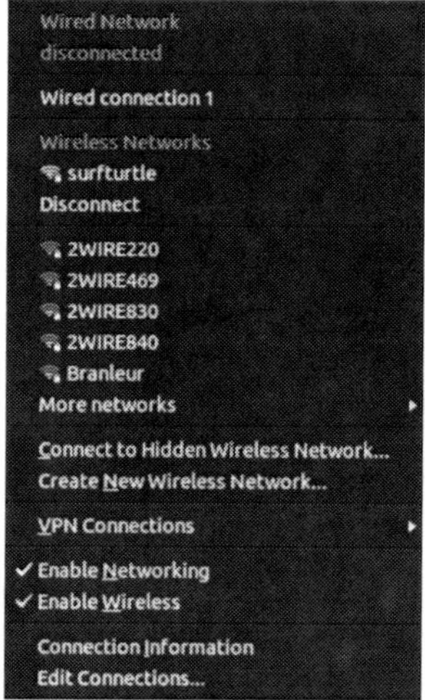

Figure 3-15: Network Manager connections menu: wired and wireless

Note: If a computer has both wired (Ethernet or dial-up) and wireless connection devices, as most laptops have, then you will see entries for both Wired and Wireless networks.

To connect to a wireless network, find its network entry in the Network Manager menu and click on it. If this the first time you are trying to connect to that network, you are prompted to enter connection information: the wireless security and passphrase. The type of wireless security used by the network will be detected and displayed for you. If it is incorrect, you can use the drop-down menu to select the correct method. The entries will change depending on the method chosen. The WPA passphrase is one of the more common methods. Figure 3-16 shows the prompt for the passphrase to a wireless network that uses the WPA security method. A checkbox lets you see the passphrase should you need to check that you are entering it correctly. Click Connect to activate the connection.

Figure 3-16: Network Manager wireless authentication

Once connected a message is displayed indicating that the connection has been established, as shown here.

When you connect to a wireless network for the first time, a configuration entry will be made for the wireless connection in the Wireless tab of the Network Connections dialog.

The very first time you make a wireless connection, you will be prompted to set up a keyring. The keyring holds your wireless connection passphrase, allowing you to connect to a wireless network without having to re-enter the network passphrase each time. You will be asked to create a keyring password for accessing the keyring. This is a one-time operation. Once the keyring is set up, any additional wireless connection passphrases will be added to it. When you first login and try to connect to a wireless network, you will be prompted for your keyring password.

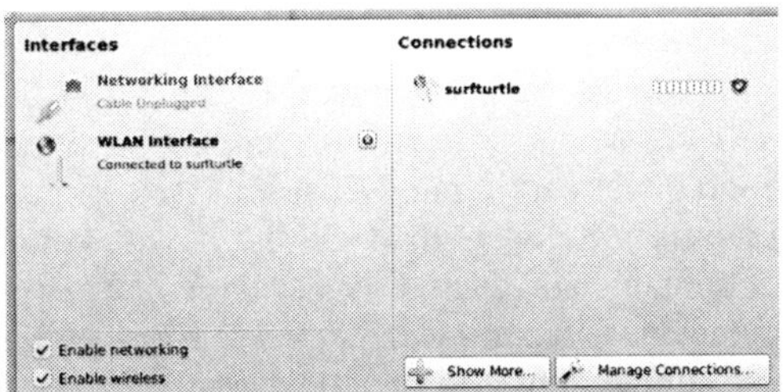

Figure 3-17: KDE Network Manager connection menu, wireless selection dialog, and panel icon

On KDE, clicking the Network Manager icon on the Plasma panel displays the KDE Network Manager widget (see Figure 3-17). Interfaces are listed on the left and connections on the right. To see a list of wireless connections, click the WLAN Interface icon on the left. Information about the WLAN interface is displayed with a list of possible wireless connections shown on the right side. Click the one you want to use to open an Add Network Connection dialog displaying the Wireless Security tab where you can choose the type of security and enter the password. If you have not already set up a KDE Wallet password, you are prompted to do so now. This will allow automatic access to the connection later. You are then connected. You can click the Show Less button to hide all connections except the active one. Click Show More to see all possible connections, allowing you to switch to a different one. The Manage Connections button opens the KDE Network Manager dialog where you can manage all your connections.

Wireless connections can also be hidden. These are wireless connections that do not broadcast an SSID, making them undetectable by an automatic scan. To connect to a hidden wireless network, you select "Connect to hidden wireless network" on the Network Manager menu (see Figure 3-18). The Connection drop-down menu will select the New entry. If you have set up any hidden connections previously, they also are listed in the Connection drop-down menu. For a New connection, enter the wireless network name and select a security method. You are prompted in either case for your network keyring password.

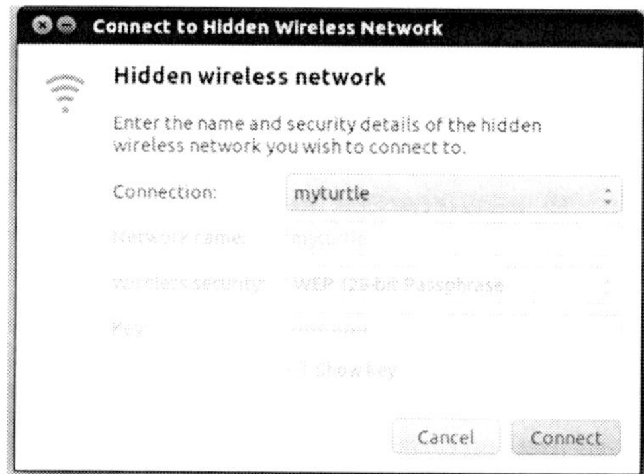

Figure 3-18: Connect to a Hidden Wireless Network

Network Manager options

The network menu also provides options for editing your connection, shutting off your connection (Enable Networking and Enable Wireless), disabling all network access (Enable Networking), or to see information about the connection (see Figure 3-19). On Ubuntu (Unity), these entries are included on theNetwork Manager menu. A computer with both wired and wireless connections will have entries to Enable Networking and Enable Wireless. Selecting Enable Wireless will disconnect only the wireless connections, leaving the wired connection active. The Enable Wireless checkbox will become unchecked and a message will be displayed telling you that your wireless connection is disconnected. Selecting Enable Networking will disable your wired connection, along with any wireless connections. Do this to work offline, without any network access.

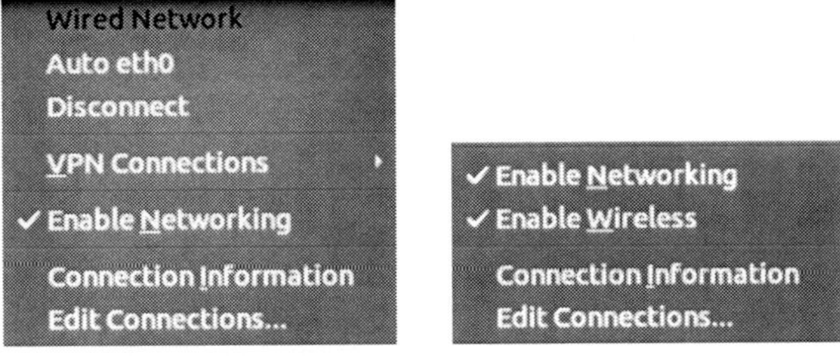

Figure 3-19: Network Manager options

A computer with only a wired network device (no wireless) will only show an Enable Networking entry. Selecting it will disconnect you from any network access, allowing you to work offline.

System Settings Network (GNOME and proxies)

GNOME provides a network dialog for basic information and network connection management, including proxy settings. It is designed to work with Network Manager, though it is still a work in progress. Click the Network icon in the System Settings dialog to open the Network dialog (see Figure 3-20). Tabs for network connections are listed to the right. Clicking on a connection tab displays information about it with connection options. You should have entries for Wired, Wireless, and Network proxy (Wireless is displayed on computers with wireless connections). The Wired tab lets you turn the wired connection on or off. The Wireless tab lets you choose a wireless network and then prompts you to enter a passphrase. The connection and security type is automatically detected. Clicking the configure button opens the NetworkManager wireless dialog for this connection, letting you add more detailed information. Instead of using a wireless network, you can choose an airplane mode wireless connection or to use your connection as a hotspot.

Figure 3-20: System Settings Network

The Proxy tab provides a Method menu with None, Manual, and Automatic options (see Figure 3-21). The Manual options lets you enter address and port information. For the Automatic option, you enter a configuration address. Click the "Apply system wide" button to apply the proxy information to all users.

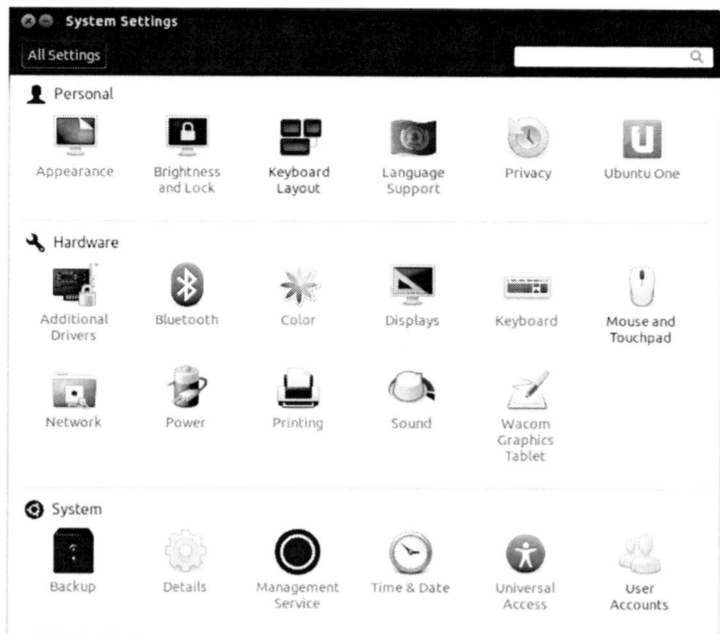

Figure 3-21: Proxy settings (System Settings Network)

To add a new connection, such as a vpn connection, click the plus button (**+**) below the network devices listing. You are prompted to choose the interface types. Then the NetworkManager configuration dialogs will start up to let you enter configuration information.

System Settings

You can configure desktop settings and perform most administrative tasks using the administration tools listed in the GNOME System Settings dialog, accessible from the session menu and the Launcher. System Settings organizes tools into Personal, Hardware, and System categories (see Figure 3-22).

Figure 3-22: System Settings dialog

Setting	Description
Additional Drivers	Added drivers such as proprietary graphics drivers (Nvidia and AMD) (See chapter 3)
Appearance	Desktop Backgrounds, Themes, and Launcher behavior configuration.
Assistive Technologies	Enables features like accessible login and keyboard screen.
Backup	Deja Dup backup tool (see chapter 14)
Bluetooth	Bluetooth detection and configuration (see Chapter 14)
Brightness and Lock	Set screen brightness and the inactivity time to dim or lock the screen.
Details	System and hardware information, default applications, defaults for removable media, and graphics information.
Displays	Change your screen resolution, refresh rate, and screen orientation.
Color	Set the color profile for a device
Keyboard	Configure repeat key sensitivity, and keys for special tasks.
Keyboard Layout	Configure your keyboard: selecting options, models, and typing breaks, accessibility features like slow, bounce, and sticky keys.
Language Support	Language selection
Management Service	Canonical's Landscape commercial management service
Mouse and Touchpad	Mouse and touchpad configuration: select hand orientation, speed, and accessibility.
Network	Lets you turn wired and wireless networks on and off. You can access an available wireless network and proxy configuration
Power	Set the power options for laptop inactivity.
Removable Media	Default options for Music CDs, DVD Videos, and picture CDs.
Sound	Configure sound effects, output volume, sound device options, input volume, and sound application settings (see Chapter 6).
Time & Date	Set the time and date, including time zone, along with clock display options (see Chapter 14).
Universal Access	Set Universal access settings for the screen reader, text size, contrast, visual alerts, screen keyboard, and keypad based mouse.
Privacy	Set or clear logging for file types and applications
Printer	Printer configuration with system-config-printer (see Chapter 16)
Ubuntu One	Ubuntu One (see Chapter 9)
User Accounts	Manage users, a GNOME 3 tool (see Chapter 14)
Wacon Graphics tablet	Wacom graphics tablet configuration

Table 3-4: Desktop System Settings

Many invoke the Ubuntu supported system tools available from previous releases such as Sound (PulseAudio) and Printing (system-config-printer). Others use the new GNOME 3 configuration and administrative tools such as Brightness, User Accounts, and Power. The Color tool lets you choose color schemes for different devices such as scanners, cameras, and printers. System Settings tools will open with an "All Settings" button at the top, which you can click to return to the System Settings dialog (see Figure 3-23). Table 3-4 lists the System Settings tools.

The Mouse and Touchpad preferences are the primary tools for configuring your mouse and touchpad (see Figure 3-23). Mouse preferences lets you choose its speed, hand orientation, and double-click times. For laptops, you can configure your touchpad, enabling touchpad clicks and edge scrolling (left side).

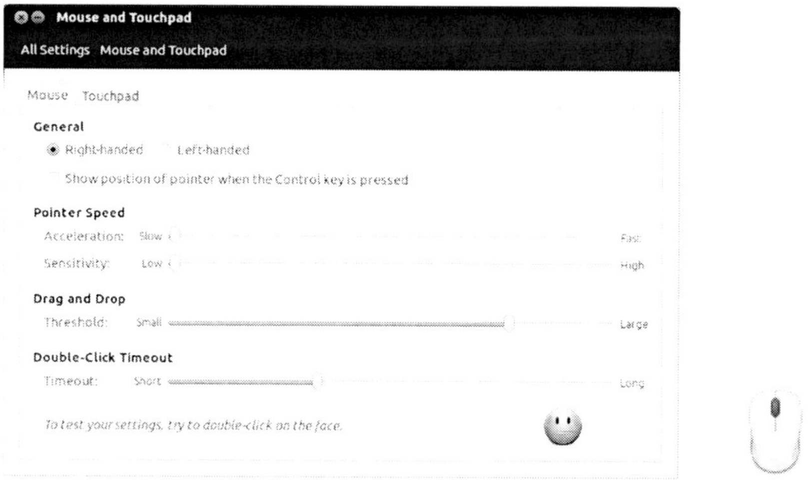

Figure 3-23: System Settings, mouse

Appearance (Backgrounds, Themes, and Launcher auto-hide)

Several appearance-related configuration tasks are combined into the Appearance tool. These include Themes and Background. You can access the Appearance tool from the Customization dash or from the System Settings dialog. The Appearance window has two tabs: Look and Behavior. The Look tab shows sections for Background and Theme (see Figure 10-24).

The Behavior tab lets you set the auto-hide behavior for the Launcher. A switch lets you turn the auto-hide feature on. You can then set the location at the left side of the screen to top left corner. You can also set the reveal sensitivity for unhiding the Launcher.

Also for the Launcher, on the Look tab, you can set the size of the Launcher items.

On the Look tab, the background section, to the right, displays a drop-down menu that lets you choose to display wallpapers, images in your Pictures folder, or to choose a color or gradient. If you choose Wallpapers, then the install backgrounds are displayed in a frame below the menu. To add your own image, click on the plus button to locate and select the image file. To remove an image, select it and click the minus button. Installed backgrounds are listed as Wallpapers.

The Pictures Folder option displays images in your Pictures folder, which you can scroll through and select one to use for your background. The Colors & Gradients entry lists color, vertical gradient, and horizontal gradient buttons. If you click the color button, a color button appear on the lower left side under the monitor image, which you can use to select your colors.

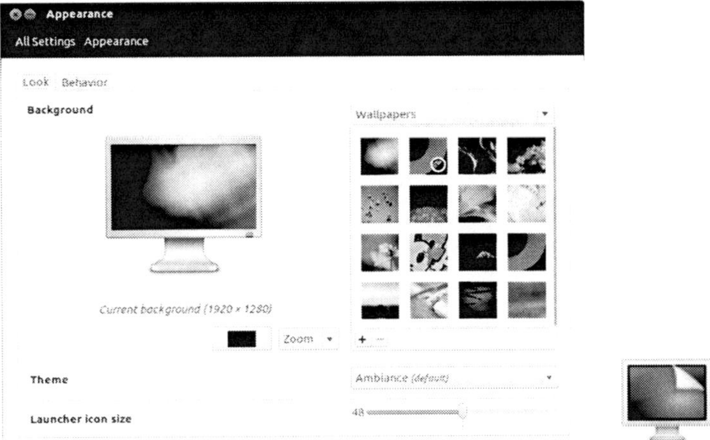

Figure 3-24: Appearance: Background and Theme

If you choose an image from the Pictures Folder listing, then a style drop-down menu and color button appear in the lower left side, below the monitor image. From the style drop-down menu, you can choose display options such as Zoom, Centered, Scaled, Tiled, or Fill Screen (located below the current background image to the left). A centered or scaled image will preserve the image proportions. Fill screen may distort it. Any space not filled, such as with a centered or scaled images, will be filled in with the desktop color. Click on the color button to open a "Pick a Color" dialog where you can select a color from a color wheel.

For gradients, two color buttons are displayed for selecting a color at each end of the gradient. If you choose a gradient from the Background drop-down menu, then two color buttons are displayed from which you can choose the two ends of the color range. In the Background menu display for gradients, you can choose a vertical or horizontal gradient, indicated by the arrows.

You use the Themes drop-down menu at the bottom of the Appearance dialog to select a theme. Themes control your desktop appearance. The Ambience theme is initially selected.

Initially only the Ubuntu backgrounds are listed. Install the **gnome-background** package to add a collection of GNOME backgrounds. You can download more GNOME backgrounds from **http://www.art.gnome.org/backgrounds**.

Details: system info and default applications and media

The Details dialog shows system information using four tabs: Overview, Default Applications, Removable Media, and Graphics. The Overview tab shows your hardware specifications (memory, CPU, graphics card chip, and free disk space) along with the host name (Device name) and the OS type (64 or 32 bit system) (see Figure 3-25). You can change the host name here if you wish. When you open the dialog, updates are checked for, and, if found, an Install Update button displayed, which open Software Updates, allowing you to update your system (see Chapter 4).

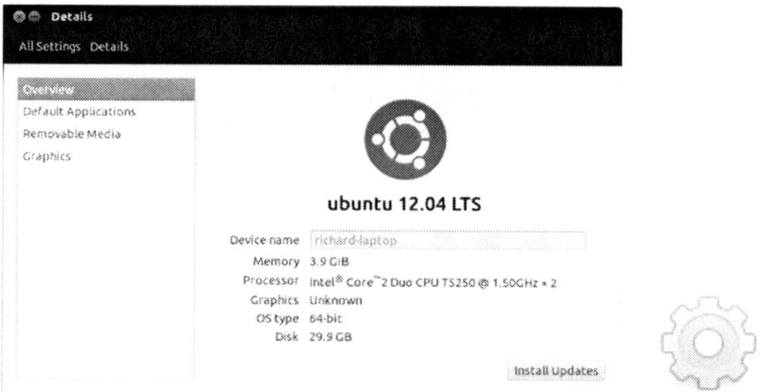

Figure 3-25: System Information Overview

The Default Applications tab lets you set default applications for basic types of files: Web, Mail, Calendar, Music, Video, and Photos (see Figure 3-26). Use the drop-down menus to choose installed alternatives such as Thunderbird instead of Evolution for Mail, or Image Viewer instead of Shotwell for Photos.

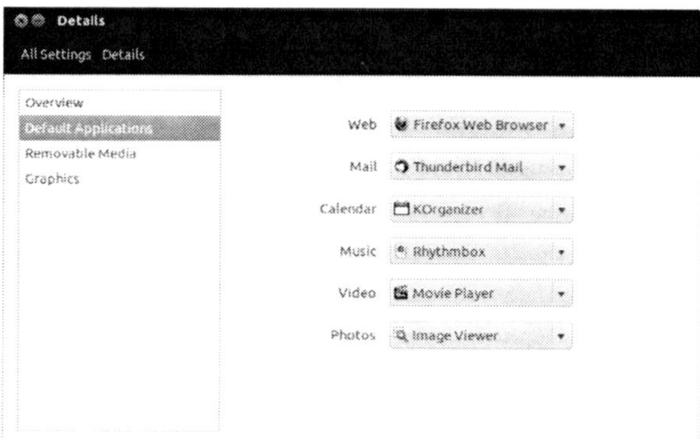

Figure 3-26: Details Default Applications

The Removable Media tab lets you specify default actions for CD Audio, DVD Video, Music Player, Photos, and Software media. You can select the application to use for the different media from drop-down menus (see Figure 3-27). These menus also include options for Ask What To Do, Do Nothing, and Open Folder. The Open Folder option will open a window displaying the files on the disc. A button labeled "Other Media" opens a dialog that lets you set up an association for less used media like Blu-Ray discs and Audio DVD. Initially the "Ask what to do" option is set for all entries. Possible options are listed for the appropriate media, like Rhythmbox Media Player for CD Audio discs and Movie Player (Totem) for DVD Video. Photos can be opened with the Shotwell Photo-manager.

For media for which there is no entry, click the Other Media button to open a dialog where you can specify media such a Blu-ray disc, Ebook reader files, and Video CDs.

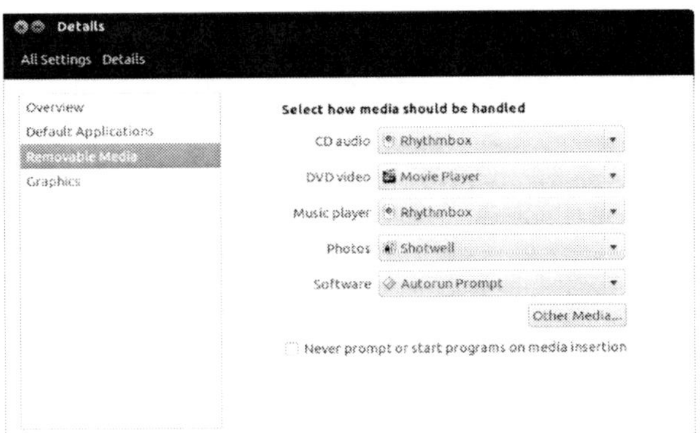
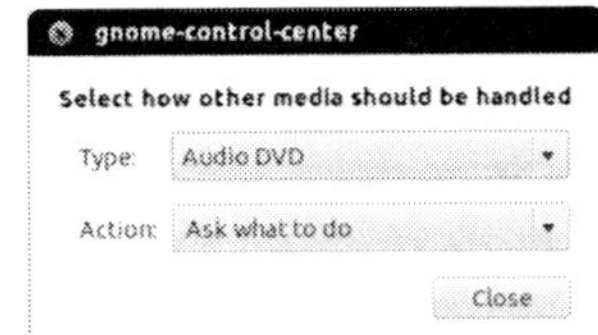

Figure 3-27: Removable Media defaults (GNOME)

When you insert removable media, such as a CD audio disc, its associated application is automatically started, unless you change that preference. If you want to turn off this feature for a particular kind of media, you can select the Do Nothing entry from its application drop-down menu. If you want to be prompted for options, use the "Ask what to do" entry. Then, when you insert a disc, a dialog with a drop-down menu for possible actions is displayed. From this menu, you can select another application or select the Do Nothing or Open Folder options.

You can turn the automatic start up off for all media by checking the box for "Never prompt or start programs on media insertion" at the bottom of the Removable Media dialog.

Privacy

The Privacy dialog lets you manage your history logs. The Record Activity switch lets you turn recording on and off (see Figure 3-28). On the Recent Items tab you can choose how long to keep activity recordings, and whether to delete history. The Files tab lets you exclude certain types of media from recording such as audio, images, and spreadsheets. You can also exclude folders from recording.

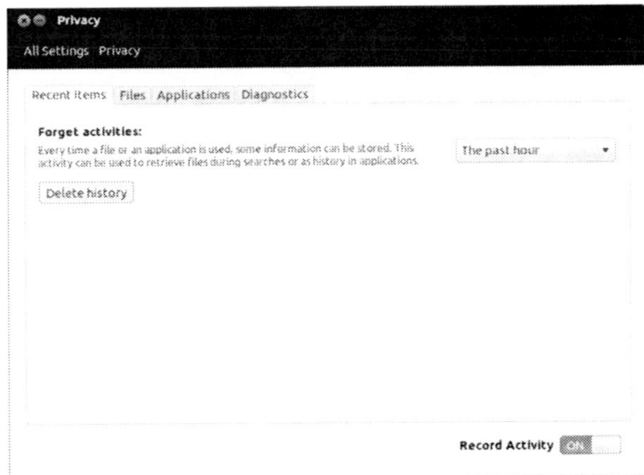

Figure 3-28: System Settings, Privacy

The Applications tab lets you select applications for which you do not want any activity logged. Diagnostics allows performance data to be sent to Ubuntu to aide in development.

Power Management

For power management, Ubuntu uses the GNOME 3 Power Manager, which makes use of Advanced Configuration and Power Interface (ACPI) support provided by a computer to manage power use. The GNOME Power Manager displays an icon on the panel showing the current power source, a battery (laptop) or lightning (desktop). Clicking on the battery icon displays a menu showing the power charge of your wireless devices, both your laptop and any other wireless devices like a wireless mouse.

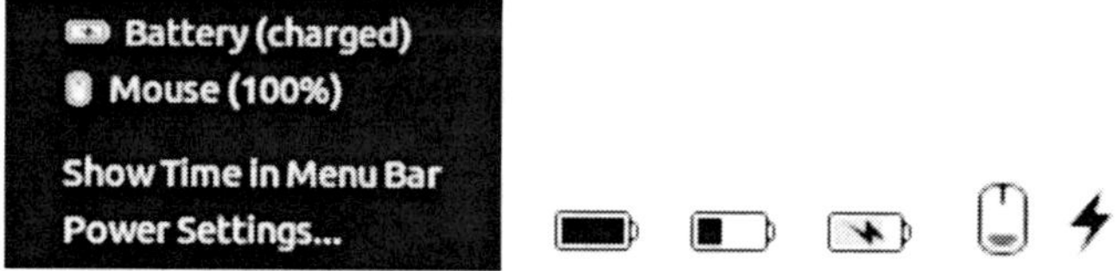

The GNOME Power manager is configured with the Power dialog, accessible as Power from the Customization tab and from System Settings. You have the options to set the suspension time out, and what action to take when the lid is closed or the power is low (see Figure 3-29). If present, battery levels for your laptop and mouse are displayed.

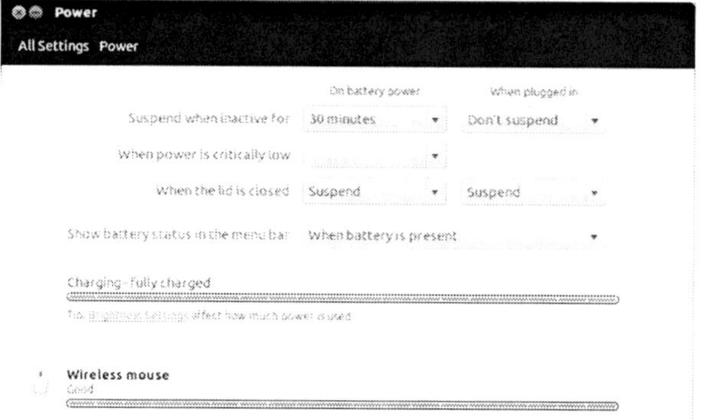

Figure 3-29: GNOME Power Manager

To see how your laptop or desktop is performing with power, you can use Power statistics, accessible from the Customization dash. The Power Statistics window displays a sidebar listing your different power devices. A right pane will show tabs with power use information for a selected device. The Laptop battery device will display three tabs: Details, History, and Statistics. The History tab will show your recent use, with graph options for Time to empty (time left), Time to full (recharging), Charge, and Rate. The Statistics tab can show charge and discharge graphs.

Brightness and lock

With Brightness and Lock, you can specify the idle time for the screen, having it turn off when not in use. You can also control whether to lock the screen or not. A Lock switch lets you turn the lock feature on or off. You can set the lock to a specific time, or when the screen turns off.

(see Figure 3-30). On a laptop, you can also set the brightness of the screen, and to dim the screen to save power.

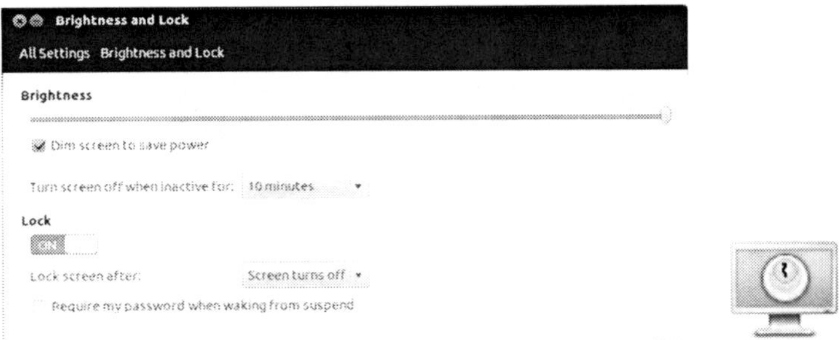

Figure 3-30: Brightness and Lock

Displays (resolution and rotation)

Any user can specify their own resolution or orientation without affecting the settings of other users. The System Settings Displays dialog provides a simple interface for setting rotation, resolution, and selecting added monitors, allowing for cloned or extended displays across several connected monitors (see Figure 3-31). From the drop-down menus, you can set the resolution and rotation. After you select a resolution, click Apply. The new resolution is displayed with a dialog with buttons that asks you whether to keep the new resolution or return to the previous one. You can use the Detect Displays button to detect any other monitors connected to your system. With multiple displays, you can turn a monitor off or mirror displays. You can also choose which display to place the Launcher on, or to have it shown on all displays. A switch turns sticky edges on and off.

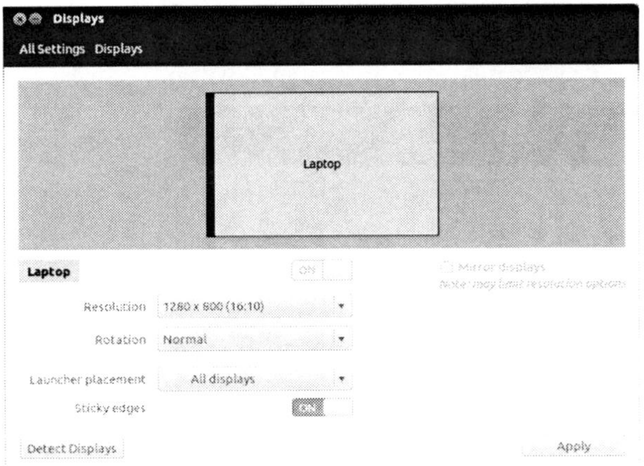

Figure 3-31: Displays

Universal Access

The Universal Access dialog in System Settings lets you configure alternative access to your interface for your keyboard and mouse actions. Four tabs set the display, sound properties, typing, and point and click features. Display lets you adjust the contrast and text size, and whether to allow use of screen reader (see Figure 3-32). Typing displays a screen keyboard and adjusts key presses. Hearing uses visual cues for alert sounds. Pointing and Clicking lets you use the keyboard for mouse operations.

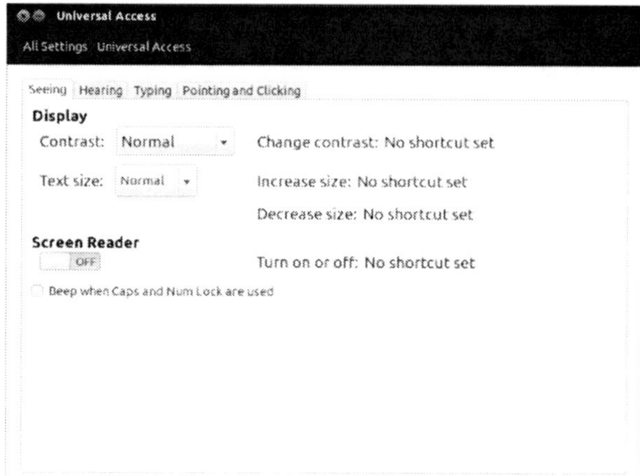

Figure 3-32: Universal Access

Keyboard

The System Settings Keyboard dialog shows tabs for typing and shortcuts. The Typing tab adjusts repeat keys and cursor blinking (see Figure 3-33). The Shortcuts tab lets you assign keys to perform tasks such as starting the Web browser or   mapping multimedia keys on a keyboard to media tasks like play and pause. Just select the task and then press the key. There are tasks for the desktop, multimedia, and window management. With window management, you can also map keys to perform workspace switching. Keys that are already assigned will be shown.

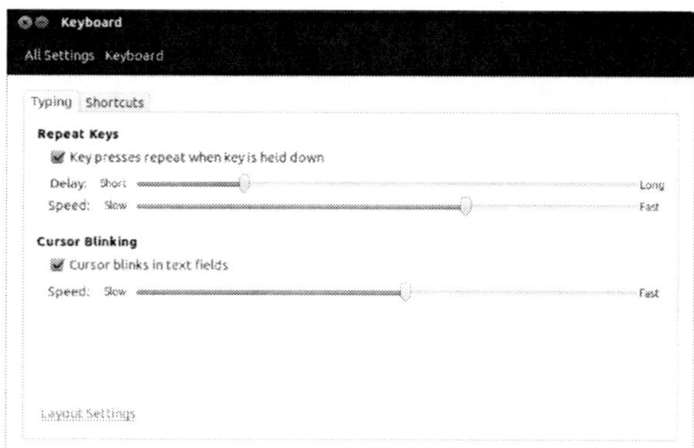

Figure 3-33: Keyboard

Keyboard Layout

The Keyboard Layout dialog choose your keyboard language and options (see Figure 3-34). The current input language source is listed and selected. Click the plus button to open a dialog listing other language layouts, which you can add. Click the keyboard button to see the keyboard layout of your currently selected input source. You can also allow different layouts for different windows.

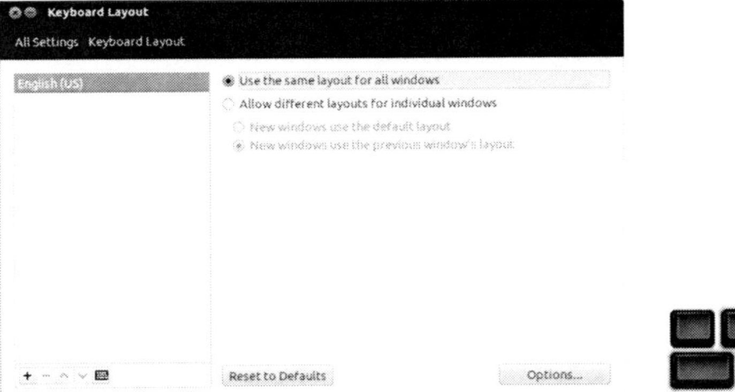

Figure 3-34: Keyboard Layout

For specialized keyboard options, click the Options button to list options such as enabling the key sequence to kill the X server (see Figure 3-35).

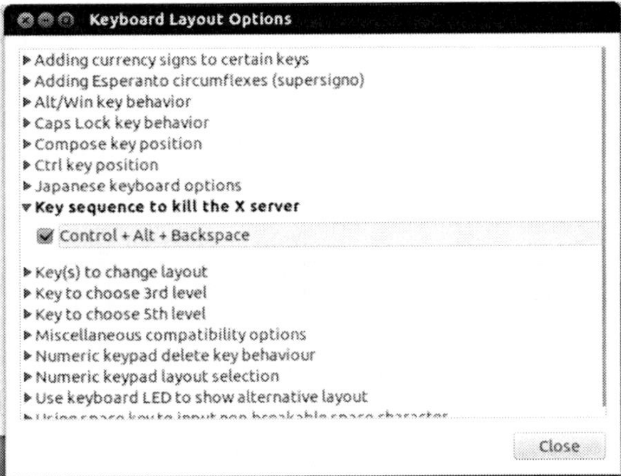

Figure 3-35: Keyboard Layout Options

Color Profiles (GNOME Color Manager)

You can manage the color for different devices using color profiles specified with the Color dialog accessible from System Settings. The Color dialog lists devices for which you can set color profiles. Click on a device to display buttons at the bottom of the screen to Add profile,

Calibrate, Remove profile, and View details. Your monitor will have a profile set up automatically. Click View Details for the color profile information (see Figure 3-36).

Click the Add Profile button to open a dialog with an Automatic Profiles menu from which can choose a color profile to use. Click the Add button to add the Profile. Available profiles include Adobe RGB, sRGB, and Kodak ProPhoto RGB. You can also import a profile from an ICC profile file of your own.

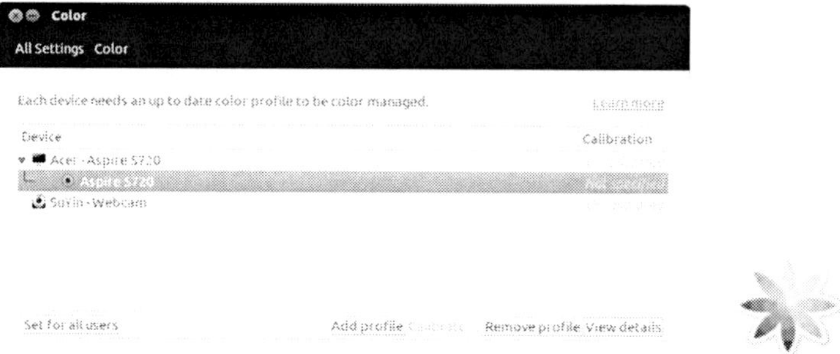

Figure 3-36: Color Management dialog

Clock: Time & Date Indicator

The Time & Date menu is located on the top panel to the right. It displays the current time and date for your region, but can be modified to display the weekday, as well as the time, date of any location in the world. The calendar shows the current date, but you can move to different months and years using the month and year scroll arrows at the top of the calendar.

Time & Date display options are set using the Time & Date dialog, which open by choosing Time & Date Settings in the Time & Date menu. The Time & Date dialog shows two tabs: Time & Date and Clock (see Figure 3-37). The time and date can be set manually or automatically from a timeserver ("Automatically from the Internet"). For manual changes, you can set the time and date directly.

Figure 3-37: Time & Date Settings dialog: Time & Date tab

Note: For a weather menu, install the **indicator-weather** package (Universe repository). You can specify location, temperature scale, and data source.

The Clock tab lets you set display options for the clock in the indicator menu bar and the clock's menu (see Figure 3-38). On the indicator menu bar the clock can show weekdays, date and month, 12 or 24 hour time, and seconds. By default, only the time is shown. For the menu, you can choose to display the monthly calendar, coming events from the Evolution calendar, and the time in other geographical locations. Both the monthly calendar and coming events options are set by default, and are shown on the clock menu (see Figure 39).

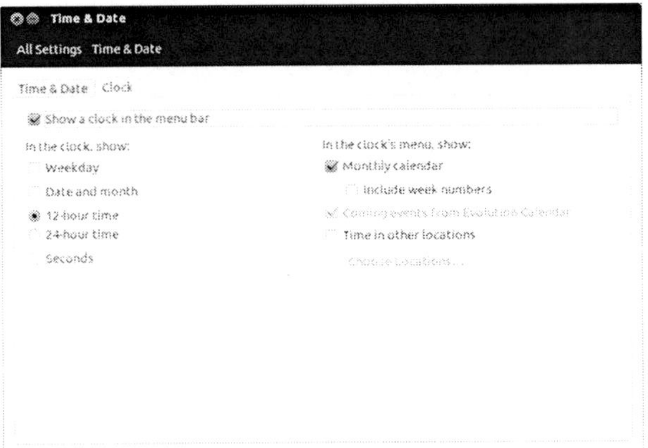

Figure 3-38: Time & Date Settings dialog: Clock tab

Figure 3-39: Time & Date indicator, showing calendar

If you want to display time in other locations, click the "Time in other locations" checkbox. The Choose Locations button then becomes active, which you click to open the Locations dialog (see Figure 3-40). Click the plus button at the bottom right to add a location entry. As you type the name of a city, a drop down menu of possible cities is displayed. Choose the one you want. The added locations are then displayed on the clock menu (see Figure 3-41).

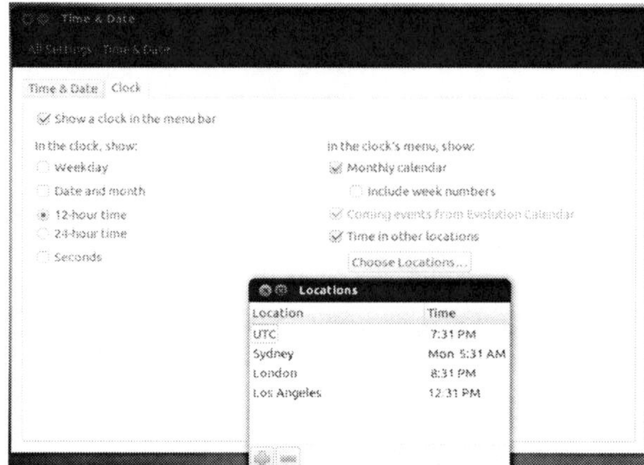

Figure 3-40: Time & Date Settings dialog (Clock tab) and Locations dialog

Time & Date is designed to work with the Evolution Calendar. Clicking on the Add Event entry in the Time & Date menu opens the Evolution Calendar. Events will be listed on the Time & Date menu. To turn off the event feature, on the Time & Date Settings dialog, Clock tab, uncheck the "Coming events from the Evolution Calendar" entry.

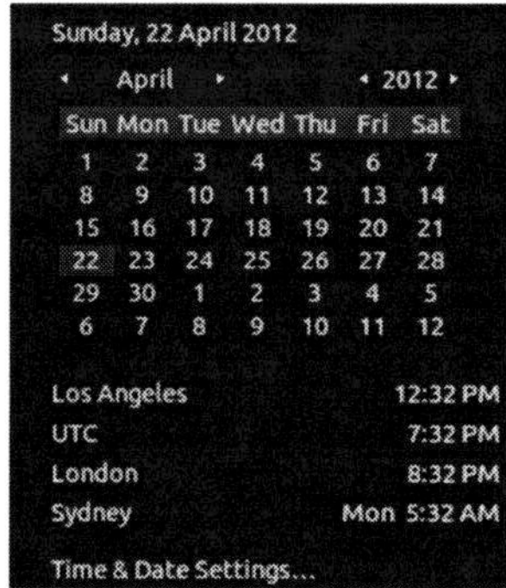

Figure 3-41: Time & Date indicator, showing locations

Searching files

Several primary search tools are available for your Ubuntu desktop: the Folders & Files dash and the file manager search.

Folders & Files (Find Files) Dash

You can use the Dash to search for files and folders. On the Dash, shortcuts click on File icon (blank page image) at the bottom of the dash to open the Files & Folders dash (see Figure 3-42). Enter the name or prefix of the file name you wish to search for in the search box, and press ENTER. The results are listed. Use the "Filter results" options to refine your search by date, type, and size.

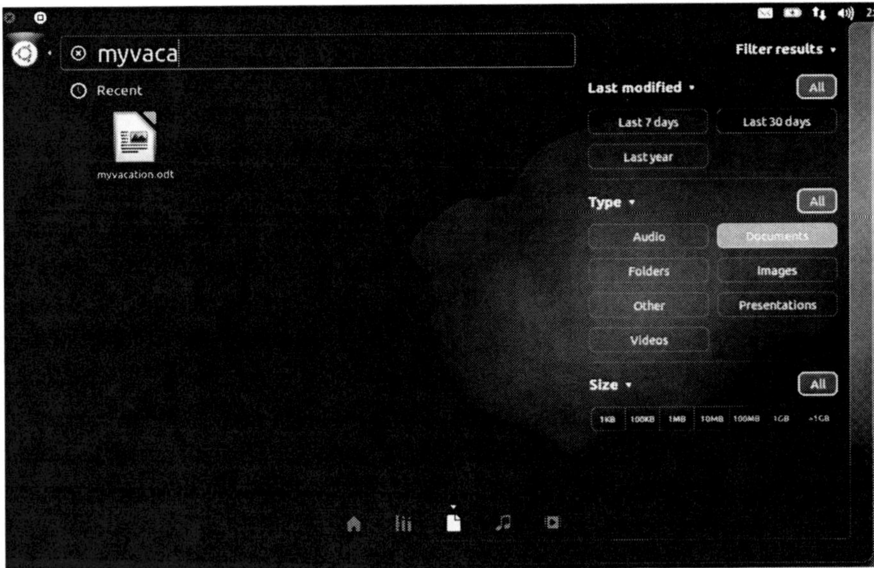

Figure 3-42: Find Files dash

File Manager Search

The file manager provides a search tool, with similar features. You can access the file manager search either from the desktop menu or from any file manager window. Choose Select Search for Files from the Go menu (desktop menu bar, click on desktop). From a file manager window, click the Search button on the toolbar (Looking glass at end) to make the URL box a Search box, or select Go | Search for files. Enter the pattern to search and press ENTER. The results are displayed (see Figure 3-43).

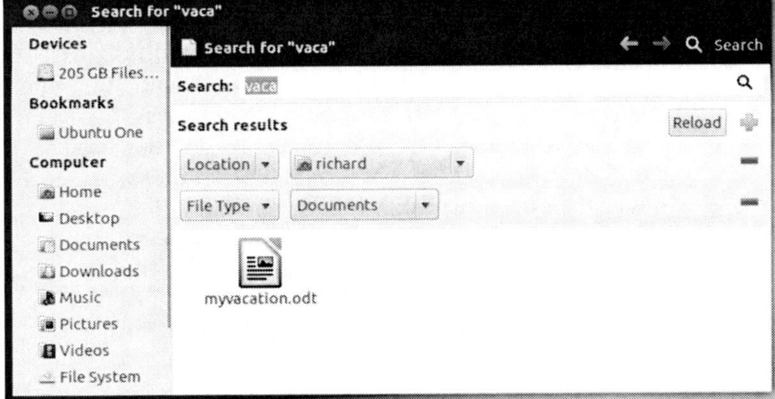

Figure 3-43: Gnome File Manager Search

Drop-down menus for location and file type will appear in the folder window, with + and - buttons for adding or removing location and file type search parameters. Click the plus + button to add more location and file type search parameters. The search begins from the folder opened, but you can specify another folder to search (a Location menu). To search multiple folders at once, click the + button to add a Location menu for each folder, and specify that folder. You can do the same for multiple file types, only files with certain types.

Accessing File Systems and Devices

From the file manager you not only have access to removable media, but you also have access to all your mounted file systems, remote and local, including any Windows shared directories accessible from Samba.

You can access your file systems and removable media using the Computer entry in the Go menu (desktop applications menu on Unity). This opens a top-level window showing icons for all removable media (mounted CD-ROMs, USB drives, and so on), your local file system, additional partitions, and your network shared resources. Double-click any icon to open a file manager window displaying its contents. The file system icon will open a window showing the top-level directory for your file system. Access will be restricted for system directories (use the **sudo** command to perform any operations on system files).

File systems on removable media will also appear automatically as Launcher items on the Launcher. A DVD/CD-ROM is automatically mounted when you insert it into your DVD/CD-ROM drive, displaying an icon for it with its label. The same kind of access is also provided for card readers, digital cameras, USB drives, and external USB/ESATA hard drives. When you attach an external USB/ESATA drive, it will be mounted automatically and opened in a file manager window. Be sure to unmount (Eject or Safely Remove Drive) the USB or external USB/ESATA drives before removing them so that data will be written.

If you have already configured associated applications for audio and video CD/DVD discs, or discs with images, sound, or video files, the disc will be opened with the appropriate application; like Shotwell for images, Banshee for audio, and Totem for DVD/video.

You can access a DVD/CD-ROM disc or USB drive from the desktop by clicking its Launcher item or by right clicking on the DVD/CD-ROM Launcher item and selecting the Open entry. A file manager window opens to display the contents of the CD-ROM disc. To eject a CD-ROM, you right-click its Launcher item icon and select Eject from the pop-up menu. The same procedure works for USB drives, using the USB drive icon, but with a "Safely Remove Drive" entry. Be sure you do not remove a mounted USB drive or floppy disk until you have first unmounted it, selecting the "Safely Remove Drive" entry in the pop-up menu. The Launcher items for USB and DVD drives with their menus are shown here

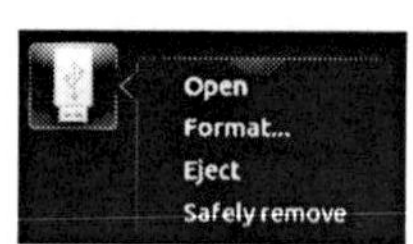

To see network resources, open the Network window using the Network entry in the Go menu. The network window will list your connected network computers. Opening these, displays the shares they provide, such as shared directories that you have access to. Drag-and-drop operations are supported for all shared directories, letting you copy files and folders between a shared directory on another computer with a directory on your system. If you have a firewall active

(Gufw or Firestarter), you first have to configure your firewall to accept Samba connections before you can browse Windows systems.

Accessing Archives from GNOME: Archive Mounter

Ubuntu supports the access of archives directly from GNOME using Archive Mounter. You can select the archive file and then right-click and select Archive Mounter to open the archive. The archive contents are listed in a Nautilus file manager window. You can extract or display the contents.

You can also use Archive Mounter to mount CD/DVD disk ISO image files as archives. You can then browse and extract the contents of the CD/DVD. Right-click on a disk ISO image file (**.iso** extension) and select "Open with Archive Mounter." The image is automatically mounted as an archive. A disk icon for the CD/DVD will appear on the desktop. It will be read only. The disk will also appear in the Computer folder as a valid disk. To unmount the disk image as an archive, right-click on its icon and select Unmount.

Burning DVD/CDs with GNOME (Brasero)

GNOME performs disc-burning operations using the Brasero Disc Burner application. Brasero is integrated into the desktop, letting you burn data disc using a Nautilus file manager window.

File Manager CD/DVD Creator interface

Using the GNOME file manager to burn data to a DVD or CD is a simple matter of dragging files to an open blank CD or DVD and clicking the Write To Disk button. When you insert and open a blank DVD/CD, a window will open labeled CD/DVD Creator. To burn files, just drag them to that window. Click the Write To Disc button when ready to burn a DVD/CD. A Brasero Disc burning setup dialog will open, which will perform the actual write operation. Also, click the Properties button to open a dialog with burning options like the burn speed.

Burning ISO images from the file manager

The GNOME file manager also supports burning ISO images using Brasero. Just double-click the ISO image file or right-click the file and select Open with Brasero. This opens the Image Burning Setup dialog, which prompts you to burn the image. Be sure first to insert a blank CD or DVD into your CD/DVD burner.

GNOME desktop CD/DVD disc operations

You can perform disc copy, erasing, and checking using the Brasero CD/DVD burner directly. Once a disc is inserted, open the Computer window from the Go menu, then right-click on its CD/DVD desktop icon to display a menu with the Copy Disc and Check Disc entries. Selecting the Copy Disc entry will start the Brasero copy dialog.

You have the option of writing to an ISO image to another disc. For the ISO image file, the Properties dialog lets you choose the folder to save the file. For copying to another disc, the Properties dialog lets you choose the burning speed and options like using burnproof or performing a simulation first. Check Disc will check the integrity of the disk, with the option of using the disc's md5 file, if available. The menu for CD/DVD RW discs will also display a Blank Disc entry, which will erase a disc.

Brasero Disc Burner application interface

For more complex DVD/CD, burning you can use the Brasero DVD/CD burner application interface. Choose Brasero Disc Burner on the Multimedia dash. Brasero supports drag-and-drop operations for creating Audio CDs. In particular, it can handle CD/DVD read/write discs, and can erase discs. It also supports multi-session burns, adding data to DVD/CD disc. Initially Brasero displays a dialog with buttons for the type of project you want to create. You can create a data or audio project, create a DVD/Video disc, copy a DVD/CD, or burn a DVD/CD image file.

For a Data project, the toolbar displays an Add button, which you use to select files and directories to be burned to your disc. You also can drag-and-drop files and folders to your data listing (right-pane). You can choose to display a side panel (View menu) which will let you select files and directories.

Private Encrypted Directories (ecryptfs)

Ubuntu provides each user with the capability of setting up a private encrypted directory. Encryption adds a further level of security. Should others gain access to your home directory, they still would not be able to read any information in your private encrypted directory.

Private directory encryption is implemented using the **ecryptfs** utilities, **ecryptfs-utils** on the Ubuntu main repository. You use the **ecryptfs-setup-private** command to set up an encrypted private directory. During setup, an **.ecryptfs** directory is created which holds your encryption keys and manages access.

```
ecryptfs-setup-private
```

You are prompted to enter your user password, and then your mount password. The mount password is the password used to recover your private directory manually. Leave blank to have one generated automatically. A directory named **.Private** is set up which is the actual encrypted directory, holding the encrypted data files. This is a dot file, with a period preceding the name. Then a directory is set up named **Private**, which will serve as a mountpoint for the **.Private** directory. For security purposes, your encrypted private directory (**.Private**) remains unmounted until your decide to access it.

The **Private** directory is located in your home directory. You can open your file browser to the home directory where you will find an icon for the Private folder. When you start up your computer and first login, the Private folder will be unmounted (lock emblem). Open the folder to display a file named "Access Your Private Data". Click on it to mount the **.Private** folder. The contents of your Private directory are then displayed. You can double-click on this icon to mount and access your Private directory contents. You will be prompted to enter your login password.

The first time you try to run the "Access Your Private Data" file, you will receive a message saying that there is no application for it. The execute permission needs to be set to allow you to run it. Ownership is set originally to the root user. Use the following command in a terminal window to change ownership. For *user* use your user name.

```
sudo chown user Access-Your-Private-Data.desktop
```

You can then right click on the file, select Properties to open the Properties dialog, and on the Permissions tab, you can click the Execute checkbox.

If you are working from the command line interface, you can mount the **.Private** directory with the **ecryptfs-mount-private** command. Do not try to run this command from within the **Private** directory.

```
mount.ecryptfs_private
```

You can later unmount it with the **ecryptfs-umount-private** command.

To create a passphrase for your private directory, you use the **ecryptfs-manager** command. This displays a simple menu for creating passphrases.

Startup Applications Preferences

On the Startup Applications Preferences dialog, you can select programs you want started automatically and de-select the ones you do not want (accessible from the Customization dash as Startup Applications and from the Session menu). Some are selected already like the Update Notifier (Software updater) and Network Manager (see Figure 3-44). Here you can choose whether to start Ubuntu One on startup and play the Login Sound. To add an application not listed, click the Add button and enter the application name and program (use Browse to select program, usually in **/usr/bin**).

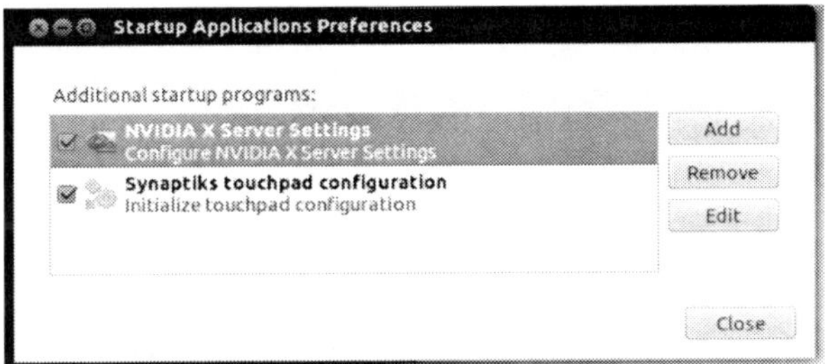

Figure 3-44: Startup Applications Preferences

Display Configuration and Additional Drivers

The graphics interface for your desktop display is implemented by the X Window System. The version used on Ubuntu is X.org (**x.org**). X.org provides its own drivers for various graphics cards and monitors. You can find out more about X.org at **www.x.org**.

X.org will automatically detect most hardware. The **/etc/X11/xorg.conf** file is no longer used for the open source drivers (**nv** and **ati**). It is still used to a limited extent by proprietary drivers, though mouse and keyboard entries are ignored. Information such as the monitor used is determined automatically. If you have an older monitor that is not correctly detected, you may have to specify monitor information by editing the **/etc/X11/xorg.conf** file.

Your display is detected automatically, configuring both your graphics card and monitor. Normally you should not need to perform any configuration yourself. However, if you have a graphics card that uses Graphics processors from a major Graphics vendor like ATI (AMD) or Nvidia, you have the option of using their driver, instead of the open source X drivers installed with

Ubuntu. Some graphics cards may work better with the vendor driver, and provide access to more of the card's features like 3D support. The open source ATI driver is **xserver-xorg-video-ati**, and the open source Nvidia driver is **xserver-xorg-video-nv** for older cards and **xserver-xorg-video-nouveau** for newer cards.

After you install Ubuntu and login, your graphic card will be detected and you will be notified that you can use a vendor driver instead for better performance. A restricted hardware notification icon is displayed on the top panel. Click on it or choose Additional Drivers from the Customization dash, or from the System Settings dialog. This invokes the jockey application, which will detect and mange the installation of needed hardware drivers (see Figure 3-45).

Select the driver entry and then click on the Activate button to use download and install the driver. Once installed the Activate button will change to a Deactivate button. You are notified to Restart your system. Close the Additional Drivers window and then restart your system. On restart, your system will then be using the vendor drivers such as ATI or Nvidia. The drives are part of the restricted repository, supported by the vendor but not by Ubuntu. They are not open source, but proprietary. This situation is beginning to change, with AMD (ATI) releasing much of its driver source code as open source.

Once installed, an examination of the Additional Drivers window will show the selected driver in use (see Figure 3-46). Should you want to remove the driver for any reason, click the Remove button. The driver will be removed and you will have to restart your system. Upon restart, the open source Xorg driver will be automatically selected and used. For Nvidia cards, the Nouveau open source drivers are used, which provides some acceleration support.

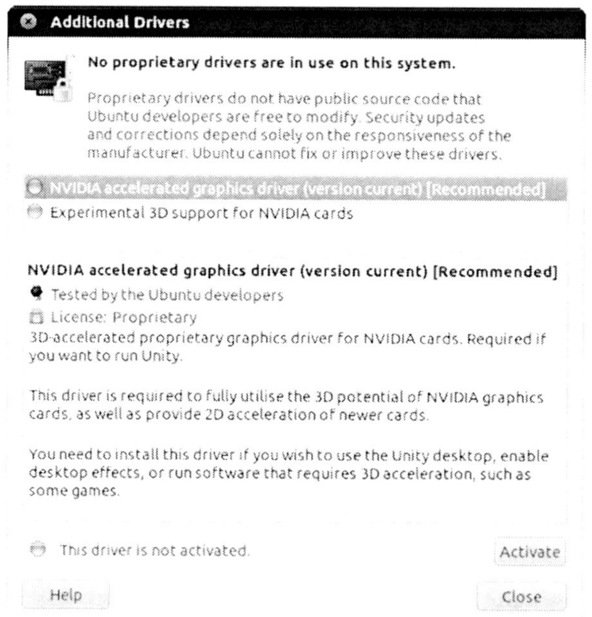

Figure 3-45: Hardware Drivers

When you install a new kernel, compatible kernel drivers for your proprietary graphics driver are generated automatically for you by the DKMS (Dynamic Kernel Module Support) utility.

When new version of the proprietary drivers becomes available, you will be notified and prompted to select the new version. A note will tell you that a different version is currently in use, and the Activate button will be displayed. Clicking it will download and install the new version.

The graphic vendors also have their own Linux-based configuration tools, which are installed with the driver. The Nvidia configuration tool is in the **nvidia-settings** package. Once installed, you will see Nvidia Server Settings in the System dash. This interface provides Nvidia vendor access to many of the features of Nvidia graphics cards like color corrections, video brightness and contrast, and thermal monitoring. You can also set the screen resolution and color depth.

ATI/AMD provides a Linux version of its Catalyst configuration tool for use on Linux, the **fglrx-amdcccle** package. Much of the ATI video drivers have now become open source, making the ATI video driver much more Linux compatible.

If you have problems with the vendor driver, you can always uninstall it. Your original Xorg open source driver will be used instead. The change over will be automatic. To uninstall the vendor driver, use the Additional Drivers dialog and un-check the vendor driver entry. After the uninstall process, you will be prompted to reboot.

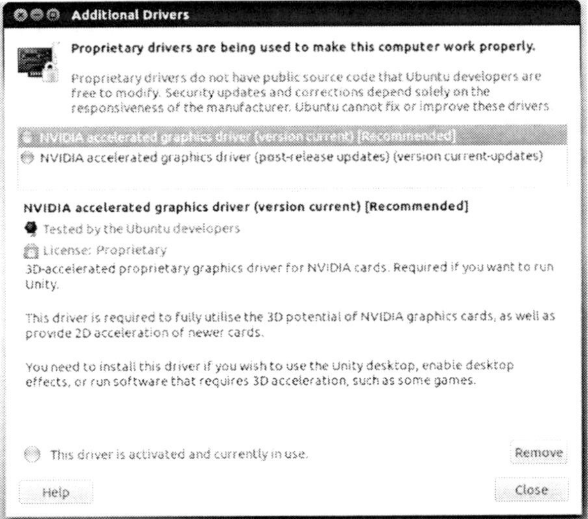

Figure 3-46: Activated Hardware Drivers

If the problem is more severe, with the display not working, you can use the GRUB menu on start up to select the recovery kernel. Your system will be started without the vendor graphics driver. You can use the "drop to shell" to enter the command line mode. From there you can use **apt-get** command-line APT tool to remove the graphics driver. The Nvidia drivers have the prefix have **nvidia**. In the following example, the asterisk will match on all the **nvidia** packages.

```
sudo apt-get remove nvidia*
```

Help Resources

A great deal of support documentation is already installed on your system, and is accessible from online sources. Table 3-2 lists Help tools and resources accessible on your Ubuntu Linux system. Both the GNOME and KDE desktops feature Help systems that use a browser-like interface to display help files. The Help browsers support the Ubuntu Help Center, which provides Ubuntu specific help.

If you need to ask a question, you can choose Help | Get online help to access the Ubuntu help support at **https://answers.launchpad.net**. and at **http:// askubuntu.com**. Here you can submit your question, and check answered questions about Ubuntu.

Ubuntu Desktop Guide

To start the Ubuntu Desktop Guide, click the desktop background, and then move the mouse to the applications menu (top bar to left), and choose "Ubuntu Help" from the Help menu. The Guide displays several links covering Ubuntu topics (see Figure 3-47). Unity topics covered include the Launcher, the Dash, indicator menus, window management, and workspace access.

You can use the right and left arrows to move through previous documentation you displayed. You can also search for topics. The search box displays the name of the current document. Clicking on the search bar lets you enter a search term. Press ENTER to display results. You can also add bookmarks for documents and search results by clicking the yellow start button at the right of the search box (or choosing "Add Bookmark" from the Bookmarks menu).

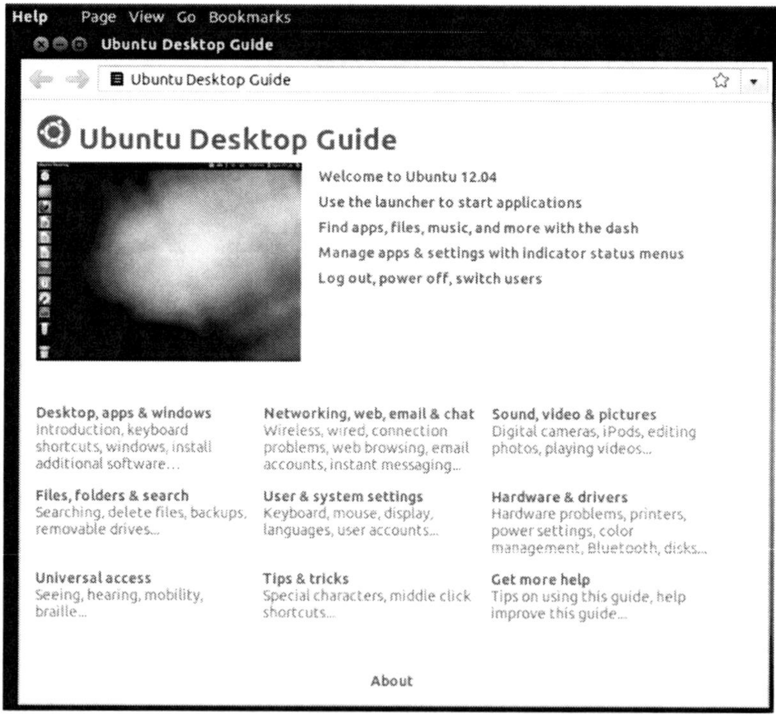

Figure 3-47: Ubuntu Desktop Guide

The pages are organized more like frequently asked questions documents, with more detailed headings designed to provide a clearer understanding of what the document is about (see Figure 3-48). The Sound, video, and pictures link opens a page with entries like "Why won't DVDs play" and "My new iPod won't work."

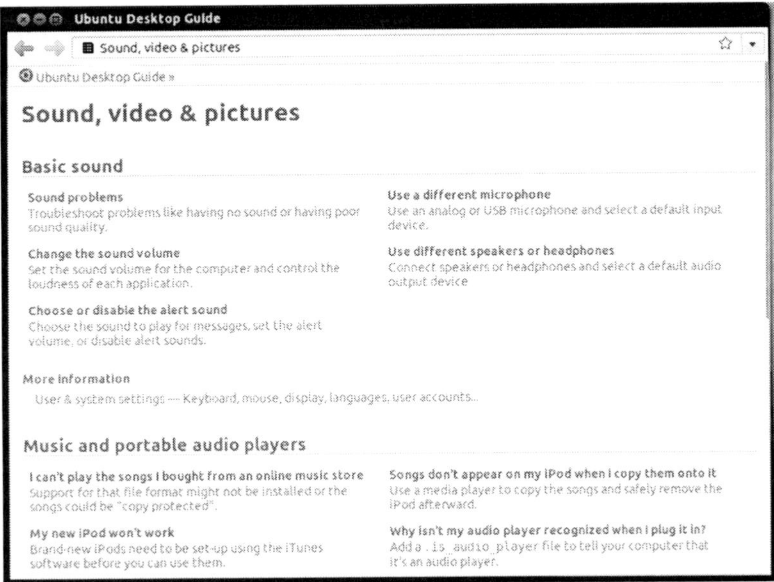

Figure 3-48: Ubuntu Desktop Guide topics

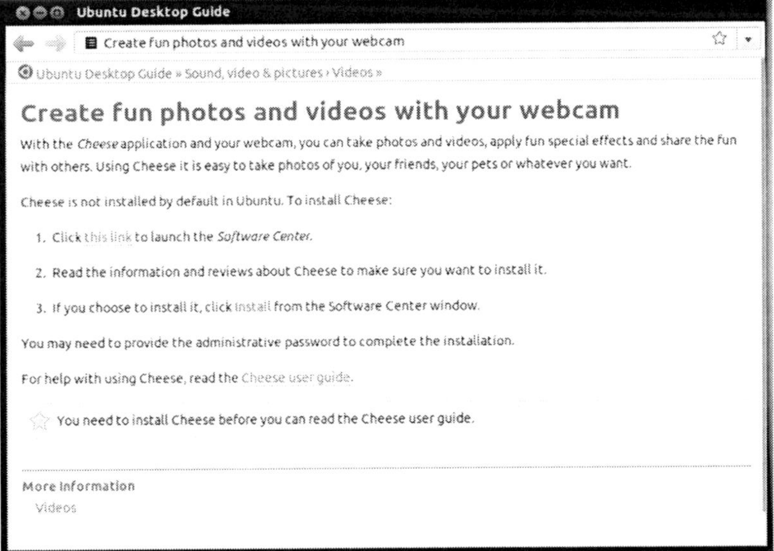

Figure 3-49: Ubuntu Desktop Guide page

Help documents will include helpful links such as an install links that opens the Ubuntu Software Center showing the software you have to install, or a link to a user guide for a relevant application (see Figure 3-49). At the bottom of most pages, a More Information section will have links for more detailed information.

If you want to see all the help documents available, choose All Documents from the Go menu. You will see application manuals including ones for the Evince Document Viewer, Empathy Internet messenger, Evolution, Disk Utility, Shared Folders, Shotwell, Simple scan, Tomboy, Synaptic package manager, Totem movie player, the Ubuntu Software Center, User Administration, and the Gedit editor (see Figure 3-50).

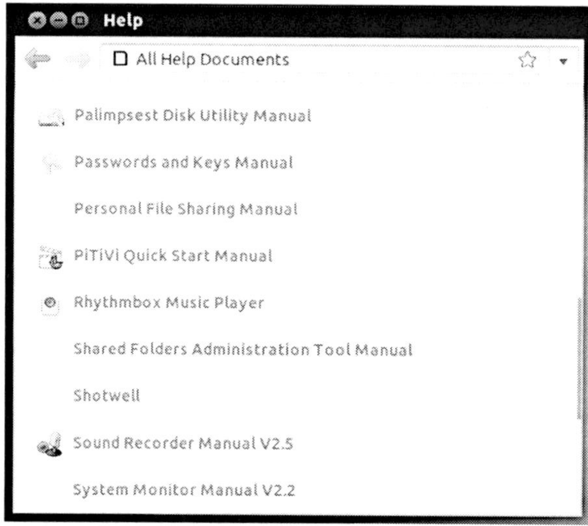

Figure 3-50: Ubuntu Help, All Documents

Context-Sensitive Help

Both GNOME and KDE, along with applications, provide context-sensitive help. Each KDE and GNOME application features detailed manuals that are displayed using their respective Help browsers. In addition, system administrative tools feature detailed explanations for each task.

Application Documentation

On your system, the **/usr/share/doc** directory contains documentation files installed by each application. Within each directory, you can usually find HOW-TO, README, and INSTALL documents for that application.

The Man Pages

You can also access the Man pages, which are manuals for Linux commands available from the command line interface, using the **man** command. Enter **man** along with the command on which you want information. The following example asks for information on the **ls** command:

```
$ man ls
```

Pressing the SPACEBAR key advances you to the next page. Pressing the **b** key moves you back a page. When you finish, press the **q** key to quit the Man utility and return to the command line. You activate a search by pressing either the slash (/) or question mark (?) keys. The / key searches forward and the ? key searches backward. When you press the / key, a line opens at the bottom of your screen, where you can enter a word to search for. Press ENTER to activate the search. You can repeat the same search by pressing the **n** key. You need not re-enter the pattern.

The Info Pages

Documentation for GNU applications, such as the gcc compiler and the Emacs editor, also exist as info pages accessible from the GNOME and KDE Help Centers. You can also access this documentation by entering the command **info** in a terminal window. This brings up a special screen listing different GNU applications. The info interface has its own set of commands. You can learn more about it by entering **info info** at the command prompt. Typing **m** opens a line at the bottom of the screen where you can enter the first few letters of the application. Pressing ENTER brings up the info file on that application.

Terminal Window

The Terminal window allows you to enter Linux commands on a command line, accessible as Terminal from the Accessories dash. It also provides you with a shell interface for using shell commands instead of your desktop. The command line is editable, allowing you to use the backspace key to erase characters on the line. Pressing a key will insert that character. You can use the left and right arrow keys to move anywhere on the line, and then press keys to insert characters, or use backspace to delete characters (see Figure 3-51). Folders, files, and executable files are color-coded: black for files, blue for folders, green for executable files, and aqua for links. Shared folders are displayed with a green background.

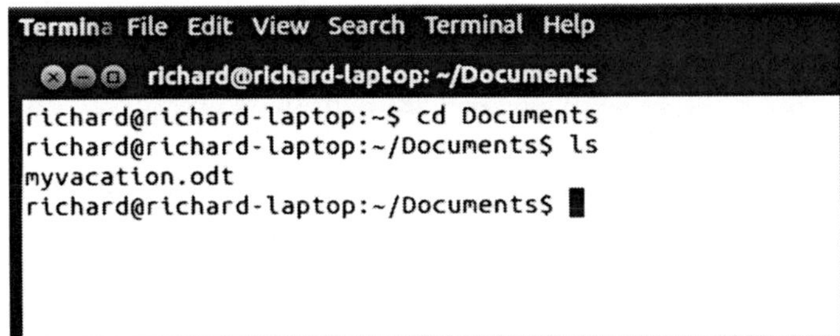

Figure 3-51: Terminal Window

The terminal window will remember the previous commands you entered. Use the up and down arrows to have those commands displayed in turn on the command line. Press the ENTER key to re-execute the currently displayed command. You can even edit a previous command before running it, allowing you to execute a modified version of a previous command. This can be helpful if you need to re-execute a complex command with a different argument, or if you mistyped a complex command and want to correct it without having to re-type the entire command. The terminal window will display all your previous interactions and commands for that session. Use the scrollbar to see any previous commands you ran and their displayed results.

You can open as many terminal windows as you want, each working in its own shell. Instead of opening a separate window for each new shell, you can open several shells in the same window, using tabs. Select Open Tab from the File menu to open a new tab (**Shift-Ctrl-t**). Each tab runs a separate shell, letting you enter different commands in each (see Figure 3-52). You can use the Tabs menu to move to different tabs, or just click on its tab to select it. The Tab menu is displayed on the toolbar only if multiple tabs are open. For a single window, the Tab menu is not shown (see Figure 3-53).

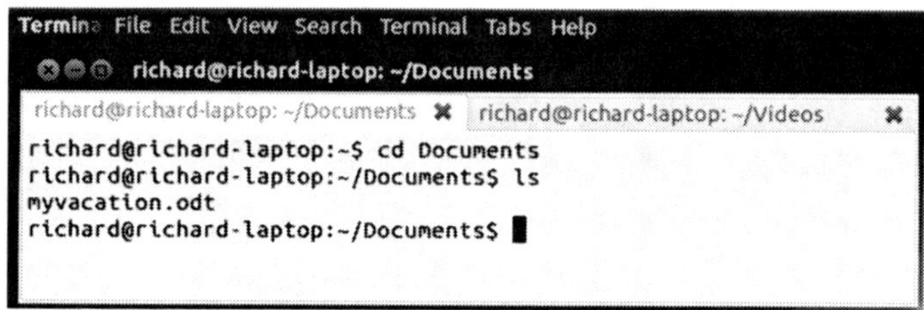

Figure 3-52: Terminal Window with tabs

The terminal window also supports desktop cut/copy and paste operations. You can copy a line from a Web page and then paste it to the terminal window (you can use the Paste entry on the Terminal window's Edit menu, or press **Shift-Ctrl-v**). The command will appear and then you can press ENTER to execute the command. This is useful for command line operations displayed on an instructional Web page. Instead of typing in a complex command yourself, just select and copy from the Web page directly, and then paste to the Terminal window. You can also perform any edits on the command if needed before executing it.

You can customize terminal windows using profiles. A default profile is set up already. You can create new ones with customized preferences. To customize your terminal window select Profile Preferences from the Edit menu. This opens a window for setting your profile options with tabs for General, Title and Command, Colors, Background, Scrolling, and Compatibility. The window title lists your current profile. This will be the **default** profile if you have not set up and selected another profile (see Figure 3-42).

To create a new profile, choose New Profile from the File menu. This opens a Profiles window listing current profiles. Click the New button to open the New Profile window where you can enter the profile name and select any profile to base it on. The default profile will be chosen initially. To edit a profile, select Profiles from the Edit menu to open the Profile window listing your profiles. Select the one you want to edit and then click the Edit button to open the Editing Profile window for that profile.

On the General tab, you can select the default size of a terminal window in text rows and columns.

The Scrolling tab specifies the number of command lines your terminal history will keep. These are the line you can move back through and select to re-execute. You can set this to unlimited to keep all the commands. You can also place the scrollbar on the right or left side.

Your terminal window will be set up to use a black background with white text. To change this you can edit the profile to change the background and text colors on the Colors tab. De-select the "Use colors from system theme" entry. This enables the "Built-in schemes" menu from which you can select a "Black on white" display. Other color combinations are also listed such as "Black on light yellow" and "Green on black." The Custom option lets you choose your own text and background colors. The colors on your open terminal window will change according to your selection, allowing you to see how the color choices will look.

Should you want a transparent or image background, use the Background tab. Initially the background will be set to solid color (the colors chosen on the Colors tab). To use an image instead select the Background image entry and then choose an image file. For a transparent background, choose the Transparent background entry and then set the amount of shading (none is completely transparent and maximum shows no transparency).

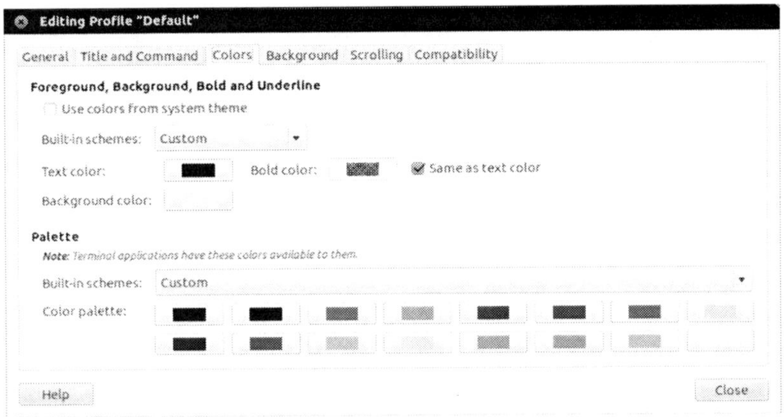

Figure 3-53: Terminal Window Profile configuration

Command Line Interface

When using the command line interface, you are given a simple prompt at which you type in a command. Even when you are using a desktop like GNOME, you sometimes need to execute commands on a command line. You can do so in a terminal window, which is accessed from the Accessories dash as Terminal. You can keep the terminal window icon on the Launcher by right clicking on it and choosing "Lock to Launcher"

Linux commands make extensive use of options and arguments. Be careful to place your arguments and options in their correct order on the command line. The format for a Linux command is the command name followed by options, and then by arguments, as shown here:

```
$ command-name options arguments
```

An *option* is a one-letter code preceded by one or two hyphens, which modifies the type of action the command takes. Options and arguments may or may not be optional, depending on the command. For example, the `ls` command can take an option, `-s`. The `ls` command displays a listing of files in your directory, and the `-s` option adds the size of each file in blocks. You enter the command and its option on the command line as follows:

```
$ ls -s
```

If you are uncertain what format and options a command uses, you can check the command syntax quickly by displaying its man page. Most commands have a man page. Just enter the **man** command with the command name as an argument.

An argument is data the command may need to execute its task. In many cases, this is a filename. An argument is entered as a word on the command line that appears after any options. For example, to display the contents of a file, you can use the **more** command with the file's name as its argument. The **less** or **more** command used with the filename **mydata** would be entered on the command line as follows:

```
$ less mydata
```

The command line is actually a buffer of text you can edit. Before you press ENTER to execute the command, you can edit the command on the command line. The editing capabilities provide a way to correct mistakes you may make when typing a command and its options. The BACKSPACE key lets you erase the character you just typed (the one to the left of the cursor) and the DEL key lets you erase the character the cursor is on. With this character-erasing capability, you can BACKSPACE over the entire line if you want, erasing what you entered. CTRL-U erases the whole command line and lets you to start over again at the prompt.

You can use the UP ARROW key to redisplay your last-executed command. You can then re-execute that command, or you can edit it and execute the modified command. This is helpful when you have to repeat certain operations, such as editing the same file. This is also helpful when you have already executed a command you entered incorrectly.

Running Windows Software on Linux: Wine

Wine is a Windows compatibility layer that will allow you to run many Windows applications natively on Linux. The actual Windows operating system is not required. Windows applications will run as if they were Linux applications, able to access the entire Linux file system and use Linux-connected devices. Applications that are heavily driver-dependent, like graphic intensive games, may not run. Others that do not rely on any specialized drivers, may run very well, including Photoshop, Microsoft Office, and newsreaders like Newsbin. For some applications, you may also need to copy over specific Windows dynamic link libraries (DLLs) from a working Windows system to your Wine Windows system32 or system directory.

You can install Wine on your system from the Ubuntu Software Center | System | Wine Microsoft Windows Compatibility Layer. The **ttf-mscorefonts-installer** for the Microsoft core fonts will also be installed. You will be prompted to accept the Microsoft end user agreement for using those fonts.

Once installed, you can access Wine applications from the Applications dash, or search on *wine*. The Wine applications include Wine configuration, the Wine software uninstaller, and Wine file browser, as well as Winetricks and notepad.

To set up Wine, start the Wine Configuration tool ("Configure Wine") to open a window with tabs for Applications, Libraries (DLL selection), Audio (sound drivers), Drives, Desktop Integration, and Graphics. On the Applications tab, you can select the version of Windows an application is designed for. The Drives tab lists your detected partitions, as well as your Windows-emulated drives, such as drive C. The C: drive is actually just a directory, **.wine/drive_c**, not a partition of a fixed size. Your actual Linux file system will be listed as the Z drive.

Once configured, Wine will set up a **.wine** directory on the user's home directory (the directory is hidden, enable Show Hidden Files in the file manager View menu to display it). Within that directory will be the **drive_c** directory, which functions as the C: drive that holds your Windows system files and program files in the Windows and Program File subdirectories. The System and System32 directories are located in the Windows directory. This is where you would place any needed DLL files. The Program Files directory holds your installed Windows programs, just as they would be installed on a Windows Program Files directory.

To install a Windows application with Wine, you right-click on the application icon in the file manager window, and then choose "Open With Wine Windows Program Loader." Alternatively, you can open a terminal window and run the `wine` command with the Windows application as an argument. The following example installs the popular Newsbin program:

```
$ wine newsbin.exe
```

Icons for installed Windows software will appear on your desktop. Just double-click an icon to start up an application. It will run normally within a Linux window, as would any Linux application.

Installing Windows fonts on Wine is a simple matter of copying fonts from a Windows font directory to your Wine **.wine/drive_c/Windows/fonts** directory. You can copy any Windows **.ttf** file to this directory to install a font.

Wine should work on both **.exe** and **.msi** files. You may have to make them executable by checking the file's Properties dialog Permissions tab's Execute checkbox. If a **.msi** file cannot be run, you may have to use the **msiexec** command with the **/a** option.

```
msiexec /a  mobireadersetup.msi
```

Tip: Alternatively, you can use the commercial Windows compatibility layer called Crossover Office. This is a commercial product tested to run certain applications like Microsoft Office. Check **http://www.codeweavers.com** for more details. Crossover Office is based on Wine, which CodeWeavers supports directly.

4. Installing and Updating Software

Ubuntu software distribution is implemented using the online Ubuntu software repositories, which contain an extensive collection of Ubuntu-compliant software. With the integration of repository access into your Linux system, you can think of that software as an easily installed extension of your current collection. You can add software to your system by accessing software repositories that support Debian packages (DEB) and the Advanced Package Tool (APT). Software is packaged into DEB software package files. These files are, in turn, installed and managed by APT. The Ubuntu Software Center provides an easy-to-use front end for installing software with just a click, accessible from the Ubuntu Software Center Launcher item and from the System dash.

The Ubuntu software repository is organized into sections, depending on how the software is supported. Software supported directly is located in the main Ubuntu repository section. Other Linux software that is most likely compatible is placed in the Universe repository section. Many software applications, particularly multimedia applications, have potential licensing conflicts. Such applications are placed in the Multiverse repository section, which is not maintained directly by Ubuntu. Many of the popular multimedia drivers and applications such as video and digital music support can be obtained from the Ubuntu Multiverse sections using the same simple APT commands you use for Ubuntu-supported software. Software from the Multiverse and Universe sections are integrated into the Ubuntu Software Center, and can be installed just as easily as Ubuntu main section software. Some drivers are entirely proprietary and supplied directly by vendors. This is the case with the Nvidia and ATI vendor-provided drivers. These drivers are placed in a restricted section, noting that there is no open source support.

You also can download source code versions of applications, then compile, and install them on your system. Where this process once was complex, it has been streamlined significantly with the use of configure scripts. Most current source code, including GNU software, is distributed with a configure script, which automatically detects your system configuration and creates a binary file that is compatible with your system.

You could download Linux software from many online sources directly, but it is always advised that you use the Ubuntu prepared package versions if available. Most software for GNOME and KDE have corresponding Ubuntu-compliant packages in the Ubuntu Universe and Multiverse sections.

Installing Software Packages

Installing software is an administrative function performed by a user with administrative access. During the Ubuntu installation, only some of the many applications and utilities available for users on Linux were installed on your system. On Ubuntu, you can install or remove software from your system with the Ubuntu Software Center, the Synaptic Package Manager, or the **apt** command. Alternatively, you could install software as separate DEB files or by downloading and compiling its source code.

APT (Advanced Package Tool) is integrated as the primary tool for installing packages. When you install a package with the Ubuntu Software Center or with the Synaptic Package Manager, APT will be invoked and will select and download the package automatically from the appropriate online repository. This will include the entire Ubuntu online repository, including the main, universe, multiverse, and restricted sections.

A DEB software package includes all the files needed for a software application. A Linux software application often consists of several files that must be installed in different directories. The application program itself is placed in a system directory such as **/usr/bin**, online manual files go in another directory, and library files go in yet another directory. When you select an application for installation, APT will install any additional dependent (required) packages. APT also will install all recommended packages by default. Many software applications have additional features that rely on recommended packages.

Note: Be careful not to mix distributions. The distribution segments of all your **sources.list** entries should be the same: precise if you are using Ubuntu 12.04, Oneiric for 11.10, and so on.

Ubuntu Package Management Software

Although all Ubuntu software packages have the same DEB format, they can be managed and installed using different package management software tools. The underlying software management tool is APT.

The Ubuntu Software Center is now the primary interface for locating and installing Ubuntu software, repository files at **/var/cache/apt**. Designed as a central software management application for handling all Ubuntu packages (replaces Add/Remove Applications tool).

APT (Advanced Package Tool) performs the actual software managements operations for all applications installed from a repository. The Ubuntu Software Center, the Synaptic Package Manager, update-manager, dpkg, and apt-get are all front ends for APT, repository files at **/var/cache/apt**.

Synaptic Package Manager is a Graphical front end for APT that manages packages, repository files at **/var/cache/apt**.

Update Manager is the Ubuntu graphical front end for updating installed software using APT.

Muon is the KDE software manager, a graphical front end for APT.

tasksel is a cursor-based screen for selecting package groups and particular servers (front end for APT). This tool will work on the command-line interface installed by the Ubuntu Server CD. You can also run it in a terminal window on a desktop (**sudo tasksel**). Use arrow keys to move to an entry, the spacebar to select, the Tab key to move to the OK button. Press ENTER on the OK button to perform your installs.

dpkg is the older command line tool used to install, update, remove, and query software packages; uses its own database, **/var/lib/dpkg**; repository files are kept at **/var/cache/apt**, same as APT.

apt-get is the primary command line tool for APT to install, update, and remove software; uses its own database, **/var/lib/apt/**; repository information at **/var/cache/apt**

aptitude is a cursor based front end for **dpkg** and **apt-get**, which uses its own database, **/var/lib/aptitude**. It is used during the Alternate CD and Ubuntu DVD (text mode) installations to select individual packages for installation.

Ubuntu Software Repositories

Four main components or sections make up the Ubuntu repository: main, restricted, universe, and multiverse. These components are described in detail at:

```
https://help.ubuntu.com/community/Repositories/Ubuntu
```

To see a listing of all packages in the Ubuntu repository see:

```
http://packages.ubuntu.com
```

To see available repositories and their sections, open Software Sources from System | Administration | Software Sources, Ubuntu Software tab.

In addition, there is a third-party repository called **medibuntu.org**, which provides several popular codecs and applications like Realplayer and the DVD Video codec. This repository has to be configured manually, as discussed later in this chapter.

```
http://www.medibuntu.org
```

Repository Components

The following repository components are included in the Ubuntu repository:

main: Officially supported Ubuntu software (canonical), includes GStreamer Good plug-ins.

restricted: Software commonly used and required for many applications, but not open source or freely licensed, like the proprietary graphics card drivers from Nvidia and ATI needed for hardware support. Because they are not open source, they are not guaranteed to work.

universe: All open source Linux software not directly supported by Ubuntu includes GStreamer Bad plug-ins.

multiverse: Linux software that does not meet licensing requirements and is not considered essential. It is not guaranteed to work. For example, the GStreamer ugly package is in this repository. Check **http://www.ubuntu.com/project/about-ubuntu/licensing**.

Repositories

In addition to the Ubuntu repository, Ubuntu maintains several other repositories used primarily for maintenance and support for existing packages. The updates repository holds updated packages for a release. The security updates repository contains critical security package updates every system will need.

Ubuntu repository: Collection of Ubuntu-compliant software packages for releases organized into main, universe, multiverse, and restricted sections.

Updates: Updates for packages in the main repository, both main and restricted sections.

Backports: Software under development for the next Ubuntu release, but packaged for use in the current one. Not guaranteed or fully tested. Backports access is now enabled by default.

Security updates: Critical security fixes for main repository software.

Partners: Third party proprietary software tested to work on Ubuntu. You need to authorize access manually.

The backports repository provides un-finalized or development versions for new and current software. They are not guaranteed to work, but may provide needed features.

There is also a third-party repository called **Medibuntu.org (http://medibuntu.org)** that is commonly used for multimedia and Web applications that have licensing issues, like the DVD Video **libdvdcss** codec for commercial DVD Video and Google Earth. You first have to configure access to this repository. Once setup, packages from this repository will be listed in the Synaptic Packages Manager and the Ubuntu Software Center, which you then can use to install them. See the following sections for configuration instructions.

Medibuntu.org   Third-party repository for software and codecs with licensing issues.

Note: Though it is possible to add the Debian Linux distribution repository, it is not advisable. Packages are designed for specific distributions Combining them can lead to irresolvable conflicts.

Ubuntu Repository Configuration file: sources.list and sources.list.d

Repository configuration is managed by APT using configuration files in the **/etc/apt** directory. The **/etc/apt/sources.list** file holds repository entries. The main and restricted sections are enabled by default. An entry consists of a single line with the following format:

```
format   URI   release   section
```

The format is normally **deb,** for Debian package format. The URI (universal resource identifier) provides the location of the repository, such as an FTP or Web URL. The release name is the official name of a particular Ubuntu distribution like precise or jaunty. Ubuntu 12.04 has the name precise. The section can be one or more terms that identify a section in that release's repository. There can be more than one term used to specify a section, like **main** and **restricted** to specify the restricted section in the Ubuntu repository. The Multiverse and Universe sections can be specified by single terms: **universe** and **multiverse**. You can also list individual packages if you want. The entry for the Precise restricted section is shown here.

```
deb http://us.archive.ubuntu.com/ubuntu/   precise   main restricted
```

Corresponding source code repositories will use a **deb-src** format.

```
deb-src http://us.archive.ubuntu.com/ubuntu/ precise main restricted
```

The update repository for a section is referenced by the **-updates** suffix, as in **precise-updates**.

```
deb http://archive.ubuntu.com/ubuntu/   precise-updates   main restricted
```

The security repository for a section is referenced with the suffix **-security**, as **precise-security**.

```
deb http://archive.ubuntu.com/ubuntu/   precise-security   main restricted
```

Both Universe and Multiverse repositories should already be enabled. Each will have an updates repository as well as corresponding source code repositories, like those shown here for Universe.

```
deb http://us.archive.ubuntu.com/ubuntu/ precise universe
deb-src http://us.archive.ubuntu.com/ubuntu/ precise universe
deb http://us.archive.ubuntu.com/ubuntu/ precise-updates universe
deb-src http://us.archive.ubuntu.com/ubuntu/ precise-updates universe
```

Comments begin with a # mark. You can add comments of your own if you wish. Commenting an entry effectively disables that component of a repository. Placing a # mark before a repository entry will effectively disable it.

Commented entries are included for the backports and Canonical partners repositories. Backports holds applications being developed for future Ubuntu releases and may not work well. Partners include companies like Adobe and Skype.

Most entries, including third-party entries for Ubuntu partners, can be managed using Software Sources. The backports entry requires that you edit the **sources.list** file. You can edit the file directly with the following command.

```
gksu gedit /etc/apt/sources.list
```

Then remove the # at the beginning of the line.

```
# deb http://us.archive.ubuntu.com/ubuntu/ precise-backports main restricted
universe multiverse
```

Repository information does not have to be added to the **sources.list** file directly. It can also be placed in a text file in the **/etc/apt/sources.list.d** directory, which APT will read as if part of the **sources.list** file. For example, to add the Medibuntu.org repository, a file is created in the **/etc/at/sources.list.d** directory, which contains the Medibuntu.org repository URL lines. This way you do not have to edit the **/etc/apt/sources.list** file. Editing such an important file always includes the risk of incorrectly changing the entries.

Software Sources managed from Ubuntu Desktop

You can manage your repositories with the Software Sources dialog, allowing you to enable or disable repository sections, as well as add new entries. This dialog edits the **/etc/apt/sources.list** file directly. Software Sources is not displayed on the dash by default. Use the Main Menu to display it on the System dash or from the System Settings dialog. You can also access the Software Sources dialog on the Ubuntu Software Center from the Edit menu, and on the Synaptic Package Manager from the Settings menu as the Repositories entry. The Software Sources dialog displays five tabs: Ubuntu Software, Other Software, Updates, Authentication, and Statistics (see Figure 4-1). The Ubuntu Software tab lists all the Ubuntu repository section entries. These include the main repository, universe, restricted, and multiverse, as well as source code. Those that are enabled will be checked. Initially all of them, except the source code, will be enabled. You can enable or disable a repository section by checking or un-checking its entry. You can select the repository server to use from the "Download from" drop-down menu.

On the Other Software tab, you can add repositories for third-party software (see Figure 4-2). The repository for Ubuntu partners will already be listed, but not checked. Check that entry if you want access software from the Partners repository such as Adobe reader. If you install

Medibuntu.org repository support, you will see Medibuntu.org entries on this tab. To add a third-party repository manually, click the Add button. This opens a dialog where you enter the complete APT entry, starting with the deb format, followed by the URL, release, and sections or packages. This is the line as it will appear in the **/etc/apt/sources.list** file. Once entered, click the Add Source button.

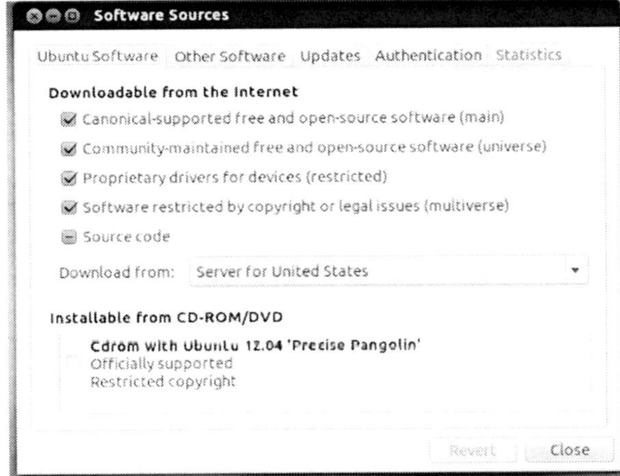

Figure 4-1: Software Sources Ubuntu Software repository sections.

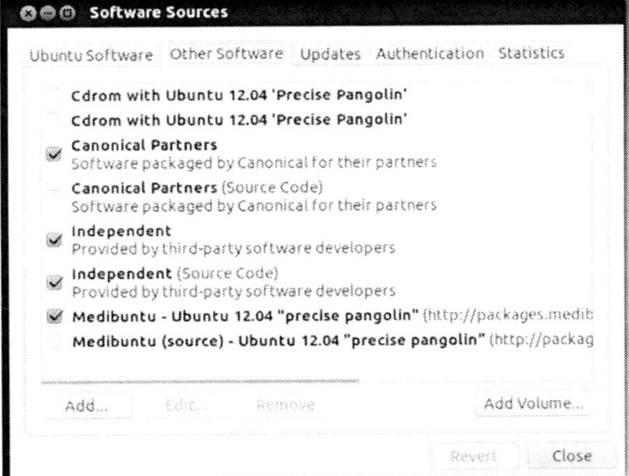

Figure 4-2: Software Sources Other Software configuration

The Updates tab lets you configure how updates are handled (see Figure 4-3). The tab specifies both your update repositories and how automatic updates are handled. You have the option to install Important Security Updates (precise-security), Recommended Updates (precise-updates), Pre-released Updates (precise-proposed), and Unsupported Updates (precise-backports). The Important Security and Recommended updates will already be selected; these cover updates for the entire Ubuntu repository. Pre-released and unsupported updates are useful if you have installed any packages from the backports or pre-release repositories.

Your system is already configured to check for updates automatically on a daily basis. You can opt not to check for updates at all by un-checking the "Check for updates" check box. You also have options for how updates are handled. You can install any security updates automatically, without confirmation. You can download updates in the background. Or you can just be notified of available updates, and then choose to install them when you want. The options are exclusive.

On this tab, you also can choose what releases to be notified of: the LTS releases only, all releases, or none.

The Authentication tab shows the repository software signature keys that are installed on your system (see Figure 4-4). Ubuntu requires a signature key for any package that it installs. Signature keys for all the Ubuntu repositories are installed, and are listed on this tab, including your CD/DVD disc. For Medibuntu.org, installing the **medibuntu-keyring** package set up the signature key for the Medibuntu.org repository, which would also be listed on this tab.

Figure 4-3: Software Sources Update configuration

Most other third party or customized repositories will provide a signature key file for you to download and import. You can add such keys manually from the Authentication tab. Click the Import Key File to open a file browser where you can select the downloaded key file. This procedure is the same as the **apt-key add** operation. Both add keys that APT then uses to verify DEB software packages downloaded from repositories before it installs them.

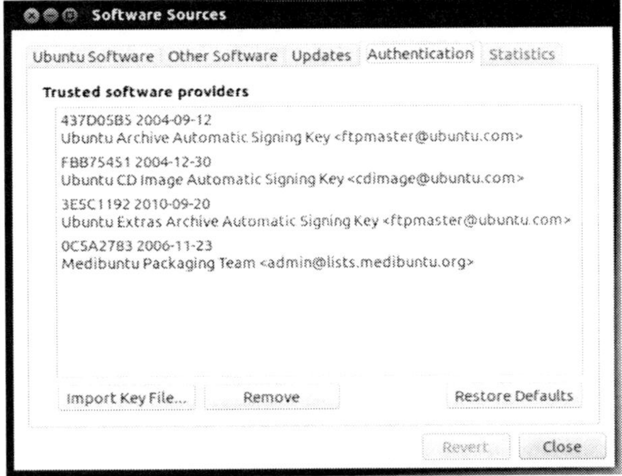

Figure 4-4: Software Sources Authentication, package signature keys

The Statistics tab lets you provide Ubuntu with software usage information, letting them know what software is being used.

After you have made changes and click the Close button, the Software Sources tool will notify you that your software package information is out of date, displaying a Reload button. Click the Reload button to make the new repositories or components available on your package managers like the Ubuntu Software Center and the Synaptic Package Manager. You also can reload your repository configuration by running **apt-get update**, clicking the Reload button on the Synaptic Package Manager, or clicking the Check button on the Update Manager.

Medibuntu.org repository configuration

For applications and codecs with licensing issues, like FFmpeg unrestricted support, Real Player, Google Earth, and the DVD Video commercial decoder (**libdvdcss**), you access the Medibuntu.org repository, **http://medibuntu.org**. Table 4-1 lists some of the applications and codec available on the Medibuntu repository.

Medibuntu stand for Multimedia, entertainment, and distractions in Ubuntu, and holds some unrestricted multimedia codecs such as unrestricted FFmpeg, and proprietary applications like Google Earth. To enable access, the **medibuntu.list** repository file, which holds the Medibuntu repository references, has to be added to the **/etc/apt/sources.list.d** directory. In addition, the Medibuntu GPG software authentication key has to be installed on your system. These tasks are usually performed on a command line in a terminal window. See the Medibuntu help page for details. You can also access this page from the Medibuntu.org Web site by clicking the Repository HowTo link.

```
https://help.ubuntu.com/community/Medibuntu
```

Once you have set up repository access, you can use the Synaptic Package Manager to download and install any of the Medibuntu packages. If you want to use the Ubuntu Software Center to install Medibuntu applications, you can use the Synaptic Package Manager first to install the **app-install-data-medibuntu** package. You will then see Medibuntu applications listed in the

Ubuntu Software Center. Packages will reside in their respective categories, such as libdvdcss in Multimedia and Google Earth in Internet.

Package	Description
aacgain	AAC normalizer for MP4 video and MP3 media files
aacplusenc	AAC encoder
acroread-fonts	Adobe Acrobat reader fonts
alsa-firmware	Proprietary firmware support for several soundcards.
app-install-data-medibuntu	Adds Medibuntu application entries to Ubuntu Software Center and the Synaptic Package Manager.
ices	Icecast streaming audio
libdvdcss2	Commercial DVD Video support
libav	Stream audio and video codecs, tools, and support (decode, encode, record, and convert): libavcodec, libavdevice, libavfilter, libavformat, libavutil. libpostproc, and libswscale.
medibuntu-keyring	Medibuntu repository digital signature key
mplayer	Version of Mplayer that uses the unrestricted FFmpeg libraries
non-free-codecs	Meta package for installing a wide range of non-free codecs at once. Installs amr, w32codecs, and the restricted-extras packages.
realplayer	RealPlayer 10 for Linux (based on Helix player)
rmconverter	Convert Real Player media
w32codecs, w64codecs	Windows media codecs

Table 4-1: Medibuntu.org codecs and applications

Medibuntu quick configuration

To configure access quickly to the Medibuntu repository, you can copy the command line from the Medibuntu.org Repository HowTo Web page (**http://medibuntu.org/repository.php** or **https://help.ubuntu.com/community/Medibuntu**) and paste it directly to a terminal window, without having to type anything. First, locate the "Adding the Repository" section on the Web page. A highlighted command line to run in a Terminal will be displayed. The commands to set up the repository, read the repository information (update), and to install the Medibuntu software key (medibuntu-keyring), have been combined into a single line using **&&** operators to connect them. The following is all one line.

```
sudo wget --output-document=/etc/apt/sources.list.d/medibuntu.list
http://www.medibuntu.org/sources.list.d/$(lsb_release -cs).list && sudo apt-get -
-quiet update && sudo apt-get --yes --quiet --allow-unauthenticated install
medibuntu-keyring && sudo apt-get --quiet update
```

Click and drag your mouse over the highlighted command line to select it.

From the Web browser Edit menu, select Copy (or press Ctrl-c).

Open a terminal window (Terminal on the Accessories dash).

Select the terminal window, then click on the Edit menu for the terminal window and select the Paste entry (or press **Shift-Ctrl-v**). The selected text from the Web page will be pasted to the terminal window. Make sure it was copied correctly. Then press the ENTER key. As these are **sudo** operations performing administrative tasks, you will be prompted for your password. A long list of APT operations will be displayed as the Medibuntu.org repository is read and the software key installed. First, the **/etc/apt/sources.list.d/medibuntu.list** file is created with the Medibuntu.org repository information. Then the Medibuntu.org software list is read. This is to obtain a reference to the **medibuntu-keyring** package, which holds the GPG software authentication key for Medibuntu.org software packages. Then the **medibuntu-keyring** package is installed, with an option to allow an unauthenticated package installed (the software authentication key is inside the package). Then the Medibuntu.org repository is read again, this time with the software authentication key, allowing for package installation.

If you want to use the Ubuntu Software Center to install Medibuntu applications, you can install the **app-install-data-medibuntu** with the following command. For bug reporting you also can install the **apport-hooks-medibuntu** package. This command also is located on the Medibuntu.org Repository HowTo page in the "Adding the Repository" section. You can cut and paste it to a terminal window to run it.

```
sudo apt-get --yes install app-install-data-medibuntu apport-hooks-medibuntu
```

Alternatively, you can use the Synaptic Package Manager to install the **app-install-data-medibuntu** package.

Note: The name given to the file containing the Medibuntu.org URL information in the **/etc/apt/sources.list.d** directory is **medibuntu.list**.

If you want, you could enter the Medibuntu.org configuration command as separate commands, as shown here.

```
sudo wget --output-document=/etc/apt/sources.list.d/medibuntu.list
http://www.medibuntu.org/sources.list.d/$(lsb_release -cs).list
sudo apt-get --quiet update
sudo apt-get --yes --quiet --allow-unauthenticated install medibuntu-keyring
sudo apt-get --quiet update
```

In the first line, the **$(lsb_release -cs)** operation provides the current distribution name, in this case **precise**.

Free (open source) and Non-free (proprietary) Medibuntu.org Software

The Medibuntu.org repository holds packages that are both open source and proprietary. The term free applies to open source packages, and non-free is used to reference proprietary packages. In this sense, non-free applies to Google Earth, which is proprietary and free applies to libdvdcss, which is open source. Should you not want any proprietary (non-free) software packages installed on your system, you can simply remove the **non-free** repository section name from the **medibuntu.list** URI line. The following command line will do this for you.

```
sudo sed -e 's/ non-free//' -i /etc/apt/sources.list.d/medibuntu.list
```

You could also just edit the **medibuntu.list** file and remove the **non-free** section name.

```
gksu gedit /etc/apt/sources.list.d/medibuntu.list
```

The URL line originally looks like this, showing both **free** and **non-free** repository section names.

```
deb http://packages.medibuntu.org/ precise free non-free
```

The edited version would have the **non-free** repository section name removed.

```
deb http://packages.medibuntu.org/ precise free
```

Medibuntu alternative repository support installation methods

You could also manually create a **medibuntu.list** file in your **/etc/apt/sources.list.d** directory, which will contain the apt source references for the Medibuntu repository. The contents of the **medibuntu.list** repository file for Ubuntu precise are available at **http://www.medibuntu.org/sources.list.d/precise.list**. Creating the file in the **/etc/apt/sources.list.d** directory requires administrative access, so you would have to use the **sudo** command. The **wget** operation downloads the **precise.list** repository file to the **/etc/apt/sources.list.d** directory.

```
sudo wget http://www.medibuntu.org/sources.list.d/precise.list
--output-document=/etc/apt/sources.list.d/medibuntu.list
```

Alternatively, you could access the **precise.list** file on your browser and download it as a text file named **precise.list**.

```
http://www.medibuntu.org/sources.list.d/precise.list
```

Then copy the file to **the /etc/apt/sources.list.d** directory as **medibuntu.list**, using the **sudo** and **cp** commands.

```
sudo cp precise.list /etc/apt/sources.list.d/medibuntu.list
```

You then have to install the Medibuntu signature key, before you can download and install any packages. The Medibuntu key is held in the **medibuntu-keyring** package, which allows you to perform package installations.

To install the key use the following command line in a terminal window, also available on the Medibuntu Repository HowTo page listed previously as the last two sudo operations in the add repository command. You can copy it from your browser and paste it to the terminal window. Use the terminal window Edit menu Paste to copy, or press **Shift-Ctrl-v**.

```
sudo apt-get --quiet update && sudo apt-get --yes --quiet --allow-unauthenticated
install medibuntu-keyring && sudo apt-get --quiet update
```

The **--allow-authentication** option allows you to install the **medibuntu.keyring** package without authentication.

You could also download the **medibuntu-keyring** package directly from the **medibuntu.org** Web site and open it with the Ubuntu Software Center installer, or save it to a file and install it later with the Ubuntu Software Center or **dpkg**.

```
http://packages.medibuntu.org/precise/medibuntu-keyring.html
```

The name of the downloaded medibuntu-keyring package is:

```
medibuntu-keyring_2008.04.20_all.deb
```

Alternatively, an easy way to install the **medibuntu-keyring** package, once you have installed Medibuntu repository support, is to use the Synaptic Package Manager. Click the Reload button to read the Medibuntu repository listing. Then search for:

```
medibuntu-keyring
```

Select the package for install and click Apply. You will be warned that it is not authenticated, but install anyway. The key will be installed. Click Reload again. You can now download and install any Medibuntu package. Install the **app-install-data-medibuntu** package to have Medibuntu packages appear in the Ubuntu Software Center.

Updating Ubuntu with Update Manager

New updates are continually being prepared for particular software packages as well as system components. These are posted as updates you can download from software repositories and install on your system. These include new versions of applications, servers, and even the kernel. Such updates may range from single software packages to whole components. Updating your Ubuntu system is a very simple procedure, using Update Manager, a graphical update interface for APT.

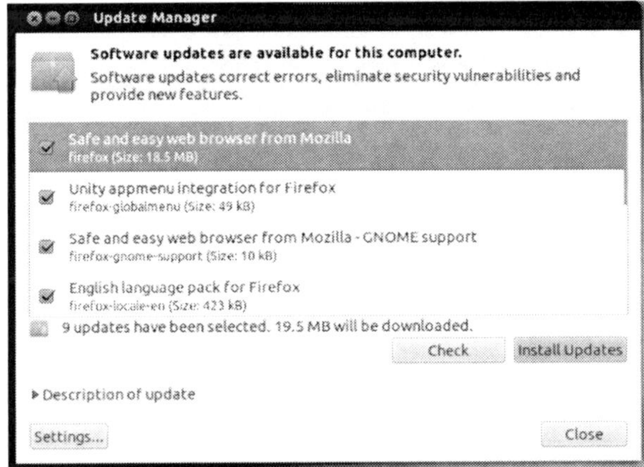

Figure 4-5: Update Manager with selected packages

When updates become available, the Session menu (power icon) displays an "Updates available" message. Click on the entry to start up the Update Manager. If there are no updates, the Session menu shows a "Software Up to Date" entry. Clicking on it still opens the Update Manager. You can also check for updates manually by choosing Update Manager from the System dash, and clicking the Check button.

You can also start the Update Manager from the Applications lens, system tools. If you have placed the Update Manager item on the Launcher, you can invoke the update from its quicklist. The item also shows the number of packages to be updated, as shown here:

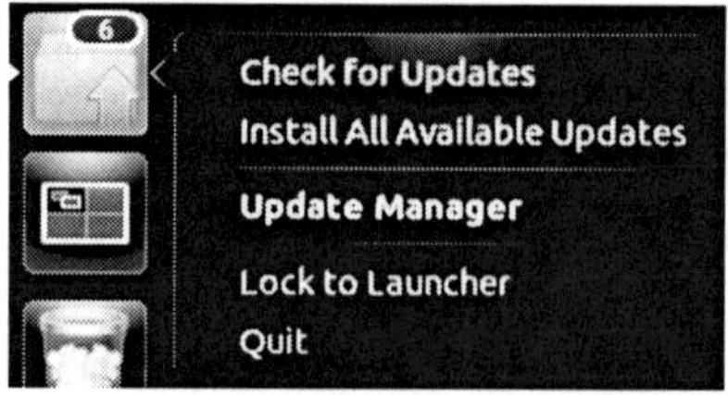

All needed updates are selected automatically when Update Manager starts up (see Figure 4-5). The check boxes for each entry lets you de-select any particular packages you do not want to update. Packages are organized according to importance, beginning with Important security updates and followed by Recommended updates. You should always install the security updates. All the APT-compatible repositories that are configured on your system will be checked for updates.

To see a detailed description of an update, select the update and then click the "Description of update" arrow at the bottom of the window (see Figure 4-6). Two tabs are displayed: Changes and Description. The Changes tab lists detailed update information, and Description provides information about the software.

Click the Install Updates button to start updating. The packages will be downloaded from their appropriate repository. Once downloaded, the packages are updated.

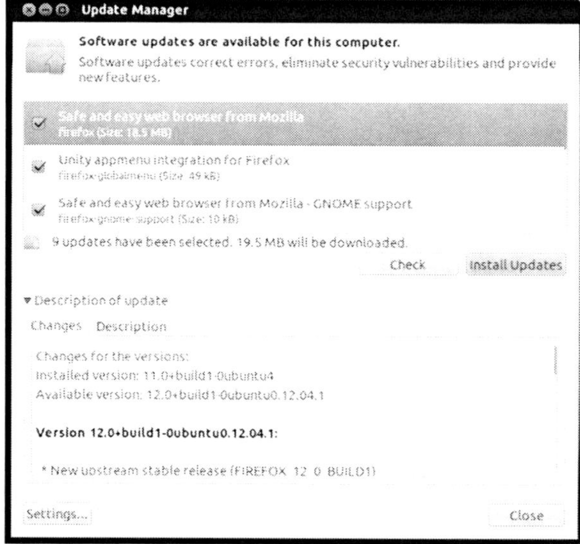

Figure 4-6: Detailed Update information

When downloading and installing, a dialog appears showing the download and install progress (see Figure 4-7). You can choose to show progress for individual files. A window will open up that lists each file and its progress. Once downloaded, the updates are installed (see Figure 4-8). Click the Details button to see install messages for particular software packages. The Update Software Launcher item will also show a progress bar for the install process and the number of updates, as shown in Figure 4-7).

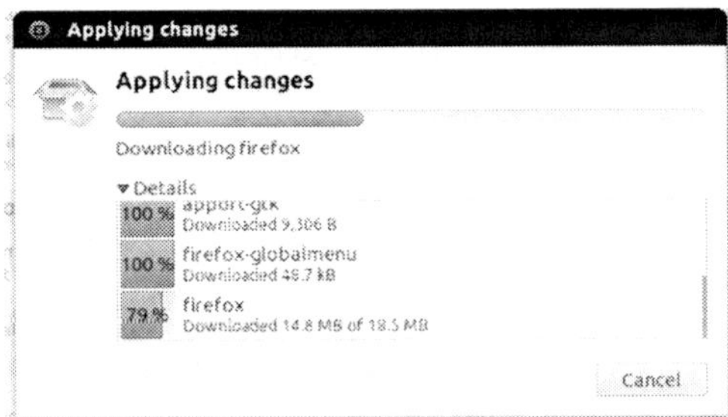

Figure 4-7: Download updates

When the update completes, Update Manager will display a message saying that your system is up-to-date. If a critical package was installed such as a new kernel, you are prompted to restart your system. The power icon will turn red as a warning and the Session menu will have the added entry "Restart required."

Figure 4-8: Install updates

Managing Packages with the Ubuntu Software Center

To perform simple installation and removal of software, you can use the Ubuntu Software Center, which is the primary supported package manager for Ubuntu. The Ubuntu Software Center is designed to be the centralized utility for managing all your software. The Ubuntu Software Center is also a store for commercial Ubuntu applications. For more details on the Ubuntu Software Center, open the Ubuntu Help dialog by choosing Help | Ubuntu Software Center Help.

You can also set up an Ubuntu Software Center account to let you check and synchronize the software you have installed on different computers using Ubuntu. The account is the same as your Ubuntu One account. Choose File | Sync Between Computers to use this feature. Your Ubuntu computers are listed with expandable software categories on a right pane. You can choose to remove software from a selected computer, and, the next time you synchronize on that computer, the software is removed.

Figure 4-9: Ubuntu Software Center

To use the Ubuntu Software Center, you click the Ubuntu Software Center icon on the Launcher or from the System dash. The Ubuntu Software Center displays a toolbar, a side panel on the left showing categories and software lists (see Figure 4-9).

The "What's New" and "Top Rated" sections at the right provide a listing of new and popular applications. Click on an icon to display its information tab where you can install the application or link to its web site. Click the More button at the top right of each section to open a full listing of new and top rated software. The "Recommended For You" feature lists applications you may be interested in based on software you have installed. Click the "Turn on Recommendations" link to turn this feature on (also, you can choose Turn On Recommendations from the View menu).

The toolbar provides forward and back buttons for moving through previously viewed software listing and search results. On the toolbar, software icons and menus let you choose the software categories you want to view or search. The All Software icon displays all available software. A drop-down menu to the right of the icon lets you limit your views and searches to certain software categories such as "Provided by Ubuntu" for Ubuntu supported software, "Canonical Partners" for software available from Ubuntu partners like Adobe, and "For Purchase" for software you can purchase.

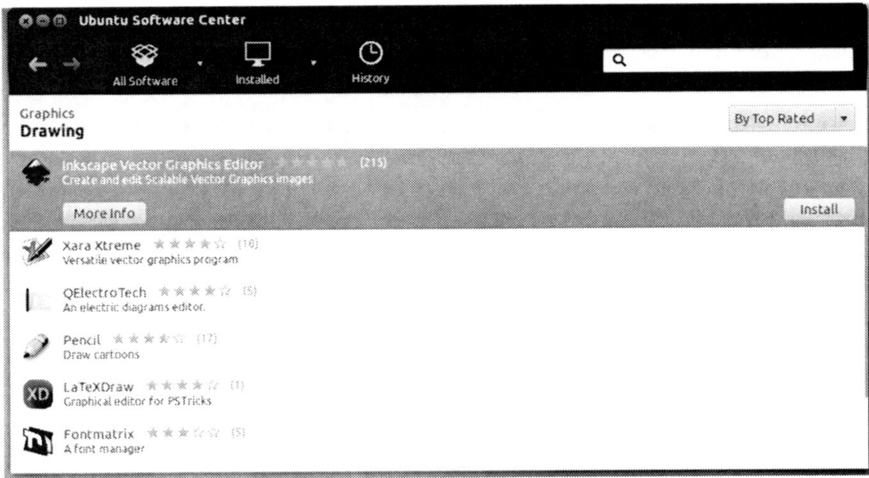

Figure 4-10: Ubuntu Software Center package listing

Clicking the All Software icon displays the listing of software categories such as Office, Graphics, Internet, and System on a left sidebar. Clicking on a category will list the available software with a brief description of each (see Figure 4-10). Some categories will have subcategories such as Drawing and Viewers for Graphics (see Figure 4-11). You can scroll down the list to find the package you want. Installed software will have a green check mark emblem displayed on their small icon. To display the sidebar of software categories again, just click on the All Software button.

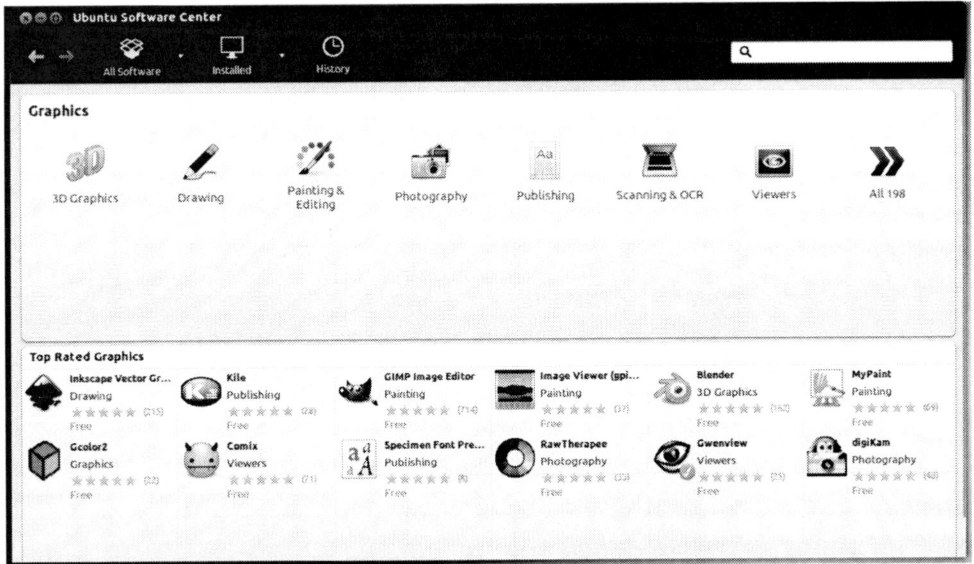

Figure 4-11: Ubuntu Software Center sub-categories

To install a package, first locate it. Once you have found your package, you can click it to display an Install button on the right side, which you click to install (see Figure 4-10). An install process entry is displayed on the left sidebar as the package is installed.

Should you want more information about a package, click the More Info button to open a new tab for that application. The application tab for an uninstalled package will have an Install button and display a detailed description of the application, along with the License and Price, if any (see Figure 4-12). For software on the Ubuntu repository, most have an Open Source license and the price is free. You can click the Website link to access the application's Web site, which may provide detailed documentation. If an application thumbnail is displayed, you can click on it to display the full image. Listed under the Add-ons heading is a list of associated software designed to work with your application. Packages installed already are marked. To install an additional software package, click on its checkbox. An Apply Changes button appears above the Add-ons list, which you then click.

The "People Also Installed" section lists applications that others users who installed the package have also installed. These popular applications similar or complimentary to the package.

Version, License, size, and update information is then listed. The update information indicates whether it is supported by the Ubuntu repository. If Canonical does not provide critical updates, the package is part of the Universe or Multiverse repositories. User reviews then follow, providing information about the software's stability and usefulness.

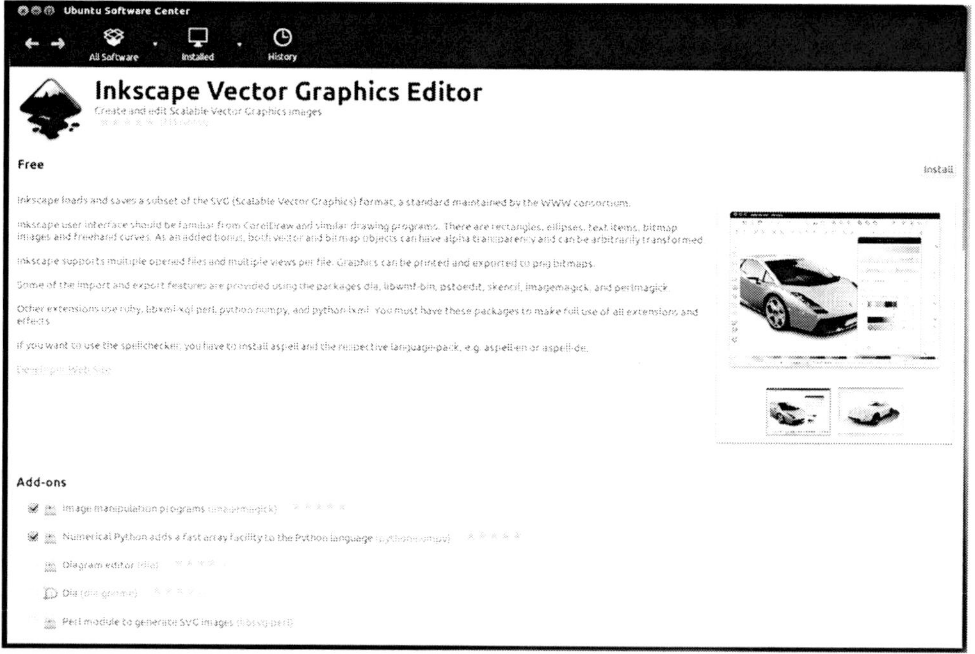

Figure 4-12: Ubuntu Software Center application

You also can install the application from this page by clicking the Install button (if the application is already installed, a Remove button is shown). You are prompted to enter your password. You also can choose the Install item on the File menu to install the application (File | Install).

A progress bar on the Info page will show the download and install progress. A "Progress" icon also appears in the toolbar. Clicking on it displays the progress bar and the package name (see Figure 4-13). When installation takes place, the Launcher item for that application is placed on the Launcher. A progress bar on the Launcher item shows the install progress (see Figure 4-13). When installation is finished, the Launcher item remains on the Launcher (locked). You can remove it if you want using its quicklist "Unlock from launcher" entry.

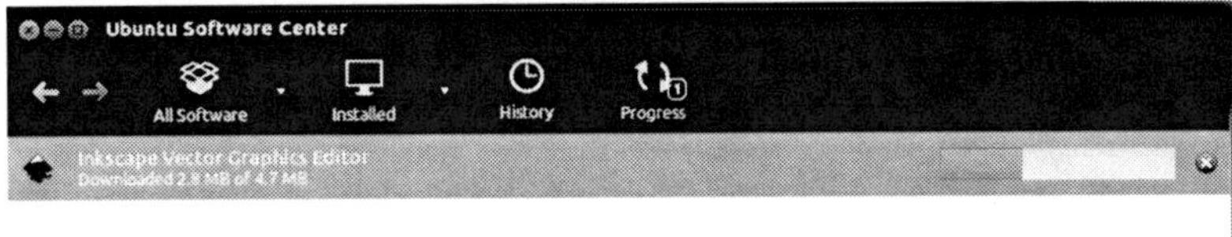

Figure 4-13: Ubuntu Software Center and Launcher item download and install progress

When finished, the application page displays a Remove button and a green check mark with the installed label and the date (see Figure 4-14). The entry in the list of applications also will have a green checkmark emblem indicating that the application is installed.

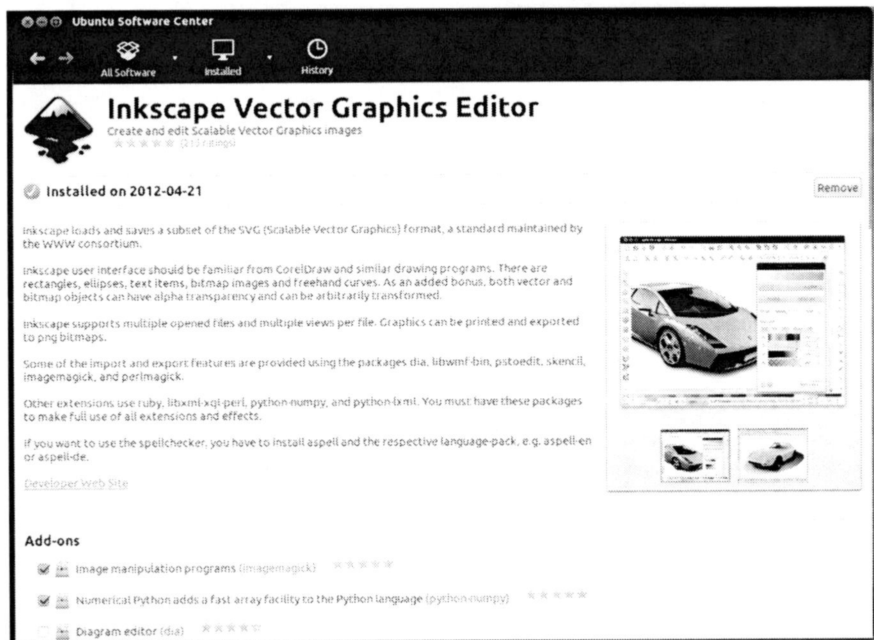

Figure 4-14: Ubuntu Software Center installed application

To remove a package, first locate it in the package lists, select it and a Remove button will appear which you can click to remove. You also can use the Remove button on the application's Info page.

You can perform a search using the Search box. The search is performed on the description and the package name. To remove the search list and return to the All Software page, click the x button icon on the right side of the search box. Searches can be carried out within categories and subcategories. To search globally, search from the "All Software" page. In Figure, 4-15 all vector related applications are listed.

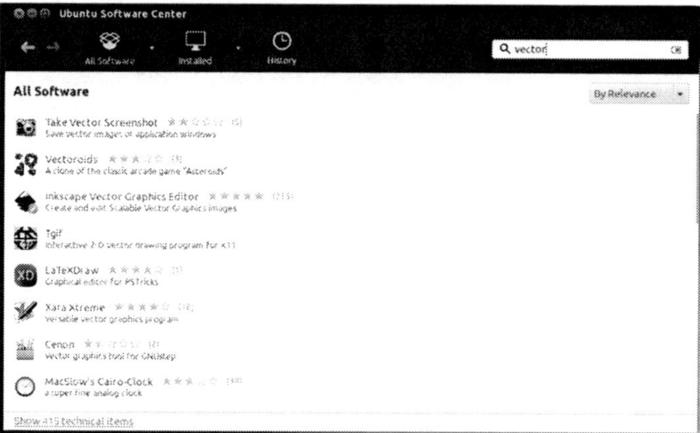

Figure 4-15: Ubuntu Software Center search

If you have selected a category and are displaying a category page like Graphics, then the search will be performed only on the packages in that category. In Figure 4-16 only vector applications in the Graphics | Drawing subcategory are listed.

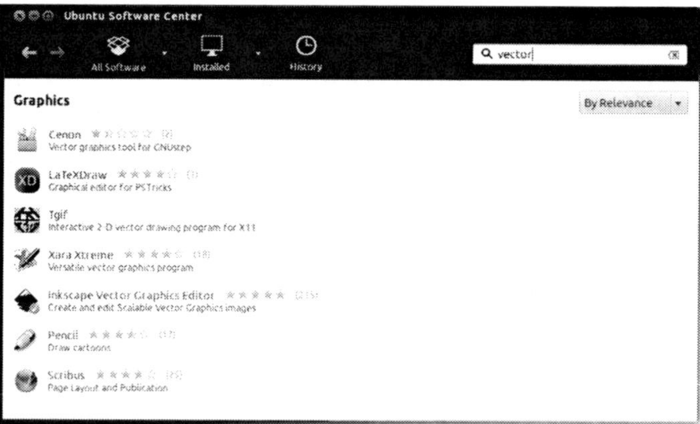

Figure 4-16: Ubuntu Software Center search within a category

On the Ubuntu Software Center toolbar, the Installed icon lists installed software, with a drop-down menu for installed Ubuntu, Partner, and Purchased software. Software categories such as Graphics and Office are listed, which you expand to show those packages installed (see Figure 4-17).

On the toolbar, the History icon displays a list of all package changes, installations, updates, and removals.

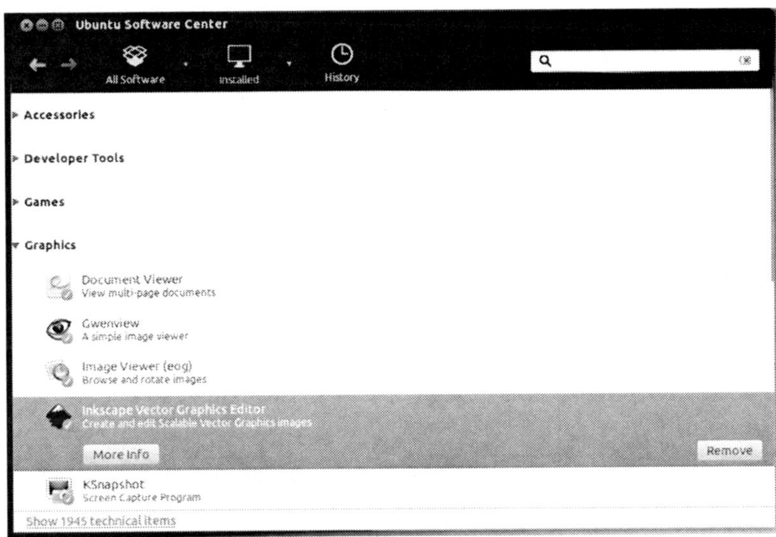

Figure 4-17: Ubuntu Software Center installed software

The Ubuntu Software Center is a front end for the APT package manager. When you install a package with the Ubuntu Software Center, APT is invoked and automatically selects and downloads the package from the appropriate online repository.

The packages listed in the Ubuntu Software Center are set up using the **app-install-data** packages, accessible through the Synaptic Package Manager. The **app-install-data** and **app-install-data-partner** packages will already be installed. These list the commonly used packages on the Ubuntu repository. In addition, you can install the **app-install-data-edubuntu** package to list edubuntu educational packages. If you have set up Medibuntu.org repository access, you can install the **app-install-data-medibuntu** package to list software applications on the Medibuntu.org repository.

Synaptic Package Manager

The Synaptic Package Manager has been replaced by the Ubuntu Software Center as the primary package manager. It is no not installed by default. Synaptic is no longer supported by Ubuntu, though support is still provided by the Ubuntu community. Packages are listed by name and include supporting packages like libraries and system critical packages. Once installed, you can access the Synaptic Package Manager on the System dash.

The Synaptic Package Manager displays three panes, a side pane for listing software categories and buttons, a top pane for listing software packages, and a bottom pane for displaying a selected package's description. When a package is selected, the description pane also displays a Get

Screenshot button. Clicking this button will download and display an image of the application, if there is one. Click the Get Changelog button to display a window listing the application changes.

Buttons at the lower left of the Synaptic Package Manager window provide options for organizing and refining the list of packages shown (see Figure 4-18). Five options are available: Sections, Status, Origin, Custom Filters, and Search results. The dialog pane above the buttons changes depending on which option you choose. Clicking the Sections button will list section categories for your software such as Base System, Communications, and Development. The Status button will list options for installed and not installed software. The Origin button shows entries for different repositories and their sections, as well as those locally installed (manual or disc based installations). Custom filters lets you choose a filter to use for listing packages. You can create your own filter and use it to display selected packages. Search results will list your current and previous searches, letting you move from one to the other.

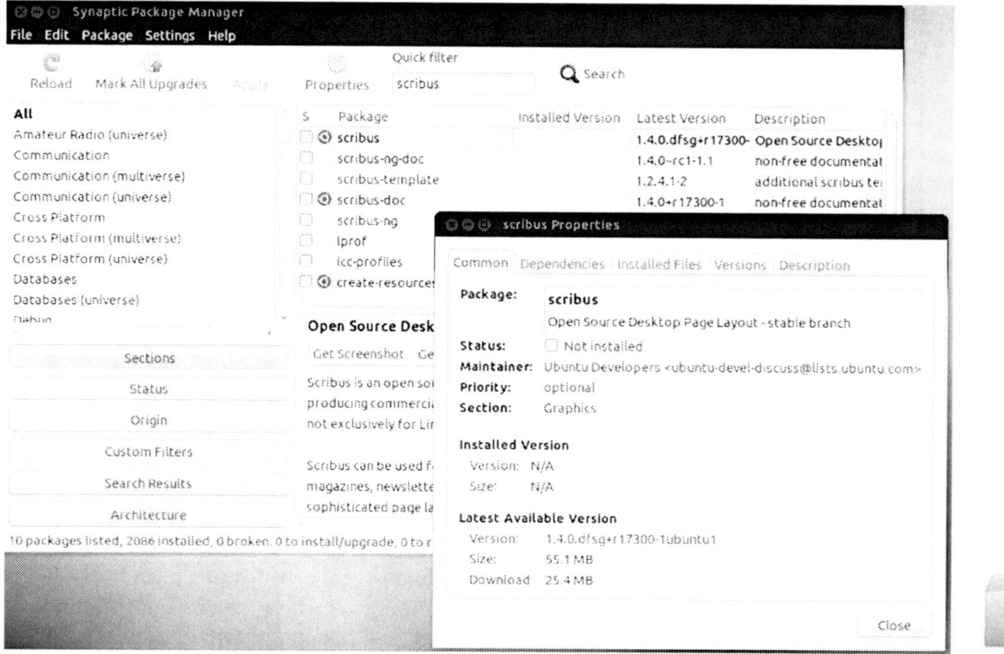

Figure 4-18: Synaptic Package Manager: Quick search

The Sections option is selected by default (see Figure 4-19). You can choose to list all packages, or refine your listing using categories provided in the pane. The All entry in this pane will list all available packages. Packages are organized into categories such as Base System, Cross Platform, and Communications. Each category is in turn subdivided by multiverse, universe, and restricted software.

To perform a quick search, enter the pattern to be searched for in the "Quick search" box and the results will appear. In Figure 4-18 the *scribus* pattern is used to locate the Scribus desktop publishing software. Quick searches will be performed within selected sections. Selecting different sections applies your quick search pattern to the packages in that section. Clicking on the Editors section with a scribus search pattern would give no results, since Scribus is not an editor package.

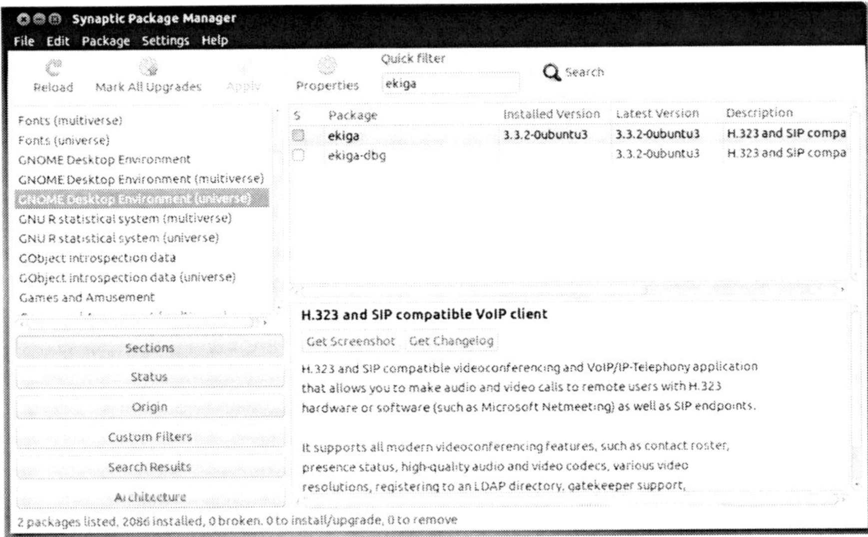

Figure 4-19: Synaptic Package Manager: Sections

Figure 4-20: Synaptic Package Manager: Status

Status entries further refine installed software as manual or as upgradeable (see Figure 4-20). Local software consists of packages you download and install manually

With the Origin options, Ubuntu-compliant repositories may further refine access according to multiverse, universe, and restricted software. A main section selects Ubuntu-supported software.

To perform more detailed searches, you can use the Search tool. Click the Search button on the toolbar to open a Search dialog with a text box where you can enter search terms. A pop-up menu lets you specify what features of a package to search such as the "Description and Name" feature. You can search other package features like the Name, the maintainer name (Maintainer), the package version (Version), packages it may depend on (Dependencies), or associated packages (Provided Packages). A list of searches will be displayed in Search Results. You can move back and forth between search results by clicking on the search entries in this listing.

Properties

To find out information about a package, select the package and click the Properties button. This opens a window with Common, Dependencies, Installed Files, Versions, and Description tabs (see Figure 4-18). The Common tab provides section, versions, and maintainer information. The Installed Files tab show you exactly what files are installed, which is useful for finding the exact location, and names for configuration files as well as commands. The Description tab displays detailed information about the software. The Dependencies tab shows all dependent software packages needed by this software, usually libraries.

Installing packages

Before installing software, you should press the Reload button to load the most recent package lists from the active repositories

To install a package, right-click on its name to display a pop-up menu and select the Mark for installation entry. Should any dependent packages exist, a dialog opens listing those packages. Click the Mark button in the dialog to mark those packages for installation. The package entry's check box will then be marked in the Synaptic Package Manager window.

Once you have selected the packages you want to install, click the Apply button on the toolbar to begin the installation process. A Summary dialog opens showing all the packages to be installed. You have the option to download the package files. The number of packages to be installed is listed, along with the size of the download and the amount of disk space used. Click the Apply button on the Summary dialog to download and install the packages. A download window will then appear showing the progress of your package installations. You can choose to show the progress of individual packages, which opens a terminal window listing each package as it is downloaded and installed.

Once downloaded, the dialog name changes to Installing Software. You can choose to have the dialog close automatically when finished. Sometimes installation requires user input to configure the software. You will be prompted to enter the information if necessary.

When you right-click a package name, you also see options for Mark Suggested for Installation or Mark Recommended for Installation. These will mark applications that can enhance your selected software, though they are not essential. If there are no suggested or recommended packages for that application, then these entries will be grayed out.

Certain software, like desktops or office suites that require a significant number of packages, can be selected all at once using metapackages. A metapackage has configuration files that select, download, and configure the range of packages needed for such complex software. For example, the **kubuntu-desktop** meta package will install the entire Kubuntu desktop (Sections | Meta Packages).

Removing packages

To remove a package, first locate it. Then right-click it and select the "Mark package for removal" entry. This will leave configuration files untouched. Alternatively, you can mark a package for complete removal, which will also remove any configuration files, "Mark for Complete Removal." Dependent packages will not be removed.

Once you have marked packages for removal, click the Apply button. A summary dialog displays the packages that will be removed. Click Apply to remove them.

The Synaptic Package Manager may not remove dependent packages, especially shared libraries that might be used by other applications. This means that your system could have installed packages that are never being used.

Search filters

You can further refine your search for packages by creating search filters. Select the Settings | Filters menu entry to open the Filters window. The Filters window shows two panes, a filter list on the left, and three tabs on the right: Status, Section, and Properties. To create a new filter, click the New button located just below the filter listing. Click the New Filter 1 entry in the filter list on the left pane. On the Status tab, you can refine your search criteria according to a package's status. You can search only uninstalled packages, include installed packages, include or exclude packages marked for removal, or search or those that are new in the repository. Initially all criteria are selected. Uncheck those you do not want included in your search. The Section tab lets you include or exclude different repository sections like games, documentation, or administration. If you are looking for a game, you could choose to include just the game section, excluding everything else. On the Properties tab, you can specify patterns to search on package information such as package names, using Boolean operators to refine your search criteria. Package search criteria are entered using the two pop-up menus and the text box at the bottom of the tab, along with AND or OR Boolean operators.

Note: For KDE you can use the Muon to install and update packages (see Chapter 11).

Ubuntu Software Center for separate DEB packages

You can also use the Ubuntu Software Center to perform an installation of a single DEB software package. Usually these packages are downloaded directly from a Web site and have few or no dependent packages. When you use your browser to download a particular package, you will be prompted to open it with Ubuntu Software Center. The Ubuntu Software Center opens to an install page for that software package, displaying information about the package and checking to see if it is compatible with your system. Click the Install button to download and install the package. It is advisable to use the Ubuntu Software Center to install a manually downloaded package.

You could also first download the package, and then later select it from your file manager window (usually the Downloads folder). Double clicking should open the package with the Ubuntu Software Center. You can also right-click and choose to open it with the Ubuntu Software Center.

In Figure 4-20, the Ubuntu Software Center tool is used to install the **libdvdcss2** library, the codec for DVD Video. The package is part of the Medibuntu.org repository, but if you did not configure access to that repository, you can use your Web browser to download and install packages directly with the Ubuntu Software Center (**http://packages.medibuntu.org/precise/**).

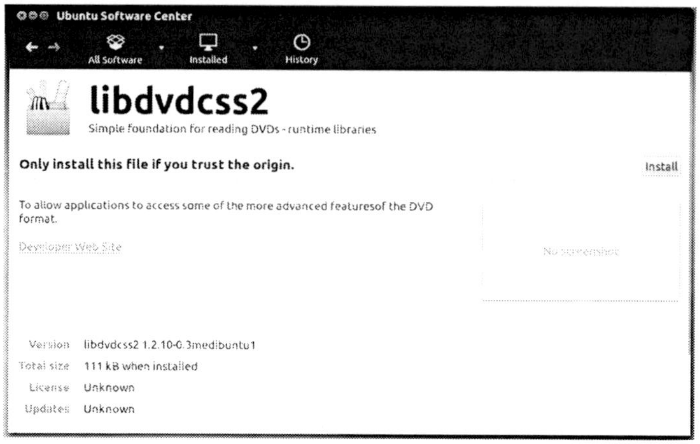

Figure 4-20: Ubuntu Software Center installer

Source code files

You can install source code files using **apt-get**. Specify the **source** operation with the package name. Packages will be downloaded and extracted.

```
sudo apt-get source mplayer
```

The **--download** option lets you just download the source package without extracting it. The **--compile** option will download, extract, compile, and package the source code into a Debian binary package, ready for installation.

With the **source** operation, no dependent packages will be downloaded. If a software packages requires any dependent packages to run, you would have to download and compile those. To obtain needed dependent files, you use the **build-dep** option. All your dependent files will be located and downloaded for you automatically.

```
sudo apt-get build-dep mplayer
```

Installing from source code requires that supporting development libraries and source code header files be installed. You can do this separately for each major development platform like GNOME, KDE, or the kernel. Alternatively, you can run the APT meta-package **build-essential** for all the Ubuntu development packages. You will have to do this only once.

```
sudo apt-get install build-essential
```

Software Package Types

Ubuntu uses Debian-compliant software packages (DEB) whose filenames have a **.deb** extension. Other packages, such as those in the form of source code that you need to compile, may come in a variety of compressed archives. These commonly have the extension **.tar.gz**, **.tgz**, or **.tar.bz2**. Packages with the **.rpm** extension are Red Hat Package software packages used on Red Hat, Fedora, SuSE and other Linux distributions that use RPM packages. They are not compatible directly with Ubuntu. You can use the **alien** utility to convert most RPM packages to DEB packages that you can then install on Ubuntu. Table 4-2 lists several common file extensions that you will find for the great variety of Linux software packages available. You can download any Ubuntu-compliant deb package as well as the original source code package, as single files, directly from **http://packages.ubuntu.com**.

Extension	File
.deb	A Debian/Ubuntu Linux package
.gz	A **gzip**-compressed file (use **gunzip** to decompress)
.bz2	A **bzip2**-compressed file (use **bunzip2** to decompress; also use the **j** option with **tar**, as in **xvjf**)
.tar	A tar archive file (use **tar** with **xvf** to extract)
.tar.gz	A **gzip**-compressed **tar** archive file (use **gunzip** to decompress and **tar** to extract; use the **z** option with **tar**, as in **xvzf**, to both decompress and extract in one step)
.tar.bz2	A **bzip2**-compressed **tar** archive file (extract with **tar -xvzj**)
.tz	A **tar** archive file compressed with the **compress** command
.Z	A file compressed with the **compress** command (use the **decompress** command to decompress)
.bin	A self-extracting software file
.rpm	A software package created with the Red Hat Software Package Manager, used on Fedora, Red Hat, Centos, and SuSE distributions

Table 4-2: Linux Software Package File Extensions

DEB Software Packages

A Debian package will automatically resolve dependencies, installing any other needed packages instead of simply reporting their absence. Packages are named with the software name, the version number, and the **.deb** extension. Check **http://www.us.debian.org/doc** for more information. File name format is as follows:

the package name

version number

distribution label and build number. Packages created specifically for Ubuntu have the ubuntu label here. Attached to it is the build number, the number of times the package was built for Ubuntu.

architecture   The type of system on which the package runs, like i386 for Intel 32-bit x86 systems, or amd64 for both Intel and AMD 64-bit systems, x86_64.

package format. This is always **deb**

For example, the package name for 3dchess is 3dchess, with a version and build number 0.8.1-16, and an architecture amd64 for a 64 bit system.

```
3dchess_0.8.1-16_amd64.deb
```

The following package has an Ubuntu label, a package specifically created for Ubuntu. The version and build number is 2.28.0, with the Ubuntu label ubuntu1. The architecture is i386 for a 32-bit system.

```
gnome-mahjongg_2.28.0ubuntu1_i386.deb
```

Managing software with apt-get

APT is designed to work with repositories, and will handle any dependencies for you. It uses **dpkg** to install and remove individual packages, but can also determine what dependent packages need to be installed, as well as query and download packages from repositories. Several popular tools for APT let you manage your software easily, like the Synaptic Package Manager, the Ubuntu Software Center, and aptitude. The Ubuntu Software Center and the Synaptic Package Manager rely on a desktop interface like GNOME. If you are using the command line interface, you can use **apt-get** to manage packages. Using the **apt-get** command on the command line you can install, update, and remove packages. Check the **apt-get** man page for a detailed listing of **apt-get** commands (see Table 4-3).

```
apt-get  command  package
```

Command	Description
update	Download and resynchronize the package listing of available and updated packages for APT supported repositories. APT repositories updated are those specified in **/etc/apt/sources.list**
upgrade	Update packages, install new versions of installed packages if available.
dist-upgrade	Update (upgrade) all your installed packages to a new release
install	Install a specific package, using its package name, not full package file name.
remove	Remove a software package from your system.
source	Download and extract a source code package
check	Check for broken dependencies
clean	Removes the downloaded packages held in the repository cache on your system. Used to free up disk space.

Table 4-3: apt-get commands

The **apt-get** command takes two arguments: the command to perform and the name of the package. Other APT package tools follow the same format. The command is a term such as **install** for installing packages or **remove** to uninstall a package. Use the **install**, **remove**, or **update** commands respectively. You only need to specify the software name, not the package's full file name. APT will determine that. To install the MPlayer package you would use:

```
sudo apt-get install mplayer
```

To make sure that **apt-get** has current repository information, use the **apt-get update** command.

```
sudo apt-get update
```

To remove packages, you use the **remove** command.

```
sudo apt-get remove mplayer
```

You can use the **-s** option to check the remove or install first, especially to check whether any dependency problems exist. For remove operations you can use **-s** to find out first what dependent packages will also be removed.

```
sudo apt-get remove -s mplayer
```

The **apt-get** command can be very helpful if your X Windows System server ever fails (your display driver). For example, if you installed a restricted vendor display driver, and then your desktop fails to start, you can start up the recovery mode, start the root shell, and use **apt-get** to remove the restricted display driver. Your former X open source display drivers would be restored automatically. The following would remove the Nvidia restricted display driver.

```
sudo apt-get remove nvidia*
```

A complete log of all install, remove, and update operations are kept in the **/var/log/dpkg.log** file. You can consult this file to find out exactly what files were installed or removed.

Configuration for APT is held in the **/etc/apt** directory. Here the **sources.list** file lists the distribution repositories from where packages are installed. Source lists for additional third-party repositories (like that for Medibuntu.org) are kept in the **/etc/sources.list.d** directory. GPG (GNU Privacy Guard) database files hold validation keys for those repositories. Specific options for **apt-get** are can be found in an **/etc/apt.conf** file or in various files located in the **/etc/apt.conf.d** directory.

Updating packages (Upgrading) with apt-get

The **apt-get** tool also lets you easily update your entire system at once. The terms update and upgrade are used differently from other software tools. In **apt-get**, the **update** command just updates your package listing, checking for packages that may need to install newer versions, but not installing those versions. Technically, it updates the package list that APT uses to determine what packages need to be updated. The term upgrade is used to denote the actual update of a software package; a new version is downloaded and installed. What is referred to as updating by **apt-get**, other package managers refer to a obtaining the list of software packages to be updated (the reload operation). In **apt-get**, upgrading is what other package managers refer to as performing updates.

TIP: The terms **update** and **upgrade** can be confusing when used with **apt-get**. The **update** operation updates the Apt package list only, whereas an **upgrade** actually downloads and installs updated packages.

Upgrading is a simple matter of using the **upgrade** command. With no package specified, using **apt-get** with the **upgrade** command will upgrade your entire system. Add the **-u** option to list packages as they are upgraded. First, make sure your repository information (package list) is up to date with the **update** command, then issue the **upgrade** command.

```
sudo apt-get update
sudo apt-get -u upgrade
```

Command Line Search and Information: dpkg-query and apt-cache tools

The **dpkg-query** command lets you list detailed information about your packages. They operate on the command line (terminal window). Use **dpkg-query** with the **-l** option to list all your packages.

```
dpkg-query -l
```

The **dpkg** command can operate as a front end for **dpkg-query**, detecting its options to perform the appropriate task. The preceding command could also be run as:

```
dpkg -l
```

Listing a particular package requires and exact match on the package name, unless you use pattern matching operators. The following command lists the **wine** package (Windows Compatibility Layer).

```
dpkg-query -l wine
```

A pattern matching operator, such as *, placed after a pattern will display any packages beginning with the specified pattern. The pattern with its operators needs to be placed in single quotation marks to prevent an attempt by the shell to use the pattern to match on filenames on your current directory. The following example finds all packages beginning with the pattern "wine". This would include packages with names such as **wine-doc** and **wine-utils**.

```
dpkg-query -l 'wine*'
```

You can further refine the results by using **grep** to perform an additional search. The following operation first outputs all packages beginning with **wine**, and from those results, the **grep** operations lists only those with the pattern *utils* in their name, such as **wine-utils**.

```
dpkg -l  'wine*' | grep 'utils'
```

Use the **-L** option to list the files that a package has installed.

```
dpkg-query  -L  wine
```

To see the status information about a package, including its dependencies and configuration files, use the **-s** option. Fields will include Status, Section, Architecture, Version, Depends (dependent packages), Suggests, Conflicts (conflicting packages), and Conffiles (configuration files).

```
dpkg-query -s  wine
```

The status information will also provide suggested dependencies. These are packages not installed, but likely to be used. For the wine package, the **ttf-mscorefonts** Windows fonts package is suggested.

```
dpkg-query  -s  wine | grep Suggests
```

Use the **-S** option to determine to which package a particular file belongs to.

```
dpkg-query  -S  filename
```

You can also obtain information with the **apt-cache** tool. Use the search command with **apt-cache** to perform a search.

```
apt-cache search wine
```

To find dependencies for a particular package, use the **depends** command.

```
apt-cache depends wine
```

To display just the package description, use the **show** command.

```
apt-cache show wine
```

Note: If you have installed Aptitude software manager, you can use the **aptitude** command with the **search** and **show** options to find and display information about packages.

Managing non-repository packages with dpkg

You can use **dpkg** to install a software package you have already downloaded directly, not with an APT enabled software tool like **apt-get**, the Ubuntu Software Center, or the Synaptic Package Manager. In this case, you are not installing from a repository. Instead, you have manually downloaded the package file from a Web or FTP site to a folder on your system. Such a situation would be rare, reserved for software not available on the Ubuntu repository or any APT enabled repository like Medibuntu.org. Keep in mind that most software is already on your Ubuntu or an APT enabled repositories. Check there first for the software package before performing a direct download and install with **dpkg**. The **dpkg** configuration files are located in the **/etc/dpkg** directory. Configuration is held in the **dpkg.cfg** file. See the **dpkg** man page for a detailed listing of options.

One situation, for which you would use **dpkg**, is for packages you have built yourself, like packages you created when converting a package in another format to a Debian package (DEB). This is the case when converting a RPM package (Red Hat Package Manager) to a Debian package format.

For **dpkg**, you use the **-i** option to install a package and **-r** to remove it.

```
sudo dpkg -i package.deb
```

The major failing for **dpkg** is that it provides no dependency support. It will inform you of needed dependencies, but you will have to install them separately. **dpkg** installs only the specified package. It is useful for packages that have no dependencies.

You use the **-I** option to obtain package information directly from the DEB package file.

```
sudo dpkg -I package.deb
```

To remove a package you use the **-r** option with the package software name. You do not need version or extension information like **.386** or **.deb**. With **dpkg**, when removing a package with dependencies, you first have to remove all its dependencies manually. You will not be able to uninstall the package until you do this. Configuration files are not removed.

```
sudo dpkg -r packagename
```

If you install a package that requires dependencies, and then fail to install these dependencies, your install database will be marked as having broken packages. In this case, APT will not allow new packages to be installed until the broken packages are fixed. You can enter the **apt-get** command with the **-f** and install options to fix all broken packages at once.

```
sudo apt-get -f install
```

Using packages with other software formats

You can convert software packages in other software formats into DEB packages that can then be installed on Ubuntu. To do this you use the **alien** tool, which can convert several different kinds of formats such as RPM and even TGZ (**.tgz**). You use the **--to-deb** option to convert to a DEB package format that Ubuntu can then install. The **--scripts** option attempts also to convert any pre or post install configuration scripts.

```
alien  --scripts  --to-deb   package.rpm
```

Once you have generated the **.deb** package, you can use **dpkg** or the Ubuntu Software Center to install it.

Part 2: Applications

Office Applications and Editors
Multimedia and Graphics
Mail and News
Internet Applications
Social Networking

ubuntu

5. Office Applications and Editors

LibreOffice

Calligra

GNOME Office

Running Microsoft Office on Linux

Document Viewers (PostScript, PDF, and DVI)

Ebook readers

PDA Access

Editors

Database Management Systems

Several office suites are now available for Ubuntu (see Table 5-1). These include professional-level word processors, presentation managers, drawing tools, and spreadsheets. The freely available versions are described in this chapter. LibreOffice is currently the primary office suite supported by Ubuntu. Calligra is an office suite designed for use with KDE. The GNOME Office suite integrates GNOME applications into a productivity suite. CodeWeavers CrossOver Office provides reliable support for running Microsoft Office Windows applications directly on Linux, integrating them with KDE and GNOME. You can also purchase commercial office suites such as Oracle Open Office from Oracle. For desktop publishing, especially PDF generation, you can use Scribus, a cross-platform tool available from the Ubuntu repository.

Web Site	Description
http://www.libreoffice.org	LibreOffice open source office suite
http://www.calligra.org	Calligra Suite, for KDE
http://live.gnome.org/GnomeOffice	GNOME Office, for GNOME
http://www.codeweavers.com	CrossOver Office (MICROSOFT Office support)
http://www.scribus.net	Scribus desktop publishing tool.

Table 5-1: Linux Office Suites

Several database management systems are also available for Linux, which include high-powered, commercial-level database management systems, such as Oracle, IBM's DB2, and Sybase. Most of the database management systems available for Linux are designed to support large relational databases. Ubuntu includes both MySQL and PostgreSQL open source databases in its distribution, which can support smaller databases. Various database management systems available to run under Linux are listed in Table 5-8 later in this chapter.

Linux also provides several text editors that range from simple text editors for simple notes to editors with more complex features such as spell-checkers, buffers, or complex pattern matching. All generate character text files and can be used to edit any Linux text files. Text editors are often used in system administration tasks to change or add entries in Linux configuration files found in the **/etc** directory or a user's initialization or application configuration files located in a user's home directory (dot files). You can also use a text editor to work on source code files for any of the programming languages or shell program scripts.

Ubuntu also supports several Ebook readers. Some such as Calibre and FBReader run natively on Linux. The Window versions of Ebook readers such as the Kindle for PC, Mobipocket, and Adobe Digital Editions run under Wine (the Windows compatibility layer for Linux), but work directly on the Ubuntu desktop.

Note: Oracle Open Office is a commercial product no longer freely available for Linux distributions.

LibreOffice

LibreOffice is a fully integrated suite of office applications developed as an open source project and freely distributed to all. It is the primary office suite for Ubuntu. LibreOffice applications are accessible from the Office dash. There are also default Launcher items for three commonly used OpenOffice applications (Writer, Calc, and Impress). LibreOffice is the open source and freely available office suite derived originally from OpenOffice. LibreOffice is supported by the Document Foundation, which was established after Oracle's acquisition of Sun, the main developer for Open Office. LibreOffice is now the primary open source office software for Linux. Oracle retains control of all the original OpenOffice software and does not cooperate with any LibreOffice development. LibreOffice has replaced OpenOffice as the default Office software for most Linux distributions.

LibreOffice includes word processing, spreadsheet, presentation, and drawing applications (see Table 5-2). Versions of LibreOffice exist for Linux, Windows, and Mac OS. You can obtain information such as online manuals and FAQs as well as current versions from the LibreOffice Web site at **http://www.libreoffice.org**. The LibreOffice suite of applications is installed as part of the Ubuntu Desktop installation.

Application	Description
Calc (Spreadsheet)	LibreOffice spreadsheet
Draw (Drawing)	LibreOffice drawing application
Writer (Word Processing)	LibreOffice word processor
Math (Formula)	LibreOffice mathematical formula composer
Impress (Presentation)	LibreOffice presentation manager
Base (Database)	Database front end for accessing and managing a variety of different databases.

Table 5-2: LibreOffice Applications

Figure 5-1: LibreOffice dialog

LibreOffice is an integrated suite of applications. You can open the writer, spreadsheet, or presentation application directly. The word processing, spreadsheet, and presentations applications are also accessible from the Launcher: Writer, Calc, and Impress. To open a dialog with buttons for accessing any of the Libre applications, click the LibreOffice icon in the Office dash (see Figure 5-1). You can also open existing office documents (Open button) and manage document templates. Buttons as the bottom of the dialog let you download new features and templates, and access the LibreOffice Web site.

Note: In most LibreOffice applications, you can select New from the File menu and select a different application if you wish.

The LibreOffice Writer word processor supports standard word processing features, such as cut and paste, spell-checker, and text formatting, as well as paragraph styles (see Figure 5-2). Context menus let you format text easily. Wizards (Letter, Web page, Fax, and Agenda) let you generate different kinds of documents quickly. You can embed objects within documents, such as using Draw to create figures that you can then drag-and-drop to the Writer document. LibreOffice Writer is compatible with earlier versions of Microsoft Word. It will read and convert Word 2003 and earlier documents to LibreOffice Writer document, preserving most features including contents, tables, and indexes. Writer documents also can be saved as Word documents.

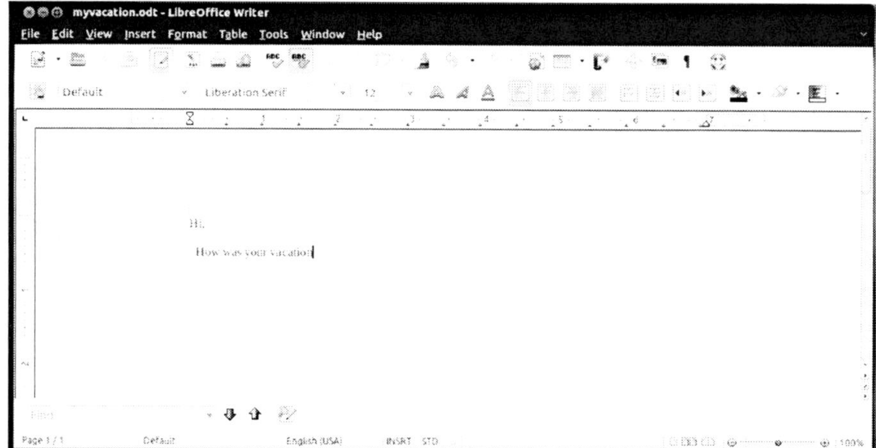

Figure 5-2: LibreOffice Writer word processor

LibreOffice provides access to many database files. File types supported include ODBC (Open Database Connectivity), JDBC (Java), MySQL, PostgreSQL, and MDB (Microsoft Access) database files. You can also create your own simple databases. Check the LibreOffice Features | Base page (**http://www.libreoffice.org/features/base/**) for detailed information on drivers and supported databases.

LibreOffice Calc is a professional-level spreadsheet. With LibreOffice Math (LibreOffice Formula), you can create formulas that you can embed in a text document. With the presentation manager (Libre Office Impress), you can create images for presentations, such as circles, rectangles, and connecting elements like arrows, as well as vector-based illustrations. Impress supports advanced features such as morphing objects, grouping objects, and defining gradients. Draw is a sophisticated drawing tool that includes 3-D modeling tools (LibreOffice Drawing). You can create simple or complex images, including animation text aligned on curves. LibreOffice also includes a printer setup tool with which you can select printers, fonts, paper sizes, and page formats.

Scribus is a desktop publishing tool (see Figure 5-3), **www.scribus.net**. Install it from the Ubuntu Software Center | Graphics | Publishing. Also available is ScribusNG, the development version with the latest features.

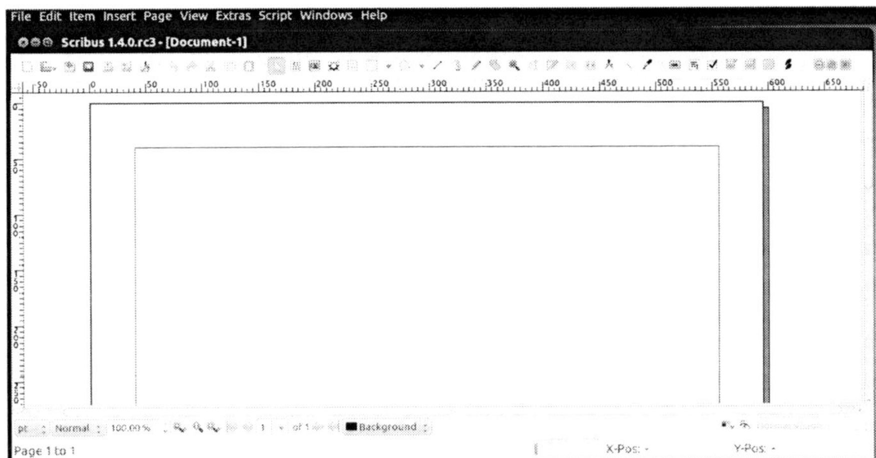

Figure 5-3: Scribus desktop publisher

Calligra

Calligra is an integrated office suite for the K Desktop Environment (KDE) consisting of several office applications, including a word processor, a spreadsheet, and graphics applications. You can download it from the Ubuntu Software Center | Office | Calligra. Calligra is the new version of KOffice, integrating many of the older applications provided by KOffice. Calligra allows components from any one application to be used in another, letting you to embed a spreadsheet from Calligra Sheets or diagrams from Karbon in a Calligra Words document. It also uses the open document format (ODF) for its files, providing cross-application standardization. There is also a Windows version available. You can obtain more information about Calligra from **http://www.calligra.org**.

Currently, Calligra includes Calligra Sheets, Calligra Flow, Calligra Words, Karbon, Krita, Plan, Calligra Stage Braindump, and Kexi (see Table 5-3). The contact application, Kontact, has been spun off as a separate project. Kontact is an integrated contact application including Kmail, Korganizer, Kaddressbook, and Knotes. Calligra Sheets is a spreadsheet, Calligra Stage is a presentation application, Karbon is a vector graphics program, and Calligra Words is a publisher-like word processor. Krita is a paint and image editor. Kexi provides database integration with Calligra applications, currently supporting PostgreSQL and MySQL.

Calligra Sheets is the spreadsheet application, which incorporates the basic operations found in most spreadsheets, with formulas similar to those used in MS Excel. You can also embed charts, pictures, or formulas using Krita and Karbon. With Calligra Stage, you can create presentations consisting of text and graphics modeled using different fonts, orientations, and attributes such as colors. Karbon is a vector-based graphics program, much like Adobe Illustrator and LibreOffice Draw. It supports the standard graphic operations such as rotating, scaling, and aligning objects. Calligra Words can best be described as a desktop publisher, with many of the features found in publishing applications. Although it is a fully functional word processor, Calligra Words sets up text in frames that are placed on the page like objects. Frames, like objects in a drawing program, can be moved, resized, and reoriented. You can organize frames into a frame set, having text flow from one to the other.

Application	Description
Braindump	Whiteboards for notes, images, and charts
Calligra Flow	Flow chart applications
Calligra Stage	Presentation application
Calligra Words	Word processor (desktop publisher)
Calligra Sheets	Spreadsheet
Karbon	Vector graphics program
Kexi	Database integration
Plan	Project management and planning
Krita	Paint and image manipulation program
Kontact (separate project)	Contact application including mail, address book, and organizer

Table 5-3: Calligra Applications

GNOME Office Applications

There are several GNOME Office applications available including AbiWord, Gnumeric, Evince, and Evolution. GNOME Office applications are part of Ubuntu and can be downloaded with the Ubuntu Software Center. You can find out more about the GNOME Office applications at **http://live.gnome.org/GnomeOffice**. A current listing for common GNOME Office applications is shown in Table 5-4. All implement the support for embedding components, ensuring drag-and-drop capability throughout the GNOME interface.

AbiWord is an open source word processor that aims to be a complete cross-platform solution, running on Mac, Unix, and Windows, as well as Linux.   It is part of a set of desktop productivity applications being developed by the AbiSource project (**http://www.abisource.com**).

Gnumeric is a professional-level GNOME spreadsheet meant to replace commercial spreadsheets. Gnumeric supports standard spreadsheet features, including auto filling and cell formatting, and an extensive number of formats. Gnumeric also supports plug-ins, making it possible to extend and customize its abilities easily.

Dia is a drawing program designed to create diagrams, such as database, circuit object, flow chart, and network diagrams. You can create elements along with lines and arcs with different types of endpoints such as arrows or diamonds. Data can be saved in XML format, making it transportable to other applications.

GnuCash (**http://www.gnucash.org**) is a personal finance application for managing accounts, stocks, and expenses.

Application	Description
AbiWord	Cross-platform word processor
Gnumeric	Spreadsheet
Evince	Document Viewer
Evolution	Integrated e-mail, calendar, and personal organizer
Dia	Diagram and flow chart editor
GnuCash	Personal finance manager
Glom	Database front end for PostgreSQL database
glabels	Label Designer
Planner	Project planner

Table 5-4: GNOME Office and Other Office Applications for GNOME

Running Microsoft Office on Linux: Wine and CrossOver

One of the concerns for new Linux users is what kind of access they will have to their Microsoft Office files, particularly Word files. The Linux operating system and many applications for it are designed to provide seamless access to Microsoft Office files. The major Linux Office suites, including Calligra, LibreOffice, and Oracle Open Office, all read and manage Microsoft Office files. In addition, these office suites are fast approaching the same level of features and support for office tasks as found in Microsoft Office.

Wine (Windows Compatibility Layer) allows you to run many Windows applications directly, using a supporting virtual windows API. See the Wine website for a list of supported applications, **http://www.winehq.org**, AppDB tab. Well-written applications may run directly from Wine, like the Newsbin newsreader. Sometimes you will have to have a working Windows system from which you can copy system DLLs needed by particular applications. You can also import Windows fonts by directly copying them to the Wine font directory. Each user can install their own version of Wine with its own simulated C: partition on which Windows applications are installed. The simulated drive is installed as **drive_c** in your **.wine** directory. The **.wine** directory is a hidden directory. It is not normally displayed with the **ls** command or the GNOME file manager (View | Show Hidden Files). You can also use any of your Linux directories for your Windows application data files instead of your simulated C: drive. These are referenced by Windows applications as the **z:** drive.

In a terminal window, using the **wine** command with an install program will automatically install that Windows application on the simulated C: drive. The following example installs Microsoft Office. Though there may be difficulties with the latest Microsoft Office versions, earlier versions, like 2007, should work fine for the most part (see **http://www.winehq.org**, AppDB tab, search on Word). Applications are rated platinum, gold, silver, bronze, and garbage. The Microsoft Office applications are silver.

When you insert the Microsoft Office CD, it will be mounted to the **/media** directory using the disk label as its folder name. Check the **/media** folder (Filesystem in the Computer window, Go | Computer) to see what the actual name is. You then run the **setup.exe** program for

Office with wine. Depending on the version of Office you have, there may be further subfolders for the actual Office **setup.exe** program. The following example assumes that the label for Office is OFFICE and that the **setup.exe** program for Office is on the top-level directory of that CD.

```
$ wine /media/OFFICE/setup.exe
```

The install program will start up and you will be prompted to enter your product key. Be sure to use only uppercase as you type. Once installed, choose Applications | Wine | Programs | Microsoft Office, and then choose the application name to start up. The application should start up normally. The application is referenced by Wine on the user's simulated **c:** drive.

The Windows My Documents folder is set up by Wine to be the user's Ubuntu Documents directory. There you will find any files saved to My Documents.

Wine is constantly being updated to accommodate the latest versions of Windows applications. However, for some applications you may need to copy DLL files from a working Windows system to the Wine Windows folder, **.wine/drive_c/windows**, usually to the **system** or **system32** directories. Though effective, Wine support will not be as stable as Crossover.

CrossOver Office is a commercial product that lets you install and run most Microsoft Office applications (Silver rating). CrossOver Office was developed by CodeWeavers, which also supports Windows web browser plug-ins as well as several popular Windows applications like Adobe Photoshop. CrossOver features both standard and professional versions, providing reliable application support. You can find out more about CrossOver Office at **http://www.codeweavers.com**.

CrossOver can be installed either for private multi-user mode or managed multi-user mode. In private multi-user mode, each user installs Windows software, such as full versions of Office. In managed multi-user mode, the Windows software is installed once and all users share it. Once the software is installed, you will see a Windows Applications menu on the main menu, from which you can start your installed Windows software. The applications will run within a Linux window, but they will appear just as if they were running in Windows.

With VMware, you can run Windows under Linux, allowing you to run Windows applications, including Microsoft Office, on your Linux system. For more information, check the VMware Web site at **http://www.vmware.com**.

Another option, for users with high-powered computers that support virtualization, is to install the Windows OS on a virtual machine using the Virtual Machine Manager (Ubuntu Software Center | System | Virtual Machine Manager). You could then install and run Windows on the virtual machine and install Microsoft Office on it.

Document Viewers, and DVI)

Though located under Graphics dash, PostScript, PDF, DVI, and ebook viewers are more commonly used with Office applications (see Table 5-5). You can install these viewers from the Ubuntu Software Center | Graphics | Viewers. Evince (PostScript, PDF and Okular can display both PostScript (**.ps**) and PDF (**.pdf**) files. Evince is the default document viewer for GNOME. It is started automatically whenever you double-click a PDF file on the GNOME desktop. Its menu entry is Document Viewer in the Graphics dash, but this is not turned on by default (use Main Menu to have the menu entry appear). Okular is the default document viewer for KDE4, with its menu entry as Applications | Graphics | Document Viewer on KDE, but as Okular on GNOME.

Viewer	Description
Evince	Document Viewer for PostScript, DVI, and PDF files
Okular	KDE4 tool for displaying PDF, DVI, and postscript files (replaces KPDF, Kghostview, and Kdvi)
xpdf	X Window System tool for displaying PDF files only
Acrobat Reader for Linux	Adobe PDF viewer and Ebook reader (Ubuntu **partner** repository, **acroread** package)
Scribus	Desktop publisher for generating PDF documents
pdfedit	Edit PDF documents
Simple Scan	GNOME Scanner interface for scanners (Applications | Graphics | Simple Scan)

Table 5-5: PostScript, PDF, and DVI viewers

Okular, Evince, and Xpdf are PDF viewers. They include many of the standard Adobe reader features such as zoom, two-page display, and full-screen mode. Alternatively, you can use Acrobat reader from Adobe (Partner repository) to display PDF files. You can install it with the Ubuntu Software Center | Office | Adobe Reader. On the Synaptic Package Manager, the name of the Adobe Acrobat Reader package is **acroread**.

All these viewers have the ability to print documents. To generate PDF documents you can use LibreOffice Writer or the Scribus desktop publisher (**http://www.scribus.net**), and to edit PDF documents you can use **pdfedit** (Ubuntu Software Center | Graphics | Viewers | PDF Editor).

Linux also supports a professional-level typesetting tool, called TeX, commonly used to compose complex mathematical formulas. TeX generates a DVI document that can be displayed by DVI viewers, several of which are available for Linux. DVI files generated by the TeX document application can be viewed by Evince and Okular.

Note: To scan documents directly, you can use Simple Scan (Graphics dash) which you can save as jpeg, png, or PDF files.

Ebook Readers: FBReader, Calibre, Adobe, and Kindle

On Ubuntu, for Ebooks you can use Calibre and FBReader directly. Under Wine, you can use the Windows versions of Adobe Digital Editions, which supports Digital Rights Management (DRM). On any Web browser, you can use the Kindle Cloud Reader.

Note: Though still under development, the Sigil ebook reader and Epub editor and converter will work on Ubuntu, **http://code.google.com/p/sigil/**. Download the Linux version. To install, make the file executable, and run from a terminal window preceded with a *./* . It is not available on a repository.

FBReader

FBReader is an open source reader that can read non-DRM ebooks, including mobipocket, html, palmdoc, chm, EPUB, text, and rtf (Ubuntu Software Center | Graphics | Viewers | E-book reader). The toolbar holds operations that move you through the text and configure your reader, adding books and setting interface preferences (see Figure 5-4). To see your selection of books click the Library Tree icon on the left. You can organize text by author or tag. On the Options window, the Library tab lets you choose where your books are stored. You also can search for public domain books from catalogs for Feedbooks, ManyBooks, and Smashwords.

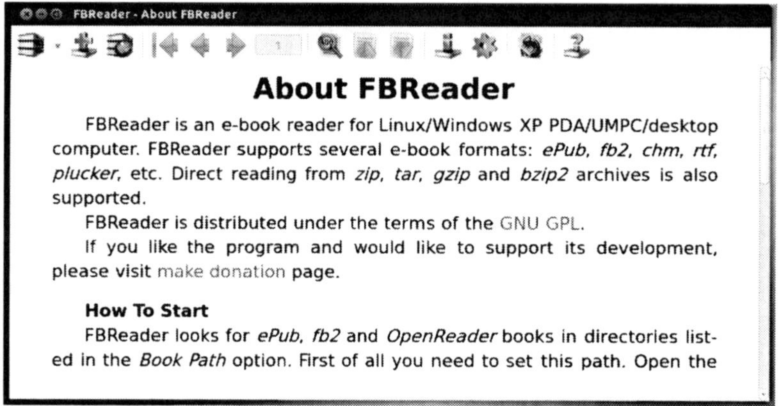

Figure 5-4: FBReader ebook reader

Calibre

Calibre reads PDF, EPUB, Lit (Microsoft), and Mobipocket Ebooks. Calibre functions as a library for accessing and managing your ebooks (see Figure 5-5). Calibre also can convert many document files and ebooks to the EPUB format, the open source standard used by Apple (iPad) and Barnes and Noble (Nook). It can take as conversion input text, HTML, TRF, and ODT (LibreOffice), as well as ebooks.

Figure 5-5: Calibre ebook reader, organizer, and converter

Adobe Digital Editions

You can run Adobe Digital Editions Ebook reader under Wine (see Figure 5-6). Be sure you have installed Wine. On your Web browser go to the Adobe Digital Editions web site and click on the Installation Technote link located below the button for the download (**http://www.adobe.com/products/digitaleditions/, Installation technote**). This page is titled "Adobe Digital Editions does not install on Windows or Mac OS". In the section "Manually install Adobe Digital Editions for Windows", the second item will have a link for downloading the Windows version, **Adobe Digital Editions 1.7.2 for Windows**. Click the link to download a file name **setup.exe**. It will download to the Download directory. Right-click on the **setup.exe** file and click Properties to open the file's Properties dialog. On the Permissions tab, click the Execute checkbox, "Allow executing file as program". On the Open With tab, choose the "Wine Windows Program Loader." Then click the Close button. Then double click on the **setup.exe** file to run it under Wine, installing the Adobe Digital Editions reader. An Adobe Digital Editions icon will appear on your desktop. Right-click on it and click Properties, and then on the Permissions tab check the Execute box. You can now run Adobe Digital Editions by double clicking its desktop icon. You can then remove the **setup.exe** file if you want.

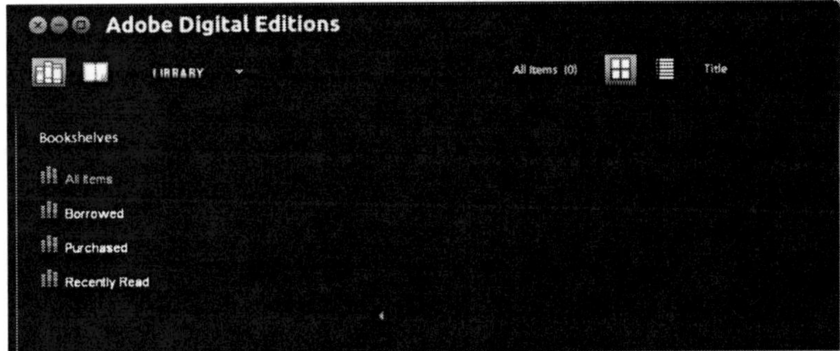

Figure 5-6: Adobe Digital Editions under Wine

Viewer	Description
Calibre	Ebook reader and library, also converts various inputs to EPUB ebooks.
E-book reader	FBReader Ebook reader
Adobe Digital Editions	Adobe Ebook Reader with DRM, Windows version works on Linux using Wine **http://www.adobe.com/products/digitaleditions**
Kindle Cloud Reader	Kindle reader on Web browser, which works on Linux **https://read.amazon.com/about**

Table 5-6: Ebook Readers

Kindle

You can now use the Kindle Cloud Reader on your Web browser to read kindle books on Ubuntu Linux (**https://read.amazon.com/about**). Simply sign in and be sure to allow storage on your computer when prompted (see Figure 5-7). The "Kindle For PC" reader currently does not work under Wine.

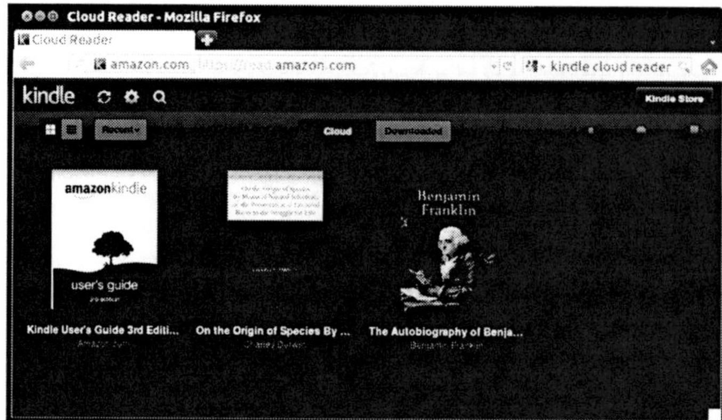

Figure 5-7: Kindle (Kindle Cloud Reader) ebook reader

PDA Access

For many PDAs, you can use the pilot tools to access your handheld device, transferring information between it and your system. You can use the J-Pilot, KPilot, and GnomePilot applications to access your PDA from your desktop.

To use your PDA on Ubuntu, you can use gnome-pilot. To access gnome-pilot, use the Control Center, which is accessible from the power menu's System Settings entry. On the Control Center dialog, choose PalmOS Devices from the Hardware section. A gnome -pilot Launcher item will appear on the Launcher, and the gnome-pilot settings dialog will open. The Conduits tab lets you enable several hot sync operations to perform automatically, including e-mail, memos, and installing files. Click the Help button for a detailed manual. When you start up gnome-pilot for the first time, you are prompted to specify the device settings. Serial is the default, but most PDA devices now use USB.

J-Pilot provides a desktop interface that lets you perform basic tasks such as synchronizing the address book and writing memos (Ubuntu Software Center | Office | J-Pilot). J-Pilot is accessible from the Office menu.

KPilot works on the KDE4 desktop, and is installed as the **kpilot** package. On the Kubuntu desktop it is accessible from Applications | Utilities | PalmPilot Tool. It will first open the Kpilot configuration window to let you set up your device, HotSync, contact, calendar, and Conduit preferences.

The **pilot-link** package holds tools you can use to access your PDA. Check **http://www.pilot-link.org** for detailed documentation and useful links. The tool name usually begins with "pilot"; for instance, **pilot-addresses** read addresses from an address book. Other tools whose names begin with "read" allow you to convert PDA device data for access by other applications; **read-expenses**, for instance, outputs expense data as standard text. One of the more useful tools is **pilot-xfer**, used to back up your PDA.

Editors

The Ubuntu desktop (GNOME and Kubuntu) supports powerful text editors with full mouse support, scroll bars, and menus. These include basic text editors such as Gedit and Kate, as well as word processors such as LibreOffice Word, Abiword, and Calligra Words. Ubuntu also provides the cursor-based editors Nano, Vim, and Emacs. Nano is the default cursor-based editor with an easy-to-use interface supporting menus and mouse selection (if run from a terminal window). *Vim* is an enhanced version of the Vi text editor used on the Unix system. These editors use simple, cursor-based operations to give you a full-screen format. Table 5-7 lists several desktop editors for Linux. Vi and Emacs have powerful editing features that have been refined over the years. Emacs, in particular, is extensible to a full-development environment for programming new applications. Later versions of Emacs and Vim, such as GNU Emacs, XEmacs, and Gvim provide support for mouse, menu, and window operations.

Application	Description
Kate	Text and program editor
Calligra Words	Desktop publisher, part of Calligra Suite
Gedit	Text editor
AbiWord	Word processor
OpenWriter	LibreOffice word processor that can edit text files
nano	Easy to use screen based editor, installed by default
GNU Emacs	Emacs editor with X Window System support
XEmacs	X Window System version of Emacs editor
gvim	Vim version with X Window System support

Table 5-7: Desktop Editors

GNOME Text Editor: Gedit

The Gedit editor is a basic text editor for the GNOME desktop. It provides full mouse support, implementing standard GUI operations, such as cut and paste to move text, and click and drag to select and move/copy text. It supports standard text editing operations such as Find and Replace. The editor is accessible from the Accessories dash as Text Editor. You can use Gedit to create and modify your text files, including configuration files. Gedit also provides more advanced features such as print preview and configurable levels of undo/redo operations, and it can read data from pipes. It features a plug-in menu that provides added functionality, and it includes plug-ins for spell checking, encryption, e-mail, and text-based Web page display.

The nano text editor

The nano editor is a simple screen-based editor that lets you visually edit your file, using arrow and page keys to move around the file. You use control keys to perform actions. **Ctrl-x** will exit and prompt you to save the file, **Ctrl-o** will save it. **Ctrl-k** will cut the current line.

You start nano with the **nano** command entered in a terminal window or on the command line interface. To edit a configuration file you will need administrative access. You would start nano with the **nano** command. Figure 5-8 shows the nano editor being used to edit the GRUB configuration file, **/etc/default/grub**.

```
sudo nano /etc/default/grub
```

```
 GNU nano 2.2.6             File: /etc/default/grub

# If you change this file, run 'update-grub' afterwards to update
# /boot/grub/grub.cfg.
# For full documentation of the options in this file, see:
#   info -f grub -n 'Simple configuration'

GRUB_DEFAULT=0
#GRUB_HIDDEN_TIMEOUT=0
GRUB_HIDDEN_TIMEOUT_QUIET=true
GRUB_TIMEOUT=10
GRUB_DISTRIBUTOR=`lsb_release -i -s 2> /dev/null || echo Debian`
GRUB_CMDLINE_LINUX_DEFAULT="quiet splash"
GRUB_CMDLINE_LINUX=""

# Uncomment to enable BadRAM filtering, modify to suit your needs
# This works with Linux (no patch required) and with any kernel that obtains
# the memory map information from GRUB (GNU Mach, kernel of FreeBSD ...)
#GRUB_BADRAM="0x01234567,0xfefefefe,0x89abcdef,0xefefefef"

                        [ Read 34 lines ]
^G Get Help   ^O WriteOut   ^R Read File  ^Y Prev Page  ^K Cut Text   ^C Cur Pos
^X Exit       ^J Justify    ^W Where Is   ^V Next Page  ^U UnCut Text ^T To Spell
```

Figure 5-8: Editing with nano

KDE Editor: Kate (KWrite)

The KDE editor Kate provides full mouse support, implementing standard GUI operations, such as cut and paste to move text, and click and drag to select and move/copy text. The editor is accessible from the Applications | Utilities menu on the KDE desktop, and from the Accessories dash on the Ubuntu desktop. Kate is an advanced editor, with such features as spell checking, font selection, and highlighting. Most commands can be selected using menus. A toolbar of icons for common operations is displayed across the top of the Kate window. A sidebar displays panels for a file list. Kate also supports multiple views of a document, letting you display segments in their own windows, vertically or horizontally. You can also open several documents at the same time, moving among them with the file list. Kate is designed to be a program editor for editing software programming/development-related source code files. Kate can format the syntax for different programming languages, such as C, Perl, Java, and XML. The Kate text editor has added features including a SQL, debugger, and highlight plugins, as well as recovery for unsaved data.

The Emacs Editor

Emacs can best be described as a working environment featuring an editor, a mailer, a newsreader, and a Lisp interpreter. The editor is tailored for program development, enabling you to format source code according to the programming language you use. Many versions of Emacs are currently available for use on Unix and Linux systems. The versions usually included with Linux distributions are either GNU Emacs or XEmacs. GNU Emacs is X Window System capable, enabling GUI features such as menus, scroll bars, and mouse-based editing operations. You can find out more information about Emacs at **http://www.emacs.org**, and for XEmacs at its Web site, **http://www.xemacs.org**.

The Emacs editor operates much like a standard word processor. The keys on your keyboard represent input characters. Commands are implemented with special keys, such as control (CTRL) keys and alternate (ALT) keys. There is no special input mode, as in Vi. You type in your text, and if you need to execute an editing command, such as moving the cursor or saving text, you use a CTRL key. You invoke the Emacs editor with the command **emacs**. You can enter the name of the file you want to edit, and if the file does not exist, it is created. In the next example, the user prepares to edit the file **mydata** with Emacs:

```
$ emacs mydata
```

The GNU Emacs editor supports basic desktop editing operations such as selection of text with click-and-drag mouse operations, cut/copy/paste, and a scroll bar for moving through text. The Mode line and Echo areas are displayed at the bottom of the window, where you can enter keyboard commands.

The Vi Editor: Vim and Gvim

The Vim editor is an enhanced version of the Vi editor. It includes all the commands and features of the Vi editor. Vi, which stands for *visual,* remains one of the most widely used editors in Linux. On Ubuntu, a basic version of Vi, called **vim-tiny**, is installed as part of the basic installation. For the full version, install the Vim package from the Ubuntu Software Center | Vi Improved.

Keyboard-based editors like Vim and Emacs use a keyboard for two different operations: to specify editing commands and to receive character input. Used for editing commands, certain keys perform deletions, some execute changes, and others perform cursor movement. Used for character input, keys represent characters that can be entered into the file being edited. Usually, these two different functions are divided among different keys on the keyboard. Alphabetic keys are reserved for character input, while function keys and control keys specify editing commands, such as deleting text or moving the cursor. Such editors can rely on the existence of an extended keyboard that includes function and control keys.

modes of operation for the keyboard: command and input modes, and a line editing mode. In command mode, all the keys on the keyboard become editing commands; in the input mode, the keys on the keyboard become input characters. Some of the editing commands, such as **a** or **i**, enter the input mode. On typing **i**, you leave the command mode and enter the input mode. Each key now represents a character to be input to the text. Pressing ESC automatically returns you to the command mode, and the keys once again become editor commands. As you edit text, you are constantly moving from the command mode to the input mode and back again. With Vim, you can use the **Ctrl-o** command to jump quickly to the command mode and enter a command, and then automatically return to the input mode. Table 5-8 lists a basic set of Vi commands to get you started.

Although you can create, save, close, and quit files with the Vi editor, the commands for each are not very similar. Saving and quitting a file involves the use of special line editing commands, whereas closing a file is a Vi editing command. Creation of a file is usually specified on the same shell command line that invokes the Vi editor. To edit a file, type **vi** or **vim** and the name of a file on the shell command line. If a file by that name does not exist, the system creates it. In effect, entering the name of a file that does not yet exist instructs the Vi editor to create that file.

The following command invokes the Vi editor, working on the file **booklist**. If **booklist** does not yet exist, the Vi editor creates it.

```
$ vim  booklist
```

Command	Description
h	Moves the cursor left one character.
l	Moves the cursor right one character.
k	Moves the cursor up one line.
j	Moves the cursor down one line.
CTRL-F	Moves forward by a screen of text; the next screen of text is displayed.
CTRL-B	Moves backward by a screen of text; the previous screen of text is displayed.
Input	*(All input commands place the user in input; the user leaves input with ESC.)*
a	Enters input after the cursor.
i	Enters input before the cursor.
o	Enters input below the line the cursor is on; inserts a new empty line below the one the cursor is currently on.
Text Selection (Vim)	
v	Visual mode; move the cursor to expand selected text by character. Once selected, press key to execute action: **c** change, **d** delete, **y** copy, **:** line-editing command, **J** join lines, **U** uppercase, **u** lowercase.
V	Visual mode; move cursor to expand selected text by line.
Delete	
x	Deletes the character the cursor is on.
dd	Deletes the line the cursor is on.
Change	*(Except for the replace command, **r**, all change commands place the user into input after deleting text.)*
cw	Deletes the word the cursor is on and places the user into the input mode.
r	Replaces the character the cursor is on. After pressing **r**, the user enters the replacement character. The change is made without entering input; the user remains in the Vi command mode.
R	First places into input mode, and then overwrites character by character. Appears as an overwrite mode on the screen but actually is in input mode.
Move	Moves text by first deleting it, moving the cursor to desired place of insertion, and then pressing the **p** command. (When text is deleted, it is automatically held in a special buffer.)
p	Inserts deleted or copied text after the character or line the cursor is on.

P	Inserts deleted or copied text before the character or line the cursor is on.
dw p	Deletes a word, and then moves it to the place you indicate with the cursor (press **p** to insert the word *after* the word the cursor is on).
yy or **Y p**	Copies the line the cursor is on.
Search	The two search commands open up a line at the bottom of the screen and enable the user to enter a pattern to be searched for; press ENTER after typing in the pattern.
/pattern	Searches forward in the text for a pattern.
?pattern	Searches backward in the text for a pattern.
n	Repeats the previous search, whether it was forward or backward.
Line Editing Commands	**Effect**
w	Saves file.
q	Quits editor; **q!** quits without saving.

Table 5-8: Vi Editor Commands

Editors in Unix were designed originally to assume a minimal keyboard with alphanumeric characters and some control characters, as well as the ESC and ENTER keys. Instead of dividing the command and input functions among different keys, the Vi editor has three separate

After executing the **vim** command, you enter Vi's command mode. Each key becomes a Vi editing command, and the screen becomes a window onto the text file. Text is displayed screen by screen. The first screen of text is displayed, and the cursor is positioned in the upper-left corner. With a newly created file, there is no text to display. When you first enter the Vi editor, you are in the command mode. To enter text, you need to enter the input mode. In the command mode, **a** is the editor command for appending text. Pressing this key places you in the input mode. Now the keyboard operates like a typewriter and you can input text to the file. If you press ENTER, you merely start a new line of text. With Vim, you can use the arrow keys to move from one part of the entered text to another and work on different parts of the text. After entering text, you can leave the input mode and return to the command mode by pressing ESC. Once finished with the editing session, you exit Vi by typing two capital *Z*s, **ZZ**. Hold down the SHIFT key and press **z** twice. This sequence first saves the file and then exits the Vi editor, returning you to the Linux shell. To save a file while editing, you use the line editing command **w**, which writes a file to the disk; **w** is equivalent to the Save command found in other word processors. You first type a colon to access the line editing mode, and then type **w** and press ENTER, **:w**.

You can use the **:q** command to quit an editing session. Unlike the **ZZ** command, the **:q** command does not perform any save operation before it quits. In this respect, it has one major constraint. If any modifications have been made to your file since the last save operation, the **:q** command will fail and you will not leave the editor. However, you can override this restriction by placing a **!** qualifier after the **:q** command. The command **:q!** will quit the Vi editor without saving any modifications made to the file in that session since the last save (the combination **:wq** is the same as **ZZ**).

To obtain online help, enter the `:help` command. This is a line editing command. Type a colon, enter the word `help` on the line that opens at the bottom of the screen, and then press ENTER. You can add the name of a specific command after the word `help`. Pressing the **F1** key also brings up online help.

As an alternative to using Vim in a command line interface, you can use gvim, which provides X Window System–based menus for basic file, editing, and window operations. Gvim is installed from the Ubuntu Software Center | Accessories | GVim. On the Synaptic Package Manager the package is called the **vim-gui-common** package, which includes several links to Gvim such as **evim**, **gview**, and **gex** (open Ex editor line). To use Gvim, you can enter the `gvim` command at a terminal prompt. The standard Vi interface is shown, but with several menu buttons displayed across the top along with a toolbar with buttons for common commands like search and file saves. All the standard Vi commands work just as described previously. However, you can use your mouse to select items on these menus. You can open and close a file, or open several files using split windows or different windows. The editing menu enables you to cut, copy, and paste text as well as undo or redo operations. In the editing mode, you can select text with your mouse with a click-and-drag operation, or use the Editing menu to cut or copy and then paste the selected text. Text entry, however, is still performed using the `a`, `i`, or `o` command to enter the input mode. Searches and replacements are supported through a dialog window. There are also buttons on the toolbar for finding next and previous instances. You can also split the view into different windows to display parts of the same file or different files. Use the **:split** command to open a window, and use **:hide** to close the current one. Use **Ctrl-w** with the up and down arrow keys to move between them. On Gvim, you use entries in the Windows menu to manage windows. Configuration preferences can be placed in the user's **.vimrc** file.

Database Management Systems

Database software can be generally organized into three categories: SQL and desktop databases. SQL-based databases are professional-level relational databases whose files are managed by a central database server program. Applications that use the database do not access the files directly. Instead, they send requests to the database server, which then performs the actual access. SQL is the query language used on these industrial-strength databases. Ubuntu includes both MySQL and PostgreSQL databases. Both are open source projects freely available for your use. Table 5-9 lists database management systems currently available for Linux.

SQL Databases (RDBMS)

SQL databases are relational database management systems (RDBMSs) designed for extensive database management tasks. Many of the major SQL databases now have Linux versions, including Oracle, Informix, Sybase, and IBM. These are commercial and professional database management systems. Linux has proved itself capable of supporting complex and demanding database management tasks. In addition, many free SQL databases are available for Linux that offer much the same functionality. Most commercial databases also provide free personal versions.

LibreOffice Base

LibreOffice provides a basic data base application, LibreOffice Base that can access many database files. You can set up and operate a simple database, as well as access and manage files from other database applications. When you start up LibreOffice Base, you will be prompted either to start a new database or connect to an existing one. File types supported include ODBC (Open Database Connectivity), JDBC (Java), Adabas D, MySQL, PostgreSQL, and MDB (Microsoft Access) database files (install the **unixodbc** and **java-libmysql** packages). You can also create your own simple databases. Check the LibreOffice Base page (**http://www.libreoffice.org/features/base/**) for detailed information on drivers and supported databases.

System	Site
LibreOffice	LibreOffice database (Ubuntu repository): **www.libreoffice.org**
PostgreSQL	The PostgreSQL database (Ubuntu repository): **www.postgresql.org**
MySQL	MySQL database (Ubuntu repository): **www.mysql.com**
Oracle	Oracle database: **www.oracle.com**
Sybase	Sybase database: **www.sybase.com**
DB2	IBM database: **http://ibm.com/software/data/db2**
Informix	Informix database: **http://ibm.com/software/data/informix**

Table 5-9: Database Management Systems for Linux

PostgreSQL

PostgreSQL is based on the POSTURES database management system, though it uses SQL as its query language. POSTGRESQL is a next-generation research prototype developed at the University of California, Berkeley. Linux versions of PostgreSQL are included in most distributions, including the Red Hat, Fedora, Debian, and Ubuntu. You can find more information on it from the PostgreSQL Web site at **http://www.postgresql.org**. PostgreSQL is an open source project, developed under the GPL license.

MySQL

MySQL, included with Ubuntu, is a true multi-user, multithreaded SQL database server, supported by MySQL AB. MySQL is an open source product available free under the GPL license. You can obtain current information on it from its Web site, **http://www.mysql.com**. The site includes detailed documentation, including manuals and FAQs.

6. Graphics and Multimedia

Ubuntu includes a wide range of graphics and multimedia applications, including simple image viewers such as the Eye of GNOME, sophisticated image manipulation programs like GIMP, music and CD players like Banshee, and Video players like Totem. Several helpful Linux multimedia sites are listed in Table 6-1. There is strong support for graphics and multimedia tasks from image management, video and DVD, to sound and music editing (see Tables 6-1, 6-4 and 6-5). Most are available on Ubuntu's multiverse and universe repositories. In addition, the Ubuntu Studio project has collected popular multimedia development software into several collections for audio, video, and graphics. The Mythbuntu project provides an Ubuntu version of MythTV for Home Theater PCs (HTPC). For information on graphics hardware and drivers, check **http://www.phoronix.com**.

Projects and Sites	Description
Advanced Linux Sound Architecture (ALSA)	The Advanced Linux Sound Architecture (ALSA) project for current sound drivers: **www.alsaproject.org**
Open Sound System	Open Sound System, drives for older devices: **www.opensound.com**
PulseAudio	PulseAudio sound interface, now the default for Ubuntu. **www.pulseaudio.org**
Phoronix	Site for the latest news and reviews of Linux hardware compatibility, including graphics cards. **www.phoronix.com**
Ubuntu Studio	Ubuntu Studio multimedia development applications and desktop, audio, video, and graphics collection installed from ubuntustudio meta packages, Meta Packages (universe) **www.ubuntustudio.org**
Mythbuntu	MythTV implementation of HTPC multimedia software, **www.mythbuntu.org**.
Medibuntu.org	Ubuntu third party repository for some third party non-free multimedia codecs and applications: **http://medibuntu.org**

Table 6-1: Linux and Ubuntu Multimedia Sites

Support for many popular multimedia operations, specifically MP3, DVD, and DivX, are not included on the Ubuntu CDs because of licensing and other restrictions. To play MP3, DVD, or DivX files, you will have to download and install support packages manually. For Ubuntu, precompiled packages for many popular media applications and libraries, such as MPlayer and XviD as well as MP3 and DVD video support, are available on the Ubuntu multiverse and universe repository sections.

Certain codecs and applications are provided by the third-party repository Medibuntu.org (**http://www.medibuntu.org**). See Chapter 4 on how to configure access to this repository. The Medibuntu.org repository provides AAC sound support, the DVD Video commercial decoder (**libdvdcss2**), the Windows multimedia codecs (**w32codecs** and **w64codecs**), and Realplayer.

Graphics Applications

The GNOME and KDE desktops support an impressive number of graphics applications, including image viewers, window grabbers, image editors, and paint tools. These tools can be found on the Graphics dash.

Tools	Description
Shotwell	GNOME digital camera application and image and video library manager (**http://www.yorba.org/shotwell/**)
F-Spot	GNOME digital camera application and image library manager (**http://www.f-spot.org**) (universe)
Cheese	GNOME Web cam application for taking pictures and videos
ubuntustudio-graphics	Ubuntu Studio meta package (Meta Packages (universe)), includes a collection of graphics applications. Use Synaptic Package Manager.
Digikam	Digital photo management tool, works with both GNOME and KDE
KDE	
Gwenview	Image browser and viewer (default for KDE)
ShowFoto	Simple image viewer, works with digiKam (**www.digikam.org**)
KSnapshot	Screen grabber
KolourPaint	Paint program
Krita	Image editor (**http://www.calligra.org/krita/**)
GNOME	
Eye of Gnome	GNOME Image Viewer
GIMP	GNU Image Manipulation Program (**www.gimp.org**)
Inkscape	GNOME Vector graphics application (**www.inkscape.org**)
gpaint	GNOME paint program
Blender	3d modeling, rendering, and animation
LibreOffice Draw	LibreOffice Draw program
X Window System	
Xpaint	Paint program
Xfig	Drawing program
ImageMagick	Image format conversion and editing tool

Table 6-2: Graphics Tools for Linux

Photo Management: Shotwell, F-Spot, and Cheese

Shotwell provides an easy and powerful way to manage, display, and import, and publish your photos and images (**http://www.yorba.org/shotwell/**). It is the default photo manager for Ubuntu 12.04. See the Shotwell user manual for full details (Help | User Manual,

http://yorba.org/shotwell/help/). Shotwell is accessible as the Shotwell Photo Manager from the Graphics dash. Shotwell also supports video files (wmv, avi, ogg, and MP4). You can use Shotwell to upload videos to Web services such as YouTube and Facebook.

You can import folders from cameras, folders, or from F-spot (see Figure 6-1). Your Pictures folder is the default library folder, whose photos are imported automatically. Adding an image file to the Pictures folder, also imports it to Shotwell. Photo thumbnails are displayed in the main right pane. The View menu lets you control the thumbnail display, allowing you to sort photos, zoom, show photo file names (Titles), or select by rating. You can adjust the size of the displayed thumbnails using a slider bar in the toolbar located at the bottom right of the Shotwell window. The small figure button to the left of the slider reduces thumbnails to their smallest size, and the large figure button to the right of the slider expands them to the largest size.

Figure 6-1: Shotwell Photo Management

To see a full screen slide show of the photos, click the slideshow button in the bottom toolbar. The slide show starts automatically. During the slideshow, moving your mouse to the center bottom of the screen displays slideshow controls for pausing and stepping through photos. The Settings button opens a dialog where you can set the display time. To end the slide show and return to the desktop, click the full screen button. The slideshow buttons are shown here.

You can also select photos to work as a desktop slideshow. Select the photos and choose File | Set as Desktop Slideshow (**Ctrl-b**).

Photos are organized automatically by the time they were taken. Dates are listed under the Events entry in the left sidebar, arranged by year, month, and date. To name a photo, right-click on it and choose Edit Title to open a dialog where you can enter the name. You can also tag photos placing them in groups, making them easier to access. To tag a photo, right-click it and choose Add Tags to open a dialog where you can enter a tag name. The tag will show up as a label for the photo. You can access photos by tags using the Tags entries in the left sidebar. For each photo, you can also set a rating indicated by five stars or less. You can also mark a photo as rejected. To rate a photo, right-click it and choose Set Rating which then lists rating options in a submenu. Use the Show Photos button in the bottom toolbar to display photos by rating. You can select several photos at once using click and drag, Ctrl-click, or Shift-click (as you would files in a file manager window), and then right click to give them the same rating (Set Rating) or same tag (Add Tags).

To search for photos, click the Find button to open a search bar, which displays a text box for entering the search pattern. Buttons to the left let you refine the search by image type, photos or videos, flagged files, and ratings.

When you select a photo or group of photos, the Rotate, Enhance, and Publish buttons in the bottom toolbar become active. The Publish button lets you publish the photo on a Web service: Facebook, Flickr, or Picasa. The Rotate button rotates the Photo (from the Photos menu you can also flip the Photo horizontally or vertically). The Enhance button will adjust the photo automatically.

You can perform more complex edits either within the Shotwell window or in full screen. To edit a photo within the Shotwell window, double click its image to display the edit toolbar, which hold Rotate, Crop, Red-eye, Adjust, and Enhance buttons. For full screen edits, select the photo and then choose View | Fullscreen (F11) to open the photo in the Shotwell photo editor (see Figure 6-2) . Move your mouse to the bottom of the screen to display edit toolbar (Rotate, Crop, Red-eye, Adjust, and Enhance buttons). You can also zoom in or out from the photo using the slider bar. The Crop button opens an adjustable border, with a menu for choosing the display proportions you may want such as HD video or postcard. The Adjust button opens a dialog for refined changes such as exposure, saturation, tint, temperature and shadows. The toolbar will keep disappearing. Click the pin button to have it displayed permanently. Edits are stored in a Shotwell database; they are not made to the original photo. To revert to the original photo, right-click and choose "Revert to Original" or choose that entry from the Photos menu.

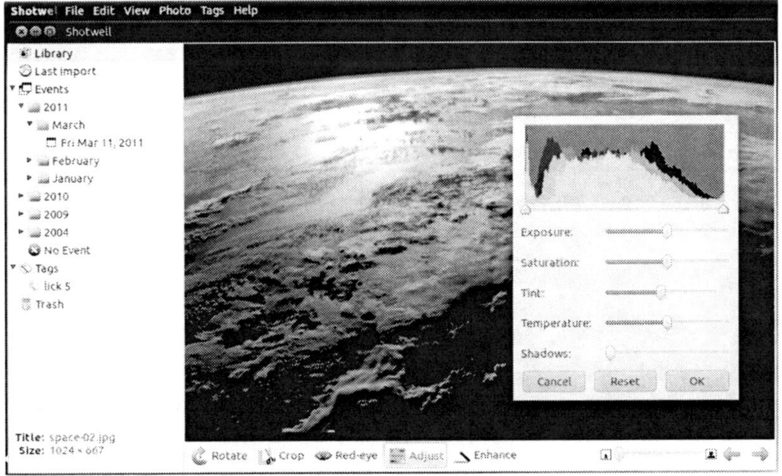

Figure 6-2: Shotwell Photo Editing

The Shotwell Preferences dialog (Edit | Preferences) lets you set the background intensity, choose a photo library folder, and select a photo editor. To open a photo with an external photo editor, right-click the photo thumbnail and select "Open With External Editor." Photos are stored in your Pictures directory under Events sub-folders by year and then month. To open a photos folder, right-click and select "Show in File Manager."

The F-Spot Photo Manager provides an easy and powerful way to manage, display, and import your photos and images (**http://www.f-spot.org**). It is part of the universe repository and no longer supported by Ubuntu directly. Photos can be organized by different categories such as events, people, and places. You can perform standard display operations like rotation or full-screen viewing, along with slide shows. Image editing support is provided. Selected photos can be burned directly to a CD. A timeline feature lets you see photos as they were taken. F-Spot includes a photo editor that provides basic adjustments and changes like rotation, red-eye correction, and standard color settings including temperature and saturation.

DigiKam (**http://www.digiKam.org**) is a KDE photo manager with many of the same features as Shotwell (Ubuntu Software Center | Graphics | Photography | digiKam). DigiKam is accessible from the Graphics dash. A side panel allows easy access by album, date, tags, or previous searches (see Figure 6-3). The program also provides image-editing capabilities, with numerous effects. The digiKam configuration (Settings menu) provides extensive options, including image editing, digital camera support, and interface configuration.

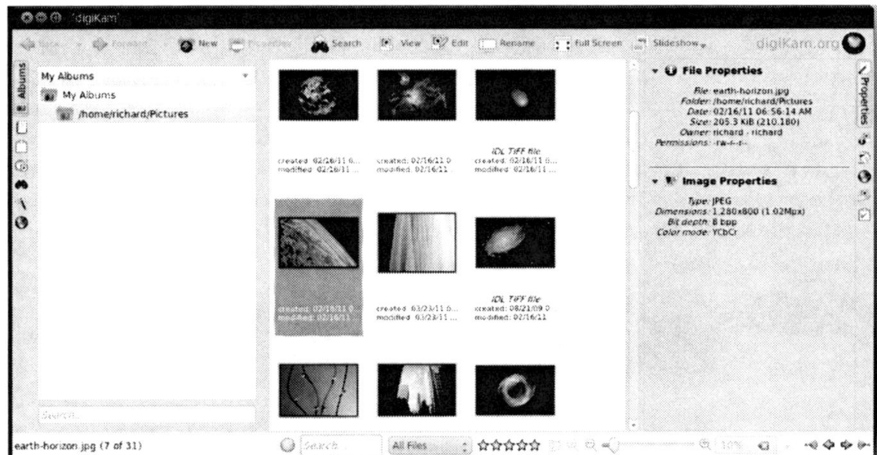

Figure 6-3: digiKam Photo Manager

Tip: The Windows version of Photoshop is supported by Wine. You can install Photoshop CS on Ubuntu using Wine. Once started, Photoshop will operate like any Linux desktop application.

Cheese is a Web cam picture-taking and video-recording tool (**http://www.gnome.org/projects/cheese**), install from the Ubuntu Software Center | Sound & Video. You can snap pictures from your Web cam and apply simple effects. Cheese is accessible as the Cheese Webcam Booth on the Multimedia dash. Click the Photo button to manage photos and the Video button to record video (located to the left). Icons of photos and video will appear on the bottom panel, which you can select for effects or removal. The effects tab will show effects that can be turned on or off for the current image. To save a photo, right click on its icon on the lower panel and select Save As from the pop-up menu.

GNOME Graphics Applications

GNOME features several powerful and easy-to-use graphics applications. The Eye of GNOME is the GNOME image viewer. It is installed by default (Ubuntu Software Center | Graphics | Viewers | Image Viewer (eog)). The image viewer provides basic image display operations such as enlargement, full screen display, rotation, and slide shows. The Image Edit button opens the Shotwell image editor (see Figure 6-4). The Eye of GNOME is accessible as "Image Viewer" on the Graphics dash. Eye of GNOME is not displayed by default on the dash, use Main Menu to have it appear, selecting Image Viewer under Applications | Graphics.

Figure 6-4: Image Viewer (Eye of Gnome)

The gThumb application is an image viewer and browser that lets you browse images using thumbnails, display them, and organize them into catalogs for easy reference.

GIMP is the GNU Image Manipulation Program, a sophisticated image application much like Adobe Photoshop (see Figure 6-5). You can use GIMP for such tasks as photo retouching, image composition, and image authoring. It supports features such as layers, channels, blends, and gradients. GIMP makes effective use of the GTK+ widget set. GIMP is accessible as the GIMP Image Editor on the Graphics dash. You can find out more about GIMP from its Web site at **http://www.gimp.org**. GIMP is freely distributed under the GNU Public License. You can install GIMP from the Ubuntu Software Center | Graphics | Painting & Editing | GIMP Image Editor.

Note: The gPhoto project provides software for accessing digital cameras (**http://www.gphoto.org**). Several front-end interfaces are provided for a core library, called **libgphoto2**, consisting of drivers and tools that can access numerous digital cameras.

Figure 6-5: GIMP

Inkscape is a Gnome based vector graphics application for SVG (Scalable Vector Graphics) images (see Figure 6-6). Inkscape is accessible as Inkscape Image Editor on the Graphics dash. It features abilities similar to professional level vector graphics applications like Adobe Illustrator. The SVG format allows easy generation of images for Web use as well as complex art. Though its native format is SVG, it can also export to the Portable Network Graphics (PNG) format. It features layers and easy object creation, including stars and spirals. A color bar lets you quickly change color fills. You can install Inkscape from the Ubuntu Software Center | Graphics | Drawing | Inkscape.

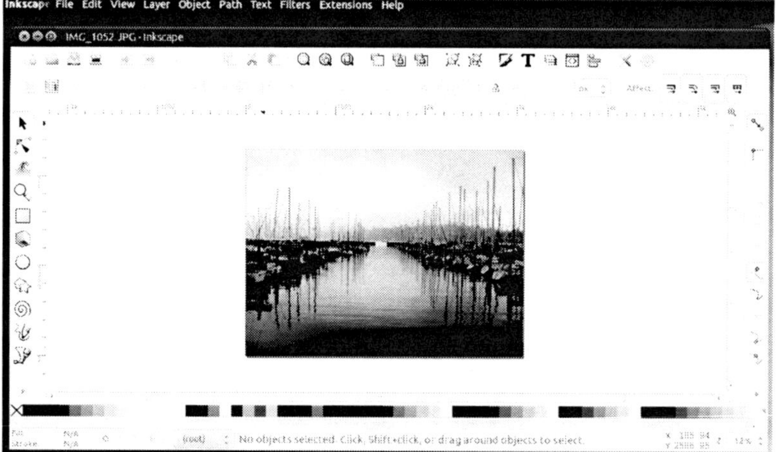

Figure 6-6: Inkscape

KDE Graphics Applications

The KDE desktop features the same variety of graphics applications found on the GNOME desktop. Many are available from the Ubuntu main repository. Most do not require a full installation of the KDE desktop. The KSnapshot program is a simple screen grabber for KDE. Gwenview is an easy-to-use image browser and viewer supporting slide shows and numerous image formats (Ubuntu Software Center | Graphics | Viewers | Gwenview). It is the default viewer for KDE, but can also be used on GNOME (see Figure 6-7). Gwenview can share photos with social networking sites directly. KolourPaint is a basic paint program with brushes, shapes, and color effects; it supports numerous image formats (Ubuntu Software Center | Graphics | Painting & Editing | KolourPaint). Krita is the Calligra professional image paint and editing application, with a wide range of features such as the ability to create web images and modify photographs (formerly known as Krayon and KImageShop).

Figure 6-7: Gwenview

X Window System Graphic Programs

X Window System–based applications run directly on the underlying X Window System. These applications tend to be simpler, lacking the desktop functionality found in GNOME or KDE applications. Most are available on the Ubuntu Universe repository. Xpaint is a simple paint program that allows you to load graphics or photographs and then create shapes, add text and colors, and use brush tools with various sizes and colors. Xfig is a drawing program. ImageMagick lets you convert images from one format to another; you can, for instance, to change a TIFF image to a JPEG image. Table 6-2 lists some popular graphics tools for Linux.

Multimedia

Many applications are available for both video and sound, including sound editors, MP3 players, and video players (see Tables 6-5 and 6-6). Linux sound applications include mixers, digital audio tools, CD audio writers, MP3 players, and network audio support. To use restricted formats such as commercial DVD and Blu-Ray see the following site.

```
https://help.ubuntu.com/community/RestrictedFormats
```

Multimedia support

A listing of popular multimedia codecs available is shown in Table 6-3. Of particular interest may be the liba52, faad2, and lame codecs for sound decoding, as well as the xvidcore, x264, libdvdcss, and libdvbpsi for video decoding.

Ubuntu provides a codec wizard that automatically detects whenever you need to install a new multimedia codec (see Figure 6-8). If you try to run a media file for which you do not have the proper codec, the codec wizard will appear, listing the codecs you need to download and install. Often there are several choices (see Figure 6-9). The codec wizard will select and install these packages for you, simplifying the process of installing the various multimedia codecs available for Linux.

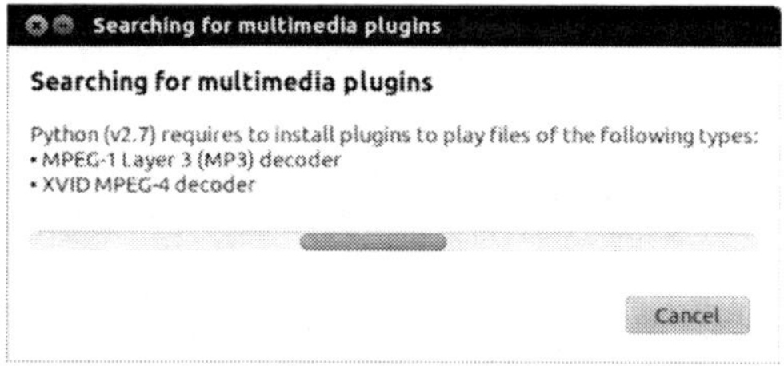

Figure 6-8: Ubuntu codec wizard prompt

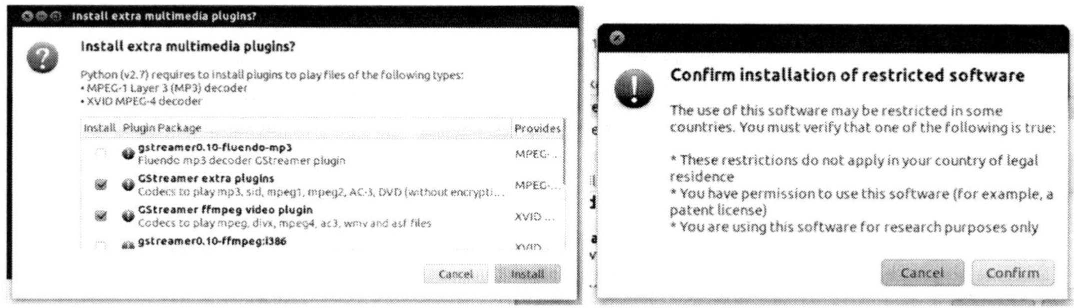

Figure 6-9: Ubuntu codec wizard selection

To install support for most of the commonly used codecs, you can install the Ubuntu restricted extras package, **ubuntu-restricted-extras**, available from the Ubuntu Software Center | System | Ubuntu Restricted Extras, or the Synaptic Package Manager (Meta Packages (multiverse) section, ubuntu-restricted-extras). This package is a meta package that will download a collection of other packages that provide support for DVD, MP3, MPEG4, DivX, and AC3, as well as Flash (non-free) and Java runtime support. It will install all the GStreamer bad, ugly, and ffmpeg packages, as well as Adobe flash and JRE packages. The Microsoft font collection (**ttf-mscorefonts**) is also included, as well as RAR archive extraction (**unrar**). You are warned that licensing for these codecs may be restricted in some countries.

Package	Description
liba52	HDTV audio (ATSC A/52, AC3)
faad	MPEG2/ 4 AAC audio decoding, high quality (faad2)
faac	MPEG2/ 4 AAC sound encoding and decoding
ffmpeg	Play, record, convert, stream audio and video. Includes digital streaming server, conversion tool, and media player.
libav extra libraries	Unrestricted multimedia libraries, includes encoders and additional formats (Medibuntu.org).
gstreamer-ffmpeg	ffmpeg plug-in for GStreamer
gstreamer-plugins-bad	Not fully reliable codecs and tools for GStreamer, some with possible licensing issues.
gstreamer-plugins-ugly	Reliable video and audio codecs for GStreamer that may have licensing issues
gstreamer-fluendo-mp3	Fully licensed MP3 codec from Fluendo for GStreamer
gstreamer-fluendo-mpegmux	Fully licensed MPEG2 TS video streams demuxing from Fluendo for GStreamer
lame	MP3 playback capability, not an official MP3 decoder
libdvbpsi	MPEG TS stream (DVB and PSI) decoding and encoding capability, VideoLAN project.
libdvdcss	DVD commercial decryption, available from **medibuntu.org** repository.
libfame	Fast Assembly MPEG video encoding
libmad	MPEG1 audio decoding (Ubuntu main repository)
libmpeg2	MPEG video audio decoding (MPEG1/2 audio and video, AC3, IFO, and VOB)
libquicktime	QuickTime playback
mt-daap	ITunes support
mpeg2dec	MPEG2 and MPEG1 playback
x264	H264/AVC encoding (high definition media)
libxvidcore4	OpenDivx codec (DivX and Xvid playback)
libsmpeg	Smpeg MPEG 1 video and audio decoder
swfdec-gnome, swfdec-mozilla	Play SWF files (FLASH)
libxine1-all-plugins	Added video/ audio playback plugins for Xine

Table 6-3: Multimedia third-party codecs

ubuntu-restricted-extras

For the Kubuntu desktop, you would also install the KDE version (the Ubuntu Software Center | System | Kubuntu Restricted Extras).

```
kubuntu-restricted-extras
```

For GStreamer supported applications like the Totem movie player, you will need a special set of packages called gstreamer-bad and gstreamer-ugly. These are installed by the **ubuntu-restricted-extras** package. On the Ubuntu Software Center, the gstreamer-bad plugins are accessible as Sound & Video | GStreamer plugins for aac, xvid, mpeg2, faad; and the gstreamer-ugly package as Gstreamer extra plugins.

The DVD video **libdvdcss** and the Windows **w32codecs/w64codecs** are available only from the Medibuntu.org repository. If you configure APT to use the Medibuntu repository, you can use the Synaptic Package Manager or the Ubuntu Software Center to download and install them. Medibuntu also provides a meta package called **non-free-codecs** that will select and install most of the codecs for you.

```
non-free-codecs
```

FFmpeg provides both restricted and unrestricted multimedia libraries. The restricted libraries are available on the Ubuntu main repository and are fully supported by Ubuntu. However, the restricted versions lack FFmpeg support for a variety of encoders and formats including h263, AAC, AMR, mp3, h264, xvid, and MPEG4. The unrestricted package versions can be downloaded from the Medibuntu.org repository and have the term "extra" inserted into the name, as in **libavcodec-extra-52** instead of **libavcodec52**. An unrestricted version of Mplayer available on Medibuntu.org uses these unrestricted versions of the FFmpeg libraries. The unstripped FFmpeg packages on Medibuntu.org are used for older pre 9.10 versions of Ubuntu.

For certified valid multimedia licensed codecs for Linux, check **http://www.fluendo.com**. You can purchase Fluendo supported and fully licensed codes for all the standard multimedia formats including DVD video, MP3, MPEG4, and AC3. You can also purchase the Fluendo DVD Player using the Ubuntu Software Center (Get Software | For Purchase | Fluendo DVD Player).

For MP3 music files, the easiest way to install the MP3 music codec is to start up the Banshee Music Player and select the Ubuntu One music store. Banshee is accessible from the Multimedia dash. You will be prompted to install the MP3 codec. Alternatively, you can install the lame codec or the licensed Fluendo codec manually (see Figure 6-5). Both are available on the universe and multi-verse repositories, though you would need to know what packages to look for. For the Fluendo codecs, search on fluendo in the Synaptic Package Manager.

GStreamer

Many GNOME-based applications make use of GStreamer, a streaming media framework based on graphs and filters (**http://gstreamer.freedesktop.org**). Using a plug-in structure, GStreamer applications can accommodate a wide variety of media types:

The Totem video player uses GStreamer to play DVDs, VCDs, and MPEG media.

Banshee and Rhythmbox provide integrated music management.

Sound Juicer is an audio CD ripper.

A GNOME CD player and sound recorder

GStreamer can be configured to use different input and output sound and video drivers and servers, using the GStreamer properties tool, the Multimedia System Selector. You can access it on the Multimedia dash. It is not displayed by default, use Main Menu to have it listed.

Note: Phonom now uses of a Gstreamer backend, which provides standard multimedia codec support for both Kubuntu and Ubuntu (GNOME and Unity).

GStreamer Plug-ins: the Good, the Bad, and the Ugly

Many GNOME multimedia applications like Totem use GStreamer to provide multimedia support. To use such features as DVD Video and MP3, you have to install GStreamer extra plug-ins. You can find out more information about GStreamer and its supporting packages at **http://gstreamer.freedesktop.org**.

GStreamer has four different support packages called the base, the good, the bad, and the ugly. The base package is a set of useful and reliable plug-ins. These are in the Ubuntu main repository. The good package is a set of supported and tested plug-ins that meets all licensing requirements. This is also part of the Ubuntu main repository. The bad package is a set of unsupported plug-ins whose performance is not guaranteed and may crash, but still meet licensing requirements. The ugly package contains plug-ins that work fine, but may not meet licensing requirements, like DVD support.

The base   Reliable commonly used plug-ins

The good   Reliable additional and useful plug-ins

The ugly   Reliable but not fully licensed plug-ins (DVD/MP3 support)

The bad   Possibly unreliable but useful plug-ins (possible crashes)

As an alternative to the ugly package, you can use Fluendo packages for MP3 and MPEG2 support, **gstreamer-fluendo-mp3** and **gstreamer-fluendo-mpegmux** (Ubuntu Software Center | Sound & Video | GStreamer fluendo MPEG2 demuxing plug-in). Another plug-in for GStreamer that you may want include is **ffmpeg** for Matroska (mkv) and OGG support. The codec wizard will automatically detect the codec you will need to use for your GStreamer application.

GStreamer MP3 Compatibility: iPod

Ubuntu provides support for your iPod and iPod Touch from your desktop directly. For your iPod and other MP3 devices to work with GNOME applications like Banshee, you are prompted to install MP3 support for GStreamer the first time you use them (**gstreamer-fluendo-mp3** (licensed MP3) or **gstreamer-plugins-ugly** packages). MP3 support is not installed initially because of licensing issues.

The **libgpod** library allows player applications like Rhythmbox, Banshee, and Amarok to play songs from your iPod. To synchronize, import, or extract data from your iPod, you can use iPod management software such as GUI for iPod, both **gtkpod** (Universe) and **gtkpod-aac** with aac and MP4 support (Multiverse). For the iPhone you can use **ifuse**.

Music Applications

Many music applications are currently available for GNOME, including sound editors, MP3 players, and audio players (see Table 6-4). You can use Banshee, Rhythmbox, and Sound Juicer to play music from different sources, and the GNOME Sound Recorder to record sound sources. Several applications are also available for KDE, including the media players Amarok and Juk, a mixer (KMix), and a CD player (Kscd). For sound and music editing you can use Jokosher.

Application	Description
Jokosher	Sound editor to create and record music and audio projects (Gstreamer).
Banshee	Music management (GStreamer)
Rhythmbox	Music management (GStreamer), default Music player with iPod support..
Sound Juicer	GNOME CD audio ripper (GStreamer)
Amarok	KDE4 multimedia audio player
Audacious	Multimedia player
Kscd	Music CD player
JuK	KDE4 Music player (jukebox) for managing music collections
GNOME CD Player	CD player
GNOME Sound Recorder	Sound recorder
XMMS	CD player
RealPlayer	RealMedia and RealAudio streaming media (**www.real.com**), download from **medibuntu.org**, the **realplayer** package.
ubuntustudio-audio	Ubuntu Studio meta package (Meta Packages (universe)), includes a collection of audio applications. Use Synaptic Package Manager.
Audex	KDE CD audio ripper (universe)
Specimen	MIDI controlled sampler (universe)
QMidiRoute	MIDI event router and filter (universe)

Table 6-4: Music players, editors, and rippers

GNOME includes sound applications like the Sound Juicer (Audio CD Extractor) and Rhythmbox. Rhythmbox is the default sound multimedia player, supporting music files, radio streams, video, and podcasts (see Figure 6-10). When you open Rhythmbox, the indicator sound menu on the top panel displays options for Rhythmbox to play or stop playing, and to move to the next or previous audio source such as a song or radio station.

KDE applications include Amarok and Juk. Amarok is the primary multimedia player for KDE but will play on the GNOME desktop (see Figure 6-11). It includes access to Internet sources, local music files, and local devices like Audio CDs. JuK (Music Jukebox) is the KDE music player for managing music collections.

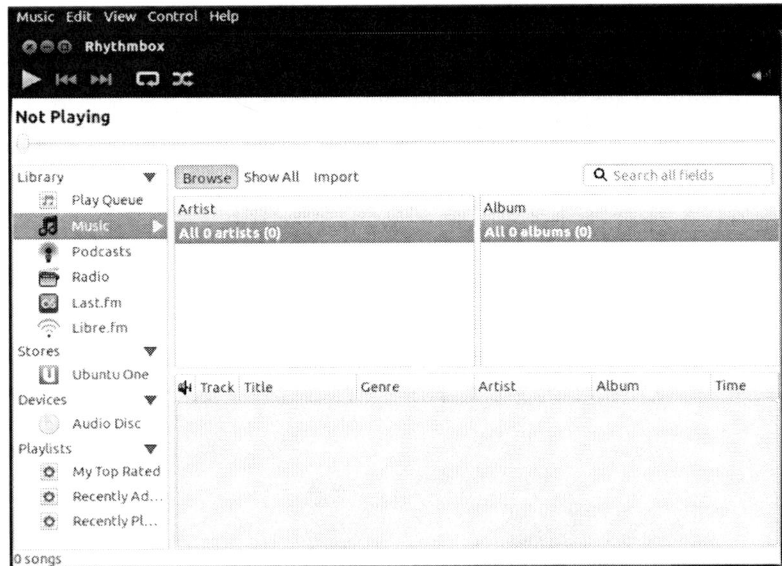

Figure 6-10: Rhythmbox GNOME Multimedia Player

Figure 6-11: Amarok KDE Multimedia Player

Due to licensing and patent issues, Ubuntu does not install MP3 support by default. MP3 playback capability has been removed from multimedia players like Banshee and Rhythmbox. The Ubuntu codec wizard will prompt you to install MP3 support when you first try to play an MP3 file, usually the Gstreamer package and the free Fluendo MP3 codec. As an alternative to MP3, you can use Ogg Vorbis compression for music files (**http://www.vorbis.com**).

Ubuntu One Music Store and Online Media

Ubuntu provides a music store where you can purchase sound files. On Rhythmbox you will find an entry for the Ubuntu Music Store in the Online Media section. If you have not installed MP3 plugins, you will be prompted to do so. Songs are stored on your Ubuntu One account, and accessible from all your Ubuntu computers.

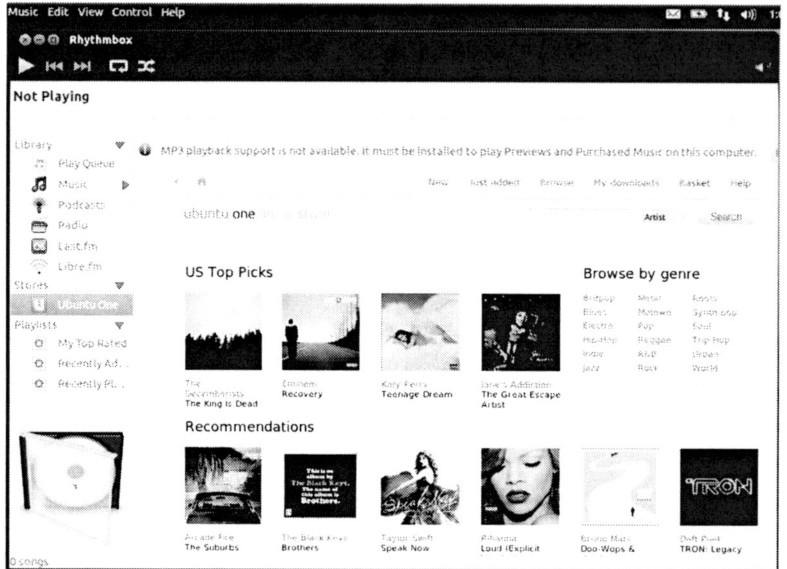

Figure 6-12: Ubuntu One Music Store

Click the Install button and the plugins will be downloaded and installed for you. The Ubuntu One Music store is then displayed (see Figure 6-12).You can choose to download particular songs, which are added to your basket. When you check out, you login to your Ubuntu One account (if you are not logged in already) and purchase the song.

Banshee also provides access to other online media stores such as the Amazon MP3 Store, Miro Guide, and Last.fm. The Internet Archive provides a digital library of audiobooks, video, concerts, books, and movies.

You can now use the Dash music lens to search your music files. On the Dash click on the music note icon at the bottom of the dash to open a music dash where you can search your music collections.

CD/DVD Burners

Several CD/DVD ripper and writer programs can be used for CD music and MP3 writing (burners and rippers). These include Sound Juicer, Brasero (see Chapter 3), and K3b (See Table 6-5). GNOME features the CD audio ripper Sound Juicer, available on the Ubuntu Software Center under the name Audio CD Extractor. You can also use Serpentine to create audio CDs. For burning DVD/CD music and data discs, you can use Brasero CD/DVD burner. The Brasero CD/DVD burner is integrated into the Ubuntu file manager. For KDE you can use K3b

Application	Description
Brasero	Full service CD/DVD burner, for music, video, and data discs.
Sound Juicer (Audio CD Extractor)	GNOME music player and CD burner and ripper
Serpentine	GNOME music CD burner and ripper.
ogmrip	DVD ripping and encoding with DivX support
K3b	KDE CD writing interface
dvdauthor	Tools for creating DVDs

Table 6-5: CD/DVD Burners

Brasero, K3b, and dvdauthor can all be used to create DVD Video discs. All use mkisofs, cdrecord, and cdda2wav DVD/CD writing programs installed as part of your desktop. OGMrip can rip and encode DVD video. DVD-Video and CD music rippers may require addition codecs installed, for which the codec wizard will prompt you.

Video Applications

Several projects provide TV, video, DivX, DVD, and DVB support for Ubuntu (see Table 6-6). Aside from GStreamer applications, there are also several third party multimedia applications you may want, also available on the Ubuntu repositories including MPlayer and VideoLan.

Projects and Players	Sites
Totem	Totem video and DVD player for GNOME using GStreamer, includes plugins for DVB, YouTube, and MythTV:
Dragon Player	Dragon Player video and DVD player for KDE4
VLC Media Player (vlc)	Network multimedia streaming. **www.videolan.org**
MPlayer	MPlayer DVD/multimedia player (fully capable version at **medibuntu.org**) **www.mplayerhq.hu**
MythTV (Mythbuntu)	Home media center with DVD, DVR, and TV capabilities **www.mythtv.org** (use the Mythbuntu version)
me-tv	TV viewer featuring DVB support
tvtime	TV viewer, **http://tvtime.sourceforge.net**
XviD	Open Source DivX, **www.xvid.org**
ubuntustudio-video	Ubuntu Studio meta package (Meta Packages (universe)), includes a collection of video applications. Use Synaptic Package Manager.
Kaffeine	KDE media player, including HDTV, DVB, DVD, CD, and network streams.
PiTiVi	Video editor
GNOME Media Player	Basic media player using Gstreamer, vlc, or xine engines.

Table 6-6: Video and DVD Projects and Applications

Video and DVD Players

Most current DVD and media players are provided on the Ubuntu repositories

Dragon Player is a KDE multimedia player, installed with KDE desktop but will play on the GNOME Ubuntu desktop (see Figure 6-112), install from the Ubuntu Software Center | Sound & Video | Dragon Player.

Fluendo DVD Player is a fully licensed DVD player, available for purchase. Install and purchase from the Ubuntu Software Center | Get Software | Sound & Video | Fluendo DVD Player.

GNOME Media Player provides a simple interface for playing media files using the xine, vlc, or Gstreamer engines. Install from Ubuntu Software Center | Get Software | Sound & Video | GNOME Media Player.

Kaffeine is a KDE multimedia player (video and dvb) (**kaffeine** package, Ubuntu main repository, install from the Ubuntu Software Center | Sound & Video | Kaffeine).

MPlayer is one of the most popular and capable multimedia/DVD players in use. It is a cross-platform open source alternative to RealPlayer and Windows Media Player (**www.mplayerhq.hu**). MPlayer uses an extensive set of supporting libraries and applications like **lirc**, **lame**, **lzo**, and **aalib**, which are also available on the Ubuntu repository. If you have trouble displaying video, be sure to check the preferences for different video devices and select one that works best (**mplayer** package, Multiverse repository). For non-free video codec support, install the Mplayer version at **medibuntu.org**.

Totem is the GNOME movie player that uses GStreamer (see Figure 6-11). To expand Totem capabilities, you need to install added GStreamer plug-ins, as discussed previously. The codec wizard will prompt you to install any needed media codecs and plugins. (**totem** package, Ubuntu main repository, installed with GNOME desktop, also from the Ubuntu Software Center | Sound & Video | Movie Player).

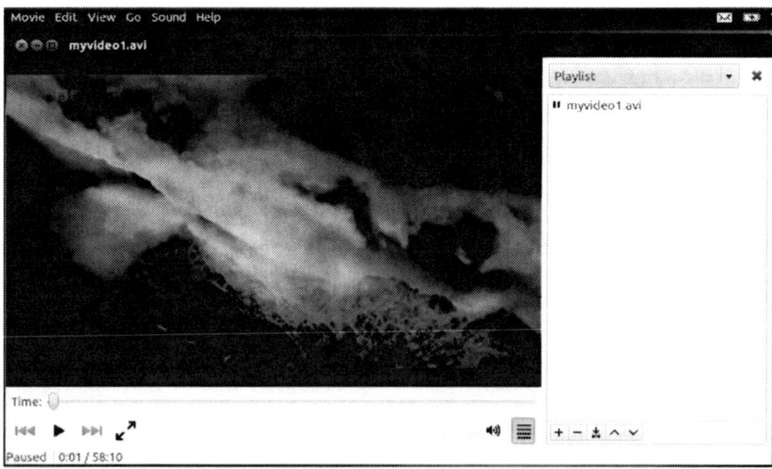

Figure 6-13: Totem Movie player

Totem Xine This is a version of Totem that uses the Xine video engine, install from the Ubuntu Software Center | Sound & Video | Movie Player Totem (xine backend). The xine backend can better handle DVD and HDTV video.

The **VideoLAN** project (**http://www.videolan.org**) offers network streaming support for most media formats, including MPEG-4 and MPEG-2. It includes a multimedia player, VLC, which can work on any kind of system (**vlc** package, Universe repository). VLC supports high-def hardware decoding. Install from the Ubuntu Software Center | Sound & Video | VLC media player.

Xine is a multipurpose video engine and for Linux/Unix systems that can play video, DVD, and audio discs. Many applications like Totem and Kaffeine use Xine support to playback DVD Video. See **http://xinehq.de** for more information. (**xine** support packages, Ubuntu main repository). For the Xine user interface, install the **xine-ui** package with the Synaptic Package Manager.

Figure 6-14: KDE Dragon Player

Figure 6-15: Kaffeine

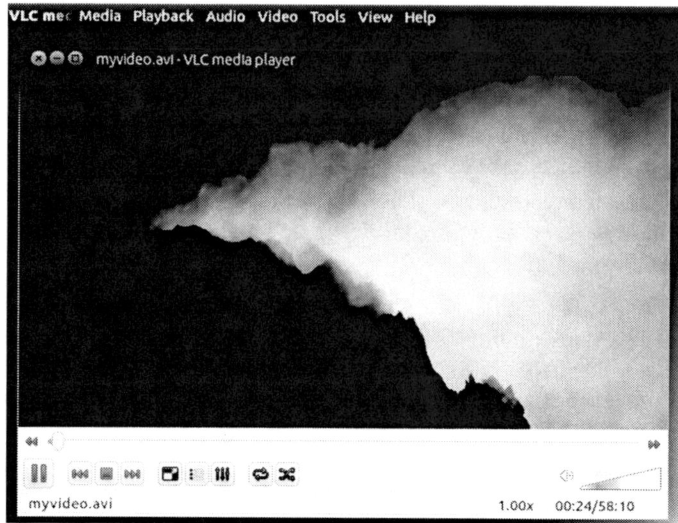

Figure 6-16: VLC Video Player (VideoLAN)

Totem Plugins

The Totem movie player uses plugins to add capabilities like Internet video streaming. YouTube support is already installed as part of the desktop, along with the BBC content viewer. Select Edit | Plugins to open the Configure Plugins window (see Figure 6-17). Choose the plugins you want. The YouTube and BBC plugins will already be selected. For added support, install the **totem-plugins-extra** package. This provides the Gromit annotation tool.

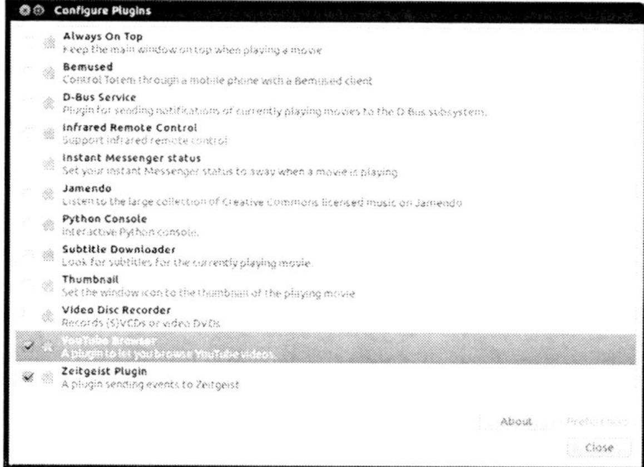

Figure 6-17: Totem Movie Player plugins

DVD Video support

Un-encrypted DVD Video support is provided by three packages available on the Ubuntu repository: **gstreamer-plugins-ugly**, **libdvdnav**, and **libdvdread**. These packages are available on the Ubuntu repository and can be installed with Synaptic Package Manager and the Ubuntu Software Center. With the **libdvdnav4** library, these players now feature full DVD menu support. The **libdvdread4** library provides basic DVD interface support, such as reading IFO files.

None of the DVD-Video applications will initially play commercial DVD-Video discs. That requires Content Scrambling System (CSS) decryption for commercial DVDs, which is provided by the **libdvdcss** package. This package is not available on the primary Ubuntu repositories. It is only available on the third-party **medibuntu.org** repository. The packages on medibuntu.org are fully compatible with Ubuntu, but the packages, due to licensing restrictions, are not considered part of the official Ubuntu software collection.

The **libdvdcss** library works around CSS decryption by treating the DVD as a block device, allowing you to use any of the DVD players to play commercial DVDs. It is also provides region-free access. See the following page for complete details.

```
https://help.ubuntu.com/community/RestrictedFormats/PlayingDVDs
```

The easiest way to install the **libdvdcss** package is to configure Medibuntu.org repository access, as described previously in chapter 4. Once configured, just use the Synaptic Package Manager or the Ubuntu Software Center to search for the **libdvdcss** package, select it and install it.

Should you not want to configure Medibuntu.org repository access, you can directly download and install the package with your Web browser using the Ubuntu Software Center. You have to be sure to select the correct architecture version (see Chapter 4).

```
http://packages.medibuntu.org/precise/libdvdcss2.html
```

Alternatively, you can use the **install-css.sh** script provided by the **libdvdread4** package. This script will download the **libdvdcss** decryption library from the **medibuntu.org** repository. Enter the following in a terminal window. You will have to provide your administrative password.

```
sudo /usr/share/doc/libdvdread4/install-css.sh
```

PiTiVi Video editor

The PiTiVi Video editor is an open source application that lets you edit your videos. It is accessible from the Multimedia dash (on Ubuntu Classic choose Applications | Sound & Video | Pitivi video Editor). Check the PiTiVi web site for more details (**http://www.pitivi.org**). You can download a quick-start manual from the Documentation page. Pitivi is a GStreamer application and can work with any video file supported by an installed GStreamer plugin. However third party playback plugins designed to be licensed officially such as Fluendo MP3 and MPEG plugins, may not be compatible. These plugins are designed to be playback only and do not provide full codec support. You should use the GStreamer Ugly plugins instead.

The PiTiVi window shows a Clip Library pane on the left, and video playback for a selected video clip on the right (see Figure 6-18). To run a video clip, right click on its icon and select Play Clip. To add a video file to the library, click the Import clips button on the tool bar. You can also drag-and-drop files directly to the Clip Library. The timeline at the bottom of the window displays the video and audio streams for the video clip you are editing, using a rule to shows your position. To edit a video, drag its icon from the Clip Library to the timeline. To trim a video you pass the mouse over the timeline video and audio streams. Trimming handles will appear that you can use to shorten the video. PiTiVi features ripple editing and rolling editing, splitting, and transitions.

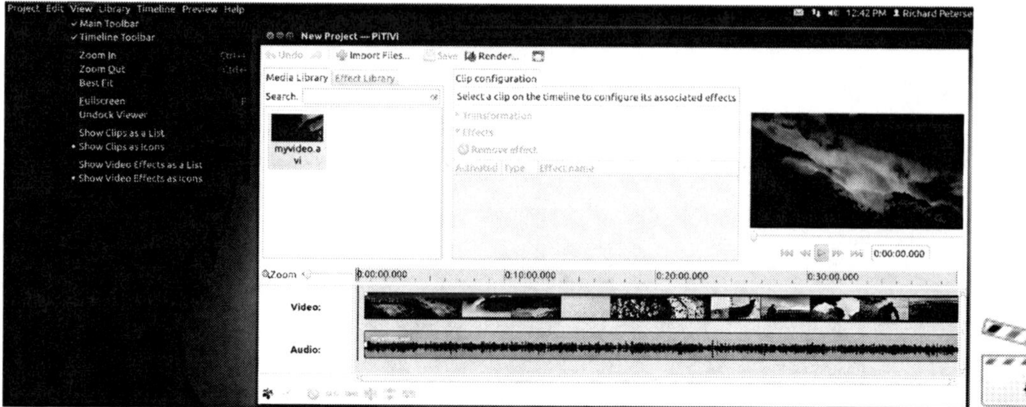

Figure 6-18: Pitivi video editor

TV Players

The following TV players are provided on Ubuntu repositories:

TV player **tvtime** works with many common video capture cards, relying on drivers developed for TV tuner chips on those cards like the Conexant chips. It can only display a TV image. It has no recording or file playback capabilities. Check **http://tvtime.sourceforge.net** for more information.

MythTV is a popular video recording and playback application on Linux systems. (Mythbuntu release, multiverse repository). See **www.mythbuntu.org** for more information.

me-tv is a DVB and HDTV video recording and playback application for Linux systems.

Kaffeine is a popular KDE video recording and playback application on Linux systems. It can also play ATSC over the air digital broadcasts.

Note: To play DivX media on Ubuntu you use the Xvid OpenDivX codec, xvidcore.

DVB and HDTV support

For DVB and HDTV reception, you can use most DVB cards as well as many HDTV cards like the pcHDTV video card (**www.pdhdtv.com**). For example, the latest pcHDTV card uses the **cx88-dvb** drivers included with the Linux kernel. The DVB kernel driver is loaded automatically. You can use the **lsmod** command to see if your DVB module is loaded.

Tip: The VideoLan (VLC) player can run HD media (x264) using your display card's native high definition decoder (hardware decoding instead of software decoding), check Tools | Preferences | Codecs | Use GPU acceleration.

Be sure you have installed the **kubuntu-restricted-extras** and **ubuntu-restricted-extras** packages, which provide support for appropriate decoders like mpeg2, FFmpeg, and A52 (ac3) (**liba52**, **libxine1-ffmpeg**, **gstreamer-ffmpeg**, and **libdvbpsi**).

For DVB broadcasts, many DVB-capable players and tools like Kaffeine and metv, as well as vdr will tune and record DVB broadcasts in t, s, and c formats. Some applications, like me-tv and Kaffeine, can scan DVB channels directly. Others may require that you first generate a **channels.conf** file. You can do this with the **w_scan** command (**w-scan** package). Then copy the generated **channels.conf** file to the appropriate applications directory. Channel scans can be output in vdr, Kaffeine, and Xine formats for use with those applications as well as others like Mplayer and MythTV. The **w_scan** command can also generate **channel.conf** entries for ATSC channels (HDTV), though not all applications can tune ATSC channels (Kaffeine and me-tv can tune HDTV as well as scan for HDTV channels). You can also use the **dvbscan** tool (**dvb-apps** package) for scanning your channels and the **azap** tool for accessing the signal directly. This tool makes use of channel frequencies kept in the **/usr/share/dvb** directory. There are files for ATSC broadcast as well as cable.

Kaffeine DVB and ATSC tuning

The Kaffeine KDE media player can scan for both DVB and ATSC channels. You will need to have a DVB or ATSC tuner installed on your system. On Kaffeine, from the Television menu choose Configure Television, and on the device tab choose the source such as ATSC. Then from the Television menu, select Channels to open a Channel dialog (see Figure 6-19). Your tuner device is selected on the Search on menu. Click on the Start scan button to begin scanning. Detected channels are listed on the "Scan results" scroll box. Select the ones you want and click Add Selected to place them in the Channels scroll box. Be sure to add the channel you want to watch on the Channel list.

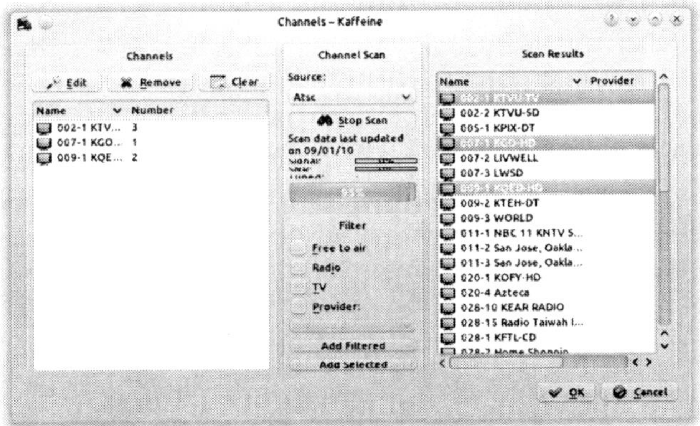

Figure 6-19: Kaffeine ATSC channel scan

You can use Kaffeine to both tune and record both DVB and ATSC HDTV channels. Kaffeine records an HDTV file as an **m2t** HDV MPEG-2 file, the High Definition Video (HDV) format used for high definition camcorders. The **m2t** files that Kaffeine generates can be played back by most video players, including Totem, Dragon Player, and vlc. To schedule a recording on

Kaffeine, click the Television tab or click Digital TV from the Start tab. From the Television menu choose Recording Schedule or click the calendar button in the lower left corner to open the Recording Schedule dialog. Click the New button to open a Schedule Entry dialog where you can name the program, select the channel, set the time and duration, and choose to repeat daily or weekly (see Figure 6-20).

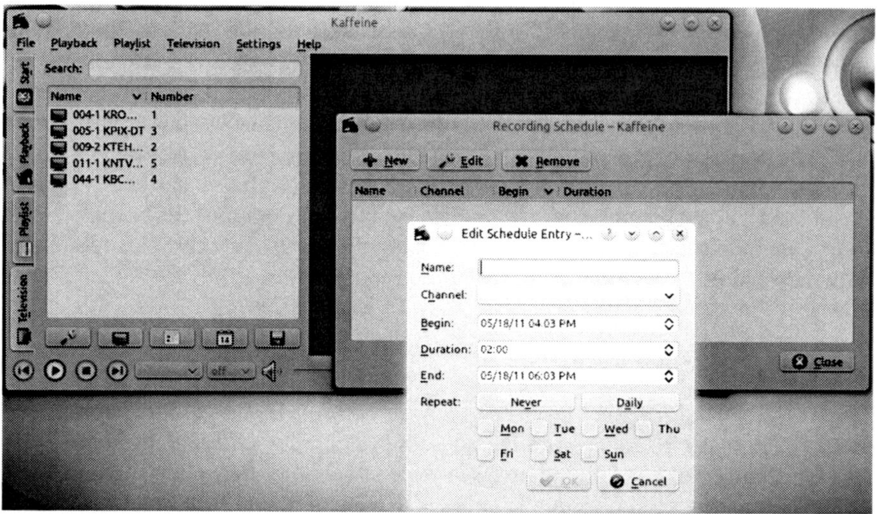

Figure 6-20: Kaffeine TV recording

MeTV DVB and ATSC tuning

MeTV can scan and record both DVB and ATSC HDTV channels. Install both the **me-tv** and **w-scan** packages. MeTV is still a work in progress, but provides a very easy interface to list and record programs. When you first start up MeTV, the MeTV scan wizard opens with options to auto scan, scan based on an initial scan file, or to use a channels.conf file. The auto scan option will scan for channels, detecting signal strength. You the select the ones you want (Ctrl-click). From the MeTV channels editor you can add or remove channels.

MeTV features an EPG listing, which makes it very easy to choose, and record programs. Right-click on the MeTV window to toggle the display of the channel programs. Click on a current program to view it, and a future program to record it. A record now button lets you record the current program.

Single click on the MeTV window to toggle between a window and full screen view. A menu at the bottom of the screen lets you record, adjust the sound, and search for programs.

Recording are saved as high-definition mpeg files to your home directory. You can play these back using any video player, including me-tv, totem, dragon player, and vlc. From the MeTV scheduled recordings dialog you can click the Add button to open a Scheduled Recording dialog where you can choose the channel, date, time, and duration.

Recording the raw transport stream

The raw transport stream (**.ts** or **.tp**) files generated by HDTV cards like PCHDTV can be viewed with an HDTV capable viewer, such as Kaffeine or the Videolan VLC media player. However, there is no player currently that records and saves a raw HDTV video stream. One solution for recording the raw HDTV video stream is to use the atsc tools provided by the PCHDTV Web site. The pcHDTV card and related cards using the Conexant c88 chips; the c88x DVB kernel module will automatically be detected and loaded. You can then use the PCHDTV atsc tools to access and record programs. From the PCHDTV site, download the **dvb-atsc-tools** package (**http://www.pchdtv.com/downloads/dvb-atsc-tools-1.0.7.tgz**). These are source code programs you will have to compile. Unzip the archive file to a directory. You can use either the **tar** command or Archive Manager.

```
tar xvjf dvb-atsc-tools-1.0.7.tgz
```

In a terminal window change to that directory issue the **make** and **make install** commands. Be sure you have already downloaded and installed the kernel development packages.

```
make
make install
```

You can then use the **dtvsignal** and **getatsc** commands to check and record HDTV receptions. The following records a channel to a file. The **-dvb 0** option is the DVB device number, usually 0, and the following number is the channel, in this case channel **12**. The output is directed by the **>** operator to a file called **my.ts**.

```
getatsc -dvb 0 12 > my.ts
```

This is an open ended process that will continue until you kill the process. To stop the recording you could do the following, which uses the **ps** command to obtain the process id (pid) for the **getatsc** process. These getatsc and kill operations can be set up as scheduled tasks (GNOME Schedule) to implement automatic recording like a DVR or VCR (see Chapter 12, Schedule for examples).

```
kill `ps -C getatsc -o pid=`
```

You could then use an application like the VLC media player, Kaffeine, or an HDTV capable Mplayer to play back the file.

Xvid (DivX) and Matroska (mkv) on Linux

MPEG-4 compressed files provide DVD-quality video with relatively small file sizes. They have become popular for distributing high-quality video files over the Internet. When you first try to play an MPEG-4, the codec wizard will prompt you to install the needed codec packages to play it. Many multimedia applications like VLC already support MPEG-4 files.

MPEG-4 files using the Matroska wrapper, also know by their file extension **mkv**, can be played on most video players including the VideoLan vlc player, Totem, Dragon Player, and Kaffeine. You will need HDTV codecs, like MPEG4 AAC sound codec, installed to play the high definition **mkv** file files. If needed, the codec wizard will prompt you to install them. For the KDE players like Dragon Player, be sure to install the kubuntu-restricted-extras package (Ubuntu Software Center | System | Kubuntu restricted extras). To manage and create MKV files you can use the **mkvtoolnix-gui** tools (the Ubuntu Software Center | Sound & Video | MKV files creator).

You use the open source version of DivX known as Xvid to play DivX video (**libxvidcore** package, Multiverse repository, the Ubuntu Software Center | Sound & Video | Gstreamer plugins for aac, xvid, mpeg2, faad). Most DivX files can be run using XviD. XviD is an entirely independent open source project, but it is compatible with DivX files. You can also download the XviD source code from **http://xvid.org**.

To convert DVD-Video files to an MPEG-4/DivX format you can use **transcode** (Multiverse repository) or the **ffmpeg extra** libraries (Medibuntu.org repository). Many DVD burners can convert DVD video files to DivX/Xvid files.

Ubuntu Multimedia Editions

Ubuntu supports two editions for multimedia applications, Ubuntu Studio for multimedia projects, and Mythbuntu for video/tv viewing and recording.

Ubuntu Studio

Ubuntu Studio features Linux software for multimedia production, including sound, music, video, and graphics applications. You can install Ubuntu Studio as its own installation or as an added desktop on your Ubuntu desktop install.

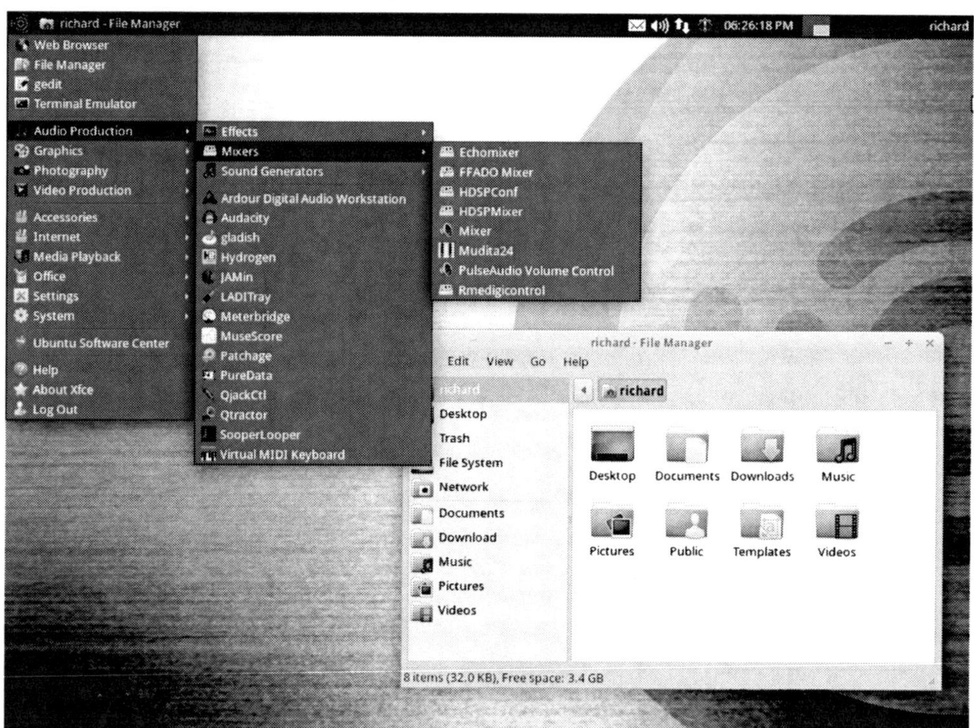

Figure 6-21: Ubuntu Studio desktop with Ubuntu Studio theme

You can download the Ubuntu Studio install DVD from **http://ubuntustudio.org**. This is an Alternate DVD that installs using the text install utility. Use the arrow keys and tabs to move the cursor, the spacebar to choose, and ENTER key to select. The install procedure is the same for the desktop.. Use the arrow keys and spacebar to select entries. Select them all for the entire collection.

To add Ubuntu Studio to your current desktop install, use the Synaptic Package Manager and find the Meta Package (universe) section. There you will find the **ubuntustudio-desktop** Meta package, which will install the complete Ubuntu Studio desktop. You also install the Ubuntu Studio software collections including **ubuntustudio-audio, ubuntustudio-graphics**, and **ubuntustudio-video**. Ubuntu studio uses its own Ubuntu Studio desktop theme with its own icons, Applications menu categories, and background image. (see Figures 6-21).

Mythbuntu

Mythbuntu is the Ubuntu version of MythTV, a linux implementation of a multimedia center for Home Theater Personal Computers (HTPC). You can download Mythbuntu from **http://mythbuntu.org**, or install on an Ubuntu desktop with **mythbuntu-desktop** Meta package. In the Synaptic Package Manager, you will find the Meta package in the Meta Packages (multiverse) section. The package will uninstall your Ubuntu desktop, replacing it with the Mythbuntu desktop.

Figure 6-22: Mythbuntu MythTV front end (Applications | Multimedia)

Installation adds several steps, one for selecting a configuration, another for your remote, and another for configuring your file sharing support.

Mythbuntu uses the XFCE desktop, which runs much more economically than either GNOME or KDE. Once installed, you can run the MythTV front end (Applications | Multimedia) to display the Mythbuntu interface for selecting media tasks like watching TV or viewing a recording. You can leave the front end by pressing the ESC key to access the Mythbuntu desktop.

To configure Mythbuntu, use the Mythbuntu Control Center, Applications | System menu (see Figure 6-24). Be sure to enable Medibuntu proprietary codec support to allow your system to play all kinds of media. To return to the Mythbuntu interface select Applications | Multimedia | MythTV front-end.

Sound Preferences

Your sound cards are detected automatically for you when you start up your system by ALSA, which is invoked by udev when your system starts up. Removable devices, like USB sound devices, are also detected. See Table 6-7 for a listing of sound device and interface tools.

Sound tool	Description
KMix	KDE sound connection configuration and volume tool
alsamixer	ALSA sound connection configuration and volume tool
amixer	ALSA command for sound connection configuration
Sound Preferences	GNOME Sound Preferences, used to select and configure your sound interface
PulseAudio	PulseAudio sound interface, the default sound interface for Ubuntu. **www.pulseaudio.org**
PulseAudio Volume Control	PulseAudio Volume Control, controls stream input, output, and playback, **pavucontrol** package.
PulseAudio Volume Meter	Volume Meter, displays active sound levels
PulseAudio Manager	Manager for information and managing PulseAudio, **pman** package
PulseAudio Preferences	Options for network access and virtual output.

Table 6-7: Sound device and interface tools

In addition to hardware drivers, sound systems also use sound interfaces to direct encoded sound streams from an application to the hardware drivers and devices. Ubuntu uses the PulseAudio server for its sound interface. PulseAudio aims to combine and consolidate all sound interfaces into a simple, flexible, and powerful server. The ALSA hardware drivers are still used, but the application interface is handled by PulseAudio. Pulse audio is installed as the default set up for Ubuntu.

Note: Sound devices on Linux are supported by hardware sound drivers. With the Ubuntu kernel, hardware support is implemented by the Advanced Linux Sound Architecture (ALSA) system. ALSA replaces the free version of the Open Sound System used in previous releases, as well as the original built-in sound drivers. You can find more about ALSA at **http://alsa-project.org**.

PulseAudio provides packages for interfacing with Gstreamer, VLC, and xmms, replacing those sound interfaces with PulseAudio. The KDE aRts interface is not supported as aRts performs its own synthesizing.

PulseAudio is cross-platform sound server, allowing you to modify the sound level for different audio streams separately. See **http://www.pulseaudio.org** for documentation and help. PulseAudio offers complete control over all your sound streams, letting you combine sound devices and direct the stream anywhere on your network. PulseAudio is not confined to a single system. It is network capable, letting you direct sound from one PC to another.

As an alternative, you can use the command-line ALSA control tool, **alsamixer**. This will display all connections and allow you to use keyboard command to select (arrow keys), mute (m key), or set sound levels (Page Up and Down). Press the ESC key to exit. The **amixer** command lets you perform the same tasks for different sound connections from the command line. To actually play and record from the command-line, you can use the **play** and **rec** commands.

Sound menu (volume control and player access)

The sound menu (speaker icon) displays volume control, media player access, and sound preferences access entries (see Figure 6-23). You can change your application's sound volume using a sliding bar. When you click on the sound volume slider, you can use your mouse scroll button to adjust the sound volume. To perform volume control for specific devices like a microphone, you use Sound Preferences, which you can access from the Customization dash as Sound, from the sound menu's Sound Preferences entry, or from the System Settings dialog as Sound.

The sound menu also provides basic access to the Rhythmbox and Banshee media players, showing the title of the current track and displaying controls to play, pause, and move to the previous and next tracks. You can also access the playlist. The sound menu is shown here.

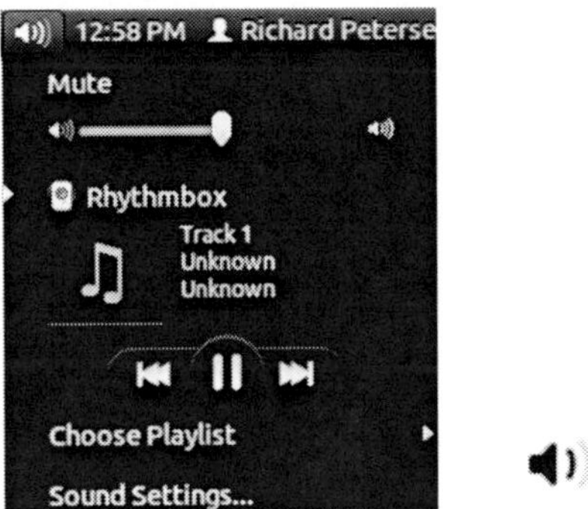

Figure 6-23: Sound Menu

Sound: PulseAudio

You configure sound devices and set volume for sound effects, input and output, and applications using GNOME sound tool. Choose Sound on the System Settings dialog or from the Customization dash. This opens the Sound dialog, which has four tabs: Sound Effects, Input, Output, and Applications (see Figure 6-24). Sound control is integrated into the Sound dialog. A sliding bar at the bottom of the window, lets you set the output volume.

The Sound Effects tab lets you choose sound alerts, such as Drip or Sonar. A sliding bar lets you set the volume for your sound alerts, or turn them off by checking the Mute checkbox.

On the Input tab, you choose the input device and set the input volume. When speaking or recording, the input level is displayed (see Figure 6-25). If you have more than one input device, they will be listed in the "Record sound from" section to the left.

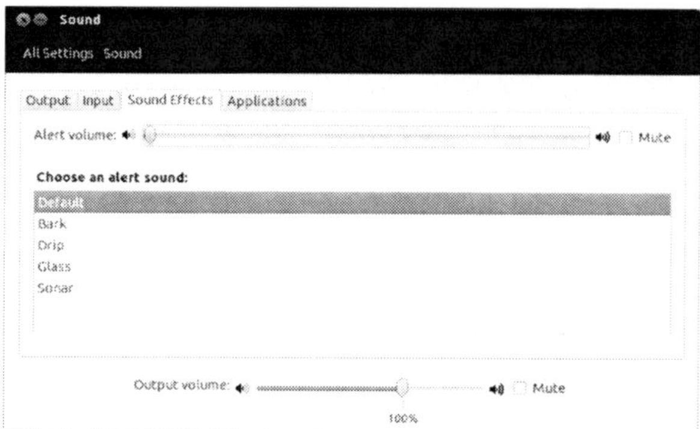

Figure 6-24: Sound Preferences

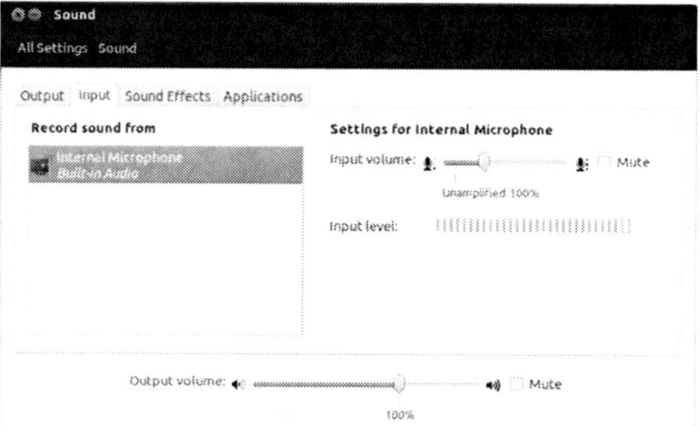

Figure 6-25: Sound Preferences: Input

On the Output tab, you can configure settings for a selected device: Digital, Headphones, and Speakers. The available settings will become active according to the device selected. For a simple Analog Stereo Output on Speakers, only a Balance setting is active (see Figure 6-26).

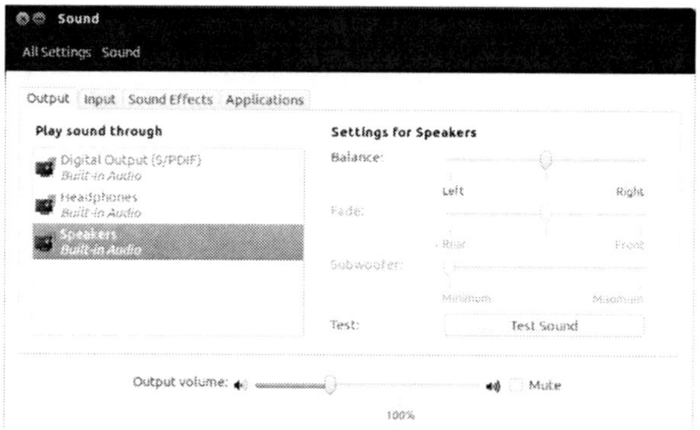

Figure 6-26: Sound Preferences: Output

A laptop may support only a simple internal audio device with left and right balance. Computers with more powerful sound devices have many more options. To test your speakers, click the Test Speakers button to open the Speakers Testing dialog with test buttons for each speaker.

The Applications tab will show applications currently using sound devices. You can set the sound volume for each (see Figure 6-27).

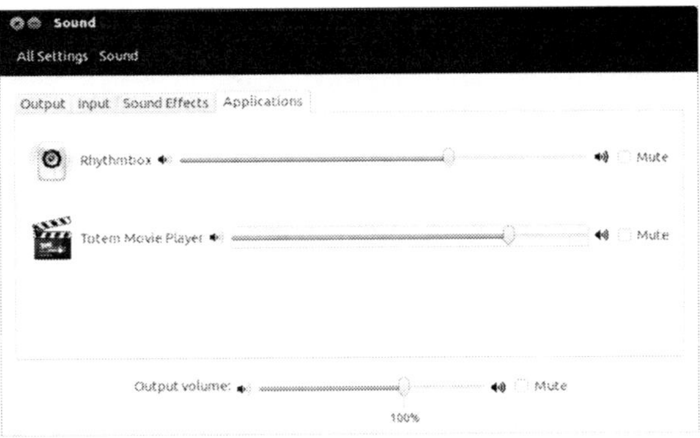

Figure 6-27: Sound Preferences: Applications

For systems with several input sound devices, the input tab will list an entry for each. Figure 6-30 shows both a TV tuner sound device and the system's internal audio device.

Sound devices that support multiple interfaces like analog surround sound 7.1 or digital SPDIF output, will display a list of interface combinations in a Mode menu. In Figure 6-25, Analog Surround 7.1 Output with Analog Stereo Input has been selected on the Output tab, which then activates settings for Fade and Subwoofer (see Figure 6-28). From the Mode menu you can choose the type of output you would, should your system support several as shown in Figure 6-29.

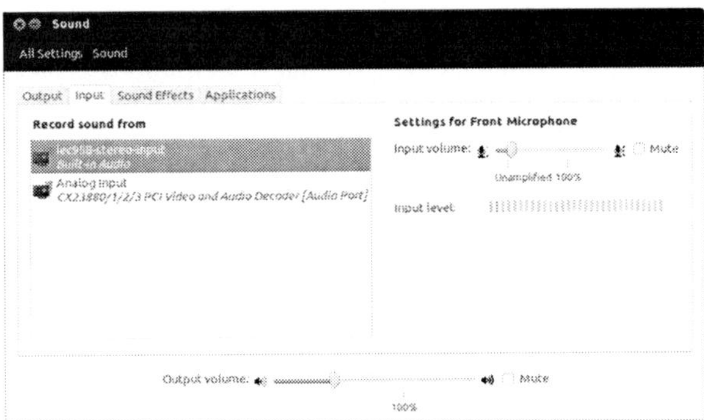

Figure 6-28: Sound Preferences: Hardware tab, multiple sound devices

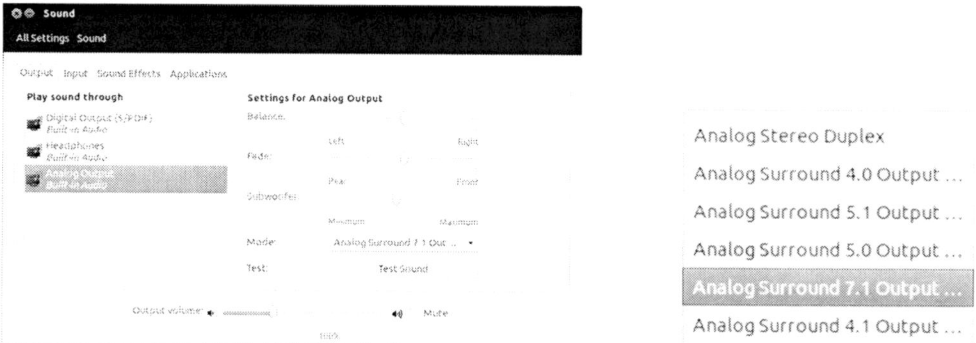

Figure 6-29: Sound Preferences: Output tab, Surround sound settings and Mode menu

Configuring digital output for Digital Output (S/PDIF) connectors is a simple matter of selecting the digital output and input entries Output and Input tabs (see Figure 6-30). Only the Balance entry will be active.

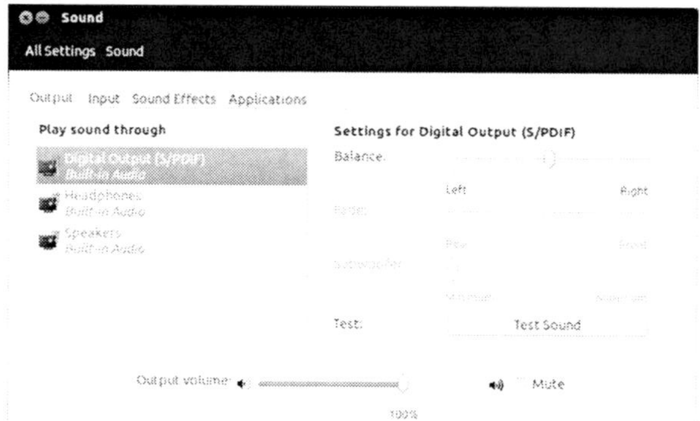

Figure 6-30: Sound Preferences: Hardware tab, Digital sound settings

Installed with Pulse Audio are the Pulse Audio utilities (**pulseaudio-utils** package). These are command line utilities for managing Pulse Audio and playing sound files (see Table 6-8). The **paplay** and **pacat** will play a sound files, **pactl** will let you control the sound server and **pacmd** lets you reconfigure it. Check the Man pages for each for more details. If you change your sound preferences frequently, you could use these commands in a shell script to make the changes, instead of having to use the preferences dialog each time. Some of these commands such as **parec** and **paplay** are links to the **pacat** command, which performs the actual tasks.

PulseAudio applications

For additional configuration abilities, you can also install the Pulse Audio applications. Most begin with the prefix **pa** in the package name. You can install them from the Ubuntu Software Center by searching PulseAudio. Most PulseAudio tools are accessible from the Multimedia dash. The PulseAudio tools and their command names are shown here.

PulseAudio Volume Control, **pavucontrol**

PulseAudio Volume Meter, **pavumeter**

PulseAudio Manager, **paman**

PulseAudio Preferences, **papref**

Sound tool	Description
pabrowse	List PulseAudio sound servers
pacat	Play, record, and configure a raw audio stream
pacmd	Generates a shell for entering configuration commands
pactl	Control a PulseAudio server, changing input and output sources and providing information about the server.
padsp	PulseAudio wrapper for OSS sound applications
pamon	Link to pacat
paplay	Playback audio. The -d option specifies the output device, the -s option specifies the server, and the --volume option sets the volume (link to pacat)
parec	Record and audio stream (link to pacat)
parecord	Record and audio stream (link to pacat)
pasuspender	Suspend a PulseAudio server
pax11publish	Access PulseAudio server credentials

Table 6-8: PulseAudio commands (command-line)

You can use the PulseAudio Volume Control tool to set the sound levels for different playback applications and sound devices (choose PulseAudio Volume Control on the Multimedia dash).

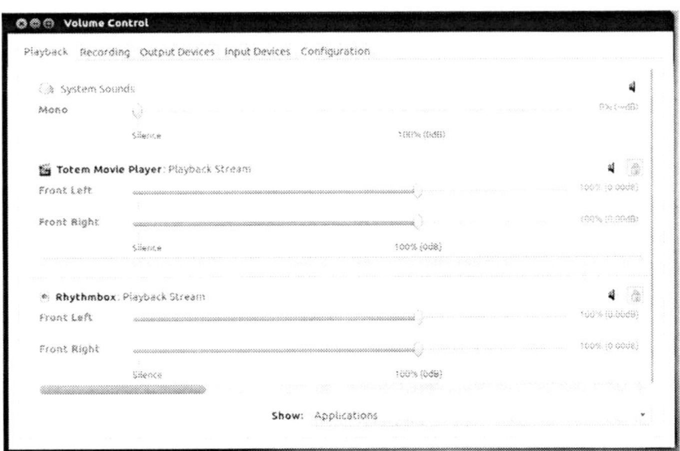

Figure 6-31: PulseAudio Volume Control, Playback

The PulseAudio Volume Control applications will show five tabs: Playback, Recording, Output Devices, Input Devices, and Configuration (see Figure 6-31). The Playback tab shows all the applications currently using PulseAudio. You can adjust the volume for each application separately.

You can use the Output tab panel to set the volume control at the source and to select different output devices like Headphones (see Figure 6-32). The volume for input and recording devices are set on the Recording and Input Devices tabs. The configuration tab lets you choose different device profiles, like selecting Digital output or Surround Sound 5.1. To find the actual name of the SPDIF output is not always obvious. You may need to run **aplay -L** in a terminal window to see what the name of the digital output device is on your system. It will be the entry with Digital in it.

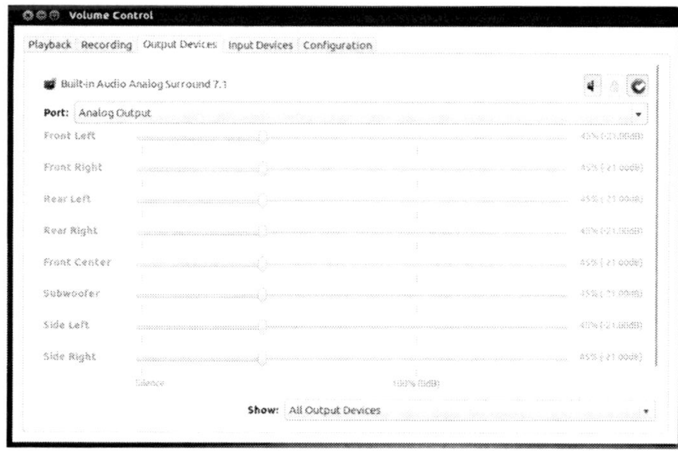

Figure 6-32: PulseAudio Volume Control, Output Devices

You can also use the PulseAudio Volume control to direct different applications (streams) to different outputs (devices). For example, you could have two sound sources running, one for video and another for music. The video could be directed through one device to headphones and the music through another device to speakers, or even to another PC. To redirect an application to a different device, right-click its name in the Playback tab. A pop-up menu will list the available devices and let you select the one you want to use.

The PulseAudio Volume Meter tool will show the actual volume of your devices.

The PulseAudio Manager will show information about your PulseAudio configuration, accessible from the Multimedia dash. The Devices tab shows the currently active sinks (outputs or directed receivers) and sources (see Figure 6-33). The Clients tab shows all the applications currently using PulseAudio for sound.

The PulseAudio Volume Control applications will show five tabs: Playback, Recording, Output Devices, Input Devices, and Configuration (see Figure 6-31). The Playback tab shows all the applications currently using PulseAudio. You can adjust the volume for each application separately.

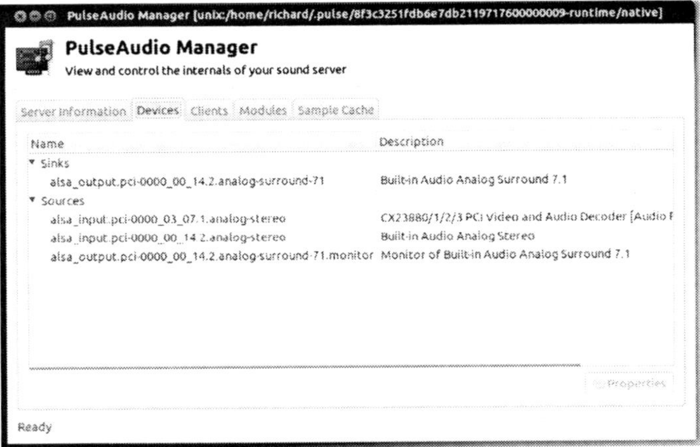

Figure 6-33: PulseAudio Manager Devices tab

x

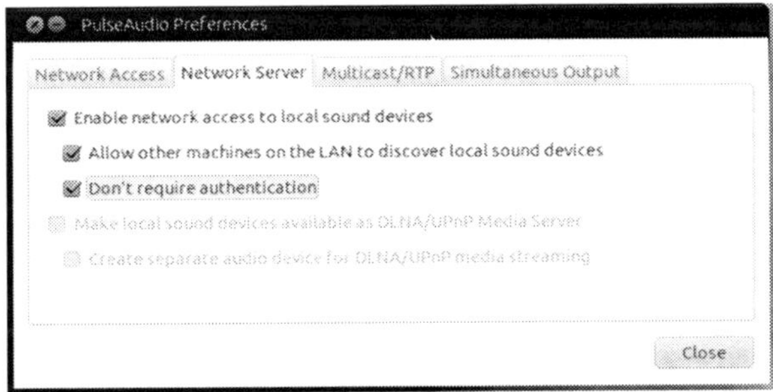

Figure 6-34: PulseAudio Preferences

Simultaneous output creates a virtual output device to the same hardware device. This lets you channel two sources onto the same output. With PulseAudio Volume Control, you could then channel playback streams to the same output device, but using a virtual device as the output for one. This lets you change the output volume for each stream independently. You could have music and voice directed to the same hardware device, using a virtual device for music and the standard device for voice. You can then reduce the music stream, or raise the voice stream.

7. Mail (email) and News

Mail Clients: Evolution, Thunderbird, Kmail

Command Line Mail Clients

Notifications of Received Mail

Accessing Mail on Remote POP Mail Servers

Usenet News

Newsreaders

News Transport Agents

Ubuntu supports a wide range of both electronic mail and news clients. Mail clients let you send and receive messages to and from other users on your system or users accessible from your network. News clients let you read articles and messages posted in newsgroups, which are open to access by all users.

Mail Clients

You can send and receive e-mail messages in a variety of ways, depending on the type of mail client you use. Although all e-mail utilities perform the same basic tasks of receiving and sending messages, they tend to use different interfaces. Some mail clients are designed to operate on a specific desktop interface such as KDE and GNOME. Several older mail clients use a screen-based interface and can be started only from the command line. For Web-based Internet mail services, such as GMail and Yahoo, you use a Web browser instead of a mail client to access mail accounts provided by those services. Table 7-1 lists several popular Linux mail clients. Mail is transported to and from destinations using mail transport agents like Sendmail, Exim, and Postfix. To send mail over the Internet, Simple Mail Transport Protocol (SMTP) is used.

Mail Client	Description
Kontact (KMail, KAddressbook, KOrganizer)	Includes the K Desktop mail client, KMail; integrated mail, address book, and scheduler
Evolution	E-mail client, **http://projects.gnome.org/evolution/**
Thunderbird	Mozilla mail client and newsreader
Sylpheed	Gtk mail and news client
Claws-mail	Extended version of sylpheed Email client
GNUEmacs and XEmacs	Emacs mail clients
Mutt	Screen-based mail client
Mail	Original Unix-based command line mail client
Squirrel Mail	Web-based mail client
gnubiff	E-mail checker and notification tool
Mail Notification	E-mail checker and notification that works with numerous mail clients, including MH, Sylpheed, Gmail, Evolution, and Mail

Table 7-1: Linux Mail Clients

Thunderbird

Thunderbird is a full-featured stand-alone e-mail client provided by the Mozilla project (**http://www.mozilla.org**). It is installed by default along with LibreOffice. Thunderbird is designed to be easy to use, highly customizable, and heavily secure. It features advanced intelligent spam filtering, as well as security features like encryption, digital signatures, and S/MIME. To protect against viruses, e-mail attachments can be examined without being run. Thunderbird supports both Internet Message Access Protocol (IMAP) and the Post Office Protocol (POP). It also functions as a newsreader and features a built-in RSS reader. Thunderbird also supports the use of the Lightweight Directory Access Protocol (LDAP) for address books. Thunderbird is an extensible application, allowing customized modules to be added to enhance its abilities. You can download extensions such as dictionary search and contact sidebars from the Web site. GPG encryption can be supported with the enigmail extension (Ubuntu main repository).

You can install Thunderbird from the Ubuntu Software Center | Internet | Mozilla Thunderbird Mail/News. It provides better integration with popular online mail services like Gmail, saved searches, and customized tags for selected messages. You can access Thunderbird from the Internet dash.

The Thunderbird interface uses a standard three-pane format, with a side pane for listing mail accounts and their mail boxes (see Figure 7-1). The top pane is the message list pane and the bottom pane shows a selected message's text. Commands can be run using the toolbar, menus, or keyboard shortcuts. You can even change the appearance using different themes. Thunderbird also supports HTML mail, displaying Web components like URLs in mail messages.

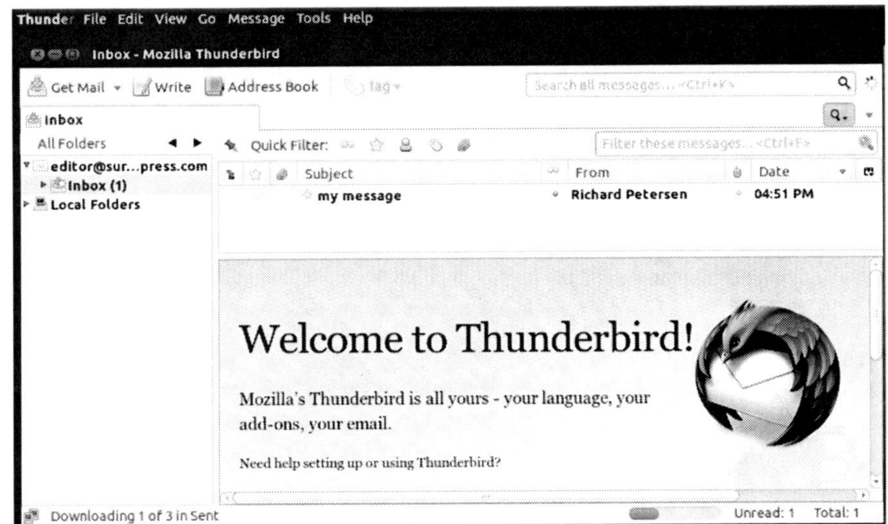

Figure 7-1: Thunderbird Email client

The message list pane shows several fields by which you can sort your messages. Some use just symbols like the Threads, Attachments, and Read icons. Clicking Threads will gather the messages into respective threads with replies grouped together. The last icon in the message list fields is a pop-up menu that lets you choose which fields to display. Thunderbird provides a variety of quick display filters, such as displaying only messages from people included in your address book and display messages with attached files. Search and sorting capabilities also include filters that can match selected patterns in any field, including subject, date, or the message body. To compose a message, click the Write button to open the Write window. The Security button lets you digitally sign and encrypt a message.

When you first start up Thunderbird, The Mail Account Setup dialog opens, which prompts you to create an e-mail account. You can add more e-mail accounts or modify current ones by selecting Account Settings from the Edit menu (Edit | Account Settings). The first page of the Mail Account Setup dialogs prompts you to enter your name, e-mail address, and password.

Thunderbird then attempts to detect and configure your email account automatically. Popular email services such as GMail (Google) and Yahoo will be detected and their incoming and outgoing mail servers configured automatically. If the user name entry is wrong you can click the User name Edit button to edit it. For more email configuration options, you can click the Manual Setup button. You can also just choose to abandon the email setup by clicking the Start Over link. If the settings are correct, click the Create Account button to create the account. The account will be accessed. If the account detection fails, you will be prompted to enter the user name and password along with the names of the incoming and outgoing mail servers for that account (see Figure 7-2). For more detailed configuration, click the Manual Setup button where you can specify the security protocol like SSL/TSL.

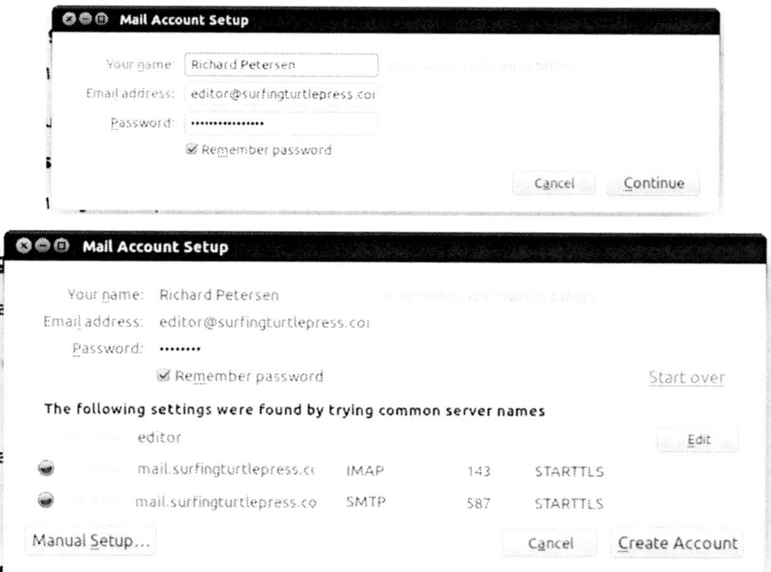

Figure 7-2: Thunderbird Email account detection

To edit an email account, select the Edit | Account Settings menu entry. In the Account Settings window, you will see an entry for your mail account, with tabs for Server Settings, Copies & Folders, Composition & Addressing, Offline & Disk Space, Synchronization & Storage, Return Receipt, and Security. The Server Settings tab has entries for your server name, port, user name, and connection and task configurations such as downloading new messages automatically. The Security tab opens the Certificate Manager, where you can select security certificates to use to digitally sign or encrypt messages.

Thunderbird provides an address book where you can enter complete contact information, including e-mail addresses, street addresses, phone numbers, and notes. Select Address Book from the Tools menu to open the Address Book window (Tools | Address Book). There are three panes: one for the address books available; another listing the address entries with field entries like name, email, and organization; and one for displaying address information. You can sort the entries by these fields. Clicking an entry will display the address information, including email address, street addresses, and phone. Only fields with values are displayed. To create a new entry in an address book, click New Contact to open a window with tabs for Contact, Private, Work, Other, and Photo. To create mailing lists from the address book entries, you click the New List button, specify the name of the list, and enter the e-mail addresses.

Once you have set up your address book, you can use its addresses when creating mail messages. On the Write window, when you start to enter an email address in the To text box, the address will auto-complete to the corresponding address in your address book. Alternatively, you can open the address book and drag-and-drop addresses to an address box on the message window.

A user's e-mail messages, addresses, and configuration information are kept in files located in the **.thunderbird** directory within the user's home directory. Backing up this information is as simple as making a copy of that directory. Messages for the different mail boxes are kept in a **Mail** subdirectory. If you are migrating to a new system, you can copy the directory from the older system. To back up the mail for any mail account, just copy the **Mail** subdirectory for that account. Though the default address books, **abook.mab** and **history.mab**, can be interchangeably copied, non-default address books need to be exported to an LDIF format and then imported to the new Thunderbird application. It is advisable to export your address books regularly to LDAP Data Interchange Format (LDIF) files as backups.

Evolution

Evolution is the primary mail client for the GNOME desktop. Though designed for GNOME, it will work equally well on KDE. Evolution is an integrated mail client, calendar, and address book. It supports numerous protocols (SMTP, POP, and IMAP). With Evolution, you can create multiple mail accounts on different servers, including those that use different protocols such as POP or IMAP. You can also decrypt Pretty Good Privacy (PGP) or GNU Privacy Guard (GPG) encrypted messages. Messages are indexed for easy searching. Junk mail filtering is provided. Evolution also provides collaboration server support like Microsoft Exchange (2000/2003) and GroupWise (Novell) and can function as an Exchange or GroupWise client. As an added feature, you can display Web calendars within evolution. See the Evolution Web site for a complete description of its features.

```
http://projects.gnome.org/evolution/
```

You can access Evolution from the Office dash. The Evolution mailer provides a simple desktop interface, with a toolbar for commonly used commands and a sidebar for shortcuts. A set of buttons on the lower left allows you to access other operations such as the calendar and contacts. The mail screen is divided into two panes, one for listing the mail headers and the other for displaying the currently selected message (see Figure 7-3). You can click any header label to sort your headers by that category. Evolution also supports the use of virtual folders that can be created by the user to hold mail that meets specified criteria. Incoming mail can be automatically distributed to a particular virtual folder.

With evolution, you can also create search folders to organize access to your messages. A search folder is not an actual folder. It simply collects links to messages based on certain search criteria. Using search folders, you can quickly display messages on a topic, or subject, or from a specific user. In effect, it performs an automatic search on messages as they arrive. To set up a search folder, select Search Folders in the Edit menu (Edit | Search Folders) and click Add to open the Add Rule window. Here you can add criteria for searches and the folders to search. You can also right-click a message header that meets criteria you want searched and select Create Rule from Message, and then select one of the Search Rule entries.

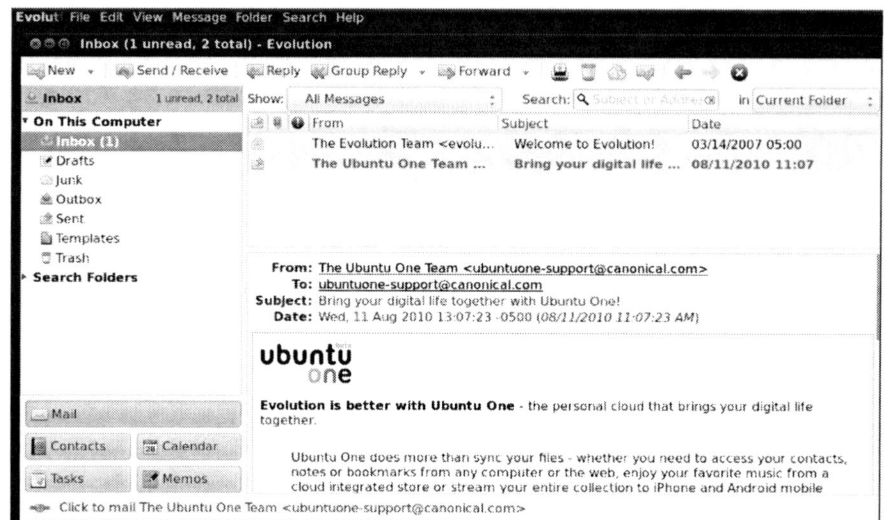

Figure 7-3: Evolution Email client

To configure Evolution, select Preferences from the Edit menu (Edit | Preferences). On the Evolution Preferences window, a sidebar shows icons for mail accounts, contacts, mail preferences, composition preference, calendar and tasks, and certificates. The Mail accounts tab displays a list of current accounts. An Add button lets you add new accounts, and the Edit button allows you to change current accounts. When editing an account, the Account Editor displays tabs for Identity, Receiving email (your incoming mail server), sending email (outgoing mail server), and security (encryption and digital signatures) among others. Mail Preferences lets you configure how Evolution displays and manages messages. The Mail Preferences Automatic Contacts tab is where you can specify that addresses of mail to which you reply should be added automatically to the Evolution Contacts list. Composer Preferences lets you set up composition features like signatures, formatting, and spell-checking. Calendar and Tasks lets you configure you calendar, specifying a type zone, work days, display options, and publishing.

Numerous plugins are available to extend Evolution's capabilities. Most are installed and enabled for you automatically, including the SpamAssassin plug-in for handling junk mail. To manage your plug-ins, select the Plugins entry in the Edit menu (Edit | Plugin) to open the Plugin Manager, with plug-ins listed in a left scroll window and configuration tabs located for a selected plug-in on the right side.

Evolution also supports filters. You can use filters to direct some messages automatically to certain folders, instead of having all incoming messages placed in the inbox folder. To create a filter, you can select the Message Filters entry in the Edit menu (Edit | Message Filters) and click Add to open the Add Rule window. You can also right-click the header of a message whose heading meets your criteria, like a subject or sender, and select Create Rule from Message and select a Filter entry for sender, subject, or recipient. On the Add Rule window, you can add other criteria and specify the action to take, like moving the message to a particular folder. You can also add other actions like assigning a score, changing the color, copying the message, or deleting it.

A user's e-mail messages, addresses, and configuration information are kept in files located in the **.evolution** directory within the user's home directory. Backing up this information is as simple as making a copy of that directory. Messages for the different mail boxes are kept in a **mail** subdirectory. If you are migrating to a new system, you can just copy the directory from the older system. To back up the mail for any given mail account, just copy the **mail** subdirectory for that account. You can also backup the address book, calendar, memos, and tasks subdirectories.

Note: The Evolution Calendar is linked to the Date and Time indicator menu on Ubuntu Unity, listing calendar events on that menu.

Evolution also supports contact operations like calendars, contact lists, and memos. On the left side pane, the bottom section displays buttons for these different functions: Mail, Contacts, Calendars, Tasks, and Memos. To see and manage your contacts, click the Contacts button on the left sidebar. The Calendar displays a browseable calendar on the left pane to move easily to a specific date (see Figure 7-4). The right pane shows a daily calendar page by the hour with sections for tasks and memos. You can set up several calendars, which you can access at the top of the right pane. A personal calendar is set up for you already. To add a new calendar, select Calendar from the New menu to open a New Calendar dialog where you can choose the type and name.

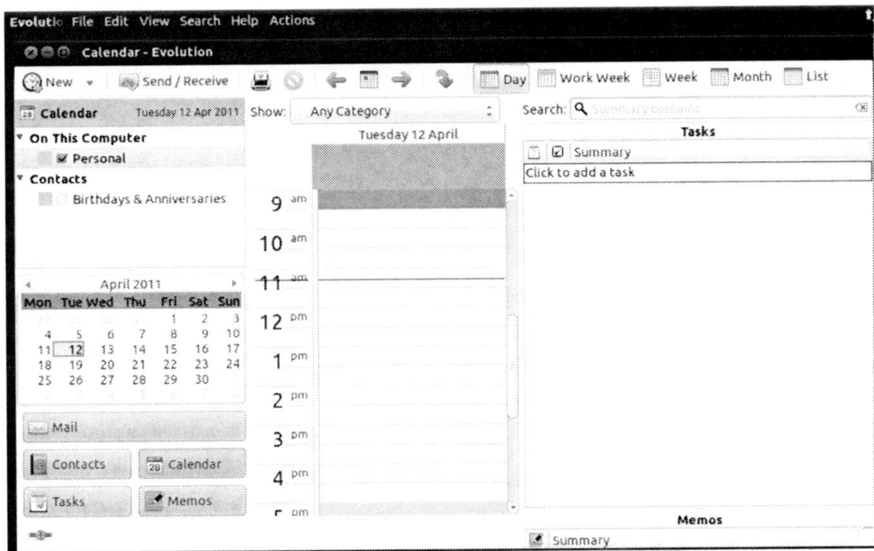

Figure 7-4: Evolution Calendar

Note: Other GNOME mail clients include sylpheed and Claws-mail (both are on the Ubuntu Universe repository). Sylpheed is a mail and news client with an interface similar to Windows mail clients. Claws-mail is an extended version of Sylpheed with many additional features (**www.claws-mail.org**).

The KDE Mail Client: KMail

The   KDE mail client, KMail, provides a full-featured desktop interface for composing, sending, and receiving e-mail messages. KMail is part of the KDE Personal Information Management suite (KDE-PIM) which also includes an address book (KAddressBook), an organizer and scheduler (KOrganizer), and a note writer (KNotes). All these components are also directly integrated on the desktop into Kontact. You can start up KMail directly, or as part of the Kontact applications (Mail). KMail, along with Kontact, KOrganizer, and KaddressBook, is accessible from the KDE Desktop Office and Internet menus. On Ubuntu Unity you can access it from the Internet dash. You can access Kontact in the Office dash. KMail is installed as part of the KDE desktop, but you can install it separately from the Ubuntu Software Center | Internet | KMail, and it will run on GNOME.

The KMail window displays three panes for folders, headers, and messages (see Figure 7-5). The lower-left pane displays your mail folders: an inbox folder for received mail, an outbox folder for mail you have composed but have not sent yet, and a sent-mail folder for messages you have previously sent. You can create your own mail folders and save selected messages in them, if you want. You can designate certain folders as favorite folders and have them listed in the Favorite Folders pane (right-click on the Favorite Folders pane and select Add Favorite Folder to choose a folder).

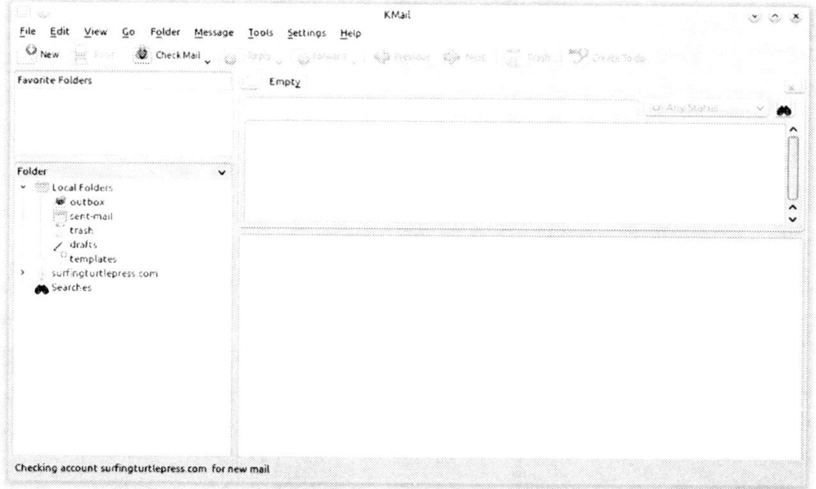
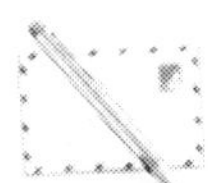

Figure 7-5: KMail

The top-right pane displays mail headers for the currently selected mail folder. To display a message, click its header. The message is then displayed in the large pane below the header list. You can also send and receive attachments, including binary files. Pictures and movies that are received are displayed using the appropriate KDE utility. If you right-click the message, a pop-up menu displays options for actions you may want to perform on it. You can move or copy it to another folder, or simply delete it. You can also compose a reply or forward the message.

To quickly set up a new email account, you can use the Account Wizard (Tools | Account Wizard). A series of dialogs will prompt you to enter the account type, account name and address, login name and password, and the incoming and outgoing servers, For more detailed configuration select the Configure Kmail entry in the Settings menu (Settings | Configure Kmail). Several tabs are available on the Configure window, which you can display by clicking their icons in the left column. To set up an account, click the Accounts icon, and then select the Receiving tab. Click the Add button to open an Add Account dialog where you can enter login, password, and host information. For secure access, KMail supports the Secure Sockets Layer (SSL), provided OpenSSL is installed. Messages can be encrypted and decoded by users. It also supports IMAP in addition to POP and SMTP protocols.

SquirrelMail

You can use the SquirrelMail Web mail tool to access mail from Internet email services using your Web browser. It will display a login screen for mail users. It features an inbox list and message reader, support for editing and sending new messages, and a plug-in structure for adding new features. You can find out more about SquirrelMail at **http://www.squirrelmail.org**. The Apache configuration file is **/etc/httpd/conf.d/squirrelmail.conf**, and SquirrelMail is installed in **/usr/share/squirrelmail**. Be sure that the IMAP mail server is also installed.

To configure SquirrelMail, you use the **config.pl** script in the **/usr/share/squirrelmail/config** directory (run in a terminal window). This displays a simple text-based menu where you can configure settings like the server to use, folder defaults, general options, and organizational preferences.

```
cd /usr/share/squirrelmail/config
./config.pl
```

To access SquirrelMail, use the Web server address with the **/squirrelmail** extension, as in **localhost/squirrelmail** for users on the local system, or **www.mytrek.com/squirrelmail** as an example for remote users.

Command Line Mail Clients

Several mail clients use a simple command line interface. They can be run without any other kind of support, such as the X Window System, desktops, or cursor support. They are simple and easy to use but include an extensive set of features and options. Two of the more widely used mail clients of this type are Mail and Mutt. Mail is the mailx mail client that was developed for the Unix system. It is considered a default mail client that can be found on all Unix and Linux systems. Mutt is a cursor-based client that can be run from the command line.

Mutt

Mutt has an easy-to-use cursor-based interface with an extensive set of features. You can find more information about Mutt from the Mutt Web site, **http://www.mutt.org**. The Mutt manual is located in the **/usr/doc** directory under Mutt. To use Mutt, enter the **mutt** command in a terminal window or on the command line.

Mail

What is known now as the Mail utility was originally created for BSD Unix and called, simply, mail. Later versions of Unix System V adopted the BSD mail utility and renamed it mailx. Now, it is simply referred to as Mail. Mail functions as a default mail client on most Unix and Linux systems. It is not installed by default on Ubuntu. Install the **bsd-mailx** package with the Synaptic Package Manager.

To send a message with Mail, type `mail` on the command line along with the address of the person to whom you are sending the message. Press ENTER and you are prompted for a subject. Enter the subject of the message and press ENTER again. At this point, you are placed in input mode. Anything you type in is considered the contents of the message. Pressing ENTER adds a new line to the text. When you finish typing your message, press CTRL-D on a line of its own to end the message. You will then be prompted to enter a user to whom to send a carbon copy of the message (Cc). If you do not want to send a carbon copy, just press ENTER. You will then see EOT (end-of-transmission) displayed after you press CTRL-D

You can send a message to several users at the same time by listing those users' addresses as arguments on the command line following the `mail` command. In the next example, the user sends the same message to both **chris** and **aleina**.

```
$ mail chris aleina
```

To receive mail, you first enter the `mail` command and press ENTER. This invokes a Mail shell with its own prompt and mail commands. A list of message headers is displayed. Header information is arranged into fields beginning with the status of the message and the message number. The status of a message is indicated by a single uppercase letter, usually **N** for new or **U** for unread. A message number, used for easy reference to your messages, follows the status field. The next field is the address of the sender, followed by the date and time the message was received, and then the number of lines and characters in the message. The last field contains the subject the sender gave for the message. After the headers, the Mail shell displays its prompt, an ampersand (**&**). At the Mail prompt, you enter commands that operate on the messages. An example of a Mail header and prompt follows:

```
$ mail
Mail version 8.2 01/15/2001. Type ? for help.
"/var/spool/mail/larisa": 3 messages 1 new 2 unread
 1 chris@turtle.mytrek. Thu Jun 7 14:17 22/554 "trip"
>U 2 aleina@turtle.mytrek Thu Jun 7 14:18 22/525 "party"
 U 3 dylan@turtle.mytrek. Thu Jun 7 14:18 22/528 "newsletter"
& q
```

Mail references messages either through a message list or through the current message marker (>). The greater-than sign (>) is placed before a message considered the current message. The current message is referenced by default when no message number is included with a Mail command. You can also reference messages using a message list consisting of several message numbers.

You use the **R** and **r** commands to reply to a message you have received. The **R** command entered with a message number generates a header for sending a message and then places you into input mode to type the message. The **q** command quits Mail. When you quit, messages you have already read are placed in a file called **mbox** in your home directory. Instead of saving messages in the **mbox** file, you can use the **s** command to save a message explicitly to a file of your choice. Mail has its own initialization file, called **.mailrc**, which is executed each time Mail is invoked, either for sending or receiving messages. Within it, you can define Mail options and create Mail aliases.

Notifications of Received Mail

As your mail messages are received, they are automatically placed in your mailbox file, but you are not automatically notified when you receive a message. You can use a mail client to retrieve any new messages, or you can use a mail monitor tool to tell you when new mail has arrived in your inbox. Several mail notification tools are also available, such as **gnubiff** and Mail Notification. Mail Notification will support Gmail, as well as Evolution (for Evolution, install the separate plug-in package). When you first log in after Mail Notification has been installed, the Mail Notification configuration window is displayed. Here you can add new mail accounts to check, such as Gmail accounts, as well as set other features like summary pop-ups. When you receive mail, a mail icon will appear on your top desktop panel. Move your cursor over it to check for any new mail. Clicking it will display the Mail Notification configuration window, though you can configure this to go directly to your e-mail application. The **gnubiff** tool will notify you of any POP3 or IMAP mail arrivals.

For command line interfaces, you can use the biff utility, which notifies you immediately when a message is received. biff automatically displays the header and beginning lines of messages as they are received. To turn on biff, you enter **biff y** on the command line. To turn it off, you enter **biff n**. To find out if biff is turned on, enter **biff** alone.

Accessing Mail on Remote Mail Servers

Most new mail clients are equipped to access mail accounts on remote servers. Mail clients, such as Evolution, KMail, Sylpheed, and Thunderbird, enable you to set up a mailbox for such an account and access a mail server to check for and download received mail. You must specify what protocol a mail server uses. This is usually either the Post Office Protocol (POP) or the IMAP protocol (IMAP). Using a mail server address, you can access your account with your username and password.

For email clients such as mail and mutt that do not provide mail server access, you can use Fetchmail to have mail from those accounts sent directly to the inbox maintained by your Linux system for your Linux account. All your mail, whether from other users on your Linux system or from remote mail accounts, will appear in your local inbox. Fetchmail checks for mail on remote mail servers and downloads it to your local inbox, where it appears as newly received mail. Enter **fetchmail** on the command line with the mail server address and any needed options. The mail protocol is indicated with the **-p** option and the mail server type, usually POP3. If your e-mail username is different from your Linux login name, you use the **-u** option and the e-mail name. Once you execute the **fetchmail** command, you are prompted for a password. The syntax for the **fetchmail** command for a POP3 mail server follows:

```
fetchmail -p POP3 -u username mail-server
```

You will see messages telling you if mail is there and, if so, how many messages are being downloaded. You can then use a mail client to read the messages from your inbox. You can run

Fetchmail in daemon mode to have it check automatically for mail. You have to include an option specifying the interval in seconds for checking mail.

```
fetchmail -d 1200
```

To have fetchmail run automatically you can set the START DAEMON option to yes in the **/etc/default/fetchmail** file. Edit the file with the **gksu gedit** command.

You can specify options such as the server type, username, and password in a **.fetchmailrc** file in your home directory. You can also include entries for other mail servers and accounts you may have. Once Fetchmail is configured, you can enter **fetchmail** with no arguments; it will read entries from your **.fetchmailrc** file. You can also make entries directly in the **.fetchmailrc** file. An entry in the **.fetchmailrc** file for a particular mail account consists of several fields and their values: poll, protocol, username, and password. The poll field refers to the mail server name. You can also specify your password, instead of having to enter it each time Fetchmail accesses the mail server.

Mailing Lists

Users on mailing lists automatically receive messages and articles sent to the lists. Mailing lists work much like a mail alias, broadcasting messages to all users on the list. Mailing lists were designed to serve specialized groups of people. Numerous mailing lists, as well as other subjects, are available for Linux. By convention, to subscribe to a list, you send a request to the mailing list address with a **–request** term added to its username. For example, to subscribe to **gnome-list@gnome.org**, you send a request to **gnome-list-request@gnome.org**.

You can use the Mailman and Majordomo programs to manage your mailing lists automatically. Mailman is the GNU mailing list manager, included with Ubuntu (**http://www.list.org**). You can find out more about Majordomo at **http://www.greatcircle.com/majordomo** and about Mailman at **http://sourceforge.net**.

MIME: /etc/mime.types

MIME (the term stands for Multipurpose Internet Mail Extensions) is used to enable mail clients to send and receive multimedia files and files using different character sets such as those for different languages. Multimedia files can be images, sound clips, or even video. Mail clients that support MIME can send binary files automatically as attachments to messages. MIME-capable mail clients maintain a file called **mailcap** that maps different types of MIME messages to applications on your system that can view or display them. For example, an image file will be mapped to an application that can display images. Your mail clients can then run that program to display the image message. A sound file will be mapped to an application that can play sound files. Most mail clients have MIME capabilities built in and use their own version of the **mailcap** file. Others use a program called metamail that adds MIME support. MIME is used not only in mail clients. Both the KDE and GNOME file managers use MIME to map a file to a particular application so that you can launch the application directly from the file.

Applications are associated with binary files by means of the **mailcap** and **mime.types** files. The **mime.types** file defines different MIME types, associating a MIME type with a certain application. The **mailcap** file then associates each MIME type with a specified application. Your system maintains its own MIME types file, usually **/etc/mime.types**.

Entries in the MIME types file associate a MIME type and possible subtype of an application with a set of possible file extensions used for files that run on a given kind of application. The MIME type is usually further qualified by a subtype, separated from the major type by a slash. For example, a MIME type image can have several subtypes such as jpeg, gif, or tiff. A sample MIME type entry defining a MIME type for JPEG files are shown here. The MIME type is image/jpeg, and the list of possible file extensions is "jpeg jpg jpe":

```
image/jpeg       jpeg jpg jpe
```

The applications specified will depend on those available on your particular system. The application is specified as part of the application type. In many cases, X Window System–based programs are specified. Comments are indicated with a **#**. The following entries associate **odt** files with the LibreOffice writer and **qtl** files with the QuickTime player.

```
application/vnd.oasis.opendocument.text    odt
application/x-quicktimeplayer              qtl
```

Though you can create your own MIME types, a standard set already is in use. The types text, image, audio, video, application, multipart, and message, along with their subtypes, have already been defined for your system. You will find that commonly used file extensions such as **.tif** and **.jpg** for TIFF and JPEG image files are already associated with a MIME type and an application. Though you can easily change the associated application, it is best to keep the MIME types already installed. The current official MIME types are listed at the IANA Web site (**http://www.iana.org**) under the name Media Types, provided as part of their Assignment Services.

S/MIME and OpenPGP/MIME are authentication protocols for signing and encrypting mail messages. S/MIME was originally developed by the RSA Data Security. OpenPGP is an open standard based on the PGP/MIME protocol developed by the PGP (Pretty Good Privacy) group. Clients like KMail and Evolution can use OpenPGP/MIME to authenticate messages. Check the Internet Mail Consortium for more information, **www.imc.org**.

Usenet News

Usenet is an open mail system on which users post messages that include news, discussions, and opinions. It operates like a mailbox to which any user on your Linux system can read or send messages. Users' messages are incorporated into Usenet files, which are distributed to any system signed up to receive them. Certain Usenet sites perform organizational and distribution operations for Usenet, receiving messages from other sites and organizing them into Usenet files, which are then broadcast to many other sites. Such sites are called backbone sites, and they operate like publishers, receiving articles and organizing them into different groups.

To access Usenet news, you need access to a news server, which receives the daily Usenet newsfeeds and makes them accessible to other systems. Your network may have a system that operates as a news server. If you are using an Internet service provider (ISP), a news server is probably maintained by your ISP for your use. To read Usenet articles, you use a newsreader, a client program that connects to a news server and accesses the articles. On the Internet and in TCP/IP networks, news servers communicate with newsreaders using the Network News Transfer Protocol (NNTP) and are often referred to as NNTP news servers. You can also create your own news server on your Linux system to run a local Usenet news service or to download and maintain the full set of Usenet articles. News transport agent applications can be set up to create such a server.

Usenet files were originally designed to function like journals. Messages contained in the files are referred to as articles. A user could write an article, post it in Usenet, and have it immediately distributed to other systems. Usenet files themselves were organized as journal publications. Because journals are designed to address specific groups, Usenet files are organized according to groups called newsgroups. When a user posts an article, it is assigned to a specific newsgroup. You can also create articles of your own, which you can then add to a newsgroup for others to read. Linux has newsgroups on various topics. Some are for discussion, and others are sources of information about recent developments. On some, you can ask for help for specific problems. A selection of some of the popular Linux newsgroups is provided here:

Newsgroup	Topic
comp.os.linux.announce	Announcements of Linux developments
comp.os.linux.admin	System administration questions
comp.os.linux.misc	Special questions and issues
comp.os.linux.setup	Installation problems
comp.os.linux.help	Questions and answers for particular problems
linux.help	Obtain help for Linux problems

Newsreaders

You read Usenet articles with a newsreader, such as KNode, Pan, Thunderbird, or tin, which enable you to select a specific newsgroup and then read the articles in it. A newsreader operates like a user interface, letting you browse through and select available articles for reading, saving, or printing. Most newsreaders employ a retrieval feature called threads that pulls together articles on the same discussion or topic. Several popular newsreaders are listed in Table 7-2.

Most newsreaders can read Usenet news provided on remote news servers that use the NNTP. Desktop newsreaders, such as KNode and Pan, have you specify the Internet address for the remote news server in their own configuration settings. Shell-based newsreaders such as **tin**, obtain the news server's Internet address from the NNTPSERVER shell variable, configured in the **.profile** file.

```
NNTPSERVER=news.domain.com
export NNTPSERVER
```

Binary Newsreaders and Grabbers

A binary newsreader can convert text messages to binary equivalents, like those found in **alt.binaries** newsgroups. There are some news grabbers, applications designed only to download binaries. The binaries are normally encoded with RAR compression, which have an **.rar** extension. To decode them you first have to install the **unrar-free** package. Binaries normally consist of several rar archive files, some of which may be incomplete. To repair them you can use Par2 recovery program. Install the **par2** and **Gpar2** packages. A binary should have its own set of par2 files also listed on the news server that you can download and use to repair any incomplete **rar** files. The principle works much the same as RAID arrays using parity information to reconstruct damaged data. You can use the Gpar2 application to manually repair rar archive files, accessible from the Accessories dash.

Newsreader	Description
Pan	GNOME Desktop newsreader
KNode	KDE Desktop newsreader
Thunderbird	Mail client with newsreader capabilities (X based)
Sylpheed	GNOME Windows-like newsreader
Slrn	Newsreader (cursor based)
Emacs	Emacs editor, mail client, and newsreader (cursor based)
tin	Newsreader (command line interface)
trn4	Newsreader (command line interface)
Newsbin	Newsreader (Windows version works under Wine)
Knews	KDE news reader
xpn	Desktop newsreader
nzb	Binary only NZB based news grabber

Table 7-2: Linux Newsreaders

The NZB grabber application works using NZB files to locate and download binaries. You first have to obtain the NZB file to use. But if you can obtain an NZB file, then NZB is by far the easiest to use. Set the server options in Tools | Options (port would be 119). Load the NZB file (File | Open) and then start the download and decode (Action | Start).

An alternative solution is to use the Windows version of the Newsbin newsreader running under Wine (Windows compatibility layer for Linux). You need to install Wine first. The current version of Newsbin runs stable and fast with Wine. Newsbin is an inexpensive commercial product. You can download and install Wine from the Ubuntu Software Center | Office | Wine Microsoft Windows Compatibility Layer. Then download Newsbin (**http://www.newsbin.com**) and install it using wine.

```
wine nb553-install.exe
```

Newsbin works on Wine and Ubuntu with no modifications needed. Newsbin will be accessible directly from an icon on your desktop as you would any application. It is advisable to disable the Message of the Day (MOTD) feature on the Options Advanced panel. You can save files on any Linux file system, as well as newsgroup downloads. The Autorar feature works effectively for binary files, automatically extracting and repairing if needed the complete binary. Your entire Linux files system along with any mounted files systems is accessible as the **z:** drive. To test Par2 files for binaries you will need to also download and install QuickPar, another windows program that works effectively on Wine (**http://www.quickpar.org.uk**). QuickPar will be accessible from Newsbin.

slrn

The **slrn** newsreader is cursor-based. Commands are displayed across the top of the screen and can be executed using the listed keys. Different types of screens exist for the newsgroup list, article list, and article content, each with its own set of commands. An initial screen lists your subscribed newsgroups with commands for posting, listing, and subscribing to your newsgroups. When you start slrn for the first time, you may have to create a **.jnewsrc** file in your home directory. Use the following command: `slrn -f .jnewsrc -create`. Also, you will have to set the **NNTPSERVER** variable and make sure it is exported.

The slrn newsreader features a utility called **slrnpull** that you can use to download articles in specified newsgroups automatically. This allows you to view your selected newsgroups offline. The slrnpull utility was designed as a simple single-user version of Leafnode; it will access a news server and download its designated newsgroups, making them available through slrn whenever the user chooses to examine them. Newsgroup articles are downloaded to the **SLRNPULL_ROOT** directory. On Ubuntu, this is **/var/spool/slrnpull**. The selected newsgroups to be downloaded are entered in the **slrnpull.conf** configuration file placed in the **SLRNPULL_ROOT** directory. In this file, you can specify how many articles to download for each group and when they should expire. To use **slrn** with **slrnpull**, you will have to configure the **.slrnrc** file to reference the **slrnpull** directories where newsgroup files are kept.

News Transport Agents

Usenet news is provided over the Internet as a daily newsfeed of articles and postings for thousands of newsgroups. This newsfeed is sent to sites that can then provide access to the news for other systems through newsreaders. These sites operate as news servers; the newsreaders used to access them are their clients. The news server software, called news transport agents, is what provides newsreaders with news, enabling you to read newsgroups and post articles. For Linux, several popular news transport agents are INN, Leafnode, Papercut, and sn. Both Papercut and Leafnode are small and simple, and useful for small networks. INN is more powerful and complex, designed with large systems in mind (see **www.isc.org** for more details).

Daily news feeds on Usenet are often large and consume much of a news server's resources in both time and memory. For this reason, you may not want to set up your own Linux system to receive such newsfeeds. If you are operating in a network of Linux systems, you can designate one of them as the news server and install the news transport agent on it to receive and manage the Usenet newsfeeds. Users on other systems on your network can then access that news server with their own newsreaders. If your network already has a news server, you need not install a news transport agent at all. You only have to use your newsreaders to access that server remotely.

You can also use news transport agents to run local versions of news for only the users on your system or your local network. To do this, install INN, Leafnode, or Papercut configure them just to manage local newsgroups. Users on your system could then post articles and read local news.

8. Internet Applications

Web Browsers: Firefox, Epiphany, Chromium, Lynx

BitTorrent: Transmission

Java for Linux

Network File Transfer: FTP

FTP Clients

Ubuntu provides powerful Web and FTP clients for accessing the Internet. Some of these applications are installed automatically and are ready to use when you first start up your Ubuntu system. Ubuntu also includes full Java development support, letting you run and construct Java applets. Web and FTP clients connect to sites that run servers, using Web pages and FTP files to provide services to users.

On your Ubuntu system, you can choose from several Web browsers, including Firefox, Rekonq, Epiphany, Chromium, and Lynx. Firefox, Rekonq, Chromium, and Epiphany are desktop browsers that provide full picture, sound, and video display capabilities. The Lynx browser is a line-mode browser that displays only lines of text.

Web browsers and FTP clients are commonly used to conduct secure transactions such as logging in to remote sites, ordering items, or transferring files. Such operations are currently secured by encryption methods provided by the Secure Sockets Layer (SSL). If you use a browser for secure transactions, it should be SSL enabled. Most browsers include SSL support. Linux distributions include SSL (OpenSSL) as part of a standard installation.

URL Addresses

An Internet resource is accessed using a Universal Resource Locator (URL). A URL is composed of three elements: the transfer protocol, the hostname, and the pathname. The transfer protocol and the hostname are separated by a colon and two slashes, *://*. The pathname begins with a single slash:

```
transfer-protocol://host-name/path-name
```

The transfer protocol is usually HTTP (Hypertext Transfer Protocol), indicating a Web page. Other possible values for transfer protocols are **ftp**, and **file**. As their names suggest, **ftp** initiates FTP sessions, whereas **file** displays a local file on your own system, such as a text or HTML file. The hostname is the computer on which a particular Web site is located. You can think of this as the address of the Web site. By convention, many hostnames begin with **www**, though not necessarily. In the next example, the URL locates a Web page called **guides.html** on the **http://tldp.org** Web site:

```
http://tldp.org/guides.html
```

If you do not want to access a particular Web page, you can leave the file reference out, and then you access the Web site's home page automatically. To access a Web site directly, use its hostname. If no home page is specified for a Web site, the file **index.html** in the top directory is used as the home page. In the next example, the user brings up the GNOME home page:

```
http://www.gnome.org/
```

The resource file's extension indicates the type of action to be taken on it. A picture has a **.gif** or **.jpeg** extension and is converted for display. A sound file has an **.au** or **.wav** extension and is played. The following URL references a **.gif** file. Instead of displaying a Web page, your browser invokes a graphics viewer to display the picture.

Note: You can install the Adobe version of the Flash plug-in for Linux from the Ubuntu Software Center | Sound & Video | Adobe Flash Plugin 10. Ubuntu also includes two free and open source versions of Flash: **swfdec** and **gnash**. The **swfdec** version is newer. Be sure the Partners repository is enabled.

Web Browsers

Popular browsers for Ubuntu include Firefox (Mozilla), Rekonq, Chromium (Google), Epiphany, and Lynx (see Table 8-1). Firefox is the default Web browser used on most Linux distributions, including Ubuntu. Rekonq is the KDE Web browser, accessible from the KDE desktop, and Epiphany is the GNOME Web browser. Chromium is the open source version of the new Google Web browser. Lynx and ELinks are command line–based browsers with no graphics capabilities, but in every other respect they are fully functional Web browsers.

Web Site	Description
Firefox	The Mozilla project Firefox Web browser, Ubuntu desktop default browser **http://www.mozilla.org**
Rekonq	KDE desktop Web browser **http://reconq.sourceforge.net**
Epiphany	GNOME Web browser **http://projects.gnome.org/epiphany/**
Chromium	Open source version of Google Chrome Web browser **http://www.crhomium.org**
lynx	Text-based command-line Web browser (Ubuntu supported) **http://lynx.isc.org**
elinks	Text-based command-line Web browser **http://elinks.or.cz**

Table 8-1: Web browsers

The Firefox Web Browser

Ubuntu uses Firefox as its primary browser (see Figure 8-1). Firefox is a streamlined browser featuring fast web access. Firefox can operate from any desktop, including GNOME, KDE, and Xfce. Firefox is installed by default with a Launcher item and an icon in both the Shortcuts and Internet dashes.

When opened, Firefox displays a navigation toolbar at the top of the screen below the title bar and tabs with a text box for entering a URL address and a series of navigation buttons for accessing web pages. On the left side are the next and previous buttons for paging through previously accessed Web pages. A home button at the right side of the navigation bar moves you to your home page. To the right of the URL text box is a refresh button for re-accessing a page. When you enter a Web page name in the text box, Firefox performs a dynamic search on previously accessed pages and displays the pages in a drop-down menu, which you can choose from. Click the drop-down menu button at the right side of the text box to display a list of previously accessed pages.

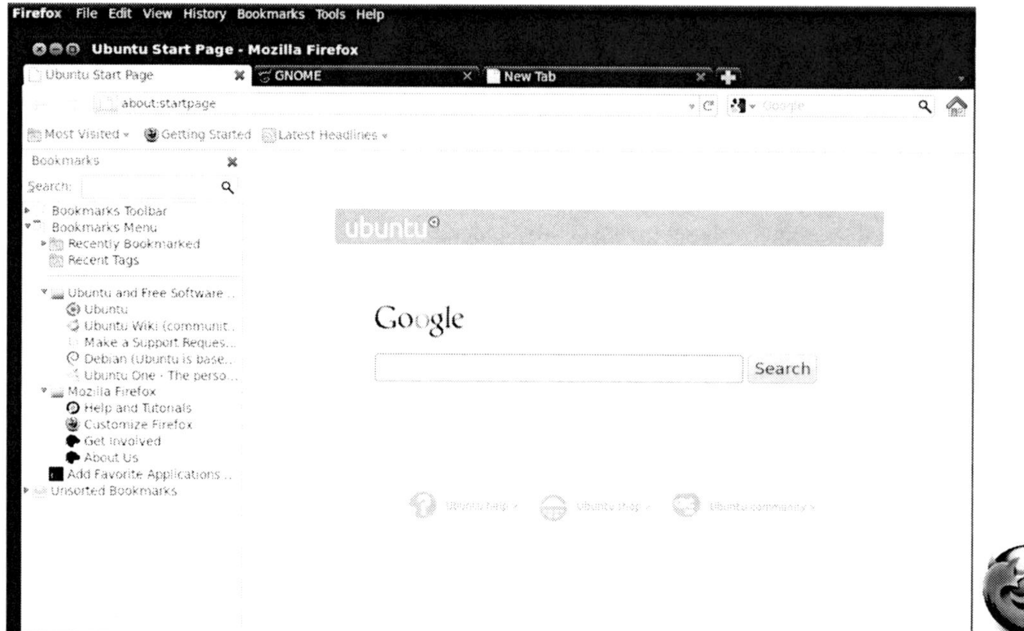

Figure 8-1: Firefox Web Browser

To the right of the URL box is a search box where you can use different search engines for searching the Web, selected sites, or particular items. A pop-up menu lets you select a search engine. Currently included are Google, Yahoo, Amazon, Wikipedia, Creative Commons, and eBay. Firefox also features button links and tabbed pages. You can drag the URL from the URL box to the button link bar to create a button with which to access the site quickly.

Menus on the top menu bar (application menu on Ubuntu Unity) provide access to such Firefox features as Tools, View, History, and Bookmarks.

For easy browsing, Firefox features tabs for displaying web pages. Tabs are listed below the title bar, with a tab set up for the current Web page. To open a new tab, click the plus button shown to the right of the tab titles. You can also press CTRL-T or select New Tab from the File menu (File | New Tab). To display a page in a tab, click on the tab title and enter a URL or choose a bookmark. You can have several tabs open at once, moving from one page to the next by clicking their tabs. You can open all your Bookmark toolbar buttons as tabs by right-clicking the Bookmark toolbar and selecting "Open All in Tabs."

Tip: Right-clicking on the Web page background displays a pop-up menu with options for most basic operations like page navigation and saving pages.

To search a current page for certain text, press CTRL-F. This opens a search toolbar at the bottom of Firefox where you can enter a search term. You have search options to highlight found entries or to match character case. Next and Previous buttons let you move to the next or previous found pattern.

When you download a file using Firefox, the download is managed by the Download Manager. You can download several files at once. Downloads can be displayed in the Download

Manager window (Tools | Downloads). You can cancel a download at any time, or pause a download, resuming it later. Right-clicking a download entry will display the site from which it was downloaded as well as the directory in which you saved the entry. By default, downloads will be saved to your Downloads directory. To remove an entry, first select it and click Remove from list.

Firefox Bookmarks and History

Firefox refers to the URLs of web pages you want to keep as bookmarks, marking pages you want to access directly. The Bookmarks menu enables you add your favorite web pages. You can also press CTRL-D to add a bookmark. You can then view a list of your bookmarks and select one to view. You can also edit your list, adding or removing bookmarks. When adding a bookmark a Page Bookmarked dialog opens with drop-down menus for folders and tags. The Folder menu is set to Bookmarks Menu folder by default. You can also select the Bookmarks Toolbar or Unsorted Bookmarks.

The History menu displays a list of previous sites you have accessed recently. The URL box also features a pop-up menu listing your previous history sites. Bookmarks and History can be viewed as sidebars, selectable from the View | Sidebar menu.

Firefox also features Bookmark toolbar that you use for frequently accessed sites. The Bookmark toolbar is displayed just above the Web page. You can drag the site address from the URL box to the Bookmark toolbar to create a button for quick access to a site. Buttons can also be folders, containing button links for several pages. Clicking a folder button will display the button links in a pop-up menu. You can also right-click on the Bookmark toolbar to open a pop-up menu with options to add entries: New Bookmark, New Folder, and New Separator. The New Bookmark entry opens a New Bookmark dialog where you can enter the bookmark name and URL address. The New Folder entry lets you create a bookmark folder where you can place bookmarks of your choosing, letting you organize your bookmarks into folders. From the Bookmark toolbar pop-up the menu, you can also sort your bookmark buttons by name. To delete a Bookmark toolbar button, right-click on it and choose Delete. You can also use the cut, copy, and paste options in the menu to move or copy a bookmark from the Bookmark sidebar to the Bookmark toolbar, and vice versa. You can also use these options to copy or move a bookmark to a folder on the Bookmark toolbar.

To manage your bookmarks, click on the Show All Bookmarks entry in the Bookmarks menu (Bookmarks | Show All Bookmarks). This opens the Library window with bookmark folders displayed in a sidebar, organized into Bookmark toolbar and Bookmark menu entries, as well as history. Bookmarks in a folder are shown in the upper-right pane, and properties for a selected bookmark in that list are displayed in the lower-right pane. The Organize menu has an option to create a new folder. The View menu lets you sort your bookmarks. The "Import and Backup" menu has options to save backups of your bookmark, as well as export your bookmark for use on other systems using Firefox. You can also import exported Firefox bookmarks from other systems. Bookmarks also maintain a Most Visited, Recently Bookmarked, and Recent Tags folders. This lets you find sites you visit most often, or those you consider important.

Firefox supports live bookmarks, which connect to sites that provide a live RSS feed. This is a page that is constantly being updated, like a news site. Live bookmarks are indicated by a live bookmark icon to the right of its address. Click this icon or select Subscribe to this Page from the Bookmark menu, to subscribe to the site (Bookmarks | Subscribe to this Page). A pop-up menu is displayed in the main window with the prompt "Subscribe to this feed using". Live Bookmarks is selected by default, but you can also choose MY Yahoo!, Bloglines, or Google. You can also choose to "Always use Live bookmarks for feeds." You can then click Subscribe Now to set up the live bookmark. This opens a dialog where you can choose to place the live bookmark, either in the Bookmark menu, or on the Bookmark toolbar. In the Bookmark toolbar, the live bookmark becomes a pop-up menu listing the active pages, with an entry at the end for the main site.

When you open the live bookmark in the Bookmark toolbar or from the live bookmark icon in its URL entry, a list of active pages is displayed. An "Open all in Tabs" entry at the bottom of the listing lets you open all the active pages at once. News pages on a site are often RSS feeds that you can set up as a live bookmark. At the Ubuntu site (**www.ubuntu.com**) the Canonical News feed link (Further information | News feed at bottom right of page) can be subscribed to as a live bookmark. When you select a subscribed site on the bookmark menu, a submenu of active pages is displayed from which you can choose. On Ubuntu, the Canonical news feed live bookmark is accessed from the "Canonical" bookmark toolbar button.

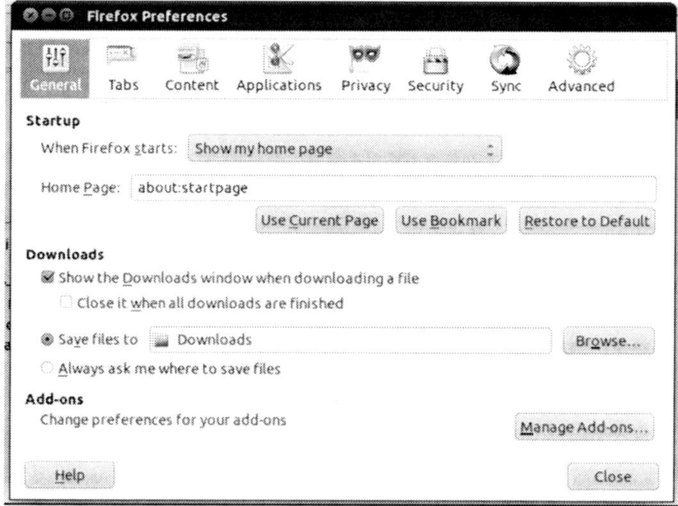

Figure 8-2: Firefox Preferences

Firefox Configuration

The Preferences dialog (Edit | Preferences) in Firefox enables you to set several different options. There are preference buttons for General, Tabs, Content, Applications, Privacy, Security, Sync, and Advanced (see Figure 8-2). On the General tab, you can set you home page, download options, and access add-on management. Tabs control tab opening and closing behavior. Content lets you set the font and font size, as well as color and language to use. You can also block pop-ups and enable java. Applications associates content with applications to run it, like video or mp3. Privacy controls history, cookies, and private data. Security is where you can remember passwords and set warning messages.

Sync is a new feature that sets up the Firefox's sync service, letting you synchronize your history, bookmarks, passwords, and open tabs on all your devices. You are first prompted to create a new account, prompting you for your email address, password, and a Firefox server. You are then provided with a sync key, which you should save.

The Advanced page has several tabs: General, Network, Update, and Encryption. The General tab provides features like spell-checking, and keyboard navigation. The Network tab has a Settings button for the Connection feature, which is where you set up your network connections such as the direct connection to the internet or proxy settings. Here you can also set up offline storage size. The encryption tab is where you can manage certificates, setting up validation methods, view certificates, and set up revocation lists.

If you are on a network that connects to the Internet through a firewall, you use the Connection Setting dialog to enter the address of your network's firewall gateway computer. The Connection Settings dialog is open from the Advanced tab's Network tab on which you click the Settings button, "Configure how Firefox connects to the Internet". Several types of firewalls exist. The most restrictive kinds of firewalls use programs called proxies, which receive Internet requests from users and then make those requests on their behalf. There is no direct connection to the Internet.

The "Manage Add-ons" button, on the Preferences General tab, opens the Add-ons window with tabs for Get Add-ons, Extensions, Themes, Languages, and Plugins. Select the "Get Add-ons" tab to see a list of tools you can add to Firefox. The "Browse All Add-ons" link opens a Web page that lists available add-ons. The Plugins panel lists all your current plugins, like QuickTime or Flash, letting you enable or disable them (see Figure 8-3).

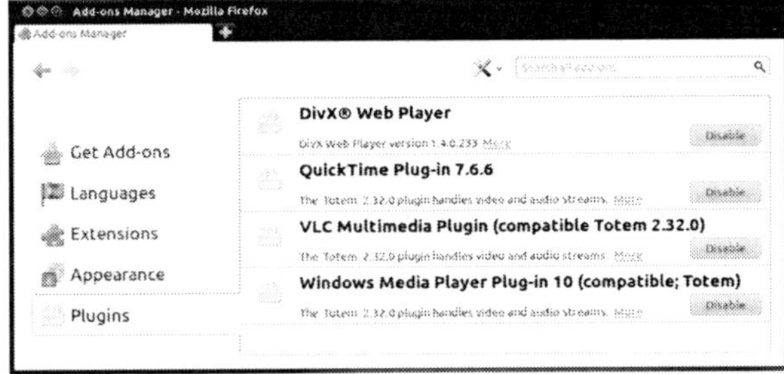

Figure 8-3: Firefox Add-ons Management

Firefox also supports profiles. You can set up different Firefox configurations, each with preferences and bookmarks. This is useful for computers like laptops that connect to different networks or are used for different purposes. You can select and create Profiles by starting the profile manager. Enter the **firefox** command in a terminal window with the **-P** option.

```
firefox -P
```

A default profile is already set up. You can create a new profile, which runs the profile wizard to prompt you for the profile name and directory to use. Select a profile to use and click Start Firefox. The last profile you used will be used the next time you start Firefox. You have the option to prompt for the profile to use at start up, or run the **firefox -P** command again to change your profile.

The Mozilla Project

The Mozilla project is an open source project based on the original Netscape browser code that provides a development framework for Web-based applications, primarily the Web browser and e-mail client. Originally, the aim of the Mozilla project was to provide an end-user Web browser called Mozilla. Its purpose has since changed to providing a development framework that anyone can use to create Web applications, though the project also provides its own. Table 8-2 lists some Mozilla resources.

Currently the framework is used for Mozilla products like the Firefox Web browser and the Thunderbird email client, as well for non-Mozilla products like Epiphany Web browser. In addition, the framework is easily extensible, supporting numerous add-ons in the form of plug-ins and extensions. The Mozilla project site is **http://www.mozilla.org**, and the site commonly used for plug-in and extension development is **http://www.mozdev.org**.

Web Site	Description
`http://www.mozilla.org`	The Mozilla project
`http://www.mozdev.org`	Mozilla plug-ins and extensions
`http://www.oreillynet.com/mozilla`	Mozilla documentation and news
`http://www.mozillazine.org`	Mozilla news and articles
`http://www.mozillanews.org`	Mozilla news and articles
`http://www.bugzilla.org`	Mozilla bug reporting and tracking system

Table 8-2: Mozilla Resources

The KDE Rekonq Web Browser

Rekonq is the new default Web browser for KDE (see **http://reconq.sourceforge.net** for more details). Rekonq is based on the WebKit layout engine, like Chrome and Apple's Safari. It provides full integration with the KDE Desktop for tasks such as editing and file management (see Figure 8-4).

A navigation bar lets you move through accessed pages on a tab, refresh a site, or enter the address of a new site. On the right side of the navigation bar is a menu button that displays Rekonq browser operations such as open, save, print, panels to display, help, and configuration (see Figure 8-5). The History and Bookmark entries can be displayed in panels to the left of the web site tabs. Rekonq also supports private browsing which keeps no history record, and a Clear Private Data option to remove browsing information and history.

Like Chrome, Rekonq is tab based. Tabs can be reordered with a click-and-drag of their tab thumbnails. To close a tab, click its x button to the right of its name. You add new tabs by clicking on the new tab button to the right of an open tab. The new tab opens to the Favorites page. Should you ever want to return to the Favorites page, just open a new tab (see Figure 8-4).

The Favorites page shows a button bar across the top that lets you choose Favorites, Closed Tabs, Bookmarks, History, and Downloads. Favorites displays icons of your favorite sites, initially showing Google, Kubuntu, KDE UserBase, and KDE Community Forums. Click the Add Favorite button to the right to add a favorite site of your own. A blank icon appears. Click on it to display a button labeled "Set to This Page" and the notice "Please open up the webpage you want to add as favorite." You then enter the site you want to use in the navigation bar and click on the "Set to This Page" button to add that page as the favorite. On the Favorites page the site previewed in the new favorites icon you set up. To remove a favorite, move to that icon and click on the red x that appears to the right of the favorite's name.

Figure 8-4: Rekonq favorites

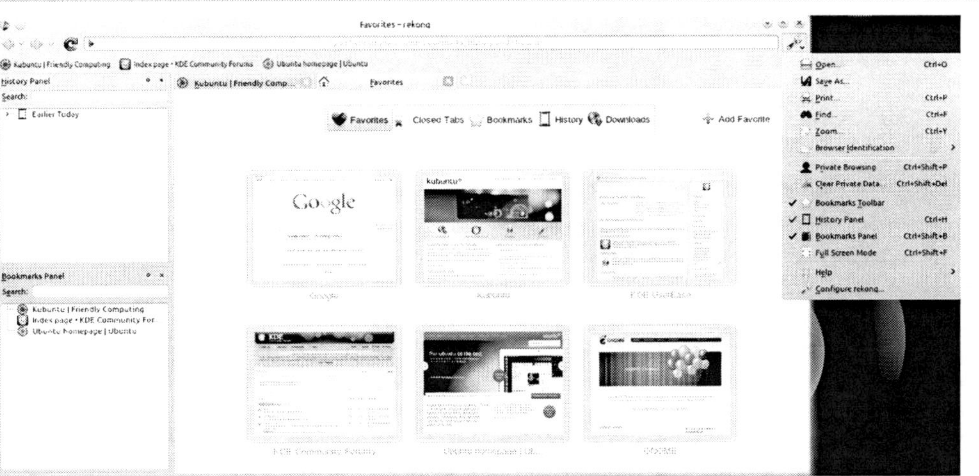

Figure 8-5: Rekonq with panels, bookmarks, and menus

The History tab displays your previous history, with a Clear Private Data button to the right, which you can click to clear your history components such as visited pages, downloads, cookies, and cached pages. To reopen closed tabs, use the Closed Tabs tab. Downloads lists your recent downloads.

You add a page as a bookmark by right-clicking on it and choosing Add Bookmark or by pressing **Ctrl-b**. The bookmark appears on the Bookmark toolbar located above the tabs (see Figure 8-5). The Bookmarks tab accessed from the Favorites page also lists your bookmarks. Click the Edit Bookmarks button to open the Bookmark Editor, which lets you organize your bookmarks, setting up folders for them, deleting bookmarks, or importing bookmarks from other browsers. You can also add new bookmarks or change the names and icons of current ones.

To configure Rekonq, select Configure Rekonq from a Rekonq window Settings menu. The General tab specifies the page displayed on Rekonq at start up, the default being a new tab page (see Figure 8-6). You can set it to your home page or last opened pages. Set your home page in the Home page URL text box. The Tabs tab determines new tab behavior such as displaying your Favorites page in a new tab or opening links in a new tab. Appearance is where you set the default font and font size. WebKit sets WebKit and Plugin settings such as image loading, java support, and storage use. Network controls your cache, cookies, and proxy settings. Ad Block filters ads, which is enabled by default. Shortcuts sets up keyboard shortcuts for Rekonq tasks like those for navigation or tab operations. Web Shortcuts lets you specify your default search provider.

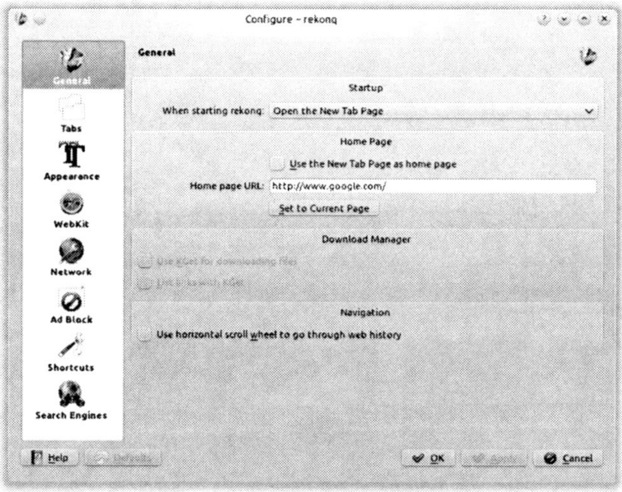

Figure 8-6: Rekonq configuration

Note: The older Konqueror Web browser is still available and you can install from the Ubuntu repository (see **http://www.konqueror.org/** for more details). It supports vertical or horizontal split views, tabbed displays, and a navigation panel. Konqueror can also operate as a file manager and FTP client.

Epiphany

Epiphany is a GNOME Web browser designed to be fast with a simple interface (see Figure 8-7). You can install Epiphany from the Ubuntu Software Center | Internet | Web Browsers page. You can find out more about Epiphany at **http://projects.gnome.org/epiphany/**. Epiphany works well as a simple browser with a clean interface. Epiphany also supports tabs for multiple Web site access.

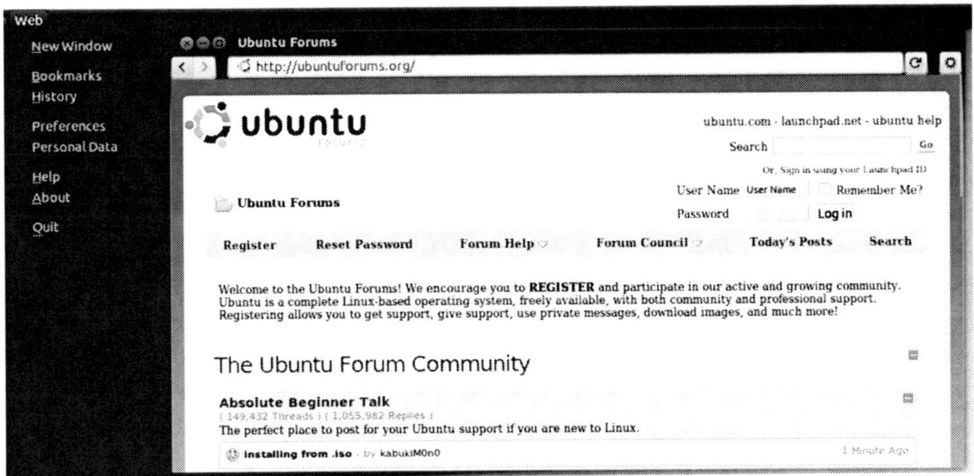

Figure 8-7: Epiphany Web browser

Chromium

Chromium is the open source version of Google's Chrome Web Browser (Ubuntu Software Center | Internet | Web Browsers | Chromium). Chromium provides easy and very secure access to the Web with full Google integration (see Figure 8-8). See **http://www.chromium.org** for more details and support.

Primacy is afforded to tabs. At the top of the Chromium window are your tabs for open Web pages, with a + button at the end to the tabs for opening a new tab. Chromium features a simple toolbar with navigation buttons and a bookmark button (start icon). To close a tab, click the x icon to the right of the tab title.

To the right of the URL box a page button displays a drop-down menu for Web page operations like search, print, and zoom. The tool button (wrench icon) display menu items for browser operations like new tabs, zoom, history, the Bookmark Manager, downloads, and extensions. To configure Chromium select Preferences from this menu to open the Chromium Preferences tab. Here you can set your home page, default search service (Basics tab), themes, password, and autofill options (Personal Stuff tab), and privacy and proxy settings (Under the hood tab).

When you open a new tab, a thumbnail listing of recently closed and most visited sites is displayed. Clicking on a thumbnail move you to that site. On a new tab, the bookmark toolbar is also displayed, which you can use to access a site.

Figure 8-8: Chromium Web browser (Google Chrome)

Lynx and ELinks: Line-Mode Browsers

Ubuntu features two line mode browsers, Lynx and Elinks, which you can use from a command line interface. Lynx is supported by Ubuntu, whereas Elinks is not. You can install both from the Ubuntu Software Center | Internet | Web Browsers page. On these browsers, a Web page is displayed as text only. A text page can contain links to other Internet resources but does not display graphics, video, or sound. Except for the display limitations, Lynx and Elinks are fully functional Web browsers. You can also use them to download files or access local pages. All information on the Web is still accessible to you. Because they do not require as much overhead as desktop-based browsers, they can operate much faster, quickly displaying Web page text. To start the Lynx browser, you enter **lynx** on the command line and press ENTER (you can also use a terminal window). ELinks includes features such as frame, form, and table support. It also supports SSL secure encryption. To start ELinks, enter the **elinks** command in a terminal window. You can find out more about lynx at **http://lynx.isc.org**, and about elinks at **http://elinks.or.cz**.

Java for Linux

To develop Java applications, use Java tools, and run many Java products, you use the Java 2 Software Development Kit (SDK) and the Java 2 Runtime Environment (JRE). The SDK is a superset of the JRE, adding development tools like compilers and debuggers. Together with other technologies like the Java API, they make up the Java 2 Platform, Standard Edition (J2SE).

Sun (now owned by Oracle) has open sourced Java as the OpenJDK project and supports and distributes Linux versions. The JRE subset can be installed as OpenJRE. They are directly supported by Ubuntu as packages on the main repository. You can install them with the Synaptic Package Manager or from the Ubuntu Software Center | Internet | OpenJDK Java 6. On Ubuntu, the **openjdk-6-jre** installs the Java runtime environment, and **openjdk-6-jdk** installs both the JRE and the Java development tools. Java packages and applications are listed in Table 8-3.

Application	Description
Java Development Kit, OpenJDK	An open source Java development environment with a compiler, interpreters, debugger, and more (include the JRE), **http://openjdk.java.net**. Included on the Ubuntu main repository **openjdk-6-jdk**
Java Runtime Environment, OpenJRE	An open source Java runtime environment, including the Java virtual machine, included on the Ubuntu main repository, **openjdk-6-jre**. **http://openjdk.java.net**
Java Platform Standard Edition (JSE)	Complete Java collection, including JRE, JDK, and API, **http://java.sun.com/javase**.
GNU Java Compiler	GNU Public Licensed Java Compiler (GCJ) to compile Java programs, **http://gcc.gnu.org/java**. Included on Ubuntu main repository, **gcj**.
Jakarta Project	Apache Software Foundation project for open source Java applications, **http://jakarta.apache.org**.
CACAO	A just-in-time (**jit**) compiler only implementation of the Java Virtual Machine (JVM), included on the Ubuntu main repository, **www.cacaojvm.org**.
Classpath	GNU license Java open source libraries, Universe repository, **www.gnu.org/software/classpath**

Table 8-3: Java Packages and Java Web Applications

Several compatible GNU packages (Java-like) are provided that allow you to run Java applets using GNU free Java support. These include GNU Java compiler (**gcj**) and the Eclipse Java compiler (**ecj**).

You also can install the Sun version of the JRE, now included in the Ubuntu multiverse repository. Use the Synaptic Package Manager and search on "sun-java6", like the **sun-java6-jre** and **sun-java6-jdk** packages. These are Debian versions packaged for installation on Ubuntu (Canonical Partners repository). Also available is CACAO, the open source GNU licensed Java Virtual Machine that uses the compiler only, instead of the interpreter, **icedtea-6-jre-cacao** and **cacao** (**www.cacaojvm.org**).

For those that want an entire open source and GNU licensed version of the Java libraries, you can install the classpath Java libraries, also available on the Ubuntu Universe repository, **www.gnu.org/software/classpath**.

BitTorrent Clients (transmission)

GNOME and KDE provide very effective BitTorrent clients. With BitTorrent, you can download very large files quickly in a shared distributed download operation where several users participate in downloading different parts of a file, sending their parts of the download to other participants, known as peers. Instead of everyone trying to access a few central servers, all peers participating in the BitTorrent operation become sources for the file being downloaded. Certain peers function as seeders, those who have already downloaded the file, but continue to send parts to those who need them.

Ubuntu will install and use the GNOME BitTorrent client, Transmission, accessible from the Internet dash. For Kubuntu you can use the Ktorrent BitTorrent client. To perform a BitTorrent download you need the BitTorrent file for the file you want to download. The BitTorrent file for the Ubuntu Alternate CD iso image is **ubuntu-12.04-alternate-amd64.iso.torrent**. When you download the file from the **http://releases.ubuntu.com** site, you will be prompted to either open it directly with Transmission or save it to a file.

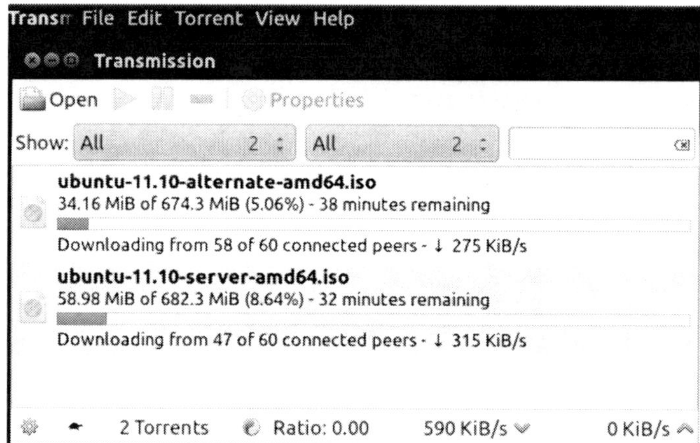

Figure 8-9: Transmission BitTorrent client

Transmission can handle several torrents at once. On the toolbar are buttons for starting, pausing, and remove a download. The Add button can be used to load a BitTorrent file (**.torrent**), setting up a download. You also can drag-and-drop a torrent file to the Transmission window. When you first open a torrent file, the Torrent Options window opens where you can specify the destination folder and the priority. The option to start the download automatically will be selected by default. Figure 8-9 shows Transmission with two BitTorrent operations set up, one of which is active. A progress bar shows how much of the file has been downloaded.

You could set up Transmission to manage several BitTorrent operations, of which only a few may be active, others paused, and still others that have finished but continue to functions as seeders. From the first drop-down menu, you can select All, Active, Downloading, Seeding, Paused, Finished, and Queued torrents. You can also choose those verifying and those that have errors. From the second menu you can choose Trackers, public or private torrents (Privacy), and select by priority (high, normal, or low).

To remove a torrent, right-click on it and select Remove. Choose Delete Files and Remove to remove what you have downloaded so far.

To see more information about a torrent, select it and then click the Properties button (see Figure 8-10). This opens a Properties window with tabs for Information, Peers, Tracker, Files, and Options. On the Information tab, the Activity section shows statistics like the progress, times, and errors, and the Details section shows the origin, comment, and locations of the download folder. Peers show all the peers participating in the download. Tracker displays the location of the tracker, the server that manages the torrent operation. Files shows the progress of the file download (a torrent could download more than one file). The Options tab lets you set bandwidth and connection parameters, limiting the download or upload, and the number of peers.

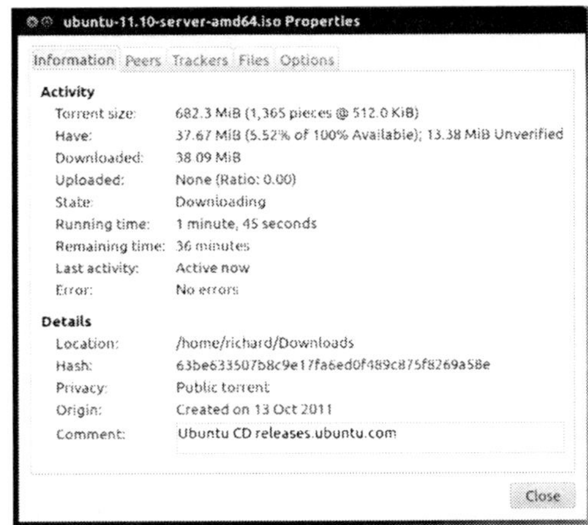

Figure 8-10: Transmission BitTorrent client properties

FTP Clients

With File Transfer Protocol (FTP) clients, you can connect to a corresponding FTP site and download files from it. These sites feature anonymous logins that let any user access their files. Basic FTP client capabilities are incorporated into the Dolphin (KDE) and Nautilus (GNOME) file managers. You can use a file manager window to access an FTP site and drag files to local directories to download them. Effective FTP clients are also now incorporated into most Web browsers, making Web browsers the primary downloading tool. Firefox in particular has strong FTP download capabilities.

Although file managers and Web browsers provide effective access to public (anonymous login) sites, to access private sites, you may need a stand-alone FTP client like curl, wget, Filezilla, gFTP, lftp, or **ftp**. These clients let you enter user names and passwords with which you can access a private FTP site. The stand-alone clients are also useful for large downloads from public FTP sites, especially those with little or no Web display support. Popular Linux FTP clients are listed in Table 8-4.

Network File Transfer: FTP

With File Transfer Protocol (FTP) clients, you can transfer extremely large files directly from one site to another (see Table 8-4). FTP can handle both text and binary files. FTP performs a remote login to another account on another system connected to you on a network. Once logged in to that other system, you can transfer files to and from it. To log in, you need to know the login name and password for the account on the remote system. Many sites on the Internet allow public access using FTP, however. Such sites serve as depositories for large files anyone can access and download. These sites are often referred to as FTP sites, and in many cases, their Internet addresses begin with the term ftp, such as **ftp.gnome.org**. These public sites allow anonymous FTP login from any user. For the login name, you use the word "anonymous," and for the password, you use your email address. You can then transfer files from that site to your own system.

FTP Clients	Description
Dolphin	KDE file manager
Nautilus	GNOME file manager
gFTP	GNOME FTP client, **gftp-gtk**
ftp	Command line FTP client
lftp	Command line FTP client capable of multiple connections
curl	Internet transfer client (FTP and HTTP)
Filezilla	Linux version of the open source Filezilla ftp client (Universe repository).

Table 8-4: Linux FTP Clients

Several FTP protocol are available for accessing sites that support them. The original FTP protocol is used for most anonymous sites. FTP transmissions can also be encrypted using SSH2, the SFTP protocol. More secure connections may use FTPS for TLS/SSL encryption. Some sites support a simplified version of FTP called File Service Protocol, FSP. FTP clients may support different protocols like gFTP for FSP and Filezilla for TLS/SSL. Most clients support both FTP and SSH2.

Web Browser–Based FTP

You can access an FTP site and download files from it with any Web browser. Browsers are useful for locating individual files, though not for downloading a large set of files. A Web browser is effective for checking out an FTP site to see what files are listed there. When you access an FTP site with a Web browser, the entire list of files in a directory is listed as a Web page. You can move to a subdirectory by clicking its entry. You can easily browse through an FTP site to download files. To download a file, click the download link. This will start the transfer operation, opening a dialog for selecting your local directory and the name for the file. The default name is the same as on the remote system. On many browsers, you can manage your downloads with a download manager, which will let you cancel a download operation in progress or remove other downloads requested. The manager will show the time remaining, the speed, and the amount transferred for the current download.

GNOME Desktop FTP: Connect to Server

The easiest way to download files is to use the built-in FTP capabilities of the GNOME file manager, Nautilus. On GNOME, the desktop file manager has a built-in FTP capability much like the KDE file manager. The FTP operation has been seamlessly integrated into standard desktop file operations. Downloading files from an FTP site is as simple as dragging files from one directory window to another, where one of the directories happens to be located on a remote FTP site. Use the GNOME file manager (Nautilus) to access a remote FTP site, listing files in the remote directory, just as local files are. In a file manager's Location bar (**Ctrl-l** or GO | Location), enter the FTP site's URL following the prefix **ftp://** and press ENTER. A dialog opens prompting you to specify how you want to connect. You can connect anonymously for a public FTP site, or connect as a user supplying your user name and password (private site). You can also choose to remember the password.

For more access options such as a secure SSH connection, windows share, and Secure Web (HTTPS), you can use the Connect to Server dialog (see Figure 8-11). To open the Connect to Server dialog, choose File | Connect to Server menu item on any file manager window, or on the Desktop applications menu. From the Service type menu you can select the service type. Entry options change accordingly, with the "FTP (with login)" adding an entry for the user name. Click the Connect button to access the site.

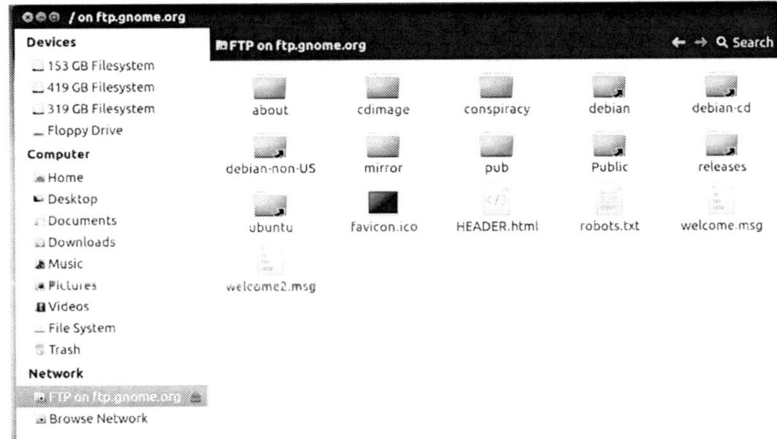
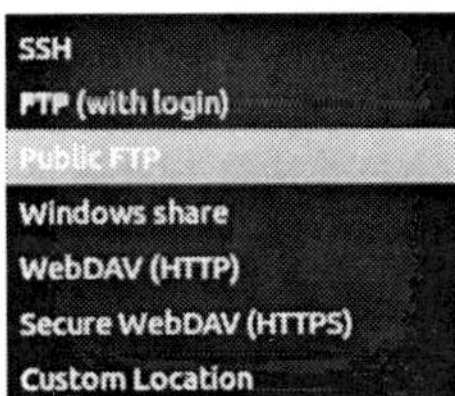

Figure 8-11: GNOME FTP access with Connect to Server and the file manager

The top directory of the remote FTP site will be displayed in a file manager window. Use the file manager to progress through the remote FTP site's directory tree until you find the file you want. Then open another window for the local directory to which you want the remote files copied. In the window showing the FTP files, select those you want to download. Then click and drag those files to the window for the local directory. As files are downloaded, a dialog appears showing the progress.

The file manager window's sidebar (Network section) will list an entry for the FTP site accessed. An eject button is shown to the right of the FTP site's name. To disconnect from the site, click this button. The FTP entry will disappear along with the FTP sites icons and file listings.

The KDE File Managers: Konqueror and Dolphin

On the KDE Desktop, the desktop file managers (Konqueror and Dolphin) have built-in FTP capability. The FTP operation has been seamlessly integrated into standard desktop file operations. Downloading files from an FTP site is as simple as copying files by dragging them from one directory window to another, with one of the directories located on a remote FTP site. On KDE, you can use a file manager window to access a remote FTP site. Files in the remote directory are listed just as your local files are. To download files from an FTP site, you open a window to access that site, entering the URL for the FTP site in the window's location box. Use the **ftp://** protocol for FTP access. Once connected, open the directory you want, and then open another window for the local directory to which you want the remote files copied. In the window showing the FTP files, select the ones you want to download. Then click-and-drag those files to the window for the local directory. A pop-up menu appears with choices for Copy, Link, or Move. Select Copy.

The selected files are then downloaded. Another window opens, showing the download progress and displaying the name of each file in turn, along with a bar indicating the percentage downloaded so far.

Filezilla

Filezilla is an open source FTP client originally implemented on Windows systems (**http://www.filezilla.org**). The Linux version for Ubuntu is available on the Ubuntu Universe repository. Use the Synaptic Package Manager to install it or install it from the Ubuntu Software Center | Internet | File Sharing | FileZilla. Once installed, you can access it from the Internet dash. The interface displays a left and right pane for local and remote folders. You navigate through folder trees, with the files of a selected folder displayed below. To download a file, right-click on a file in the Remote site pane (right) and select Download. To upload, right-click on the file in the Local site pane (left) and select Upload. Text boxes at the top let you specify the host, username, password, and port. A Quick connect dropdown menu will connect to a preconfigured site.

To configure a remote site connection use the Site Manager (File | Site Manager). In the Site Manager window, click on the New Site button to create a new site connection. Four configuration tabs become active: General, Advanced, Transfer settings, and Charset. On the General tab, you can specify the host, user, password, and account. The server type drop down menu lets you specify a particular FTP protocol like SFTP for SSH encrypted transmissions or FTPS for TLS/SSL encryption.

gFTP

The gFTP program is a simpler GNOME FTP client designed to let you make standard FTP file transfers. The package name for gFTP is **gftp-gtk**, located in the Ubuntu main repository. You can install it from Ubuntu Software Center | Internet | File Sharing | gFTP. You can access it from the Internet dash.

The gFTP window consists of several panes. The top-left pane lists files in your local directory, and the top-right pane lists your remote directory. Subdirectories have folder icons preceding their names. The parent directory can be referenced by the double period entry (**..**) with an up arrow at the top of each list. Double-click a directory entry to access it. The pathnames for all directories are displayed in boxes above each pane. A drop down menu to the far right lets you specify the FTP protocol to use such as FTP for a standard transmission, SSH2 for SSH encrypted connections, and FSP for File Service Protocol transmissions.

Two buttons between the panes are used for transferring files. The left arrow button, <-, downloads selected files in the remote directory, and the right arrow button, ->, uploads files from the local directory. To download a file, click it in the right pane and then click the left arrow button, <-. When the file is downloaded, its name appears in the left pane, your local directory. Menus across the top of the window can be used to manage your transfers. A connection manager enables you to enter login information about a specific site. You can specify whether to perform an anonymous login or provide a username and password. Click Connect to connect to that site. A drop-down menu for sites lets you choose the site you want. Interrupted downloads can be restarted later.

wget

The wget tool lets you access Web and FTP sites for particular directories and files. Directories can be recursively downloaded, letting you copy an entire Web site. The **wget** command takes as its option the URL for the file or directory you want. Helpful options include **-q** for quiet, **-r** for recursive (directories), **-b** to download in the background, and **-c** to continue downloading an interrupted file. One of the drawbacks is that your URL reference can be very complex. You have to know the URL already. You cannot interactively locate an item as you would with an FTP client. The following would download the Ubuntu Install DVD in the background.

```
wget -b ftp://cdimages.ubuntu.com/releases/precise/release/ubuntu-12.04-dvd-amd64.iso
```

With the Gnome Wget tool (**gwget**) you can run wget downloads using a desktop interface.

curl

The **curl** Internet client operates much like **wget**, but with much more flexibility. With curl, you can specify multiple URLs on its command line. You can also use braces to specify multiple matching URLs, like different Web sites with the same domain name. You can list the different Web site host names within braces, followed by their domain name (or vice versa). You can also use brackets to specify a range of multiple items. This can be very useful for downloading archived files that have the same root name with varying extensions, like different issues of the same magazine. **curl** can download using any protocol, and will try to intelligently guess the protocol to use if none is provided. Check the **curl** man page for more information.

ftp

The **ftp** client uses a command line interface, and it has an extensive set of commands and options you can use to manage your FTP transfers. It is the original FTP client used on Unix and Linux systems. See the **ftp** man page for more details. Alternatively, you can use **sftp** for more secure access. The **sftp** client has the same commands as **ftp**, but provides SSH (Secure SHell) encryption. Also, if you installed the Kerberos clients (**krb5-clients**), a Kerberized version of ftp is setup, which provides for secure authentication from Kerberos servers. It has the same name as the **ftp** client (an **ftp** link to Kerberos **ftp**) and the same commands.

You start the **ftp** client by entering the command `ftp` at a shell prompt. If you want to connect to a specific site, you can include the name of that site on the command line after the **ftp** keyword. Otherwise, you need to connect to the remote system with the ftp command `open`. You are then prompted for the name of the remote system with the prompt "(to)". When you enter the remote system name, ftp connects you to the system and then prompts you for a login name. After entering the login name, you are prompted for the password. In the next example, the user connects to the remote system **garnet** and logs in to the **robert** account:

```
$ ftp
ftp> open
(to) garnet
Connected to garnet.berkeley.edu.
220 garnet.berkeley.edu FTP server ready.
```

```
Name (garnet.berkeley.edu:root): robert
password required
Password:
user robert logged in
ftp>
```

Once logged in, you can execute Linux commands on either the remote system or your local system. You execute a command on your local system in ftp by preceding the command with an exclamation point. Any Linux commands without an exclamation point are executed on the remote system. One exception exists to this rule. Whereas you can change directories on the remote system with the **cd** command, to change directories on your local system, you need to use a special ftp command called **lcd** (local **cd**). In the next example, the first command lists files in the remote system, while the second command lists files in the local system:

```
ftp> ls
ftp> !ls
```

The ftp program provides a basic set of commands for managing files and directories on your remote site, provided you have the permission to do so. You can use **mkdir** to create a remote directory, and **rmdir** to remove one. Use the **delete** command to erase a remote file. With the **rename** command, you can change the names of files. You close your connection to a system with the **close** command. You can then open another connection if you want. To end the ftp session, use the **quit** or **bye** command.

```
ftp> close
ftp> bye
Good-bye
$
```

To transfer files to and from the remote system, use the **get** and **put** commands. The **get** command receives files from the remote system to your local system, and the **put** command sends files from your local system to the remote system. In a sense, your local system gets files *from* the remote and puts files *to* the remote. In the next example, the file **weather** is sent from the local system to the remote system using the **put** command:

```
ftp> put weather
PORT command successful.
ASCII data connection
ASCII Transfer complete.
ftp>
```

lftp

The **lftp** program is an enhanced FTP client with advanced features such as the abilities to download mirror sites and to run several FTP operations in the background at the same time. You can install it from Ubuntu Software Center | System | Sophisticated command-line FTP/HTTP client programs|

It uses a command set similar to that for the ftp client. You use **get** and **mget** commands to download files, with the **-o** option to specify local locations for them. Use **lcd** and **cd** to change local and remote directories.

When you connect to a site, you can queue commands with the **queue** command, setting up a list of FTP operations to perform. With this feature, you could queue several download operations to a site. The queue can be reordered and entries deleted if you wish. You can also connect to several sites and set up a queue for each one. The **mirror** command lets you maintain a local version of a mirror site. You can download an entire site or just update newer files, as well as removing files no longer present on the mirror.

You can tailor lftp with options set in the **.lftprc** file. System-wide settings are placed in the **/etc/lftp.conf** file. Here, you can set features like the prompt to use and your anonymous password. The **.lftp** directory holds support files for command history, logs, bookmarks, and startup commands. The lftp program also supports the **.netrc** file, checking it for login information.

9. Social Networking

Messaging Menu

Broadcast Messages: Gwibber

Instant Messenger: Empathy and Pidgin

VoIP: Ekiga and Skype

KDE Social Desktop

Ubuntu One

Ubuntu provides integrated social networking support for broadcasting, IM (Instant Messenger), and VoIP (Voice over Internet). User can communicate directly with other users on your network (see Table 9-5). These applications are installed automatically and are ready to use when you first start up your Ubuntu system. The Messaging menu lets you access your social networking applications directly. To access broadcast services like Twitter and Facebook, you also can use the Gwibber application, broadcasting short messages across the Internet. Instant messenger (IM) clients allows users on the same IM system to communicate anywhere across the Internet. With Voice over the Internet Protocol applications, you can speak over Internet connections.

The Messaging menu

The messaging menu lets you access messaging tasks for email, instant messenger, and broadcasting applications using Empathy, Thunderbird, and Gwibber (see figure 9-1). You can also access your Ubuntu One account. For Empathy instant messaging, you can set your status (available, away, busy, invisible, and offline). Selecting Chat opens the Empathy instance messenger. In the Broadcast section, Update Status opens a broadcast message box where you can enter a message to send on Twitter or Facebook. You can also check messages, replies, and private messages on Gwibber. In the Mail section, Compose New Message opens Thunderbird with a new message window. When a new email, chat, or broadcast message arrives, the message menu icon will turn blue.

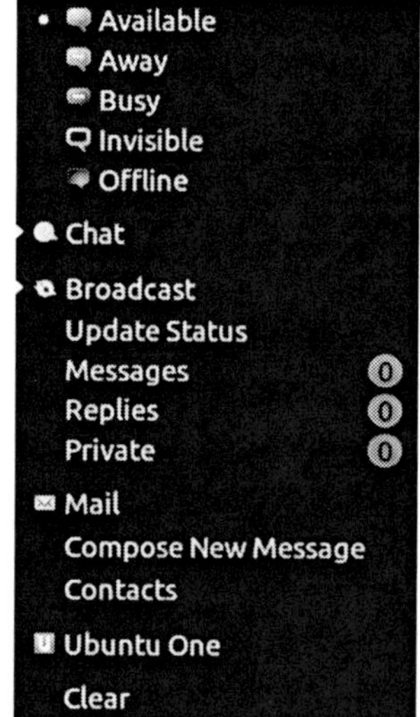

Figure 9-1: Messaging Menu

For applications that are not configured yet, a setup entry is listed, such as "Set Up Broadcast Account" for configuring Gwibber and "Set Up Mail" to configure Thunderbird (see Figure 9-2). Once configured, the menu entries let you access the applications to perform messaging tasks such as sending email and checking broadcast messages.

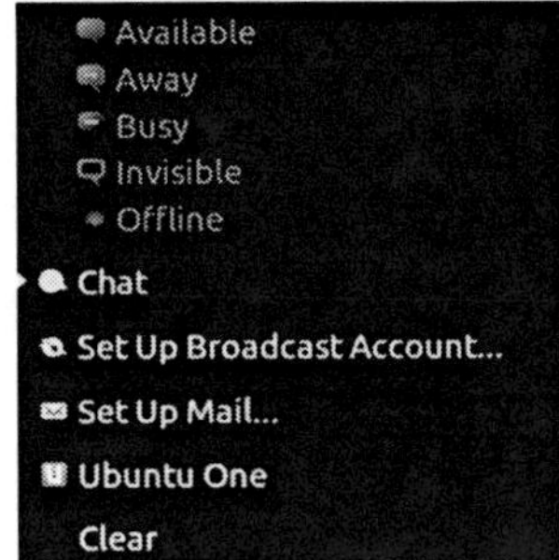

Figure 9-2: Messaging Menu (unconfigured)

Broadcast Services

Ubuntu provides integrated support for social broadcasts (micro-blogging) based on the Gwibber project. You access broadcast accounts using the Gwibber Social Client, accessible from the Internet dash. The first time you use Gwibber, the "Broadcast Accounts" dialog is opened first letting you add a broadcast service. The Gwibber window will then open (see Figure 9-3). : Gwibber

The toolbar lists icons for Home, Messages, Replies, Private Messages, Attachments, Searches, Users, and New Message. A triangle below the icon indicates the currently selected one. The Home icon lists postings from your authorized services as they arrive (see Figure 9-3). Searches displays a search box. Users lets you search for and select users on Twitter.

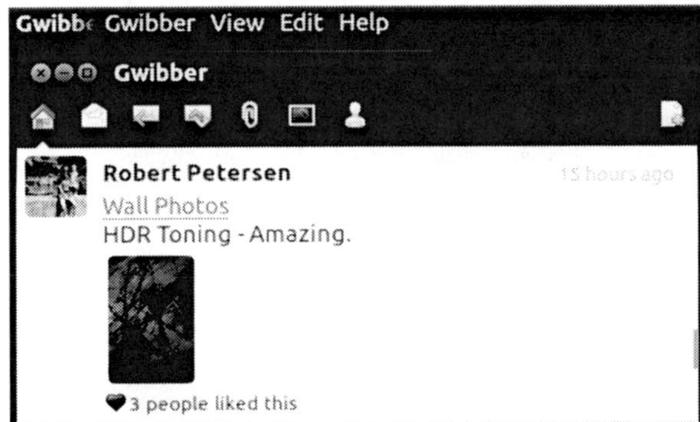

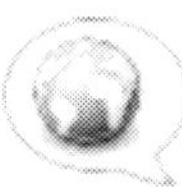

Figure 9-3: Gwibber broadcast messages

To send a message, click the New Message icon to open a text box where you can enter the message. Icons for the available services will be listed below the text box. Click the service you want to send the message with. Clicking toggles a service on and off. As you type, the number of remaining available characters to the right will count down. When ready click the Send button.

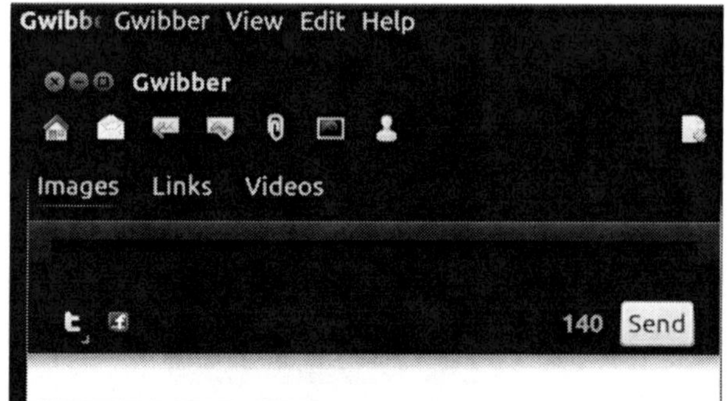

Figure 9-4: Gwibber messaging

If you have no accounts configured, Gwibber will open a Broadcast Accounts dialog (see Figure 9-5). You can add or edit accounts later by selecting Account from the Edit menu (Edit | Accounts) on the Social broadcast message window. On the Broadcast Accounts dialog, click the plus button (+) below the list of accounts to open a pane with an "Add new account for" menu and an Add button. From the menu, you can select the type of service you want such as Twitter, Identica, or Facebook. Click the Add button to display the configuration entries for your selection. The Account Settings section shows account status options you can select and appearance features like the message color (Account Color). Then click the Authorize button to open an authorization page for that service, usually requesting your email and password. Once authorized the service will appear in the list of accounts to the left.

To configure Gwibber, select Preferences from the Edit menu to display the Broadcast Messaging Preferences dialog with tabs for Options and Messages. There are options for notifications and update frequency. For messages you can choose to show your real name or shorten pasted URLs.

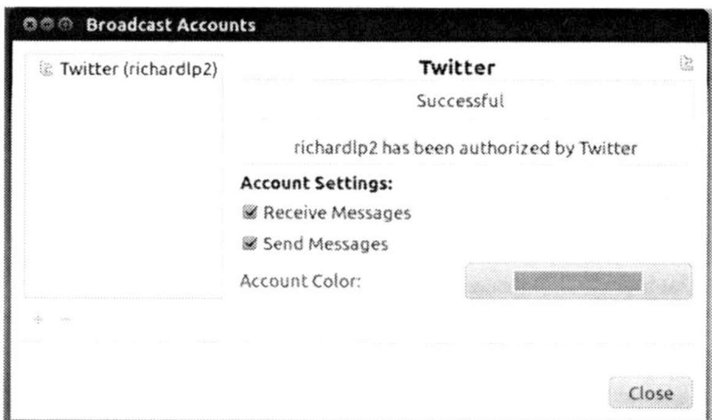

Figure 9-5: Gwibber broadcast accounts

Instant Messenger: Empathy, Kopete, and Pidgin

Instant messenger (IM) clients allow users on the same IM service to communicate anywhere across the Internet (see Table 9-1). Currently some of the major IM services are AIM

(AOL), Microsoft Network (MSN), Yahoo, ICQ, and Jabber. Some use an XML protocol called XMPP, Extensible Messaging and Presence Protocol (**www.xmpp.org**).

Clients	Description
Ekiga	VoIP application
Skype	VoIP application (Partner repository)
empathy	GNOME 2.24 instant messenger
Kopete	KDE 4 instant messenger client
Pidgin	Older instant messenger client used in previous releases and still available.
Jabber	Jabber IM client (XMPP)
Finch	Command line cursor-based IM client
Konversation	KDE IRC client

Table 9-1: Instant Messenger, Talk, and VoIP Clients

The Messaging menu will display active IM options on its menu: Available, Away, Busy, Invisible, and Offline (see Figure 9-1). A dot appears next to the currently active option. You can use this menu to change your IM status quickly.

Empathy

Ubuntu 12.04 uses Empathy as the default IM application. Empathy is the GNOME replacement for Pidgin. Empathy is based on the Telepathy framework, which is designed to provide IM support to any application that wants an IM capability. All major IM services are supported, including Facebook Chat, Google Talk, AIM, myspace, Windows Live (MSN), zephyr, Jabber (XMPP), ICQ, and Yahoo.

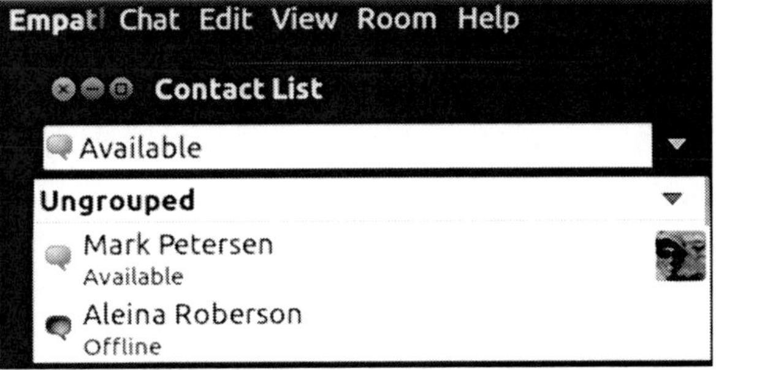

Figure 9-6: Empathy IM Client

Empathy is accessible from the Internet dash (see Figure 9-6). Click the Add button on the Accounts dialog to add new accounts (Edit | Accounts). If you have no accounts configured, the "Messaging and VoIP Accounts Assistant" wizard starts up. You are first prompted to specify if you already have an account from another chat application, if you want to create a new account, or if you just want to see who is nearby. For a new account, you select a type, ID, and password, and then on the following screen your personal information. For an account from another chat service you have options such as Facebook, Google Talk, AIM, and MSN. Should you add more accounts, the accounts dialog adds a new entry. You then choose the protocol (chat service) and provide the login information (see Figure 9-7). The login information will be different according to the chat service you choose

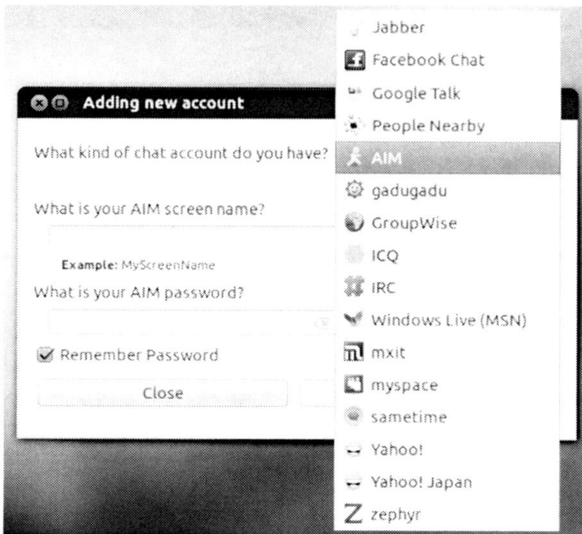

Figure 9-7: Empathy IM Client account set up

Facebook requires only a username and password. Others, such as MSN and AIM have an advanced expansion set of entries where you can specify the server and port. A drop down menu on the Contact List window lets you select your status, like Available, Busy, Away, Invisible, or Offline. You can specify a custom message for a particular status.

Telepathy provides IM support with connection managers, making IM services easy to maintain and add. Current connection managers include telepathy-gabble for Jabber/XMPP, telepathy-idle for IRC, telepathy-butterfly for MSN, telepathy-salut for local network (link-local) XMPP connections, telepathy-sofiasip for SIP, and telepathy-haze for Pidgin's Yahoo, AIM, and other support (libpurple) (**http://telepathy.freedesktop.org**).

Pidgin

Pidgin is the older IM application used on previous Ubuntu releases. You can install it if you want (Ubuntu Software Center | Internet | Chat | Pidgin Internet Messenger). Pidgin is a multi-protocol IM client that works with most IM protocols including AIM, MSN, Jabber, Google Talk, ICQ, IRC, Yahoo, MySpaceIM, and more. Pidgin will be accessible from the Internet dash. Pidgin will open a Buddy List window with menus for Buddies, Accounts, Tools, and Help (see Figure 9-8). Use the Buddies menu to send a message or join a chat. The Accounts menu lets you configure and add accounts. The Tools menu provides configuration features such as preferences, plugin selection, privacy options, and sound.

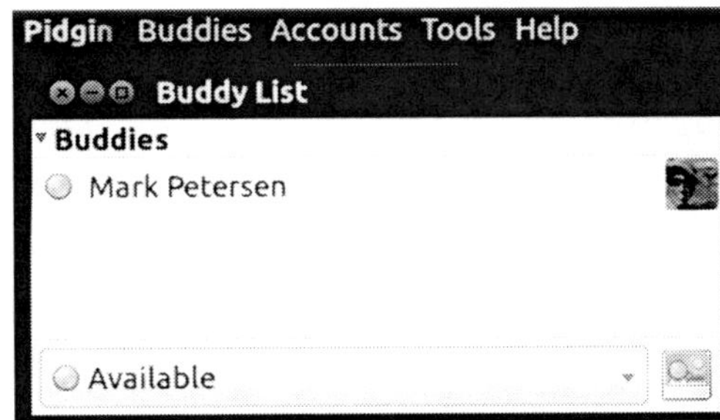

Figure 9-8: Pidgin Buddy List

The first time you start Pidgin, the Add Account window is displayed with Basic, Advanced, and Proxy tabs for setting up an account. Later you can edit the account by selecting it in the Accounts window (Accounts | Manage) and clicking the Modify button.

To create a new account, select Manage Accounts from the Accounts menu (Accounts | Manage). This opens the Accounts dialog, which lists your current accounts. Click the Add button to open the Add Account dialog with a Basic, Advanced, and Proxy tabs. On the Basic panel, you choose the protocol from a pop-up menu that shows items such as AIM, Bonjour, MySpaceIM, Yahoo!, and IRC, and then enter the appropriate account information. You can also select a buddy icon to use for the account. On the Advanced tab, you specify the server and network connection settings. Many protocols will have a server entered already. The configuration entries for both the Basic and Advanced tabs will change depending on the protocol. On the Proxy tab you can enter specific proxy server host and connection information, should your network use a proxy.

To edit an existing account, click on its entry in the Accounts menu and select Edit Account to open a Modify Account dialog with the same Basic, Advanced, and Proxy tabs. Make your changes and click Save. You can also select Accounts | Manage Accounts to open the Accounts dialog where you can select the accounts you want to modify.

To configure your setup, select Preferences from the Tools menu (Tools | Preferences) to open the Preferences dialog where you can set options for logging, sounds, themes, and the interface display. You can find out more about Pidgin at **http://pidgin.im**. Pidgin is a GNOME front end that used the libpurple library for is actual IM tasks (formerly libgaim). The libpurple library is used by many different IM applications such as Finch.

Kopete

For KDE you can use Kopete, the KDE Instant Messenger client. Kopete features a simple interface with a Status menu for selecting your availability such as Available, Away, and Busy. You can also add a new status, giving it your own name and message. All the major services are supported, including XMPP, Google Talk, AIM, ICQ, and MSN Messenger. See the Kopete Handbook, accessible from the Help menu for detailed instructions.

VoIP Applications

Ubuntu provides two popular VoIP applications: Ekiga, which is open source, and Skype, which is proprietary (available through the Partners repository).

Ekiga

Ekiga is GNOME's VoIP application providing Internet IP Telephone and video conferencing support (see Figure 9-9), **http://www.ekiga.org**. Ekiga supports both the H.323 and SIP (Session Initiation Protocol) protocols. It is compatible with Microsoft's NetMeeting. H.323 is a comprehensive protocol that includes the digital broadcasting protocols such as digital video broadcast (DVB) and H.261 for video streaming, as well as the supporting protocols like the H.450 series for managing calls. You can access Ekiga from the Internet dash. Ekiga has panel status icons that display circles indicating Online, Away, and Do Not Disturb.

Figure 9-9: Ekiga VoIP

To use Ekiga you will need a SIPaddress. You can obtain a free address from **http://www.ekiga.org**. You will first have to subscribe to the service. When you first start Ekiga, the Ekiga Configuration Assistant prompts you to configure your connection (SIP address, Callout account if you wish, connection type, and audio and video devices). Here you can provide information like contact information, your connection method, sound driver, and video device. Use the address book to connect to another Ekiga user. A white pages directory lets you search for people who are also using Ekiga.

Skype

Skype is an Ubuntu supported package software package which you can install from the Ubuntu Software Center | System | VOIP and instant messaging client (search on Skype). Skype is now part of the Ubuntu Partner repository.

Once installed, you can access Skype from the Internet dash. When you first start Skype, you are asked to accept a user agreement. The interface is similar to the Windows version (see Figure 9-10). A Skype panel icon will appear on the panel, once you start Skype. You can use it to access Skype throughout your session. Click to open Skype and right-click to display a menu from which you can change your status, sign out, access options, list contact groups, and start a conference call. The panel icon changes according to your status.

Also, the **pidgin-skype** package provides a Skype plugin, which will let you use Ubuntu applications like Pidgin, Finch, and Empathy to operate through Skype connections.

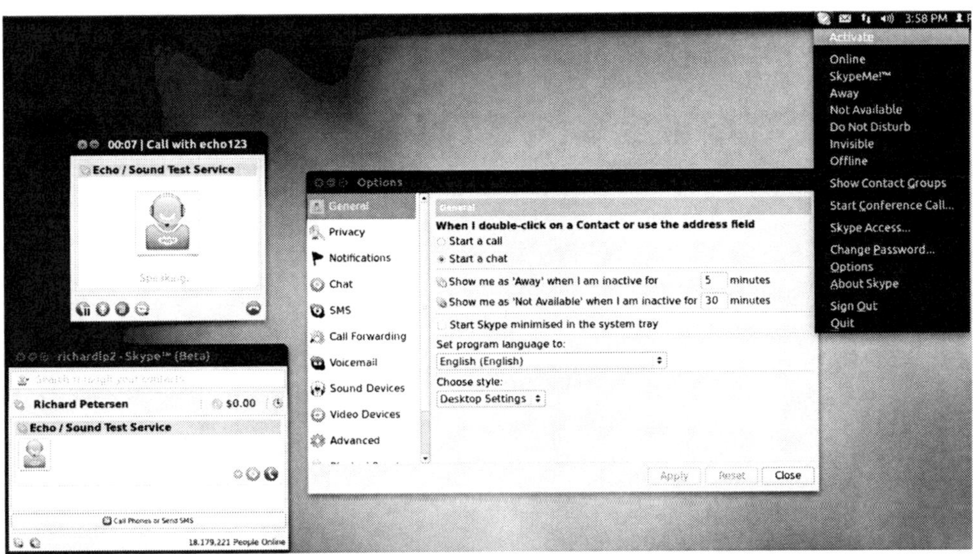

Figure 9-10: Skype VoIP and panel icon

KDE Social Desktop

KDE provides a set of Internet applications as part of the KDE Social Desktop initiative. The social desktop is based on a Web API called the Open Collaboration Services (OCS) that allows applications to interface easily with Internet services like blogging and twitter (**http://freedesktop.org/wiki/Specifications/open-collaboration-services**). KDE provides a data engine for Plasma widgets supporting social desktop features. In effect, it establishes an open source method for social networking. In addition, the Geolocation data engine allows plasmoids to detect and respond to user geographic locations. Currently the social desktop supports plasmoids for microblogging, knowledge bases, messaging, and social networking (see Figure 9-11). For Facebook, add the Facebook plasmoid.

The Microblogging plasmoid (KDE uBlog) is initially displayed on the desktop with a Configure button. Click the button to open the Microblogging Settings dialog. The Kubuntu service is selected by default using the **identi.ca** microblogging site. You can configure access to Twitter by selecting the twitter service instead from the Service URL drop-down menu. Once configured, the uBlog plasmoid will display an emblem for the service and a text box for entering messages. For Facebook, add the Facebook plasmoid.

You configure Social Desktop support by opening System Settings and choosing Account Details in the "Common Appearance and Behavior" section, and then choose the Social Desktop tab (see Figure 9-11). Here you select a provider (currently there is only one, openDesktop.org). On the Login tab, enter your user name and password, for new users use the Register tab to create an openDesktop.org account. You can then use openDesktop plasmoids including Community, which lets you detect the location of friends, and Social News, which lists latest news of social users. On the Community configuration dialog, you specify your location. The Geolocation engine will detect your system's location automatically. The Community plasmoid also detects the location of other KDE users near you, the Nearby tab. You can choose to add one as a friend and send a message. Moving your mouse over a name displays a person icon for add and removing the person as a friend, and a mail icon for sending a message. Clicking on the name displays information about the user.

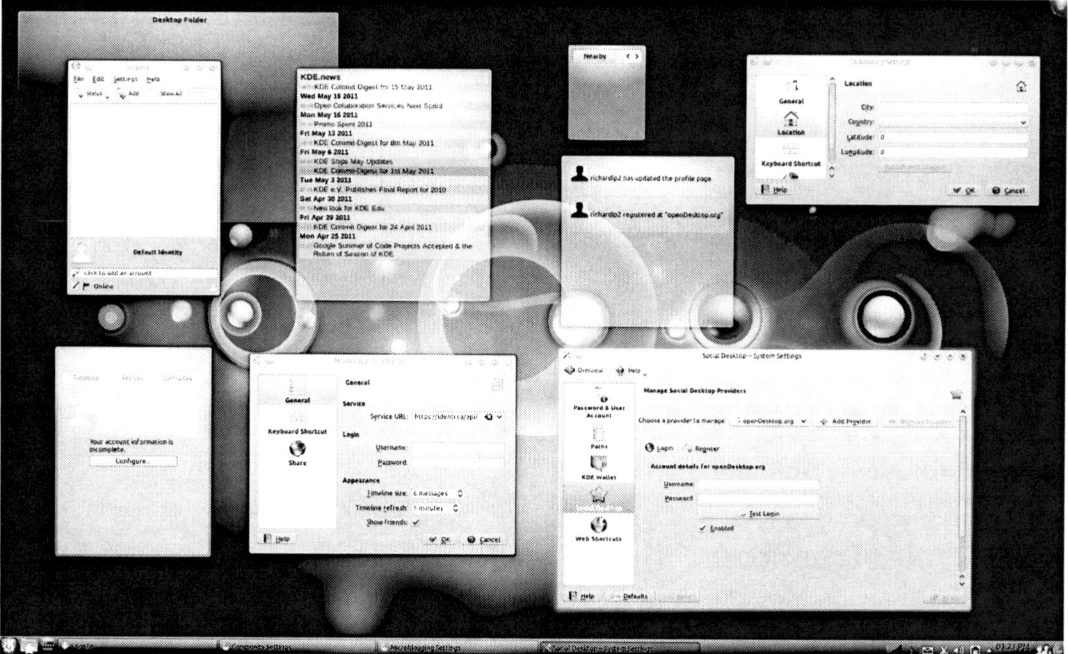

Figure 9-11: KDE Social Desktop (microblogging, IM, and location detection)

Ubuntu One

Ubuntu One is a suite of online services provided by Canonical. Ubuntu One is designed as a cloud server, making Ubuntu resources available to users everywhere. The service provides synchronization and sharing of files, like picture or word-processing files, and the synchronization of application data like notes and contacts, the Ubuntu One Music Store, and mobile device synchronization. The sharing feature allows you to share data with other registered Ubuntu One users. Application data synchronization will save the same data on all your Ubuntu computers. Currently Tomboy notes synchronization is supported, but other applications may be supported later (Evolution synchronization is no longer supported). For synchronization and sharing 5 GIGs are free. You can purchase 20 GIGs per month for 3 dollars (**https://one.ubuntu.com/services**). See the following site for documentation, including tutorials, as well as to sign up for the service.

```
https://one.ubuntu.com/
```

For tutorials on using Ubuntu One for file sharing, notes, contacts, bookmarks, and configuration see:

```
https://wiki.ubuntu.com/UbuntuOne/Tutorials
```

Features include:

Synchronizing and sharing files: Store, synchronize, and share files. Files will be stored on the Ubuntu One servers and downloaded automatically to other computers you have set up for the Ubuntu One service. You can also share folders and files with other Ubuntu One users. This makes file sharing and collaboration very easy.

Contacts: Contacts can be held on Ubuntu One for online access and editing, synchronizing with all your computers. You can access and download your Facebook contacts.

Notes: Edit and create Tomboy notes that will synchronize with the Tomboy notes applications on all your computers.

Storage is provided by Amazon S3 (Amazon Simple Storage Service) on the Amazon EC2 cloud. Connections use a new protocol called u1storage. Though the Ubuntu One client is open source, the Ubuntu One server software is proprietary, though full documentation will be available.

Note: Kubuntu supports Own Cloud, the KDE remote file server. Own Cloud is part of the KDE Social Desktop. It provides services similar to Ubuntu One such as storing files, synchronizing with your computers, backups, versioning, and sharing. You can set up your own server, or use a hosted server.

Ubuntu One set up

Ubuntu One software is easily installed on Ubuntu 12.04. You just need to set up access. Check the Ubuntu One installation tutorial at:

```
https://one.ubuntu.com/help/tutorial/installation-and-setup-on-ubuntu-1204-
precise/
```

To set up access to your Ubuntu One account go to Ubuntu One Control Panel, which you can open from the Ubuntu One launcher item or the Messaging menu as Ubuntu One. The Ubuntu One launcher item is an orange icon showing the U character (see Figure 9-12). Initially, Ubuntu One is not installed on your computer. A dialog prompts you to install it (see Figure 9-12).

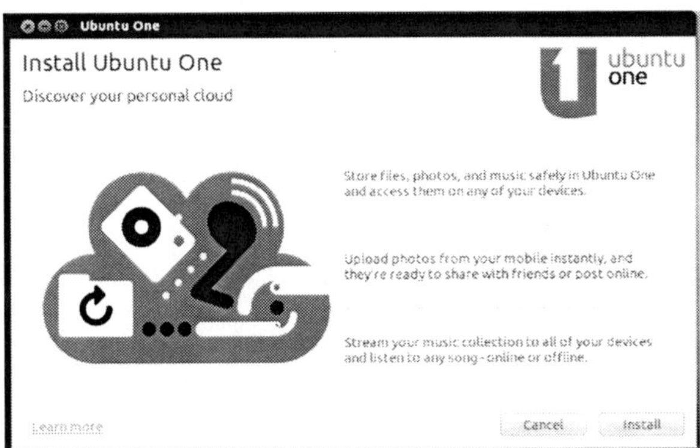

Figure 9-12: Ubuntu One installation

The first time you open the Ubuntu One, a dialog prompts you to sign in to an existing account or to sign up for a new one (see Figure 9-13). You can click the Learn More button for more information.

Figure 9-13: Ubuntu One set up

If you do not have an Ubuntu One account, click the "I don't have an account yet- sign me up" button to open the "Ubuntu Single Sign On" dialog where you can enter your email address, password, and verification characters (see Figure 9-14). If you have difficulty entering the verification characters, click the refresh link to generate a new one. Click the "Set Up Account" button to open the a dialog prompting you for a verification code. Upon entering your verification code you are signed into Ubuntu One.

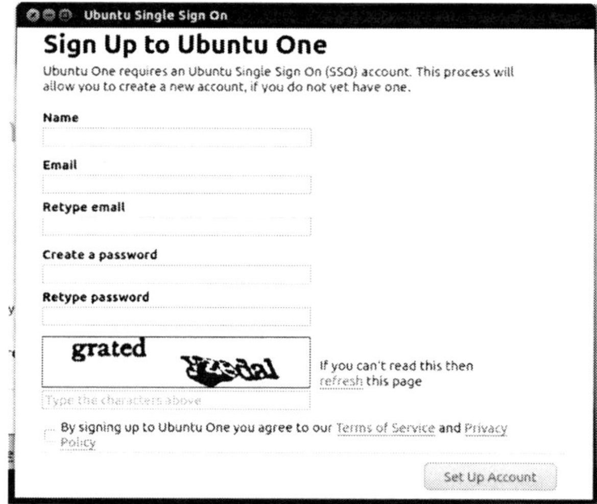

Figure 9-14: Create Ubuntu One account

Figure 9-15: Ubuntu Single Sign On

Should you have an account already, click the "Sign me up with my existing account" link to open the "Ubuntu Single Sign On" dialog where you can enter your email address and password (see Figure 9-15).

You can then choose folders that you want synced with the cloud on your computer (see Figure 9-16). The local folders in your home directory are listed. Choose the ones you want copied to the cloud by clicking their check box and the clicking the "Add a folder from this computer" button. Then click the Finish button.

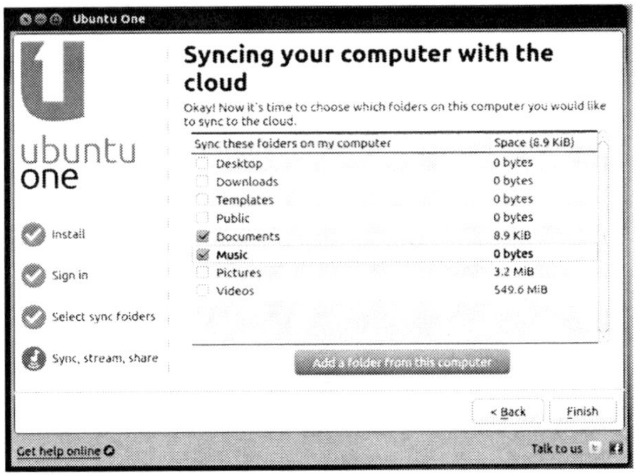

Figure 9-16: Ubuntu One select sync folders

You can also sign on or create an account from the Ubuntu One sign on page at the Ubuntu One Web site (see Figure 9-17). If you already have an account, enter your email address and password. If you do not have an account click the New account button.

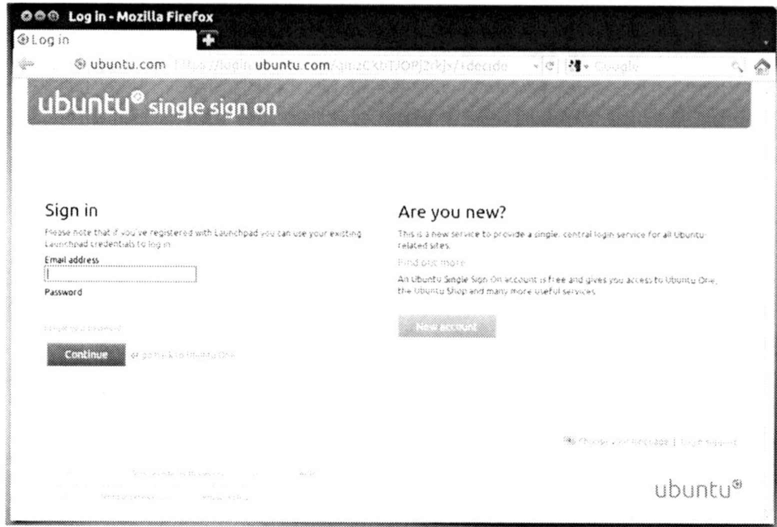

Figure 9-17: Ubuntu One sign in (Web site)

When you first sign up, you are set up with at free 5 GB plan. You can upgrade to a 20 GB plan for 3.00 per month. On the Ubuntu One Control Panel's Account tab, click the "Buy storage and plans" link.

Ubuntu One Control Panel

Use the Ubuntu One control panel to connect your computer to Ubuntu One, select supported services, and link to your online Ubuntu One account. To access the Ubuntu One control panel, click the Ubuntu One Launcher item, or on the Messaging menu choose Ubuntu One. On a computer already added to your Ubuntu One service, you will be connected to your Ubuntu One service automatically.

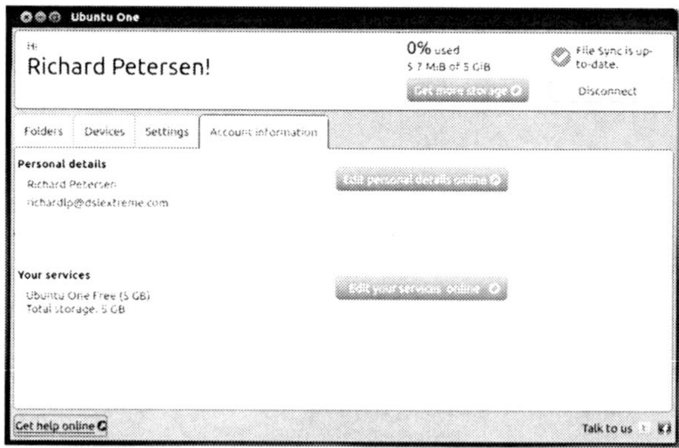

Figure 9-18: Ubuntu One Control Panel, Account Information

Note: Ubuntu One will start automatically once configured. De-select the Ubuntu One entry in Startup Applications Preferences (System | Preferences menu) to not have it start up.

The Ubuntu One Control Panel shows four tabs: Account Information, Folders, Devices, and Settings. At the top of the dialog is the file sync status and the percent of storage used (see Figure 9-18).

The Account Information tab shows your name, email address, and current service (see Figure 9-18). The "Edit personal details online" link will access your account login page on your Web browser where you can configure your account name and password (**https://login.ubuntu.com**). The "Edit your services online" link opens your Ubuntu One service page (**https://one.ubuntu.com/account**).

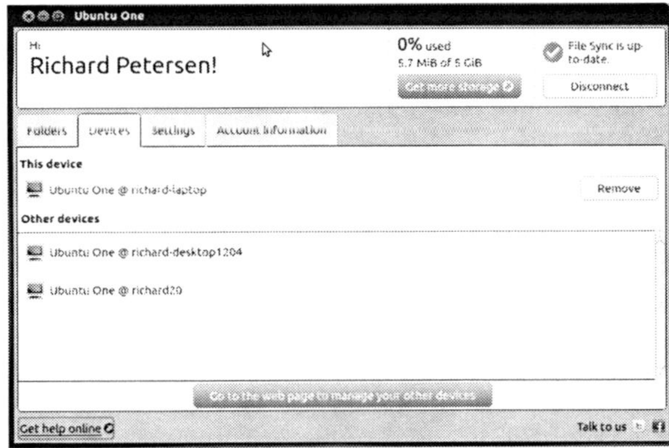

Figure 9-19: Ubuntu One Control Panel: Devices

To manage Ubuntu computers on your Ubuntu One service, open Ubuntu One Control Panel and choose the Devices tab (see Figure 9-19). If you do not want your computer connected you can click the Remove button. You also have the option to limit bandwidth usage for uploads and downloads.

On the Settings tab you can choose file sync settings and the upload and download speeds.

Ubuntu One Folder, Folder Synchronization, and Sharing

Check the Ubuntu Tutorial on file sharing for instructions on how to use Ubuntu one to save and synchronize files to your Ubuntu one account.

```
https://one.ubuntu.com/help/tutorial/install-and-setup-file-sync/
```

A folder named Ubuntu One is set up on your home folder. This folder is synchronized already with your Ubuntu One service. Any folders or files you create or place in your "Ubuntu One" folder are uploaded to your account automatically.

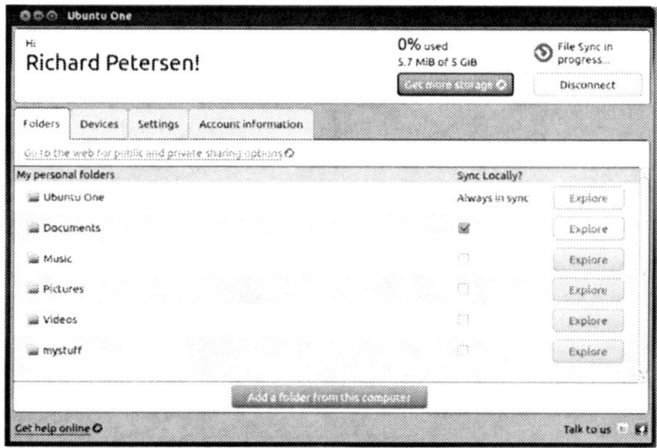

Figure 9-20: Ubuntu One Control Panel: Cloud Folders

You also can choose to have the contents of other folders uploaded to your account. The GNOME desktop file manager, Nautilus, provides integrated support for the folder synchronization. You can choose to synchronize any of your existing folders, by right-clicking on a folder and selecting "Ubuntu One | Synchronize This Folder".

Though the Ubuntu One Folder is always synced when connected, you can choose whether or not to synchronize other folders. On the Ubuntu Control Panel, on the Cloud Folders tab, the Documents, Music, Pictures, and any other Ubuntu One folders you may have set up are listed. To Sync a folder on your current computer, click the folder's Sync locally check box (see Figure 9-20).

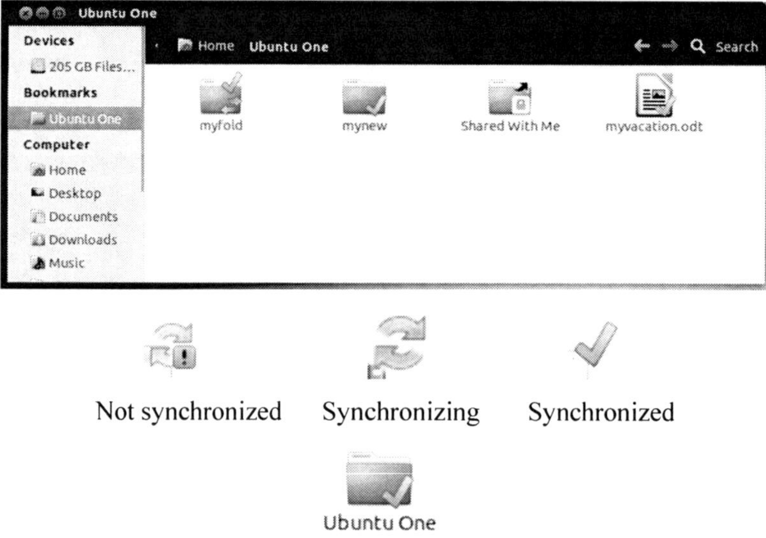

Figure 9-21: Ubuntu One folder

The Ubuntu one folder and its contents display emblems showing their update status (see Figure 9-21). The same emblems apply to the folder and file contents of additional synchronized folders, but the emblems are not displayed on the synchronized folder icons. If all the files are up-to-date, a green check mark is displayed. To check your overall synchronization status check the Ubuntu Preferences Dialog (Messaging menu | Ubuntu One) which will show the current status.

When the file in the Ubuntu One folder or in an additional synchronized folder are modified, the Ubuntu One client detects the changed files and uploads them to the Ubuntu One server, which then uploads the changed files automatically to your corresponding Ubuntu One folder and, in turn, downloads to the synchronized folders on your other Ubuntu One computers.

If you want to shut down the automatic uploading manually, you can open the Ubuntu One Control Panel dialog and click the Disconnect link on the Devices tab in the upper right corner. The link will change to a Connect button, which you can use to re-connect later.

Figure 9-22: Ubuntu One file and folder sharing

Your Ubuntu One folder and synchronized folders are synced automatically with your corresponding folders on your other computers. When synched, each computer will have the same set files and folders in their Ubuntu One folder and synchronized folders, with a master copy maintained on the Ubuntu One servers (cloud). If you add a file to an Ubuntu One folder or a synchronized folder on one computer, it will be uploaded to the Ubuntu One server automatically and then download to the corresponding folders on all your computers. Changing a file in an Ubuntu One folder or synchronized folder on one computer will change the corresponding copy in folders on your other computers, as well as on the master copy maintained on the server. The same synching process applies to deletion. Removing a file from an Ubuntu One folder or a synchronized folder on one computer, will remove them from all others.

You can also share a folder within an Ubuntu One folder or synchronized folder with other Ubuntu One users. Right-click on the folder to share, and select "Ubuntu One | Share" to open a dialog where you enter the email address of the Ubuntu One user to share with (see Figure 9-22). An email will be sent to the user requesting that the user accept sharing the folder. The user then logs into his or her Ubuntu One account and chooses to accept the shared folder, adding it to the "Folders shared with me" section of the Files tab. The same procedure works for other users sharing their folders with you. Those shared folders will show up on your Ubuntu One folders, and on the "Folders shared with me" section of your account Files tab. Previously used email addresses are listed in your Recently used and A-Z tabs. The share name is set to the name of the folder, but you can change it if you wish.

Managing your Ubuntu One service on the Ubuntu One site

To manage your Ubuntu One service from your Web browser, access the Ubuntu One Web site (**https://one.ubuntu.com**), and click the Sign in link at the upper right to open the Ubuntu single sing on page. You are prompted to enter your email address and password.

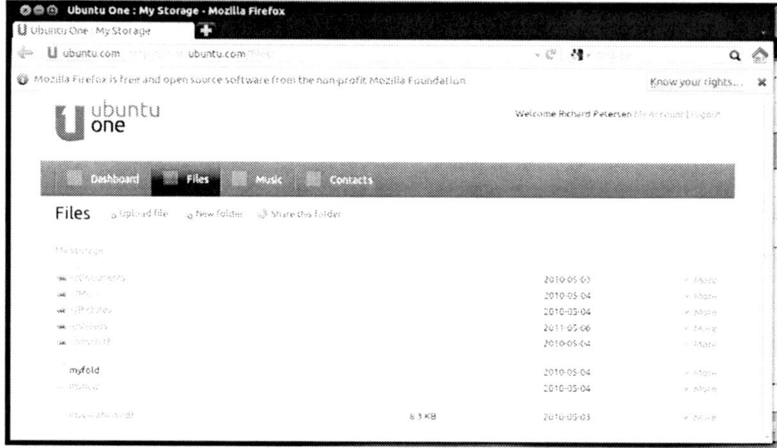

Figure 9-23: Ubuntu One online Files

Your Ubuntu one page displays tabs for Dashboard, Files, and Contacts. The Dashboard tab shows the amount of space you have used, notes and contact summaries, and service status. On the Files, and Contact pages you can configure and make changes to your stored files and folders, add or remove notes, and enter or update contacts. All Ubuntu One connected computers with Ubuntu One access activated for synchronized folders, Evolution mail, and notes will be automatically updated with any changes you make.

Files

The Files tab shows your synchronized folders (My synced folders), folders in your Ubuntu One folder (Folders), files in your Ubuntu One folder (Files), and folders shared with others (Folders shared with me) (see Figure 9-23). To the right of each entry is the time it was last updated, and a More link. Clicking on the More link will display options you can configure for the file or folder. For your synchronized folders, you have the option to share the folder. For folders in the Ubuntu One folder, you also can delete the folder. For an individual file in the Ubuntu One folder, you can download the file, delete it, or publish it on the Ubuntu site. The folder names are links, which when you click them, will open the folder contents on a new page. If you click a file name, it will be downloaded to the **/etc/tmp** folder and opened in its appropriate application on your system as a read-only file.

Links below the My Storage heading let you upload a file, create a new folder, or share a folder. On the main Files tab, these operations will work on the Ubuntu One folder. Clicking the "New folder" link will let you create a new folder in the Ubuntu One folder. The "Share this folder" link will share all the items in your Ubuntu One folder. To perform operations on just a particular folder, click on its name to open it in a new page. The "Upload file" link will upload files to that folder, "New folder" will create a subdirectory within that folder, and "Share this folder" will share this file only.

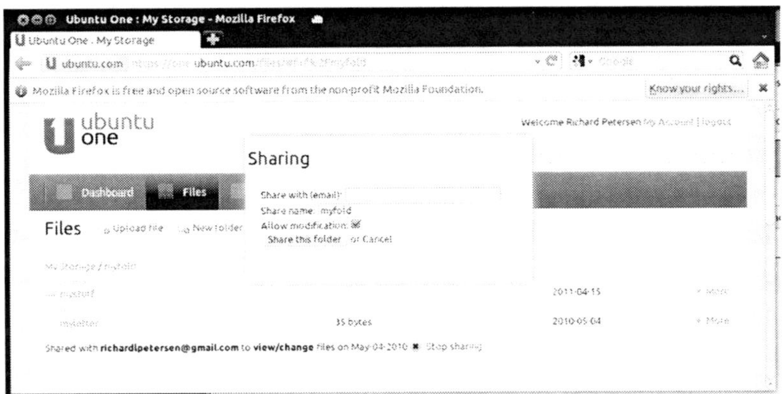

Figure 9-24: Ubuntu One sharing

All the Ubuntu One folders on your computers will be synched accordingly. The "Folders shared with me" section displays files and folders that other Ubuntu One users are sharing with you. Copies are also downloaded to your Ubuntu One folders and synched when changed automatically.

On the Files tab, you can also specify a folder to share with another Ubuntu user. You open the folder and then click the Sharing link at the top right of the page. A dialog opens that prompts you to enter the email address of the Ubuntu One user (see Figure 9-24). You can specify whether the sharing should be read only, preventing the other user from changing contents of the folder. On your Files tab, the folders you are sharing with others will be displayed in blue.

The other user is then sent an email asking if they want to accept the shared folder and providing a link to open a browser with and Accept Share button, which the user clicks to have your shared folder downloaded to their Ubuntu One folder. The shared folder will be listed in the user's "Folders shared with me" section, with a pencil emblem to show if it is writeable.

Contacts

On the Contacts tab, you can manage your contact database. You can manage contacts from several sources including your desktop, facebook, and Ubuntu One Mobile. Click on the Desktop button o import Facebook contacts. The "Add contact" link at the top of the page opens a dialog where you can enter contact information such as name, phone, address, email, IM, and personal and work information.

Synching Tomboy Notes

The Ubuntu One service supports synching your notes. No matter what computer or computing device you are using, you always can have access to your Notes. The Note service operates through the Tomboy Notes application.

To enable the service, first open Tomboy Notes, accessible from the Accessories dash, and then open the Preferences dialog (Edit | Preferences) and click the Synchronization tab. From the Service drop-down menu, select Ubuntu One, and click the Save button (see Figure 9-26).

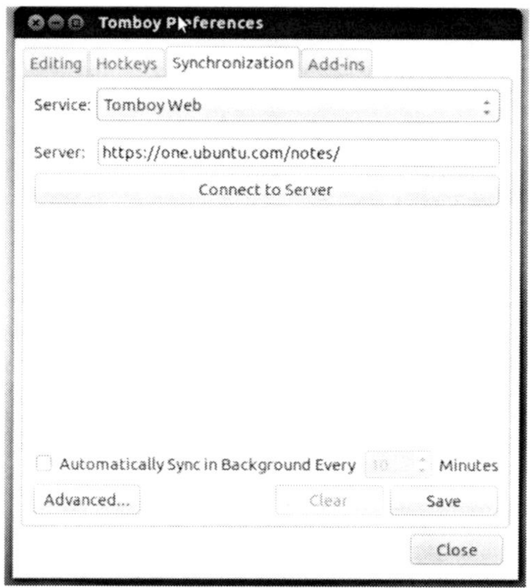

Figure 9-25: Ubuntu One Tomboy Preferences

Tomboy is now synchronized with notes on Ubuntu One (see Figure 9-26).

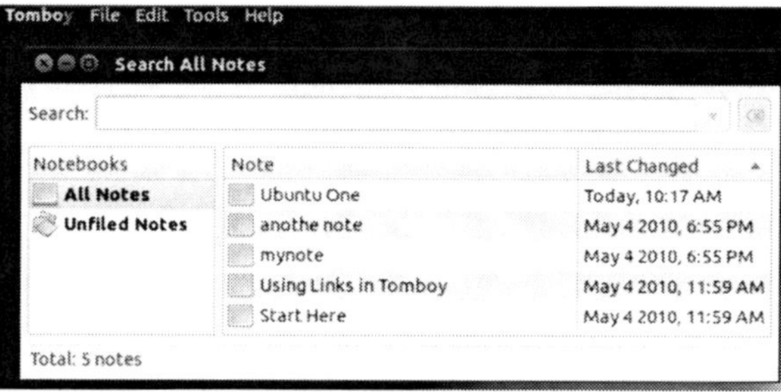

Figure 9-26: Ubuntu One Tomboy Notes

Any notes you write on Tomboy will be copied and synchronized to any of your Ubuntu computers whose Tomboy Notes are also configured to use your Ubuntu One service.

Part 3: Desktops

Ubuntu Desktop

KDE

The Shell

10. Ubuntu Desktop

Ubuntu Unity

Unity 2D

Launcher

Indicator Menus

Application Menu

Workspaces

Dash

Lenses

Quicklists

The Nautilus File Manager

The Ubuntu desktop features a user interface called Unity. As discussed in Chapter 3, check the Ubuntu Desktop Guide for a help and documentation. From the desktop Help menu, choose the Ubuntu Help. The Ubuntu desktop still uses the Nautilus file manager as well as many of the same GNOME desktop configuration tools (see Chapter 3). The Unity desktop is based on GNOME 3. The Unity desktop and the Nautilus file manager are examined in this chapter.

Ubuntu Unity

Unity is designed to make the best use of screen space, placing a launcher on the left side to free up vertical space, making the window title bar and menu bar part of the top panel, along with indicator menus for Network Manager, sound volume, messaging, time and date, the User Switcher, and the Session menu (see Figure 10-1). The Unity interface features a Launcher for applications and tasks, with icons for the dash, the home folder, the Firefox browser, LibreOffice applications (Writer, Calc, and Impress), the Ubuntu Software Center, and Ubuntu One. There are also icons for accessing workspaces and the trash.

Unity requires a 3D accelerated graphics capability: Intel, Nvidia, or AMD. You may have to first login to the Ubuntu 2D desktop, which provides a 2D version of Unity and does not need an accelerated graphics driver. Then install the hardware video drivers (System dash | Additional Drivers).

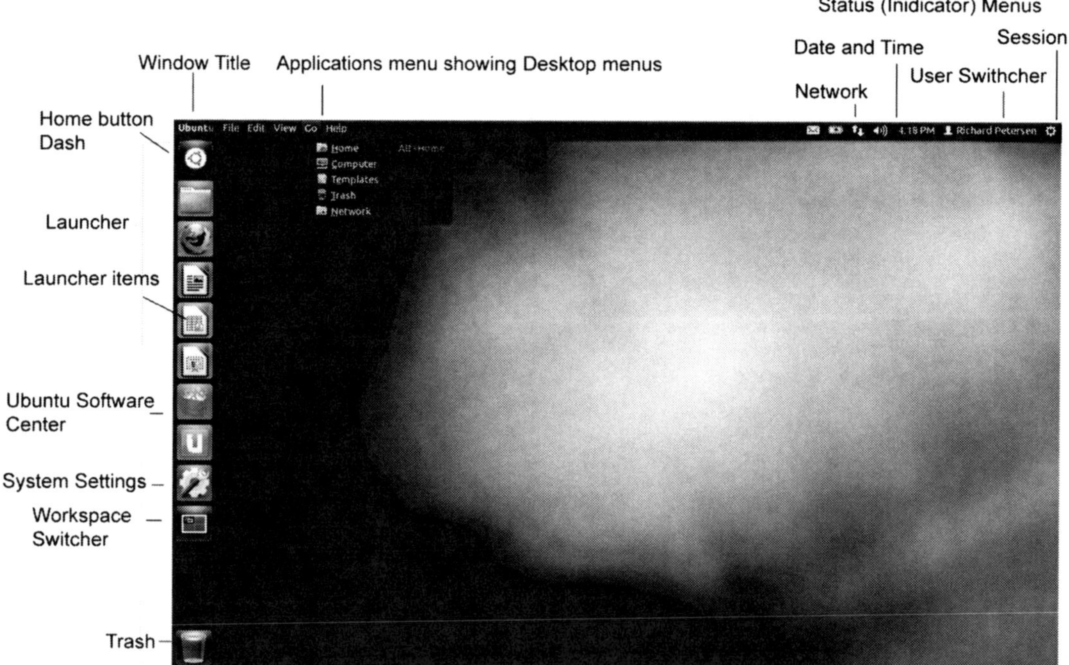

Figure 10-1: Ubuntu Unity desktop

The top panel displays the applications menu, and the indicator menus. The left side of the top panel is the application menu, showing the menu bar for the currently selected open window. When you click on the desktop background, the applications menu show the desktop menu bar, showing the menus File, Edit, View, Go, and Help. The Go menu provides entries for the Computer and Network windows, as well as the Trash and Home Folder.

Note: Unity uses Compiz as its window manager, making use of a special Unity plugin to run Unity. This means that you should not try to configure any Compiz features on Unity other than the Ubuntu Unity Plugin.

The left side of the top panel is the application menu, showing the menu bar for the currently selected open window. When you click on a window, its title is displayed on the Unity top panel applications bar. When you move your mouse to the top panel, that window's menu bar is displayed (see Figure 10-2).

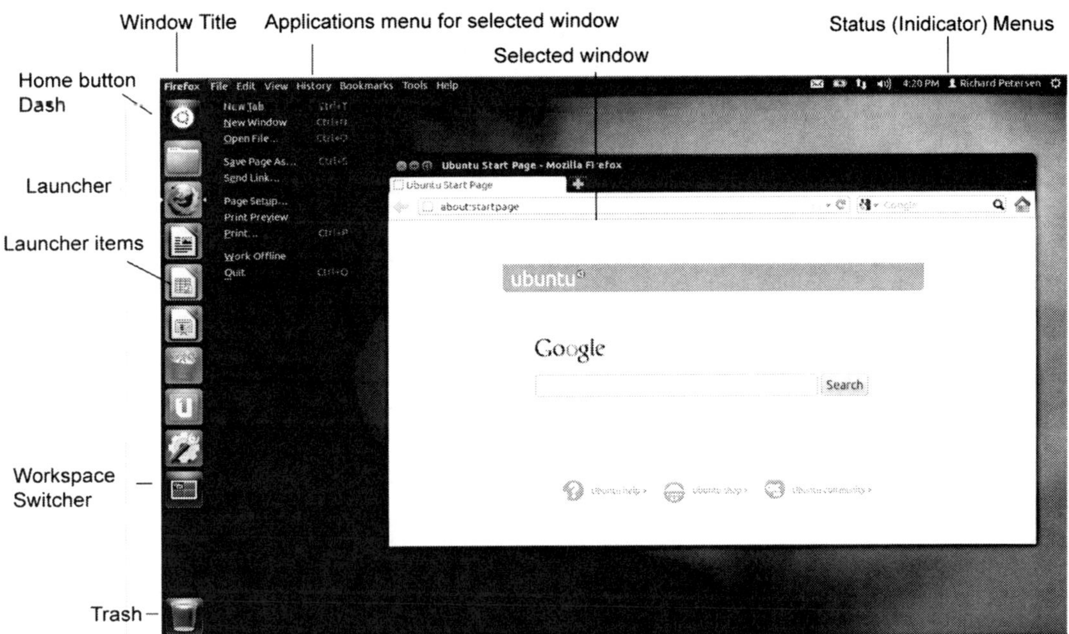

Figure 10-2: Ubuntu Unity interface with window

The right side of the top bar holds indicator menus for the network manager, sound volume, messaging, date and time, User switcher, and the Session menu (shut down options).

Unity 2D

As a default backup to Unity, Ubuntu installs the Unity 2D desktop, which provides a non-accelerated version of Unity. The interface and features are much the same, with the Launcher, indicator menus, and the dash. Unity 2D will run on the xorg open source graphics drivers, though it will lack some Unity capabilities. Unity 2D is also based on GNOME 3.0.

To re-order a Launcher item, you **Ctrl**-click on the item to select it and then you can move it through the list.

The desktop applications menu is not available.

Accelerated graphics features are not available such as move windows between workspaces on the Workspace switcher.

Keyboard and Mouse Shortcuts

Check the Ubuntu Desktop Guide's Keyboard Shortcuts page in the "Desktop, apps & windows" section for a listing of commonly used keyboard shortcuts. The meta key is also referred to as the super key, and is the Windows key on most keyboards. You can also check the "Unity keyboard/mouse shortcuts" page at the **http://askubuntu.com** site for a listing of Unity keyboard shortcuts and mouse operations. A listing is provided in Table 10-1.

http://askubuntu.com/questions/28086/unity-keyboard-mouse-shortcuts

Keys	Description
Launcher	
Meta key	Opens the dash, press again to close the dash
Meta key hold	If the Launcher is hidden, then press and hold the meta key momentarily to display the Launcher. The Launcher is hidden if a window occupies the left side of the desktop or is maximized.
Meta key hold and item number	When you hold the meta key down, numbers appear on all the launcher items. You can use that number to open or focus the corresponding launcher item. Works only for the first 10 items, which are numbered beginning with 1, with 0 used for the 10th item.
Meta+Shift key and item number	Opens a new instance of an item. When you hold the meta key down with the Shift key, numbers appear on all the launcher items. You can use that number to open a new instance of the corresponding launcher item. Works for the first 10 items, beginning with 1, with 0 used for the 10th item.
Meta-a	Open Applications dash
Meta-f	Open Files & Folders dash
Meta-t	Open the trash window
Alt-F1	Use keyboard to access launcher items, selecting first launcher item to start. Use up and down arrow keys navigate. Press Enter to launch an application. The right arrow displays a launcher quicklist
Ctrl-Alt-t	Opens a terminal window.
Dash	
Meta	Opens the Dash
Arrow keys	Use arrow keys will navigate items displayed on the dash or the launcher
Enter	Launch a selected item on the Launcher or Dash
Alt-F2	Opens the dash showing just a text box where you can enter a command to be run. Use up and down arrow keys to select previously entered commands.
Ctrl-Tab	Move to the next lens.

Ctrl-Shift-Tab	Move to the previous next lens.
Panel	
F10	Opens the first menu on the panel, use the left/right arrows keys to move to the next menu, including application and status (indicator) menus. If no windows are open, the first status menu is displayed. Use arrow keys to navigate menus, and Enter to choose an entry. Press Esc to close a menu.
Alt	Displays the applications menu bar on the top panel for the active window.
Workspaces	
Meta-s	Open workspaces.
Meta-w	Expo mode, zoom out on all windows in all workspaces.
Shift-Alt-*uparrow*	Expo mode, zoom out on windows in the current workspace.
Meta-d	Toggles minimize and restore for all windows.
Ctrl-Alt-*arrows*	Move to a new workspace.
Ctrl-Alt-Shift-*arrows*	Move window to a new workspace.
Ctrl-Alt-L	Lock the screen.
Windows	
Alt-Tab	Switch between windows
Alt-Shift-Tab	Switch between windows, backwards
Alt-`	Switch between windows for the same application
Ctrl-Meta-*uparrow*	Maximize current window
Ctrl-Meta-*downarrow*	Minimize current window
Window Position	Cycling through the same key will change the window size
Ctrl-Alt-Numpad 0	Maximize window.
Ctrl-Alt-Numpad 1	Place window in the bottom left corner of the screen.
Ctrl-Alt-Numpad 2	Place window in the bottom half of the screen.
Ctrl-Alt-Numpad 3	Place window in the bottom right corner of the screen.
Ctrl-Alt-Numpad 4	Place window on the left side of the screen.
Ctrl-Alt-Numpad 5	Center/Maximize the window in the middle of the screen.
Ctrl-Alt-Numpad 6	Place window on the right side of the screen.
Ctrl-Alt-Numpad 7	Place window in top left corner of screen.
Ctrl-Alt-Numpad 8	Place window in top half of screen.
Ctrl-Alt-Numpad 9	Place window in top right corner of screen.

Table 10-1: Unity Keyboard Shortcuts

There are certain mouse operations you can use on the Launcher, windows, and the top panel (see Table 10-2) such as scrolling through the Launcher items and maximizing a window by dragging it to the top panel.

Mouse actions	Effects
Launcher	
Middle click on an application's launcher item	Open a new instance of the application in a new window.
Click and drag a launcher item to the right, and back to the launcher	Reorder a launcher item on the launcher. Make a movement to the right to move the icon off the launcher, and move it back to the Launcher at the new position.
Drag an icon into the trash	Remove an item from the Launcher. The application remains installed
Scroll the mouse while over the Launcher	Scrolls through the icons if there are more items than those displayed on the screen
Window Management	
Drag a window to the top panel	Maximize the window.
Double click a window's titlebar	Maximize the window.
Middle click on Maximize button	Maximize Window Vertically.
Right click on Maximize button	Maximize Window Horizontally
Click to the right of the applications menu bar and drag the top panel down	Restore (unmaximize) a maximized window (full screen).
Double click on the top panel to the right of the application menu bar	Restore (unmaximize) a maximized window (full screen).
Middle click on the top panel to the right of the applications menu bar	Cycle between maximized windows for this workspace
Dragging a Window to the left or right side of the screen (when mouse meets the side of the screen)	Auto tile the window to that side of the screen.
Middle click on the top panel to the right of the applications menu bar	Send the current maximized window behind all other windows.

Table 10-2: Unity Mouse operations

Unity Launcher

The Launcher is used to launch commonly used applications (locked) and open applications, as well as access to the dash, your home folder, workspaces, the trash, and open windows. These are represented using launcher items (icons). Open applications are listed after the locked applications and before the workspace switcher. When you close an unlocked application, its Launcher item is removed from the Launcher.

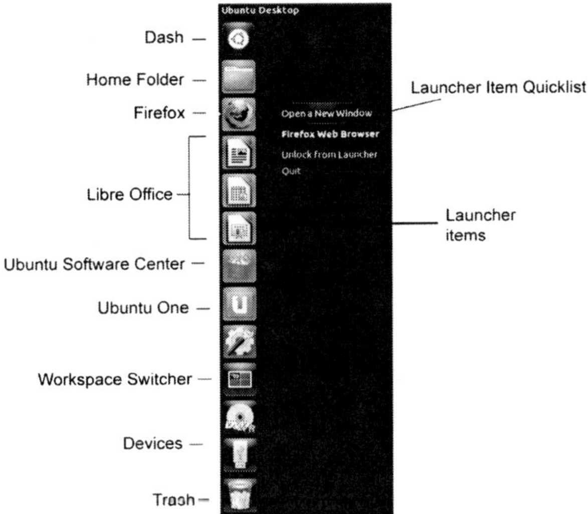

Figure 10-3: Unity Launcher

Opening a launcher item

To open an application from the launcher, left click on its launcher item. Once opened, clicking on the launcher item makes that application the active window.

To launch a launcher item using the keyboard, press and hold the meta key to display a number on each launcher button, and then press the number of the application you want to start.

To open a new instance of an application with a new window, you can middle click on the item (middle mouse button, usually the scroll button or both left and right button's simultaneously). There may also be an "Open in new window" entry in the item's quicklist menu, as there is for Firefox. Right-click on a Launcher item to display the quicklist menu. You could also use an application's "Open in new window" entry (if there is one) in that application's File menu, just as you would with any GNOME window.

Open Applications and Launcher items

When an application is open, a small white triangle appears on the left side of its Launcher item on the Launcher. As shown here for the Firefox Launcher item, a Firefox window is open.

If the application becomes the active window, a white triangle appears on the right side of its Launcher item. This means that an application that is the active window, will display two white triangles on its Launcher item, one on the left (open) and one on the right (active). As shown here for the Firefox Launcher item, a Firefox window is open and it is the active window.

Should there be more than one instance of an application open, such as several folder windows or browser windows, additional white triangles appear on the left side of the Launcher item. For two instances, there are two triangles, for three or more instances there will be three triangles. As shown here for the Firefox and Home Folder Launcher items, at least three or more folder windows are open, and two Firefox windows are open with one of them being the active window.

Launcher Quicklists

When you right-click on a launcher item, a pop-up menu appears, which lists possible actions you can perform such as starting an application or opening a file manager window. Initially most quicklists will have only a few entries such as the application title, a lock or unlock entry, and an option to open the application. If the application is open, then a Quit entry is added. Some items such as Firefox and Libre Writer have additional actions such as Firefox's "Open in New Window" and Libre Writer's "New Document", as shown here. The file manager quicklist will list your default folders, as well as any of your bookmarked folders. See the section "Customizing Launcher Quicklists" to see how you can add quicklist entries and create customized launcher items.

An application Launcher item can be locked to the Launcher, keeping it there for easy access. The default items are already locked to the launcher. Whenever you install a new application, its Launcher item is also locked to the Launcher by default. When you open an application, its Launcher item appears on the Launcher, and remains there until you close the application. You can manually lock it to the Launcher by right clicking on it to display its quicklist and choose "Lock to Launcher." You can use this entry to keep the launcher items for your commonly used applications retained by the Launcher. To later remove it, choose "Unlock from Launcher" as shown here.

Devices on the Launcher

Devices such as USB devices CD/DVD discs are detected automatically and launcher items displayed for them in the Unity launcher and on the desktop. To remove a USB device or CD/DVD disc, right-click on its icon on the Launcher and select Eject or Safely Remove (as shown here). The device will also show up as an icon on the desktop, which you can right-click on to display a menu with entries to eject and safely remove.

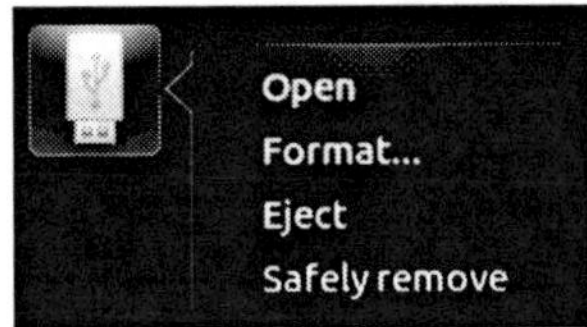

Navigating and accessing the Launcher

If the number of launcher items exceeds the amount that can be displayed on the screen at once, you can move your mouse to the launcher and use your scroll button to scroll through the launcher items. You can also click and drag on the launcher to move the entire list up and down.

When you open an application in full screen mode or move a window to the left side of the screen, the launcher hides. To make the launcher reappear you can move your mouse to the left edge of the screen, pushing on the edge. You can also display the launcher using your keyboard by pressing and holding the meta key (Windows key).

You can configure the hiding feature of the Launcher using the System Setting's Appearance tool's Behavior tab. On the Look tab, you can configure the size of Launcher items. For more refined configuration, you can use the Compiz Config Settings Manager's Unity plugin as described in the following section on Configuring the Launcher.

Adding and removing application items to the Launcher

When you open an application from the dash, an icon for it appears on the Launcher. When you minimize a window, you can maximize it again by clicking its launcher button. When you close your application, the launcher button disappears. Should you want the launcher button to remain, giving you easy access to the application, you can right click on the launcher button and choose the "Lock to Launcher" entry from the pop-up menu. This makes the launcher a pinned item.

To add an application to the launcher from the dash, drag the applications icon on the dash to the launcher. This will lock the item to the Launcher, keeping it there permanently. You can remove it later by right clicking and choosing "Unlock from Launcher" from its quicklist.

To change a launcher item's position on the launcher, you can either click and drag it through the column of items (you will see its position moving), or click and drag it out of the launcher to the right and then back into the launcher to the new position, all in one motion.

To remove a locked launcher item, right click on the button and click on the "Unlock from Launcher" entry from the pop-up menu. You can also drag the launcher item to the trash.

If an installed application is not displayed on the dash, first check the MainMenu application to see if the application you are looking for is not checked as displayed on the menus. For applications like the Evince Document Viewer (Applications | Graphics | Document Viewer), Shared Folders, and Software Sources (System | Administration, and System Preferences), you first have to use MainMenu to check the applications, making them visible for the Unity Dash. You then have to logout and log back in.

Configuring the Launcher

To configure the auto-hide behavior of the Launcher, you use the Behavior tab on the System Setting's Appearance tool (see Figure 10-4). A switch lets you turn the auto-hide feature on. You can then set the location at the left side of the screen to top left corner. You can also set the reveal sensitivity for unhiding the Launcher.

You can set the size of the Launcher items on the Look tab using the "Launcher icon size" slider at the bottom of the dialog. The default size is 48.

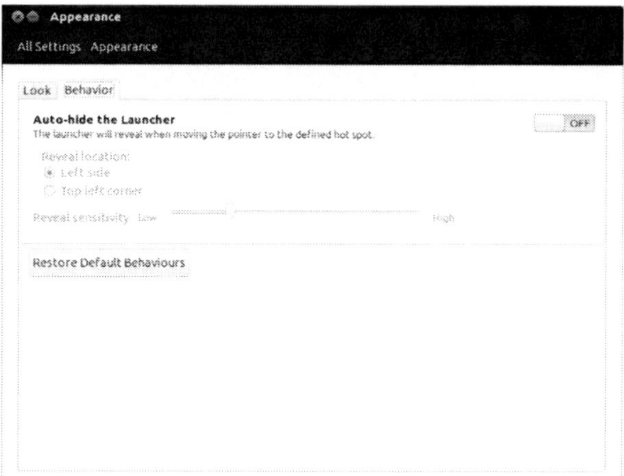

Figure 10-4: System Settings Appearance Behavior tab for the Launcher

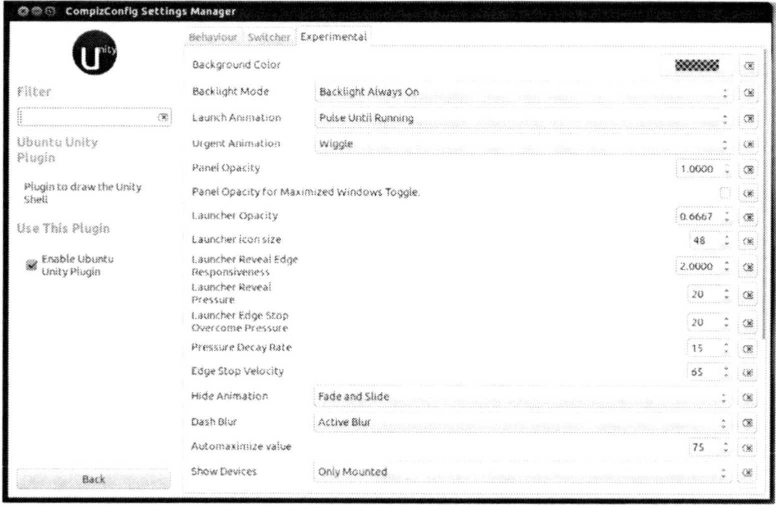

Figure 10-5: Ubuntu Unity Plugin on Compiz (CompizConfig Settings Manager)

For more additional Launcher configuration, you use the CompizConfig Settings Manager's Unity plugin. You first have to install the CompizConfig Settings Manager. Then open the CompizConfig Settings Manager on the Customization dash. Carefully click the Ubuntu Unity

Plugin in the Desktop section. The Unity plugin displays three tabs: Behavior, Switcher, and Experimental. The Switcher tab lets you choose what keys to use for the windows switcher. To have changes take effect, logout and login again to restart the window manager (see Figure 10-5). You should not make any other changes on the CompizConfig Settings Manager to any plugin other than Ubuntu Unity Plugin.

You can also configure the hiding feature of the Launcher on the Ubuntu Unity plugin's Behavior tab's "Hide launcher" menu. You can turn hiding off, choose autohide, or hide based on windows placement: Never, Autohide, Dodge windows, Dodge active windows. The autohide feature hides the Launcher until you move your mouse to the left side edge of the screen. You can also choose the keys to use to show the launcher and time needed to hold the mouse at the left edge before the Launcher will appear (Reveal mode).

Windows

Windows on Unity operate much as they do on GNOME, with similar maximizing, minimizing, and workspace operations. You still use the window buttons on the left side of the window title bar to minimize, maximize, and close a window.

Window Sliders

One key feature for windows is the slider (see Figure 10-6). The slider is reduced to thin color bar on the left and bottom sides of the window when not in use. To use the slider, move your mouse over this bar. The slider expands to a slider button that you can use scroll through the window. Click and drag on the slider button to move it. When you are finished and move your mouse away, the slider button disappears and is reduced to a simple color bar.

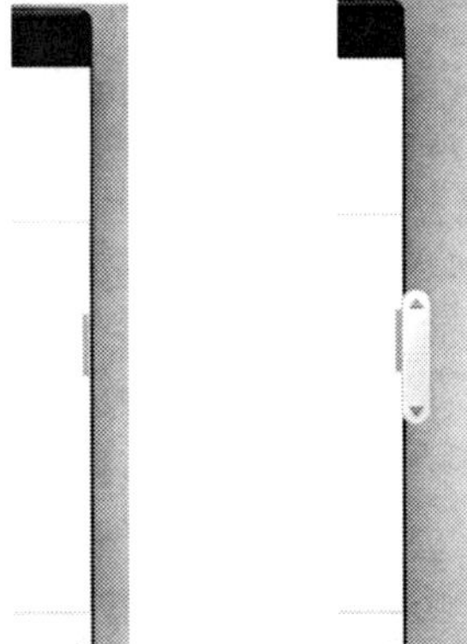

Figure 10-6: Window Slider (inactive and active)

Minimizing, Maximizing, and Closing Windows

To maximize a window you can double-click on the title bar, click and drag the title bar to the top of the screen, or click on it's maximize button (square image) on the left side of the title bar. You can also right-click on the title bar and choose the Maximize entry from the pop-up menu. The maximized window shows the window buttons places on the top panel between the home button and the applications menu bar (see Figure 10-7).

To unmaximize a window, drag its title bar down and away from the top bar, or click on it's maximize button on the left side of the title bar (square image).

To move a window, click and drag on its title bar. You can also press the Alt key with a mouse click and drag to move a window. You can also right-click on the title bar and choose the Move entry from the pop-up menu.

From the keyboard, you can press the Alt-space keys to display the window menu for that window, and then press x to maximize, n to Minimize, and m to move a window.

Figure 10-7: Unity maximized window

To minimize a window, you can click the window's minimize button (minus sign) on the left side of the title bar. Minimized windows are reduced to icons on the launcher. To restore a minimized window, click on its launcher item. If the window is not maximized, you can also right-click on the title bar and choose the Minimize entry from the pop-up menu. From the keyboard, you can also press Alt-tab to display images of the open windows and then click on the one you want, or continue to press Alt-tab to move to the window you want.

To close a window, click the window close button (the x character) on the left side of the title bar. You can also right-click on the title bar and choose the Close entry from the pop-up menu. From the keyboard, you can press Alt+F4, or press Alt+space to display the window menu and then press c to choose the Close entry.

Resize and tiling Windows

You can resize a window vertically, horizontally, or both at the same time. To resize in both directions at once, move the mouse to any corner of the window until it becomes a corner-pointer, an arrow with a right-angle pointer image. You can then click-and drag to the size you want. For horizontal changes, move the mouse to the left or right side edge of the window until it changes to a side-pointer, an arrow with a line image. The same operation works for vertical changes at the top or bottom of the window.

Ubuntu Unity supports window snapping. Moving the window to the right or left edge of the screen (when the mouse reaches the edge) expands the window to take up that side of the screen. Moving the window to the top panel maximizes the window to the use the full screen, with the window menu bar and buttons using the top panel.

You can also tile two windows so that one takes up one-half the screen, and the other uses the other half. Drag a window to left side (click and drag the title bar, or Alt-click on the window). When your mouse pointer meets the edge of your screen, the entire left side of the screen is highlighted. When you release your mouse, the window snaps to display on the entire left side of the screen. The same operation works for the right side. To restore the window to its previous size, simply drag it down away from the edge.

Switching Windows

Applications that have more than one window open will have several white triangles displayed on the left side of its Launcher icon. To see just the open windows for that application, click on the launcher item. Those windows are zoomed and displayed next to each other on the desktop (see Figure 10-8). You can then click on the one you want to move to. For example, if you have several folders open, white triangles for each appear on the Launcher home folder icon. Click on the home folder icon to display a zoomed image of each folder. Then click on the one you want to move to.

Figure 10-8: Zoomed windows for same application (click Launcher item)

You can also switch between windows using the Alt-Tab key to display the window switcher (see Figure 10-9). Open windows are displayed using their Launcher icons in the center of the screen. Use the Alt-Tab key to select the one you want.

You can also press the meta key (Windows key) with the w key to zoom out a display of all open windows in all workspaces (Expo mode), and then use the arrow keys to move to the window you want, or click on it with your mouse (see Figure 10-10). Use Shift-Alt-*uparrow* to display only the windows in the current workspace.

Figure 10-9: Window switcher (Alt-tab)

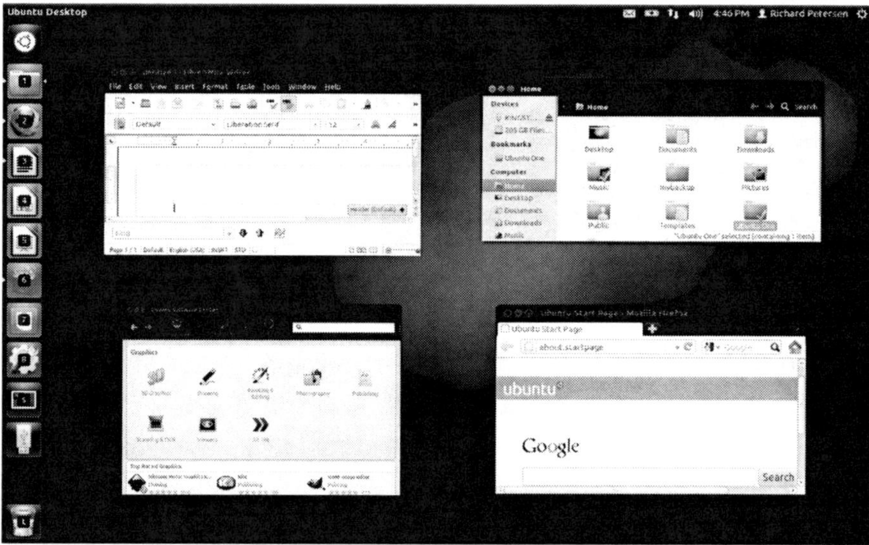

Figure 10-10: Zoomed windows for all open windows (Meta-w)

Workspaces

The workspaces launcher displays your workspaces (virtual desktops) as squares covering the entire screen (see Figure 10-11). All the open windows in each workspace are displayed. You can reposition them or move them from one workspace to another. To move windows from one workspace to another by simply drag them to the other workspaces.

Initially, Unity sets up four workspaces, 2 columns and 2 rows. Double click on a square to move to that workspace. To move to another workspace, click the workspaces icon again, and then double-click on another workspace.

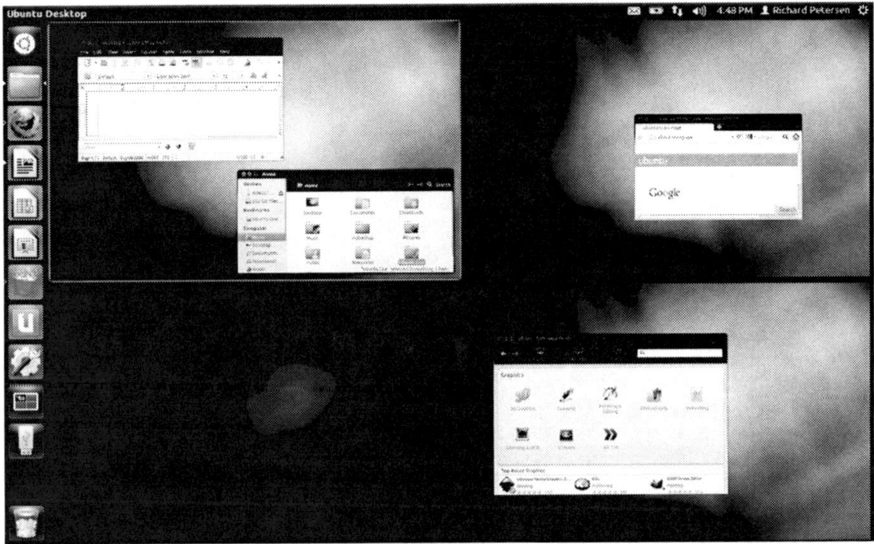

Figure 10-11: Unity Workspace Switcher

From the keyboard, you can also use the **Ctrl+Alt-***arrow* keys to move quickly to a different workspace (Compiz desktop wall). Small images of the workspaces is displayed in the center of the screen, with the current one highlighted (See Figure 10-12). Use the up, down, right, and left arrows to move through the workspace images, with the one selected being highlighted.

To move a window to a different workspace, open the workspace launcher, and simply click and drag that window to a different workspace. To quickly move a window to another workspace, you can use **Ctrl+Alt+Shift+***arrow* keys, with the up, down, left, right arrow keys moving the window to the next workspace. You can also right-click on the title bar and choose one of the Move to Workspace entries. The "Move to Another Workspace" entry displays a submenu listing all workspaces.

The Ubuntu Desktop Guide (Windows and Workspaces | What is a workspace, and how will it help me?) recommends a way to change the number of workspaces. You use the **gconftool-2** to set the vsize and hsize parameters for the Compiz window manager. Open a terminal window (in the Accessories dash), and enter the following for the vertical number of workspaces (vsize).

```
gconftool2 --type=int --set /apps/compiz-1/general/screen0/optons/vsize 2
```

Use hsize for the horizontal number of workspaces.

```
gconftool2 --type=int --set /apps/compiz-1/general/screen0/optons/hsize 2
```

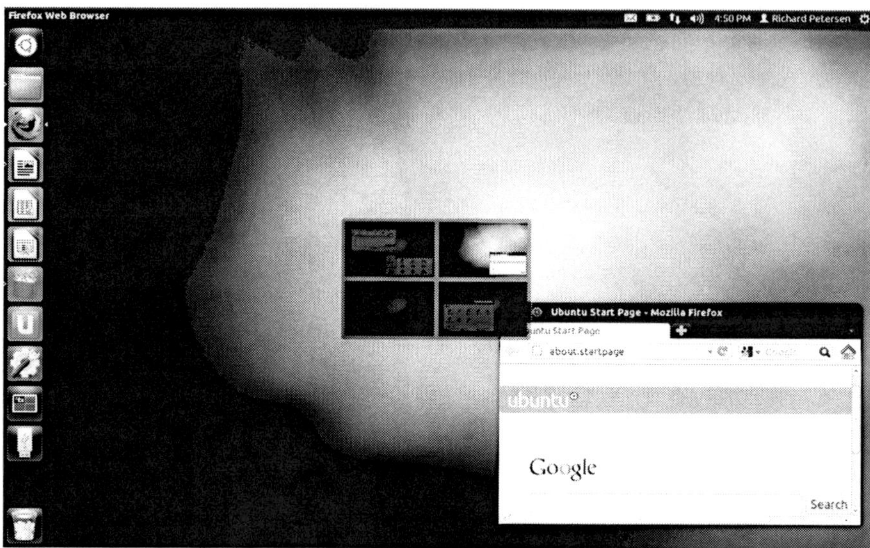

Figure 10-12: Workspace switcher (Ctrl+Alt+*arrow*)

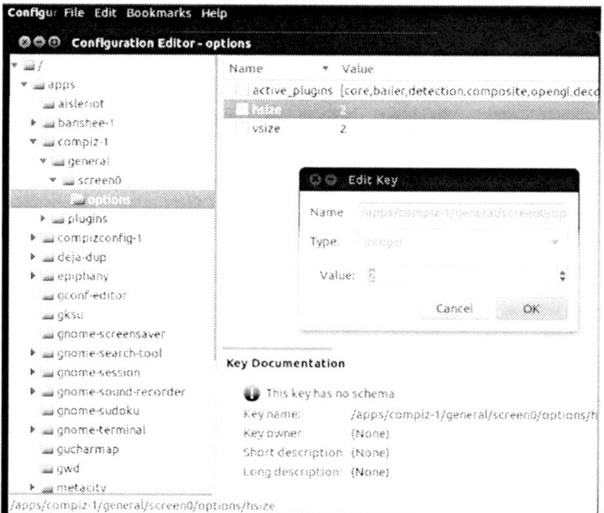

**Figure 10-13: Changing number of workspaces on Unity with the GNOME
Configuration Editor**

Alternatively, you can use the GNOME Configuration Editor to change the number of
workspaces. First, install the Configuration Editor (**gconf-editor**) package. You can then choose
Configuration Editor on the System dash. On the configuration tree at the left side of the
Configuration Editor window, expand apps | compiz-1 | general | screen0, and then click options
(see Figure 10-13). On the right pane, you can change the hsize and vsize entries to change the

number of workspaces. Double click on the vsize or hsize entries to open a dialog that allows you to change the number. To have 6 workspaces, you could change the number of hsize entries from 2 to 3, with the vsize remaining 2. To set up four workspaces as a single row, you would set hsize to 4 and vsize 1.

Desktop menus and application menu

If you click on the desktop background, and then move your mouse to the top bar (left side), the application menu will display the desktop menu: File, Edit, View, Go, and Help (see Figure 10-14). Be sure to first open an application after logging in. The File menu has create folder and document entries similar to the ones displayed if you right-click on the desktop. The View menu lets you organize your desktop. The Go menu works much the similar to the Places menu in previous releases, with entries for Home, Computer, Network, Trash, and Templates.

Should you open a file manager window, the same set of menus is displayed with an added Bookmarks menu. The menus have more options for managing files and folders. The Bookmarks menu lets you access the primary home folder such as Documents and Pictures. You can also add Bookmarks from any file manager window and they are displayed on the Bookmarks menu.

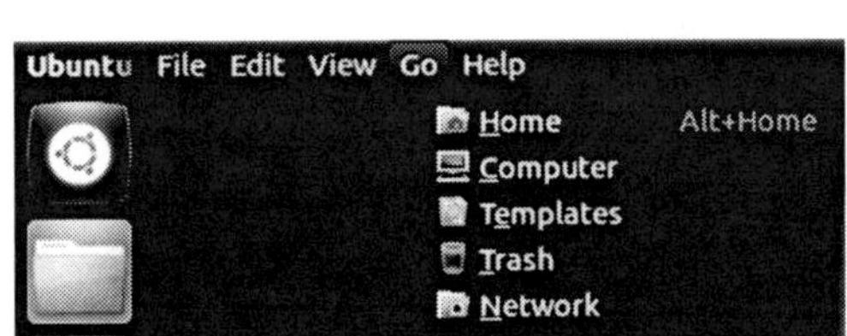
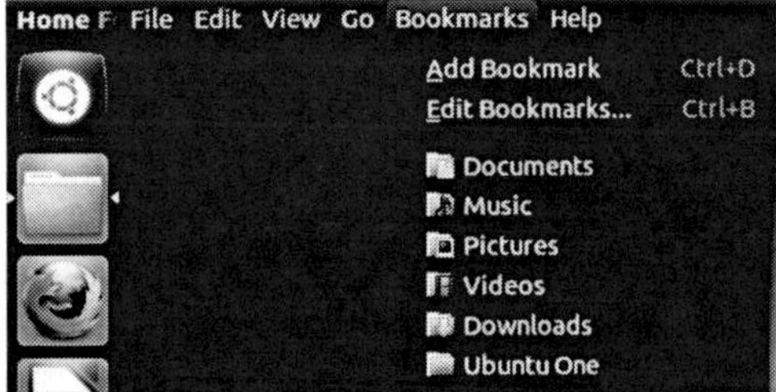

Figure 10-14: Desktop and File Manager Menus on the Applications menu bar

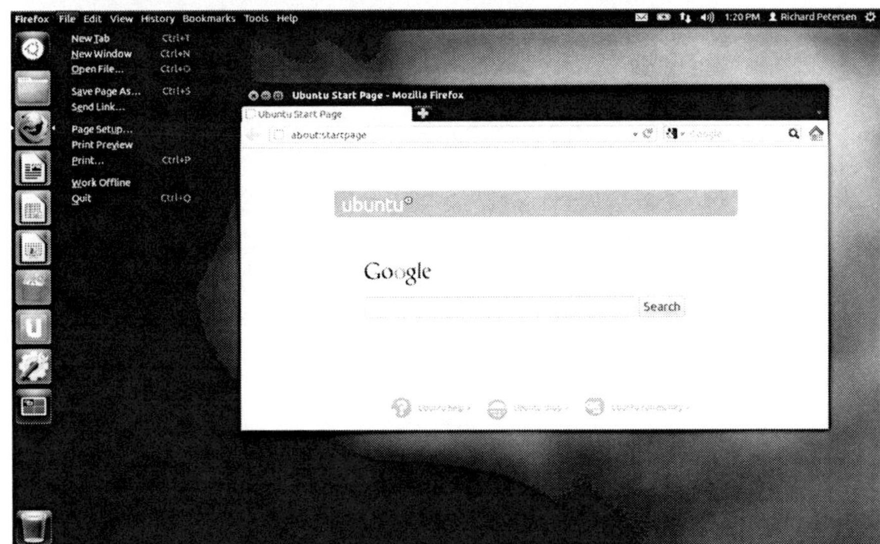

Figure 10-15: Active window's menu bar on the top panel Applications menu bar

The application menu displays the name of the currently selected window. If that window is used for an application, which has a menu bar, then, when you move your mouse to the left side of the top bar, that application's menu bar is displayed (see Figure 10-15). The applications menu displays the menu bar for the currently active window. For example, if the window for Firefox is active, when you move your mouse to the application menu, it displays the Firefox menu bar. When you click on a different application window, that application's menu bar becomes the applications menu on the top bar. This means that menu bars are no longer displayed on the application window. This is also true for the Nautilus file manager, whose menu bar is displayed as the application menu, not in the file manager window.

Dash

Applications and files can be accessed easily using the Unity dash, which provides quick search capability as well as access to commonly used applications. To open the Unity dash, click the Dash home icon (Ubuntu logo) on the Launcher, to display the Dash home dash consisting of a search bar (see Figure 10-16). You can also press the meta key to start the dash. To close the dash, click the close button (**x**) at the left side of top panel or press the ESC key. To expand the dash to the full screen, click the square image at the top left side of the panel.

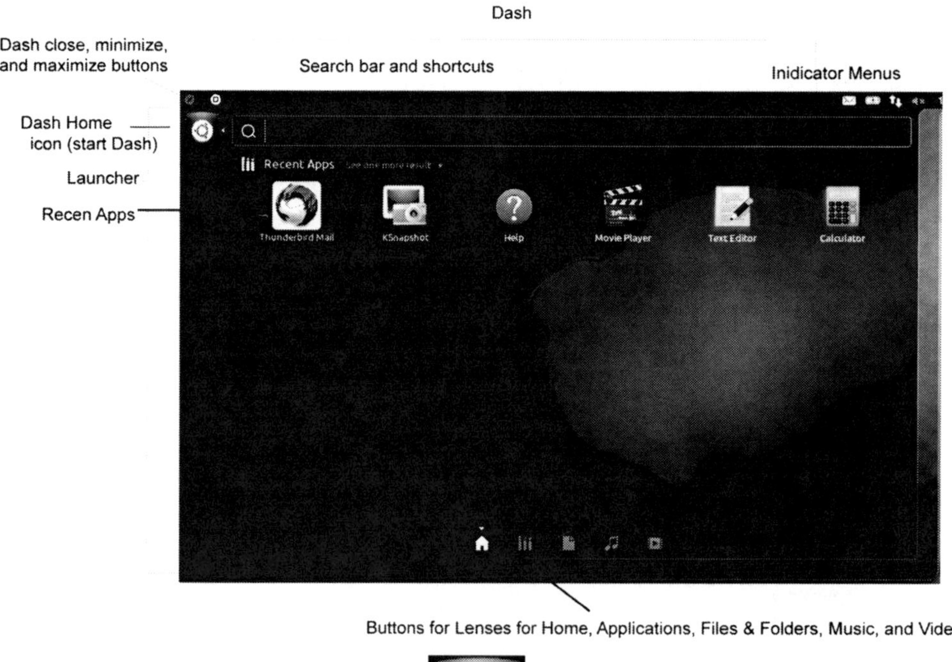

Figure 10-16: Unity Dash

Dash Search Bar

You can use the search bar to quickly search for an application by pattern. The search is dynamic. As you enter a pattern, matching applications are displayed, refining the search as you enter more of the pattern. The pattern will match on any part of the application name. In Figure 10-17, the pattern "me" matches on both "Messaging and VoIP" and the "Keyboard Input Methods."

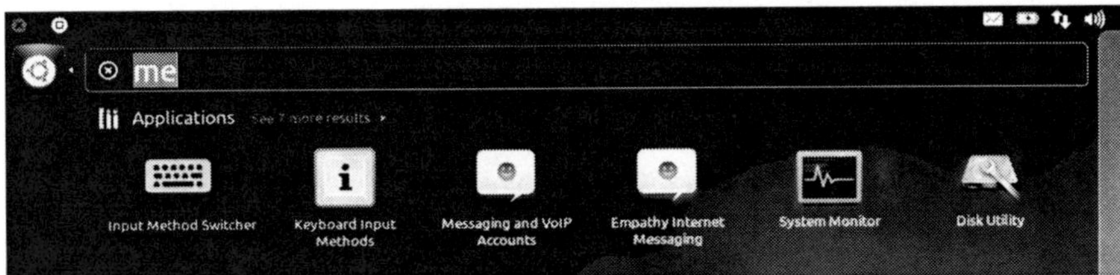

Figure 10-17: Dash search

The search bar is a global search bar, meaning that it searches for both applications and files and folders. Entering the pattern "doc" will display both an Applications section showing document related applications such as LibreOffice, and display a Files & Folders section showing the Documents folder (see Figure 10-18).

By default, a search will display a single row of results. If there are more results, a More Results link is displayed, which as can click to see the remaining results.

Pressing the ENTER key will select and run the first item in the search results. If it is an application, that application will start up. If it is a folder, the folder is opened.

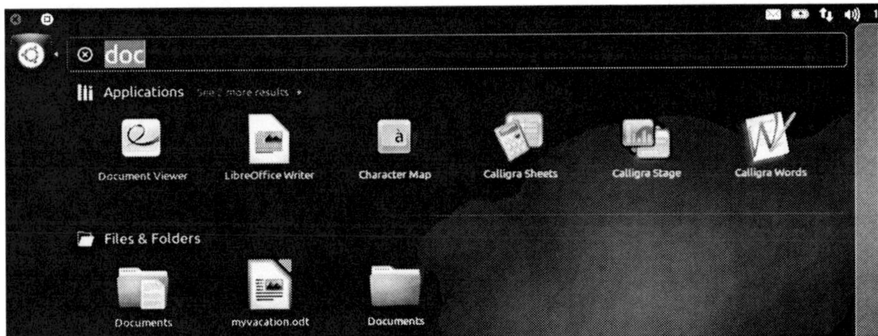

Figure 10-18: Dash search results

Dash lenses

A dash lens lets you access different kinds of objects on your system such as applications, files and folders, and your music and videos collections. Access to several lenses is located at the bottom of the dash, represented by the home, applications, document, music note, and video play buttons, as shown here:

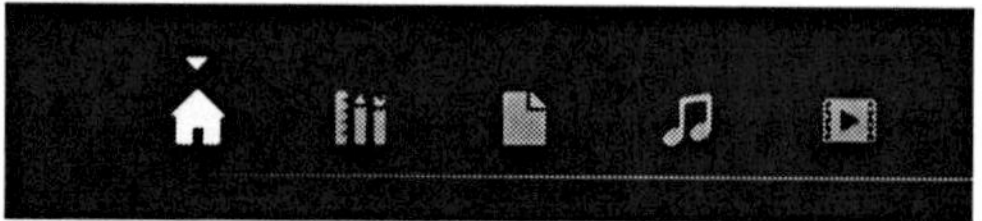

You can quickly move from one lens to another with the Ctrl-Tab keys, once the dash is open. The Ctrl-Shift-Tab keys move backwards.

The home button opens the Dash home dash showing the global search box. The applications button opens the applications search dash. The documents button opens a Files & Folders search dash for searching your file system. The music note button lets you search your music collection. The video play button opens a video dash listing both your videos and those available from online sources such as Amazon and You Tube.

You can also access lenses by right-clicking on the dash icon on the Launcher to open a quicklist showing entries for the Dash Home, Applications, Files & Folder, Music, and Video lenses, as shown above:

Any grouping can be configured as a lens. See **https://wiki.ubuntu.com/Unity/Lenses** for detailed configuration information. Lens configuration files have the extension **.lens** and are located at **/usr/share/unity/lenses**.

Note: Maximizing a window moves its close, minimize, and downsize buttons to the application menu. The launcher at the side is hidden, until you move your mouse there.

Dash Home

The Dash Home lens shows your recently used applications and files (see Figure 10-19). If you have performed a search, which you have not cleared, that search will be re-displayed instead of the recently used applications and files.

Files & Folders lens

The Files & Folders lens provides a quick search capability for your home folder and access to your home folder subfolders such as Documents and Pictures (see Figure 10-20).   You can access it as Find Files on the Dash Home lens or from the document button at the bottom of a dash. The Files & Folders dash shows a Folders segment, which shows folder icons for your primary home folders: Documents, Music, Pictures, Videos, and Downloads. Clicking on a folder opens it using the Nautilus file manager. The dash also shows your most recently used files and folders, as well as folders you have bookmarked. A search box lets you search for file and folders in your home folder. To the left of the search box is an expandable "Filter results" menu that lest you search by modification, type and size. Types include documents, folders, images, audio, video, presentations, and other. You can choose more than one criteria at a time, refining your search. Click on a selected button to deselect it.

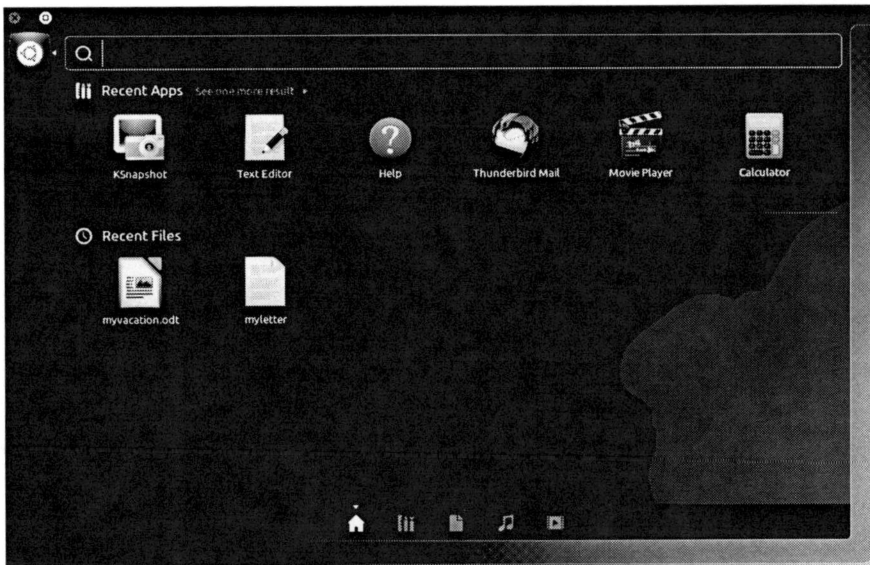

Figure 10-19: Dash Home

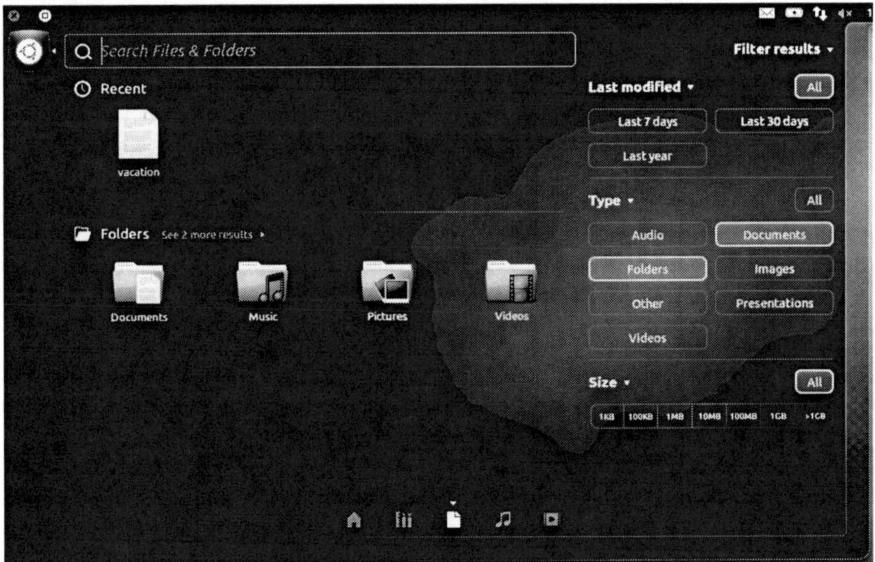

Figure 10-20: Files & Folders lens

Applications lens

The Applications dash can be opened from the Dash Home dash with the More Apps icon, or from the books button at the bottom of a dash. Applications are arranged into several segments such as Recently Used, Installed, and Apps Available for Download (see Figure 10-21). The Installed segment shows a few of your installed applications, with a link to display all of them. You can search for an application by pattern using the search box at the top of the dash.

Figure 10-21: Applications lens

To the right of the search box is a "Filter results" expansion arrow for accessing application categories. Initially it is set to All Applications. User applications can be found in categories similar to those used in previous releases such as Office, Internet, and Graphics. There are also Science & Engineering, Media, and Education categories. Media replaces the Sound & Video category used in previous releases. Most preference tools are located in Customization, and system administration tools can be found in the System category. The Customization category tends to become extensive as it includes both desktop configuration dialogs and system tools. Some tools are located in both Customization and System, such as System Settings and the Ubuntu Software Center. You can choose more than one category at a time, expanding your search. Click on a selected category again to deselect it, narrowing the search. The Applications Filter is shown in Figure 10-21.

A search will display both installed applications and those available for download and installation from the Ubuntu repositories, making un-installed applications much more accessible. Clicking on the icon will open the Ubuntu Software Center to that application, letting you install the application immediately. For example, a search on ink will display the Inkscape Vector Graphics Editor in an "Apps Available for Download" segment. Clicking on the icon opens the Ubuntu Software Center to the Inkscape dialog, letting you click the Install button to install Inkscape directly.

Music and Video lens

The Music lens displays your music files. Filter results lets you refine searches by decade, genre, and source (see Figure 10-22). The source can be Banshee or Rhythmbox music applications.

The video lens displays your videos, both those on your system and those available from online sources. The filter lets you choose sources such as Amazon, YouTube Education, TED Talks, and Bing Video (see Figure 10-22).

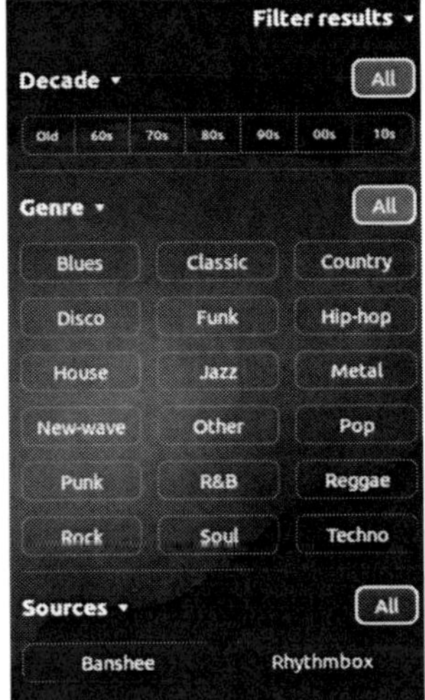
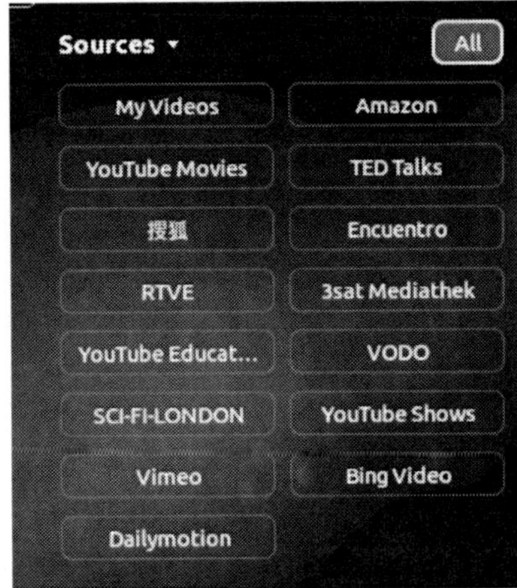

Figure 10-22: Music and Video lens filters

Indicator Menus

Indicator menus provide a standard interface for applications and system tools to interact with the Unity desktop (see Figure 10-23). Indicator menus are used in place of applets, which are no longer supported in ether Unity or GNOME 3. Your Unity desktop initially displays several system indicator menus: Session, User Switcher, Date & Time, messaging, sound volume and Network Manager (see Table 10-3). Ubuntu Unity indicator buttons display colors for a certain status (red for system actions, orange for system warnings, blue for new information, green for approved, and grey for no status). For example, the Session menu icon (Power image) will turn red if your system requires a restart to complete updates. The Messaging menu icon (envelope image) will turn blue if your mailer or IM receives new messages.

Applications can also use indicator menus. For example, the messaging menu handles chat (Empathy), micro-blogs (Twitter), mail, and Ubuntu One status and notifications. Other applications such as tomboy notes and transmission also can add their own indicator menus. In effect, instead of using panel applets, applications now use indicator menus. There is no equivalent of the Add to Panels used in previous releases.

Figure 10-23: Indicator menus

To add the universal access menu, open the Keyboard Preferences dialog (Customization dash), and on the Accessibility tab click "Accessibility features can be toggled with keyboard shortcuts."

Status button	Status menu	Description
Bluetooth icon	Bluetooth	Send or receive files with Bluetooth (hidden if not Bluetooth device detected)
Battery icon	Battery	Battery charge status (hidden if no battery, or fully charged)
Network icon	Network	Network Manager, entries to connect to wired, wireless, mobile, and VPN networks
Sound icon	Sound	Volume control, control default media player (Banshee), and access Sound preferences
Messaging icon	Messaging	Messaging applications such as email, microblogs, and IM. Set IM and microblogging status (social networking)
10:12 AM	Clock	Date & Time, with calendar, and access to Evolution calendar events.
Richard Petersen	User Switcher	Switch users and access user account configuration (Users). Configure access to online accounts
Session icon	Session	Lists entries for configuration tools and power operations. Entries include Lock Screen and Guest Session. For power operations you can log out, suspend, and shut down the system. You can access tools such as System Settings, Displays, Update Manager, Startup Applications, and Printers.

Table 10-3: System Indicator Menus

Custom indicator menus

There are several custom indicator menus available from the Universe repository that support many popular tasks such a weather, system load, cpu frequency, hardware sensors, and radio tray. Currently available on the Ubuntu Universe repository are the Weather Indicator (**indicator-weather** package) , System Load indicator (**indicator-multiload** package), Glipper clipboard manager (**glipper** package), and StackApplet to monitor Stack Exchange sites (**stackapplet** package). Many of the custom indicators require access to the developer's repository using a ppa entry set in the Software Sources dialog, Other Software tab, Add button. Check the Ask Ubuntu page for indicators for more detailed information.

```
http://askubuntu.com/questions/30334/list-of-application-
indicators?page=1&tab=votes#tab-top
```

HUD (Heads-Up Display) for searching menus

Ubuntu features a Heads-Up Display (HUD) for quickly searching for entries in the menus of the current application. The search also includes the indicator menus. Press the Alt key to open the HUD search box, with the icon of the current application to the left. Enter in a search pattern, and a list of matching menus entries is displayed. Choose the one you want, and then press ENTER. In Figure 10-24, the file manager menus are searched.

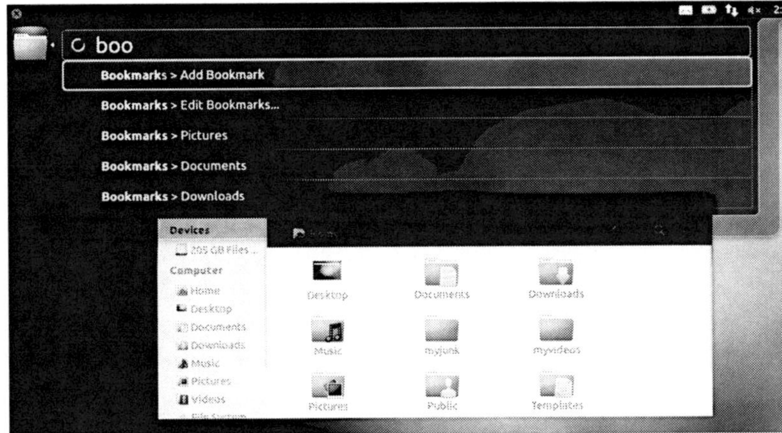

Figure 10-24: HUD menu search

Adding Computer and Network folders to the Launcher and Quicklists

A few specialized folders and applications are not visible either from the Dash or through the MainMenu application. These include certain Go folders such as Computer and Network. You could simply open them and then bookmark them, which adds their entries to the home folder quicklist. Should you want them to be separate Launcher items, you can manually create separate launcher files for them.

To place computer and network on the launcher, you copy the Nautilus Home desktop file from the **/usr/share/applications** folder to your **.local/share/applications** folder, changing the name to **nautilus-computer** or **nautilus-network**. You may have to create an **applications** folder in your **.local/share** directory. For the Computer folder open a terminal and then use a **cp** command to copy the **nautilus-home.desktop** file from the **/usr/share/applications** folder to your **.local/share/applications** folder as **nautilus-computer.desktop**.

```
cp /usr/share/applications/nautilus-home.desktop .local/share/applications/nautilus-
computer.desktop
```

For the network folder, change the name to **nautilus-network.desktop** folder.

```
cp /usr/share/applications/nautilus-home.desktop .local/share/applications/nautilus-
network.desktop
```

To configure a launcher item, you would edit the new applications desktop files in the **/usr/share/applications** folder. The following would edit the Home Folder desktop file (**nautilus-home.desktop**).

```
cd /usr/share/applications
gedit nautilus-computer.desktop
```

Change the Name from "Home Folder" to Computer and the Exec command (fourth line) to invoke **computer:**. Be sure to include the colon. You can also change the icon if you wish.

```
Name=Computer
Exec=nautilus computer:
Icon=computer
```

Also, be sure to change the "Open in a New Window " entry in the [Desktop Action Window] section, as shown here:

```
[Desktop Action Window]
Name=Open a New Window
Exec=nautilus computer:
OnlyShowIn=Unity
```

For the **nautilus-network.desktop** file, you would use the name Network and invoke nautilus with **network:**.

```
Name=Network
Exec=nautilus network:
Icon=network-workgroup

Name=Open a New Window
Exec=nautilus network:
```

Then open your home folder, and from the View menu choose Show Hidden Files to list the **.local** folder. Then access the **.local/share/applications** folder. There you will find the **nautilus-computer-desktop** and **nautilus-network.desktop** files. Simply drag them to the launcher. You can then access your network shares and computer file systems from the launcher. (see Figure 10-25). By default, they are locked to the Launcher. To remove them from the Launcher, right-click and choose the "Unlock from Launcher" entry.

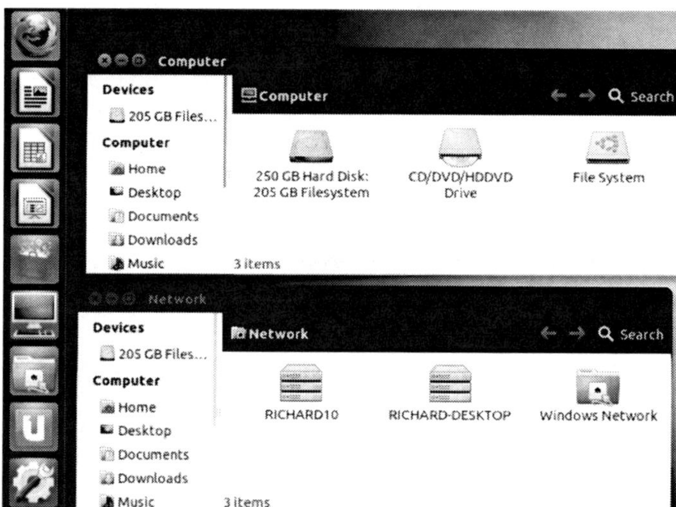

Figure 10-25: Computer and Network item on the Launcher

You could also simply add Computer and Network entries to the Home Folder launcher's quicklist, or to any other Launcher item's quicklist. The entries are placed in Desktop Action segments, referenced by an Actions command. The entries are shown here.

```
Actions=Computer;Network;

[Desktop Action Computer]
Name=Computer
```

```
Exec=nautilus --no-desktop computer:
OnlyShowIn=Unity

[Desktop action Network]
Name=Network
Exec=nautilus --no-desktop network:
OnlyShowIn=Unity
```

Adding Launchers to the Desktop

To add an application launcher to the desktop, you have to place the application launcher file in your **Desktop** folder. An application launcher file has the extension **.desktop** and can be found in the **/usr/share/applications** folder and in your **.local/share/applications** folder. You will have to know the name of the desktop file and perform the copy operation from a terminal window using the **cp** command. For example, the Image Viewer application's launcher file is named **eog.desktop**. The name eog stands for Eye of GNOME , which is the official name for the Image Viewer application. The following copies the **eog.desktop** file to your local Desktop folder, where ~ will reference your home folder.

```
cp /usr/share/applications/eog.desktop  ~/Desktop
```

Then change the permission on the copy to allow execution (open the Desktop folder, right-click on the file, choose properties, and then click the executable check box on the Permission tab). You can also use a simple **chmod** command in a terminal window with the option **755** for read, write, and execute for the owner, and read and execute for all others.

```
cd Desktop
chmod 755 eog.desktop
```

Customizing Launcher Quicklists

The Unity Launcher API discusses how to configure your launcher items to include quicklists, counters, urgency, and progress bars.

```
https://wiki.ubuntu.com/Unity/LauncherAPI
```

The feature most users may want to configure is the static quicklist. The quicklist adds menu items to the launcher item's menu, displayed when you right-click on a launcher item. The Unity API The Unity FAQ shows how to modify the home folder launcher to include a quicklist for your home folder favorite places.

To configure a launcher item's quicklist, you add quicklist entries to the application's desktop file. To make changes system wide to all launchers, you would edit the applications desktop file in the **/usr/share/applications** folder, as an administrative user. The following would edit the Home Folder desktop file (**nautilus-home.desktop**).

```
sudo gedit  /usr/share/applications/nautilus-home.desktop
```

If you want to change the launcher just for your account, create version of your applications desktop files in your **.local/share/applications** folder. A simple way to do this is to copy the system desktop files from the **/usr/share/applications** folder.
For the home folder desktop file, you would copy the **nautilus-home.desktop** file to your home folder's **.local/share/applications** folder.

```
cp /usr/share/applications/nautilus-home.desktop  ~/.local/share/applications
```

Edit the copied file.

```
gedit .local/share/applications/nautilus-home.desktop
```

If the desktop file is not already on the launcher, click and drag it from the **./local/share/applications** folder, or the **/usr/share/applications** folder, to the launcher.

Home Folder Quicklist

Should you want to add entries manually, without using bookmarks, you can configure the Nautilus quick list directly.

Decide whether to make system-wide changes or to make a copy of the **nautilus-home.desktop** file to modify on your account (see previous section).

Be sure the **OnlyShowIn** directive allows display on Unity.

```
OnlyShowIn=GNOME;Unity;
```

If you keep the same name for the desktop file (**nautilus-home.desktop**), then your modified version will also include the local folder entries such as Documents and Pictures. If you use a different name for the desktop file, such as **myhome.desktop** instead of **nautilus-home.desktop**, then the local folder entries are not included.

To simply add entries to the quicklist, add a new Desktop Actions section for each entry. Then add the section name to the Actions command.

Figure 10-26: Home Folder Launcher Quicklist

In each Desktop Action section place Name, Exec, and OnlyShowIn entries. Specify the text to be displayed as the menu entry (Name), the application command to run (Exec) along with any options, and the environment to show it in (OnlyShowIn), which is Unity. In the following example, a "My Videos" entry is added after the "Open in New Window" entry. The text displayed is "My Videos." The application run is nautilus with the option myvideos, which will open the nautilus file manager at the myvideos folder. The OnlyShowIn option is always set to Unity.

```
Actions=Window;myvideos;

[Desktop Action Window]
Name=Open a New Window
Exec=nautilus
OnlyShowIn=Unity
```

```
[Desktop Action myvideos]
Name=My Videos
Exec=nautilus myvideos
OnlyShowIn=Unity
```

Add a Desktop Action section for each folder you want listed, and add the action names to the Actions command.

Should you want a separate desktop launcher that does not include the local folders, you would simply create a desktop file with a different name, such as **mynautilus.desktop**.

```
[Desktop Action myfolders]
```

The complete set of definitions for the modified **nautilus-home.desktop** is shown here.

```
[Desktop Entry]
Name=Home Folder
Comment=Open your personal folder
TryExec=nautilus
Exec=nautilus %U
Icon=user-home
Terminal=false
StartupNotify=true
Type=Application
Categories=GNOME;GTK;Core;
OnlyShowIn=GNOME;Unity;
X-GNOME-Bugzilla-Bugzilla=GNOME
X-GNOME-Bugzilla-Product=nautilus
X-GNOME-Bugzilla-Component=general
X-Ubuntu-Gettext-Domain=nautilus
Actions=Window;myvideos;

[Desktop Action Window]
Name=Open a New Window
Exec=nautilus
OnlyShowIn=Unity

[Desktop Action myvideos]
Name=My Videos
Exec=nautilus myvideos
OnlyShowIn=Unity
```

Ubuntu Software Center Quicklist

A helpful quicklist modification is to add entries for the Update Manager and Software Sources to the Ubuntu Software Center launcher item menu (see Figure 10-27). Edit the **ubuntu-software-center.desktop** file. Add the quicklist definitions to the end of the file.

To make changes system wide to all launchers, you would edit the applications desktop file in the **/usr/share/applications** folder, as an administrative user. The following would edit the Ubuntu Software Center desktop file (**ubuntu-software-center.desktop**).

```
sudo gedit /usr/share/applications/ubuntu-software-center.desktop
```

Figure 10-27: Ubuntu Software Center Launcher Quicklist

If you want to change the launcher just for your account, create versions of the **ubuntu-software-center.desktop** file in your **.local/share/applications** folder. A simple way to do this is to copy the file from the **/usr/share/applications** folder, as shown here.

```
cp /usr/share/applications/ubuntu-software-center.desktop ~/.local/share/applications/
```

Edit the copied file.

```
gedit .local/share/applications/ubuntu-software-center.desktop
```

Add in quicklist entries for the menu entries you want displayed, such as Software Sources. First, add an Actions entry at the end of the file with name you want to give to the Actions section, such as source.

```
Actions=sources;
```

Then define Desktop Action Window encased in brackets.

```
[Desktop Action sources]
```

Then specify the text to be displayed as the menu entry (Name), the application command to run (Exec) along with any options, and the environment (OnlyShowIn), which is Unity. In this case, the text displayed is "Software Sources." The application run is **software-properties-gtk** with the **gksu** command, which opens the Software Sources dialog with administrative permission. The OnlyShowIn option is always set to Unity.

```
[Desktop Action sources]
Name=Software Sources
Exec=gksu software-properties-gtk
OnlyShowIn=Unity
```

Libre Office Quicklist

Instead of showing the three LibreOffice launchers (Writer, Calc, and Presentation), you could simply show the LibreOffice starter launcher for the LibreOffice starter dialog, and add a quicklist for the LibreOffice applications (see Figure 10-28).

To customize your launcher in this way, first copy the **libreoffice-startcenter.desktop** file to your **.local/share/applications** folder. Notice that **.local** is a hidden folder and begins with a period, **.local**. Open a terminal (Terminal in the Accessories dash) and enter the following copy command.

```
cp /usr/share/applications/libreoffice-startcenter.desktop ~/.local/share/applications/
```

Figure 10-28: Libre Office Launcher Quicklist

Then edit the local copy.

```
gedit .local/share/applications/libreoffice-startcenter.desktop
```

Add in quicklist entries for the menu entries you want displayed, such as Software Sources. First, add an Actions entry at the end of the file with name you want to give to the Actions sections, such as writer, calc, impress, math, and draw.

Separate each with a semicolon.

```
Actions=writer;impress,calc,math,draw
```

Then define Desktop Action sections encased in brackets.

```
[Desktop Action writer]
Name=Writer
Exec=libreoffice -writer %U
OnlyShowIn=Unity

[Desktop Action impress]
Name=Impress
Exec=libreoffice -impress %U
OnlyShowIn=Unity

[Desktop Action calc]
Name=Calc
Exec=libreoffice -calc %U
OnlyShowIn=Unity

[Desktop Action math]
Name=Math
Exec=libreoffice -math %U
OnlyShowIn=Unity

[Desktop Action draw]
Name=Draw
Exec=libreoffice -draw %U
OnlyShowIn=Unity
```

Once you have made the changes, you need to place the desktop file on the launcher. Open your home folder. From the View menu, choose Show Hidden files. The **.local** folder is now displayed. Open the **.local** folder, the **share** folder, and then **applications** folder

(**.local/share/applications**). There you will see the **libreoffice-startcenter.desktop** file. Drag it to the launcher. The LibreOffice starter launcher item is now displayed with the quicklist for all the LibreOffice applications.

Accessing Web pages with quicklists

You could also use quicklists to open Web pages. The Exec entry would reference a Web browser command such as **chromium-browser** or the **xdg-open** command, which opens the default browser. The following quicklist definition opens the Ubuntu web site.

```
[Desktop Action ubuntuweb]
Name=Ubuntu Web site
Exec=xdg-open http://www.ubuntu.com
OnlyShowIn=Unity
```

The next definition opens the Google Web site with the Chromium browser.

```
[Desktop Action googleweb]
Name=Google Web site
Exec=chromium-browser https://www.google.com
OnlyShowIn=Unity
```

Be sure to add the section names to the Actions command.

```
Actions=ubuntuweb;googleweb;
```

Managing Services with quicklists

To manage a service such as the Samba or Apache servers, you would use the **gksu** command with the **service** command and the server scripts with a specified option such as start, stop, and restart. The following restarts the Samba server using the Samba service scripts **smbd** and **nmbd**.

```
[Desktop Action samba]
Name=Restart Samba
Exec=gksu service smbd restart && gksu service nmbd restart
OnlyShowIn=Unity
```

Be sure to add the section name to the Actions command.

```
Actions=samba;
```

Creating a custom desktop launcher and quicklist

You can also create your own desktop file with a custom quicklist, which you can add to the Launcher (see Figure 10-29).

The desktop file has the extension **.desktop** and includes a [Desktop Entry] definition. For personal use only, place the file in the **.local/share/applications** folder, and for system-wide use place it in the **/etc/usr/share/applications** folder. The following example shows a **myfavorites.desktop** file with quicklists for tasks commonly used.

Figure 10-29: Favorites Launcher Quicklist

```
 [Desktop Entry]
Name=myfavorites
X-GNOME-FullName=My Favorites
Comment=Some of my favorites tasks
Icon=emblem-favorite
Terminal=false
Type=Application
StartupNotify=true

Actions=UbuntuSite;Computer;Network;SambaRestart

[Desktop Action UbuntuSite]
Name=Ubuntu Web site
Exec=xdg-open http://www.ubuntu.com
OnlyShowIn=Unity

[Desktop Action Computer]
Name=Computer
Exec=nautilus --no-desktop computer:
OnlyShowIn=Unity

[Desktop Action Network]
Name=Network
Exec=nautilus --no-desktop network:
OnlyShowIn=Unity

[Desktop Action SambaRestart]
Name=Restart Samba
Exec=gksu service smbd restart && gksu service nmbd restart
OnlyShowIn=Unity
```

The Nautilus File Manager

Nautilus the GNOME file manager that supports the standard features for copying, removing, and deleting items as well as setting permissions and displaying items. Nautilus also lets you set up customized views of file listings, enabling you to display images for directory icons and run component applications within the file manager window.

Nautilus was designed as a desktop shell in which different components can be employed to add functionality. An image viewer can display images. The GNOME compliant media player can run sound and video files. Files can be archived, as well as extracted from archives.

Home Folder Sub-folders and Bookmarks

Ubuntu uses the Common User Directory Structure (xdg-user-dirs at **http://freedesktop.org**) to set up sub-folders in the user home directory. Folders will include **Documents**, **Music**, **Pictures**, **Downloads**, and **Videos**. These localized user folders are used as defaults by many desktop applications. Users can change their folder names or place them within each other using the GNOME file browser. For example, Music can be moved into **Documents**, **Documents/Music**. Local configuration is held in the **.config/user-dirs.dirs** file. System-wide defaults are set up in the **/etc/xdg/user-dirs.defaults** file. The icons for these folders are displayed in figure 10-30.

Figure 10-30: Nautilus file manager home folders

The folders are also default bookmarks. You can access a bookmarked folder directly from the either the Nautilus window sidebar or from the Bookmarks menu. You can also add your own bookmarks for folders by opening the folder and choosing Add Bookmark from the Bookmarks menu. Your folder will appear in the Bookmarks section of the Nautilus sidebar and on the Bookmarks menu, as well as on the Nautilus Launcher icon's quicklist (right-click). Use the Edit Bookmarks dialog to remove bookmarks.

In the Launcher, the Home Folder item quicklist now includes entries for default and custom bookmarks (see Figure 10-31). You can easily add your own folders by bookmarking them. They will appear in the quicklist along with the default folders.

Figure 10-31: Home Folder Launcher Quicklist

Nautilus Windows

When you click the folder for your home folder item on the Launcher or choose Home Folder form the desktop Go menu, a file manager window opens showing your home folder. On Ubuntu Unity, the file manager menu bar is located on the Unity application menu (see Figure 10-

32). The file manager window displays several components, including a toolbar, a location bar, and a sidebar (see Figure 10-32). The sidebar displays Places items showing your file systems and home folder sub-folders. The main pane (to the right) displays the icons or listing of files and sub-folders in the current working folder. A status bar at the bottom of the window displays information about a selected file or folder. You can choose to display or hide the status bar, sidebar, and main toolbar by selecting their entries in the View menu.

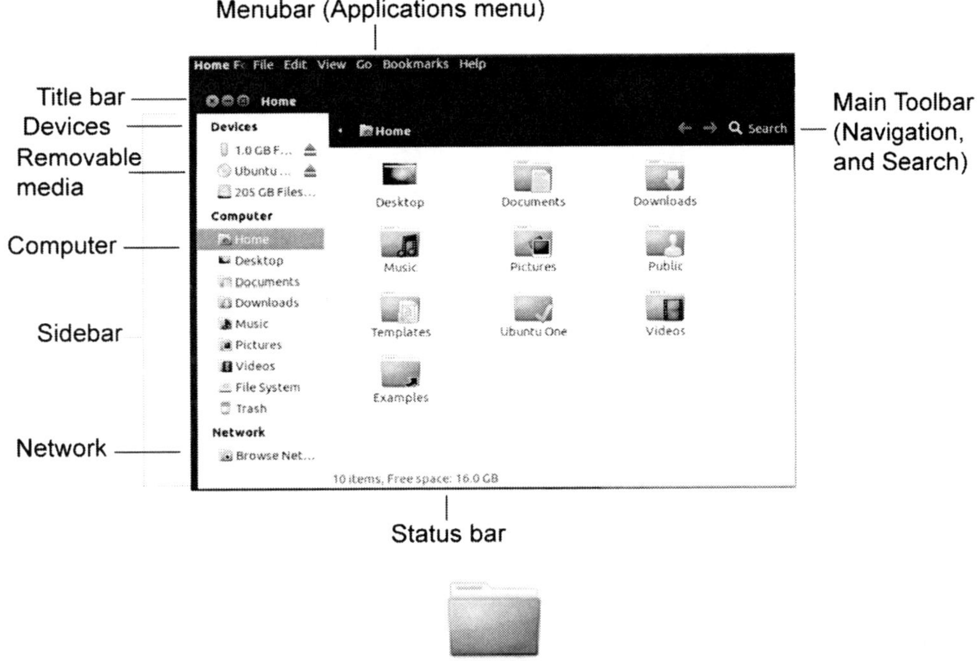

Figure 10-32: Nautilus file manager window on Unity with Menu bar in Applications menu

When you open a new folder, the same window is used to display it, and you can use the Forward and Back arrows to move through previously opened folders. The main toolbar displays buttons for your folder and its parent folders. You can click on a folder button to move to it directly. It also can display a location URL text box instead of buttons, where you can enter the location of a folder, either on your system or on a remote system. Press **Ctrl-L** or from the GO menu select Location (GO | Location). When you access another folder, you revert back to the folder button location bar.

For a less cluttered window you can choose not to display the main toolbar, side pane, location bar, or status bar (see Figure 10-33). Open any folder and from the View menu you can choose the Main Toolbar, Side Pane, Location Bar, or Status Bar entries to uncheck them.

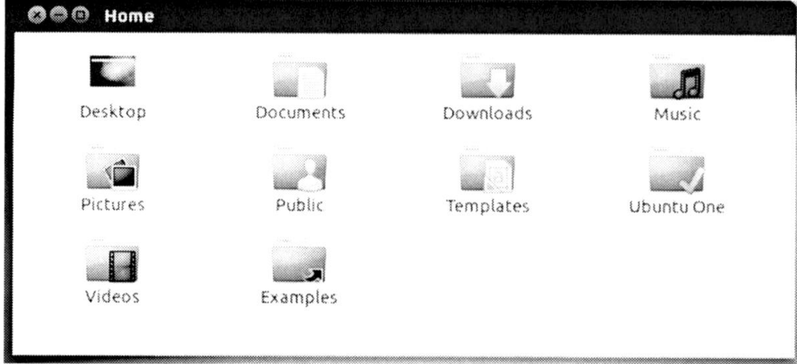

Figure 10-33: Nautilus file manager window simplified

Nautilus Side Pane: Tree, History, and Notes

The Nautilus sidebar provides two different views you can select from View | Sidebar menu: Places and Tree. The Places view shows file system locations that you would normally access: devices, computer folders, and network folders. Selecting the File System location places you at top of the file system, letting you move to any accessible part of it. The Tree view displays a tree-based hierarchical view of the folders and files on your system, highlighting the one you have currently selected. You can use this tree to move to other directories and files. The tree maps all the folders on your system, starting from the root folder, as well as your network folders. You can expand or shrink any folder. Select a folder by clicking the folder name. The contents of that folder are then displayed.

Tabs and Extra Pane

The GNOME file manager supports tabs with which you can open up several folders in the same file manager window. To open a tab, select New Tab from the File menu or press **Ctrl-t**. You can use the entries in the Tabs menu to move from one tab to another, or to rearrange tabs. You can also use the Ctrl-PageUp and Ctrl-PageDown keys to move from one tab to another. Use the Shift-Ctrl-PageUp and Shift-Ctrl-PageDown keys to rearrange the tabs. To close a tab, click its close **x** button on the right side of the tab (see Figure 10-34).

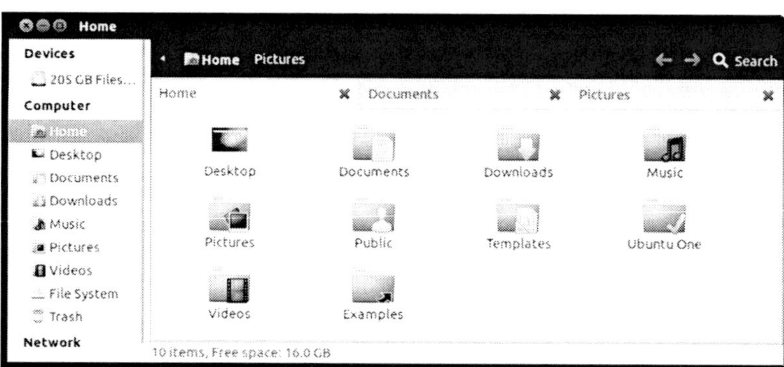

Figure 10-34: Nautilus file manager window with tabs

To access two folders at the same time within the same file manager window, you can choose to add a pane. Choose View | Extra Pane or press F3 to open a new pane, use the same actions to close the pane. The extra pane is useful if you want to copy or move files and sub-folders from one folder to another. Each pane can have tabs, letting you move quickly between folders.

Menu Item	Description
Create Folder	Creates a new subdirectory in the directory.
Create Document	Creates a new document using installed templates.
Ubuntu One	Displays a submenu to share, synchronize, and publish a folder, as well as hide the Ubuntu One emblem or copy the Web link.
Arrange Items	Displays a submenu to arrange files by name, size, type, date, or emblem.
Organize by Name	Arrange files by name
Paste	Pates files that you have copied or cut, letting you move or copy files between folders, or make duplicates.
Zoom In	Provides a close-up view of icons, making them appear larger.
Zoom Out	Provides a distant view of icons, making them appear smaller.
Normal Size	Restores view of icons to standard size.
Properties	Opens the Properties dialog for the directory

Table 10-5: Nautilus File Manager Pop-up Menu

Displaying Files and Folders

You can view a directory's contents as icons, a compact list, or as a detailed list, which you can choose from the View menu: Icons, List, and Compact. Use the control keys to change views quickly: **Ctrl-1** for Icons, **Ctrl-2** for list, and **Ctrl-3** for compact. The List view provides the name, permissions, size, date, owner, and group. Buttons are displayed for each field across the top of the main pane. You can use these buttons to sort the list according to that field. For example, to sort the files by date, click the Date button, to sort by size, click Size.

To sort items in the Icon view, select the Arrange Items entry in the View menu and then select a layout option (View | Arrange Items | By *layout*). Certain types of file icons will display previews of their contents—for example, the icons for image files will display a small version of the image. A text file will display in its icon the first few words of its text.

The View | Zoom In entry enlarges your view of the window, making icons bigger, and Zoom Out reduces your view, making them smaller. Normal Size restores them to the standard size. You can also use the **Ctrl-+** and **Ctrl--** keys to zoom in and out.

Nautilus Pop-up Menu

You can click anywhere on the empty space on the main pane of a file manager window to display a pop-up menu with entries for managing and arranging your file manager icons (see Table 10-5). To create a new folder, select Create Folder. The Arrange Items entry displays a submenu with entries for sorting your icons by name, size, type, modification date, and emblems. The

Manually entry lets you move icons wherever you want on the main pane. You can also paste files you have cut or copied to move or copy them between folders, or make duplicates. Use the Zoom in and Zoom out entries to change the icon size for the folders and files in the current directory.

The "Ubuntu One | Synchronize This Folder" entry will make the folder an Ubuntu One managed folder, uploading its contents to the Ubuntu One server, and copying it to corresponding folders on all your Ubuntu One enabled computers. You have to have Ubuntu One configured and running (see Chapter 9).

Note: If you move a file to a directory on another partition it will be copied instead of moved.

Navigating in the file manager

The Nautilus file manager operates similarly to a Web browser, using the same window to display opened directories. It maintains a list of previously viewed directories, and you can move back and forth through that list using the toolbar buttons. The left arrow button moves you to the previously displayed directory, and the right arrow button moves you to the next displayed directory. Use the sidebar to access your storage devices (USB, CD/DVD disc, and attached hard drives). From the sidebar, you can also access mounted network folders. On the Computer section of the sidebar, you can access your home folders, trash, and the file system. The File System entry opens your root (top) system directory.

To open a subdirectory, you can double-click its icon or single-click the icon and select Open from the File menu (File | Open). If you want to open a separate Nautilus window for that directory, right-click the directory's icon and select "Open In New Window." To open the folder in a new tab, select "Open in New Tab."

Figure 10-35: File Manger Launcher item and quicklist for copy operations

Managing Files

As a GNOME-compliant file manager, Nautilus supports desktop drag-and-drop operations for copying and moving files. To move a file or directory, drag-and-drop from one directory to another as you would on Windows or Mac interfaces. The move operation is the default drag-and-drop operation in GNOME. To copy a file to a new location, press the Ctrl key as you drag-and-drop.

When you copy a large file, the file manger Launcher item show a program bar for the copy operation (see Figure 10-35). Also, the file manager quicklist adds two entries: Show Copy Dialog and Cancel All In-progress Actions.

Using a file's pop-up menu

You can also perform remove, rename, and link creation operations on a file by right-clicking its icon and selecting the action you want from the pop-up menu that appears (see Table 10-6). For example, to remove an item, right-click it and select the Move To Trash entry from the pop-up menu. This places it in the Trash directory, where you can later delete it. To create a link, right-click the file and select Make Link from the pop-up menu. This creates a new link file that begins with the term "Link."

Menu Item	Description
Open	Opens the file with its associated application. Directories are opened in the file manager. Associated applications are listed.
Open In A New Tab	Opens a file or directory in a new tab in the same window.
Open In A New Window	Opens a file or directory in a separate window.
Open With Other Application	Selects an application with which to open this file. An Open With dialog opens listing possible applications.
Cut Copy	Entries to cut and copy the selected file.
Make Link	Creates a link to that file in the same directory.
Rename (F2)	Renames the file.
Copy To	Copy a file to the Home Folder, Desktop, or to a folder displayed in another pane in the file manager window.
Move To	Move a file to the Home Folder, Desktop, or to a folder displayed in another pane in the file manager window.
Move To Trash	Moves a file to the Trash directory, where you can later delete it.
Ubuntu One	Displays a submenu to share, synchronize, and publish a folder, as well as hide the Ubuntu One emblem or copy the Web link.
Send To	Email the file
Compress	Archives file using File Roller.
Sharing Options	Displays the Folder Sharing dialog (Samba and NFS).
Properties	Displays the Properties dialog.

Table 10-6: The Nautilus File and Directory Pop-Up Menu

Renaming Files

To rename a file, you can either right-click the file's icon and select the Rename entry from the pop-up menu, or click its icon and press the F2 function key. The name of the icon will be highlighted in a color background, encased in a small text box. You can overwrite the old one, or edit the current name by clicking a position in the name to insert text, as well as use the backspace key to delete characters. You can also rename a file by entering a new name in its Properties dialog box (Basic tab).

Grouping Files

You can select a group of files and folders by clicking the first item and then hold down the SHIFT key while clicking the last item, or by clicking and dragging the mouse across items you want to select. To select separated items, hold the CTRL key down as you click the individual icons. If you want to select all the items in the directory, choose the Select All entry in the Edit menu (Edit | Select All). You can then copy, move, or even delete several files at once. To select items that have a certain pattern in their name, choose Edit | Select Items Matching to open a dialog where you can enter the pattern (**Ctrl-s**). Use the * character to match partial patterns, as in ***let*** to match on all file names with the pattern "let" in them. The pattern **my*** would match on file names beginning with the "my" pattern, and ***.png** would match on all PNG image files (the period indicates a file name extension).

Opening Applications and Files MIME Types

You can start any application in the file manager by double-clicking either the application itself or a data file used for that application. If you want to open the file with a specific application, you can right-click the file and select one of the Open With entries. One or more Open with entries will be displayed for default and possible application, like "Open with gedit" for a text file. If the application you want is not listed, you can select "Open with Other Application" to open an "Open With dialog listing available applications. Drag-and-drop operations are also supported for applications. You can drag a data file to its associated application icon (say, on the desktop); the application then starts up using that data file.

To change or set the default application to use for a certain type of file, you open a file's Properties dialog and select the Open With tab. Here you can choose the default application to use for that kind of file. Possible applications will be listed, organized as the default, recommended, related, and other categories. Click on the one you want to change to the default and click the "set as default" button. Once you choose the default, it will appear in the Open With list for this file.

For example, to associate BitTorrent files with the original BitTorrent application, you would right-click any BitTorrent file (one with a **.torrent** extension), select the Properties entry, and then select the Open With tab. A list of installed applications is displayed, such as Transmission, Ktorrent, and BitTorrent. Click BitTorrent to use the original BitTorrent application, and then click Close. BitTorrent is now the default application for all **.torrent** files.

If you want to add an application to the Open With menu, click the "Show other applications" button to list possible applications. Select the one you want and click the Add button. If there is an application on the Open With tab you do not want listed in the Open With menu items, right-click on it, and choose **Forget association**.

File and Directory Properties

In a file's Properties dialog, you can view detailed information on a file and set options and permissions (see Figure 10-36). A file's Properties dialog has three tabs: Basic, Permissions, and Open With. Folders will have an additional share tab. The Basic tab shows detailed information such as type, size, location, and date modified. The type is a MIME type, indicating the type of application associated with it. The file's icon is displayed at the top with a text box showing the file's name. You can edit the filename in the Name text box, changing that name. If you want to change the icon image used for the file or folder, click the icon image (next to the name) to open a Select Custom Icon dialog to browse for the one you want. The **/usr/share/pixmaps** directory holds the set of current default images, though you can select your own images (click **pixmaps** entry in the Places sidebar). Click an image file to see its icon displayed in the right pane. Double-click to change the icon image.

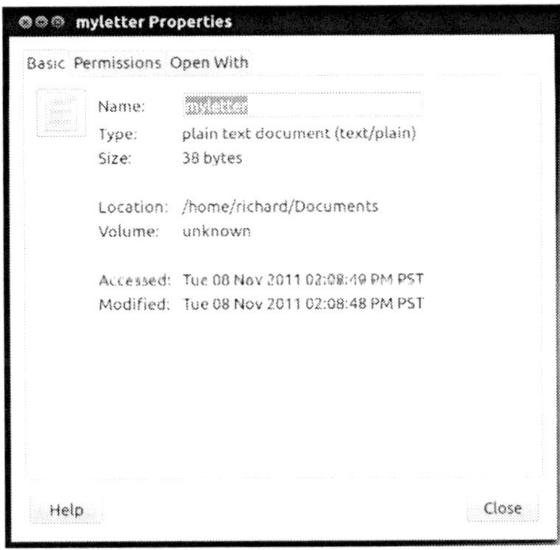

Figure 10-36: File properties on Nautilus

The Permissions tab for files shows the read, write, and execute permissions for owner, group, and others, as set for this file. You can change any of the permissions here, provided the file belongs to you. You configure access for the owner, the group, and others, using drop-down menus. You can set owner permissions as Read Only or Read And Write. For group and others, you can also set the None option, denying access. Clicking on the group name displays a menu listing different groups, allowing you to select one to change the file's group. If you want to execute this as an application you check the "Allow executing file as program" entry. This has the effect of setting the execute permission.

The Open With tab for files lists all the applications associated with this kind of file. You can select the one you want to use as the default. This can be particularly useful for media files, where you may prefer a specific player for a certain file, or a particular image viewer for pictures.

Certain kind of files will have additional tabs, providing information about the file. For example, an audio file will have an Audio tab listing the type of audio file and any other information like a song title or compression method used. An image file will have an Image tab listing the resolution and type of image. A video file will contain an Audio/Video tab showing the type of video file along with compression and resolution information.

The Permissions tab for folders operates much the same way, but it includes two access entries: Folder Access and File Access. The Folder Access entry controls access to the folder with options for None, List Files Only, Access Files, and Create And Delete Files. These correspond to read, read and execute permissions given to directories. The File Access entry lets you set permissions for all those files in the directory. They are the same as for files: for the owner, Read or Read and Write; for the group and others, the entry adds a None option to deny access. To set the permissions for all the files in the directory accordingly (not just the folder), you click the "Apply Permissions To Enclosed Files" button.

The Share tab for folders allows you to share folders as network shares. If you have Samba or NFS, these will allow your folders and files to be shared with users on other systems. You have the option to specify whether the shared folder or file will be read only or allow write access. To allow write access check the "Allow other to create and delete files in this folder" entry. To open access to all users, check the Guest access entry.

Nautilus Preferences

You can set preferences for your Nautilus file manager in the Preferences dialog, accessible by selecting the Preferences item in any Nautilus file manager window's Edit menu (Edit | Preferences).

The Views tab allows you to select how files are displayed by default, such as the list, icon, or compact view. You also can set default zoom levels for icon, compact, and list views.

Behavior lets you choose how to select files, manage the trash, and handle scripts.

Display lets you choose what added information you want displayed in an icon caption, like the size or date.

The List Columns tab lets you choose both the features to display in the detailed list and the order in which to display them. In addition to the already-selected Name, Size, Date, and Type, you can add permissions, group, MIME type, and owner.

The Preview tab lets you choose whether you want small preview content displayed in the icons, like beginning text for text files.

Tip: To display a Delete option on the file menus, on the Behavior tab of the File Management Preferences click the "Include a Delete Command that bypasses Trash" entry in the Trash section.

Nautilus as a FTP Browser

Nautilus works as an operational FTP browser. You can use the Connect to Server entry on the File menu to open a "Connect to Server" dialog where you can enter the URL for the FTP site (you do not need to specify **ftp://**). The Service Type drop-down menu lists different kinds of FTP access. The default is "Public FTP" used for anonymous logins used for most public FTP sites. In the folder entry you can specify a directory on the site if you want. For a private FTP site you can use "FTP (with login)" which will display a User Name entry. For a shared Windows folder chose "Windows share" which displays entries for the share, folder, user name, and domain. For those sites requiring SSH encryption, you would use SSH.

Folders on the FTP site will be displayed, and you can drag files to a local directory to download them. You can navigate through the folders as you would with any Nautilus folder, opening directories or returning to parent directories. To download a file, just drag it from the ftp window to a local directory window. A small dialog will appear showing download progress. To upload a file, just drag it from your local folder to the window for the open ftp directory. Your file will be uploaded to that ftp site (if you have permission to do so). You can also delete files on the site's directories.

GNOME

The Network Object Model Environment, also known as GNOME, is a powerful and easy-to-use environment consisting primarily of a desktop and a set of GUI tools with which program interfaces can be constructed. GNOME is designed to provide a flexible platform for the development of powerful applications. Currently, GNOME is supported by several distributions and is the primary interface for Ubuntu. GNOME is free and released under the GNU Public License. The GNOME 3.2 desktop can be downloaded and installed from the Universe repository as **gnome**. It is not supported by Ubuntu.

You can find out more about GNOME at its Web site, **www.gnome.org**. The Web site provides online documentation, such as the GNOME User's Guide and FAQs. For detailed documentation, check the GNOME documentation site at **http://library.gnome.org**.

GTK+ is the widget set used for GNOME applications. The GTK+ widget set is entirely free under the Lesser General Public License (LGPL). The LGPL enables developers to use the widget set with proprietary software, as well as free software (the GPL would restrict it to just free software). The drag-and-drop functionality supports drag-and-drop operations with other widget sets that support these protocols, such as Qt used for KDE.

11. Kubuntu (KDE)

The KDE Desktop

Kickoff menu

Plasma

Dashboard

Activities

KWin: Desktop Effects

KDE File Manager: Dolphin

Web and FTP Access

KPackageKit Software Manager

KDE System Settings

KDE Directories and Files

The K Desktop Environment (KDE) is a desktop that includes the standard desktop features, such as a window manager and a file manager, as well as an extensive set of applications that cover most Linux tasks. The KDE version of Ubuntu is called Kubuntu and is available as a separate Desktop CD and as the **kubuntu-desktop** and **kubuntu-full** meta-packages on the Ubuntu Software Center. The KDE desktop is developed and distributed by the KDE Project, which is a large open group of hundreds of programmers around the world. KDE is open source software provided under a GNU Public License and is available free of charge along with its source code. KDE development is managed by the KDE Core Team.

Numerous applications written specifically for KDE are accessible from the desktop. These include editors, photo and paint image applications, sound and video players, and office applications. Such applications usually have the letter *K* as part of their name, for example Calligra Words or KMail. On a system administration level, KDE provides several tools for managing your system such as the KPackageKit software manager, the kde-config-cron task scheduler, and the KDE system monitor. KDE applications also feature a built-in Help application. KDE includes support for the office application suite Calligra, which includes a presentation application, a spreadsheet, an illustrator, and a word processor, among other components. In addition, an integrated development environment (IDE), called KDevelop, is available to help programmers create KDE-based software.

Web Site	Description
`http://www.kde.org`	KDE Web site
`http://www.kubuntu.org`	Kubuntu site
`http://www.kde-apps.org`	KDE software repository
`http://techbase.kde.org`	KDE developer site
`http://qt.nokia.com/`	Site for Qt libraries
`http://www.calligra.org`	Calligra Suite
`http://www.kde-look.org`	KDE desktop themes, select KDE entry
`http://lists.kde.org`	KDE mailing lists

Table 11-1: KDE Web Sites

The K Desktop Environment (KDE)

KDE, initiated by Matthias Ettrich in October 1996, is designed to run on any Unix implementation, including Linux, Solaris, HP-UX, and FreeBSD. The official KDE Web site is **http:://www.kde.org**, which provides news updates, download links, and documentation. Several KDE mailing lists are available for users and developers, including announcements, administration, and other topics. A great many software applications are currently available for KDE at **http://www.kde-apps.org**. Development support and documentation can be obtained at the KDE Techbase site at **http://techbase.kde.org**. Most applications are available on the Ubuntu repositories and can be installed directly from KPackageKit, the Synaptic Package Manager, and the Ubuntu Software Center. Various KDE Web sites are listed in Table 11-1.

New versions of KDE are released frequently, sometimes every few months. KDE releases are designed to enable users to upgrade their older versions easily. Your Ubuntu software updater will automatically update KDE from Ubuntu repositories, as updates become available.

KDE uses as its library of GUI tools the Qt library, developed and supported by Nokia (**http://qt.nokia.com**). Qt is considered one of the best GUI libraries available for Unix/Linux systems. Using Qt has the advantage of relying on a commercially developed and supported GUI library. Nokia provides the Qt libraries as Open Source software that is freely distributable.

KDE 4

The KDE 4 release is a major reworking of the KDE desktop. KDE 4.6.2 is included with the Kubuntu 12.04 distribution. Check the Kubuntu and KDE sites for detailed information on KDE 4, including the visual guide.

```
http://kde.org/announcements/4.0/
```

For features added with KDE 4.5, check:

```
http://kde.org/announcements/4.5/
```

For features added with KDE 4.7 (current Kubuntu edition), check:

```
http://kde.org/announcements/4.7/
```

Every aspect of KDE has been reworked with KDE4. There is a new files manager, desktop, theme, panel, and configuration interface. KDE Window manager supports advanced compositing effects and Oxygen artwork for user interface theme, icons, and windows.

The primary component of the KDE4 desktop is the Plasma desktop shell. Plasma has containments and plasmoids. Plasmoids operate similar to applets in GNOME 2.3, small applications running on the desktop or panel. Plasmoids operate within containments. On KDE4, there are two Plasma containments, the panel and the desktop. In this sense, the desktop and the panel are features of an underlying Plasma operation. They are not separate programs. Each has their own set of plasmoids.

Each containment has a toolbox for configuration. The desktop has a toolbox at the top right corner, and panels will have a toolbox on the right side. The panel toolbox includes configuration tools for sizing and positioning the panel. Kubuntu also supports Activities, multiple plasma desktop containments, each with their own set of plasmoids.

Kubuntu 12.04

The Kubuntu edition of Ubuntu installs KDE as the primary desktop from the Kubuntu install disc. Kubuntu 12.04 officially supports and installs KDE 4.8.1. The latest feature include with Kubuntu 12.04 are discussed at:

```
http://www.kubuntu.org/news/12.04-release
```

Changes with 12.04 include:

Kubuntu uses KDE 4.8: **http://www.kubuntu.org/news/12.04-release** and **http://www.kde.org/announcements/4.8/**

Performance improvement for KWin

Activities management has a new user interface, making it easier to associate applications with activities.

Search on KDE has unified the KFind and Dolphin search into a simplified search bar.

Dolphin supports faceted browsing, a filter panel to perform searches using file meta data.

Samba file sharing for folders is supported from dolphin directly.

New language selector and printer configuration bug fixes

Phonom now uses a Gstreamer backend, which provides standard multimedia codec support for both Kubuntu and Ubuntu.

GTK (GNOME and Unity) applications that run on KDE can now make use of the KDE Oxygen artwork (theme).

The **kubuntu-full** set of packages, provided with the Kubuntu DVD or downloadable as a meta package, provides an extensive set of KDE applications.

Installing Kubuntu

You can download the Kubuntu Desktop discs from the Kubuntu site at:

```
http://www.kubuntu.org/
```

You can also download the discs directly from **http://releases.ubuntu.com**.

```
http://releases.ubuntu.com/kubuntu/precise/
```

You can obtain the DVD disc for Kubuntu from **http://cdimages.ubuntu.com**

```
http://cdimages.ubuntu.com/kubuntu/releases/precise/release/
```

You can also add Kubuntu as a desktop to an Ubuntu desktop installation (GNOME and Unity). KDE includes numerous packages. Instead of trying to install each one, you should install KDE using its meta packages on the Ubuntu Software Center: **kde-standard** or **kde-full** (on the Synaptic Package Manager use **kubuntu-desktop** or **kubuntu-full**). The full version provides more applications.

```
kde-standard
kde-full
```

You will be prompted to keep the LightDM display manager for logins, though you can change to KDM, the KDE Display Manager. Once installed, KDE will then become an option you can select from the Sessions menu on the Login screen as "KDE Plasma Workspace."

If you are installing Kubuntu from the Kubuntu CD, you will follow the same steps as those used for the Ubuntu Desktop CD: language, keyboard, partition (Disk Setup), time zone, user and host name (User Info). Installation will begin as soon as you choose the partition configuration. The artwork will be different but the tasks will be the same. The Keyboard screen shows an actual image of the keyboard you choose. The "Prepare disk space" screen (partitioning) shows Before and After images of your hard disk partitions both at the bottom of the screen.

The initial install screen is similar to the Ubuntu Alternate CD, with options for "Try Kubuntu without installing", "Install Kubuntu", "Check disc for defects", " Test memory", and "Boot from first hard disk." The "Try Kubuntu without installing" option starts up a Live Kubuntu session from the CD. Function keys provide options for help, language, keymap, modes, accessibility, and other options. The modes menu allows use of a driver update disc or an OEM install. The "Other Options" menu displays the boot options, one of which is "Free software only" which installs open source software only.

Note: Kubuntu has its own restricted package, **kubuntu-restricted-extras**, for multimedia codecs.

KDM

If you are using the KDM to login, a login greeter is displayed at the center of the screen where you can enter your user name and password (see Figure 11-1). Power and Session (down arrow) menus are displayed at the bottom left of the login greeter with the date to the right. The Session menu lets you change the desktop interface. The Power menu has entries for Switch User, Restart X Server, Remote Login, Console Login, and Shutdown. The Shutdown entry will open a dialog with selections to either Restart or Turn Off the computer.

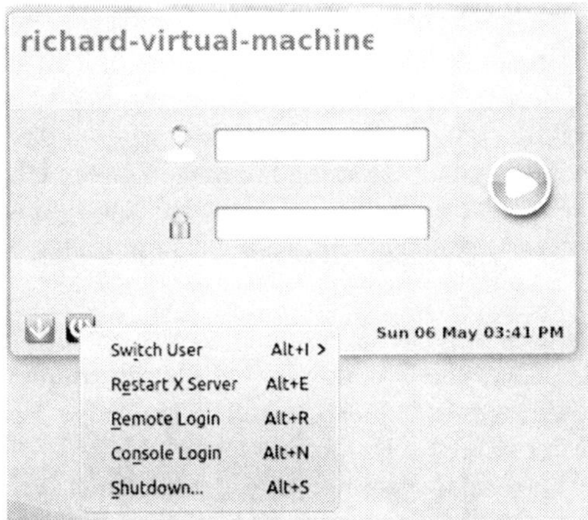

Figure 11-1: KDE Display Manager (KDM), login screen

Upon entering your user name and password and pressing ENTER or clicking the play icon, your KDE session starts up. The login box displays the login splash screen showing the login progress.

You can change the theme of the login greeter using the Login Screen tool (System Settings, Login Screen in the System Administration section). On the theme tab you can download and install new login themes (Get New Themes button), and then select the one you want to use. Click apply to use the new theme. If you want to customize your login background, you can turn off themed greeter on the General tab and then use the Background tab to use your own background image.

Configuration and Administration Access with KDE

KDE uses a set of menus and access points than differ from those in GNOME to access system administration tools. There are also different ways to access KDE configuration tasks, as well as KDE system administration tools not available through GNOME.

On the KDE menu (Kickoff), you can access GNOME and Ubuntu system administration tools from both the Applications | System entries. Here you will find Ubuntu desktop (GNOME) administration tools like Users and Groups, Printing, Login Screen (GNOME), and the Synaptic Package Manager.

Following are the menus available for system configuration and administration:

System Settings   Accessible from the Kickoff menu at Computer | System Settings and from Favorites | System Settings, this is the comprehensive KDE configuration tool, which lists all the KDE configuration tools for managing your KDE desktop, file manager, and system, as well as KDE's own system administration tools that could be used instead of the GNOME tools.

Settings   This collection of system tools is accessible from Applications | Settings. On a mixed desktop with the Ubuntu desktop (GNOME) installed, this is smaller collection of Ubuntu desktop (GNOME) administrative tools such as Ubuntu One, Users and Groups, Samba (system-config-samba), and Time and Date.

System   Accessible from Applications | System, this is collection of both Ubuntu and Kubuntu administration tools. On a mixed desktop with the Ubuntu desktop (GNOME) installed, this is a collection of system tools corresponding to those found in your GNOME System | Administration menu (System and Customization dashes), including the Ubuntu Software Center and the Synaptic Package Manager. Many Ubuntu tools, including Printing and Login Screen are listed here. You will also find Kubuntu tools such as KPackageKit for software management, K3b disc burner, the KDE system monitor, and the KConsole terminal window.

If you are using Kubuntu only, keep in mind that Kubuntu will use the KDE system administration tools if available, not the Ubuntu GNOME based counterparts. Instead of GNOME's **users-admin** you would use userconfig to manage users and groups. For network connections, you would use KNetworkManager, the KDE version of Network Manager. For Printing you use system-config-printer-kde, the KDE version of system-config-printer. On a system that uses only Kubuntu, for Software management and installation you use KDE KPackageKit manager instead of the Synaptic Package Manager or the Ubuntu Software Center. The system administration tools are accessible from the Applications | System menu.

The administration tools issue can be confusing. If you installed Ubuntu using the Ubuntu desktop CD, then GNOME is installed with all the Ubuntu GNOME administration tools. If you then later add the Kubuntu desktop then you will be able to access both the GNOME administration tools and the KDE administration tools.

If, instead, you installed directly from a Kubuntu CD, then only Kubuntu is installed and you have access only to the KDE administration tools. Should you later decide to install the GNOME desktop (ubuntu-desktop) then the Ubuntu GNOME administration tools will become available. You can still install specific GNOME based administration tools using the KPackageKit software manager, in which case the required supporting GNOME libraries will be also installed. You can then run these administration tools from your KDE desktop.

The KDE Desktop

One of KDE's aims is to provide users with a consistent integrated desktop (see Figure 11-2). KDE provides its own window manager (KWM), file manager (Dolphin), program manager, and desktop and panel (Plasma). You can run any other X Window System–compliant application, such as Firefox, in KDE, as well as any GNOME application. In turn, you can also run any KDE application, including the Dolphin file manager in GNOME. The KDE 4 desktop features the Plasma desktop shell with new panel, menu, and widgets, and adds dashboard and activities functions. Keyboard shortcuts are provided for many desktop operations, as well as plasmoid tasks (see Table 11-2).

The desktop supports drag-and-drop and copy-and-paste operations. With the copy-and-paste operation, you can copy text from one application to another. You can even copy and paste from a Konsole terminal window.

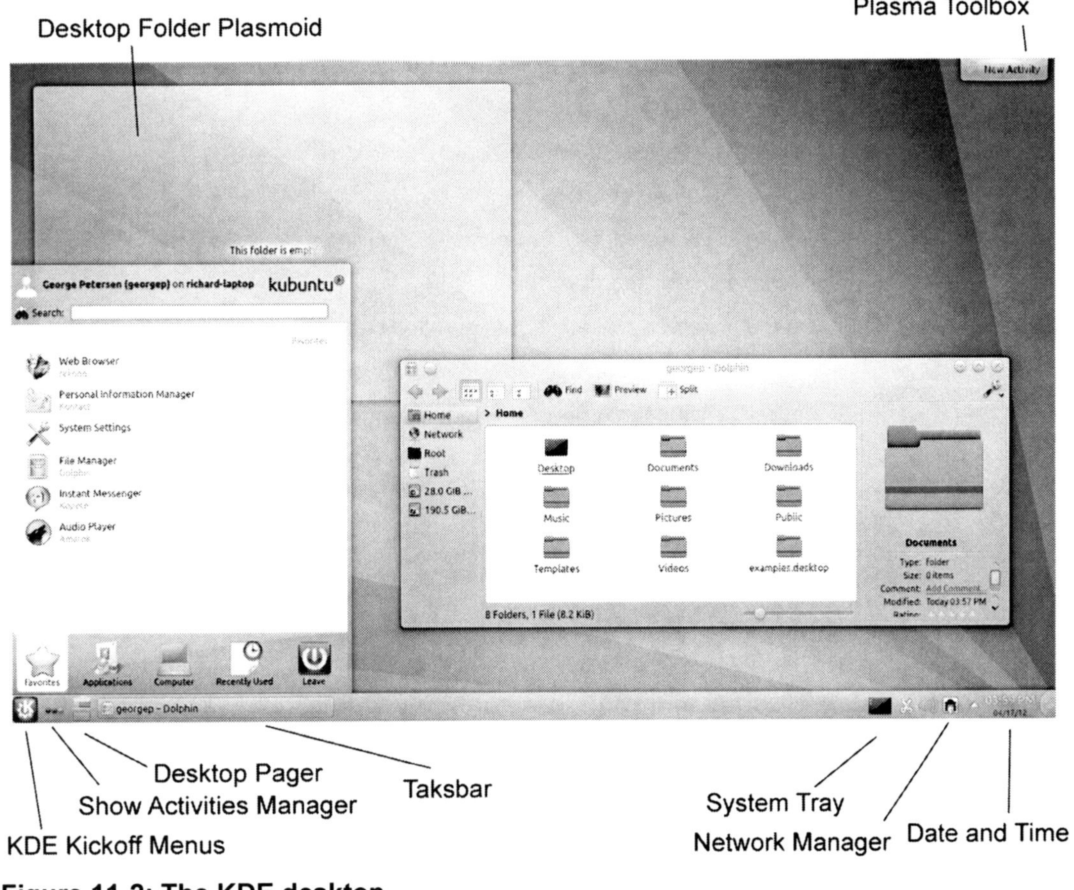

Figure 11-2: The KDE desktop

You can place access to any directories on the desktop by simply dragging their icons from a file manager window to the desktop. A small menu will appear with options for Folder View or Icon. To create just an icon on the desktop select the Icon entry. The Folder View option sets up a Folder View plasmoid for the folder, similar to the Desktop Folder shown in Figure 11-2. Items in the folder are displayed within the folder plasmoid as a menu from which you can make a selection.

Keys	Description
Alt-F1	Kickoff menu
Alt-F2	Krunner, command execution, entry can be any search string for a relevant operation, including bookmarks and contacts, not just applications.
up/down arrows	Move among entries in menus, including Kickoff and menus
left/right arrows	Move to submenus menus, including Kickoff and Quick Access submenus menus
ENTER	Select a menu entry, including a Kickoff or QuickAccess
PageUp, PageDown	Scroll up fast
Alt-F4	Close current window
Alt-F3	Window menu for current window
Ctrl-Alt -F6	Command Line Interface
Ctrl-Alt -F8	Return to desktop from command line interface
Ctrl-r	Remove a selected plasmoid
Ctrl-s	Open a selected plasmoid configuration settings
Ctrl-a	Open the Add Widgets window to add a plasmoid to the desktop
Ctrl-l	Lock your widgets to prevent removal, adding new ones, or changing settings
Alt-Tab	Cover Switch or Box Switch for open windows
Ctrl-F8	Desktop Grid
Ctrl-F9	Present Windows Current Desktop
Ctrl-F10	Present Windows All Desktops
Ctrl-F11	Desktop Cube for switching desktops

Table 11-2: Desktop, Plasma, and KWin Keyboard Shortcuts

To configure your desktop, you use the Workspace Appearance and Behavior tools in the System Settings window (Favorites | System Settings). These include Workspace Appearance, Desktop Effects, Desktop Search, Default Applications, Accessibility, and Window Behavior. Workspace Appearance lets you choose themes and window decorations. Desktop Effects is where set window effects and animation. Windows Behavior controls window display features like taskbars, virtual desktops, title bar actions, and screen edge actions. Fonts and Icons are set in the Applications Appearance dialog located in the Common Appearance and Behavior section.

The KDE Help Center

The KDE Help Center provides a browser-like interface for accessing and displaying both KDE Help files and Linux Man and info files (see Figure 11-3). You can start the Help Center by selecting its entry at the bottom of the Kickoff Applications menu. The Help window displays a sidebar that holds three tabs, one listing contents, one providing a glossary, and one for search options (boolean operators, scope, and number of results). The main pane displays currently selected documents. A help tree on the contents tab in the sidebar lets you choose the kind of Help documents you want to access. Here you can choose KDE manuals, Man pages (UNIX manual pages), or info documents (Browse info Pages), or even application manuals (Application Manuals). Online Help provides links to KDE Web sites such as the KDE user forum and the KDE tech base sites. The Kubuntu Documentation entry has the Kubuntu System Documentation index, which provides basic configuration and overviews of different topics such as networking, media management, and Office and Productivity. Click the "Table of Contents" button to open a listing of all KDE help documents, which you can browse through and click on to open.

A navigation toolbar enables you to move through previously viewed documents. KDE Help documents contain links you can click to access other documents. The Back and Forward commands move you through the list of previously viewed documents. The KDE Help system provides an effective search tool for searching for patterns in Help documents, including Man and info pages. Click the Find button on the toolbar or choose the Find entry from the Edit menu, to open a search box at the bottom of the Help window where you can enter a pattern to search on the current open help document. The Options menu lets you refine your search with regular expressions, case sensitive queries, and whole words only matches.

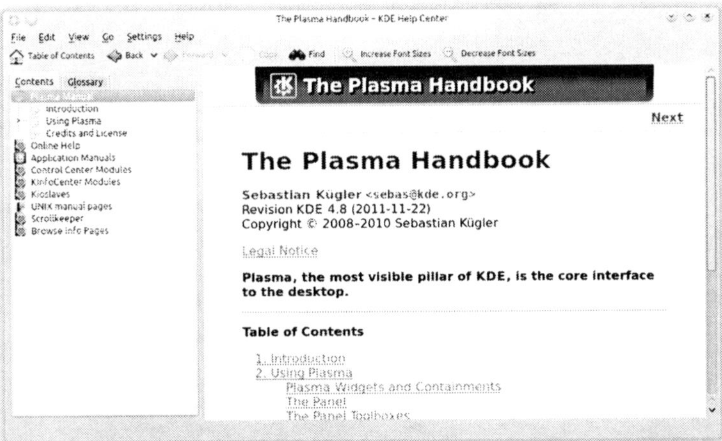

Figure 11-3: KDE Help Center

Desktop Backgrounds (Wallpaper)

The background (wallpaper) is set from the desktop menu directly, not from the System Settings window. Right-click on the desktop background to display the desktop menu and then select Desktop Settings to open the Desktop Settings dialog (see Figure 11-4). The background is called wallpaper in KDE and can be changed in the View tab. You can select other wallpaper from the wallpaper listing or select your own image by clicking the Open button. You can add more wallpaper by clicking the Get New Wallpaper button to open a "Get Hot New Stuff" dialog, which lists and downloads wallpaper posted on the **www.kde-look.org** site (see Figure 11-5). Each wallpaper entry shows an image, description, and rating. Buttons at the upper right of the dialog let you view the entries in details (list) or icon mode. Click the Install button to download the wallpaper and add it to your Desktop Setting's View tab. The wallpaper is downloaded and the Install button changes to Uninstall. You can refine the wallpaper listing by size (category), newest, rating, and popularity (most downloads). To remove a wallpaper, you can select installed wallpapers to find the entry quickly. You can also search by pattern for a wallpaper such as baseball or sky.

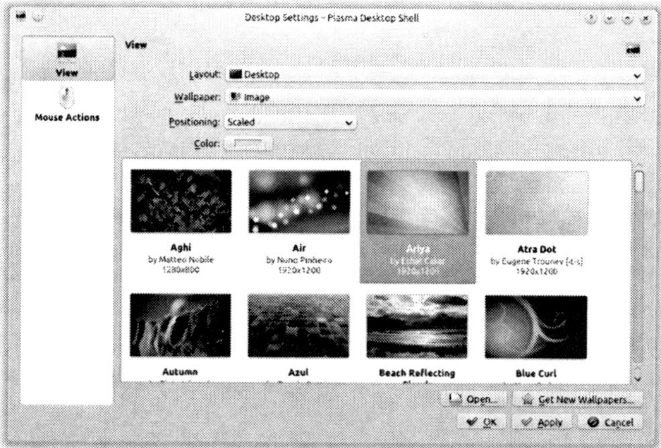

Figure 11-4: Desktop Settings, wallpaper

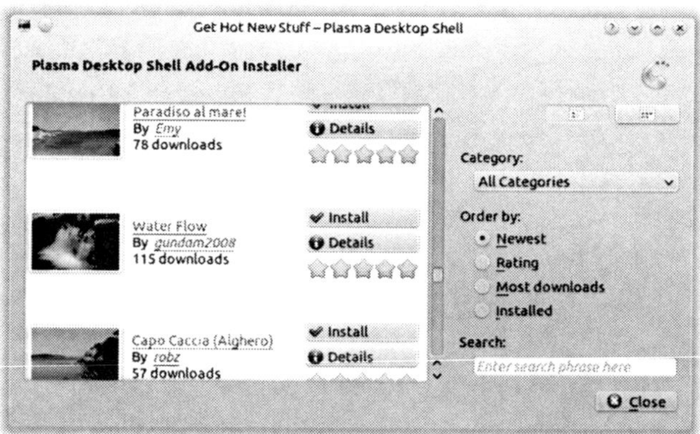

Figure 11-5: Desktop Settings, Get New Wallpapers

Themes

For your desktop, you can also select a variety of different themes, icons, and window decorations. A theme changes the entire look and feel of your desktop, affecting the appearance of desktop elements, such as scroll bars, buttons, and icons. Themes and window decorations are provided for workspaces. Access the System Settings dialog from the KDE Favorites menu or the Applications | Settings menu. On the System Settings dialog, click the Workspace Appearance icon in the "Workspace Appearance and Behavior" section. The Workspace Appearance dialog lets you choose window decorations, cursor themes, desktop themes, and splash screen (start up) themes. The Desktop Themes tab lists installed themes letting you choose the one you want. Click the Get New Themes button to opens a Get Hot New Stuff dialog listing desktop themes from **http://www.kde-look.org** (see Figure 11-6). Click a theme's Install button to download and install the theme. From the Window Decorations tab, you can select window decoration themes. Click the Get New Decorations button to download new decorations. The Splash Screen tab lists installed splash screen themes to choose. Click the Get New Themes button to install new ones.

Icons styles are chosen using Applications Appearance in System Settings dialog's "Common Appearance and Behavior section", System Settings | Applications Appearance. From the Icons tab, you can select an icon set or click the Get New Themes button to download new sets.

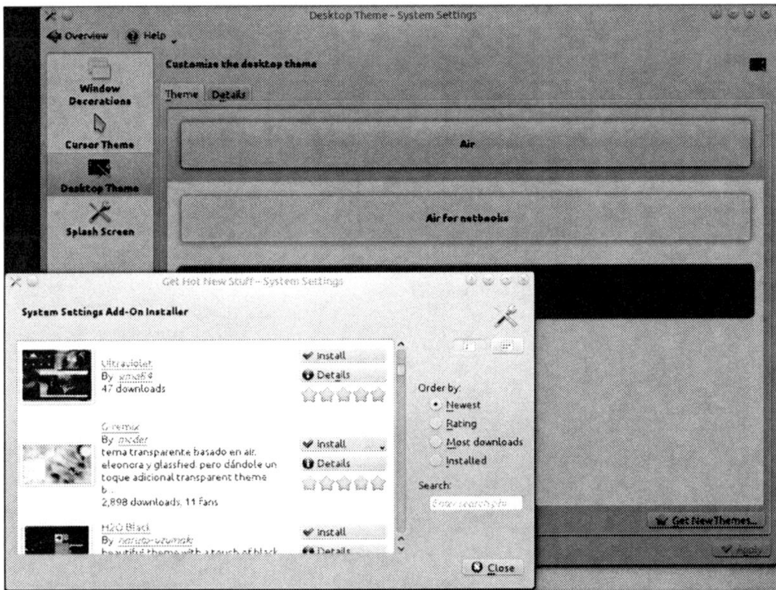

Figure 11-6: System Settings | Workspace Appearance | Desktop Theme, Get New Themes

Leave KDE

To leave KDE, you first click the Leave tab on the KDE Kickoff menu (see Figure 11-7). Here you will find options to logout, lock, switch user, sleep, shutdown, and restart. There are Session and System sections. The Session section has entries for Logout, Lock, and Switch User. The System section features system-wide operations, including Shutdown, Restart, and Sleep.

When you select a leave entry, a dialog for that action appears on the desktop, which you then click. The Shutdown entry will display a Shutdown dialog.

You can also right-click anywhere on the desktop and select the Leave entry from the pop-up menu (see Figure 11-8). If you leave any KDE applications or windows open when you quit, they are restored automatically when you start up again. If you just want to lock your desktop, you can select the Lock entry on the Kickoff Leave menu, and your screen saver will appear. To access a locked desktop, click on the screen and a box appears prompting you for your login password. When you enter the password, your desktop re-appears.

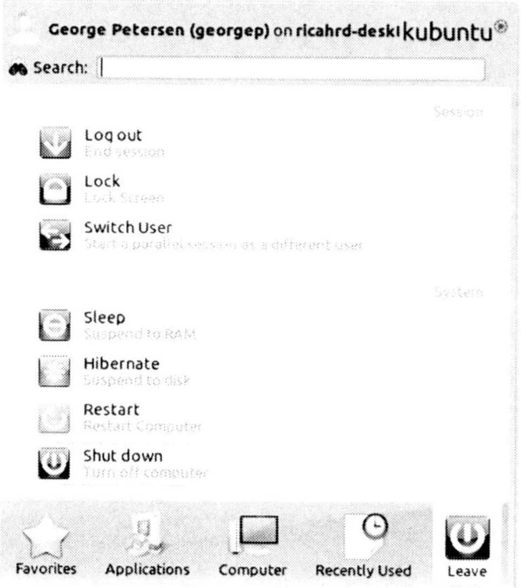

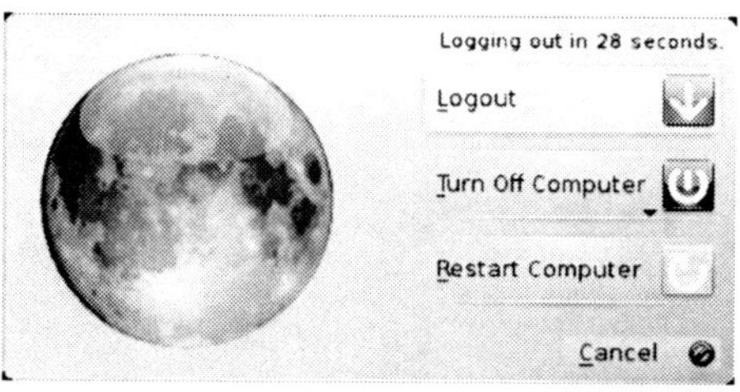

Figure 11-7: The Kickoff menu Leave

Figure 11-8: The desktop menu Leave

KDE Kickoff menus

The KickOff application launcher (see Figure 11-9) organizes menu entries into tabs that are accessed by icons at the bottom of the Kickoff menu. There are tabs for Favorites, Applications, Computer, Recently Used, and Leave. You can add an application to the Favorites tab by right-clicking on the application's Kickoff entry and selecting Add to Favorites. To remove an application from the Favorites menu, right-click on it and select Remove from Favorites. The Applications tab shows application categories. Click the Computer tab to open a window with all your fixed and removable storage. The Recently Used tab shows recently accessed documents and applications. KickOff also provides a Search box where you can search for a particular application, instead of paging through menus. As you move through sub-tabs, they are listed at the top of the Kickoff menu, below the search box, allowing you to move back to a previous tab quickly. Click on a tab name to move directly to that tab.

To configure KDE, you use the KDE System Settings referenced by the System Settings item in the Favorites, Computer, or Applications | Settings tabs.

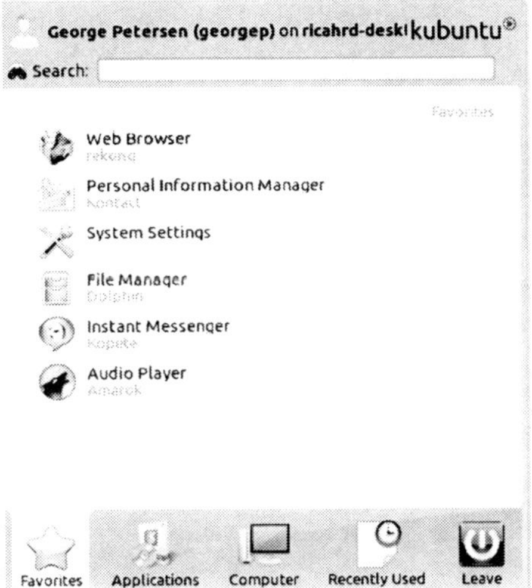

Figure 11-9: The Kickoff menu Favorites

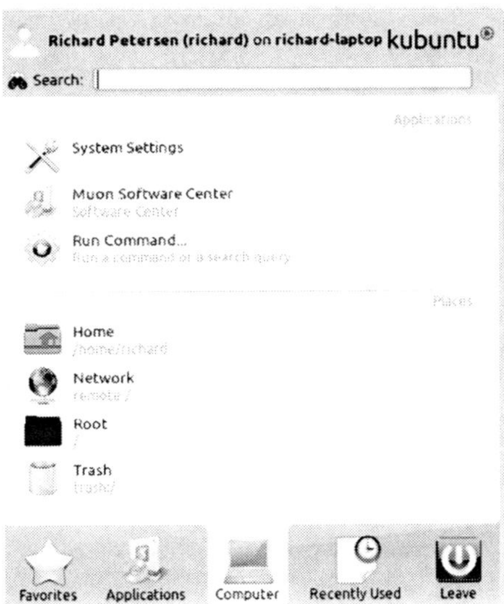

Figure 11-10: The Kickoff menu Computer

The Computer menu has Applications and Places sections (see Figure 11-10). The Applications section has an entry for System Settings. The Places section is similar to the Places menu in GNOME, with entries for your home folder, root folder and the trash, as well as removable devices like USB drives and DVD/CD discs. The root folder is the same as the system folder on GNOME, the top level directory in the Linux file system.

The Applications menu has most of the same entries as those found on GNOME (see Figure 11-11). You can find entries for categories such as Internet, Graphics, and Office. These menus list both GNOME and KDE applications you can use. However, some of the KDE menus contain entries for alternate KDE applications, like KMail on the Internet menu. Other entries will invoke the KDE version of a tool, like the Terminal entry in the System menu, which will invoke the KDE terminal window, KConsole. There is no Preferences menu.

Figure 11-11: The Kickoff menu Applications

Krunner

For fast access to applications, bookmarks, contacts, and other desktop items, you can use Krunner. The Krunner plasmoid operates as a search tool for applications and other items. To find an application, enter a search pattern and a listing of matching applications is displayed. Click on an application entry to start the application. For applications where you know the name, part of the name, or just its basic topic, Krunner is a very fast way to access the application. To start Krunner, press Alt-F2, or right-click on the desktop to display the desktop menu and select "Run Command." Enter the pattern for the application you want to search for and press enter. The pattern "software" or "package" would display both an entry for the KPackageKit software manager and the Synaptic Package Manager (if installed). Entering the pattern "office" displays entries for all the LibreOffice applications (see Figure 11-12).

Clicking the wrench button opens tabs for configuring Krunner. The User Interface tab provides position and style options. You can search by command or task. The plugins tab lists the plugins for searching applications, widgets, and bookmarks, as well as providing capabilities such a running shell commands and opening files. The question mark opens a dialog listing search features such a searching for devices, applications, commands, and widgets.

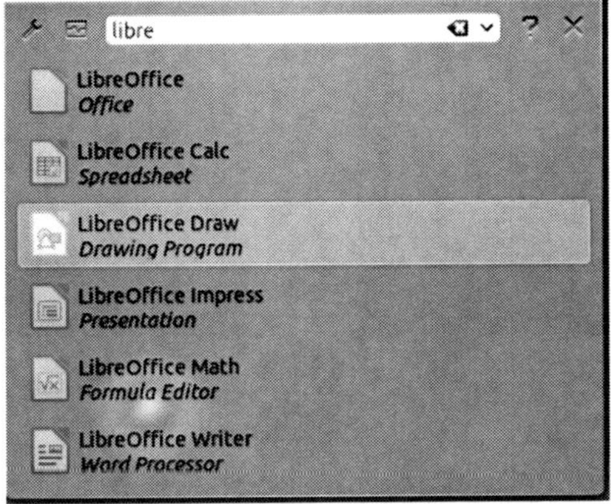

Figure 11-12: Krunner application search

Removable Devices: Device Notifier

Installed on the system tray to the right is the Device Notifier. When you insert a removable device like a CD/DVD disc or a USB drive, the New Device Notifier briefly displays a dialog showing all your removable devices, including the new one. The Device Notifier icon is displayed on the system tray. You can click on the New Device Notifier any time to display this dialog. Figure 11-13 shows the New Device Notifier displayed on the panel and its panel icon. The New Device Notifier is displayed only if at least one removable device is attached.

Removable devices are not displayed as icons on your desktop. Instead, to open the devices, you use the New Device Notifier. Click on the Device Notifier icon in the panel to open its dialog. The devices is unmounted initially with an unmount button displayed. Click on this button to mount the device. An eject button is then displayed which you can later use to unmount and eject the device. Opening the device with an application from its menu will mount the device automatically. Clicking on the eject button for a DVD/CD disc will physically eject it. For a USB drive, the drive will be unmounted and prepared for removal. You can then safely remove the USB drive.

To open a device, click on its entry in the New Device Notifier, like one for your DVD/CD disc or your USB drive. If there is more than one application that can use this device, a menu is displayed showing the options (see Figure 11-13). For a CD/DVD disc, you have the options to open the disc with the file manager, copy it with the K3b application, or download photos from it with Gwenview (should there be photos). You can open a USB drive with either Gwenview (photos) or the file manager, showing its contents. As you install more applications that can use a device, the applications will be added to the menu.

Removable media are also displayed on the File manager window's side pane. You can choose to eject removable media from the file manager instead of from the Device Notifier by right-clicking on the removable media entry and select "Safely remove" from the popup menu.

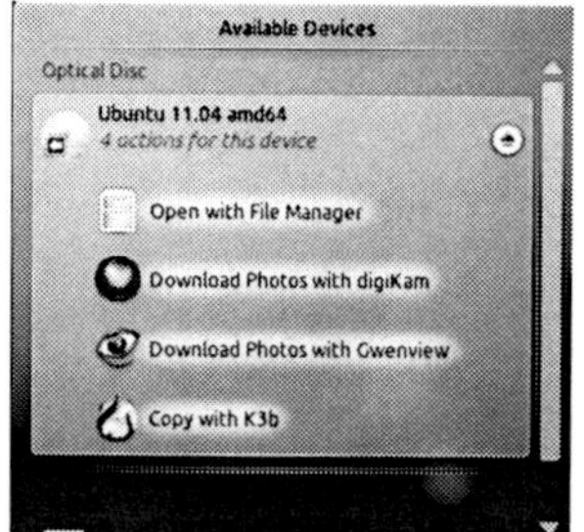
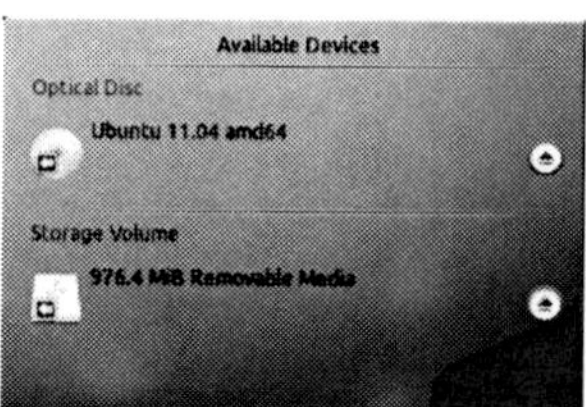

Figure 11-13: Device Notifier and its panel plasmoid icon

Network Manager

On KDE the Network Manager plasma widget provides panel access for Network Manager (see Chapter 3 for KDE Network Manager connections). This is the same Network Manager application, but adapted to the KDE interface. Clicking on the plasmoid icon in the panel opens dialog listing your current available connections (see Figure 11-14). The network image changes for wireless and wired connections. Wireless and Ethernet connections are displayed.

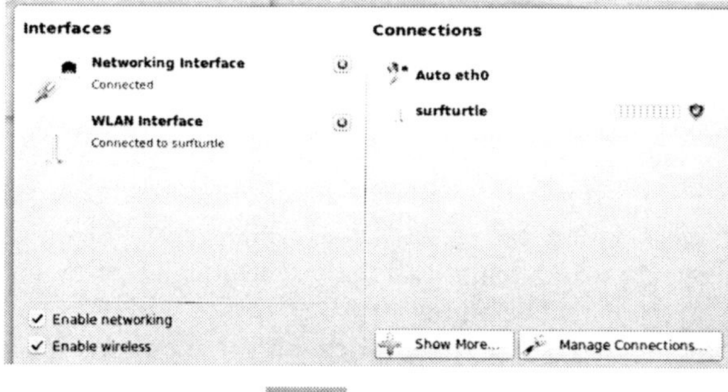

Figure 11-14: Network Manager connections and plasmoid wired and wireless icons.

To configure your connections manually, click on Manage Connections to open the Network Manager Network Connections window (KDE interface) with the same tabs for wired, wireless, mobile broadband, VPN, and DSL as described in Chapter 16.

Desktop Plasmoids

The KDE desktop features the Plasma desktop that supports plasmoids. Plasmoids are integrated into the desktop on the same level as windows and icons. Just as a desktop can display windows, it can also display plasmoids. Plasmoids can take on desktop operations, running essential operations, even replacing to a limited extent the need for file manager windows. The dashboard tool can hide all other desktop items, showing just the plasmoids.

When you first login, your desktop will show one plasmoid, the Desktop folder view (see Figure 11-15).

Figure 11-15: Initial Kubuntu screen with Desktop folder plasmoid

Managing desktop plasmoids

When you pass your mouse over a plasmoid, its sidebar is displayed with buttons for resizing, refreshing, settings, and closing the plasmoid (see Figure 11-16). Click and drag the resize button to change the plasmoid size. Clicking the settings button (wrench icon) opens that plasmoid's settings dialog (see Figure 11-17).

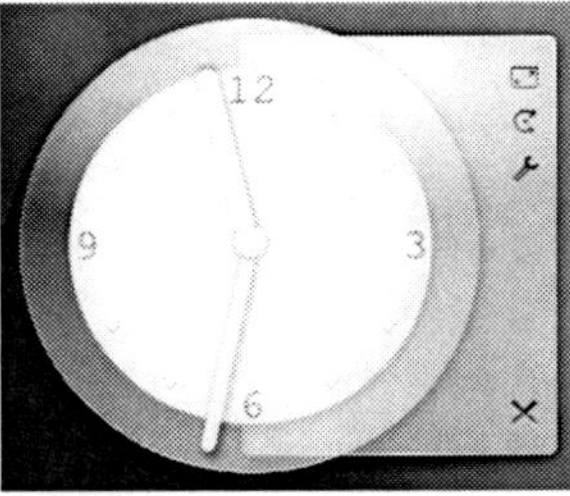

Figure 11-16: Clock Plasmoid with task sidebar

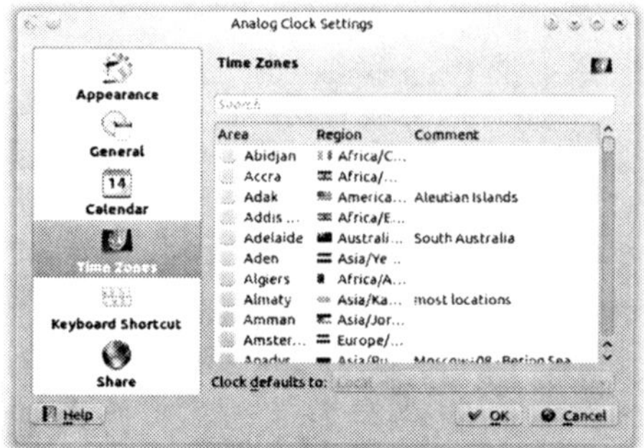

Figure 11-17: Clock Plasmoid Configuration

To add a widget (plasmoid) to the desktop, right-click anywhere on the desktop and select Add Widgets from the pop-up menu. This opens the Add Widgets dialog across the bottom of the desktop that lists widgets you can add (see Figure 11-18). Clicking on the Categories button opens a pop-up menu with different widget categories like Date and Time, Online Services, and Graphics. Use the slider and arrow button below the widgets to move through them. Double-click or drag a widget to add it to the desktop. You can enter a pattern to search for a widget using the search box located to the left of the categories button (top left).

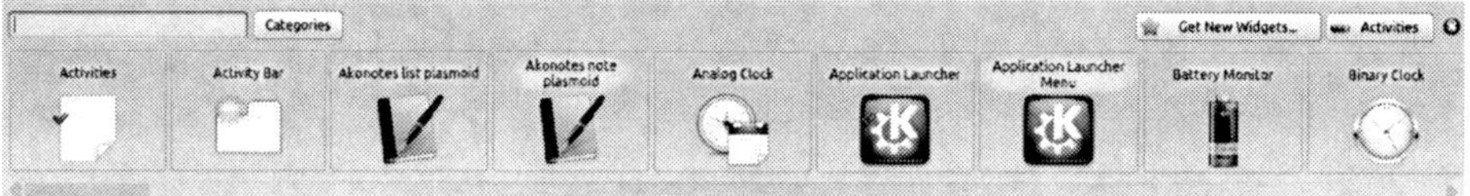

Figure 11-18: Adding a plasmoid: Add Widgets

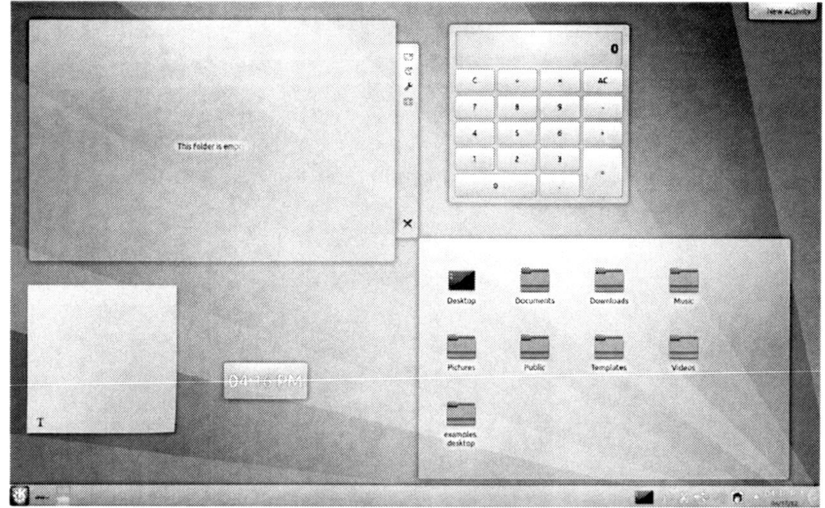

Figure 11-19: Desktop window, Folder View, Calculator, Digital clock, and Notetaker plasmoids.

Figure 11-19 shows the desktop folder, digital clock, leave a note, calculator, and folder view plasmoids. The desktop folder plasmoid is just a folder view plasmoid set to the desktop folder. When you add a Folder View plasmoid, it will default to your home folder.

Dashboard

The dashboard is designed to display plasmoids (applets) only. It hides all windows and icons, showing all your desktop plasmoids. To start the dashboard, press Ctrl-F12. You can also add a "Show Widget Dashboard" widget to your panel or desktop. When in use, the screen will display the Widget Dashboard label at the top (see Figure 11-20). To return to the desktop press Ctrl-F12 again or click the close button on the Widget Dashboard label at the top of the screen. Also, any plasmoid that interacts directly with the desktop like the opening a folder in the folder plasmoid or clicking a desktop icon, will return you to the desktop automatically.

Activities

KDE is designed to support multiple activities. Activities are different plasma containments, each with its set of plasmoids. An activity is not the same as virtual desktop. Virtual desktops affect windows, displaying a different set of windows on each desktop. An activity has its own set of plasmoids (widgets). Technically, each activity is a Plasma containment that has its own collection of plasmoids. You can switch to a different activity (containment) and display a different collection of plasmoids on your desktop.

Figure 11-20: The Dashboard (Ctrl-F12, or Show Widget Dashboard)

An activity is a way to set up as a set of widgets (plasmoids) for a certain task. You could have one activity for office work, another for news, and yet another for media. Each activity could have its own set of appropriate widgets, like clock, calculator, dictionary, and document folder for an office activity. A media activity might have a Now Playing plasmoid for audio, Picture Frame for photos, and News for latest news. You can also choose a certain type of activity based on activity templates. KDE provides the desktop, folder view, search and launch, photo layout, and newspaper templates, though you can download more. The desktop template provides a desktop interface, the folder view is a full screen view of one folder, "search and launch" displays application and task icons, and the newspaper layout template displays widgets in columns. Your original desktop is already configured as a desktop activity based on the desktop template.

Multiple activities are managed using the Activities toolbar, which is accessed through the Activities entry on the desktop toolbox menu or the Show Activities Manager button on the lower left side of the panel. Both are shown here.

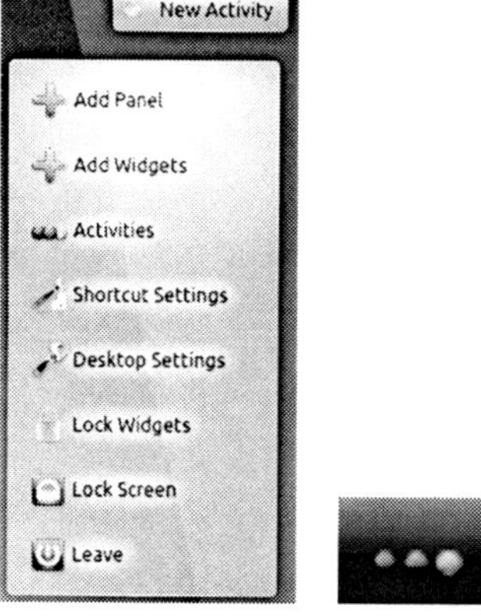

To add an activity, click the "Activities" entry in the toolbox or desktop menus, or click the Activities button on the lower left side of the panel. An activities toolbar is displayed listing your activities (see Figure 11-21). An activity icon for your desktop will already be displayed. Click the Create Activity button to add a new activity. From the pop-up menu, you can choose an empty desktop, a clone of the current activity, or choose from templates of different kinds of activities: Desktop Icons, Grid Desktop, Grouping Desktop, Newspaper Layout, Folder View, Photos Activity, and Search and Launch. The "Get New Templates" entry lets you download additional templates. A New Activity icon then appears on the activity toolbar (see Figure 11-22). To switch to another activity, click its icon.

Figure 11-21: Activity toolbar and icons

Initially, an activity's name is New Activity. To change the name click on the configuration emblem on the icon located to the lower right. The activity editing mode then lets you edit the activity name, with Apply and Cancel buttons to the right (see Figure 11-22). To change the icon image, click on the icon to open a "Select Icon" dialog where you can choose an image. Once you have made your changes, click the Apply button.

To add widgets to an activity, first click the activity to make it the current activity, and then click the Add Widgets button to display the Widgets toolbar. Widgets you add are placed in the current activity.

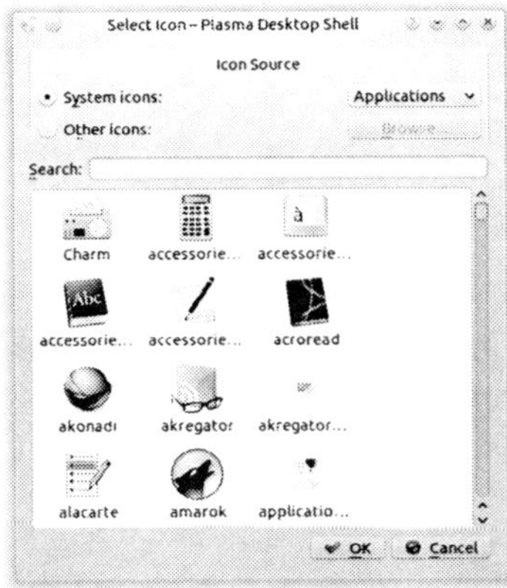
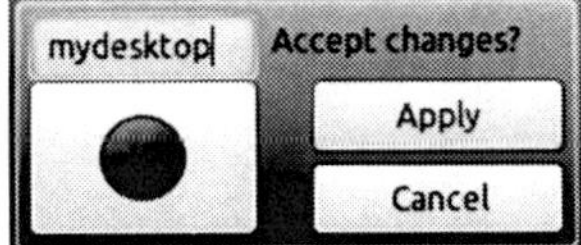

Figure 11-22: Changing an activity

To disable (stop) an activity, click its screen emblem in the upper right corner of its activity icon (a small white square). A red x is displayed and a Play button appears in the center of the icon as shown here. To re-activate the activity, click the play button.

When you stop an activity, a red x replaces the screen emblem. To remove an activity, first make sure it is stopped, and then click the red x on the activity icon. A remove dialog appears with a Remove button, which you can click to remove the activity.

To switch from one activity to another, first display the Activities toolbar by choosing Activities from the desktop toolbox menu (right-click on desktop). Then click on the activity icon you want (see Figure 11-23). The new Activity becomes your screen (see Figure 11-24). To change to another activity, open the Activities toolbar again, and click the activity icon you want. Your original desktop is the first icon.

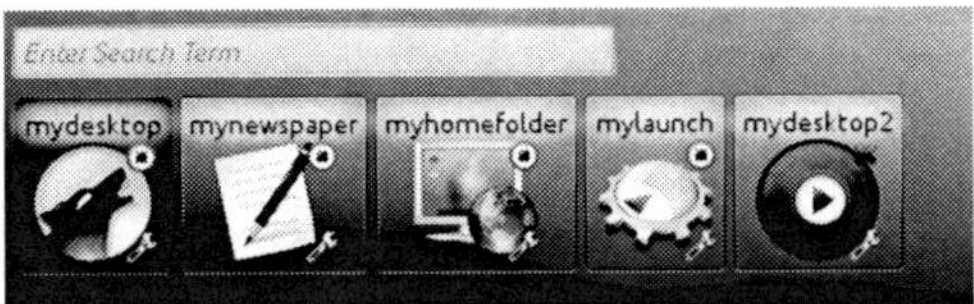

Figure 11-23: Activity icons

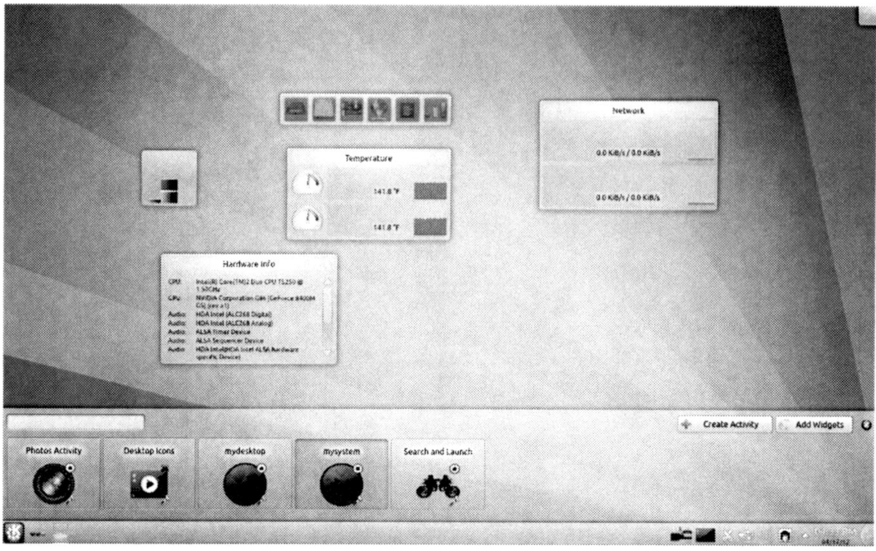

Figure 11-24: Activity toolbar and screen of selected activity

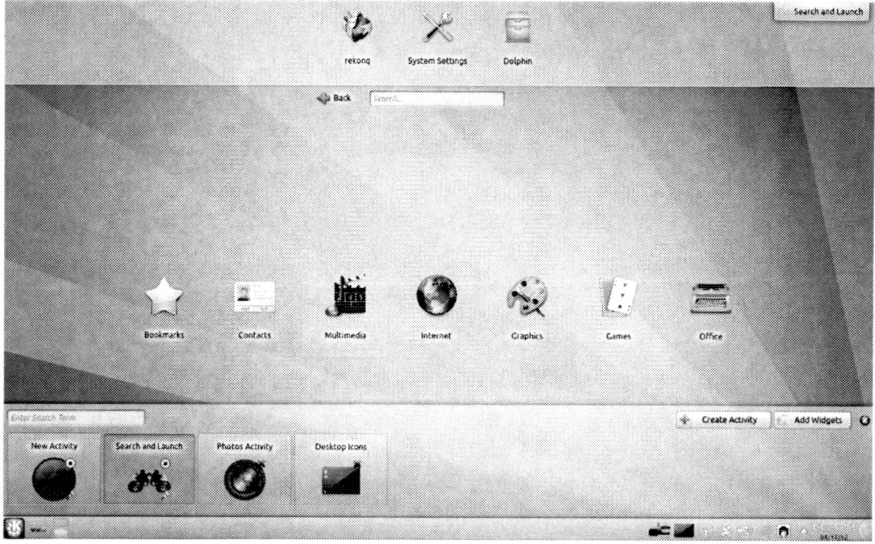

Figure 11-25: Activity search and launch

A Folder View activity functions like a file manager window, displaying a particular folder on the desktop. To configure a Folder View activity, right-click to display the desktop menu and choose Folder View Settings to display the Desktop Settings dialog. Icons are added for Location, Display, and Filter. On the Location tab, you can display the desktop folder, a place like the Home folder, or a folder of your choosing. On the Display tab you set display features such as arrangement, sorting, and size. The Filter tab lets you display files of certain types or name patterns.

A Search and Launch activity sets up an interface containing icons for tasks and application groups such as Bookmarks, Contacts, Multimedia Graphics, Office, and Internet (see Figure 11-25). To configure a Search and Launch activity, right-click to display the desktop menu and choose Configure Search and Launch to display the Desktop Settings dialog. The Desktop Settings dialog has additional Search plugins and Main Menu tabs. On the Main Menu you can add or remove application group and task icons.

A Newspaper Layout activity simply displays widgets in two columns. To configure a Newspaper activity, right-click to display the desktop menu and choose Configure Page to display the Desktop Settings dialog.

To move easily between activities, you can add the Activity bar widget, either to the panel or to the desktop. On the panel the Activity bar displays buttons for each activity. Click to move to a different activity. On the desktop the Activity bar displays a dialog with an arrow button for move from one activity to another.

KDE Windows

A KDE window has the same functionality you find in other window managers and desktops. You can resize the window by clicking and dragging any of its corners or sides. A click-and-drag operation on a side extends the window in that dimension, whereas a corner extends both height and width at the same time. The top of the window has a title bar showing the name of the window, the program name in the case of applications, and the current directory name for the file manager windows. The active window has the title bar highlighted. To move the window, click the title bar and drag it where you want. Right-clicking the window title bar displays a pop-up menu with entries for window operations, such as closing or resizing the window. The shade option will roll up the window to the title bar. Within the window, menus, icons, and toolbars for the particular application are displayed.

You can configure the appearance and operation of a window by selecting the Configure Window Behavior entry from the Window menu (right-click the title bar). Here you can set appearance (Windows), button and key operations (Actions), the focus policy such as a mouse click on the window or just passing the mouse over it (Focus), and how the window is displayed when moving it (Moving). All these features can be configured also using the System Setting's Window Behavior tool in the Workspace Appearance and Behavior section.

Opened windows are shown as buttons on the KDE taskbar located on the panel. The taskbar shows buttons for the different programs you are running or windows you have open. This is essentially a docking mechanism that lets you change to a window or application by clicking its button. When you minimize a window, it is reduced to its taskbar button. You can then restore the window by clicking its taskbar button.

To the right of the title bar are three small buttons for minimizing, maximizing, or closing the window (down, up, and x symbols). You can switch to a window at any time by clicking its taskbar button. You can also maximize a window by dragging it to the top edge of the screen.

From the keyboard, you can use the ALT-TAB key combination to display a list of current open windows. Holding down the ALT key and sequentially pressing TAB moves you through the list.

A window can be displayed as a tile on one half of the screen. Another tile can be set up for a different window on the other side of the screen, allowing you to display two windows side by side on the full screen (see Figure 11-26). You can tile a window by dragging it to the side of the screen (over the side edge to the middle of the window). A tile outline will appear. Add a second tile by moving a window to the other side edge. You can add more windows to a tile by moving them to that edge. Clicking on a window's taskbar button will display it on its tile.

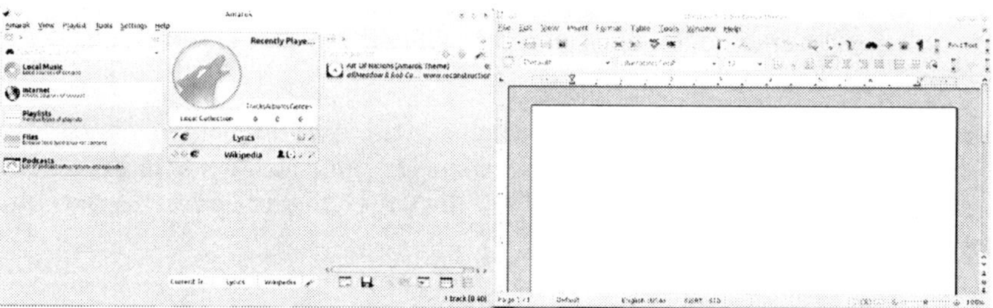

Figure 11-26: Window tiles

You can also group windows, displaying them as tabs within a single window. To add a window to a group, right-click on its title bar and choose the "Move window to group" to display a submenu of open windows. Select the one you want to group the window with. The grouped windows are displayed as tabs within a single window. To remove a window from a group, right-click on the title bar and select the "Remove from group" entry.

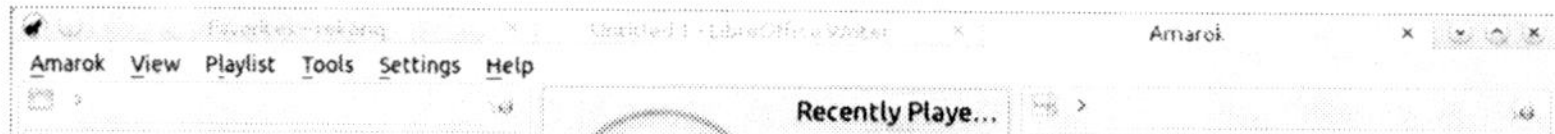

You can also add a widow to a group by moving its title bar with the middle mouse button (hold both right and left mouse buttons at once) to the title bar of another window. The title bar will become detached as you move it. Figure 11-27 shows a Rekonq, Amarok, and LibreOffice Writer application windows grouped as tabs into a single window.

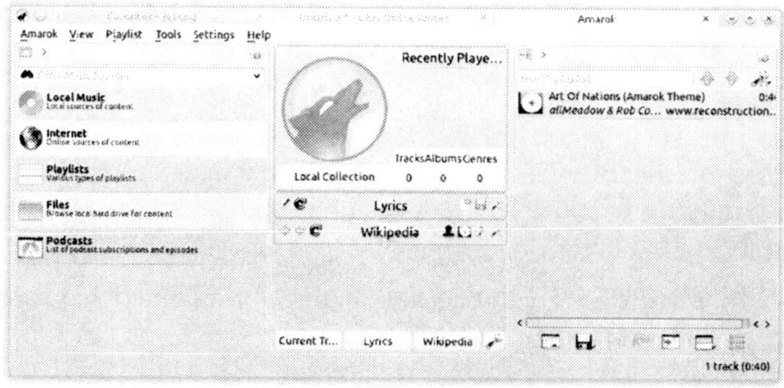

Figure 11-27: Window group, tabs within a single window

You can drag a window group to the side edge to tile it, showing the tabbed group as a tile. You can also maximize the group by dragging its window to the top edge.

Applications

You can start an application in KDE in several ways. If an entry for it is in the Kickoff Applications menu, you can select that entry to start the application. You can right-click on any application entry in the Applications menu to display a pop-up menu with "Add to Panel" and "Add to Desktop" entries. Select either to add a shortcut icon for the application to the desktop or the panel. You can then start an application by single clicking its desktop or panel icon.

An application icon on the desktop is implemented as desktop plasmoid. Passing the mouse over the application icon on the desktop displays a sidebar with the wrench icon for the icon settings. This opens a Setting window with tabs for general, permissions, application, and preview. On the general tab, you can select an icon image and set the displayed name. The application tab references the actual application program file with possible options. Permissions set standard access permissions by the owner, group, or others.

You can also run an application by right-clicking on the desktop and selecting select Run Command (or press ALT-F2) which will display the Krunner tool consisting of a box to enter a single command. Previous commands can be accessed from a pop-up menu. You need only enter a pattern to search for the application. Results will be displayed in the Krunner window. Choose the one you want.

Virtual Desktops: Desktop Pager

KDE supports virtual desktops, extending the desktop area on which you can work. You could have a Web browser running on one desktop and be using a text editor in another. KDE can support up to 16 virtual desktops, though the default is 4. Your virtual desktops can be displayed and accessed using the KDE Desktop Pager located on the left side of the panel. The KDE Desktop Pager represents your virtual desktops as miniature screens showing small squares for each desktop. It works much like the GNOME Workspace Switcher. On Ubuntu, by default, there are 4 squares, one on top of the other. To move from one desktop to another, click the square for the destination desktop. The selected desktop will be highlighted. Just passing your mouse over a desktop image on the panel will open a message displaying the desktop number along with the windows open on that desktop.

If you want to move a window to a different desktop, first open the window's menu by right-clicking the window's title bar. Then select the To Desktop entry, which lists the available desktops. Choose the one you want.

You can also configure KDE so that if you move the mouse over the edge of a desktop screen, it automatically moves to the adjoining desktop. You need to imagine the desktops arranged next to each. You enable this feature by enabling the "Switch desktop on edge" feature in the System Settings | Workspace Behavior | Screen Edges tab. This feature will also allow you to move windows over the edge to an adjoining desktop.

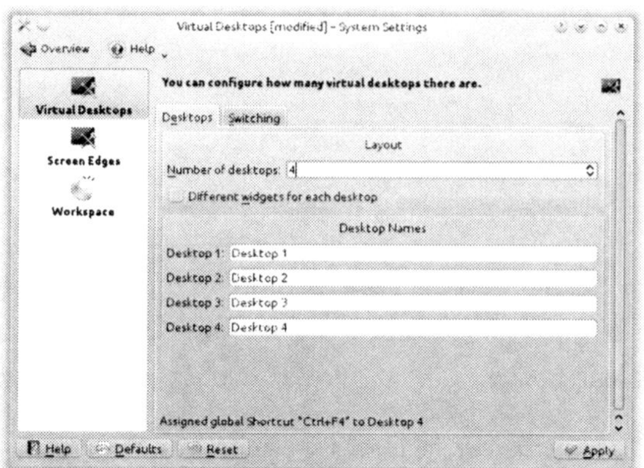

Figure 11-28: Virtual desktop configuration (Workspace Behavior) and Pager plasmoid icon.

To change the number of virtual desktops, you right-click on the Desktop Pager on the panel, and the select the Pager Settings entry in the pop-up menu to open the Pager Settings window, and choose the Virtual Desktops tab, which displays entries for your active desktops. You can also access the Virtual Desktops tab from System Settings | Workspace Behavior in the "Workspace Appearance and Behavior" section (see Figure 11-28). By default, Kubuntu will set up four virtual desktops for you. The text box labeled "Number of Desktops" controls the number of active desktops. Use the arrows or enter a number to change the number of active desktops. You can change any of the desktop names by clicking an active name and entering a new one. Choosing to display four desktops shows then stacked as shown here.

To change how the pager displays desktops on the panel, right-click and choose Pager Settings. Here you can configure the pager to display numbers or names for desktops. You can also decide on the number of rows to use. Choosing just one row would display the desktops side by side as shown here.

Tip: Use CTRL key in combination with a function key to switch to a specific desktop: for example, CTRL-F1 switches to the first desktop and CTRL-F3 to the third desktop.

KDE Panel

The KDE panel, located at the bottom of the screen, provides access to most KDE functions (see Figure 11-29). The panel is a specially configured Plasma containment, just as the desktop is a Plasma containment. The panel includes icons for menus, folder windows, specific programs, and virtual desktops. These are plasmoids that are configured for use on the panel. At the left end of the panel is a button for the Kickoff menu, a KDE *K* icon.

To add an application to the panel, right-click on its entry in the Kickoff menu to open a pop-up menu and select Add to Panel.

Figure 11-29: KDE panel

To add a widget to the panel, right-click on any panel widget on the panel to open a pop-up menu and select Panel Options submenu from which you can select the Add Widgets entry. This opens the Add Widgets window that lists widgets you can add to the panel (see Figure 11-30). A drop-down menu at the top of the window lets you see different widget categories like Date and Time, Online Services, and Graphics. You can also see recently used widgets as well as set up favorite widgets.

Note: To open the Add Widgets dialog, you can click on the panel toolbox at the right side of the panel and click the Add widgets button

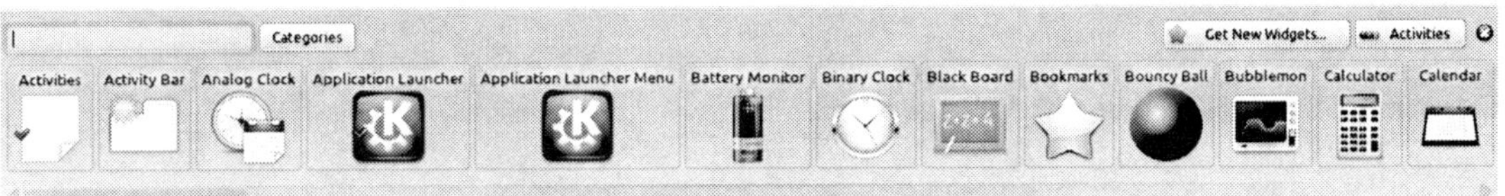

Figure 11-30: KDE Add Widgets for panel

The Plasma panel supports several kinds of Windows and Tasks widgets including the taskbar, system tray, and pager. The system tray holds widgets for desktop operations like update notifier, the clipboard (klipper), power (battery) detection, device notifier, sound settings (kmix), and network manager (see Figure 11-31). The left side of the system tray has a border and the right side has an arrow for a pop-up menu, as shown here.

The pop-up menu (arrow icon) on the right side of the system tray displays widgets that may not be in use such as printers and the file indexing service, as shown here.

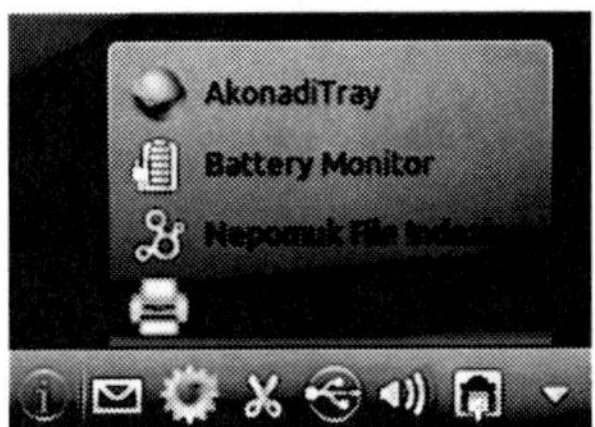

To configure the system tray, right-click on the left-side system tray border and choose System Tray Settings to open the system tray configuration dialog where you can decide what items to display or entries to make visible or remove.

Figure 11-31: KDE panel system tray, panel plasmoids, and panel toolbox

To the right of the system tray is the digital clock. To the left are added widgets such as the show desktop and jobs widget (i icon). Figure 11-33 shows, from left to right, show desktop, notifications and jobs, the system tray (update notifier, clipboard, device notifier, sound volume, network manager, and pop-up menu for printers and file indexing), and the digital clock.

KDE Panel Configuration

To configure a panel, changing its position, size, and display features, you use the panel's toolbox, located at the right side of the panel. Click on it to open an additional configuration panel with buttons for adding widgets, moving the panel, changing its size and position, and a More Settings menu for setting visibility and alignment features. Figure 11-32 shows the configuration panel as it will appear on your desktop. Figure 11-33 provides a more detailed description, including the More Settings menu entries.

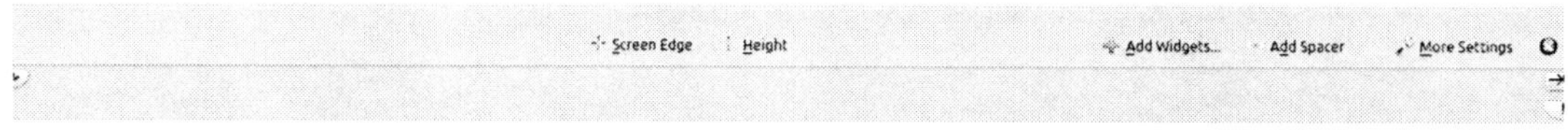

Figure 11-32: KDE Panel Configuration

With the configuration panel activated, you can also move plasmoids around the panel. Clicking on a plasmoid will overlay a movement icon, letting you then move the plasmoid icon to a different location on the panel.

The lower part of the configuration panel is used for panel position settings. On the left side is a slider for positioning the panel on the edge of the screen. On the right side are two sliders for the minimum (bottom) and maximum (top) size of the panel.

The top part of the panel has buttons for changing the location and the size of the panel. The Screen Edge button lets you move the panel to another side of the screen (left, right, top, bottom). Just click and drag. The height button lets you change the panel size, larger or smaller.

The Add Widgets button will open the Add Widgets dialog letting you add new plasmoids to the panel.

The Add Spacer button adds a spacer to separate widgets. Right click on the spacer to set a flexible size option or to remove the spacer.

The More Setting menu lets you set Visibility and Alignment features. You can choose an AutoHide setting that will hide the panel until you move the mouse to its location. The "Windows can cover" option lets a window overlap the panel. For smaller panels, you can align to the right, left, or center of the screen edge. The More Settings menu also has an entry to remove the panel. Use this entry to delete a panel you no longer want.

When you are finished with the configuration, click the red x icon the upper right side.

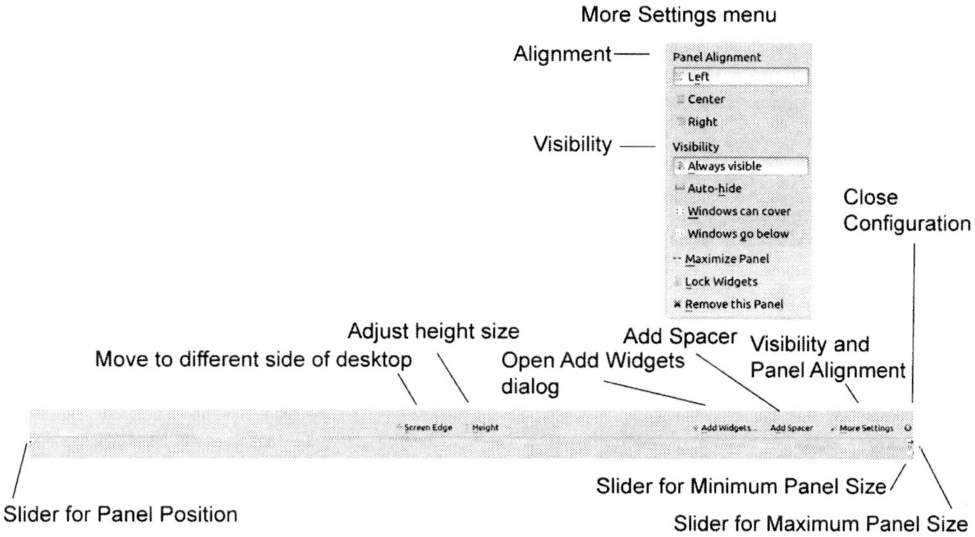

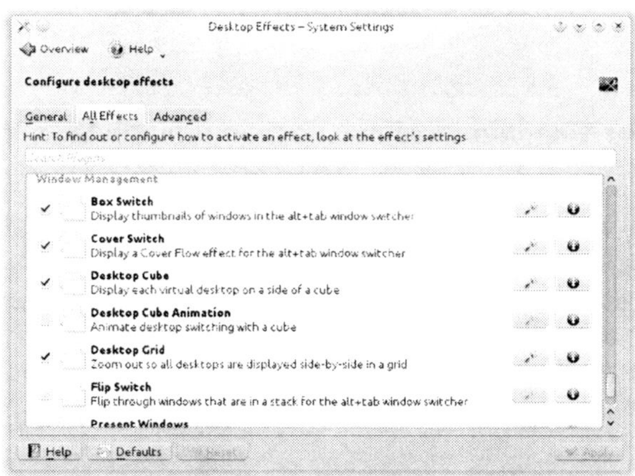

Figure 11-33: KDE Panel Configuration details and display features

KWin - Desktop Effects

KWin desktop effects can be enabled on the System Settings Desktop Effects dialog in the Workspace Appearance and Behavior section (System Settings | Desktop Effects). The switching effects for windows and desktops can be selected on the Desktop Effects tab. For window switching you can choose Cover Switch, Box Switch, Flip Switch, and Present Windows. For desktop switching you can choose Slide, Fade Desktop, and Desktop Cube Animation. The All Effects tab will list all available effects (see Figure 11-34).

Figure 11-34: Desktop Effect selection and configuration

The more dramatic effects are found in the Windows Management section. Desktop Effects requires the support of a capable graphics chip (GPU). You may have to install the proprietary graphics driver (Applications | System | Additional Drivers). Installation is the same as that for GNOME, as discussed in Chapter 3.

Several Windows effects are selected by default, depending on whether your graphics card can support them. A check mark is placed next to active effects. If there is wrench icon in the effects entry, it means the effect can be configured. Click on the icon to open its configuration dialog. For several effects, you use certain keys to start them. The more commonly used effects are Taskbar Thumbnail, Cover Switch, Desktop Grid, Present Windows, and Desktop Cube. The keys for these effects are listed in Table 11-3.

KEY	Operation
ALT-TAB	Cover Switch or Box Switch for open windows
CTRL-F8	Desktop Grid (use mouse to select a desktop)
CTRL-F9	Present Windows Current Desktop
CTRL-F10	Present Windows All Desktops
CTRL-F11	Desktop Cube (use mouse or arrow keys to move, ESC to exit)

Table 11-3: KWin desktop effects keyboard shortcuts

Most effects will occur automatically. The Taskbar Thumbnails effect displays a live thumbnail of a window on the taskbar as your mouse passes over it, showing its name, desktop, and image (see Figure 11-35).

Figure 11-35: Taskbar Thumbnails effect, showing thumbnails of minimized applications

On the Desktop Effects dialog's General tab, in the Common Settings section, you can choose the window switching effect you want to use from the "Effect for window switching" drop down menu. These include Box Switch, Present Windows, Cover Switch, and Flip Switch. The Alt-Tab keys implement the effect you have chosen. Continually pressing the Tab key while holding down the Alt key moves you through the windows. Box Switch displays windows in a boxed dialog, whereas Cover switch arranges unselected windows stacked to the sides, and Flip switch arranges the windows to one side (Figures 11-36 and 11-379).

The Present Windows effect displays images of your open windows on your screen with the selected one highlighted (see Figure 11-38). You can use your mouse to select another. This provides an easy way to browse your open windows. You can also use Ctrl-F9 to display windows on your current virtual desktop statically and use the arrow key to move between them. Use Ctrl-F10 to display all your open windows across all your desktops. Press the ESC key to return to the desktop.

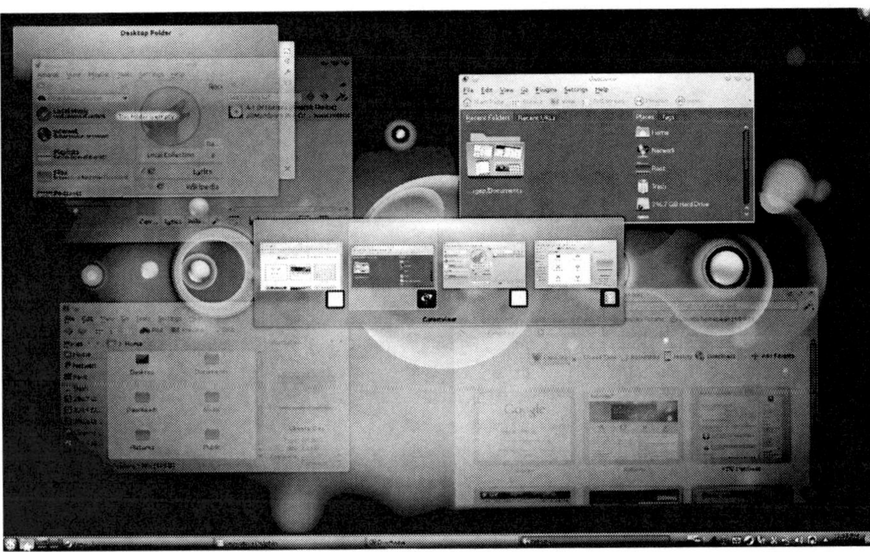

Figure 11-36: Box Switch - Alt-Tab

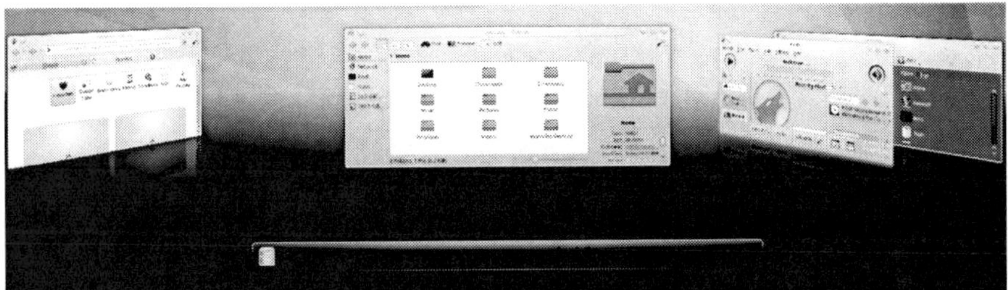

Figure 11-37: Cover Switch - Alt-Tab (Box Switch disabled)

On the Desktop Effects dialog's All Effects tab you can enable additional windows management features. Desktop Grid will show a grid of all your virtual desktops (Ctrl-F8), letting you see all your virtual desktops on the screen at once (see Figure 11-39). You can then move windows and open applications between desktops. Clicking on a desktop makes it the current one. The plus and minus keys allow you to add or remove virtual desktops.

Desktop Cube will show a cube of all your virtual desktops, letting you move to different desktops around a cube (see Figure 11-40). Stop at the side you want to select. Press Ctrl-11 to start the Desktop Cube. You can then move around the cube with the arrow keys or by clicking and dragging your mouse. When you are finished press the ESC key to return you the desktop.

Figure 11-38: Present Windows (Windows effects) Alt-Tab, or Ctrl-F9 for current desktop and Ctrl-f10 for all desktops

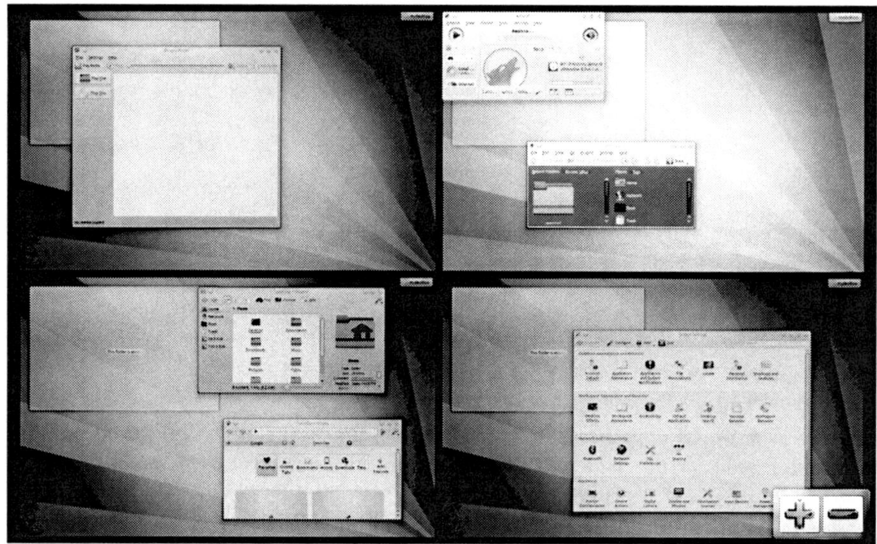

Figure 11-39: Desktop Grid - Ctrl-F8

Desktop Cube Animation will use cube animation whenever you switch to a different desktop using the Desktop Pager.

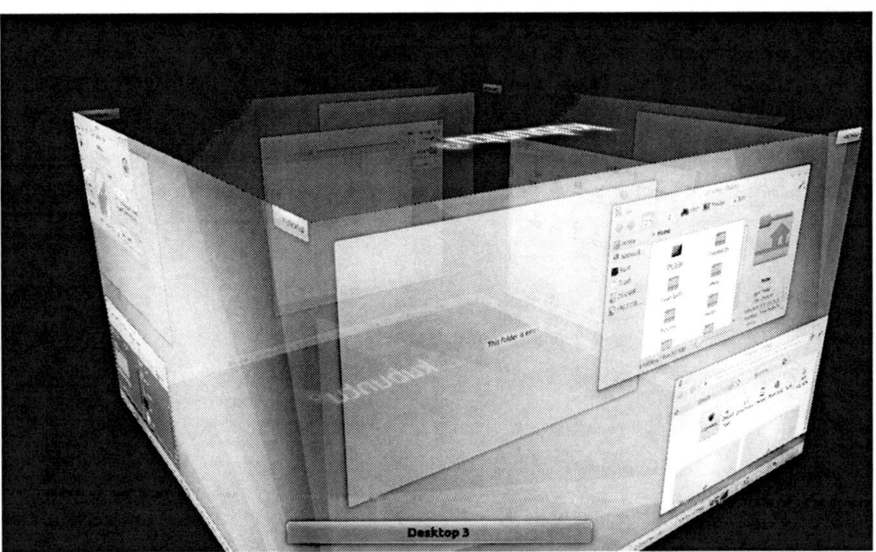

Figure 11-40: Desktop Cube - Ctrl-F11, drag-mouse or right/left arrow keys

KDE File Manager: Dolphin

Dolphin is KDE's dedicated file manager (see Figure 11-41). A navigation bar shows the current directory either in a browser or edit mode. In the browse mode it show icons for the path of your current directory, and in the edit mode it shows the path name in a text-editable box.

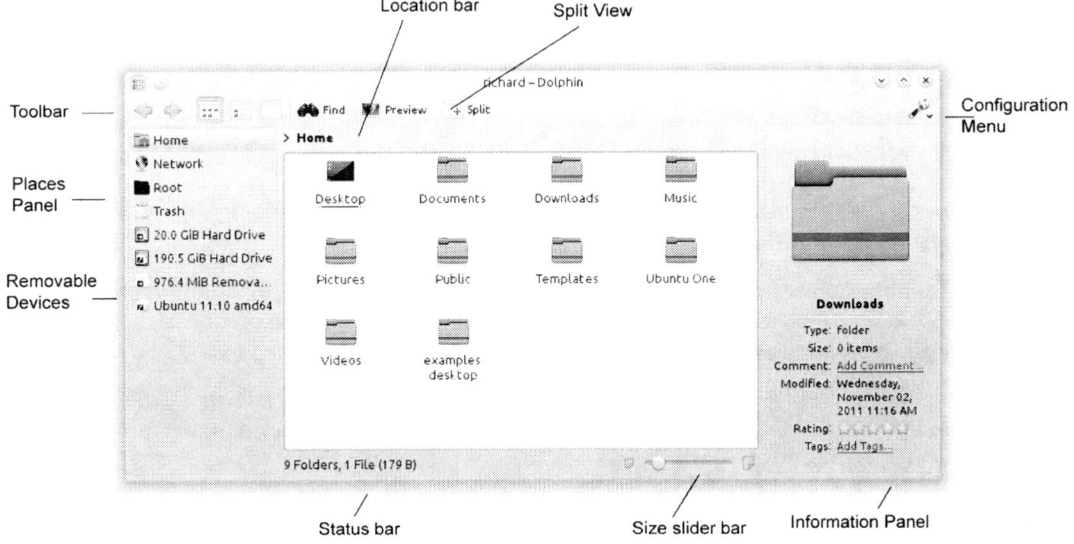

Figure 11-41: The KDE file manager (dolphin)

You can use either to move to different folders and their subfolders. Use the **Ctrl-l** key or click to the right of the folder buttons to use the edit mode. You can also choose View | Location Bar | Editable Location (the **Ctrl-l** key will toggle between the edit and browser modes). Clicking on the check mark at the end of the editable text box, returns you to the browser mode.

With KDE 4.7, the Dolphin menubar has been removed and instead, the menus are displayed when clicking the configuration button on the right side of the toolbar (see Figure 11-42).

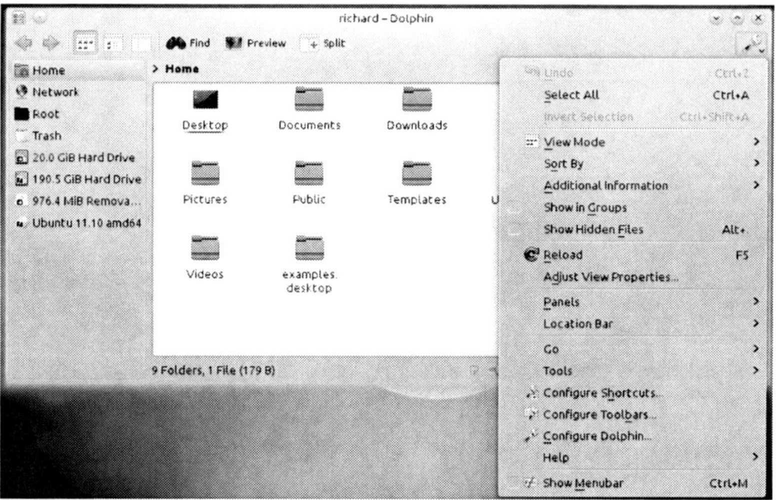

Figure 11-42: The KDE file manager menus

You can open a file either by clicking it or by right-clicking it and choosing the "Open With" submenu to list applications to open it with. If you want to just select the file or folder, you need to hold down the CTRL key while you click it. A single-click will open the file. If the file is a program, that program starts up. If it is a data file, such as a text file, the associated application is run using that data file. Clicking a text file displays it with the Kate editor, while clicking an image file displays it with the GwenView image viewer. Selecting a DEB package opens it with the Muon Software Center, which you can then use to install the package. If you want to use a double-click instead to open a file or folder, you can set the Double-click option on the Dolphin Preferences dialog Navigation tab (Settings | Configure Dolphin).

If Dolphin cannot determine the application to use, it opens a dialog box prompting you to enter the application name. You can click the Browse button on this box to use a directory tree to locate the application program you want.

Dolphin can display panels to either side (Dolphin refers to these as panels, though they operate more like stand alone tabs). The Places panel will show icons for often-used folders like Home, Network, and Trash, as well as removable devices. To add a folder to the Places panel, just drag it there. The files listed in a folder can be viewed in several different ways, such as icons, detailed listing (Details), and columns (View | View Mode menu). See Table 11-4 for keyboard shortcuts.

You can display additional panels by selecting them from the View | Panels submenu (see Figure 11-45). The Information panel displays detailed information about a selected file or folder, and the Folders panel displays a directory tree for the file system. The Search panel displays filter criteria for a search, such as file type, size, and date (see Figure 11-50). The panels are detachable from the file manager window (see Figure 11-43). Be sure to choose "Unlock Panels" the panels in the Panels menu to make them detachable.

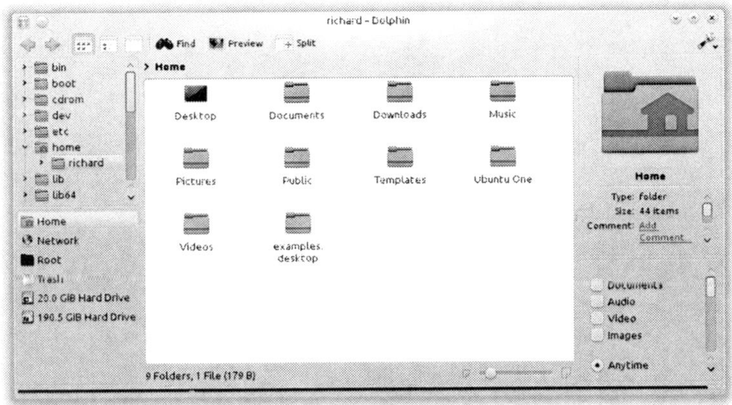

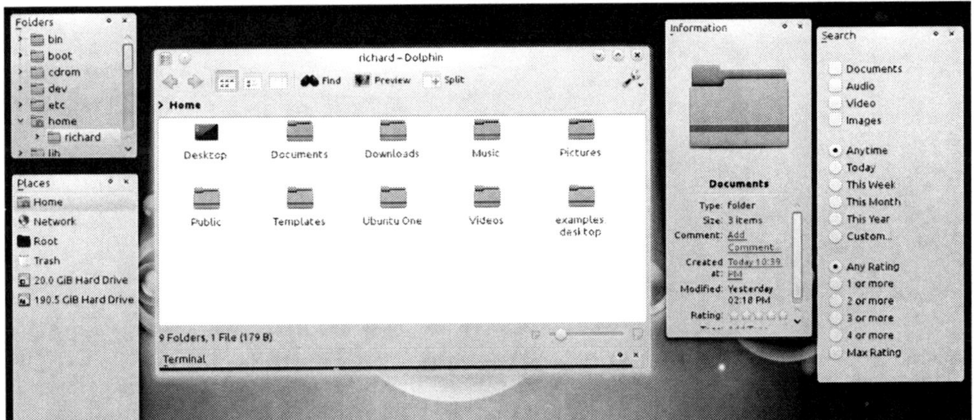

Figure 11-43: The KDE file manager with sidebars, attached and detached

Dolphin supports split views, where you can open two different folders in the same window. Click the Split button in the toolbar. You can then drag folder and files from one folder to the other (see Figure 11-44).

Dolphin also supports file sharing with Samba. To share a folder, right-click on the folder icon and choose Properties to open the Properties dialog. Then on the Share tab you can choose to share the folder with Samba (Microsoft Windows). You can also set permissions for users: Read Only, Full Control, and Deny (See Figure 11-45). For the Everyone entry you would usually set the permission to Read Only.

Figure 11-44: The KDE file manager with split views

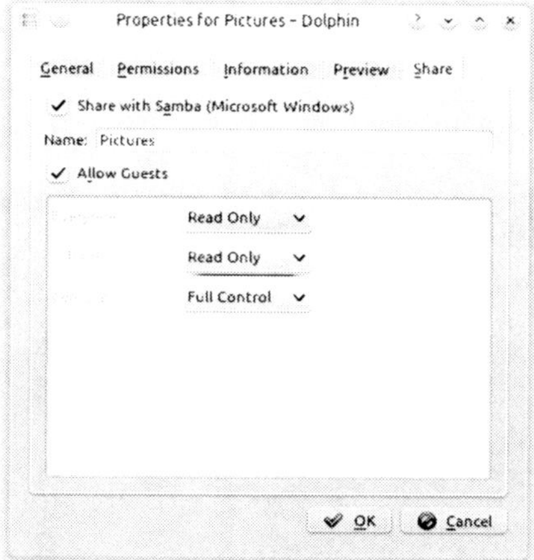

Figure 11-45: The KDE file manager share dialog for folders

To configure Dolphin, click Configure Dolphin from the Setting menu to open the Dolphin Preferences dialog with tabs for Startup, View Modes, Navigation, Services, Trash, and General. On the Startup tab, you can specify features like the split view and the default folder to start up with. On the View Modes tab you can set display features for the different display modes (Icons, Details, and Column), like the icon size, font type, and arrangement. The Navigation tab sets features like the double-click for selection. The Services tab is where you specify actions supported for different kinds of files, like play a DVD with Dragon Player, install a true type font file, or display Tiff image files. The Trash tab lets you configure trash settings like deleting items in the trash after a specified time and setting the maximum size of the trash. The General tab has sub-tabs for Behavior, Previews, Context Menu, and Status Bar. The Behavior tab is where you can enable tool tips, set confirmation prompts for file deletion or closing multiple tabs, and display the selection marker. Preview lets you choose which type of files to preview. The image, jpeg, and directories types are already selected.

Keys	Description
ALT-LEFT ARROW, ALT-RIGHT ARROW	Backward and Forward in History
ALT-UP ARROW	One directory up
ENTER	Open a file/directory
LEFT/RIGHT/UP/DOWN ARROWS	Move among the icons
PAGE UP, PAGE DOWN	Scroll fast
CTRL-C	Copy selected file to clipboard
CTRL-V	Paste files from clipboard to current directory
CTRL-S	Select files by pattern
CTRL-L	URI text box location bar
CTRL-F	Find files
CTRL-Q	Close window

Table 11-4: KDE File Manager Keyboard Shortcuts

Navigating Directories

Within a file manager window, a single-click on a folder icon moves to that folder and displays its file and sub-folder icons. To move back up to the parent folder, you click the back arrow button located on the left end of the navigation toolbar. A single-click on a folder icon moves you down the folder tree, one folder at a time. By clicking the back arrow button, you move up the tree. The Navigation bar can display either the folder path for the current folder or an editable location box where you can enter in a pathname. For the folder path, you can click on any displayed folder name to move you quickly to an upper level folder. To use the location box, click to the right of the folder path. The Location box is displayed. You can also select Show Full Location in the View | Navigation Bar menu (or press Ctrl-L). The navigation bar changes to an editable text box where you can type a path name. To change back to the folder path click the check mark to the right of the text box.

Like a Web browser, the file manager remembers the previous folder it has displayed. You can use the back and forward arrow buttons to move through this list of prior folder. You can also use several keyboard shortcuts to perform such operations, like Alt-backarrow to move up a folder, and the arrow keys to move to different icons.

Copy, Move, Delete, Rename, and Link Operations

To perform an operation on a file or folder, you first have to select it by clicking the file's icon or listing. To select more than one file, hold down the CTRL key down while you click the files you want. You can also use the keyboard arrow keys to move from one file icon to another.

To copy and move files, you can use the standard drag-and-drop method with your mouse. To copy a file, you locate it by using the file manager. Open another file manager window to the folder to which you want the file copied. Then drag-and-drop the File icon to that window. A pop-up menu appears with selections for Move Here, Copy Here, or Link Here. Choose Copy Here. To move a file to another directory, follow the same procedure, but select Move Here from the pop-up menu. To copy or move a folder, use the same procedure as for files. All the folder's files and sub-folders are also copied or moved. Instead of having to select from a pop-up menu, you can use the corresponding keys: **Ctrl** for copy, **Shift** for move, and **Ctrl-Shift** for link, same as for GNOME.

To rename a file, Ctrl-click its icon and press F2, or right-click the icon and select Rename from the pop-up menu. A dialog opens where you can enter the new name for the file or folder.

You delete a file either by selecting it and deleting it or placing it in the Trash folder to delete later. To delete a file, select it and then choose the Delete entry in the File menu, File | Delete (also SHIFT-DEL key). To place a file in the Trash folder, drag-and-drop it to the Trash icon on the Places panel, or right-click the file and choose "Move To Trash" from the pop-up menu. You can later open the Trash folder and delete the files. To delete all the files in the Trash folder, right-click the Trash icon in Dolphin file manager Places panel, and select Remove Trash from the pop-up menu. To restore files in the Trash bin, open the Trash window and right click on the file to restore and select Restore.

Each file or directory has properties associated with it that include permissions, the filename, and its directory. To display the Properties dialog for a given file, right-click the file's icon and select the Properties entry. On the General tab, you see the name of the file displayed. To change the file name, replace the name there with a new one. Permissions are set on the Permissions tab. Here, you can set read, write, and execute permissions for user, group, or other access to the file. The Group entry enables you to change the group for a file.

Search Bar, Filter Bar, and Search Panel

KDE has combined the former KFind and Dolphin search tools into one simplified search bar. KDE also supports a filter bar to search files and folders in the current folder. You can also use the Filter Panel to refine searches by meta data such as type, date, ratings, and tags.

Search Bar

To search for files, click the Find button on the icon bar to open the search bar, which displays a search text box. You can also choose Find from the Edit menu, or press Ctrl-f. The search bar displays a search text box where you enter the pattern of the file or folder you are searching for. Click the red x button to the left to close the find bar, and use the black x button in the text box to clear the search pattern.

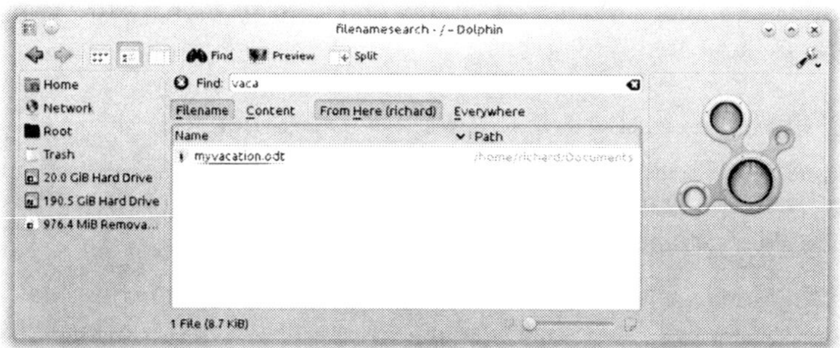

Figure 11-46: The KDE Search Bar

Buttons below the search box provide options to qualify the search. The Filename button (the default) searches on the file name. The Content button will search the contents of text files for the pattern. The "From Here" button searches the user's home folders, and the Everywhere button (the default) searches the entire file system (see Figure 11-46).

The search results are displayed in the main pane. You can click a file to have it open with its appropriate application. Text files are displayed by the Kate text editor, images by GwenView, and applications are run. The search program also enables you to save your search results for later reference (click the Save button to the right). When you are finished searching, click the Close button.

When you pass your mouse over an icon listed in the Query Results, information about it is displayed on the information panel to the right. Links are shown for adding tags and comments. Right-clicking on this panel lets you open a configure dialog where you can specify what information to display.

The search operation makes use of the KDE implementation of Nepomuk Semantic Desktop's metadata indexing, a powerful desktop indexer that makes using of file information, user tags and comments on the file, and file usage associations like the email used to send a file as email attachment. The Nepomuk project aims to implement a semantic desktop, organizing desktop information so it can be accessed easily and shared collaboratively.

To manage the Nepomuk file indexing, open the Nepomuk Indexing Controller from the system tray. You can choose to resume or suspend indexing. To configure Nepomuk, choose System Settings | Workspace Appearance and Behavior | Desktop Search (also you can also choose Configure File Indexing from the Nepomuk system tray entry). This opens the Desktop Search control module, with tabs for Basic Settings, Desktop Query, Backup, and Advanced Settings. On the Basic Settings tab you can enable the Strigi desktop search, which can search files by content.

Filter Bar

For a quick search of the current folder, you can activate the Filter bar (Tools | Show Filter Bar or **Ctrl-i**), which opens a Filter search box at the bottom of the window. Enter a pattern and only those file and directory names containing that pattern are displayed. Click the x button at the right of the Filter box to clear it (see Figure 11-47).

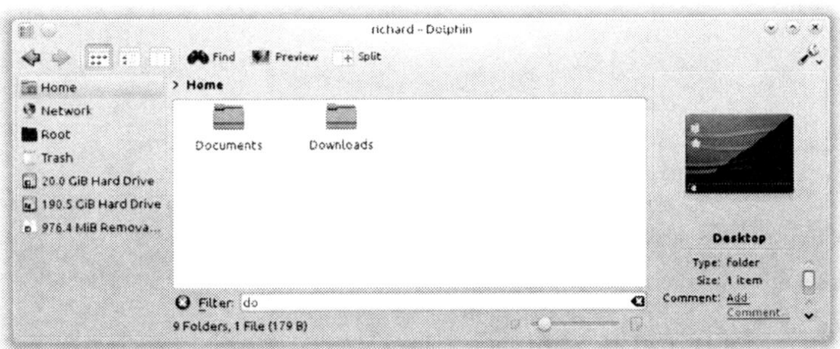

Figure 11-47: The KDE Filter Bar

Search Panel

You can also perform faceted browsing using the Search panel (View | Panels | Search). The Search panel lets you search by meta data such as Documents, Audio, Video, Image, the time and date, the file ratings, and tags (see Figure 11-48). The Custom link in the Time and Date entries opens a calendar, which you can use to select a specific date. The Search panel works with both the search and filter bars. Before you can use the Search Panel, you need to enable Nepomuk file indexing (Nepomuk Indexing Controller on the system tray).

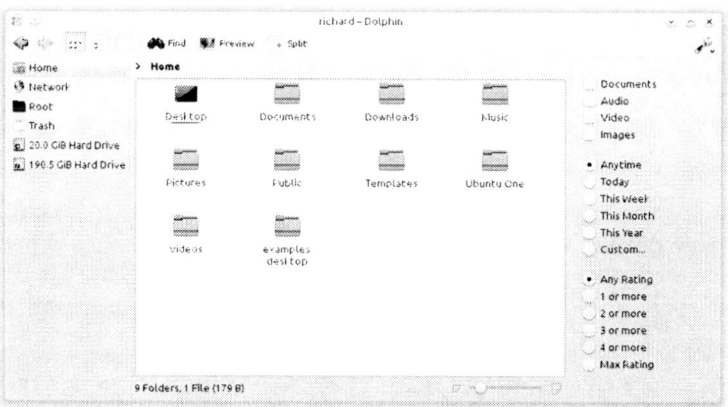

Figure 11-48: The KDE Search Panel

KDE Software Management: Muon Software Center

For software management, you can use the Ubuntu Software Center, accessible from Applications | System | Software Center. You can also use the Muon Software Center. You can access the Muon Software Center from Applications | System | Software Management.

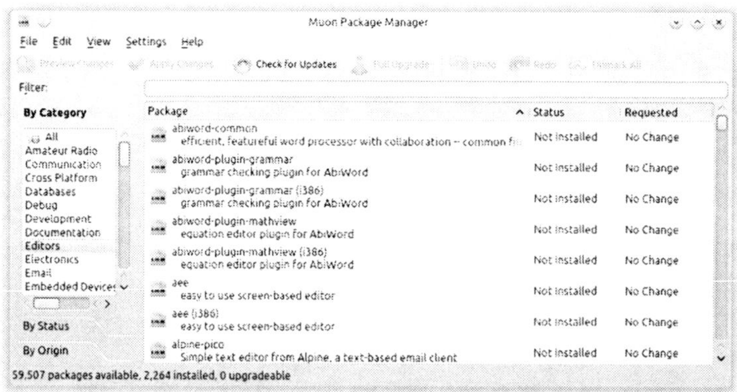

Figure 11-49: Muon Software Center: package categories

The Software Management dialog provides a sidebar with filter tabs for category, status (installed and not installed), and origin (Ubuntu). The right pane displays a listing of the selected software. You can also search using the search box above the package listing. (see Figure 11-49). Clicking on a category, lists packages in that category. A package lists its, name, status, and requested change.

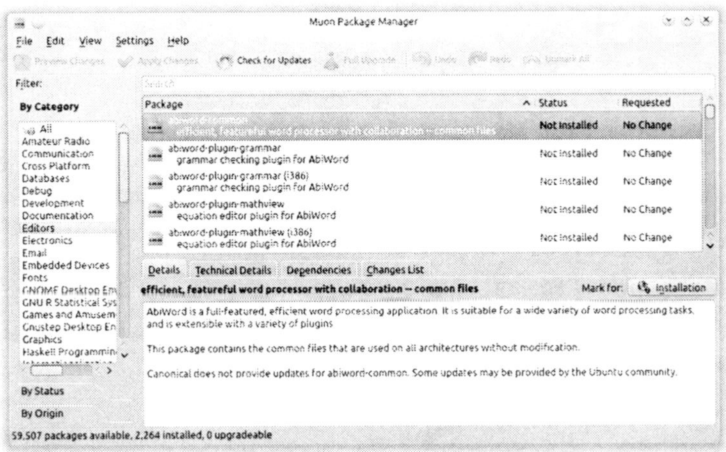

Figure 11-50: Muon Software Center: selected package

Upon clicking a package entry, information about that package is displayed in the lower half of the right pane, with tabs for Details, Technical Details, Dependencies, and Changes List (see Figure 4-12). Click the installation button to the right, to mark the package for installation. For installed packages, a Removal button is displayed.

To perform your marked installed and remove operations, click the Apply Changes button on the top toolbar. The Preview Changes buttons let you review and modify changes. From the Settings menu, you can choose "Configure Software Sources" to select repositories. From the View menu, you can see the history of your changes by date.

Icon-Only Task Manager

On the KDE panel you can add a Icon-Only Task Manager widget that operates much like the Ubuntu Launcher. You could have it work as another widget on your pane, or create a new panel that has only this Icon-Only Task Manager widget on it. You could then position the new panel to the left screen side, providing a tool that operates similar the Ubuntu Launcher. Increase the width of the panel to increase the icon sizes. Figure 11-51 shows a side panel with the Icon-Only Task Manager, showing icons for the Rekonq Web browser, Dolphin file manager, Calligra Words, and LibreOffice calc.

Figure 11-51: Icon-only Task Manager on a separate side panel

When you open an application, its icon is added to the Icon-Only Task Manager. To have the icon remain, right click and click the checkbox for "Show A Launcher When Not Running" (see Figure 11-52). To remove an icon, right click and choose "Remove this Launcher." You can manually move the position of an icon by clicking and dragging it.

To start a new instance of an application, right click and choose "Start New Instance."

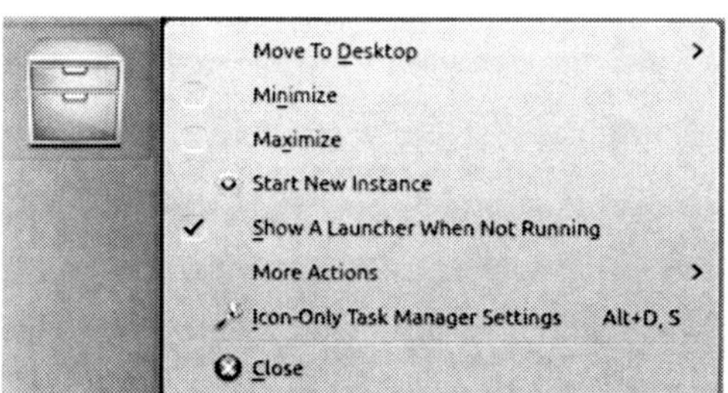

Figure 11-52: Icon-only Task Manager menus

Passing the mouse over a launcher icon displays a preview of any open windows for that application (see Figure 11-53). If several windows are open for that application, they are also previewed. Each preview has a close box (upper right x), which you can use to close the window. Media applicaitons will also show buttons for playing media. An icon for an application with multiple windows open also shows a plus sign that you can click to display a present windows screen showing only the windows for that application, and letting you choose the one you want.

The panel could be shortened as well as have other widgets added such as the pager and device notifier, providing similar functionality as the Ubuntu launcher.

To configure the Icon-Only Task Manager, right click on the panel and choose Icon Only Task Manager Settings (see Figure 11-54). On the Appearance tab you can set features such as the style, set the size, rows, and sorting.

The style is set to the workspace theme, but you can also set it to the Indicator or Indicator with backgrounds (see Figure 11-55), which displays the icon much like the Ubuntu Launcher items. Indicators are shown for the current window and multiple open windows.

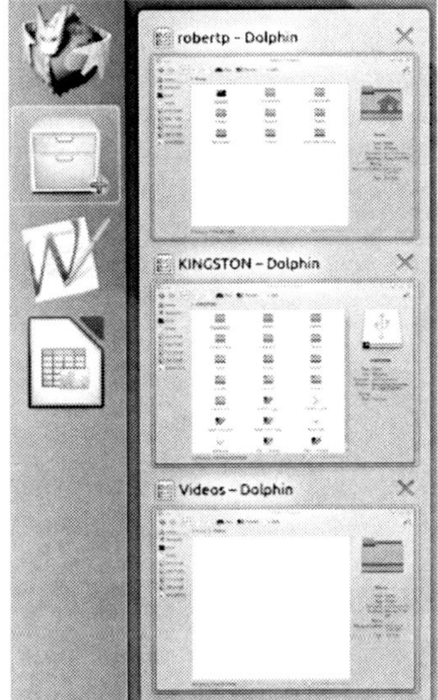

Figure 11-53: Icon-only Task Manager previews for single and multiple windows

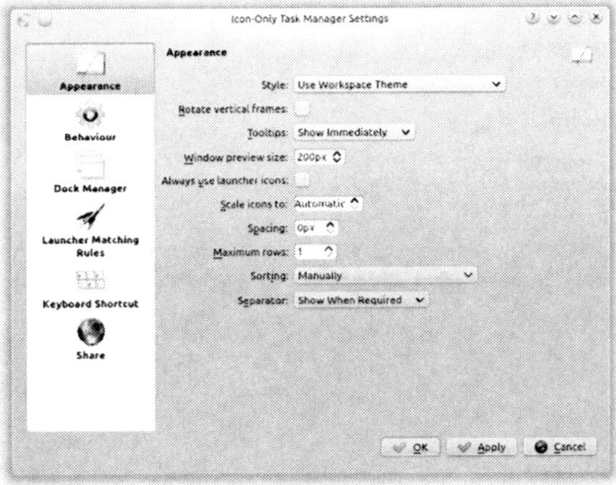

Figure 11-54: Icon-only Task Manager settings

On the Behavior tab, you can set features like showing job progress, media controls on media application previews (tooltips), and the function of the middle click button. For icons with multiple windows open (Group click action) you could use a pop-up menu listing the windows instead of the present windows operation.

The Launcher Matching Rules tab shows icons you had to manually associate with a specific application. If you start an application whose icon cannot be automatically determined, you are prompted to choose the launcher.

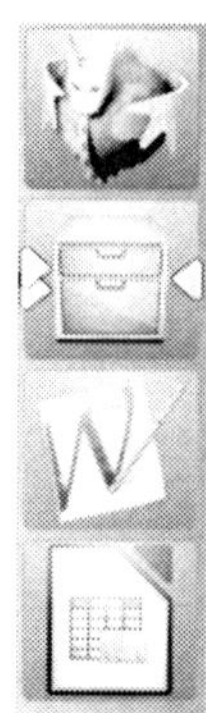

Figure 11-55: Icon-only Task Manager Indicator with backgrounds style

KDE Configuration: KDE System Settings

With the KDE configuration tools, you can configure your desktop and system, changing the way it is displayed and the features it supports. The configuration dialogs are accessed on the System Settings window (See Figure 11-56). On Kubuntu, you can access System Settings from the System Settings entry in the Kickoff Favorites menu, or from Applications | Settings | System Settings. You should use the KDE System Settings tools to configure your KDE desktop.

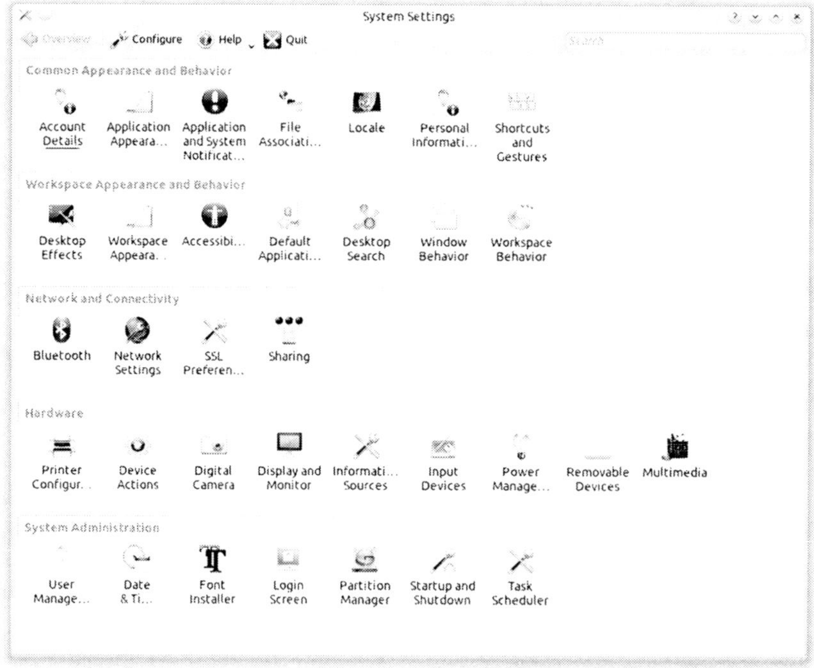

Figure 11-56: KDE System Settings

The System Settings window shows system dialog icons arranged in several sections: Common Appearance and Behavior, Workspace Appearance and Behavior, Network and Connectivity, Hardware, and System Administration. Click an icon to display a dialog with a sidebar icon list for configuration tabs, with the tab selected shown on the right. The selected tab may also have sub-tabs (see Figure 11-57).

The Network and Connectivity section holds icons for configuring the networking, Bluetooth connections, and sharing. The Common Appearance and Behavior section has icons for personal information, account details, shortcuts, file associations, and your location. Workspace Appearance and Behavior lets you set desktop effects, themes, accessibility, default applications, desktop search, and windows features. System Administration lets you set the settings for user management, the date and time, installing fonts, software management (KPackageKit), start up and shut down (sessions), and login screen (KDM, not GDM). Hardware lets you set the printer configuration, power management, multimedia devices (sound), your display resolution, and information sources (KDE Solid settings for power, network, and Bluetooth management).

Alternatively, you can display the System Settings window using the classic tree format. Click the System Settings Configure button to open the configuration dialog, and select Classic tree on the General tab. Setting sections are displayed as expandable trees on the left pane, with packages for a selected section displayed to the right.

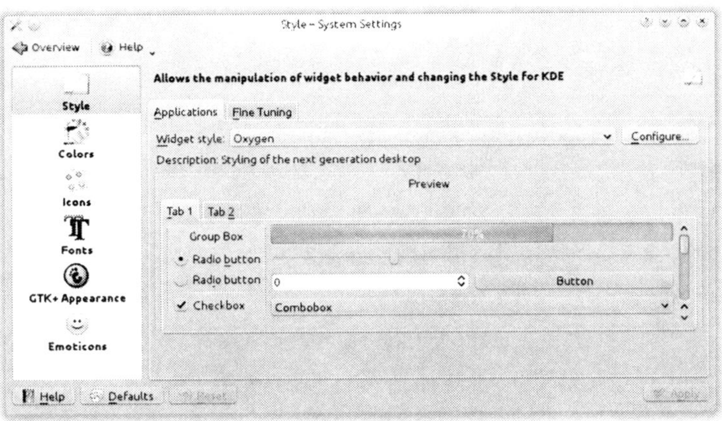

Figure 11-57: KDE System Settings | Application Appearance, Style

KDE Directories and Files

When KDE is installed on your system, its system-wide application, configuration, and support files may be installed in the same system directories as other GUIs and user applications (see Table 11-5). On Ubuntu, KDE is installed in the standard system directories with some variations, such as **/usr/bin** for KDE program files, **/usr/lib/kde4**, which holds KDE libraries, and **/usr/include/kde**, which contains KDE header files used in application development.

The **.kde** directory holds files and directories used to maintain your KDE desktop. As with GNOME, the **Desktop** directory holds KDE desktop files whose icons are displayed on the desktop. Configuration files are located in the **.kde/share/config** directory. Here you can find the general configuration files for different KDE components: **kwinrc** holds configuration commands for the window manager, **kmailrc** for mail, and **kdeglobals** for keyboard shortcuts along with other global definitions. You can place configuration directives directly in any of these files; **.kde/share/mimelnk** holds the desktop files for the menu entries added by the user. The **.kde/share/apps** directory contains files and directories for configuring KDE applications, including **calligra**, **kmail**, and even **Rekonq**.

The directories located in **share** directory contain files used to configure system defaults for your KDE environment (the system **share** directory is located at **/usr/share**). The **share/apps** directory contains files and directories set up by KDE applications; **share/config** contains the configuration files for particular KDE applications. These are the system-wide defaults that can be overridden by users' own configurations in their own **.kde/share/config** directories. The **share/icons** directory holds the default icons used on your KDE desktop and by KDE applications. The user's home directory, the **.kde** directory holds a user's own KDE configuration for the desktop and its applications.

System KDE Directories	Description
`/usr/bin`	KDE programs
`/usr/lib/kde4`	KDE libraries
`/usr/include/kde`	Header files for use in compiling and developing KDE applications
`/usr/share/config`	KDE desktop and application configuration files
`/usr/share/mimelnk`	Desktop files used to build the main menu
`/usr/share/apps`	Files used by KDE applications
`/usr/share/icons`	Icons used in KDE desktop and applications
`/usr/share/doc`	KDE Help system
User KDE Directories	**Description**
`.kde/AutoStart`	Applications automatically started up with KDE
`.kde/share/config`	User KDE desktop and application configuration files for user-specified features
`.kde/share/apps`	Directories and files used by KDE applications
`.kde/share/config/plasma-appletsrc`	Plasma applet configuration

Table 11-5: KDE Installation Directories

12. Shells

The Command Line

History

Filename Expansion: *, ?, [ ]

Standard Input/Output and Redirection

Linux Files

The File Structure

Listing, Displaying, and Printing Files

Managing Directories: mkdir, rmdir, ls, cd, pwd

File and Directory Operations: find, cp, mv, rm, ln

The *shell* is a command interpreter that provides a line-oriented interactive and non-interactive interface between the user and the operating system. You enter commands on a command line; they are interpreted by the shell and then sent as instructions to the operating system (the command line interface is accessible from Gnome and KDE through a Terminal windows – Applications/Accessories menu). You can also place commands in a script file to be consecutively executed much like a program. This interpretive capability of the shell provides for many sophisticated features. For example, the shell has a set of file expansion characters that can generate filenames. The shell can redirect input and output, as well as run operations in the background, freeing you to perform other tasks.

Shell	Web Site
`www.gnu.org/software/bash`	BASH Web site with online manual, FAQ, and current releases
`www.gnu.org/software/bash/manual/bash.html`	BASH online manual
`www.zsh.org`	Z shell Web site with referrals to FAQs and current downloads.
`www.tcsh.org`	TCSH Web site with detailed support including manual, tips, FAQ, and recent releases
`www.kornshell.com`	Korn shell site with manual, FAQ, and references

Table 12-1: Linux Shells

Several different types of shells have been developed for Linux: the Bourne Again shell (BASH), the Korn shell, the TCSH shell, and the Z shell. All shells are available for your use, although the BASH shell is the default. You only need one type of shell to do your work. Ubuntu Linux includes all the major shells, although it installs and uses the BASH shell as the default. If you use the command line shell, you will be using the BASH shell unless you specify another. This chapter discusses the BASH shell, which shares many of the same features as other shells.

You can find out more about shells at their respective Web sites as listed in Table 12-1. In addition, a detailed online manual is available for each installed shell. Use the **man** command and the shell's keyword to access them, **bash** for the BASH shell, **ksh** for the Korn shell, **zsh** for the Z shell, and **tsch** for the TSCH shell. For example, the command **man bash** will access the BASH shell online manual.

Note: You can find out more about the BASH shell at **www.gnu.org/software/bash**. A detailed online manual is available on your Linux system using the **man** command with the **bash** keyword.

The Command Line

The Linux command line interface consists of a single line into which you enter commands with any of their options and arguments. From GNOME or KDE, you can access the command line interface by opening a terminal window (Applications | Accessories | Terminal). Should you start Linux with the command line interface, you will be presented with a BASH shell command line when you log in.

By default, the BASH shell has a dollar sign (**$**) prompt, but Linux has several other types of shells, each with its own prompt (like **%** for the C shell). The root user will have a different prompt, the **#**. A shell *prompt,* such as the one shown here, marks the beginning of the command line:

```
$
```

You can enter a command along with options and arguments at the prompt. For example, with an **-l** option, the **ls** command will display a line of information about each file, listing such data as its size and the date and time it was last modified. In the next example, the user enters the **ls** command followed by a **-l** option. The dash before the **-l** option is required. Linux uses it to distinguish an option from an argument.

```
$ ls -l
```

If you wanted only the information displayed for a particular file, you could add that file's name as the argument, following the **-l** option:

```
$ ls -l mydata
-rw-r--r-- 1 chris weather 207 Feb 20 11:55 mydata
```

Tip: Some commands can be complex and take some time to execute. When you mistakenly execute the wrong command, you can interrupt and stop such commands with the interrupt key—CTRL-C.

You can enter a command on several lines by typing a backslash just before you press ENTER. The backslash "escapes" the ENTER key, effectively continuing the same command line to the next line. In the next example, the **cp** command is entered on three lines. The first two lines end in a backslash, effectively making all three lines one command line.

```
$ cp -i \
mydata \
/home/george/myproject/newdata
```

You can also enter several commands on the same line by separating them with a semicolon (;). In effect the semicolon operates as an execute operation. Commands will be executed in the sequence in which they are entered. The following command executes an **ls** command followed by a **date** command.

```
$ ls ; date
```

You can also conditionally run several commands on the same line with the **&&** operator. A command is executed only if the previous command is true. This feature is useful for running several dependent scripts on the same line. In the next example, the **ls** command is run only if the **date** command is successfully executed.

```
$ date && ls
```

TIP: Command can also be run as arguments on a command line, using their results for other commands. To run a command within a command line, you encase the command in back quotes.

Command Line Editing

The BASH shell, which is your default shell, has special command line editing capabilities that you may find helpful as you learn Linux (see Table 12-2). You can easily modify commands you have entered before executing them, moving anywhere on the command line and inserting or deleting characters. This is particularly helpful for complex commands.

Movement Commands	Operation
CTRL-F, RIGHT-ARROW	Move forward a character
CTRL-B, LEFT-ARROW	Move backward a character
CTRL-A or HOME	Move to beginning of line
CTRL-E or END	Move to end of line
ALT-F	Move forward a word
ALT-B	Move backward a word
CTRL-L	Clear screen and place line at top
Editing Commands	**Operation**
CTRL-D or DEL	Delete character cursor is on
CTRL-H or BACKSPACE	Delete character before the cursor
CTRL-K	Cut remainder of line from cursor position
CTRL-U	Cut from cursor position to beginning of line
CTRL-W	Cut previous word
CTRL-C	Cut entire line
ALT-D	Cut the remainder of a word
ALT-DEL	Cut from the cursor to the beginning of a word
CTRL-Y	Paste previous cut text
ALT-Y	Paste from set of previously cut text
CTRL-Y	Paste previous cut text
CTRL-V	Insert quoted text, used for inserting control or meta (Alt) keys as text, such as CTRL-B for backspace or CTRL-T for tabs
ALT-T	Transpose current and previous word
ALT-L	Lowercase current word
ALT-U	Uppercase current word
ALT-C	Capitalize current word
CTRL-SHIFT-_	Undo previous change

Table 12-2: Command Line Editing Operations

You can press CTRL-F or the RIGHT ARROW key to move forward a character, or the CTRL-B or LEFT ARROW key to move back a character. CTRL-D or DEL deletes the character the cursor is on, and CTRL-H or BACKSPACE deletes the character preceding the cursor. To add text, you use the arrow keys to move the cursor to where you want to insert text and type the new characters.

You can even cut words with the CTRL-W or ALT-D key and then press the CTRL-Y key to paste them back in at a different position, effectively moving the words. As a rule, the CTRL version of the command operates on characters, and the ALT version works on words, such as CTRL-T to transpose characters and ALT-T to transpose words. At any time, you can press ENTER to execute the command. For example, if you make a spelling mistake when entering a command, rather than reentering the entire command, you can use the editing operations to correct the mistake. The actual associations of keys and their tasks, along with global settings, are specified in the **/etc/inputrc** file.

The editing capabilities of the BASH shell command line are provided by Readline. Readline supports numerous editing operations. You can even bind a key to a selected editing operation. Readline uses the **/etc/inputrc** file to configure key bindings. This file is read automatically by your **/etc/profile** shell configuration file when you log in. Users can customize their editing commands by creating an **.inputrc** file in their home directory (this is a dot file). It may be best to first copy the **/etc/inputrc** file as your **.inputrc** file and then edit it. **/etc/profile** will first check for a local **.inputrc** file before accessing the **/etc/inputrc** file. You can find out more about Readline in the BASH shell reference manual at **www.gnu.org/manual/bash**.

Command and Filename Completion

The BASH command line has a built-in feature that performs command line and file name completion. Automatic completions can be effected by pressing the TAB key. If you enter an incomplete pattern as a command or filename argument, you can press the TAB key to activate the command and filename completion feature, which completes the pattern. A directory will have a forward slash (/) attached to its name. If more than one command or file has the same prefix, the shell simply beeps and waits for you to press the TAB key again. It then displays a list of possible command completions and waits for you to add enough characters to select a unique command or filename. For situations where you know multiple possibilities are likely, you can just press the ESC key instead of two TABs. In the next example, the user issues a **cat** command with an incomplete filename. When the user presses the TAB key, the system searches for a match and, when it finds one, fills in the filename. The user can then press ENTER to execute the command.

```
$ cat pre <tab>
$ cat preface
```

The automatic completions also work with the names of variables, users, and hosts. In this case, the partial text needs to be preceded by a special character, indicating the type of name. A listing of possible automatic completions follows:

Filenames begin with any text or /.

Shell variable text begins with a $ sign.

User name text begins with a ~ sign.

Host name text begins with a @.

Commands, aliases, and text in files begin with normal text.

Variables begin with a **$** sign, so any text beginning with a dollar sign is treated as a variable to be completed. Variables are selected from previously defined variables, like system shell variables. User names begin with a tilde (~). Host names begin with a @ sign, with possible names taken from the **/etc/hosts** file. For example, to complete the variable HOME given just $HOM, simply press a tab key.

```
$ echo $HOM <tab>
$ echo $HOME
```

If you entered just an **H**, then you could press TAB twice to see all possible variables beginning with H. The command line is redisplayed, letting you complete the name.

```
$ echo $H <tab> <tab>
$HISTCMD $HISTFILE $HOME $HOSTTYPE HISTFILE $HISTSIZE $HISTNAME
$ echo $H
```

You can also specifically select the kind of text to complete, using corresponding command keys. In this case, it does not matter what kind of sign a name begins with.

Command (CTRL-R for listing possible completions)	Description
TAB	Automatic completion
TAB TAB or ESC	List possible completions
ALT-/, CTRL-R-/	Filename completion, normal text for automatic
ALT-$, CTRL-R-$	Shell variable completion, $ for automatic
ALT-~, CTRL-R-~	User name completion, ~ for automatic
ALT-@, CTRL-R-@	Host name completion, @ for automatic
ALT-!, CTRL-R-!	Command name completion, normal text for automatic

Table 12-3: Command Line Text Completion Commands

For example, the pressing ALT-~ will treat the current text as a user name. Pressing ALT-@ will treat it as a host name, and ALT-$, as a variable. Pressing ALT-! will treat it as a command. To display a list of possible completions, press the CTRL-X key with the appropriate completion key, as in CTRL-X-$ to list possible variable completions. See Table 12-3 for a complete listing.

History

The BASH shell keeps a *history list,* of your previously entered commands. You can display each command, in turn, on your command line by pressing the UP ARROW key. Press the DOWN ARROW key to move down the list. You can modify and execute any of these previous commands when you display them on the command line.

Tip: The ability to redisplay a command is helpful when you have already executed a command you had entered incorrectly. In this case, you would be presented with an error message and a new, empty command line. By pressing the UP ARROW key, you can redisplay the previous command, make corrections to it, and then execute it again. This way, you would not have to enter the whole command again.

History Events

In the BASH shell, the *history utility* keeps a record of the most recent commands you have executed. The commands are numbered starting at 1, and a limit exists to the number of commands remembered—the default is 500. The history utility is a kind of short-term memory, keeping track of the most recent commands you have executed. To see the set of your most recent commands, type **history** on the command line and press ENTER. A list of your most recent commands is then displayed, preceded by a number.

```
$ history
1 cp mydata today
2 vi mydata
3 mv mydata reports
4 cd reports
5 ls
```

History Commands	Description
CTRL-N or DOWN ARROW	Moves down to the next event in the history list
CTRL-P or UP ARROW	Moves up to the previous event in the history list
ALT-<	Moves to the beginning of the history event list
ALT->	Moves to the end of the history event list
ALT-N	Forward Search, next matching item
ALT-P	Backward Search, previous matching item
CTRL-S	Forward Search History, forward incremental search
CTRL-R	Reverse Search History, reverse incremental search
fc *event-reference*	Edits an event with the standard editor and then executes it **Options** -l List recent history events; same as **history** command -e *editor event-reference* Invokes a specified editor to edit a specific event
History Event References	
!*event num*	References an event with an event number
!!	References the previous command
!*characters*	References an event with beginning characters
!?*pattern*?	References an event with a pattern in the event
!-*event num*	References an event with an offset from the first event
!*num-num*	References a range of events

Table 12-4: History Commands and History Event References

Each of these commands is technically referred to as an event. An *event* describes an action that has been taken—a command that has been executed. The events are numbered according to their sequence of execution. The most recent event has the highest number. Each of these events can be identified by its number or beginning characters in the command.

The history utility lets you reference a former event, placing it on your command line so you can execute it. The easiest way to do this is to use the UP ARROW and DOWN ARROW keys to place history events on the command line, one at a time. You need not display the list first with **history**. Pressing the UP ARROW key once places the last history event on the command line. Pressing it again places the next history event on the command line. Pressing the DOWN ARROW key places the previous event on the command line.

You can use certain control and meta keys to perform other history operations like searching the history list. A meta key is the ALT key, and the ESC key on keyboards that have no ALT key. The ALT key is used here. Pressing ALT-< will move you to the beginning of the history list; ALT-N will search it. CTRL-S and CTRL-R will perform incremental searches, display matching commands as you type in a search string. Table 12-4 lists the different commands for referencing the history list.

Tip: If more than one history event matches what you have entered, you will hear a beep, and you can then enter more characters to help uniquely identify the event.

You can also reference and execute history events using the ! history command. The ! is followed by a reference that identifies the command. The reference can be either the number of the event or a beginning set of characters in the event. In the next example, the third command in the history list is referenced first by number and then by the beginning characters:

```
$ !3
mv mydata reports
$ !mv my
mv mydata reports
```

You can also reference an event using an offset from the end of the list. A negative number will offset from the end of the list to that event, thereby referencing it. In the next example, the fourth command, **cd mydata**, is referenced using a negative offset, and then executed. Remember that you are offsetting from the end of the list—in this case, event 5—up toward the beginning of the list, event 1. An offset of 4 beginning from event 5 places you at event 2.

```
$ !-4
vi mydata
```

To reference the last event, you use a following !, as in ! !. In the next example, the command ! ! executes the last command the user executed—in this case, **ls**:

```
$ !!
ls
mydata today reports
```

Filename Expansion: *, ?, [ ]

Filenames are the most common arguments used in a command. Often you will know only part of the filename, or you will want to reference several filenames that have the same extension or begin with the same characters. The shell provides a set of special characters that search out, match, and generate a list of filenames. These are the asterisk, the question mark, and brackets (`*`, `?`, `[]`). Given a partial filename, the shell uses these matching operators to search for files and expand to a list of filenames found. The shell replaces the partial filename argument with the expanded list of matched filenames. This list of filenames can then become the arguments for commands such as `ls`, which can operate on many files. Table 12-5 lists the shell's file expansion characters.

Common Shell Symbols	Execution
ENTER	Execute a command line.
;	Separate commands on the same command line.
`` `command` ``	Execute a command.
$ (command)	Execute a command.
[]	Match on a class of possible characters in filenames.
\	Quote the following character. Used to quote special characters.
|	Pipe the standard output of one command as input for another command.
&	Execute a command in the background.
!	Reference history command.
File Expansion Symbols	**Execution**
*	Match on any set of characters in filenames.
?	Match on any single character in filenames.
[]	Match on a class of characters in filenames.
Redirection Symbols	**Execution**
>	Redirect the standard output to a file or device, creating the file if it does not exist and overwriting the file if it does exist.
>!	The exclamation point forces the overwriting of a file if it already exists.
<	Redirect the standard input from a file or device to a program.
>>	Redirect the standard output to a file or device, appending the output to the end of the file.
Standard Error Redirection Symbols	**Execution**
2>	Redirect the standard error to a file or device.
2>>	Redirect and append the standard error to a file or device.
2>&1	Redirect the standard error to the standard output.

Table 12-5: Shell Symbols

Matching Multiple Characters

The asterisk (*) references files beginning or ending with a specific set of characters. You place the asterisk before or after a set of characters that form a pattern to be searched for in filenames.

If the asterisk is placed before the pattern, filenames that end in that pattern are searched for. If the asterisk is placed after the pattern, filenames that begin with that pattern are searched for. Any matching filename is copied into a list of filenames generated by this operation.

In the next example, all filenames beginning with the pattern "doc" are searched for and a list generated. Then all filenames ending with the pattern "day" are searched for and a list is generated. The last example shows how the * can be used in any combination of characters.

```
$ ls
doc1 doc2 document docs mydoc monday tuesday
$ ls doc*
doc1 doc2 document docs
$ ls *day
monday tuesday
$ ls m*d*
monday
$
```

Filenames often include an extension specified with a period and followed by a string denoting the file type, such as **.c** for C files, **.cpp** for C++ files, or even **.jpg** for JPEG image files. The extension has no special status and is only part of the characters making up the filename. Using the asterisk makes it easy to select files with a given extension. In the next example, the asterisk is used to list only those files with a **.c** extension. The asterisk placed before the **.c** constitutes the argument for **ls**.

```
$ ls *.c
calc.c main.c
```

You can use * with the **rm** command to erase several files at once. The asterisk first selects a list of files with a given extension, or beginning or ending with a given set of characters, and then it presents this list of files to the **rm** command to be erased. In the next example, the **rm** command erases all files beginning with the pattern "doc":

```
$ rm doc*
```

Caution: Use the * file expansion character carefully and sparingly with the **rm** command. The combination can be dangerous. A misplaced * in an **rm** command without the **-i** option could easily erase all the files in your current directory. The **-i** option will first prompt you to confirm whether the file should be deleted.

Matching Single Characters

The question mark (?) matches only a single incomplete character in filenames. Suppose you want to match the files **doc1** and **docA**, but not the file **document**. Whereas the asterisk will match filenames of any length, the question mark limits the match to one extra character. The next example matches files that begin with the word "doc" followed by a single differing letter:

```
$ ls
doc1 docA document
$ ls doc?
doc1 docA
```

Matching a Range of Characters

Whereas the * and ? file expansion characters specify incomplete portions of a filename, the brackets ([]) enable you to specify a set of valid characters to search for. Any character placed within the brackets will be matched in the filename. Suppose you want to list files beginning with "doc", but only ending in *1* or *A*. You are not interested in filenames ending in *2* or *B,* or any other character. Here is how it is done:

```
$ ls
doc1 doc2 doc3 docA docB docD document
$ ls doc[1A]
doc1 docA
```

You can also specify a set of characters as a range, rather than listing them one by one. A dash placed between the upper and lower bounds of a range of characters selects all characters within that range. The range is usually determined by the character set in use. In an ASCII character set, the range "a-g" will select all lowercase alphabetic characters from *a* through *g,* inclusive. In the next example, files beginning with the pattern "doc" and ending in characters *1* through *3* are selected. Then, those ending in characters *B* through *E* are matched.

```
$ ls doc[1-3]
doc1 doc2 doc3
$ ls doc[B-E]
docB docD
```

You can combine the brackets with other file expansion characters to form flexible matching operators. Suppose you want to list only filenames ending in either a **.c** or **.o** extension, but no other extension. You can use a combination of the asterisk and brackets: * [co]. The asterisk matches all filenames, and the brackets match only filenames with extension **.c** or **.o**.

```
$ ls *.[co]
main.c  main.o  calc.c
```

Matching Shell Symbols

At times, a file expansion character is actually part of a filename. In these cases, you need to quote the character by preceding it with a backslash (\) to reference the file. In the next example, the user needs to reference a file that ends with the ? character, called **answers?**. The **?** is, however, a file expansion character and would match any filename beginning with "answers" that has one or more characters. In this case, the user quotes the **?** with a preceding backslash to reference the filename.

```
$ ls answers\?
answers?
```

Placing the filename in double quotes will also quote the character.

```
$ ls "answers?"
answers?
```

This is also true for filenames or directories that have white space characters like the space character. In this case, you could either use the backslash to quote the space character in the file or directory name, or place the entire name in double quotes.

```
$ ls My\ Documents
My Documents
$ ls "My Documents"
My Documents
```

Generating Patterns

Though not a file expansion operation, { } is often useful for generating names that you can use to create or modify files and directories. The braces operation only generates a list of names. It does not match on existing filenames. Patterns are placed within the braces and separated with commas. Any pattern placed within the braces will be used to generate a version of the pattern, using either the preceding or following pattern, or both. Suppose you want to generate a list of names beginning with "doc", but ending only in the patterns "ument", "final", and "draft". Here is how it is done:

```
$ echo doc{ument,final,draft}
document docfinal docdraft
```

Since the names generated do not have to exist, you could use the { } operation in a command to create directories, as shown here:

```
$ mkdir {fall,winter,spring}report
$ ls
fallreport springreport winterreport
```

Standard Input/Output and Redirection

The data in input and output operations is organized like a file. Data input at the keyboard is placed in a data stream arranged as a continuous set of bytes. Data output from a command or program is also placed in a data stream and arranged as a continuous set of bytes. This input data stream is referred to in Linux as the standard input, while the output data stream is called the standard output. A separate output data stream reserved solely for error messages, called the standard error.

Because the standard input and standard output have the same organization as that of a file, they can easily interact with files. Linux has a redirection capability that lets you easily move data in and out of files. You can redirect the standard output so that, instead of displaying the output on a screen, you can save it in a file. You can also redirect the standard input away from the keyboard to a file, so that input is read from a file instead of from your keyboard.

When a Linux command is executed that produces output, this output is placed in the standard output data stream. The default destination for the standard output data stream is a device—in this case, the screen. *Devices,* such as the keyboard and screen, are treated as files. They receive and send out streams of bytes with the same organization as that of a byte-stream file. The screen is a device that displays a continuous stream of bytes. By default, the standard output will send its data to the screen device, which will then display the data.

For example, the `ls` command generates a list of all filenames and outputs this list to the standard output. Next, this stream of bytes in the standard output is directed to the screen device. The list of filenames is then printed on the screen. The `cat` command also sends output to the standard output. The contents of a file are copied to the standard output, whose default destination is the screen. The contents of the file are then displayed on the screen.

Command	Execution
ENTER	Execute a command line.
;	Separate commands on the same command line.
command *opts args*	Enter backslash before carriage return to continue entering a command on the next line.
`` `command` ``	Execute a command.
Special Characters **for Filename Expansion**	**Execution**
*	Match on any set of characters.
?	Match on any single characters.
[]	Match on a class of possible characters.
\	Quote the following character. Used to quote special characters.
Redirection	**Execution**
command > filename	Redirect the standard output to a file or device, creating the file if it does not exist and overwriting the file if it does exist.
command < filename	Redirect the standard input from a file or device to a program.
command >> filename	Redirect the standard output to a file or device, appending the output to the end of the file.
command `2>` *filename*	Redirect the standard error to a file or device
command `2>>` *filename*	Redirect and append the standard error to a file or device
command `2>&1`	Redirect the standard error to the standard output in the Bourne shell.
command `>&` *filename*	Redirect the standard error to a file or device in the C shell.
Pipes	**Execution**
command | *command*	Pipe the standard output of one command as input for another command.

Table 12-6: The Shell Operations

Redirecting the Standard Output: > and >>

Suppose that instead of displaying a list of files on the screen, you would like to save this list in a file. In other words, you would like to direct the standard output to a file rather than the screen. To do this, you place the output redirection operator, the greater-than sign (**>**), followed by the name of a file on the command line after the Linux command. Table 12-6 lists the different ways you can use the redirection operators. In the next example, the output of the `ls` command is redirected from the screen device to a file:

```
$ ls -l *.c > programlist
```

The redirection operation creates the new destination file. If the file already exists, it will be overwritten with the data in the standard output. You can set the `noclobber` feature to prevent overwriting an existing file with the redirection operation. In this case, the redirection operation on an existing file will fail. You can overcome the `noclobber` feature by placing an exclamation point after the redirection operator. You can place the `noclobber` command in a shell configuration file to make it an automatic default operation. The next example sets the `noclobber` feature for the BASH shell and then forces the overwriting of the **oldarticle** file if it already exists:

```
$ set -o noclobber
$ cat myarticle >! oldarticle
```

Although the redirection operator and the filename are placed after the command, the redirection operation is not executed after the command. In fact, it is executed before the command. The redirection operation creates the file and sets up the redirection before it receives any data from the standard output. If the file already exists, it will be destroyed and replaced by a file of the same name. In effect, the command generating the output is executed only after the redirected file has been created.

In the next example, the output of the `ls` command is redirected from the screen device to a file. First the `ls` command lists files, and in the next command, `ls` redirects its file list to the **listf** file. Then the `cat` command displays the list of files saved in **listf**. Notice the list of files in **listf** includes the **listf** filename. The list of filenames generated by the `ls` command includes the name of the file created by the redirection operation—in this case, **listf**. The **listf** file is first created by the redirection operation, and then the `ls` command lists it along with other files. This file list output by `ls` is then redirected to the **listf** file, instead of being printed on the screen.

```
$ ls
mydata intro preface
$ ls > listf
$ cat listf
mydata intro listf preface
```

Tip: Errors occur when you try to use the same filename for both an input file for the command and the redirected destination file. In this case, because the redirection operation is executed first, the input file, because it exists, is destroyed and replaced by a file of the same name. When the command is executed, it finds an input file that is empty.

You can also append the standard output to an existing file using the **>>** redirection operator. Instead of overwriting the file, the data in the standard output is added at the end of the file. In the next example, the **myarticle** and **oldarticle** files are appended to the **allarticles** file. The **allarticles** file will then contain the contents of both **myarticle** and **oldarticle**.

```
$ cat myarticle >> allarticles
$ cat oldarticle >> allarticles
```

The Standard Input

Many Linux commands can receive data from the standard input. The standard input itself receives data from a device or a file. The default device for the standard input is the keyboard. Characters typed on the keyboard are placed in the standard input, which is then directed to the Linux command. Just as with the standard output, you can also redirect the standard input, receiving input from a file rather than the keyboard. The operator for redirecting the standard input is the less-than sign (**<**). In the next example, the standard input is redirected to receive input from the **myarticle** file, rather than the keyboard device (use CTRL-D to end the typed input). The contents of **myarticle** are read into the standard input by the redirection operation. Then the **cat** command reads the standard input and displays the contents of **myarticle**.

```
$ cat < myarticle
hello Christopher
How are you today
$
```

You can combine the redirection operations for both standard input and standard output. In the next example, the **cat** command has no filename arguments. Without filename arguments, the **cat** command receives input from the standard input and sends output to the standard output. However, the standard input has been redirected to receive its data from a file, while the standard output has been redirected to place its data in a file.

```
$ cat < myarticle > newarticle
```

Redirecting the Standard Error: >&, 2>, |&

When you execute commands, it is possible for an error to occur. You may give the wrong number of arguments or some kind of system error could take place. When an error occurs, the system will issue an error message. Usually such error messages are displayed on the screen along with the standard output. Error messages are placed in another standard byte stream called the standard error. In the next example, the cat command is given as its argument the name of a file that does not exist, **myintro**. In this case, the **cat** command will simply issue an error. Redirection operators are listed in Table 18-6.

```
$ cat myintro
cat : myintro not found
```

Because error messages are in a separate data stream from the standard output, this means that if you have redirected the standard output to a file, error messages will still appear on the screen for you to see. Though the standard output may be redirected to a file, the standard error is still directed to the screen. In the next example, the standard output of the **cat** command is redirected to the file **mydata**. The standard error, containing the error messages, is still directed toward the screen

```
$ cat myintro > mydata
cat : myintro not found
```

Like the standard output, you can also redirect the standard error. This means that you can save your error messages in a file for future reference. This is helpful if you need to save a record of the error messages. Like the standard output, the standard error's default destination is the display. Using special redirection operators, you can redirect the standard error to any file or device that you choose. If you redirect the standard error, the error messages will not be displayed on the screen. You can examine them later by viewing the contents of the file in which you saved them.

All the standard byte streams can be referenced in redirection operations with numbers. The numbers 0, 1, and 2 reference the standard input, standard output, and standard error respectively. By default an output redirection, **>**, operates on the standard output, 1. You can modify the output redirection to operate on the standard error by preceding the output redirection operator with the number 2, **2>**. In the next example, the **cat** command again will generate an error. The error message is redirected to the standard byte stream represented by number 2, the standard error.

```
$ cat nodata 2> myerrors
$ cat myerrors
cat : nodata not found
```

You can also append the standard error to a file by using the number 2 and the redirection append operator, **>>**. In the next example, the user appends the standard error to the **myerrors** file, which then functions as a log of errors.

```
$ cat nodata 2>> myerrors
$ cat compls 2>> myerrors
$ cat myerrors
cat : nodata not found
cat : compls not found
$
```

To both redirect the standard output as well as the standard error, you would need a separate redirection operation and file for each. In the next example, the standard output is redirected to the file **mydata**, and the standard error is redirected to **myerrors**. If nodata were to exist, then **mydata** would hold a copy of its contents.

```
$ cat nodata 1> mydata 2> myerrors
cat myerrors
cat : nodata not found
```

If, however, you want to save a record of your errors in the same file as that used for the redirected standard output, you need to redirect the standard error into the standard output. You can reference a standard byte stream by preceding its number with an ampersand. **&1** references the standard output. You can use such a reference in a redirection operation to make a standard byte stream a destination file. The redirection operation **2>&1** redirects the standard error into the standard output. In effect, the standard output becomes the destination file for the standard error. Conversely the redirection operation **1>&2** would redirect the standard input into the standard error.

Pipes: |

You may encounter situations in which you need to send data from one command to another. In other words, you may want to send the standard output of a command to another command, rather than to a destination file. Suppose you want to send a list of your filenames to the printer to be printed. You need two commands to do this: the **ls** command to generate a list of filenames and the **lpr** command to send the list to the printer. In effect, you need to take the output of the **ls** command and use it as input for the **lpr** command. You can think of the data as flowing from one command to another. To form such a connection in Linux, you use what is called a pipe.

The pipe operator (|, the vertical bar character) placed between two commands forms a connection between them. The standard output of one command becomes the standard input for the other. The pipe operation receives output from the command placed before the pipe and sends this data as input to the command placed after the pipe. As shown in the next example, you can connect the **ls** command and the **lpr** command with a pipe. The list of filenames output by the **ls** command is piped into the **lpr** command.

```
$ ls | lpr
```

You can combine the **pipe** operation with other shell features, such as file expansion characters, to perform specialized operations. The next example prints only files with a **.c** extension. The **ls** command is used with the asterisk and ".c" to generate a list of filenames with the **.c** extension. Then this list is piped to the **lpr** command.

```
$ ls *.c | lpr
```

In the preceding example, a list of filenames was used as input. What is important to note is that pipes operate on the standard output of a command, whatever that might be. The contents of whole files or even several files can be piped from one command to another. In the next example, the **cat** command reads and outputs the contents of the **mydata** file, which are then piped to the **lpr** command:

```
$ cat mydata | lpr
```

Linux has many commands that generate modified output. For example, the **sort** command takes the contents of a file and generates a version with each line sorted in alphabetic order. The **sort** command works best with files that are lists of items. Commands such as **sort** that output a modified version of its input are referred to as filters. Filters are often used with pipes. In the next example, a sorted version of **mylist** is generated and piped into the **more** command for display on the screen. The original file, **mylist**, has not been changed and is not sorted. Only the output of **sort** in the standard output is sorted.

```
$ sort mylist | more
```

The standard input piped into a command can be more carefully controlled with the standard input argument (-). When you use the dash as an argument for a command, it represents the standard input.

Linux Files

You can name a file using any letters, underscores, and numbers. You can also include periods and commas. Except in certain special cases, you should never begin a filename with a period. Other characters, such as slashes, question marks, or asterisks, are reserved for use as special characters by the system and should not be part of a filename. Filenames can be as long as 256 characters. Filenames can also include spaces, though to reference such filenames from the command line, be sure to encase them in quotes. On a desktop like GNOME or KDE you do not need to use quotes.

You can include an extension as part of a filename. A period is used to distinguish the filename proper from the extension. Extensions can be useful for categorizing your files. You are probably familiar with certain standard extensions that have been adopted by convention. For example, C source code files always have a **.c** extension. Files that contain compiled object code have an **.o** extension. You can make up your own file extensions. The following examples are all valid Linux filenames. Keep in mind that to reference the name with spaces on the command line, you would have to encase it in quotes as "New book review":

```
preface
chapter2
9700info
New_Revisions
calc.c
intro.bk1
New book review
```

Special initialization files are also used to hold shell configuration commands. These are the hidden, or dot, files, which begin with a period. Dot files used by commands and applications have predetermined names, such as the **.mozilla** directory used to hold your Mozilla data and configuration files. Recall that when you use **ls** to display your filenames, the dot files will not be displayed. To include the dot files, you need to use **ls** with the **-a** option.

The **ls -l** command displays detailed information about a file. First the permissions are displayed, followed by the number of links, the owner of the file, the name of the group to which the user belongs to, the file size in bytes, the date and time the file was last modified, and the name of the file. Permissions indicate who can access the file: the user, members of a group, or all other users. The group name indicates the group permitted to access the file object. The file type for **mydata** is that of an ordinary file. Only one link exists, indicating the file has no other names and no other links. The owner's name is **chris**, the same as the login name, and the group name is **weather**. Other users probably also belong to the **weather** group. The size of the file is 207 bytes, and it was last modified on February 20 at 11:55 A.M. The name of the file is **mydata**.

If you want to display this detailed information for all the files in a directory, simply use the **ls -l** command without an argument.

```
$ ls -l
-rw-r--r-- 1 chris weather 207 Feb 20 11:55 mydata
-rw-rw-r-- 1 chris weather 568 Feb 14 10:30 today
-rw-rw-r-- 1 chris weather 308 Feb 17 12:40 monday
```

All files in Linux have one physical format, a byte stream, which is simply a sequence of bytes. This allows Linux to apply the file concept to every data component in the system. Directories are classified as files, as are devices. Treating everything as a file allows Linux to organize and exchange data more easily. The data in a file can be sent directly to a device such as a screen because a device interfaces with the system using the same byte-stream file format used by regular files.

This same file format is used to implement other operating system components. The interface to a device, such as the screen or keyboard, is designated as a file. Other components, such as directories, are themselves byte-stream files, but they have a special internal organization. A directory file contains information about a directory, organized in a special directory format. Because these different components are treated as files, they can be said to constitute different *file types*. A character device is one file type. A directory is another file type. The number of these file types may vary according to your specific implementation of Linux. Five common types of files exist, however: ordinary files, directory files, first-in first-out (FIFO) pipes, character device files, and block device files. Although you may rarely reference a file's type, it can be useful when searching for directories or devices.

Although all ordinary files have a byte-stream format, they may be used in different ways. The most significant difference is between binary and text files. Compiled programs are examples of binary files. However, even text files can be classified according to their different uses. You can have files that contain C programming source code or shell commands, or even a file that is empty. The file could be an executable program or a directory file. The Linux **file** command helps you determine what a file is used for. It examines the first few lines of a file and tries to determine a classification for it. The **file** command looks for special keywords or special numbers in those first few lines, but it is not always accurate. In the next example, the **file** command examines the contents of two files and determines a classification for them:

```
$ file monday reports
monday: text
reports: directory
```

If you need to examine the entire file byte by byte, you can do so with the **od** (octal dump) command, which performs a dump of a file. By default, it prints every byte in its octal representation. However, you can also specify a character, decimal, or hexadecimal representation. The **od** command is helpful when you need to detect any special character in your file or if you want to display a binary file.

The File Structure

Linux organizes files into a hierarchically connected set of directories. Each directory may contain either files or other directories. In this respect, directories perform two important functions. A *directory* holds files, much like files held in a file drawer, and a directory connects to other directories, much as a branch in a tree is connected to other branches. Because of the similarities to a tree, such a structure is often referred to as a *tree structure*.

The Linux file structure branches into several directories beginning with a root directory, /. Within the root directory, several system directories contain files and programs that are features of the Linux system. The root directory also contains a directory called **home** that contains the home directories of all the users in the system. Each user's home directory, in turn, contains the directories the user has made for their own use. Each of these can also contain directories. Such nested directories branch out from the user's home directory.

Note: The user's home directory can be any directory, though it is usually the directory that bears the user's login name. This directory is located in the directory named **/home** on your Linux system. For example, a user named **dylan** will have a home directory called **dylan** located in the system's **/home** directory. The user's home directory is a subdirectory of the directory called **/home** on your system.

Home Directories

When you log in to the system, you are placed within your home directory. The name given to this directory by the system is the same as your login name. Any files you create when you first log in are organized within your home directory. Within your home directory, you can create more directories. You can then change to these directories and store files in them. The same is true for other users on the system. Each user has a home directory, identified by the appropriate login name. Users, in turn, can create their own directories.

You can access a directory either through its name or by making it your working directory. Each directory is given a name when it is created. You can use this name in file operations to access files in that directory. You can also make the directory your working directory. If you do not use any directory names in a file operation, the working directory will be accessed. The working directory is the one from which you are currently working. When you log in, the working directory is your home directory, which usually has the same name as your login name. You can change the working directory by using the **cd** command to move to another directory.

Directory	Function
/	Begins the file system structure, called the *root*.
/home	Contains users' home directories.
/bin	Holds all the standard commands and utility programs.
/usr	Holds those files and commands used by the system; this directory breaks down into several subdirectories.
/usr/bin	Holds user-oriented commands and utility programs.
/usr/sbin	Holds system administration commands.
/usr/lib	Holds libraries for programming languages.
/usr/share/doc	Holds Linux documentation.
/usr/share/man	Holds the online Man files.
/var/spool	Holds spooled files, such as those generated for printing jobs and network transfers.
/sbin	Holds system administration commands for booting the system.
/var	Holds files that vary, such as mailbox files.
/dev	Holds file interfaces for devices such as the terminals and printers (dynamically generated by udev, do not edit).
/etc	Holds system configuration files and any other system files.

Table 12-7: Standard System Directories in Linux

Pathnames

The name you give to a directory or file when you create it is not its full name. The full name of a directory is its *pathname*. The hierarchically nested relationship among directories forms paths, and these paths can be used to identify and reference any directory or file uniquely or absolutely. Each directory in the file structure can be said to have its own unique path. The actual name by which the system identifies a directory always begins with the root directory and consists of all directories nested below that directory.

In Linux, you write a pathname by listing each directory in the path separated from the last by a forward slash. A slash preceding the first directory in the path represents the root. The pathname for the **chris** directory is **/home/chris**. If the **chris** directory has a subdirectory called

reports, then the full the pathname for the **reports** directory would be **/home/chris/reports**. Pathnames also apply to files. When you create a file within a directory, you give the file a name. The actual name by which the system identifies the file, however, is the filename combined with the path of directories from the root to the file's directory. As an example, the pathname for **monday** is **/home/chris/reports/monday** (the root directory is represented by the first slash). The path for the **monday** file consists of the root, **home**, **chris**, and **reports** directories and the filename **monday**.

Pathnames may be absolute or relative. An *absolute pathname* is the complete pathname of a file or directory beginning with the root directory. A *relative pathname* begins from your working directory; it is the path of a file relative to your working directory. The working directory is the one you are currently operating in. Using the previous example, if **chris** is your working directory, the relative pathname for the file **monday** is **reports/monday**. The absolute pathname for **monday** is **/home/chris/reports/monday**.

The absolute pathname from the root to your home directory can be especially complex and, at times, even subject to change by the system administrator. To make it easier to reference, you can use the tilde (~) character, which represents the absolute pathname of your home directory. You must specify the rest of the path from your home directory. In the next example, the user references the **monday** file in the **reports** directory. The tilde represents the path to the user's home directory, **/home/chris**, and then the rest of the path to the **monday** file is specified.

```
$ cat ~/reports/monday
```

System Directories

The root directory that begins the Linux file structure contains several system directories that contain files and programs used to run and maintain the system. Many also contain other subdirectories with programs for executing specific features of Linux. For example, the directory **/usr/bin** contains the various Linux commands that users execute, such as **lp**r. The directory **/bin** holds system level commands. Table 12-7 lists the basic system directories.

Listing, Displaying, and Printing Files: ls, cat, more, less, and lpr

One of the primary functions of an operating system is the management of files. You may need to perform certain basic output operations on your files, such as displaying them on your screen or printing them. The Linux system provides a set of commands that perform basic file-management operations, such as listing, displaying, and printing files, as well as copying, renaming, and erasing files. These commands are usually made up of abbreviated versions of words. For example, the **ls** command is a shortened form of "list" and lists the files in your directory. The **lpr** command is an abbreviated form of "line print" and will print a file. The **cat**, **less**, and **more** commands display the contents of a file on the screen. Table 12-8 lists these commands with their different options. When you log in to your Linux system, you may want a list of the files in your home directory. The **ls** command, which outputs a list of your file and directory names, is useful for this. The **ls** command has many possible options for displaying filenames according to specific features.

Displaying Files: cat, less, and more

You may also need to look at the contents of a file. The `cat` and `more` commands display the contents of a file on the screen. The name `cat` stands for *concatenate*.

```
$ cat mydata
computers
```

The `cat` command outputs the entire text of a file to the screen at once. This presents a problem when the file is large because its text quickly speeds past on the screen. The `more` and `less` commands are designed to overcome this limitation by displaying one screen of text at a time. You can then move forward or backward in the text at your leisure. You invoke the `more` or `less` command by entering the command name followed by the name of the file you want to view (`less` is a more powerful and configurable display utility).

```
$ less mydata
```

When `more` or `less` invoke a file, the first screen of text is displayed. To continue to the next screen, you press the F key or the SPACEBAR. To move back in the text, you press the B key. You can quit at any time by pressing the Q key.

Command or Option	Execution
`ls`	This command lists file and directory names.
`cat` *filenames*	This filter can be used to display a file. It can take filenames for its arguments. It outputs the contents of those files directly to the standard output, which, by default, is directed to the screen.
`more` *filenames*	This utility displays a file screen by screen. Press the SPACEBAR to continue to the next screen and **q** to quit.
`less` *filenames*	This utility also displays a file screen by screen. Press the SPACEBAR to continue to the next screen and **q** to quit.
`lpr` *filenames*	Sends a file to the line printer to be printed; a list of files may be used as arguments. Use the **-P** option to specify a printer.
`lpq`	Lists the print queue for printing jobs.
`lprm`	Removes a printing job from the print queue.

Table 12-8: Listing, Displaying, and Printing Files

Printing Files: lpr, lpq, and lprm

With the printer commands such as `lpr` and `lprm`, you can perform printing operations such as printing files or canceling print jobs (see Table 12-8). When you need to print files, use the `lpr` command to send files to the printer connected to your system. In the next example, the user prints the **mydata** file:

```
$ lpr mydata
```

If you want to print several files at once, you can specify more than one file on the command line after the `lpr` command. In the next example, the user prints out both the **mydata** and **preface** files:

```
$ lpr mydata preface
```

Printing jobs are placed in a queue and printed one at a time in the background. You can continue with other work as your files print. You can see the position of a particular printing job at any given time with the **lpq** command, which gives the owner of the printing job (the login name of the user who sent the job), the print job ID, the size in bytes, and the temporary file in which it is currently held.

If you need to cancel an unwanted printing job, you can do so with the **lprm** command, which takes as its argument either the ID number of the printing job or the owner's name. It then removes the print job from the print queue. For this task, **lpq** is helpful, for it provides you with the ID number and owner of the printing job you need to use with **lprm**.

Managing Directories: mkdir, rmdir, ls, cd, pwd

You can create and remove your own directories, as well as change your working directory, with the **mkdir**, **rmdir**, and **cd** commands. Each of these commands can take as its argument the pathname for a directory. The **pwd** command displays the absolute pathname of your working directory. In addition to these commands, the special characters represented by a single dot, a double dot, and a tilde can be used to reference the working directory, the parent of the working directory, and the home directory, respectively. Taken together, these commands enable you to manage your directories. You can create nested directories, move from one directory to another, and use pathnames to reference any of your directories. Those commands commonly used to manage directories are listed in Table 12-9.

Creating and Deleting Directories

You create and remove directories with the **mkdir** and **rmdir** commands. In either case, you can also use pathnames for the directories. In the next example, the user creates the directory **reports**. Then the user creates the directory **articles** using a pathname:

```
$ mkdir reports
$ mkdir /home/chris/articles
```

You can remove a directory with the **rmdir** command followed by the directory name. In the next example, the user removes the directory **reports** with the **rmdir** command:

```
$ rmdir reports
```

To remove a directory and all its subdirectories, you use the **rm** command with the **-r** option. This is a very powerful command and could be used to erase all your files. You will be prompted for each file. To remove all files and subdirectories without prompts, add the **-f** option. The following example deletes the **reports** directory and all its subdirectories:

```
rm -rf reports
```

Displaying Directory Contents

You have seen how to use the **ls** command to list the files and directories within your working directory. To distinguish between file and directory names, however, you need to use the **ls** command with the **-F** option. A slash is then placed after each directory name in the list.

```
$ ls
weather reports articles
$ ls -F
weather reports/ articles/
```

The `ls` command also takes as an argument any directory name or directory pathname. This enables you to list the files in any directory without first having to change to that directory. In the next example, the `ls` command takes as its argument the name of a directory, **reports**. Then the `ls` command is executed again, only this time the absolute pathname of **reports** is used.

```
$ ls reports
monday tuesday
$ ls /home/chris/reports
monday tuesday
$
```

Command	Execution
`mkdir` *directory*	Creates a directory.
`rmdir` *directory*	Erases a directory.
`ls -F`	Lists directory name with a preceding slash.
`ls -R`	Lists working directory as well as all subdirectories.
`cd` *directory name*	Changes to the specified directory, making it the working directory. **cd** without a directory name changes back to the home directory: **$ cd reports**
`pwd`	Displays the pathname of the working directory.
directory name / *filename*	A slash is used in pathnames to separate each directory name. In the case of pathnames for files, a slash separates the preceding directory names from the filename.
`..`	References the parent directory. You can use it as an argument or as part of a pathname: **$ cd ..** **$ mv ../larisa oldarticles**
`.`	References the working directory. You can use it as an argument or as part of a pathname: **$ ls .**
`~/`*pathname*	The tilde is a special character that represents the pathname for the home directory. It is useful when you need to use an absolute pathname for a file or directory: **$ cp monday ~/today**

Table 12-9: Directory Commands

Moving Through Directories

The `cd` command takes as its argument the name of the directory to which you want to move. The name of the directory can be the name of a subdirectory in your working directory or the full pathname of any directory on the system. If you want to change back to your home directory, you need to enter only the `cd` command by itself, without a filename argument.

```
$ cd reports
$ pwd
/home/chris/reports
```

Referencing the Parent Directory

A directory always has a parent (except, of course, for the root). For example, in the preceding listing, the parent for **reports** is the **chris** directory. When a directory is created, two entries are made: one represented with a dot (.), and the other with double dots (..). The dot represents the pathnames of the directory, and the double dots represent the pathname of its parent directory. Double dots, used as an argument in a command, reference a parent directory. The single dot references the directory itself.

You can use the single dot to reference your working directory, instead of using its pathname. For example, to copy a file to the working directory retaining the same name, the dot can be used in place of the working directory's pathname. In this sense, the dot is another name for the working directory. In the next example, the user copies the **weather** file from the **chris** directory to the **reports** directory. The **reports** directory is the working directory and can be represented with the single dot.

```
$ cd reports
$ cp /home/chris/weather .
```

The .. symbol is often used to reference files in the parent directory. In the next example, the **cat** command displays the **weather** file in the parent directory. The pathname for the file is the .. symbol (for the parent directory) followed by a slash and the filename.

```
$ cat ../weather
raining and warm
```

Tip: You can use the **cd** command with the .. symbol to step back through successive parent directories of the directory tree from a lower directory.

File and Directory Operations: find, cp, mv, rm, ln

As you create more and more files, you may want to back them up, change their names, erase some of them, or even give them added names. Linux provides several file commands that you can use to search for files, copy files, rename files, or remove files (see Tables 12-5). If you have a large number of files, you can also search them to locate a specific one. The commands are shortened forms of full words, consisting of only two characters. The **cp** command stands for "copy" and copies a file, **mv** stands for "move" and renames or moves a file, **rm** stands for "remove" and erases a file, and **ln** stands for "link" and adds another name for a file, often used as a shortcut to the original. One exception to the two-character rule is the **find** command, which performs searches of your filenames to find a file. All these operations can be handled by the GUI desktops, like GNOME and KDE.

Searching Directories: find

Once a large number of files have been stored in many different directories, you may need to search them to locate a specific file, or files, of a certain type. The **find** command enables you to perform such a search from the command line. The **find** command takes as its arguments directory names followed by several possible options that specify the type of search and the criteria for the search; it then searches within the directories listed and their subdirectories for files that meet these criteria. The **find** command can search for a file by name, type, owner, and even the time of the last update.

```
$ find directory-list -option criteria
```

The **-name** option has as its criteria a pattern and instructs **find** to search for the filename that matches that pattern. To search for a file by name, you use the **find** command with the directory name followed by the **-name** option and the name of the file.

```
$ find directory-list -name filename
```

Command or Option	Execution
find	Searches directories for files according to search criteria. This command has several options that specify the type of criteria and actions to be taken.
-name *pattern*	Searches for files with the *pattern* in the name.
-lname *pattern*	Searches for symbolic link files.
-group *name*	Searches for files belonging to the group *name*.
-gid *name*	Searches for files belonging to a group according to group ID.
-user *name*	Searches for files belonging to a user.
-uid *name*	Searches for files belonging to a user according to user ID.
-mtime *num*	Searches for files last modified *num* days ago.
-context *scontext*	Searches for files according to security context (SE Linux).
-print	Outputs the result of the search to the standard output. The result is usually a list of filenames, including their full pathnames.
-type *filetype*	Searches for files with the specified file type. File type can be **b** for block device, **c** for character device, **d** for directory, **f** for file, or **l** for symbolic link.
-perm *permission*	Searches for files with certain permissions set. Use octal or symbolic format for permissions.
-ls	Provides a detailed listing of each file, with owner, permission, size, and date information.
-exec *command*	Executes command when files found.

Table 12-10: The find Command

The **find** command also has options that merely perform actions, such as outputting the results of a search. If you want **find** to display the filenames it has located, you simply include the **-print** option on the command line along with any other options. The **-print** option is an action that instructs **find** to write to the standard output the names of all the files it locates (you can also use the **-ls** option instead to list files in the long format). In the next example, the user searches for all the files in the **reports** directory with the name **monday**. Once located, the file, with its relative pathname, is printed.

```
$ find reports -name monday -print
reports/monday
```

The **find** command prints out the filenames using the directory name specified in the directory list. If you specify an absolute pathname, the absolute path of the found directories will be output. If you specify a relative pathname, only the relative pathname is output. In the preceding example, the user specified a relative pathname, **reports**, in the directory list. Located filenames were output beginning with this relative pathname. In the next example, the user specifies an absolute pathname in the directory list. Located filenames are then output using this absolute pathname.

```
$ find /home/chris -name monday -print
/home/chris/reports/monday
```

Tip: Should you need to find the location of a specific program or configuration file, you could use **find** to search for the file from the root directory. Log in as the root user and use **/** as the directory. This command searched for the location of the **more** command and files on the entire file system: **find / -name more -print**.

Searching the Working Directory

If you want to search your working directory, you can use the dot in the directory pathname to represent your working directory. The double dots would represent the parent directory. The next example searches all files and subdirectories in the working directory, using the dot to represent the working directory. If your working directory is your home directory, this is a convenient way to search through all your own directories. Notice that the located filenames that are output begin with a dot.

```
$ find . -name weather -print
./weather
```

You can use shell wildcard characters as part of the pattern criteria for searching files. The special character must be quoted, however, to avoid evaluation by the shell. In the next example, all files (indicated by the asterisk, *) with the **.c** extension in the **programs** directory are searched for and then displayed in the long format using the **-ls** action:

```
$ find programs -name '*.c' -ls
```

Locating Directories

You can also use the **find** command to locate other directories. In Linux, a directory is officially classified as a special type of file. Although all files have a byte-stream format, some files, such as directories, are used in special ways. In this sense, a file can be said to have a file type. The **find** command has an option called **-type** that searches for a file of a given type. The **-type** option takes a one-character modifier that represents the file type. The modifier that represents a directory is a **d**. In the next example, both the directory name and the directory file type are used to search for the directory called **travel**:

```
$ find /home/chris -name travel -type d -print
/home/chris/articles/travel
$
```

File types are not so much different types of files as they are the file format applied to other components of the operating system, such as devices. In this sense, a device is treated as a type of file, and you can use **find** to search for devices and directories, as well as ordinary files. Table 12-10 lists the different types available for the **find** command's **-type** option.

You can also use the find operation to search for files by ownership or security criteria, like those belonging to a specific user or those with a certain security context. The **-user** option lets to locate all files belonging to a certain user. The following example lists all files that the user **chris** has created or owns on the entire system. To list those just in the users' home directories, you would use **/home** for the starting search directory. This would find all those in a user's home directory as well as any owned by that user in other user directories.

```
$ find / -user chris -print
```

Copying Files

To make a copy of a file, you simply give **cp** two filenames as its arguments (see Table 12-11). The first filename is the name of the file to be copied—the one that already exists. This is often referred to as the *source file*. The second filename is the name you want for the copy. This will be a new file containing a copy of all the data in the source file. This second argument is often referred to as the *destination file*. The syntax for the **cp** command follows:

```
$ cp source-file destination-file
```

Command	Execution
cp *filename filename*	Copies a file. **cp** takes two arguments: the original file and the name of the new copy. You can use pathnames for the files to copy across directories:
cp -r *dirname dirname*	Copies a subdirectory from one directory to another. The copied directory includes all its own subdirectories:
mv *filename filename*	Moves (renames) a file. The **mv** command takes two arguments: the first is the file to be moved. The second argument can be the new filename or the pathname of a directory. If it is the name of a directory, then the file is literally moved to that directory, changing the file's pathname:
mv *dirname dirname*	Moves directories. In this case, the first and last arguments are directories:
ln *filename filename*	Creates added names for files referred to as links. A link can be created in one directory that references a file in another directory:
rm *filenames*	Removes (erases) a file. Can take any number of filenames as its arguments. Literally removes links to a file. If a file has more than one link, you need to remove all of them to erase a file:

Table 12-11: File Operations

In the next example, the user copies a file called **proposal** to a new file called **oldprop**:

```
$ cp proposal oldprop
```

You could unintentionally destroy another file with the `cp` command. The `cp` command generates a copy by first creating a file and then copying data into it. If another file has the same name as the destination file, that file is destroyed and a new file with that name is created. By default Ubuntu configures your system to check for an existing copy by the same name (`cp` is aliased with the `-i` option). To copy a file from your working directory to another directory, you need to use that directory name as the second argument in the `cp` command. In the next example, the **proposal** file is overwritten by the **newprop** file. The **proposal** file already exists.

```
$ cp newprop proposal
```

You can use any of the wildcard characters to generate a list of filenames to use with `cp` or `mv`. For example, suppose you need to copy all your C source code files to a given directory. Instead of listing each one individually on the command line, you could use an * character with the **.c** extension to match on and generate a list of C source code files (all files with a **.c** extension). In the next example, the user copies all source code files in the current directory to the **sourcebks** directory:

```
$ cp *.c sourcebks
```

If you want to copy all the files in a given directory to another directory, you could use * to match on and generate a list of all those files in a `cp` command. In the next example, the user copies all the files in the **props** directory to the **oldprop** directory. Notice the use of a **props** pathname preceding the * special characters. In this context, **props** is a pathname that will be appended before each file in the list that * generates.

```
$ cp props/* oldprop
```

You can, of course, use any of the other special characters, such as ., **?**, or **[]**. In the next example, the user copies both source code and object code files (**.c** and **.o**) to the **projbk** directory:

```
$ cp *.[oc] projbk
```

When you copy a file, you can give the copy a name that is different from the original. To do so, place the new filename after the directory name, separated by a slash.

```
$ cp filename directory-name/new-filename
```

Moving Files

You can use the `mv` command either to either rename a file or to move a file from one directory to another. When using `mv` to rename a file, you simply use the new filename as the second argument. The first argument is the current name of the file you are renaming. If you want to rename a file when you move it, you can specify the new name of the file after the directory name. In the next example, the **proposal** file is renamed with the name **version1**:

```
$ mv proposal version1
```

As with `cp`, it is easy for `mv` to erase a file accidentally. When renaming a file, you might accidentally choose a filename already used by another file. In this case, that other file will be erased. The `mv` command also has an **-i** option that checks first to see if a file by that name already exists.

You can also use any of the special characters to generate a list of filenames to use with **mv**. In the next example, the user moves all source code files in the current directory to the **newproj** directory:

```
$ mv *.c newproj
```

If you want to move all the files in a given directory to another directory, you can use * to match on and generate a list of all those files. In the next example, the user moves all the files in the **reports** directory to the **repbks** directory:

```
$ mv reports/* repbks
```

Note: The easiest way to copy files to a CD-R/RW or DVD-R/RW disc is to use the built-in Nautilus burning capability. Just insert a blank disk, open it as a folder, and drag-and-drop files on to it. You will be prompted automatically to burn the files.

Copying and Moving Directories

You can also copy or move whole directories at once. Both **cp** and **mv** can take as their first argument a directory name, enabling you to copy or move subdirectories from one directory into another (see Table 12-11). The first argument is the name of the directory to be moved or copied, and the second argument is the name of the directory within which it is to be placed. The same pathname structure used for files applies to moving or copying directories.

You can just as easily copy subdirectories from one directory to another. To copy a directory, the **cp** command requires you to use the **-r** option, which stands for "recursive." It directs the **cp** command to copy a directory, as well as any subdirectories it may contain. In other words, the entire directory subtree, from that directory on, will be copied. In the next example, the **travel** directory is copied to the **oldarticles** directory. Now two **travel** subdirectories exist, one in **articles** and one in **oldarticles**.

```
$ cp -r articles/travel oldarticles
$ ls -F articles
/travel
$ ls -F oldarticles
/travel
```

Erasing Files and Directories: the rm Command

As you use Linux, you will find the number of files you use increases rapidly. Generating files in Linux is easy. Applications such as editors, and commands such as **cp**, can easily be used to create files. Eventually, many of these files may become outdated and useless. You can then remove them with the **rm** command. The **rm** command can take any number of arguments, enabling you to list several filenames and erase them all at the same time. In the next example, the file **oldprop** is erased:

```
$ rm oldprop
```

Be careful when using the **rm** command, because it is irrevocable. Once a file is removed, it cannot be restored (there is no undo). With the **-i** option, you are prompted separately for each file and asked whether you really want to remove it. If you enter **y**, the file will be removed. If you enter anything else, the file is not removed. In the next example, the **rm** command is instructed to erase the files **proposal** and **oldprop**. The **rm** command then asks for confirmation for each file. The user decides to remove **oldprop,** but not **proposal**.

```
$ rm -i proposal oldprop
Remove proposal? n
Remove oldprop? y
$
```

Links: the ln Command

You can give a file more than one name using the **ln** command. You might do this because you want to reference a file using different filenames to access it from different directories. The added names are often referred to as *links.* Linux supports two different types of links, hard and symbolic. Hard links are literally another name for the same file, whereas symbolic links function like shortcuts referencing another file. Symbolic links are much more flexible and can work over many different file systems, while hard links are limited to your local file system. Furthermore, hard links introduce security concerns, as they allow direct access from a link that may have public access to an original file that you may want protected. Links are usually implemented as symbolic links.

Symbolic Links

To set up a symbolic link, you use the **ln** command with the **-s** option and two arguments: the name of the original file and the new, added filename. The **ls** operation lists both filenames, but only one physical file will exist.

```
$ ln -s original-file-name added-file-name
```

In the next example, the **today** file is given the additional name **weather**. It is just another name for the **today** file.

```
$ ls
today
$ ln -s today weather
$ ls
today weather
```

You can give the same file several names by using the **ln** command on the same file many times. In the next example, the file **today** is assigned the names **weather** and **weekend**:

```
$ ln -s today weather
$ ln -s today weekend
$ ls
today weather weekend
```

If you list the full information about a symbolic link and its file, you will find the information displayed is different. In the next example, the user lists the full information for both **lunch** and **/home/george/veglist** using the **ls** command with the **-l** option. The first character in the line specifies the file type. Symbolic links have their own file type, represented by an **l**. The file type for **lunch** is **l**, indicating it is a symbolic link, not an ordinary file. The number after the term "group" is the size of the file. Notice the sizes differ. The size of the **lunch** file is only 4 bytes. This is because **lunch** is only a symbolic link—a file that holds the pathname of another file—and a pathname takes up only a few bytes. It is not a direct hard link to the **veglist** file.

```
$ ls -l lunch /home/george/veglist
lrw-rw-r-- 1 chris group 4 Feb 14 10:30 lunch
-rw-rw-r-- 1 george group 793 Feb 14 10:30 veglist
```

To erase a file, you need to remove only its original name (and any hard links to it). If any symbolic links are left over, they will be unable to access the file. In this case, a symbolic link would hold the pathname of a file that no longer exists.

Hard Links

You can give the same file several names by using the **ln** command on the same file many times. To set up a hard link, you use the **ln** command with no **-s** option and two arguments: the name of the original file and the new, added filename. The **ls** operation lists both filenames, but only one physical file will exist.

```
$ ln original-file-name added-file-name
```

In the next example, the **monday** file is given the additional name **storm**. It is just another name for the **monday** file.

```
$ ls
today
$ ln monday storm
$ ls
monday storm
```

To erase a file that has hard links, you need to remove all its hard links. The name of a file is actually considered a link to that file—hence the command **rm** that removes the link to the file. If you have several links to the file and remove only one of them, the others stay in place and you can reference the file through them. The same is true even if you remove the original link—the original name of the file.

Part 4: Administration

System Tools
System Administration
Network Connections
Printing

13. System Tools

GNOME System Monitor

Scheduling Tasks

Log Viewer

Disk Usage Analyzer

Virus Protection

Hardware Sensors

Disk Utility

System Settings

Plymouth

Useful system tools as well as user specific configuration tools can be found in the Accessories, System, and the Customization dashes (see Table 13-1). The System dash holds tools like the System Monitor, whereas the Customization holds user specific tools for customizing your desktop and device usage such as Disk Utility (see Chapter 3). In particular, mouse and keyboard configurations are handled by GNOME or KDE directly (Customization). The Accessories dash holds specialized tools like the ClamTK Virus Scanner (Virus Scanner) and the Disk Usage Analyzer.

Ubuntu System Tools	Name	Description
gnome-system-monitor	System Monitor	GNOME System Monitor
gnome-system-log	Log File Viewer	GNOME system log viewer
gnome-terminal	Terminal	GNOME Terminal Window
baobab	Disk Usage Analyzer	Disk usage analyzer with graphic representation
gnome-nettool	Network Tools	Network analysis
gnome-schedule	Scheduled tasks	GNOME cron schedule manager (Universe repository)
KDE task scheduler	Task Scheduler	KDE schedule manager(KDE desktop only)
ClamTK	Virus Scanner	Clam Virus scanner
Disk Utility	Disk Utility	Udisks utility for managing hard disks and removable drives

Table 13-1: Ubuntu System Tools

GNOME System Monitor

Ubuntu provides the GNOME System Monitor for displaying system information and monitoring system processes, accessible from the System dash. There are four tabs; System, Processes, Resources, and File Systems (see Figure 13-1). The System tab shows key system information beginning with the computer name, Ubuntu software information (the Ubuntu release version number and name, the version of the Linux kernel, and the GNOME release in use), Hardware information (amount of memory and the type of CPU on your system) and the System Status which lists available disk space. The Resources tab displays graphs for CPU History, Memory and Swap History, and Network History. If your system has a multi-core CPU, the CPU History graph shows the usage for each CPU. The Memory and Swap Memory graph shows the amount of memory in use. The Network History graph displays both the amount of sent and received data, along with totals for the current session. The File Systems tab lists your file systems, where they are mounted, and their type, as well as the amount of disk space used and how much is free. Double clicking on a file system entry will open that file system in a file manager window.

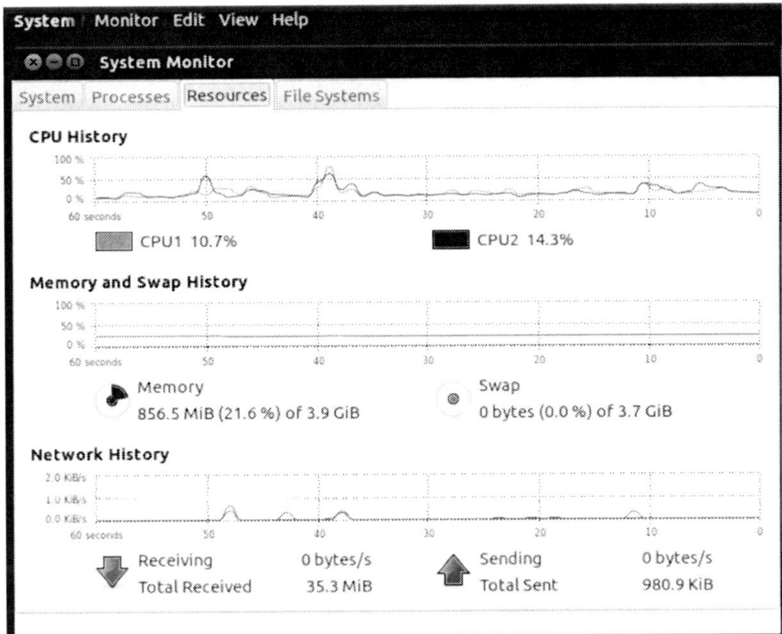
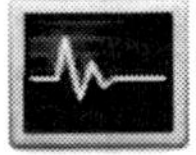

Figure 13-1: GNOME System Monitor: Resources

The Processes tab lists your processes, letting you sort and search processes. You can use field buttons to sort by name (Process Name), process ID (ID), percentage of use (%CPU), and memory used (Memory), among others. The View menu lets you select all processes, just your own (My Processes), or active processes. You can stop any process by selecting it and then clicking the End Process button (lower-right corner) or selecting the End Process entry in the Edit menu. The Edit menu displays actions you can take on a selected process such as stopping (Stop Process), ending (End Process), killing (Kill Process), and continuing a process (Continue Process), as well as changing the priority of the process (Change Priority). You can also right-click a process entry to displays the same set of actions. The Memory Maps display, selected from the View menu, shows information on virtual memory, inodes, and flags for a selected process. You can also select the memory map option from the process's pop-up menu. The Open Files option for a selected process (right-click pop-up menu or View | Open Files menu) opens a dialog listing all the files, sockets, and pipes the process is using.

Managing Processes

Should you have to force a process or application to quit, you can use the Gnome System Monitor Processes tab to find, select, and stop the process. You should be sure of the process you want to stop. Ending a critical process could cripple your system. Application processes will bear the name of the application, and you can use those to force an application to quit. Ending processes manually is usually performed for open ended operations that you are unable to stop normally. In Figure 13-2, the Firefox application has been selected. Clicking the End Process button on the lower right will then force the Firefox Web browser to end.

The Edit menu provides several other options for managing a selected process: stop, continue, end, kill, and change priority. You can also right-click on a process entry to display a pop-up menu with the same options. There are corresponding keyboard keys for each option. The stop and continue operations work together. You can stop (pause) a process, and then later start it again with the continue option. The end process stops a process safely, whereas a kill option forces an immediate end to the process. The end process option is preferred, but if it does not work, you can use the kill process option. Change priority can give a process a lower or higher priority, letting it run faster or slower.

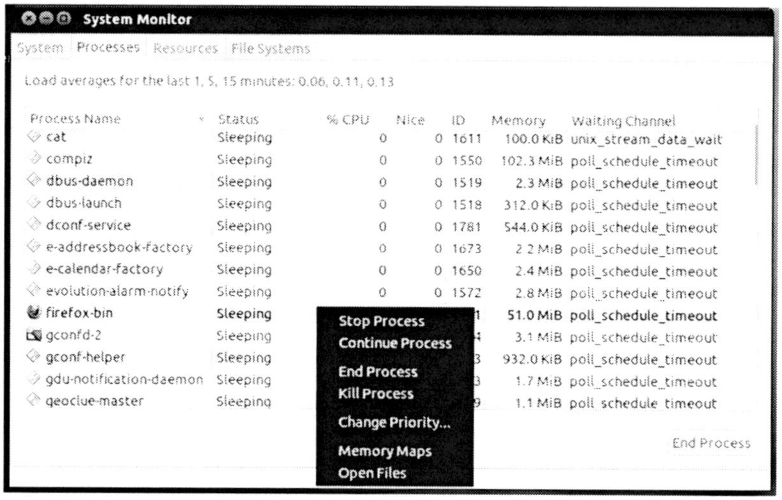

Figure 13-2: GNOME System Monitor: Processes

You can also use the **kill** command in a terminal window to end a process. The **kill** command takes as its argument a process number. Be sure you obtain the correct one. Use the **ps** command to display a process id. Entering in the incorrect process number could cripple your system. The **ps** command with the **-C** option searches for a particular application name. The **-o pid=** option will display only the process id, instead of the process id, time, application name, and tty. Once you have the process id, you can use the **kill** command with the process id as its argument to end the process.

```
$ ps -C firefox -o pid=
5555
$ kill 5555
```

One way to insure the correct number is to use the **ps** command to return the process number directly as an argument to a **kill** command. In the following example, an open-ended process was started to record a program from channel 12 from a digital video broadcast device, using the **getatsc** command. An open-ended process is one that will continue until you stop it manually.

```
getatsc -dvb 0 12 > my.ts
```

The process is then ended by first executing the **ps** command to obtain the process id for the **getatsc** process (back quotes), and then using that process id in the **kill** command to end the process. The **-o pid=** option displays only the process id.

```
kill `ps -C getatsc -o pid=`
```

System Testing

Ubuntu provides a hardware testing utility to check your hardware and report any problems. You are encouraged to set up an account at **http://www.launchpad.net** where you can send your results. You can access System Testing from the Customization dash. Each major hardware device to be tested is listed. You can de-select any you do not want to test. (see Figure 13-4). Devices tested include disks, sound, display, video, mouse and keyboard (Peripherals), and network connections.

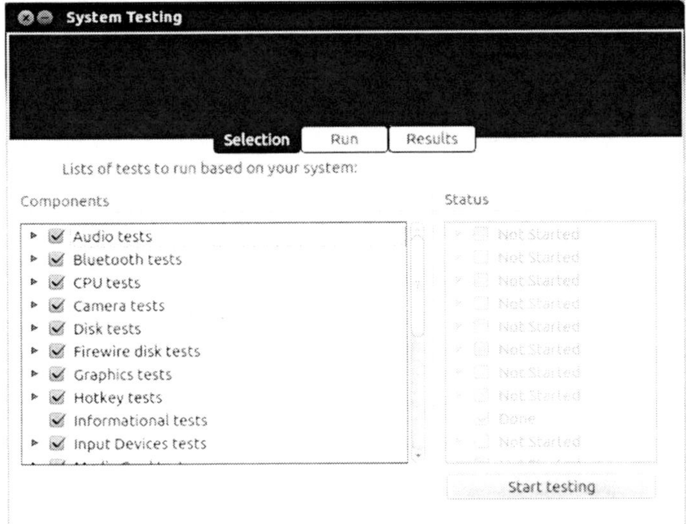

Figure 13-4: System Testing

Scheduling Tasks

Scheduling regular maintenance tasks, such as backups, is managed by the **cron** service and implemented by a **cron** daemon. These tasks are listed in the **crontab** file. The **cron** daemon constantly checks the user's **crontab** file to see if it is time to take these actions. Any user can set up a **crontab** file of their own. An administrative user can set up a **crontab** file to take system administrative actions, such as backing up files at a certain time each week or month.

Creating cron entries can be a complicated task, using the **crontab** command to make changes to crontab files in the **/etc/crontab** directory. Instead you can use several desktop cron scheduler tools to set up cron actions. Two of the more useful tools are the KDE task scheduler and GNOME Schedule, which provide an easy to use interface for creating scheduled commands.

GNOME Schedule

GNOME Schedule provides a desktop interface for managing scheduled tasks (Universe repository). You can install it from the Ubuntu Software Center | System | Scheduled tasks. Once installed (**gnome-schedule** package) you can access it from the System dash as Scheduled tasks.

The "Configure Scheduled Tasks" window opens, listing your scheduled tasks and displaying a toolbar for managing them (See Figure 13-5).

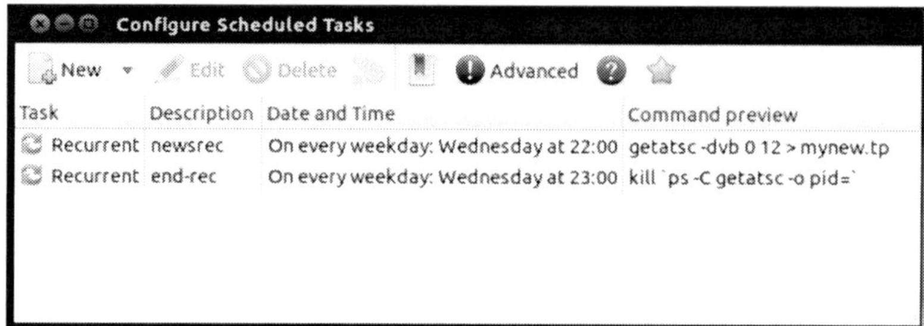

Figure 13-5: GNOME Schedule

Use the New button to schedule a task. You are first asked if you want to create the task as a recurrent item, one time task, or from a template (you can also choose this option from the New icon's drop down menu on the toolbar). The Create a New Scheduled Task window opens where you can specify the time and date, and whether to repeat the task weekly or monthly (see Figure 13-6). You can use the Basic button to set defaults for Every minute, hour, day, month, week, or even on reboot. To specify a particular time, click the Advanced entry to activate the Minute, Hour, Day, Month, and Weekday entries. You can make entries directly or use the Edit button to specify particular days or recurrent ones. For example, for the Month you can specify every month, a particular month, or a range of months. Click Add to add the task. The task will then appear on the Scheduled Tasks window. On the Scheduled Tasks window you can click the Advanced button to see the actual cron entries created by GNOME Schedule.

Figure 13-6: Schedule new task

To delete a task, just select the entry in the Scheduled Tasks window and click the Delete button. To run a task immediately, select the task and click the Run task button.

The template feature lets you set up a new schedule with information for a previous one, using the same or similar commands but different time. Click the Template button to add a new template (the icon on the toolbar before Advanced). This opens a window similar to the Create task window. You can also create templates from existing tasks. Edit the task by selecting it in the Configure Scheduled Tasks window and clicking the Edit button. Then click the "Add as template" button. Once you have created the template you can use it to create scheduled tasks. When creating a task, from the initial New menu, choose "A task from a predefined template". This opens the Choose template window. Clicking the "Use template" button opens the Create task window where you can modify your task.

KDE Task Scheduler

On KDE you can use the KDE Task Scheduler to set up user and system-level scheduled tasks (install the **kde-config-cron** package). You access the Task Scheduler on the System Settings window in the System Administration section as Task Scheduler. The Task Scheduler window will list your scheduled tasks. Task can be either personal or system-wide. Click the New Task button to open a New Task window where you can enter the command to run, add comments, and then specify the time in months, days, hours, and minutes from simple arranged buttons. On the Task Scheduler window, you can select a task and use the side buttons to modify it, delete the task, run it now, or print a copy of it. For tasks using the same complex commands or arguments, you can create a variable, and then use that variable in a command. Variables are listed in the Environment Variables section. To use a variable in a scheduled task, precede its name with the $ character when you enter the command. Entering just the $ symbol in the Command text box will display a drop-down list of pre-defined system variables you can use like **$PATH** and **$USER**.

Log File Viewer

Various system logs for tasks performed on your system are stored in the **/var/log** directory. Here you can find logs for mail, news, and all other system operations, such as Web server logs (see Figure 13-7). This usually includes startup tasks, such as loading drivers and mounting file systems. If a driver for a device failed to load at startup, you find an error message for it here. Logins are also recorded in this file, showing you who attempted to log in to what account. The **/var/log/mail.log** file logs mail message transmissions and news transfers.

To view logs you can use the GNOME Log Viewer accessible as Log File Viewer on the System and Customization dashes. A side panel lists different logs. Selecting one displays the log to the right. For **/var/log/syslog**, select **syslog**. You can also choose to display messages in this file just for a specific date.

Figure 13-7: Log Viewer

Disk Usage Analyzer

The disk usage analyzer lets you see how much disk space is used and available on all your mounted hard disk partitions (see Figure 13-8). You can access it from the Accessories dash.

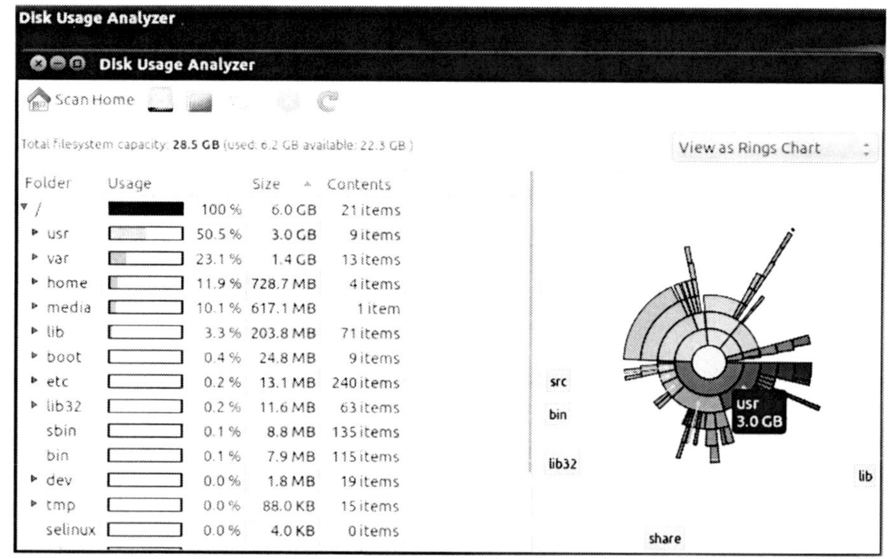

Figure 13-8: Disk Usage Analyzer, Applications | Accessories | Disk Usage Analyzer

It will also check all LVM and RAID arrays. Usage is shown in a simple graph, letting you see how much overall space is available and where it is. You can scan your home directory (Scan Home), your entire file system (disk drive icon), a particular folder (folder icon), or a remote folder (remote folder icon). When you scan a directory or the file system, disk usage for your directory is analyzed and displayed in the left pane. Each files system is shown with a graph for its usage, as well as its size and the number of top-level directories and files. Then the directories are shown, along with their size and contents (files and directories).

A representational graph for the disk usage on is displayed on the right pane. The graph can be either a Ring Chart or a Treemap. The Ring Chart is the default. Choose the one you want from the View drop down menu. For the Ring Chart, directories are shown, starting with the top level directories at the center and moving out to the subdirectories. Passing your mouse over a section in the graph displays its directory name and disk usage, as well as all its subdirectories. The Treemap chart shows a box representation, with greater disk usage in larger boxes, and subdirectories encased within directory boxes.

Virus Protection

For virus protection, you can use the Linux version of ClamAV, which uses a GNOME front-end called ClamTK, **www.clamav.org**. This Virus scanner is included on the Ubuntu main repository. You can install ClamTK from the Ubuntu Software Center | Accessories | Virus Scanner. The supporting ClamAV packages (System category) will also be selected and installed for you (clamav-base and clamav-freshclam). You can also install ClamAV using the Synaptic Package Manager, choose the clamav, clamav-base, clamav-freshclam (online virus definitions), and ClamTK packages (Klamav for KDE); selecting just ClamTK will automatically select the other clamav packages for installation.

If you have no regular access to the internet you can install the **clamav-data** package for a basic set of virus definition. The **clamav-freshclam** package retrieves current virus definitions from the ClamAV servers. For ClamAV to check your mail messages automatically, you need to install the ClamAV scanner daemon (**clamav-daemon** package).

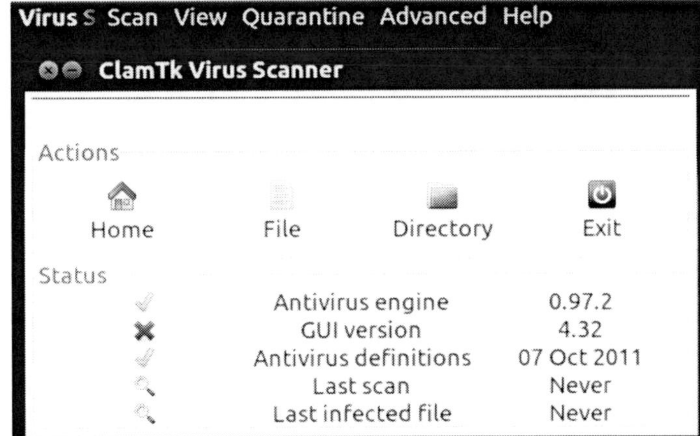

Figure 13-9: The ClamTK tool for ClamAV virus protection.

You can access ClamTK from the Accessories and System dashes as Virus Scanner. With ClamTK, you can scan specific files and directories, as well as your home directory (see Figure 13-9). Searches can be recursive, including subdirectories. You also have the option to check configuration files (Scan hidden). You can also perform quick or recursive scans of your home directory. Infected files are quarantined.

When you first start ClamTK the AV Setup Wizard should start up displaying an Antivirus Signatures window with buttons for choosing how to update the antivirus signatures, either as a Single user or System Wide. Then click the Save button to save your preferences. You can run the wizard again from Advanced | Rerun AV setup wizard.

Your virus definitions will be updated automatically. If you want to check manually for virus definitions, you need to run **ClamTK** with administrative access. Open a terminal window and enter the following. You will be prompted for your user password. You can then go to the Help menu and select "Check for Updates" to open the Updates dialog. Then select Signature updates and click the "Check for updates button" to your definitions.

```
gksu clamtk
```

Hardware Sensors

Another concern with many users is the temperatures and usage of computer components. You install different software packages to enable certain sensors (see Table 13-2).

Sensor application	Description
lm-sensors	Detects and accesses computer (motherboard) sensors like CPU and fan speed. Run **sensors-detect** once to configure.
hddtemp	Detects hard drive temperatures (also detected by Disk Utility)
Disk Utility	Disk Utility provides SMART information for hard disks showing current hard disk temperatures as well as detailed disk health information and checks.
Psensor	Application to detect and display system and hard drive temperatures.
Xsensors	Application to detect and display system temperatures and fans.

Table 13-2: Sensor packages and applications

For CPU, system, fan speeds, and any other motherboard supported sensors, you use Psensor, Xsensors, or the **lm-sensors**service. Psensors installs the hddtemp hard drive temperature server and displays your CPU, graphics card, and hard drive temperatures. You can set temperature thresholds for alerts. Xsensors displays your CPU temperature.

If not already installed, install the **lm-sensors** package. Then you have to configure your sensor detection. In a terminal window enter following and press ENTER to answer yes to the prompts:

```
sudo sensors-detect
```

Disk Utility (System dash) lets you know your hard disk temperature. Disk Utility uses Udisks to access SMART information about the disk drive, including the temperature and overall health. Open Disk Utility, select the hard disk to check, and then, on the right pane, click on the

"SMART Data" link located middle right. A hard disk dialog opens showing the disk temperature along with other details.

Disk Utility and Udisks

Disk Utility is a Udisks supported user configuration interface for your storage media, such as hard disks, USB drives, and DVD/CD drives (**gnome-disk-utility** package, installed by default). Tasks supported include disk labeling, mounting disks, disk checks, and encryption. You can also perform more advanced tasks like managing RAID and LVM storage devices, as well as partitions. Disk Utility is accessible on Unity from the Customization dash. Users can use Disk Utility to format removable media like USB drives. Disk Utility is also integrated into Nautilus, letting you format removable media directly.

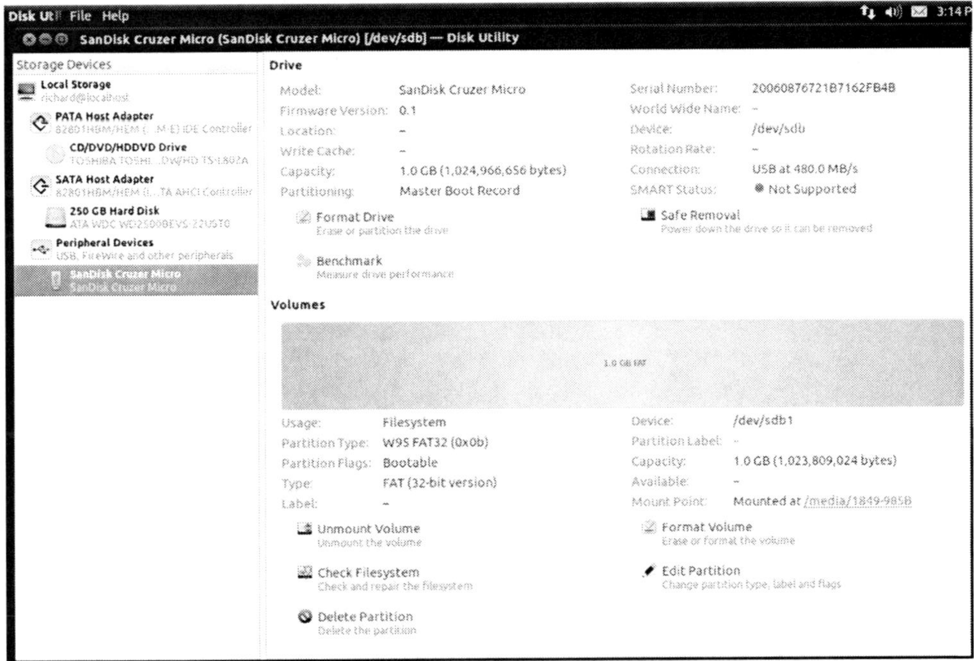

Figure 13-11: Disk Utility

Note: Udisks and Upower were named DeviceKit-disks and DeviceKit-power in previous releases.

The Disk Utility window shows a sidebar with entries for your storage media (see Figure 13-11). The storage media is organized into a tree with the host adapters at the top level, and their storage devices listed beneath. Clicking on an entry displays information for the media on the right pane.

Warning: Disk Utility will list your fixed hard drives and their partitions, including the partitions on which your Ubuntu Linux system is installed. Be careful not to delete or erase these partitions.

If you select a hard disk device, information about the hard disk is displayed on the right pane in the Drive section, such as the model name, firmware version, serial number, size, device name, and SMART status (see Figure 13-12). There are icons in this section for tasks you can perform on the hard drive: Format, Benchmark, and SMART Data.

Figure 13-12: Disk Utility, hard drive

The Volumes section on the hard disk pane shows the partitions set up on the hard drive (see Figure 13-15). Partitions are displayed in graphical icon bar, which displays each partitions size and location on the drive. Clicking on a partition entry on the graphical icon bar displays information about that partition such as the file system type, device name, partition label, and partition size. The Mount Point entry displays a "Mounted at:" link consisting of the path name where the file system is mounted. You can click on this path name to open a folder with which you can access the file system. Icons are displayed for allowable tasks like formatting, deleting, or unmounting a file system. The "Edit Partition" icon lets you change the partition label, type, and flags. The "Check Filesystem" icon will let you repair a file system. If you are formatting a partition, like that on removable media, you can specify the file system type to use (see Figure 13-13). Certain partitions like extended and swap partition display limited information and have few allowable tasks.

For more detailed hardware information about a hard drive, you can click on the "SMART Data" icon in the Drives section. This opens a SMART data dialog with hardware information about the hard disk (see Figure 13-14) including temperature, power cycles, bad sectors, and the overall health of the disk. The Attributes sections lists SMART details such as the Read Error Rate, Spinup time, temperature, and write error rate.

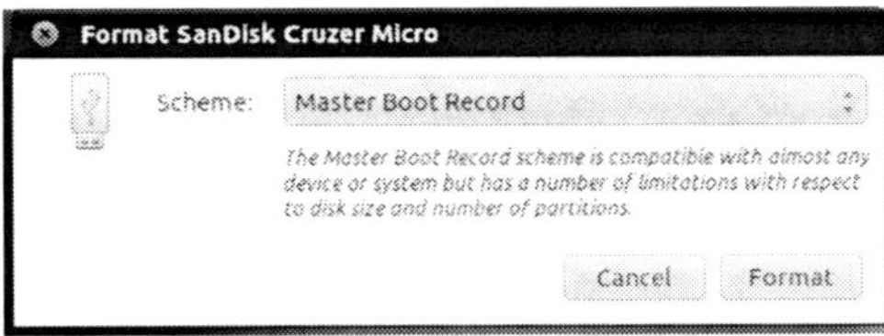

Figure 13-13: Disk Utility: Format disk dialog

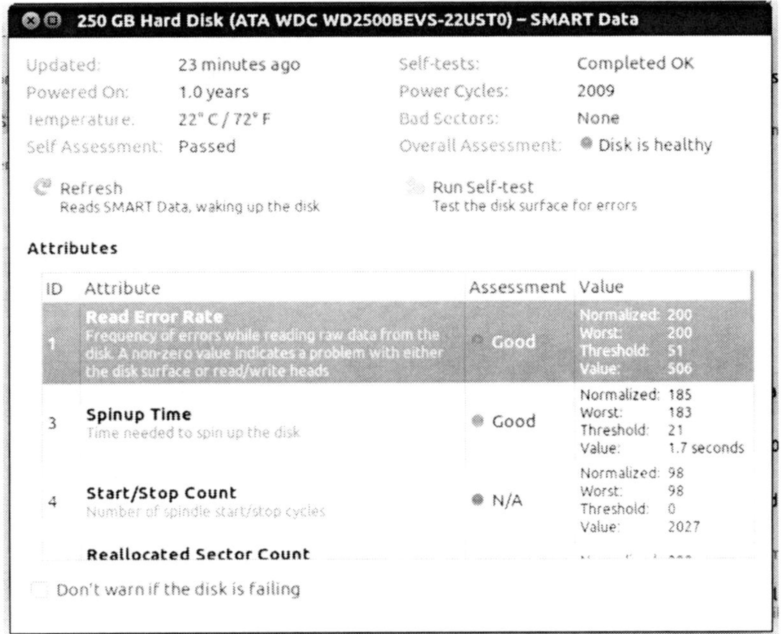

Figure 13-14: Disk Utility: Hard Disk hardware SMART data

Plymouth

Plymouth provides a streamlined, efficient, and faster graphical boot that does not require X server support. It relies on the kernel's Kernel Modesettings (KMS) feature that provides direct support for basic graphics. With the Direct Rendering Manager driver Plymouth can make use of different graphical plugins. KMS support is currently provided for ATI, Nvidia, and Intel graphics cards. The Nvidia hardware driver does not fully support KMS, but the Nouveau Nvidia open source driver does.

The Plymouth Ubuntu logo theme is installed by default. You can install others like solar, glow, or kubuntu-logo. The theme packages begin with the prefix **plymouth-theme**. You can search for them on the Synaptic Package Manager. You can also install them from the Ubuntu Software Center | System | graphical boot animation and logger (search on Plymouth).

Choosing a Plymouth theme to use involves using the Debian alternatives system designed to designate an application to use when there are several alternative versions to select. A link is set up for the application to use in the **/etc/alternatives** directory. For Plymouth this link is named **default.plymouth**. You can choose a Plymouth theme by entering the **update-alternatives** command with the **--config** option, the **default.plymouth** link, and the **sudo** command in a terminal window as shown here.

```
sudo update-alternatives --config default.plymouth
```

This displays a numbered menu listing your installed themes. An asterisk indicates the current theme. Enter the number of the theme you want to use. The **default.plymouth** link is then set to the theme you choose. When your system starts up again, it will use that Plymouth theme.

Some of the non-Ubuntu themes may hang on start up. In that case, you can edit the boot kernel line to remove the **splash** option and then boot to your system (see Chapter 3). Then use **update-alternatives** to change your Plymouth theme.

14. System Administration

Ubuntu Administrative Tools

Controlled Administrative Access

Users and Groups

Bluetooth

File System Access

Shared Folders and Samba

GRUB Bootloader

Editing Configuration Files Directly

Backup Management

Most administrative configurations tasks are performed for you automatically. Devices like printers, hard drive partitions, and graphics cards are detected and set up for you. There are cases where you may need to perform tasks manually like adding new users and installing software. Such administrative operations can be performed with user-friendly system tools. Most administration tools are listed on the System and Customization dash.

TIP: If you have difficulties with your system configuration, check the **http://ubuntuforums.org** site for possible solutions. The site offers helpful forums ranging from desktop and installation problems to games, browsers, and multimedia solutions. Also, check the support link at **www.ubuntu.com** for documentation and mailing lists.

Ubuntu Administration Tools	Description
Ubuntu Software Center	Software management using online repositories
Update Manager	Update tool using Ubuntu repositories
Synaptic Package Manager	Software management using online repositories (no longer supported by Ubuntu, available on the Universe repository)
Network Manager	Detects, connects, and configures your network interfaces
clock	GNOME Time & Date tool (see Chapter 3)
User Accounts	GNOME 3 User configuration tool
users-admin	Older User and Group configuration tool, install gnome-system-tools.
system-config-printer	Printer configuration tool
system-config-samba	Configures your Samba server. User level authentication support.
shares-admin	Configures NFS network support, install gnome-system-tools
gnome-language-selector	Selects a language to use (Language on Customization dash)
Gufw	Configures your network firewall
Deja-dup	Backup tool using rsync

Table 14-1: Ubuntu Administration Tools

Ubuntu Administrative Tools

On Ubuntu, administration is handled by a set of specialized administrative tools, such as those for user management and printer configuration (see Table 14-1). To access the desktop-based administrative tools, you log in as a user who has administrative access. You created this user when you first installed Ubuntu. On the Ubuntu desktop (Unity) System administrative tools are accessed from the System dash and from the System Settings dialog. Here you will find tools to set the time and date, manage users, configure printers, and install software. User Accounts lets you create and modify users. Printing lets you install and reconfigure printers. All tools provide easy-to-use and intuitive desktop interfaces. Tools are identified by simple descriptive terms, whereas their actual names normally begin with terms such as *system-config*. For example, the printer configuration tool is listed as Printing, but its actual name is **system-config-printer**.

Ubuntu uses the GNOME administrative tools with KDE counterparts, administrative tools adapted from the Fedora distribution supported by Red Hat Linux, and independent tools developed by open source projects. PolicyKit is used for device authorizations, and the Ubuntu Software Center provides software management. Fedora tools have the prefix *system-config*. The Printing administrative tool is Fedora's **system-config-printer**. A Samba desktop tool is now available for Ubuntu, which is the Fedora **system-config-samba** tool. The Fedora **system-config-lvm** tool provides a simple and effective way to manage LVM file systems. In addition, Virus protection is handled by third party application, ClamAV. The Synaptic Package Manager is available, but no longer supported. The older GNOME administrative tools such as Users and Groups are also available, but not installed by default (**gnome-system-tools** package).

Note: Many configuration tasks can also be handled on the command line, invoking programs directly. To use the command line, select the Terminal entry in the Accessories dash to open a terminal window with a command line prompt. You will need administrative authorization, so precede the application name with the **sudo** or the **gksu** command.

Controlled Administrative Access

To access administrative tools, you have to login as a user who has administrative permissions. The user that you created during installation is given administrative permissions automatically. Log in as that user. When you attempt to use an administrative tool, a dialog opens prompting you to enter your user password. This is the password for the user you logged in as. Some tools will open without authorization but remain locked, preventing any modifications. These tools, like "User Accounts" have an Unlock button you can press to gain access. You can use the User Accounts tool to grant or deny particular users administrative access.

To perform system administration operations, you must first have to have access rights enabling you to perform administrative tasks. There are several ways to gain such access: login as a sudo supported user (**gksu** is the graphical version of **sudo**), unlocking an administrative tool for access (PolicyKit authorization), and logging in as the root user. PolicyKit is the preferred access method and is used on many administrative tools. The **sudo** granted access method was used in previous Ubuntu releases, and is still used for many tasks including software upgrade and installation. The root user access is still discouraged, but provides complete control over the entire system.

PolicyKit: Provides access only to specific applications and only to users with administrative access for that application. Requires that the specific application be configured for use by PolicyKit. Ubuntu 12.04 uses a new version of PolicyKit called policykit-1 (Ubuntu repository). It is not to be confused with the original version, which is named simply policykit (Universe repository). Though the original policykit is still available for use on Ubuntu, it is not supported, whereas policykit-1 is installed by default and fully supported.

sudo and **gksu**: Provides access to any application will full administrative authorization. It imposes a time limit to reduce risk. The **gksu** command is used for graphical administrative tools like the Synaptic Package Manager. You will still need to use **sudo** to perform any command-line Linux commands at the root level like moving files to an administrative directory or running the **service** command to start or stop servers.

root user access, **su**: Provides complete direct control over the entire system. This is the traditional method for accessing administrative tools. It is disabled by default on Ubuntu, but can be enabled. The **su** command will allow any user to login as the root user if they know the root user password.

PolicyKit

PolicyKit will control access to certain applications and devices. It is one of the safest ways to grant a user direct access. PolicyKit configuration and support is already set up for you. A new version of PolicyKit, PolicyKit-1, is now used for PolicyKit operations. Configuration files for these operations are held in **/usr/share/polkit-1**. There is, yet, no desktop tool to use to configure these settings. The desktop tool, **policykit-gnome**, is still available, but applies to the older version of PolicyKit, which held configuration files in the **/usr/share/PolicyKit** directory.

Note: External hard drives, such as USB connected hard drives, are mounted automatically

Difficulties occur if you want to change the authorization setting for certain actions, like mounting internal hard drives. Currently, you can change the settings by manually editing the configuration files in the **/usr/share/polkit-1/actions** directory, but this is risky. To make changes you first have to know the action to change and the permission to set. The man page for **polkit** will list possible authorizations. The default authorizations are **allow_any** for anyone, **allow_inactive** for a console, and **allow_active** for an active console only (user logged in). These authorizations can be set to the following specific values:.

auth_admin	Administrative user only, authorization required always
auth_admin_keep	Administrative user only, authorization kept for a brief period
auth_self	User authorization required
auth_self_keep	User authorization required, authorization kept for a brief period
yes	Always allow access
no	Never allow access

You will need to know the PolicyKit action to modify and the file to edit. The action is listed in the PolicyKit dialog that prompts you to enter the password (expand the Details arrow) when you try to use an application. The file name will be the first segments of the action with the suffix "policy" attached. For example, the action for mounting internal drives is:

```
org.freedesktop.udisks.filesystem-mount-system-internal
```

Its file is:

```
org.freedesktop.udisks.policy
```

The file is located in the **/usr/share/polkit-1/actions** directory. Its full path name is:

```
/usr/share/polkit-1/actions/org.freedesktop.udisks.policy
```

Users with administrative access, like your primary user, can mount internal partitions on your hard drives automatically. However, users without administrative access require authorization using an administrative password before they can mount a partition (see Figure 14-13). Should you want to allow non-administrative users to mount partitions without an authorization request, the **org.freedesktop.udisks.policy** file in the **/usr/share/polkit-1** directory has to be modified to change the **allow_active** default for **filesystem-mount-system-internal** action from **auth_admin_keep** to **yes**. The **auth_admin_keep** option requires administrative authorization.

Enter the following to edit the **org.freedesktop.udisks.policy** file in the **/usr/share/polkit-1/actions** directory:

```
sudo gedit /usr/share/polkit-1/actions/org.freedesktop.udisks.policy
```

Locate the **action id** labeled as:

```
<action id ="org.feedesktop.udisks.filesystem-mount-system-internal">
  <description>Mount a system-internal device</description>
```

This is usually the second action id. At the end of that action section, you will find the following entry. It will be located within a defaults subsection, <defaults>.

```
<allow_active>auth_admin_keep</allow_active>
```

Replace **auth_admin_keep** with **yes**.

```
<allow_active>yes</allow_active>
```

Save the file. non-administrative users will no longer have to enter a password to mount internal partitions.

sudo and gksu

The sudo service provides administrative access to specific users. You have to be a user on the system with a valid username and password that has been authorized by the sudo service for administrative access. This allows other users to perform specific super user operations without having full administrative level control. You can find more about sudo at **http://www.sudo.ws**.

gksu

You can use the **gksu** command in place of **sudo** to run graphical applications with administrative access. The **gksu** tool is a front end to **sudo** (another name for **gksu** is **gksudo**). The **gksu** tool will prompt you to enter your password, assuming you are logged in as a user that has sudo authorized administrative access (See Figure 14-1).

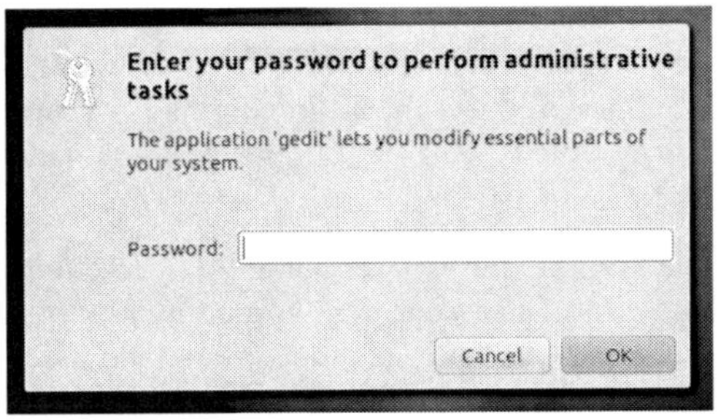

Figure 14-1: gksu prompt for access to administrative tools

You can enter the **gksu** command in a terminal window with the application as an argument, or set up an application launcher with **gksu** as the command. The following example will start up the Gedit editor with administrative access, allowing you to edit system configuration files directly (see Figure 14-2).

```
gksu gedit
```

Many administrative tools invoke applications using gksu, as in **gksu synaptic**. You will see this command in the Launcher tab in the application's properties window. If you run **gksu** directly without any application specified, it will prompt you to enter the application. You could set up a GNOME or KDE application launcher for an application with the **gksu** command prefixing the application command.

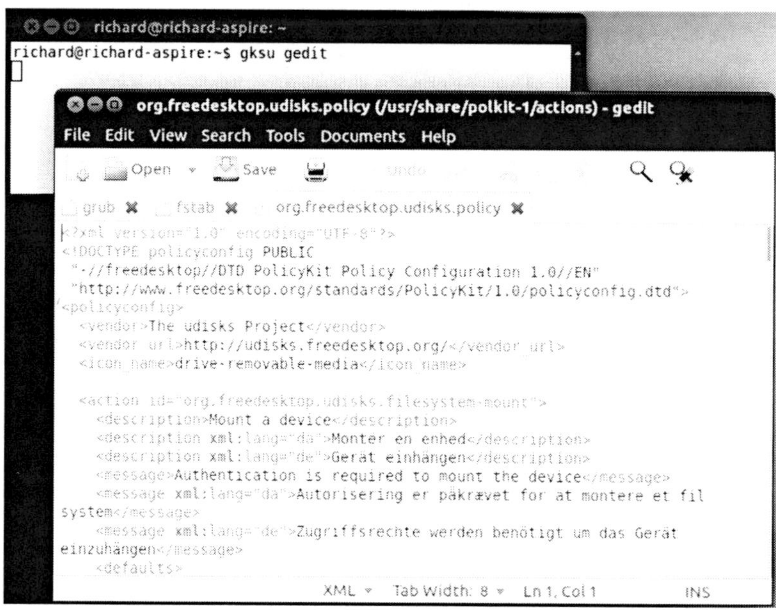

Figure 14-2: Invoking Gedit with gksu command

sudo command

Some administrative operations require access from the command line in the terminal window. For such operations, you would use the **sudo** command. You can open a terminal window from Accessories dash. For easier access, you can pin the Terminal launcher item to the Launcher (right-click and choose "Lock to Launcher").

To use **sudo** to run an administrative command, you precede the command with the **sudo** command. You are then prompted to enter your password. You will be issued a time-restricted ticket to allow access. The following example sets the system date using the **date** command.

```
sudo date 0406145908
password:
```

You can also use the sudo command to run an application with administrative access. From the terminal window, you would enter the sudo command with the application name as an argument. For example, to use the **nano** editor to edit a system configuration file, you would start **nano** using the **sudo** command in a terminal window, with the **nano** command and the file name as its arguments. This starts up **nano** editor with administrator privileges. The following example will allow you to edit the **/etc/fstab** file to add or edit file system entries. You will be prompted for your user password.

```
sudo nano /etc/fstab
```

sudo configuration

Access for **sudo** is controlled by the **/etc/sudoers** file. This file lists users and the commands they can run, along with the password for access. If the NOPASSWD option is set, then users will not need a password. The ALL option, depending on the context, can refer to all hosts on your network, all root-level commands, or all users. See the Man page for **sudoers** for detailed information on all options.

```
man sudoers
```

To make changes or add entries, you have to edit the file with the special sudo editing command **visudo**. This invokes the nano editor (see Chapter 5) to edit the **/etc/sudoers** file. Unlike a standard editor, **visudo** will lock the **/etc/sudoers** file and check the syntax of your entries. You are not allowed to save changes unless the syntax is correct. If you want to use a different editor, you can assign it to the EDITOR shell variable. Use Ctrl-x to exit and Ctrl-o to save. Be sure to invoke **visudo** with the **sudo** command to gain authorized access.

```
sudo visudo
```

A **sudoers** entry has the following syntax:

```
user    host=command
```

The *host* is a host on your network. You can specify all hosts with the ALL term. The *command* can be a list of commands, some or all qualified by options such as whether a password is required. To specify all commands, you can also use the ALL term. The following gives the user george full root-level access to all commands on all hosts:

```
george  ALL = ALL
```

In addition, you can let a user run as another user on a given host. Such alternate users are placed within parentheses before the commands. For example, if you want to give **george** access to the **beach** host as the user **mydns**, you use the following:

```
george beach = (mydns) ALL
```

To give **robert** access on all hosts to the time tool, you would use

```
robert ALL=/usr/bin/time-admin
```

To specify a group name, you prefix the group with a **%** sign, as in **%mygroup**. This way, you can give the same access to a group of users. By default **sudo** will grant access to all users in the **admin** group. These are user granted administrative access. The ALL=(ALL) ALL entry allows access by the administrative group users to all hosts as all users to all commands.

```
%admin   ALL=(ALL)    ALL
```

With the NOPASSWD option, you can allow members of a certain group access without a password. A commented **sudo** group is provided in the **/etc/sudoers** file.

```
%sudo   ALL=NOPASSWD:   ALL
```

Though on Ubuntu sudo is configured to allow **root** user access, Ubuntu does not create a **root** user password. This prevents you from logging in as the **root** user, rendering the sudo root permission useless. The default **/etc/sudoers** file does configure full access for the root user to all commands. The ALL=(ALL) ALL entry allows access by the root to all hosts as all users to all commands. If you where to set up a root password for the root user, the root user could then login and have full administrative access.

```
root    ALL=(ALL)   ALL
```

If you want to see what commands you can run, you use the **sudo** command with the **-l** option. The **-U** option to specifies a particular user. In the following example the user richard has full administrative access.

```
$ sudo -U richard -l

User richard may run the following commands on this host:
   (ALL) All
```

Root User Access: root, su, and terminal administrative access

Should you need to run several administrative commands from the command line on your desktop, you can run the terminal window with a **gksu** command, prompting you first to enter your password. You can run as many administrative commands as you want without having to provide authorization for each one.

Figure 14-3: Terminal with administrative access

You can access the root user from any normal terminal window using the **sudo** command on the **su** command. The **su** command is the superuser command. Superuser is another name for **root** user. A user granted administrative access by **sudo**, could then become the **root** user. The following logs into the root user.

```
sudo su
```

Ubuntu is designed never to let anyone directly login as the root user. The **root** user has total control over the entire system. Instead certain users are given administrative access with which they can separately access administrative tools, performing specific tasks. Even though a **root** user exists, a password for the root user is not defined, never allowing access to it.

You can activate the root user by using the **passwd** command to create a root user password. Enter the **passwd** command with the **root** user name in a **sudo** operation.

```
sudo passwd root
```

You are prompted for your administrative password, and then prompted by the **passwd** command to enter a password for the **root** user. You are then prompted to repeat the password.

```
Enter new UNIX password:
Retype new UNIX password:
passwd: password updated successfully
```

You can then log in with the **su** command as the root user, making you the superuser (you still cannot login as the root user from the GDM login window). Because a superuser has the power to change almost anything on the system, such a password is usually a carefully guarded secret, changed very frequently, and given only to those whose job it is to manage the system. With the correct password, you can log in to the system as a system administrator and configure the system any way you want.

```
su root
```

The **su** command alone will assume the root username.

```
su
```

The **su** command can be used to login to any user, provided you have that user's password.

To exit from an **su** login operation, just enter **exit**.

```
exit
```

User Accounts (GNOME 3)

You can configure and create user accounts using the User Accounts tool accessible from System Settings and the Customization dash. User Accounts does not provide any way to control groups, and its user configuration is limited. If you want group control and more configuration options, you can install the GNOME Users and Groups application, which is part of the **gnome-system-tools** package.

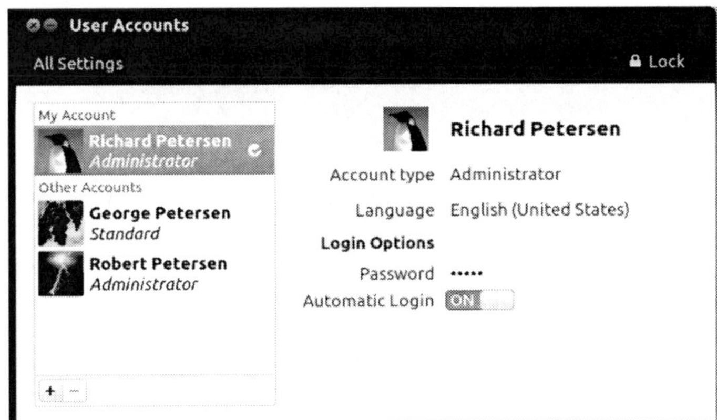

Figure 14-4: Users

The User Accounts dialog displays two panes, a left scrollable pane for a list of users, showing their icon and login name, and a right pane showing information about a selected user (see Figure 14-4). Below the left pane are plus (+) and minus (−) buttons for adding and deleting users.

PolicyKit controls administrative access for the Users tool. When you first click a task button such as the plus or minus, an Authenticate dialog will open and prompt you to enter your user password. You will also be prompted to authenticate if you try to change a user password, account type, icon, or name.

When you add a new account, a dialog opens letting you set the account type (standard or administrator), the full name of the user, and the user name (see Figure 14-5). For the user name you can enter a name or choose from a recommended list of options. Click Create to create the user. The new account appears on the right pane showing the name, icon, account type, language, password, and an automatic login option.

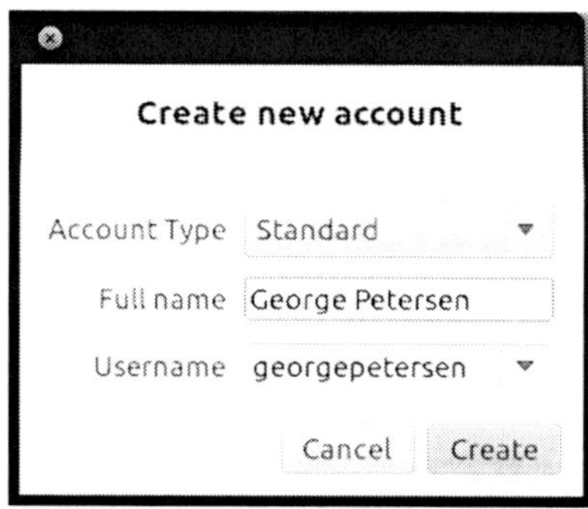

Figure 14-5: Users: new users

The account remains inactive until you specify a password (see Figure 14-6). Click on the password entry to open a dialog open where you can enter the new password (see Figure 14-7). To the right of the New password text box is a password generator button that will list possible passwords. Once the password is selected, the account becomes enabled.

Figure 14-6: Users: inactive user

To choose and icon, click on the icon image to open a icon selection dialog. Choose the one you want or locate an image of your own.

You can change the account type, language, password, and icon by clicking on their entries. You will be prompted for authorization.

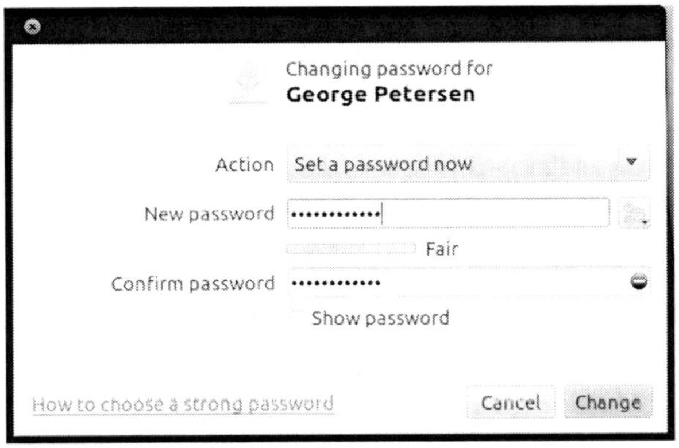

Figure 14-7: Users: password dialog

Users and Groups

Alternatively, you can install (**gnome-system-tools**) and then use the older "Users and Groups" application (users-admin), accessible from "User and Groups" on the System dash. This opens a User Settings window, which displays two panes, a left scrollable pane for a list of users, showing their icon and login name, and a right pane showing information about a selected user. Below the left pane are buttons for adding and deleting users. At the bottom of the right pane are buttons for Managing Groups and for a selected user's Advanced Settings.

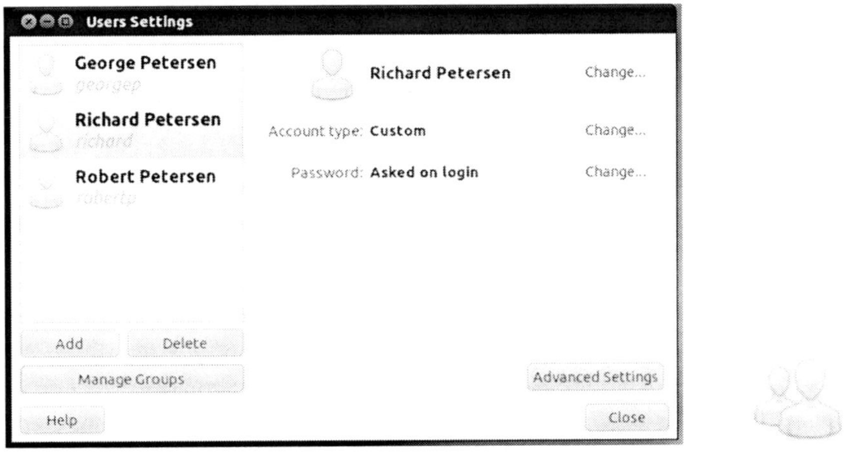

Figure 14-8: Users and Groups

When you start up the users-admin application, only read access is allowed, letting you scroll through the list of users, but not make any changes or add new ones (see Figure 14-8). Read only access is provided to all users. Users will be able to see the list of users on your system, but they cannot modify their entries, add new ones, or delete current users. Administrative access is required to perform these operations.

PolicyKit controls administrative access for the users-admin tool. When you first click a task button such as Add, Delete, or Advanced Settings, an Authenticate dialog will open and prompt you to enter your user password. You will also be prompted to authenticate if you click a Change link to change a user password, account type, or name.

To change settings for a user, select the user in the User Settings window. On the left pane the user name, account type and password access are listed with a Change link to the right of each. Clicking on a Change link lets you change that property. When you click a Change link, an authentication dialog will prompt you to enter an administrative user password. To change a user name, click the Change link to the right of the user name to open the "Change User Name and Login" dialog with a text box for entering the new name.

To change a user password, you would click the Change link to the right of the Password entry to open the "Change User Password" dialog with entries for the current password and the new password (see Figure 14-9). You can also choose to generate a random password.

Figure 14-9: User Settings: Change User Password dialog

An account type can be Administrator, Desktop User, or Custom. When you click the Change link for the Account type, the "Change User Account Type" dialog opens with options for each (see Figure 14-11).

For more detailed configuration, you click the Advanced Settings button to open the "Change Advanced User Settings" dialog, which has tabs for Contact Information, User Privileges, and Advanced (see Figure 14-11). On the Contact tab, you can add basic contact information if you wish for an office address, as well as work and home phones.

On the User Privileges tab you can control device access and administrative access (see Figure 14-8). You can restrict or allow access to CD-ROMs, scanners, and external storage like

USB drives. You can also determine whether the user can perform administrative tasks. The "Administer the system" check box is left unchecked by default. If you want to allow the user to perform administration tasks, be sure to check this box.

Figure 14-10: User Settings: Change User Account Type

The Advanced tab lets you select a home directory, the shell to use, a main group, and a user ID. Defaults are already chosen for you. A home directory in the name of the new user is specified and the shell used is the BASH shell. Normally you would not want to change these settings, though you might prefer to use a different shell, like the C-Shell. For the group, the user has a group with its own user name (same as the short name).

Figure 14-11: Users and Groups: Change User Privileges

Should to you decide to delete a user, you are prompted to keep or delete the user's home directory along with the user's files.

New Users

To create a new user, click the Add button in the Users Settings window to open a "Create New User" dialog where you can enter the user name. A short name is automatically entered for you using the user's first name and the first letter of the last name. You can change the short name if you wish, but it must be in lowercase. The short name is also the name of the new user main group (see Figure 14-12). The new user is then added to the User Settings window.

The "Change User Password" dialog is then displayed with entries for the new password and confirmation. You can also choose to use a randomly generated password instead (see Figure 14-13). Click the Generate button generate a password.

Figure 14-12: Users and Groups: Create New User

Figure 14-13: Users and Groups: new user password

If you decide not to enter a password (click Cancel), the account will remain disabled. To enable it later, you click on the Enable Account button to open the "Change User Password" dialog where you add the password.

The Account type is set initially to Desktop user, restricting access by the new user. Should you want to enable administrative access for this user, click the Change link to the right of the Account type entry to open the "Change User Account Type" dialog where you can change the account type to Administrator (see Figure 14-10). To set more specific privileges and for key user configuration settings such as the home directory and user id, click the Advanced Settings button to open the "Change Advanced User Settings" dialog with Contact Information, User Privileges, and Advanced tabs (see Figure 14-11).

Alternatively, you can use the **useradd** command in a terminal window or command line to add user accounts and the **userdel** command to remove them. The following example adds the user **dylan** to the system:

```
$ useradd dylan
```

Groups

To manage groups, click the Manage Groups button in the Users Settings window. This opens a Group Settings window that lists all groups (see Figure 14-14). To add or remove users to or from a group, click the group name in the Group Settings window and click Properties. You can then check or uncheck users from the Group Members listing.

To add a new group, click the Add Group button in the Group Settings window to open a New Group dialog where you can specify the group name, its id, and select the users to add to the group (see Figure 14-15). If you want to remove a group, just select its entry in the Groups Settings window and click the Delete button.

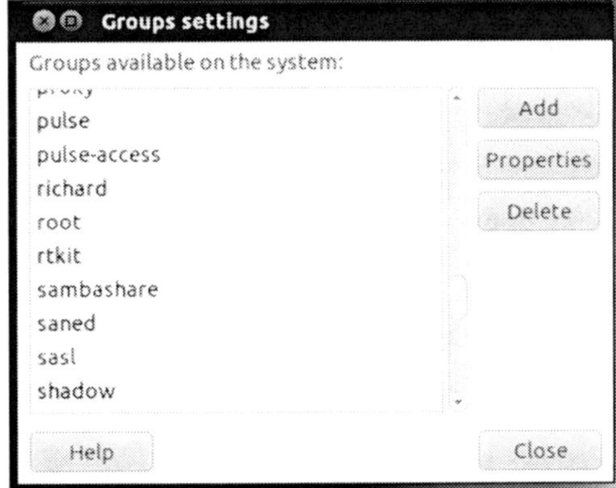

Figure 14-14: Users and Groups: Groups settings

Figure 14-15: Group Properties: Group Users panel

Passwords

The easiest way to change your password is to use the User Accounts dialog available from System Settings as User, from the User Switcher menu as User Accounts, and from the System dash. Select your user name, and then click the button to the right of the Password label to open the Change User Password dialog (see Figure 14-7).

Alternatively you can use the **passwd** command. In a terminal window enter the **passwd** command. The command prompts you for your current password. After entering your current password and pressing ENTER, you are then prompted for your new password. After entering the new password, you are asked to reenter it. This makes sure you have actually entered the password you intended to enter.

```
$ passwd
Old password:
New password:
Retype new password:
$
```

Managing Services

Many administrative functions operate as services that need to be turned on. They are daemons, constantly running and checking for requests for their services. When you install a service, its daemon is normally turned on automatically. You can start, start, and restart a service from a terminal window using the **service** command with the service name. Service scripts are located in the **/etc/init.d/** directory. To restart the Samba file sharing service you would use the following command.

```
sudo service samba restart
```

File System Access

Various file systems can be accessed on Ubuntu easily. Any additional internal hard drive partitions on your system, both Linux and Windows NTFS, will be detected automatically, but not mounted. In addition, you can access remote Windows shared folders and make your shared folders accessible.

Access to Internal Linux File Systems

Ubuntu will detect other Linux file systems (partitions) on all your internal hard drives automatically. Entries for these partitions are displayed on a file manager's Places sidebar and in the Computer window (Go | Computer). Initially they are not mounted. Administrative users can mount internal partitions by clicking on its entry or icon, which mounts the file system and displays its icon both in the Computer window and on the Launcher. A file manager window opens displaying the top-level contents of the file system. The file system is mounted under the **/media** directory in a folder named with the file system (partition) label, or, if unlabeled, with the device UUID name.

Non-administrative users (user you create and do not specify as administrators), cannot mount internal partitions unless the task is authenticated using an administrative user's password. An authorization window will appear similar to that shown in Figure 14-16. You will be asked to choose a user that has administrative access from a drop-down menu, and then enter that user's password. If there is only one administrative user, that user is selected automatically and you are prompted to enter that user's password. Whenever you start up your system again, you will still have to mount the file system, again providing authorization.

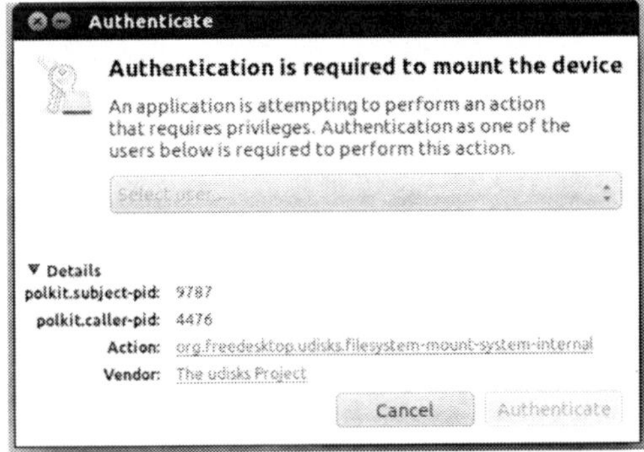

Figure 14-16: Mount authorization request for non-administrative users

Access to Windows NTFS File Systems on Local Drives

If you have installed Ubuntu on a dual-boot system with Windows 7, Vista, or XP. Linux NTFS file system support is installed automatically. Your NTFS partitions are mounted using Filesystem in Userspace (FUSE). The same authentication control used for Linux file systems applies to NTFS file systems. Icons for the NTFS partitions will be displayed in the Computer window (Go | Computer). If you are a user with administrative access, then, when you double-click on the file system icon, the file system is mounted. If you are a user without administrative access, you will be asked to choose a user that has administrative access from a drop-down menu, and then enter that user's password, providing authorization (see Figure 14-13). The NTFS file system is then mounted with icons displayed in the Computer widow and on the Launcher. The partitions will be mounted under the **/media** directory with their UUID numbers or labels used as folder names. The NTFS partitions are mounted using **ntfs-3g** drivers.

Access to Local Network Shared File Systems (Windows)

Shared Windows folders and printers on any of the computers connected to your local network are automatically accessible from your Ubuntu desktop (Go | Network). The DNS discovery service (Avahi) automatically detects hosts on your home or local network and will let you access directly any of their shared folders. When you double-click on the file system icon, you will be asked to provide authorization, as in Figure 14-17, specifying the domain and password.

To access the shared network folders, select Network from the Go menu to open the Network window (see Figure 14-18). You can also choose "Browse Network" in the Network section of the file manager sidebar. Your connected computers will be listed. If you know the name of the Windows computer you want to access, just click on its icon, otherwise, click on the Windows network icon to see just the Windows machines. Once selected, the shared folders are shown. You can then access a shared folder and it will be mounted automatically on your desktop. The Network section of the file manager sidebar will show an entry for the folder with an Eject button for un-mounting it. Figure 14-19 shows the **myshareddata** shared folder on a Windows system mounted on the Network window.

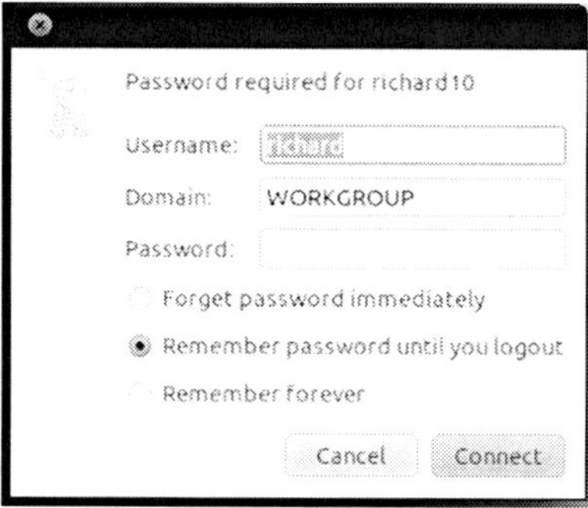

Figure 14-17: Network authorization

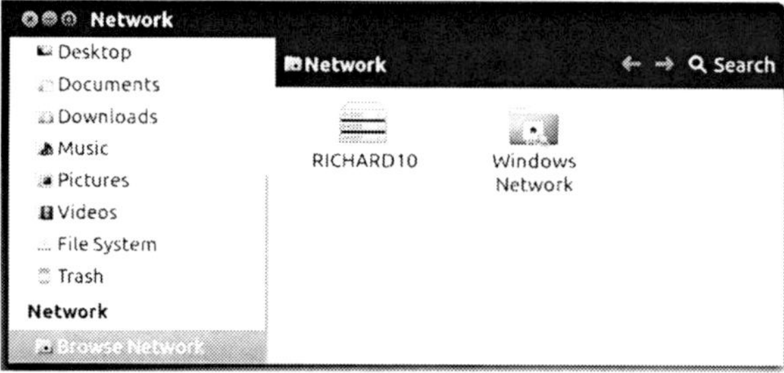

Figure 14-18: Network window

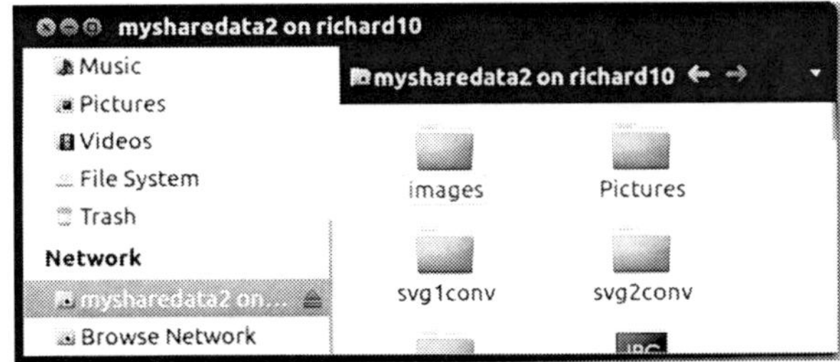

Figure 14-19: Mount remote Windows shares

Other local computers cannot access your shared folders until you install a sharing server, Samba for Windows systems and NFS for Linux/Unix systems. Should you attempt to share a directory, a notice is displayed prompting you to install the sharing service (Samba and NFS). Be sure also to allow firewall access for Samba and desktop browsing (see Chapter 14, Firewalls).

Shared Folders for your network

To share a folder on your Ubuntu system, right-click on it and select Sharing Options. This opens a window where you can allow sharing, and whether to permit modifying, adding, or deleting files in the folder (see Figure 14-20). You can also use the Share tab on the file's properties dialog (see Figure 14-23). You can allow access to anyone who does not also have an account on your system (guest). Once you have made your selections, click the Create Share button. You can later change the sharing options if you want.

For a user to create a share, they have to have permission to do so. New users are not given this permission by default. On the Users and Groups's Advanced dialog's Privileges tab set the "Share files with the local network" option.

Figure 14-20: Folder Sharing Options

To allow access by other users, permissions on the folder will have to be changed. You are prompted to allow Nautilus to make these changes for you. Just click the "Add the permissions automatically" button (see Figure 14-21).

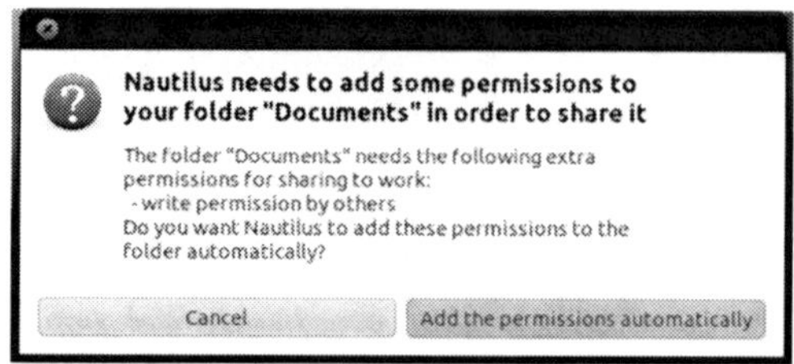

Figure 14-21: Folder Sharing permissions prompt

Note: If you are running a firewall, be sure to configure access for the NFS and Samba services, including browsing support (Go | Network). Otherwise access to your shared folders by other computers may be blocked (see Chapter 14).

Folders that are shared display a sharing emblem next to their icon on a file manager window.

Documents

To allow other computers to access your folders be sure the sharing servers are installed, Samba for Windows systems and NFS (**nfs-kernelserver**) for Linux/Unix systems. The servers are configured automatically for you and run. You will not be able to share folders until these servers are installed. If your sharing servers are not installed, you will be prompted to install them the first time you try to share a folder (see Figure 14-22). Click the Install service button. The Samba servers will be downloaded and installed. You are then prompted to restart your desktop session. Click the Restart session button. You are placed in the GDM login screen. Login again and then open the folder sharing dialog for the folder you want to share (Sharing Options).

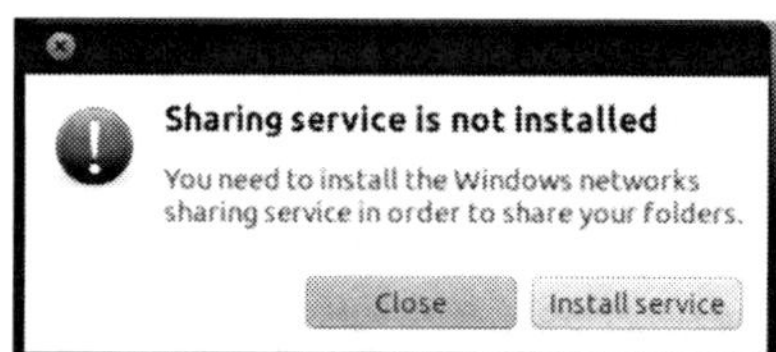
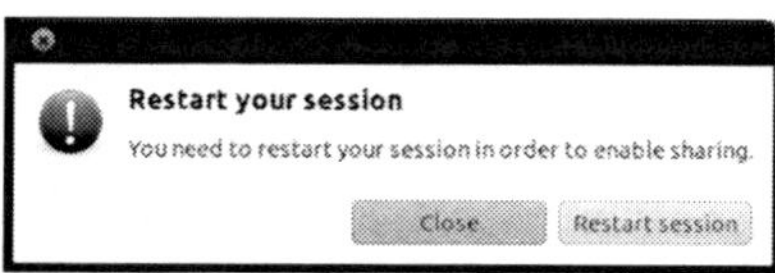

Figure 14-22: Prompt to install sharing service (Samba and NFS)

You can also install the Samba server directly with the Synaptic Package Manager (**samba** package) and from the Ubuntu Software Center | System | SMB/CIFS file, print, and login server for Unix (samba). Two servers are installed and run using the **smbd** and **nmbd** service scripts in the **/etc/init.d** directory (the **samba** service script is not longer used). The **smbd** server is the Samba server, and the **nmbd** server is the network discovery server.

Should the Samba server fail to start, you can start it manually in a terminal window with the commands:

```
sudo service nmbd start
sudo service smbd start
```

You can check the current status with the **status** option and restart with the **restart** option:

```
sudo service nmbd status
sudo service smbd status
```

When first installed, Samba imports the user accounts already configured on your Ubuntu system. Corresponding Windows users with the same user name and password as an Ubuntu account on your Ubuntu system are connected automatically to the Ubuntu shared folders. Should the Windows user have a different password, that user is prompted on Windows to enter a user name and password. This is an Ubuntu user name and password. In the case of a Windows user with the same user name but different password, the user would enter in the same user name with Ubuntu user password, not the Windows password.

Access is granted to all shares by any user. Should you want to implement restricted access by specific users and passwords, you have to configure user level access using a Samba configuration tool such as system-config-samba, as discussed in the next section.

To change the sharing permissions for a folder later, open the folder's Properties window and then select the Share tab. When you make a change, a Modify Share button is displayed. Click it to make the changes. In Figure 14-23 Guest access is added to the Pictures folder.

Figure 14-23: Folder Share panel

Configuring Samba user-level access with system-config-samba

More secure access by Windows systems to your Ubuntu shared folders can be configured using the **system-config-samba** tool. You can install it with the Synaptic Package Manager and from the Ubuntu Software Center | Samba. You can then access it from the Customization dash as Samba. With system-config-samba you can set up user level access, requiring Samba user passwords to allow access to shares. (see Figure 14-24). For more information about Samba, install the **samba-doc** package and access **file:/usr/share/doc/samba-doc/htmldocs/index.html**.

Samba Server Configuration

You will first have to configure the Samba server, designating users that can have access to shared resources like directories and printers. On the Samba Preferences menu, select Server Settings to open the Server Settings dialog.

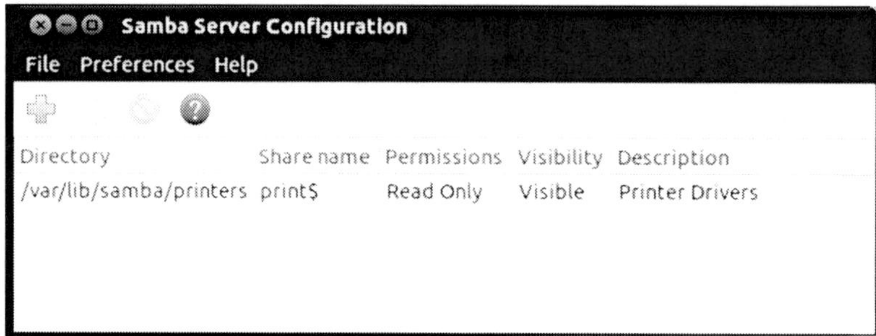

Figure 14-24: Samba server configuration with system-config-samba

On the Basic tab enter the name of your Windows network workgroup (see Figure 14-25). The default names given by Windows are MSHOME or WORKGROUP. Use the workgroup name already given to your Windows network. For home networks, you can decide on your own. Just make sure all your computers use the same workgroup name. On a Windows system, the Control Panel's System application will show you the Windows workgroup name. The description is the name you want displayed for your Samba server on your Windows systems. Windows 7 home networks will work with Samba without any special configuration.

Figure 14-25: Samba Server Settings, Basic tab

On the Security tab you can select the kind of authentication you want to use. By default User security is selected (see Figure 14-26). You could also use share or server security. These are more open, but both have been deprecated and may be dropped in later versions.

The authentication mode specifies the access level, which can be user, share, server, ADS, or domain. User-level access restricts access by user password, whereas share access opens access to any guest. Normally, you would elect to encrypt passwords, rather than have them passed over your network in plain text. The Guest user is the name of the account used to allow access to shares or printers that you want open to any user, without having to provide a password. The pop-up menu will list all your current users, with "No Guest Account" as the selected default. Unless you want to provide access by everyone to a share, you would not have a Guest account.

Figure 14-26: Samba Server Settings, Security tab

Samba Users

For user authentication, you associate a Windows user with a particular Linux account. Select Samba Users in the Preferences menu to open the Samba Users dialog (see Figure 14-27). Ubuntu users set up on your system when you installed Samba are listed already, using their user names and password for access by Windows users. If you want to add a new Samba user, click Add User to open the Create New Samba User window where you select the Unix Username from a pop-up menu, and then enter the Windows Username and the Samba password to be used for that user (see Figure 14-28). The Unix Username menu lists all the users on your Samba server. Samba maintains its own set of passwords that users on other computers will need to access a Samba share. When a Windows user wants to access a Samba share, they will have to provide their Samba password. If you use a Windows user name with spaces, enclose it within quotes.

Figure 14-27: Samba Users

Once you create a Samba user, its name will appear in the list of Samba users on the Samba Users window. To later modify or delete a Samba user, Use the same Samba Users window, select the user from the list, and click the Edit User button to change entries like the password, or click the Delete User button to remove the Samba user.

Note: If a password prompt prevents you from accessing a Windows share on Windows 7 from your Ubuntu system, you may have to uninstall the "Windows Live Sign In Assistant" on your Windows 7 system.

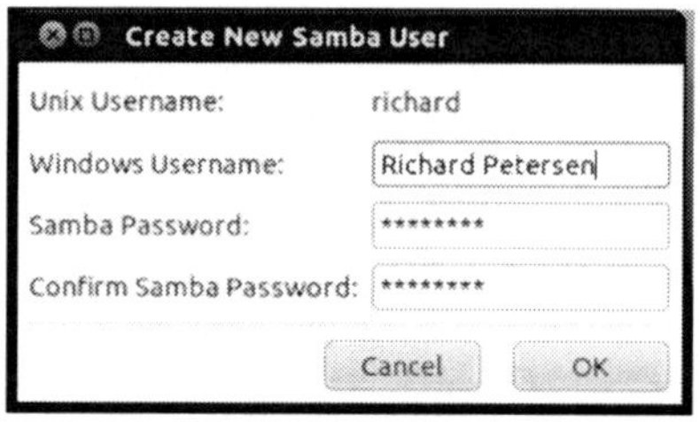

Figure 14-28: Create a new samba user

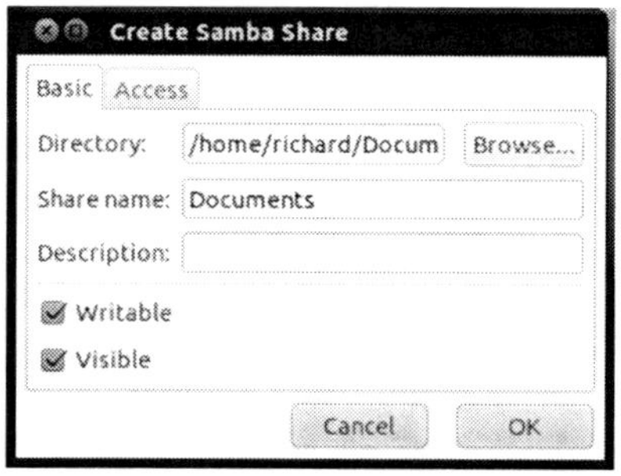

Figure 14-29: New Samba Share, Basic tab

Samba Shares

To set up a simple share, click Add Share in the Samba Server Configuration window, which opens a Create Samba Share window (see Figure 14-29).

Figure 14-30: Samba share, Access tab

On the Basic tab you select the Linux directory to share (click Browse to find it), and then specify whether it will be writable and visible.

On the Access tab you can choose to open the share to everyone, or just for specific users (see Figure 14-30). All Samba users on your system are listed with check boxes where you can select those you want to give access.

Your new share is then displayed in the Samba Server Configuration window (see Figure 14-31). The share's directory, share name, its visibility, read/write permissions, and description are shown. To modify a share later, click on its entry and then click on the Properties button (or double-click). This opens an Edit samba share window with the same Basic and Access tabs you used to create the share.

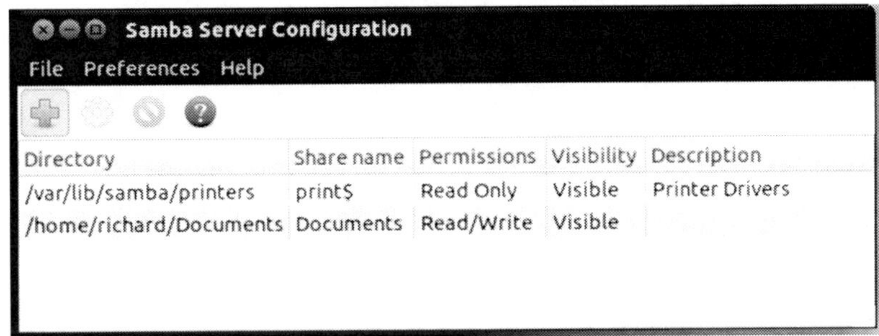

Figure 14-31: Samba with shares

Configuring Samba and NFS access with Shared Folders (shares-admin)

You can also configure access to Samba (Windows shares) and NFS (Unix/Linux shares) using the GNOME shares-admin tool, which is part of the **gnome-system-tools** package (Universe repository). One installed, it is still not visible on the Dash. You can run it from a terminal window using the following command.

```
shares-admin
```

Alternatively, you can use the Main Menu tool (alacarte, Universe repository) to make it visible (Other category). It is then accessible as Shared Folders on the dash.

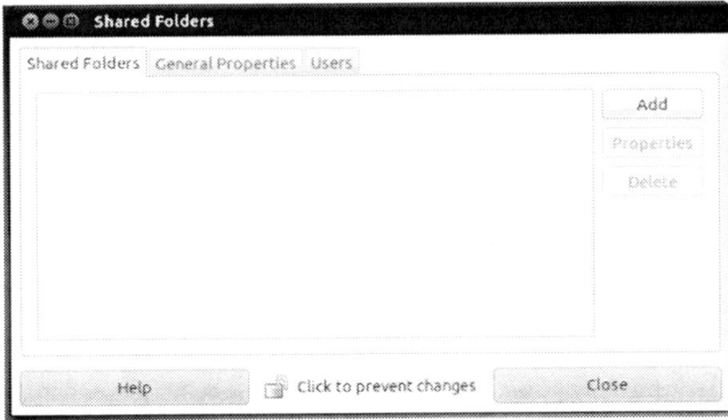

Figure 14-32: Shared Folders

The Shared Folders dialog displays three tabs: Shared Folders, General Properties, and Users (see Figure 14-32). On the General tab you specify the Windows workgroup name, and a WINS server is there is one (see Figure 14-33).

Shared Folders is not as refined as system-config-samba, which can configure user access to specific shares. On Shared Folders, user access can be configured, but for all the shares. Use the Users tab to specify which user can have access to the shared folders (see Figure 14-34).

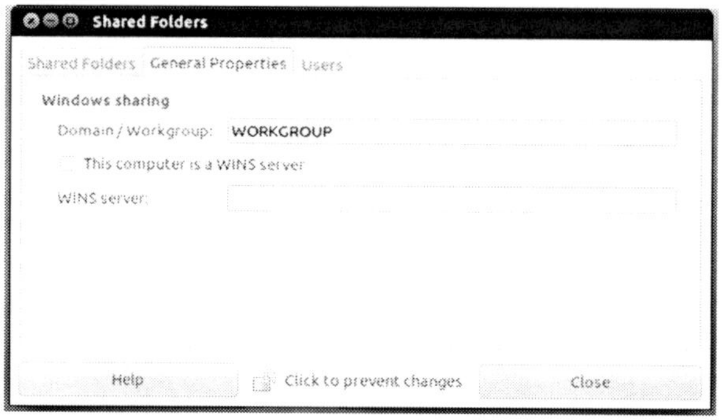

Figure 14-33: Shared Folders General tab, workgroup name

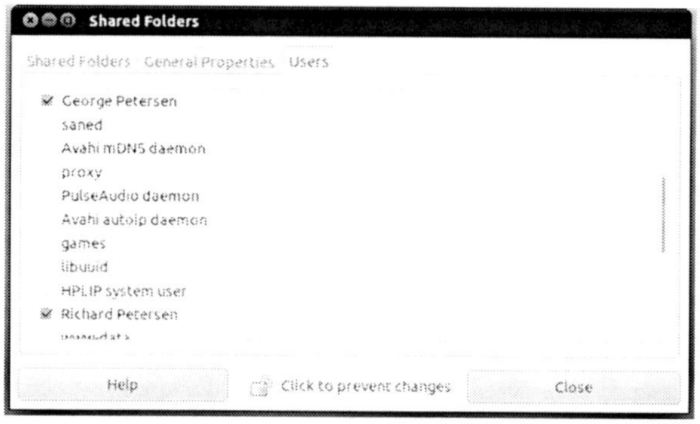

Figure 14-34: Shared Folders User tab

The Shared Folders tab lists your Samba and NFS shares. To add or edit shares, first click the "Click to make changes" lock button at the bottom of the dialog, which prompts you to enter your password. To add a share click the Add button on the Shared Folders tab to open a Share Folder dialog where you specify the folder, the share server (Samba or NFS), the share name, and whether it is read only or writable (see Figure 14-35).

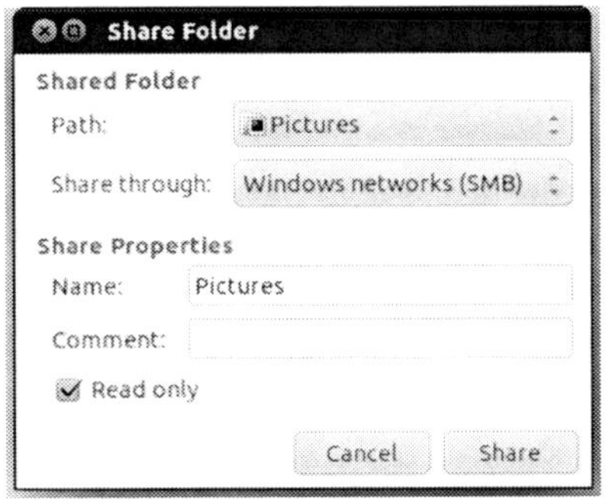

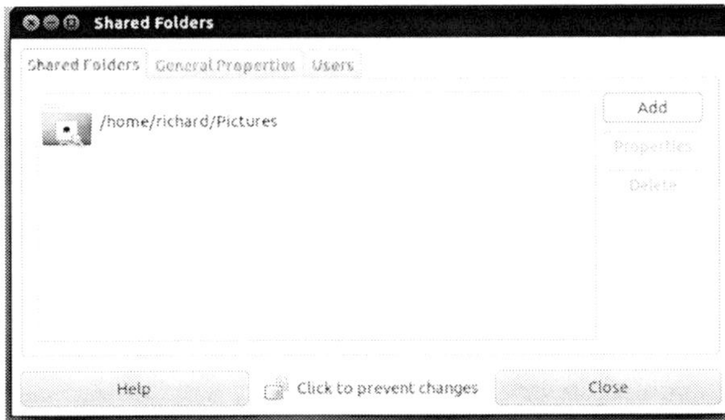

Figure 14-35: Samba with Shared Folders

Once added, the share folder appears on the Shared Folders tab (see Figure 14-36).

Figure 14-36: Shared Folders with share

To add shares for Unix/Linux systems, the Share Folder dialog lets you specify hosts that will have access to the share. Clicking the Add button opens the "Add allowed hosts" dialog where you can enter the host name (see Figure 14-37).

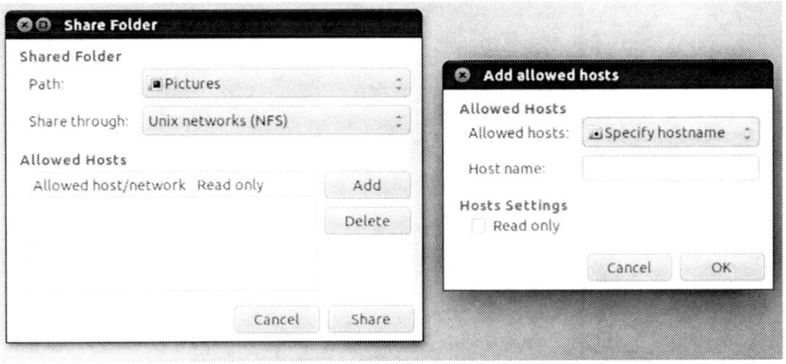

Figure 14-37: Shared Folders for NFS

File and Folder Permissions

On the desktop, you can set a directory or file permission using the Permissions tab in its Properties window (see Figure 14-38). For Files, right-click the icon or entry for the file or directory in the file manager window and select Properties. Then select the Permissions tab. Here you will find pop-up menus for read and write permissions, along with rows for Owner, Group, and Other. You can set owner permissions as Read Only or Read And Write. For the group and others, you can also set the None option, denying access. The group name expands to a pop-up menu listing different groups; select one to change the file's group. If you want to execute this file as an application (say, a shell script) check the Allow Executing File As Program entry. This has the effect of setting the execute permission

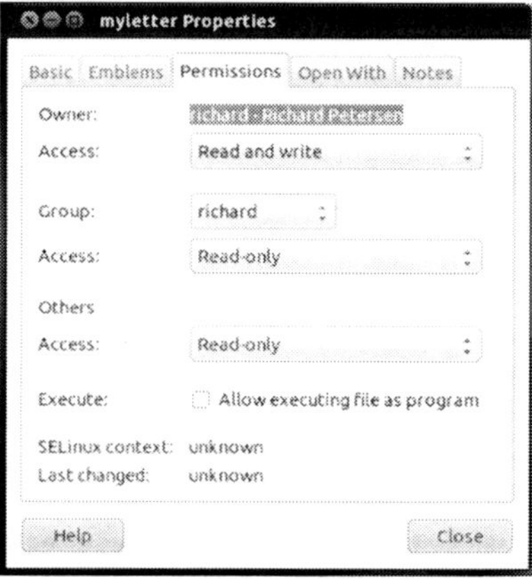

Figure 14-38: File Permissions

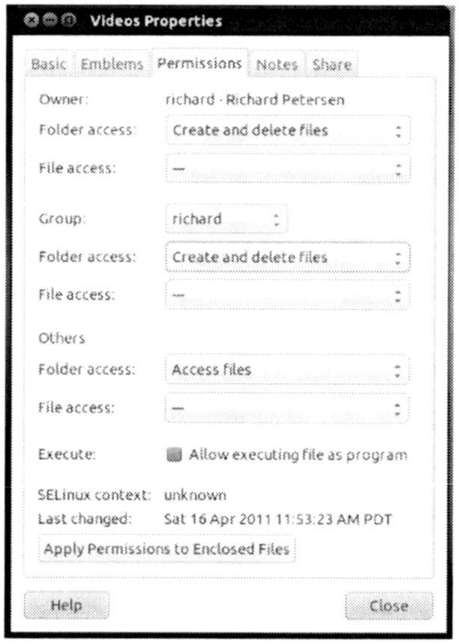

**Figure 14-39: Folder Permissions

The Permissions tab for directories operates much the same way, but it displays two access entries, Folder Access and File Access (see Figure 14-39). The Folder Access entry controls access to the folder with options for List Files Only, Access Files, and Create And Delete Files. These correspond to the read, read and execute, and read/write/execute permissions given to directories. The File Access entry lets you set permissions for all those files in the directory. They are the same as for files: for the owner, Read or Read and Write; for the group and others, the entry adds a None option to deny access. To set the permissions for all the files in the directory accordingly (not just the folder), click the "Apply Permissions To Enclosed Files" button.

Automatic file system mounts with /etc/fstab

Though most file systems are automatically mounted for you, there may be instances where you need to have a file system mounted manually. Using the mount command you can do this directly, or you can specify the mount operation in the **/etc/fstab** file to have it mounted automatically. Ubuntu file systems are uniquely identified with their UUID (Universally Unique IDentifier). These are listed in the **/dev/disk/by-uuid** directory (or with the **sudo blkid** command). In the **/etc/fstab** file, the file system disk partitions are listed as a comment, and then followed by the actual file system mount operation using the UUID. The following example mounts the file system on partition **/dev/sda3** to the **/media/sda3** directory as an **ext4** file system with default options (**defaults**). The UUID for device **/dev/sda3** is b8c526db-cb60-43f6-b0a3-5c0054f6a64a.

```
# /dev/sda3
UUID=b8c526db-cb60-43f6-b0a3-5c0054f6a64a /media/sda3 ext4 defaults 0 2
```

You can also identify your file system by giving it a label. You can use the **ext2label** command to label a file system. In the following **/etc/fstab** file example, the Linux file system labeled **mydata1** is mounted to the **/mydata1** directory as an **ext4** file system type.

/etc/fstab

```
# /etc/fstab: static file system information.
#
# <file system> <mount point>     <type>   <options>        <dump>  <pass>
proc             /proc             proc     defaults          0       0
# /dev/sda2
UUID=a179d6e6-b90c-4cc4-982d-a4cfcedea7df / ext4 defaults,errors=remount-ro 0 1
# /dev/sda3
UUID=b8c526db-cb60-43f6-b0a3-5c0054f6a64a /media/sda3  ext3 defaults 0 2
# /dev/sda1
UUID=48b96071-6284-4fe9-b364-503817cefb74  none  swap  sw        0 0
/dev/fd0        /media/floppy0  auto        rw,user,noauto,exec  0 0
LABEL=mydata1 /mydata1          ext4        defaults             1 1
```

Should you have to edit your **/etc/fstab** file, you can use the **gksu** command with the **gedit** editor on your desktop. In a terminal window enter the following command. You will be first prompted to enter your password.

```
gksu gedit /etc/fstab
```

To mount a partition manually, use the **mount** command and specify the type with the **-t** option. Use the **-L** option to mount by label. List the file system first and then the directory name to which it will be mounted. For a NTFS partition you would use the type **ntfs**. For partitions with the Ext4 file system you would use **ext4**, and for older Linux partitions you would use **ext3**. The mount option has the format:

```
mount -t type  file-system  directory
```

The following example mounts the **mydata1** file system to the **/mydata1** directory

```
mount -t ext4  -L mydata1  /mydata1
```

Bluetooth

Ubuntu Linux provides Bluetooth support for both serial connections and BlueZ protocol–supported devices. Bluetooth is a wireless connection method for locally connected devices such as keyboards, mice, printers, and even PDAs and Bluetooth-capable cell phones. You can think of it as a small local network dedicated to your peripheral devices, eliminating the need for wires. Bluetooth devices can be directly connected through serial ports or through specialized Bluetooth cards connected to USB ports or inserted in a PCI slot. BlueZ is the official Linux Bluetooth protocol and is integrated into the Linux kernel. The BlueZ protocol was developed originally by Qualcomm and is now an open source project, located at **http://bluez.sourceforge.net**. It is included with Ubuntu in the bluez-utils and bluez-libs packages, among others. Check the BlueZ site for a complete list of supported hardware, including adapters, PCMCIA cards, and serial connectors.

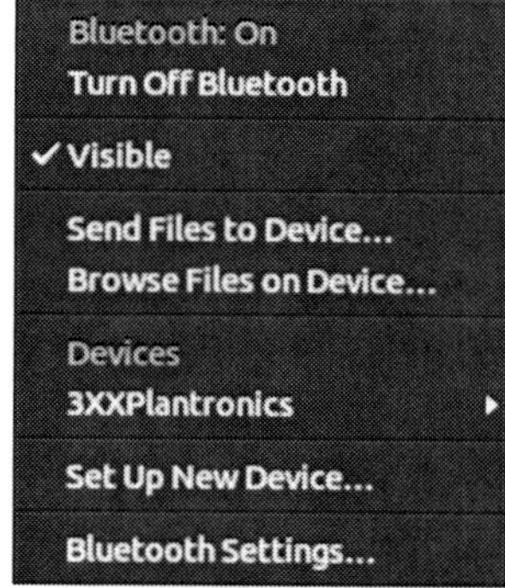

Figure 14-40: Bluetooth menu and icons

Figure 14-41: Bluetooth Preferences (System Settings)

If you have Bluetooth devices attached to your system, the Bluetooth menu is displayed on your top panel. Click it to display a menu of options for your Bluetooth devices (see Figure 14-40), along with detected Bluetooth devices. The "Setup new device" entry starts the Bluetooth New Device Wizard, which will detect your connected devices. The Send and Browse files entries lets you manage files on a Bluetooth device. The Preferences option displays the Bluetooth dialog window. You can also access Bluetooth dialog from the Customization dash or from the System Settings dialog.

The Bluetooth dialog lists any connected Bluetooth devices (see Figure 14-41). A Bluetooth switch at the top let you turn Bluetooth on or off. At the top right detected Bluetooth adaptors are listed for which you can switch visibility on or off. Detected devices are listed in the Devices frame on the left. Selecting a device displays its type and address, as well as a connection switch you can use to turn the device on or off.

Many devices, such as headsets, will be detected automatically when you connect to your system, requesting a pin number. You can add a device manually by clicking the plus button below the Devices list on the Bluetooth dialog to start up the Bluetooth New Device Wizard, detecting a new device (you choose "Set up new device" on the Bluetooth menu). The wizard performs a search and setup of a device. The "Devices search" dialog that will search for connected devices (see Figure 14-42). From the "Device type" drop-down menu you can select a type of device. The Pin options button opens a dialog where you can choose a pin number.

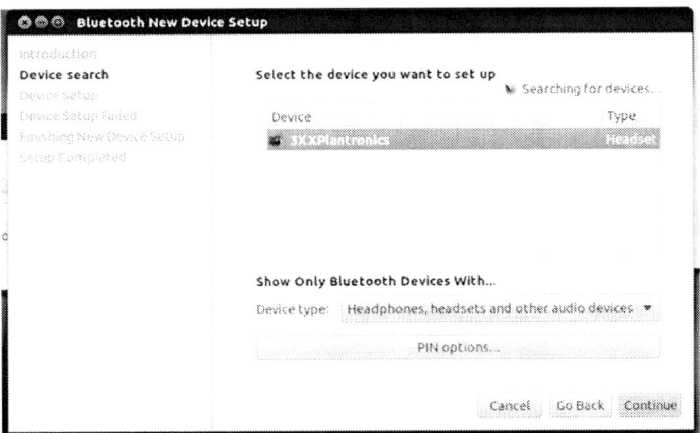

Figure 14-42: Bluetooth Setup Device Wizard

DKMS

DKMS is the Dynamic Kernel Module Support originally developed by DELL. DKMS enabled device drivers can be generated automatically whenever your kernel is updated. This is helpful for proprietary drivers like the Nvidia and ATI proprietary graphics drivers (the X11 open source drivers, Xorg, are automatically included with the kernel package). In the past, whenever you updated your kernel, you also had to download and install a separate proprietary kernel module compiled just for that new kernel. If the module was not ready, then you could not use a proprietary driver. To avoid this problem, DKMS was developed which uses the original proprietary source code to create new kernel modules as they are needed. When you install a new kernel, DKMS then detects the new configuration and compiles a compatible proprietary kernel module for your new kernel. This action is fully automatic and entirely hidden from the user.

On Ubuntu both the Nvidia and ATI proprietary graphics drivers are DKMS enable packages that are managed and generated by the DKMS service. The generated kernel modules are placed in the **/lib/modules/**/*kernel-version*/**kernel/updates** directory. When you install either graphics proprietary package, their source code is downloaded and used to create a graphics driver for use by your kernel. The source code is placed in the **/usr/src** directory. The DKMS configuration files and build locations for different DKMS enabled software are located in subdirectories in the **/var/lib/dkms** directory. The subdirectories will have the module name like **fglrx** for the ATI proprietary driver and **NVIDIA** for the Nvidia drivers.

DKMS configuration files are located in the **/etc/dkms** directory. The **/etc/dkms/framework.conf** file holds DKMS variable definitions for directories that DKMS uses like the source code and kernel module directories. The **/etc/init.d/dkms_autoinstaller** is a script the runs the DKMS operations to generate and install a kernel module. DKMS removal and install directives for kernel updates are maintained in the **/etc/kernel** directory.

Should DKMS fail to install and update automatically, you can perform the update manually using the **dkms** command. The **dkms** command with the **build** action creates the kernel module, and then the **dkms** command with the **install** action installs the module to the appropriate kernel module directory. The **-m** option specifies the module you want to build and the **-k** option is the kernel version (use **uname -r** to display your current kernel version). Drivers like Nvidia and ATI release new versions regularly (ATI every month). You use the **-v** option to specify the driver version you want. See the man page for **dkms** for full details.

```
sudo dkms build -m fglrx -v 8.543 -k 2.6.27-7-generic
sudo dkms install -m fglrx -v 8.543 -k 2.6.27-7-generic
```

Editing Configuration Files Directly

Though the administrative tools will handle all configuration settings for you, there may be times when you will need to make changes by editing configuration files directly. Most system configuration files are text files located in the **/etc** directory. To change any of these files, you will need administrative access, requiring you use the **gksu** or **sudo** commands.

You can use any standard editor such as nano or Vi to edit these files, though one of the easiest ways to edit them is to use the Gedit editor on the GNOME desktop. In a terminal window, enter the **gksu** command with the **gedit** command. You will be prompted for the root user password. The Gedit window then opens (see Figures 14-2 and 14-3 near the beginning of this chapter). Click Open to open a file browser where you can move through the file system to locate the file you want to edit.

```
gksu gedit
```

Caution: Be careful when editing your configuration files. Editing mistakes can corrupt your configurations. It is advisable to make a backup of any configuration files you are working on first, before making major changes to the original.

Gedit will let you edit several files at once, opening a tab for each. You can use Gedit to edit any text file, including ones you create yourself. Two commonly edited configuration files are

/etc/default/grub and **/etc/fstab**. The **/etc/fstab** file lists all your file systems and how they are mounted, and **/etc/default/grub** file is the configuration file for your Grub 2 boot loader.

You also can specify the file to edit when you first start up gedit.

```
sudo gedit /etc/default/grub
```

User configuration files, dot files, can be changed by individual users directly without administrative access. An example of a user configuration file is the **.profile** file, which configures your login shell. Dot files like **.profile** have to be chosen from the file manager window, not from the Gedit open operation. First configure the file manager to display dot files by opening the Preferences dialog (select Preferences in the Edit menu of any file manager window), then check the Show Hidden Files entry, and close the dialog. This displays the dot files in your file manager window. Double-click the file to open it in Gedit.

GRUB 2

The Grand Unified Bootloader (GRUB) is a multiboot boot loader used for most Linux distributions. Linux and Unix operating systems are known as multiboot operating systems and take arguments passed to them at boot time. With GRUB, users can select operating systems to run from a menu interface displayed when a system boots up. Use arrow keys to move to an entry and press ENTER. If, instead you need to edit an entry, press **e**, letting you change kernel arguments or specify a different kernel. The **c** command places you in a command line interface. Provided your system BIOS supports very large drives, GRUB can boot from anywhere on them. For detailed information on Grub2 on Ubuntu, check the Ubuntu Grub2 Wiki at:

```
https://wiki.ubuntu.com/Grub2
```

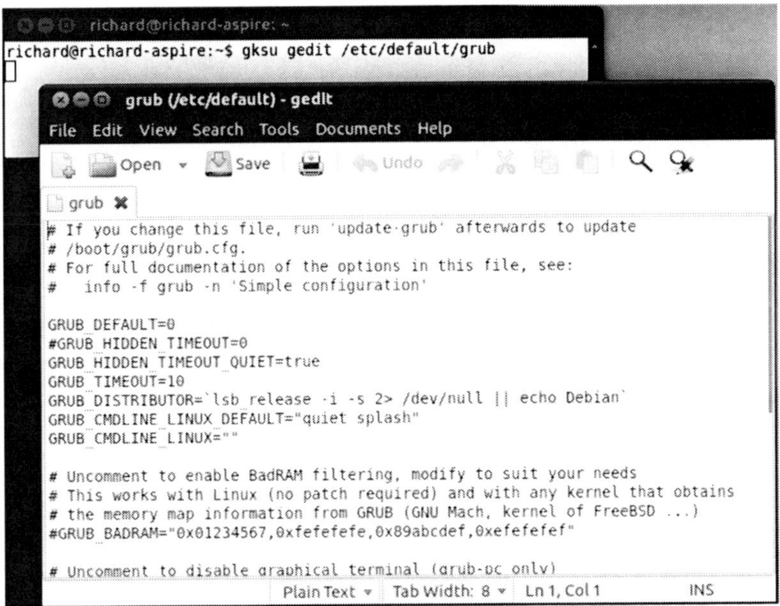

Figure 14-43: Editing the /etc/default/grub file

Check the GRUB Man page for GRUB options. GRUB is a GNU project with its home page at **http://www.gnu.org/software/grub**, the manual at **http://grub.enbug.org/Manual**, and Wiki at **http://grub.enbug.org**. The Ubuntu forums have several helpful thread on using Grub2 on Ubuntu, **http://ubuntuforums.org**. Search on Grub2.

Grub2 detects and generates a menu for you automatically. You do not have to worry about keeping a menu file updated. All your operating systems and Ubuntu kernels are detected when the system starts up, and a menu to display them as boot options is generated at that time.

With Grub2, configuration is placed in user-modifiable configuration files held in the **/etc/default/grub** file and in the **/etc/grub.d** directory. There is a Grub2 configuration file called **/boot/grub/grub.cfg**, but this file is generated by Grub each time the system starts up, and should never be edited by a user. Instead you edit the **/etc/default/grub** file to set parameters like the default operating system to boot. To create your own menu entries, you create entries for them in the **/etc/grub.d/40_custom** file.

Grub options are set by assigning values to Grub options in the **/etc/default/grub** file. You can edit the file directly to change these options (see Figure 14-43). To edit the file with the Gedit editor, open a terminal window and enter the following command. You will be prompted to enter your password.

```
gksu gedit /etc/default/grub
```

You can then edit the file carefully. The **grub** file used on Ubuntu 12.04 is shown here:

/etc/default/grub

```
# If you change this file, run 'update-grub' afterwards to update
# /boot/grub/grub.cfg.

GRUB_DEFAULT=0
#GRUB_HIDDEN_TIMEOUT=0
GRUB_HIDDEN_TIMEOUT_QUIET=true
GRUB_TIMEOUT="10"
GRUB_DISTRIBUTOR=`lsb_release -i -s 2> /dev/null || echo Debian`
GRUB_CMDLINE_LINUX_DEFAULT="quiet splash"
GRUB_CMDLINE_LINUX=""

# Uncomment to enable BadRAM filtering, modify to suit your needs
# This works with Linux (no patch required) and with any kernel that obtains
# the memory map information from GRUB (GNU Mach, kernel of FreeBSD ...)
#GRUB_BADRAM="0x01234567,0xfefefefe,0x89abcdef,0xefefefef"

# Uncomment to disable graphical terminal (grub-pc only)
#GRUB_TERMINAL=console

# The resolution used on graphical terminal
# note that you can use only modes which your graphic card supports via VBE
# you can see them in real GRUB with the command `vbeinfo'
#GRUB_GFXMODE=640x480

# Uncomment if you don't want GRUB to pass "root=UUID=xxx" parameter to Linux
#GRUB_DISABLE_LINUX_UUID=true
```

```
# Uncomment to disable generation of recovery mode menu entrys
#GRUB_DISABLE_LINUX_RECOVERY="true"

# Uncomment to get a beep at grub start
#GRUB_INIT_TUNE="480 440 1"
```

For dual boot systems (those with both Ubuntu and Windows or Mac), the option users are likely to change is GRUB_DEFAULT which set the operating system or kernel to boot automatically if one is not chosen. The option uses a line number to indicate an entry in the Grub boot menu, with numbering starting from 0 (not 1). First, check your Grub menu when you boot up (press any key on boot to display the Grub menu for a longer time) and then count to where the entry of the operating system you want to make the default is listed. If the Windows entry is at 4th, which would be line 3 (counting from 0), to make it the default you would set the GRUB_DEAULT option to 3.

```
GRUB_DEFAULT=3
```

Should the listing of operating systems and kernels change (adding or removing kernels), you would have to edit the **/etc/default/grub** file again and each time a change occurs. A safer way to set the default is to configure GRUB to use the **grub-set-default** command. First edit the **/etc/default/grub** file and change the option for GRUB_DEFAULT to **saved**.

```
GRUB_DEFAULT=saved
```

Then update GRUB.

```
sudo update-grub
```

The **grub-set-default** command takes as its option the number of the default you want to set (numbering from 0), or the name of the kernel or operating system. The following sets the default to 0, the first kernel entry.

```
sudo grub-set-default 0
```

For a kernel name or operating system, you can use the name as it appears on the GRUB menu (enclosing the name in quotes), such as:

```
sudo grub-set-default  'Windows XP (loader) (on /dev/sda1)'
```

The GRUB_TIMEOUT option sets the number of seconds Grub will wait to allow a user to access the menu, before booting the default operating system. The default options used for Ubuntu kernels are listed by the GRUB_CMDLINE_LINUX_DEFAULT option. Currently these include the **splash** and **quiet** options to display the Ubuntu emblem on start up (**splash**), but not the list of startup tasks being performed (**quiet**).

Once you have made your changes, you have to run the **update-grub** command with **sudo**, as noted in the first line of the **/etc/default/grub** file. Otherwise your changes will not take effect. This command will generate a new **/etc/grub/grub.cfg** file, which determines the actual Grub 2 configuration.

```
sudo update-grub
```

You add your own Grub2 boot entries by placing them in the **/etc/grub.d/40_custom** file. The file is nearly empty except for an initial **exec tail** command that you must take care not to change. Samples of added entries are shown on the Ubuntu Grub2 Wiki,

https://wiki.ubuntu.com/Grub2. After you make your additions to the **40_custom** file, you have to run **sudo update-grub** to have the changes take effect.

When the GRUB package is updated by Ubuntu, you will be given the choice to keep your current local version or use the maintainer's version. Keeping the local version is selected by default. However, unless you have extensively customized your configuration, it is always advisable to select the maintainer's version. The maintainer's version is the most up-to-date. If you had made any changes previously to the **/etc/default/grub** file, you will have to edit that file and make the same changes again, such as setting the default operating system to load. Be sure to run **sudo update-grub** to make the changes take effect.

Backup Management: Ubuntu One, rsync, BackupPC, and Amanda

Backup operations have become an important part of administrative duties. Several backup tools are provided on Linux systems, including Amanda and the traditional dump/restore tools, as well as the **rsync** command used for making individual copies. You can even use the Ubuntu One service for limited backups. The new Deja Dup is a front end for the duplicity backup tool, which uses rsync to generate backup archives. Deja Dup is the recommended default backup tool, available from the System Settings dialog as Backup. Amanda provides server-based backups, letting different systems on a network back up to a central server. BackupPC provides network and local backup using configured **rsync** and **tar** tools. The dump tools let you refine your backup process, detecting data changed since the last backup. Table 14-2 lists Web sites for Linux backup tools.

Website	Tools
`http://rsync.samba.org`	rsync remote copy backup
`https://launchpad.net/deja-dup` `http://www.nongnu.org/duplicity`	Deja Dup front end for duplicity which uses rsync to perform basic backups
`http://www.amanda.org`	Amanda network backup
`http://dump.sourceforge.net`	dump and restore tools
`http://backuppc.sourceforge.net`	BackupPC network or local backup using configured rsync and tar tools.

Table 14-2: Backup Resources

Online backup using Ubuntu One

Though a synchronization service for connected Ubuntu computers, the Ubuntu One file and folder synchronization service provides, in effect, a current online backup for specific files and folders in the user's Ubuntu One folder or a designated synchronized folder. If your system fails, you can restore those folders and files by simply enabling the Ubuntu One service on your new system. The backup operations apply only to the file and folders in the user's Ubuntu One directory, not to any other data. The advantage to using Ubuntu One is that it is automatic. Simply drag a file to the Ubuntu One folder (or modify it in that folder), and the Ubuntu One service will detect the change and perform the upload for you. See Chapter 8 for more information on Ubuntu One,

https://one.ubuntu.com. You can also use Deja Dup to place backup files on your Ubuntu One account.

Note: The Ubuntu one file synchronization and sharing service operates like DropBox. For more advanced file synchronization and backup features like versioning, you may want to consider DropBox for Linux, **http://www.getdropbox.com/install?os=lnx**.

Deja Dup

Deja Dup is a front end for the duplicity backup tool, which uses rsync to generate backup archives (**http://www.nongnu.org/duplicity/**). You can access Deja Dup from the System Settings dialog or from the System dash as Backup. Initially you are prompted to either restore your files or to show your backup settings (see Figure 14-44). Clicking on restore performs an immediate restore operation. If you encrypted your backups, you have to provide the encryption password.

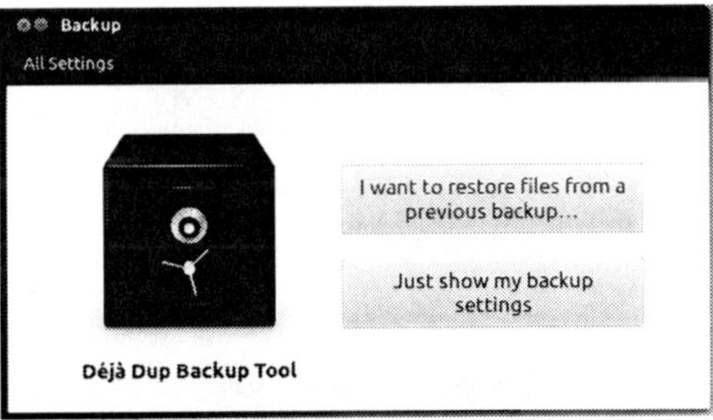

Figure 14-44: Deja Dup initial System Settings backup dialog

The deja-dup settings dialog show tabs for Overview, Storage, Folders, and Schedule (see Figure 14-45). The Overview tab provides information about your backup configuration, showing the folders to backup, those ignored, and the dates of the last and next backups. A switch allows you to turn automatic backups on and off. Click the Help button to display the Deja Dup manual.

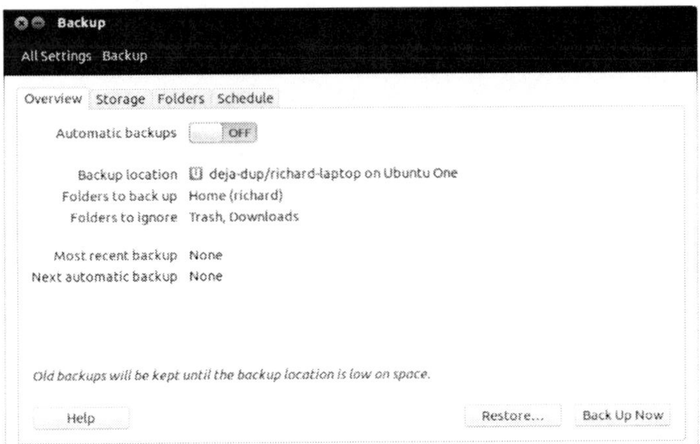

Figure 14-45: Deja Dup settings: overview

The Storage tab lets you specify a location to store your backups (see Figure 14-46). By default, this is set to Ubuntu One, which backs up to your Ubuntu One account. You can choose different locations to use instead, such as an FTP account, Amazon S3 cloud account, SSH server, Samba (Windows) share, or a local folder. Choose the one you want from the "Backup location" menu. With each choice, you are prompted for the appropriate configuration information (see Figure 14-47).

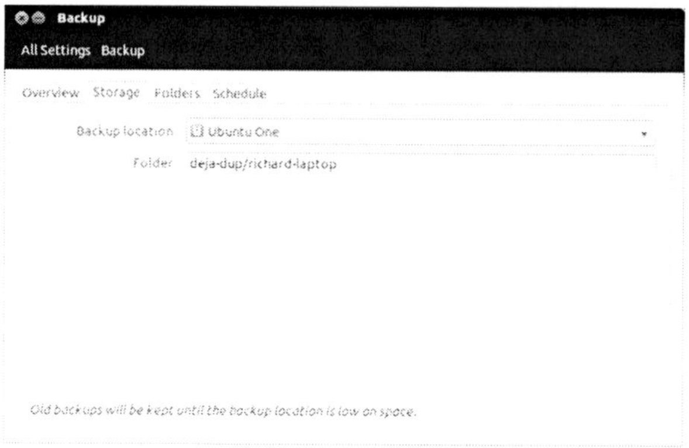

Figure 14-46: Deja Dup settings: storage

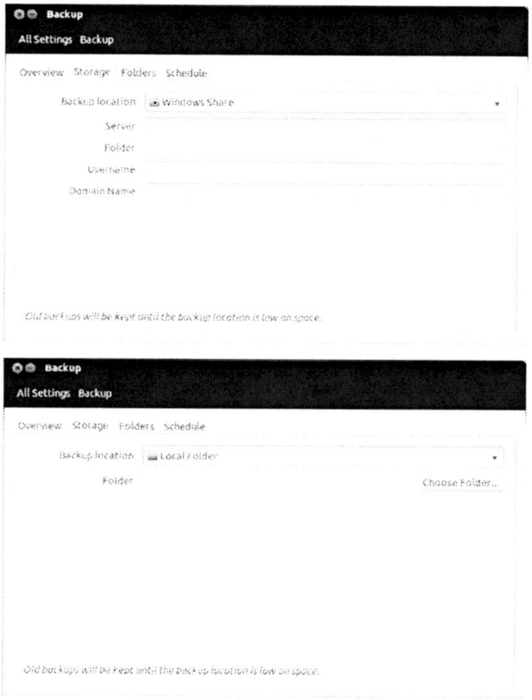

Figure 14-47: Deja Dup settings: storage for WIndows share and Local folder

The Folders tab lets you specify folders you want to backup and folders to ignore (see Figure 14-48). Click the plus button (**+**) at the bottom of the folders list to add a new folder for backup. Do the same to specify folders to ignore. The minus button removes folders from the list.

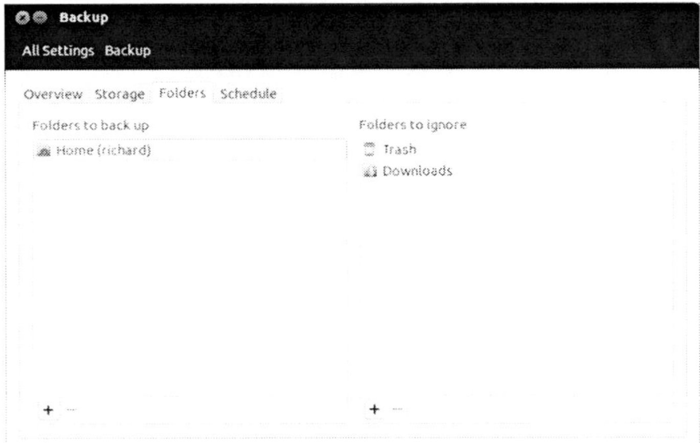

Figure 14-48: Deja Dup settings: backup folders

On the Schedule tab, you specify the frequency of your backups, and how long to keep them (see Figure 14-49). Backups can be performed daily, weekly, every two weeks, or monthly. They can be kept for a week, month, several months, a year, or forever.

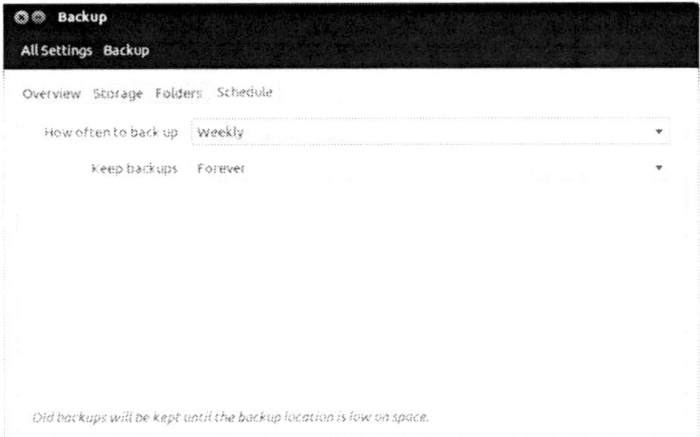

Figure 14-49: Deja Dup settings: backup times

When you perform a backup, you are prompted to backup with or without encryption. For encrypted backups, you are prompted to enter a password, which you will need to restore the files (see Figure 14-50).

Figure 14-50: Deja Dup backup: encryption

When restoring you are prompted to specify the location you are backing up from, the backup date to restore from, and whether to restore to the original location or a specific folder.

Figure 14-51: Deja Dup restore

Individual Backups: archive and rsync

You can back up and restore particular files and directories with archive tools like **tar**, restoring the archives later. For backups, **tar** is used usually with a tape device. To schedule automatic backups, you can schedule appropriate **tar** commands with the **cron** utility. The archives can be also compressed for storage savings. You can then copy the compressed archives to any medium, such as a DVD disc, a floppy, or tape. On GNOME you can use File Roller (Archive Manager) to create archives easily (Accessories dash). The Archive Manager menu entry is not displayed initially, use Main Menu to have it displayed Accessories dash.

File Roller also supports LZMA compression, a more efficient and faster compression method. On Archive Manager, when creating a new archive, select "Tar compressed with lzma (.tar.lzma)" for the Archive type. When choosing Create Archive from Nautilus file manager window on selected files, on the Create Archive dialog, choose the **.lzma** file type for just compression, and the **.tar.lzma** type for a compressed archive.

If you want to remote-copy a directory or files from one host to another, making a particular backup, you can use **rsync**, which is designed for network backups of particular directories or files, intelligently copying only those files that have been changed, rather than the contents of an entire directory. In archive mode, it can preserve the original ownership and permissions, providing corresponding users exist on the host system. The following example copies the **/home/george/myproject** directory to the **/backup** directory on the host **rabbit**, creating a corresponding **myproject** subdirectory. The **-t** specifies that this is a transfer. The remote host is referenced with an attached colon, **rabbit:**

```
rsync -t /home/george/myproject   rabbit:/backup
```

If, instead, you wanted to preserve the ownership and permissions of the files, you would use the **-a** (archive) option. Adding a **-z** option will compress the file. The **-v** option provides a verbose mode.

```
rsync -avz  /home/george/myproject   rabbit:/backup
```

A trailing slash on the source will copy the contents of the directory, rather than generating a subdirectory of that name. Here the contents of the **myproject** directory are copied to the **george-project** directory.

```
rsync -avz  /home/george/myproject/   rabbit:/backup/george-project
```

The **rsync** command is configured to use Secure Shell (SSH) remote shell by default. You can specify it or an alternate remote shell to use with the **-e** option. For secure transmission you can encrypt the copy operation with SSH. Either use the **-e ssh** option or set the **RSYNC_RSH** variable to ssh.

```
rsync -avz -e ssh  /home/george/myproject   rabbit:/backup/myproject
```

You can copy from a remote host to the host you are on.

```
rsync -avz  lizard:/home/mark/mypics/  /pic-archice/markpics
```

You can also run rsync as a server daemon. This will allow remote users to synchronize copies of files on your system with versions on their own, transferring only changed files rather than entire directories. Many mirror and software FTP sites operate as rsync servers, letting you update files without have to download the full versions again. Configuration information for rsync as a server is kept in the **/etc/rsyncd.conf** file.

Tip: Though it is designed for copying between hosts, you can also use **rsync** to make copies within your own system, usually to a directory in another partition or hard drive. Check the **rsync** Man page for detailed descriptions of each.

BackupPC

BackupPC provides an easily managed local or network backup of your system or hosts on a system using configured rsync or tar tools. There is no client application to install, just configuration files. BackupPC can back up hosts on a network, including servers, or just a single system. Data can be backed up to local hard disks or to network storage such as shared partitions or storage servers. You can configure BackupPC using your Web page configuration interface. This is the host name of your computer with the **/backuppc** name attached, like **http://richard1/backuppc**. Detailed documentation is installed at **/usr/share/doc/BackupPC**. You can find out more about BackupPC at **http://backuppc.sourceforge.net**. You can install BackupPC using the Synaptic Package Manager, Utilities section, and from the Ubuntu Software Center | System | backuppc. Canonical provides critical updates.

BackupPC uses both compression and detection of identical files to reduce the size of the backup, allowing several hosts to be backed up in limited space. Once an initial backup is performed, BackupPC will only back up changed files, reducing the time of the backup significantly.

BackupPC has its own service script with which you start the BackupPC service, **/etc/init.d/backuppc**. Configuration files are located at **/etc/BackupPC**. The **config.pl** file holds BackupPC configuration options and the **hosts** file lists hosts to be backed up.

Amanda

To back up hosts connected to a network, you can use the Advanced Maryland Automatic Network Disk Archiver (Amanda) to archive hosts. Amanda uses **tar** tools to back up all hosts to a single host operating as a backup server. Backup data is sent by each host to the host operating as the Amanda server, where they are written out to a backup medium such as tape. With an Amanda server, the backup operations for all hosts become centralized in one server, instead of each host having to perform its backup. Any host that needs to restore data simply requests it from the Amanda server, specifying the file system, date, and filenames. Backup data is copied to the server's holding disk and from there to tapes. Detailed documentation and updates are provided at **http://www.amanda.org**. For the server, be sure to install the amanda-server package, and for clients you use the amanda-clients package. You can install Amanda using the Synaptic Package Manager, Utilities (universe) section, and from the Ubuntu Software Center | System | amanda. Canonical does not provide critical updates.

15. Network Connections

Ubuntu will automatically detect and configure your network connections with Network Manager. Should the automatic configuration either fail or be incomplete for some reason, you can use Network Manager to perform a manual configuration (on Ubuntu choose Network Connections on the Customization dash or Edit Connections from the Network Manager menu). If you want to make a simple dial-up modem connection you can use WvDial. Your network will also need a firewall. UFW (with the Gufw interface) or Firestarter is recommended. Table 15-1 lists several network configuration tools. You can also use the GNOME Network dialog (System Settings) for quick wireless and wired connections, as well as proxy configuration (see Chapter 3).

Network Connections: Dynamic and Static

If you are on a network, you may need to obtain certain information to configure your connection interface. Most networks now support dynamic configuration using either the older Dynamic Host Configuration Protocol (DHCP) or the new IPv6 Protocol and its automatic address configuration. In this case, you need only check the DHCP entry in most network configuration tools. If your network does not support DHCP or IPv6 automatic addressing, or you are using a static connection (DCHP and IPv6 connections are dynamic), you will have to provide detailed information about your connection. For a static connection, you enter your connection information manually such as your IP address and DNS servers, whereas in a dynamic connection this information is provided automatically to your system by a DHCP server or generated by IPv6 when you connect to the network. For DHCP, a DHCP client on each host will obtain the information from a DHCP server serving that network. IPv6 generates its addresses directly from the device and router information such as the device hardware MAC address.

Network Configuration Tool	Description
Network Manager	Automates wireless and wired network connection, selection, and notification (System | Preferences | Network Connections). Used for all network connections including wired, wireless, mobile broadband, VPN, and DSL.
Network (System Settings)	GNOME Network connection preferences, allowing quick connection to wired and wireless networks. Use to set up proxy configuration. Uses Network Manager for network configuration.
ufw	Sets up a network firewall.
Gufw	GNOME interface for UFW firewall
Firestarter	Sets up a network firewall.
wvdial	PPP dial-up modem connection

Table 15-1: Ubuntu Network Configuration Tools

In addition, if you are using a dynamic DSL, ISDN, or a modem connection, you will also have to supply provider, login, and password information, and specify whether your system is dynamic or static. You may also need to supply specialized information such as DSL or modem compression methods or dialup number.

You can obtain most of your static network information from your network administrator or from your ISP (Internet Service Provider). You would need the following information:

The device name for your network interface   For LAN and wireless connections, this is usually an Ethernet card with the name **eth0** or **eth1**. For a modem, DSL, or ISDN connection, this is a PPP device named **ppp0** (**ippp0** for ISDN).

Hostname   Your computer will be identified by this name on the Internet. Do not use localhost; that name is reserved for special use by your system. The name of the host should be a simple word, which can include numbers, but not punctuation such as periods and backslashes. On a small network, the hostname is often a single name. On a large network that could have several domains, the hostname includes both the name of the host and its domain.

Domain name   This is the name of your network.

The Internet Protocol (IP) address assigned to your machine   This is needed only for static Internet connections. Dynamic connections use the DHCP protocol to assign an IP address for you automatically. Every host on the Internet is assigned an IP address. Small and older network addresses might still use the older IPv4 format consisting of a set of four numbers, separated by periods. The IP protocol version 6, IPv6, uses a new format with a complex numbering sequence that is much more automatic.

Your network IP address   Static connections only. This address is similar to the IP address, but lacks any reference to a particular host.

The netmask   IPv4 Static connections only. This is usually 255.255.255.0 for most networks. If, however, you are part of a large network, check with your network administrator or ISP.

The broadcast address for your network, if available (optional)   IPv4 Static connections only. Usually, your broadcast address is the same as your IP address with the number 255 added at the end.

The IP address of your network's gateway computer   Static connections only. This is the computer that connects your local network to a larger one like the Internet.

Name servers   The IP address of the name servers your network uses. These enable the use of URLs.

NIS domain and IP address for an NIS server   Necessary if your network uses an NIS server (optional).

User login and password information   Needed for dynamic DSL, ISDN, and modem connections.

Network Manager

Network Manager detects your network connections automatically, both wired and wireless. It uses the automatic device detection capabilities of udev to configure your connections. Should you instead need to configure your network connections manually, you also use Network Manager to enter the required network connection information. Network Manager operates as a daemon with the name Network Manager. It will automatically scan for both wired and wireless connections. Information provided by Network Manager is made available to other applications. The Network Manager monitors your network connection, indicating its current status on the indicator (status) menu on the top panel.

Network Manager is designed to work in the background, providing status information for your connection and switching from one configured connection to another as needed. For an initial configuration, it detects as much information as possible about a new connection.

Network Manager is also user specific. When a user logs in, wireless connections the user prefers will start up (wired connections are started automatically).

Network Manager menu

Basic network connection operations are discussed in Chapter 3.

Network Manager displays a Network menu on the right side of the Ubuntu desktop's top panel. The Network Manager icon will vary according to the type of connection. An Ethernet (wired) connection displays two arrows (other desktop themes may display two computer monitors, one in front of the other). A wireless connection displays a staggered wave graph (see Figure 15-1). If the connection is not active, an empty wave graph is shown. If you have both a wired and wireless connection, and the wired connection is active, the wired connection icon is used.

Figure 15-1: Network Manager wired, wireless, and disconnect icons.

On Ubuntu Unity click on the network menu to list network options. Options include editing your connection, shutting off your connection (Enable Networking and Enable Wireless), and to see information about the connection (see Figure 15-2). A computer with both wired and wireless connections will have entries to Enable Networking and Enable Wireless. Selecting Enable Wireless will disconnect only the wireless connections, leaving the wired connection active. The Enable Wireless checkbox will become unchecked and a message is displayed telling you that your wireless connection is disconnected. Selecting Enable Networking will disable your wired connection, along with any wireless connections. Do this to work offline, without any network access.

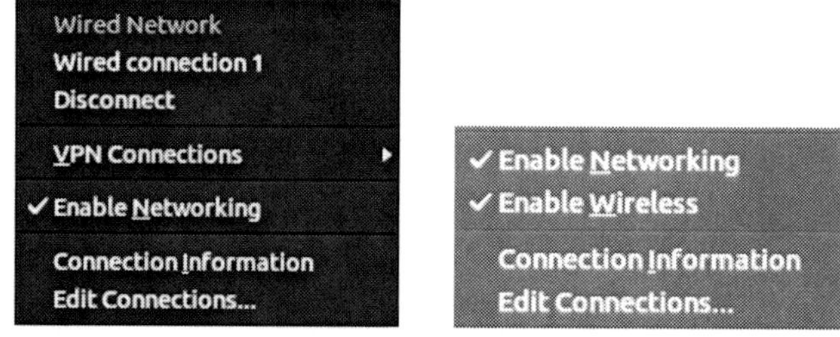

Figure 15-2: Network Manager options

A computer with only a wired network device (no wireless) will only show an Enable Networking entry. Selecting it disconnects you from any network access, allowing you to work offline.

Network Manager manual configuration for all network connections

Should you need to edit any network connection, wired or wireless, you choose Edit Connections from the Network menu (see Figure 15-2). This opens Network Manager's Network Connections window as shown in Figure 15-3. Established connections are listed, with Add, Edit, and Delete buttons for adding, editing, and removing network connections. Your current network connections should be listed, having been detected automatically. In the Figure 15-3 a wired Ethernet connection referred to as **Wired connection 1** is listed, the first Ethernet connection. This is an automatic configuration set up by Network Manager when it automatically connected to the wired network.

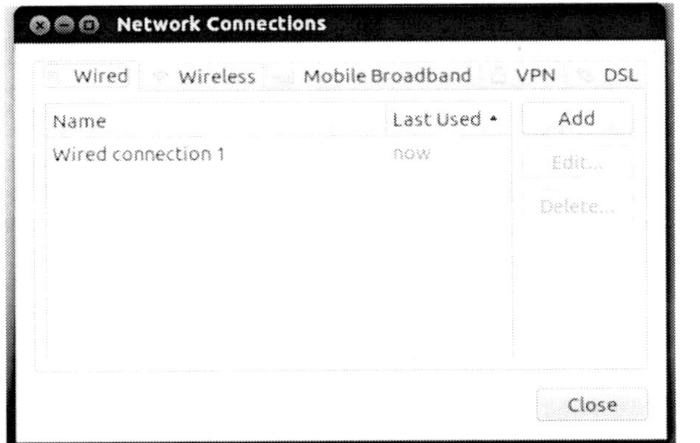

Figure 15-3: Network configuration

On the Network Connections window there are five tabs: Wired, Wireless, Mobile Broadband, VPN, and DSL.

Wired: The wired connection is used for the standard IPv4 and IPv6 Ethernet connections, featuring support for DHCP and manual Ethernet settings.

Wireless: The Wireless tab is where you enter in wireless configuration data like your ESSID, password, and encryption method.

Mobile Broadband: The mobile broadband tab is the wireless 3G configuration's, with selection for the service you are using. For manual configuration a 3G configuration wizard is provided.

VPN: The VPN tab lets you specify a virtual private network. Be sure the VPN support packages for Network Manager are installed on your system.

DSL: The DSL tab lets you set up a direct DSL connection.

Each tab will list their configured network connections. Click on the Add or Edit buttons to configure a new network connection of that type, or edit an existing one.

All configuration editing dialogs display an option at the bottom of the dialog to allow you to make your configuration available to all users, the "Available to all users" check box. In effect, this option implements a system wide network connection configuration.

Wired Configuration

To edit a wired connection, select the connection and click the Edit button on the Wired tab. This opens an Editing window as shown in Figure 15-4. The Add button is used to add a new connection and opens a similar window, with no settings.

Figure 15-4: DHCP Wired Configuration

Figure 15-5: Manual IPv4 Wired Configuration

There are four tabs: Wired, 8.02.1x Security, IPv4 Settings, and IPv6 Settings. The Wired tab lists the MAC hardware address and the MTU. The MTU is usually set to automatic. Figure 15-4 shows the standard default configuration for a wired Ethernet connection using DHCP.

The IPv4 and IPv6 Settings tabs let you select the kind of protocol your wired connection uses. A check box at the bottom of the dialog lets you require the given protocol to complete the connection. The IPv4 and IPv6 have different entries. The IPv4 options are:

Automatic (DHCP): DHCP connection, address information is blocked out.

Automatic (DHCP) addresses only: DHCP connection that lets you specify your DNS server addresses.

Manual: Enter your IP, network, and gateway addresses along with your DNS server addresses and your network domain name.

Link-local only: IPv6 private local network. All address entries are blocked out.

Shared to other computers: All address entries are blocked out.

Figure 15-6: Manual IPv6 Wired Configuration

The IPv6 options are:

Ignore: Do not use IPv6.

Automatic: IPv6 automatic address detection (similar to DHCP).

Automatic, addresses only: Use IPv6 to determine network addresses, but not DNS (domain) information. You can enter the DNS server addresses and search domains manually.

Manual: Enter your IP, network, and gateway addresses along with your DNS server addresses and your network domain name. IPv6 addresses use an address and a prefix.

Link-local only: IPv6 private local network. All address entries are blocked out.

Figure 15-5 shows the manual configuration entries for an IPv4 wired Ethernet connection. Click the Add button to enter the IP address, network mask, and gateway address. Then enter the address for the DNS servers and your network search domains. The Routes button will open a window where you can manually enter any network routes. Figure 15-6 shows the manual configuration for an IPv6 connection, with address and prefix entries for the address.

The 802.1 tab allows you to configure 802.1 security, if your network supports it (see Figure 15-7).

Figure 15-7: 802.1 Security Configuration

Wireless Configuration

Wireless connections are listed on the Network Connections window's Wireless tab. To add or edit a wireless connection, you use the Add or Edit buttons on the Wireless tab. When you click the Edit button, the Editing window opens with tabs for your wireless information, security, IPv4, and IPv6 settings (See Figure 15-8). On the Wireless tab you specify your SSID, along with your Mode and MAC address.

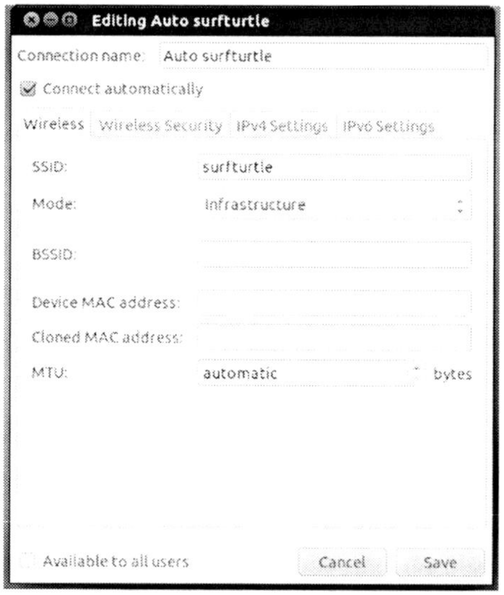

Figure 15-8: Wireless configuration

On the Wireless Security tab you enter your wireless connection security method (see Figure 15-9). The commonly used method, WEP, is supported, along with WPA personal. The

WPA personal method only requires a password. More secure connections like Dynamic WEP and Enterprise WPA are also supported. These will require more configuration information such as authentication methods, certificates, and keys.

On the IPv4 Settings tab you enter your wireless connection's network address settings. This tab is the same as the IPv4 Setting on the Wired connection (see Figures 15-5). You have the same options: DHCP, DHCP with DNS addresses, Manual, Link-local only, and Shared. If your wireless connection uses the IPv6 protocol, you would use the IPv6 Settings tab, also the same as IPv6 Settings on a wired connection (see Figure 15-6).

Note: For the command line interface you can use the **iwconfig** tools to configure and access your wireless connections.

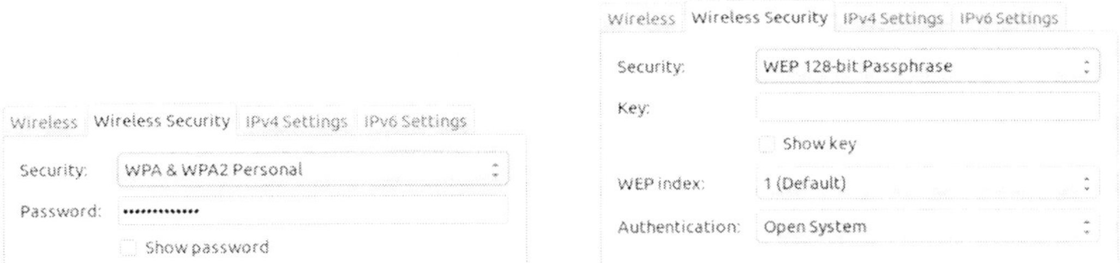

Figure 15-9: Wireless Security: WEP and WPA

DSL Configuration

To add or edit a direct DSL connection, you click the Add or Edit buttons on the Network Connections window's DSL tab. The DSL connection window opens, showing tabs for DSL configuration and for wired, PPP, and IPv4 network connections. On the DSL tab you enter your DSL user name, service provider, and password (see Figure 15-10). A wired connection requires a MAC address and MTU byte amount. The PPP tab is the same as that used for Mobile Broadband, and IPv4 is the same as the IPv4 Settings tab used for Wired, Wireless, and Mobile Broadband connections (see Figure 15-5).

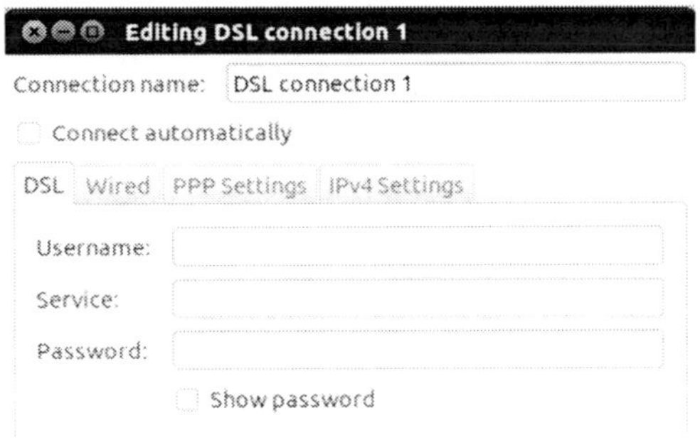

Figure 15-10: DSL manual configuration

Mobile Broadband: 3G Support

Mobile Broadband 3G connections are listed in the Mobile Broadband tab. For a new broadband connection, click the Add button. A 3G wizard starts up to help you set up the appropriate configuration for your particular 3G service (see Figure 15-11). Configuration steps are listed on the left pane. If your device is connected, you can select it from the drop-down menu on the right pane. On the next step you choose your country. The 3G wizard then displays a service provider window listing 3G service providers (see Figure 15-12). You then select the billing plan. For the last step you are asked to confirm your selections.

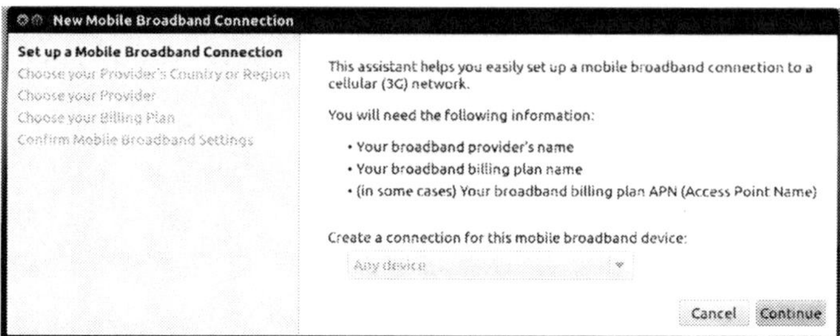

Figure 15-11: 3G Wizard

Once a service is selected, you can further edit the configuration by clicking its entry in the Mobile Broadband tab and clicking the Edit button. The Editing window opens with tabs for Mobile Broadband, PPP, IPv4 settings. On the Mobile Broadband tab you can enter your number, user name, and password. Advanced options include the APN, Network, and PIN(see Figure 15-13). The APN should already be entered.

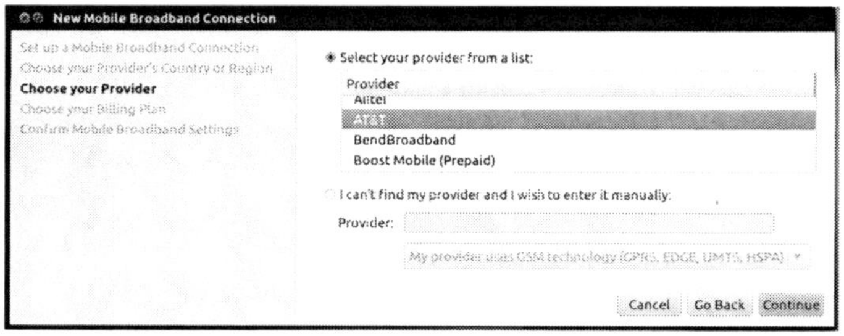

Figure 15-12: 3G Provider Listings

PPP Configuration

For either Wireless Broadband or DSL connections you also can specify PPP information. The PPP tab is the same for both (See Figure 15-14). There are Authentication, Compression, and the Echo sections. Check which features are supported by your particular PPP connection. For Authentication, click the Configure Methods button to open a dialog listing possible authentication methods. Check the ones your connection supports.

Figure 15-13: 3G configuration

Network Manager VPN

On the Network Manager menu, the VPN Connection entry submenu will list configured VPN connections for easy access. The Configure VPN entry will open the Network Connections window to the VPN tab where you can then add, edit, or delete VPN connections. The Disconnect VPN entry will end the current active VPN connection.

Several VPN services are available. The PPTP service for Microsoft VPN connections is installed by default, **network-manager-pptp**. Other popular VPN services include OpenVPN, Cisco Concentrator, and Strongswan (IPSec). For Network Manager support be sure to install the corresponding Network Manager plugin for these services. The plugin packages begin with the name **network-manager**. To use the **openvpn** service, first install the **openvpn** software along with the **network-manager-openvpn** plugin (Universe repository). For Cisco Concentrator based VPN, us the **network-manager-vpnc** plugin, and for Cisco OpenConnect use **network-manager-openconnect**. Strongswan uses the **network-manager-strongswan** plugin. To see a list of available VPN services search on vpn in the Ubuntu Software Center or in the Synaptic Package Manager.

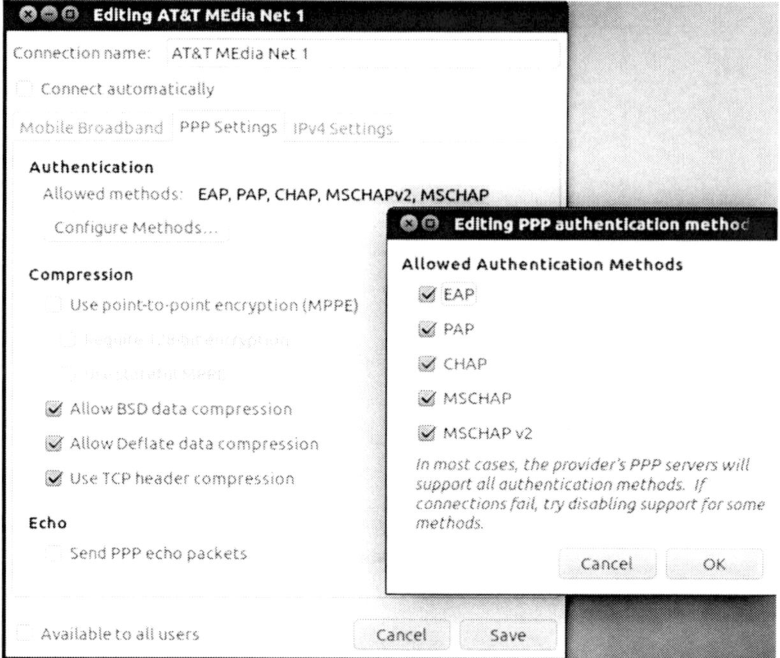

Figure 15-14: PPP Configuration

To add a VPN connection click on the Add button in the Network Connections window VPN tab. You are prompted to choose a VPN Connection Type, which you can select from the drop down menu. Options will vary according to the number of VPN Network Manager plugins you have installed (see Figure 15-15).

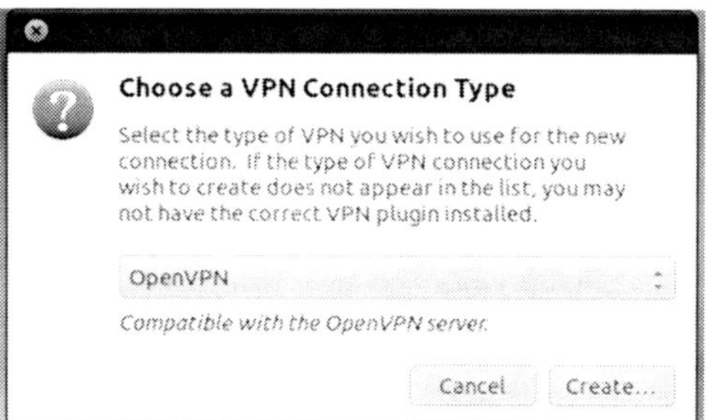
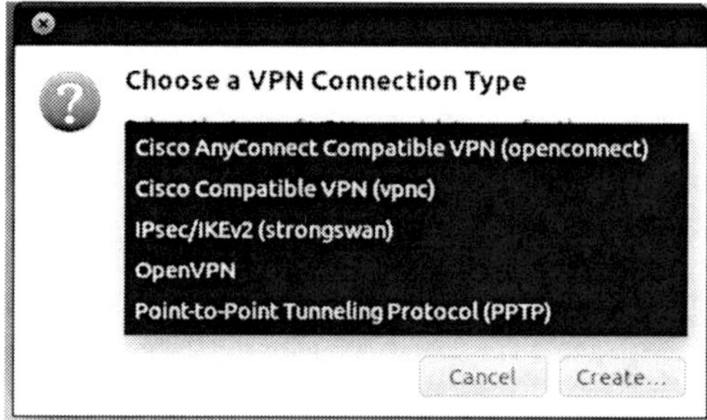

Figure 15-15: VPN Connection Type

The "Editing VPN connection" dialog then opens with two tabs: VPN and IPv4 Settings. On the VPN tab you enter VPN connection information such as the gateway address and any additional VPN information that may be required. For an OpenVPN connection you will need to provide the authentication type, certificates, and keys (see Figure 15-16). Clicking on the Advanced button opens the Advanced Options dialog. An OpenVPN connection will have tabs for General, Security, and TLS Authentication. On the Security tab you can specify the cipher to use.

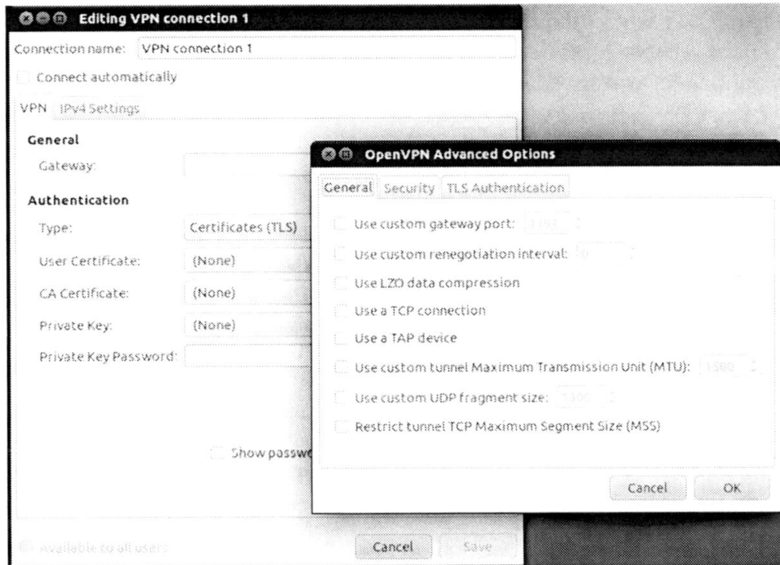

Figure 15-16: VPN configuration (openvpn)

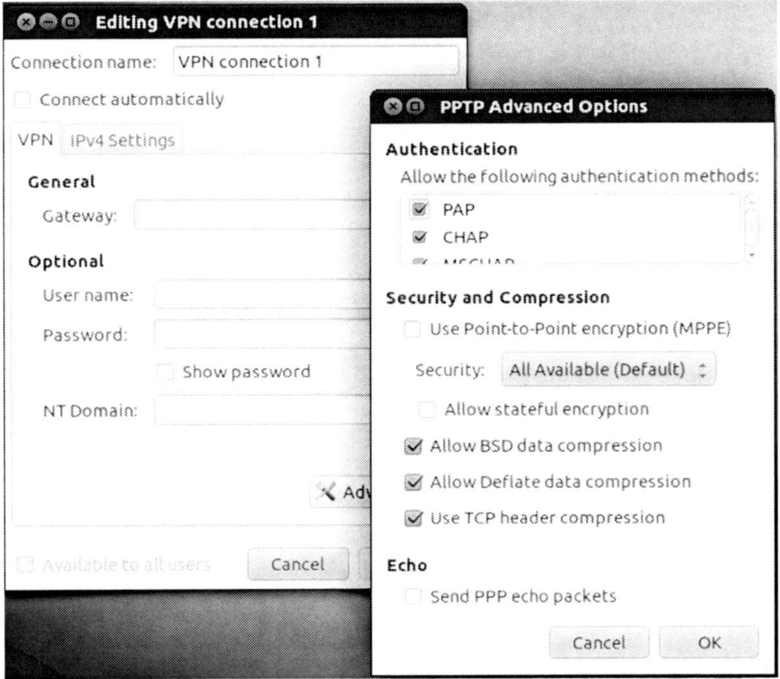

Figure 15-17: VPN configuration (pptp)

Options will differ depending on the type of VPN connection you choose. The PPTP connection used on Microsoft networks requires only a gateway address on the VPN tab. Advanced options let you specify the authentication method and security options (see Figure 15-17). Like OpenVPN, a Strongswan IPSec connection also requires certificates and keys. It does not have an Advanced Options dialog. The IPv4 tab lets you specify your DNS servers if you want. The Cisco Connector connection only requires a group name and password. You also can specify the encryption method, domain, and user name.

Network Manager wireless router, using your wireless connection as a wireless router.

You can also set up your wireless connection as a wireless router for your own wireless network. The "Create New Wireless Network" entry in the network menu opens a dialog letting you set up your computer as a wireless router that other computers can connect to (see Figure 15-18). Enter a Network name, select the kind of wireless security you want to use, and enter a password for accessing the network. You will be prompted to enter your keyring password.

Figure 15-18: Create New Wireless Network

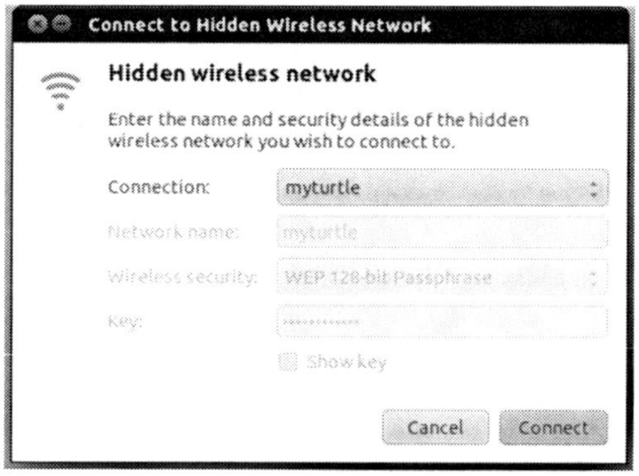

**Figure 15-19: Connect to a Hidden network

The wireless network you created will not perform any SSID broadcasting. You access it through the "Connect to Hidden Wireless network" entry on the network menu. This opens the "Hidden wireless network" window (see Figure 15-19). Your new wireless network will be listed in the Connection drop-down menu. When you select it, the network name and security information is displayed.

Dial-up PPP Modem Access: wvdial

For direct dial-up PPP modem connections, you can use the wvdial dialer, an intelligent dialer that not only dials up an ISP service but also performs login operations, supplying your username and password. The wvdial tool runs on the command line using the wvdial command, and on the desktop with the GNOME PPP application (Ubuntu Software Center | Internet | GNOME PPP). The wvdial program first loads its configuration from the **/etc/wvdial.conf** file. In this file, you can place modem and account information, including modem speed, ISP phone number, username, and password.

Variable	Description
Inherits	Explicitly inherits from the specified section. By default, sections inherit from the [Dialer Defaults] section.
Modem	The device wvdial should use as your modem. The default is **/dev/modem**.
Baud	The speed at which wvdial communicates with your modem. The default is 57,600 baud.
Init1...Init9	Specifies the initialization strings to be used by your modem; wvdial can use up to 9. The default is "ATZ" for Init1.
Phone	The phone number you want wvdial to dial.
Area Code	Specifies the area code, if any.
Dial Prefix	Specifies any needed dialing prefix—for example, 70 to disable call waiting or 9 for an outside line.
Dial Command	Specifies the dial operation. The default is "ATDT".
Login	Specifies the username you use at your ISP.
Login Prompt	If your ISP has an unusual login prompt, you can specify it here.
Password	Specifies the password you use at your ISP.
Password Prompt	If your ISP has an unusual password prompt, you can specify it here.
Force Address	Specifies a static IP address to use (for ISPs that provide static IP addresses to users).
Auto Reconnect	If enabled, wvdial attempts to reestablish a connection automatically if you are randomly disconnected by the other side. This option is on by default.

Table 15-2: Variables for wvdial

The **wvdial.conf** file is organized into sections, beginning with a section label enclosed in brackets. A section holds variables for different parameters that are assigned values, such as `username = chris`. The default section holds default values inherited by other sections, so you need not repeat them. Table 15-2 lists the wvdial variables.

You can use the **wvdialconf** utility to create a default **wvdial.conf** file, detecting your modem and setting default values for basic features automatically. You can then edit the **wvdial.conf** file and modify the Phone, Username, and Password entries entering your dial-up information. Remove the preceding semicolon (**;**) to unquote the entry. Any line beginning with a semicolon is ignored as a comment.

```
wvdialconf
```

You can also create a named dialer. This is helpful if you have different location or services you log in to.

To start wvdial, enter the command **wvdial** in a terminal window, which then reads the connection configuration information from the **/etc/wvdial.conf** file; wvdial dials the location and initiates the PPP connection, providing your username and password when requested.

```
wvdial
```

You can set up connection configurations for any number of connections in the **/etc/wvdial.conf** file. To select one, enter its label as an argument to the **wvdial** command, as shown here:

```
wvdial mylocation
```

Firewalls

Like all Linux systems, Ubuntu implements a firewall using IPtables. You can choose from several different popular firewall management tools. Ubuntu provides a firewall management tool called the Uncomplicated Firewall (ufw). You can also choose to use other popular management tools like Firestarter or Fwbuilder. Both ufw and Firestarter are covered in this chapter. Search Synaptic Package Manager for "firewall" to see a more complete listing.

Port number	Service
135,137,138,and 445	Samba ports and Microsoft discovery service (445): 135 and 445 use the TCP Protocol, and 137 and 138 use the UDP protocol.
139	Netbios-ssn
22	Secure SHell, ssh
2049	NFS, Linux and Unix shares
631	IPP, Internet Printing Protocol, access to remote Linux/Unix printers
21	FTP
25	SMTP, forward mail
110	POP3, receive mail
143	IMAP, receive mail

Table 15-3: Service ports

Important Firewall Ports

Commonly used services like Linux and Windows file sharing, FTP servers, BitTorrent, and Secure SHell remote access, use certain network connection ports on your system (see Table

15-3). A default firewall configuration will block these ports. You have to configure your firewall to allow access to the ports these services use before those services will work.

For example, to access a Windows share, you not only have to have the Samba service running, but also have to configure your firewall to allow access on ports 135, 137, 138, the ports Samba services use to connect to Windows systems, and port 445 used for Microsoft network discovery. In particular, to allow direct access to the detected shares on your system (Avahi), you have to allow access on port 139. Most can be selected easily as preconfigured items in firewall configuration tools, like Gufw and Firestarter. Some, though, may not be listed.

Setting up a firewall with ufw

The Uncomplicated Firewall, ufw, is the supported firewall application for Ubuntu. It provides a simple firewall that can be managed with the Gufw desktop interface or with **ufw** commands. Like all firewall applications, ufw uses IPtables to define rules and run the firewall. The ufw application is just a management interface for IPtables. The IPtables rule files are held in the **/etc/ufw** directory. Default IPtables rules are kept in **before** and **after** files, with added rules in user files. Firewall configuration for certain packages will be placed in the **/usr/share/ufw.d** directory. The ufw firewall is started up using the **/etc/init.d/ufw** script. You can find out more about ufw at the Ubuntu Firewall site at **https://wiki.ubuntu.com/UncomplicatedFirewall** and at the Ubuntu firewall section in the Ubuntu Server Guide at **http://doc.ubuntu.com**. The Server Guide also shows information on how to implement IP Masquerading on ufw.

Gufw

Gufw provides an easy to use GNOME interface for managing your ufw firewall. A simple interface lets you add rules, both custom and standard. You can install Gufw from the Ubuntu Software Center | Internet | Firewall configuration, or from the Synaptic Package Manager (Universe repository, **gufw** package). On Unity, search on firewall and choose Firewall Configuration on the System dash.

Figure 15-20: Gufw

Gufw will initially open with the firewall disabled with no ports configured. The application is locked initially. Click the unlock button in the lower right corner of the window. The Status button is set to off and the shield image will be gray. To enable the firewall, just click the left side of the Status button, setting the status to on. The shield image will be colored and the firewall rules will be listed. Figure 15-20 shows the firewall enabled and several rules listed such as access to the SSH port (22). Rules for both IPv4 and IPv6 (**v6**) network protocols are listed.

The Gufw dialog has two sections, Actual Status and Rules. The Firewall section has "Incoming" and "Outgoing" drop down menus for setting the default firewall rules. Options are Deny, Reject, or Allow, and are applied to incoming and outgoing traffic respectively. By default, incoming traffic is denied (Deny), and outgoing traffic is allowed (Allow). Rules you specified in the Rules section will make exceptions, allowing only certain traffic in or out. Should you select the Allow option the firewall accepts all incoming traffic. In this case you should set up rules to deny access to some traffic, otherwise the firewall becomes ineffective, allowing access to all traffic.

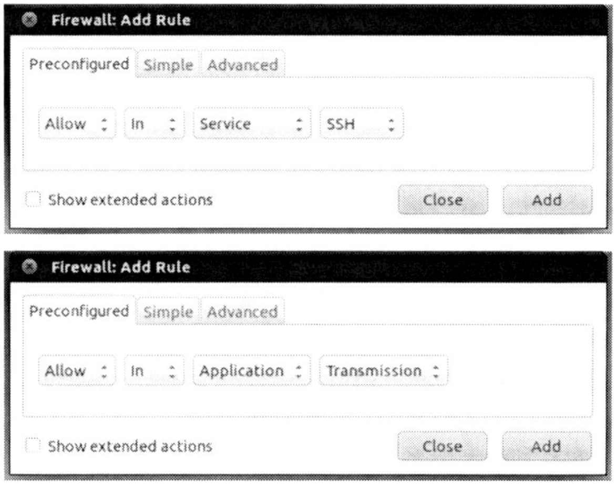

Figure 15-21: Gufw Preconfigured rules

To add a rule, click the plus button (**+**) on the lower left corner to open the "Add rule" dialog, which has three tabs for managing rules: Preconfigured, Simple, and Advanced. The Preconfigured tab provides four drop-down menus: the first for the rule (Allow, Deny, Reject, and Limit), the second for the traffic direction (In or Out), the third for the type of application (Program or Service), and the fourth for the particular application or service for the rule. Should you select Program, then the third menu lists programs such as the Transmission BitTorrent application. If you select Service, then services like SSH, Samba, and FTP are listed. If you allow all outgoing connections you will not have to specify any Out rules. You will only need rules for incoming traffic.

To allow connections for trusted service like SSH, you select Allow on the first menu, Service on the second, and then SSH on the third. Then click the Add button. A port entry will then appear in the Rules section. In Figure 15-18 the SSH service has been selected and then added, showing up in the Rules section as "22 ALLOW IN Anywhere."

Services can also be blocked. To prevent access by the FTP service, you would first select Deny, then Service, and then the FTP entry.

Click the "Show extended actions" check box to display menus for logging and the rule position (rank), starting from 0.

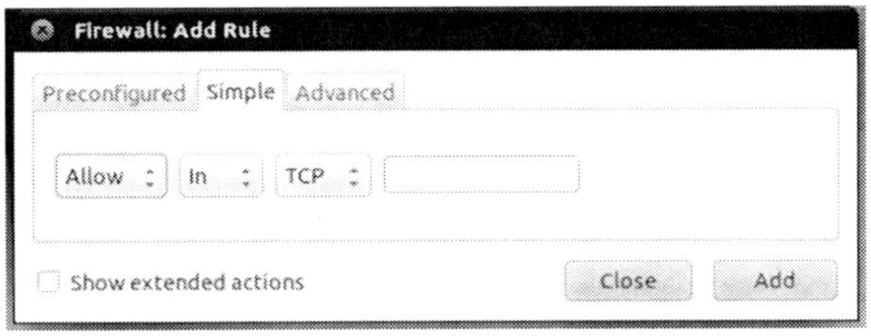

Figure 15-22: Gufw Simple rules

Besides Allow and Deny, you can also choose a Limit option. The Limit option will enable connection rate limiting, restricting connections to no more than 6 every 30 seconds for a given port. This is meant to protect against brute force attacks.

Should there be no preconfigured entry, you can use the Simple tab to allow access to a port (see Figure 15-22). The first menu is for the rule (Allow, Deny, Reject, and Limit), the second for traffic direction (In and Out), and the third is for the protocol (TCP, UDP, or both). In the following text box you enter the port number.

On the Advanced tab you can enter more complex rules. You can set up allow or deny rules for tcp or udp protocols, and specify the host and port. In Figure 15-23 the broadcast access for Samba on port 137 is set (to anywhere from port 137).

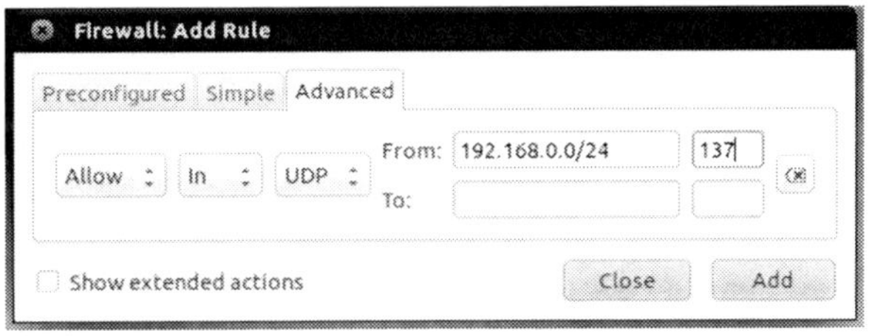

Figure 15-23: Gufw Advanced rules

If you should want to remove a rule, select it in the Rules section and then click the minus button on the lower left corner (–). To remove several rules, click and press Shift-click or use Ctrl-click to select a collection of rules, and then click the minux button.

ufw commands

You can also manage your ufw firewall using **ufw** commands entered on a command line in a Terminal window. A **ufw** command requires administrative access and must be run with the **sudo** command. To check the current firewall status, listing those services allowed or blocked, use the **status** command.

```
sudo ufw status
```

If the firewall is not enabled, you first will have to enable it with the **enable** command.

```
sudo ufw enable
```

You can restart the firewall, reloading your rules, using the **service** command with the **restart** option.

```
sudo service ufw restart
```

You can add rules using allow and deny rules and their options as listed in Table 15-4. To allow a service, specify the allow rule and the service name. This is the name for the service listed in the **/etc/services** file. For connection rate limiting, use the **limit** option in place of **allow**. The following allows the ftp service.

```
sudo ufw allow ftp
```

Commands	Description
enable | disable	Turn the firewall on or off
status	Display status along with services allowed or denied.
logging on | off	Turn logging on or off
default allow | deny	Set the default policy, allow is open, whereas deny is restrictive
allow *service*	Allow access by a service. Services are defined in **/etc/services**, which specify the ports for that service.
allow *port /protocol*	Allow access on a particular port using specified protocol.
deny *service*	Deny access by a service
delete *rule*	Delete an installed rule, use allow, deny, or limit and include rule specifics.
proto *protocol*	Specify protocol in allow, deny, or limit rule
from *address*	Specify source address in allow, deny, or limit rule
to *address*	Specify destination address in allow, deny, or limit rule
port *port*	Specify port in allow, deny, or limit rule for from and to address

Table 15-4: UFW firewall operations

If the service you want is not listed in **/etc/services**, and you know the port and protocol it uses, you can specify the port and protocol directly. For example, the Samba service uses port 445 and protocol tcp (among others, see Table 15-3).

```
sudo ufw allow 445/tcp
```

The status operation shows what services the firewall rules allow currently.

```
sudo ufw status
To                      Action          From
21:tcp                  ALLOW           Anywhere
21:udp                  ALLOW           Anywhere
445:tcp                 ALLOW           Anywhere
```

To remove a rule, prefix it with the **delete** command.

```
sudo ufw delete allow 445/tcp
```

More detailed rules can be specified using address, port, and protocol commands. These are very similar to the actual IPtables commands. Packets to and from particular networks, hosts, and ports can be controlled. The following denies ssh access (port 22) from host 192.168.03.

```
sudo ufw deny proto tcp from 192.168.03 to any port 22
```

ufw rule files

The rules you add are placed in the **/lib/ufw/user.rules** file as IPtables rules. ufw is just a front end for **iptables-restore**, which will read this file and set up the firewall using **iptables** commands. **ufw** will also have **iptables-restore** read the **before.rules** and **after.rules** files in the **/etc/ufw** directory. These files are considered administrative files that include needed supporting rules for your IPtables firewall. Administrators can add their own IPtables rules to these files for system specific features like IP Masquerading. The **before.rules** file will specify a table with the * symbol, as in ***filter** for the netfilter table. For the NAT table you would use ***nat**. At the end of each table segment, a COMMIT command is needed to instruct ufw to apply the rules. Rules use **-A** for allow and **-D** for deny, assuming the **iptables** command.

Default settings for ufw are placed in **/etc/default/ufw**. Here you will find the default INPUT, OUTPUT, and FORWARD policies specified by setting associated variables, like DEFAULT_INPUT_POLICY for INPUT and DEFAULT_OUTPUT_POLICY for OUTPUT. The DEFAULT_INPUT_POLICY variable is set to DROP, making DROP the default policy for the INPUT rule. The DEFAULT_OUTPUT_POLICY variable is set to ACCEPT, and the DEFAULT_FORWARD_POLICY variable is set to DROP. To allow IP Masquerading, DEFAULT_FORWARD_POLICY would have to be set to ACCEPT. These entries set default policies only. Any user rules you have set up would take precedence.

Setting Up Your Firewall with Firestarter

Ubuntu also provides the Firestarter firewall configuration tool with which you can set up your firewall. You can install Firestarter from the Ubuntu Software Center | Internet | Firestarter. You can use either Gufw or Firestarter, but not both at the same time. On Unity you can choose Firestarter from the System dash, and on GHOME choose System | Administration | Firestarter. The first time you start up Firestarter the Firewall Wizard starts up which prompts you for your network device and Internet connection sharing information (see Figure 15-24). Much of the configuration is automatic. If you are using a local home or work network, you may have to add rules for services like Samba Windows network access or the network address of your local network. After the Welcome screen, the Network device setup panel lets you select your network device (Ethernet connection or modem) and whether to use DHCP to detect your address information.

Figure 15-24: Firestarter setup wizard

The Internet connection sharing setup panel is used if your computer operates like a gateway for other computers (most networks use a router instead). You will most likely just skip it. A final screen prompts you to start the firewall now, with a button to save your configuration. Click the Save button.

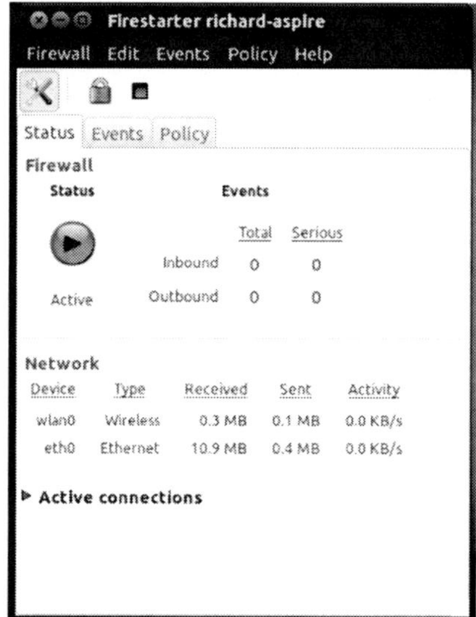

Figure 15-25: Firestarter Firewall

Firestarter will then start up with a window titled with your computer name. There are three panels: Status, Events, and Policy (see Figure 15-25). The toolbar entries will change with each panel selected. The Status panel lets you start and stop your firewall using the Stop/Start Firewall button. Its status is shown as a play or stop icon in the Status segment of the Status panel. The Events segment of this panel shows inbound and outbound traffic, and the Network segment lists your network devices along with device information like the number of packets received, sent, and average activity. An expansion list shows Active connections. Here you can see what kind of connection is active, like Samba or Internet connections.

The Events tab lists any rejected connections, Blocked Connections. The Save, Clear, and Reload buttons on the toolbar let you save the event log, clear it, or reload to see the latest events.

The Policy tab shows rules for allowing host and service connections (see Figure 15-23). The Editing menu lets you show Inbound traffic or Outbound traffic policies. On this tab you can add your own rules for inbound or outbound hosts. The toolbar shows Add Rule (+), Remove Rule (-), Edit Rule (wrench icon), and Apply Rule (checkmark) buttons. After adding a rule, you can have it applied immediately by clicking the Apply Policy item in the Policy menu (Policy | Apply Policy).

Figure 15-26: Firestarter Policy panel

For Inbound Traffic, when you can set up rules for connections, services, or forwarding. There will be segments for each. Click on the segment first, and then click on the Add Rule button (+), or right-click and choose Add Rule. The dialog is different depending on the type of rule you are setting up. For a connection, the Add Rule dialog will let you enter the host, IP address, or network from which you can receive connections.

For a service, you can select the service to allow from a pop-up menu, along with the port, as well as whether to allow access by anyone or from a specific host or network (see Figure 15-27). By default all inbound traffic is denied, unless explicitly allowed by a rule. If you were setting up a firewall for just your personal computer connected to a network, you would enter a rule for the local network address. You could also set up rules to allow access by services like Samba or BitTorrent.

For the Samba desktop file browsing service (Go | Network), you have to allow external broadcasts and add a rule to allow connections from your local network. A local home network will use the private network address, 192.160.0.0/24. Add a rule in the "Allow connections from host" section for Inbound traffic policy for this address (see Figure 15-26). Then on the Firestarter

Preferences dialog (Edit | Preferences), select the Advanced Options tab and de-select the "Block broadcasts from external network" option.

The Outbound Traffic is more complex. Here you can set either a permissive or restrictive policy. The permissive is selected by default. The permissive entry will still reject blacklisted hosts and services, and the restrictive entry will allow white listed hosts and services. Each has both a connection and service segment, just like the Inbound connections, with the same options.

If permissive is selected, you will allow all outbound traffic, except those you specifically deny. For this configuration, you can create Deny rules for certain hosts and services. When setting up a Deny rule for a service you can choose a service from a pop-up menu, and specify its port. You can then reject either anyone using this service, or specify a particular host or network. For a connection, you simply specify the host, IP address, or network that can connect. The connection rules act like your own blacklist, listing hosts or network you will not allow yourself or others to connect to.

If restrictive, you deny all outbound traffic, except those you specifically allow. In this case, you can set up Allow rules to allow connections by certain hosts and services, rejecting everything else. The restrictive option is not normally used, as it would cut off any connections from your computer to the Internet, unless you added a rule to permit the connection.

Figure 15-27: Firestarter, choosing a service to permit

To configure your Firestarter firewall, select the Edit | Preferences menu entry. This opens a Preference window where you can set either Interface or Firewall settings. For the Interface settings you can set either the Events logged or the Policy. The Events tab lets you eliminate logging of unwanted events, like redundant events or events from specific hosts or ports. The Policy tab has an option to let you apply changes immediately.

For Firewall Settings, you have tabs for Network Settings, ICMP Filtering, ToS Filtering, and Advanced Options. Network Settings just selects your network device. Here you could change your network device between Ethernet, wireless, or modem. The ICMP filtering tab blocks ICMP packet attacks. Options allow certain ICMP packets through, like Unreachable to notify you of an unknown site. The Type of Service tab lets you prioritize your packets by both the kind of service and maximized efficiency. For the kind of service you can choose either workstations, servers, or the X Window System. For maximized efficiency you can choose reliability, throughput, or interactivity. Workstations and throughput are selected by default. The Advanced options tab lets you select the drop method (silent or error reported), the Broadcast traffic rejection policy for internal and external connections (External broadcasts are blocked by default), and traffic validation block reserved addresses.

GNOME Nettool

The GNOME Nettool utility (**gnome-nettool**) provides a GNOME interface for network information tools like the ping and traceroute operations as well as Finger, Whois, and Lookup for querying users and hosts on the network (see Figure 15-28). Nettool is installed by default and is accessible from System | Administration | Network Tools. The first tab, Devices, describes your connected network devices, including configuration and transmission information about each device, such as the hardware address and bytes transmitted. Both IPv4 and IPv6 host IP addresses are listed.

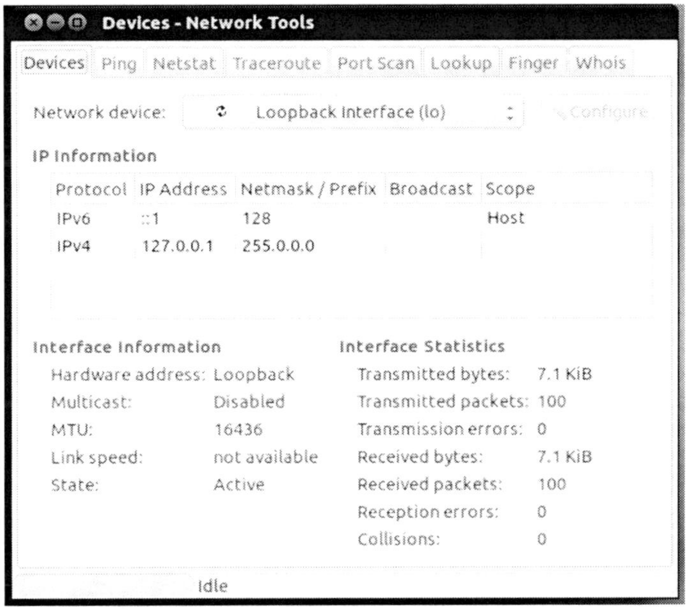

Figure 15-28: Gnome network tool

You can use the ping, finger, lookup, whois, and traceroute operations to find out status information about systems and users on your network. The ping operation is used to check if a remote system is up and running. You use finger to find out information about other users on your network, seeing if they are logged in or if they have received mail. The traceroute tool can be used to track the sequence of computer networks and systems your message passed through on its way to you. Whois will provide domain name information about a particular domain, and Lookup will provide both domain name and IP addresses. Netstat shows your network routing (addresses used) and active service (open ports and the protocols they use). Port Scan lists the ports and services they use on a given connection (address); use 12.0.0.1 for your local computer.

16. Printing

system-config-printer

Editing Printer Configuration

Printer Classes

Adding New Printers Manually

Remote Printers

Most printers are USB printers that are detected and configured automatically. For these printers you perform little if any configuration. For remote printers, you use the Ubuntu Printing utility to detect and configure access. Older printers you can configure manually in just few steps. The Ubuntu Linux printer drivers provide a complete set of configuration options for your printer such as paper size, print quality, and page sequence.

Automatic printer detection

Printers are detected and configured automatically. For removable printers, like a USB printer, a printer icon will appear on the panel as soon as you connect your USB printer as your printer is detected and configured. If a driver is available for your printer, it will be selected automatically for you and a setup message will appear. If the driver is not available, a Missing printer driver notification is displayed. Then a New Printer dialog opens where you can choose your driver.

system-config-printer

To change your configuration or to add a remote printer, you can use the printer configuration tool, system-config-printer. This utility enables you to select the appropriate driver for your printer, as well as set print options such as paper size and print resolutions. You can configure a printer connected directly to your local computer or a printer on a remote system on your network. You can start system-config-printer on Unity by choosing Printing in the System dash.

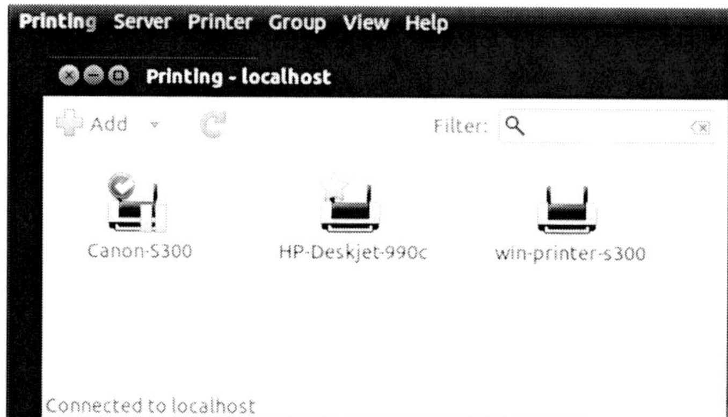

Figure 16-1: system-config-printer tool

The Printing configuration window displays icons for installed printers (see Figure 16-1). The menu bar has menus for Server configuration and selection, Printer features like its properties and the print queue, printer groups, and viewing printers by group and discovered printers. A toolbar has buttons for adding new printers manually and refreshing print configuration. A Filter search box lets you display only printers matching a search pattern. Click on the broom icon in the search box to clear the pattern. Clicking on the Looking glass icon in the File search box will display a pop-up menu that will let you search on Name, Description, Location, and Manufacturer/Model. You can save searches as a search group. You can also use the search results to create a printer group.

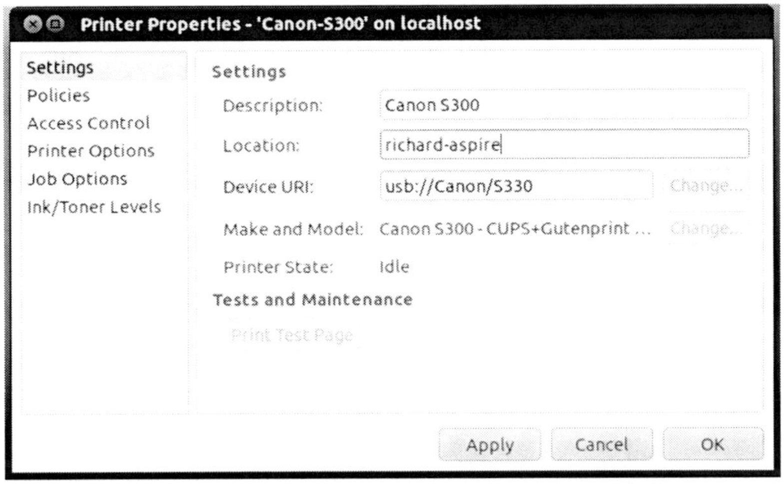

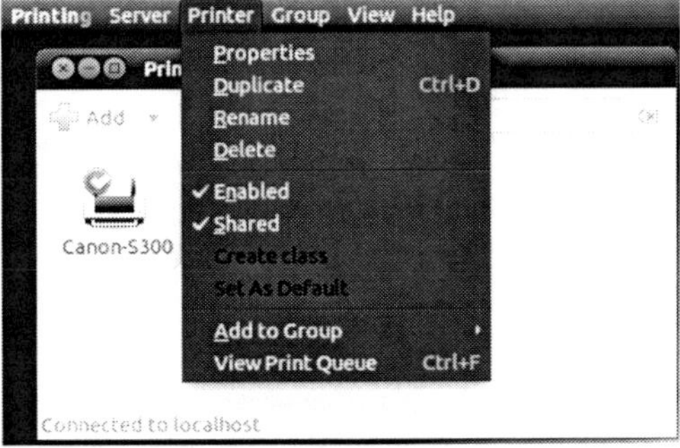

Figure 16-2: Printer properties window

To see the printer settings such as printer and job options, access controls, and policies, double-click on the printer icon or right-click and select Properties. The Printer Properties window opens up with six tabs: Settings, Policies, Access Control, Printer Options, Job Options, and Ink/Toner Levels (see Figure 16-2).

Figure 16-3: Printer configuration window Printer menu

The Printing configuration window Printer menu lets you rename the printer, enable or disable it, and make it a shared printer. Select the printer icon and then click the Printer menu (see Figure 16-3). You can also display the Printer menu by right-clicking on a printer icon. The Delete entry will remove a printer configuration. Use the Set As Default entry to make the printer a system-wide or personal default printer. The properties entry opens the printer properties window for that printer. You can also access the print queue for the selected printer. If the printer is already a default, the Set As Default entry is shaded out.

When print jobs are waiting in the print queue, a printer icon will appear on the top panel. Clicking on this icon opens the Document Print Status window listing the print jobs. You can also open this window from the system-config-printer's Printer menu, View Print Queue item (Printer | View Print Queue). On the Document Print Status window, you can change a job's queue position as well as stop or delete a job (see Figure 16-4). From the job menu you can cancel, hold (stop), release (restart), or reprint a print job. Reprint is only available if you have set the preserve jobs option in the printer settings Advanced dialog. You can also authenticate a job. From the View menu you can choose to display just printed jobs and refresh the queue.

Figure 16-4: Printer queue

To check the server settings, select Settings from the Server menu. This opens a new window showing the CUPS printer server settings (see Figure 16-5). The Advanced expand button displays job history and browser server options. If you want to allow reprinting, then select the "Preserve job files (allow reprinting)" option.

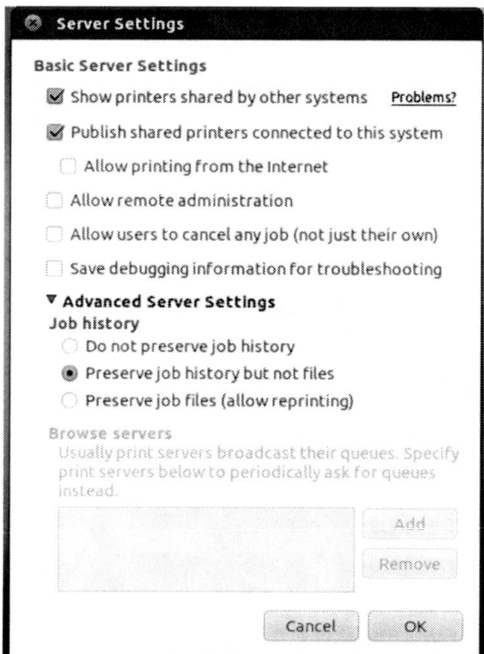

Figure 16-5: Server Settings

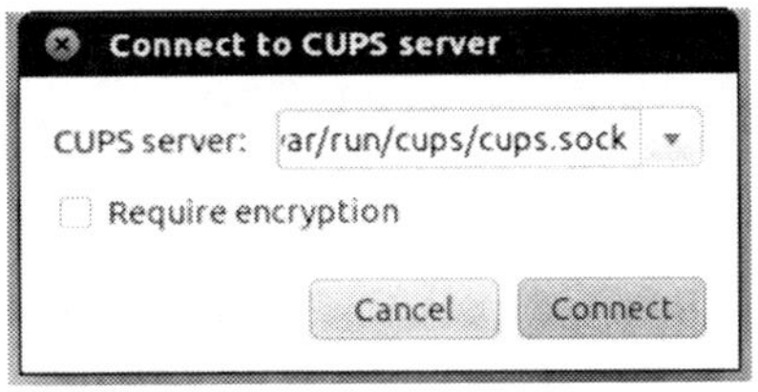

Figure 16-6: Selecting a CUPS server

To select a particular CUPS server, select the Connect entry in the Server menu. This opens a "Connect to CUPS Server" window with a drop down menu listing all current CUPS servers from which to choose (see Figure 16-6).

Editing Printer Configuration

To edit an installed printer, double click its icon in the Printer configuration window, or right-click and select the Properties entry. This opens a Printer Properties window for that printer. A sidebar lists configuration tabs. Click on one to display that tab. There are configuration tabs for Settings, Policies, Access Control, Printer Options, Job Control, and Ink/Toner Levels (see Figure 16-8).

Once you have made your changes, you can click Apply to save your changes and restart the printer daemon. You can test your printer using the Tests and Maintenance tasks on the Settings tab. The Print Test Page prints a page, whereas the Print Self-Test Page also checks the printer hardware such as ink-jet heads.

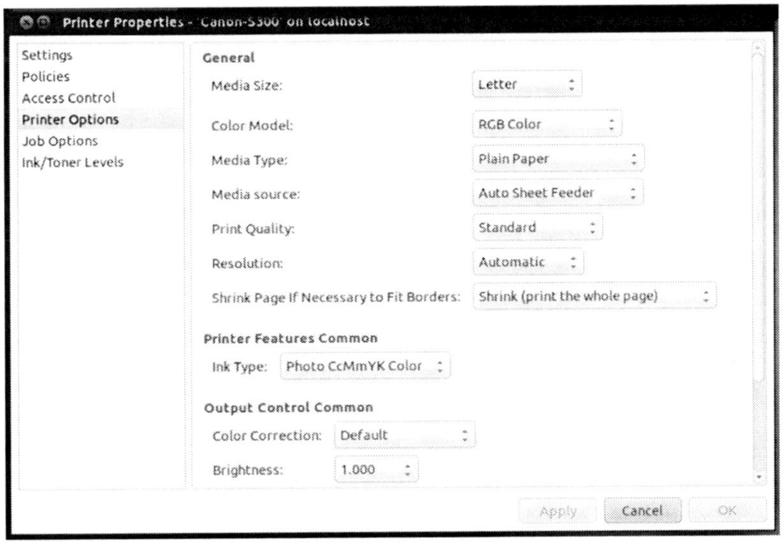

Figure 16-7: Printer Options

On the Settings tab you can change configuration settings like the driver and the printer name, and run test pages (see Figure 16-2). Should you need to change the selected driver, click on the Change button next to the Make and Model entry to open printer model and driver windows like those described in the "Add new printer manually" section. There you can specify the model and driver you want to use, even loading your own driver. Should you have to change the device URI (location and protocol), you can click the Change button to the right of the Device URI entry to open a "Change Device URI" dialog.

The Policies tab lets you enable and disable the printer, determine if it is to be shared, and whether to let it accept jobs or not (you also can enable or share the printer from the Printer menu). You can also specify an error policy, which specifies whether to retry or abort the print job, or stop the printer should an error occur. You can choose to print banners at the start or end indicating the level of security for a document, like confidential and secret.

The Access Control tab lets you to deny access to certain users.

The Printer Options tab is where you set particular printing features like paper size and type, print quality, and the input tray to use (see Figure 16-7).

On the Job Options tab you can select default printing features (see Figure 16-8) such as the number of copies, orientation, and single or double sided printing. Options are arranged into three categories: Common Options, Image Options, and Text Options. Only the more common options are displayed. Each category has an expand button that will display all the options for that category. Double sided, output order, and media are all expanded options in the Common Options category.

The Ink/Toner Levels tab will display Ink or Toner levels for supported printers, along with status messages.

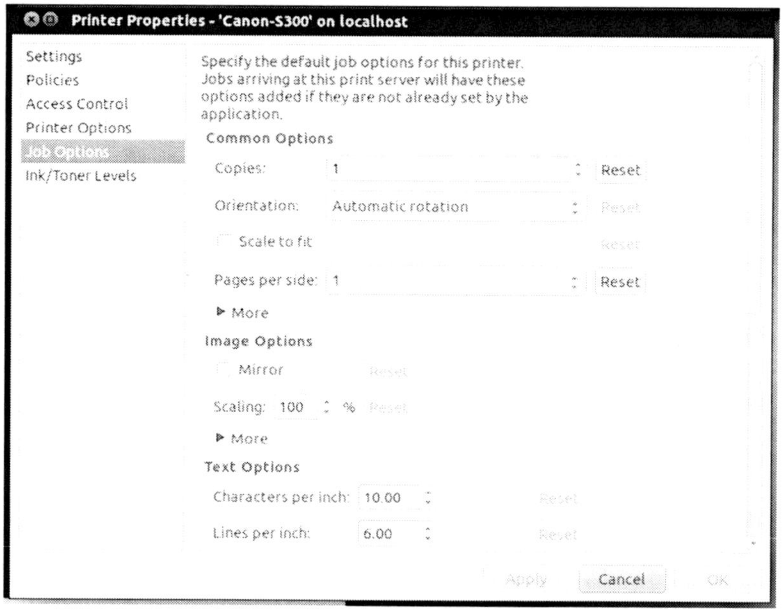

Figure 16-8: Jobs Options

Default System-wide and Personal Printers

To make a printer the default printer, either right-click on the printer icon and select "Set As Default", or single click on the printer icon and then from the Printer configuration window's Printer menu select the "Set As Default" entry (see Figure 16-3). A Set Default Printer dialog open with options for setting the system-wide default or setting the personal default (see Figure 16-9). The system-wide default printer is the default for the system served by your CUPS server.

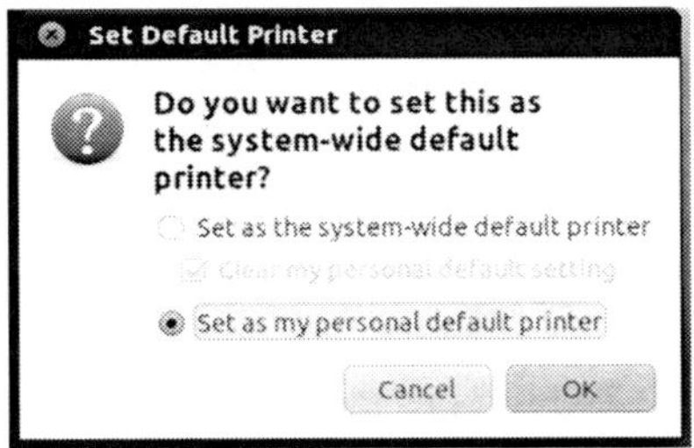

Figure 16-9: Set Default Printer

The system-wide default printer will have a green check mark emblem on its printer icon in the Printing configuration window.

Should you wish to use a different printer yourself (user specific) as your default printer, you can designate it as your personal default. To make a printer your personal default, select the entry "Set as my personal default printer" in the Set Default Printer dialog. A personal emblem, a yellow star, will appear on the printer's icon in the Printer configuration window. In Figure 16-10, the Canon-S300 printer is the system-wide default, whereas the HP-DeskJet printer is the personal default.

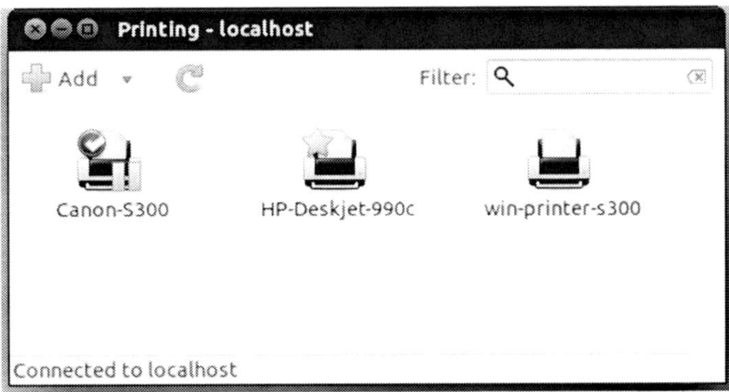

Figure 16-10: System-wide and personal default printers

Printer Classes

The Class entry in the Server | New menu lets you create a printer class. You can access the New menu from the Server menu or from the Add button. This feature lets you select a group of printers to print a job instead of selecting just one. That way, if one printer is busy or down, another printer can be selected automatically to perform the job. Installed printers can be assigned to different classes. When you click the Class entry in the New menu, a New Class window opens. Here you can enter the name for the class, any comments, and the location (your host name is entered by default). The next screen lists available printers on right side (Other printers) and the printers you assigned to the class on the left side (Printers in this class). Use the arrow button to add or remove printers to the class. Click Apply when finished. The class will appear under the Local Classes heading on the Printing configuration window. Tabs for a selected class are much the same as for a printer, with a members tab instead of a print control tab. In the Members tab you can change which printers belong to the class

Adding New Printers Manually

Printers are detected automatically, though in the case of older printers and network printers, you may need to add the printer manually. In this case click the Add button and select Printer. A New Printer window opens displaying a series of dialog boxes where you select the connection, model, drivers, and printer name with location.

On the Select Device dialog, you select the appropriate printer connection information. Connected local printer brands will already be listed by name, such as Canon. For remote printers you specify the type of network connection, like "Windows printers via Samba" for printers connected to a Windows system, "AppSocket/HP Direct" for HP printers connected directly to your network, and the "Internet Printing Protocol (ipp)" for printers on Linux and Unix systems on your network. These connections are displayed under the Network Printer heading. Click the expansion arrow to display them.

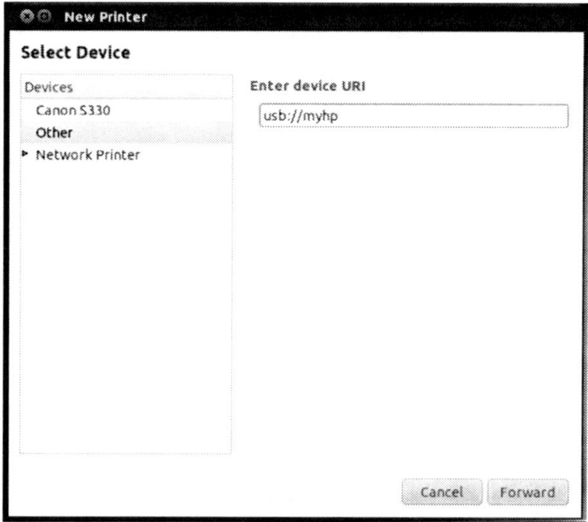

Figure 16-11: Selecting a new printer connection

For most connected printers, your connection is usually determined by udev, which now manage all devices. A USB printer will simply be described as a USB printer, using the usb URI designation (see Figure 16-11 and 16-3). For an older local printer, you may have to choose the port the printer is connected to, such as LPT1 for the first parallel port used for older parallel printers, or

Serial Port #1 for a printer connected to the first serial port. To add a USB printer manually, you would select other and enter the URI consisting of the prefix **usb://** and the name you want to give to the printer, like **usb://myepson**.

A search is conducted for the appropriate driver, including downloadable drivers. If the driver is found, the Choose Driver screen is displayed with the appropriate driver manufacturer already selected for you. You need only click the forward button. On the next screen, also labeled Choose Driver, the printer models and drivers files are listed and the appropriate one already selected for you. Just click the Forward button. The Describe Printer screen is then displayed where you can enter the Printer Name, Description, and Location. These are ways you can personally identify a printer. Then click Apply.

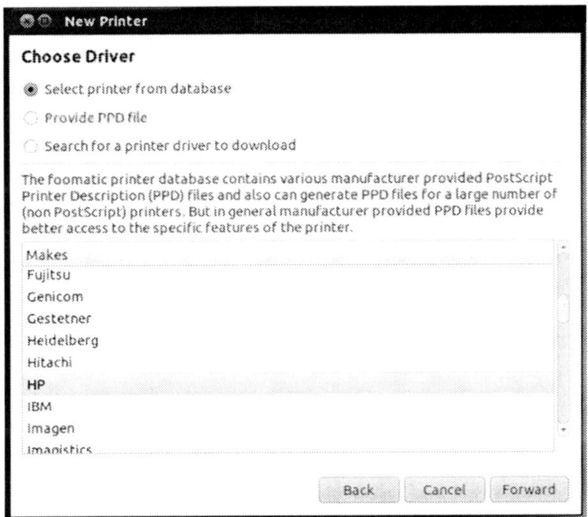

Figure 16-12: Printer manufacturer for new printers

If the printer driver is not detected or detected incorrectly, then, on the Choose Driver screen you have the options to choose the driver from the printer database, from a PPD driver file, or from a search of the OpenPrinting online repository. The selection display will change according to which option you choose.

The database option lists possible manufacturers. Use your mouse to select the one you want (see Figure 3-12).

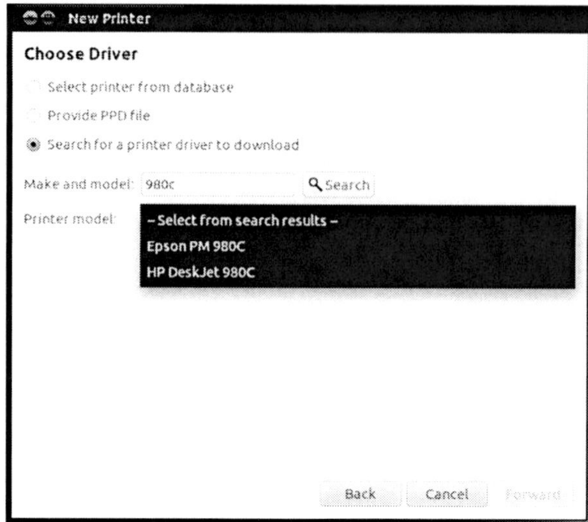

Figure 16-13: Searching for a printer driver from the OpenPrinting repository

The search option displays a search box for make and model. Enter both the make (printer manufacturer) and part of the model name (See figure 3-13). The search results will be available in the Printer model drop down menu. Select the one you want. Then click Forward.

The PPD file option displays a file location button that opens a Select file dialog you can use to locate the PPD file on your system.

Figure 16-14: Printer Model and driver for new printers using local database

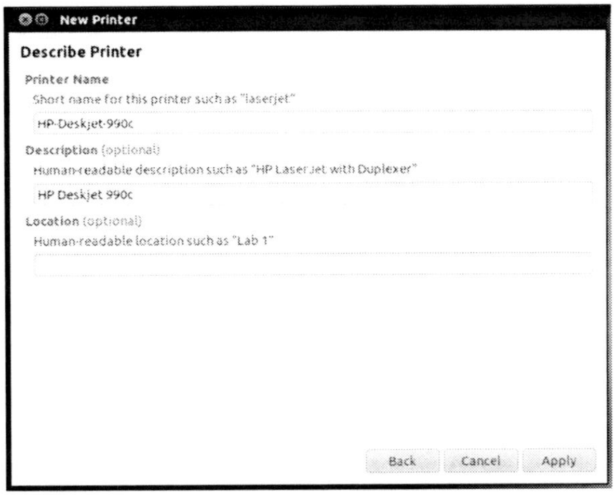

Figure 16-15: Printer Name and Location for new printers

If you are selecting a printer from the database, then, on the next screen you select that manufacturer's model along with its driver (see Figure 16-14). For some older printer, though the driver can be located on the online repository, you will still choose it from the local database (the drivers are the same). The selected drivers for your printer will be listed. If there are added options for your printer, the Installable Options screen lists them allowing you to check the ones you want.

You then enter your printer name and location (see Figure 16-15). These will be entered for you using the printer model and your system's host name. You can change the printer name to anything you want. When ready, click Apply. You are then prompted to print a test page. An icon for your printer is then displayed in the Printing configuration window. You are now ready to print.

Remote Printers

You can use system-config-printer to set up a remote printer on Linux, UNIX, or Windows networks. When you add a new printer or edit one, the New Printer dialog will list possible remote connection types under the Network entry. When you select a remote connection entry, a pane will be displayed to the right where you can enter configuration information.

A printer location is referenced using special URI protocols. For a locally attached USB printer, the USB URI is **usb**. For another CUPS printer on a remote host, the protocol used is **ipp**, for Internet Printing Protocol, whereas for a Windows printer, it would be **smb**. Older UNIX or Linux systems using LPRng would use the **lpd** protocol.

To find any connected printers on your network automatically, click the Find Network Printer entry. Your network is search and the detected printers displayed as entries under the Network Printer heading (see Figure 16-16).

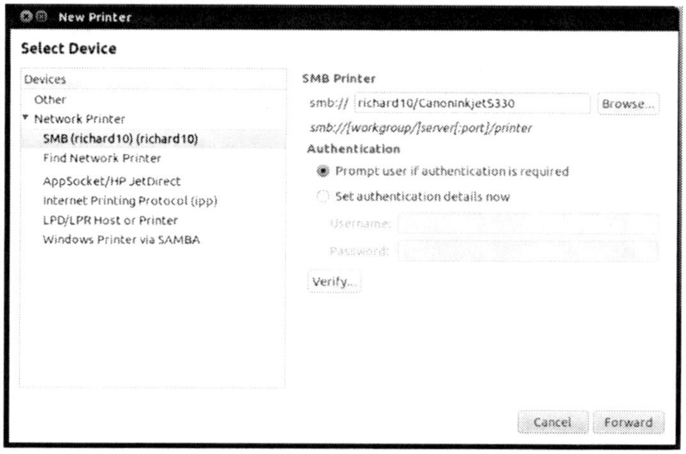

Figure 16-16: Finding a network printer

To configure a specific type of printer, choose from the available entries. For a remote Linux or UNIX printer, select either Internet Printing Protocol (ipp), which is used for newer systems, or LPD/LPR Host or Printer, which is used for older systems. Both panes display entries for the Host name and the queue. For the Host name, enter the hostname for the system that controls the printer. For an Apple or HP jet direct printer on your network, select the AppSocket/HP jetDirect entry.

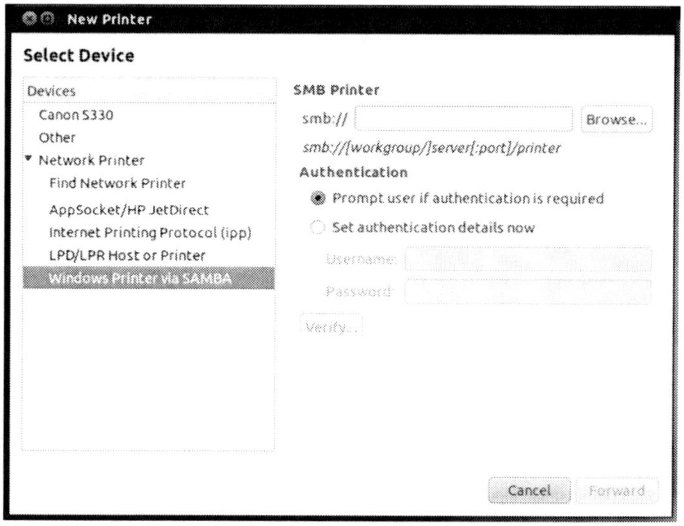

Figure 16-17: Selecting a Windows printer

A "Windows printer via Samba" printer is one located on a Windows network (see Figure 16-17). You need to specify the Windows server (host name or IP address), the name of the share, the name of the printer's workgroup, and the username and password. The format of the printer SMB URL is shown on the SMP Printer pane. The share is the hostname and printer name in the **smb** URI format *//workgroup/hostname/printername.* The workgroup is the windows network workgroup that the printer belongs to. On small networks there is usually only one. The hostname is the computer where the printer is located. The username and password can be for the printer resource itself, or for access by a particular user. The pane will display a box at the top where you can enter the share host and printer name as a **smb** URI.

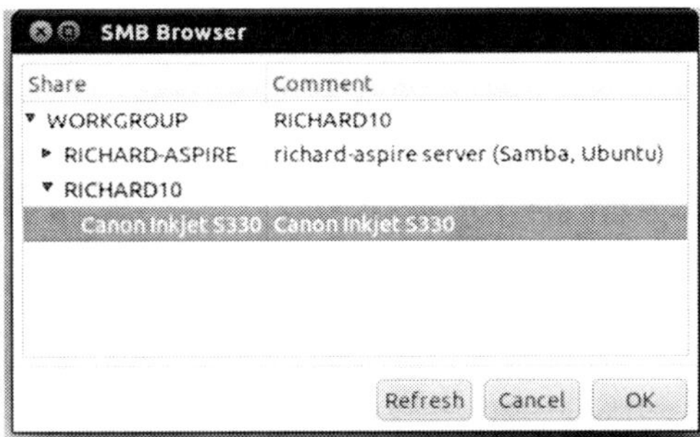

Figure 16-18: SMB Browser, selecting a remote windows printer

Instead of entering the URI for a printer manually, you can use the Browse button to choose from a list of detected Windows printers on your network. Click the Browse button to open a SMB Browser window, where you can select the printer from a listing of Windows hosts (see Figure 16-18). For example, if your Windows network is WORKGROUP, then the entry WORKGROUP will be shown, which you can then expand to list all the Windows hosts on that network (if your network is MSHOME, then that is what will be listed). If you are using a firewall, be sure to turn it off before browsing a Windows workgroup for a printer, unless the firewall is already configured to allow Samba access.

When you make your selection, the corresponding URI will show up in the **smb://** box (See Figure 16-19). You also can enter in any needed Samba authentication, if required, like user name or password. Check "Authentication required" to allow you to enter the Samba Username and Password.

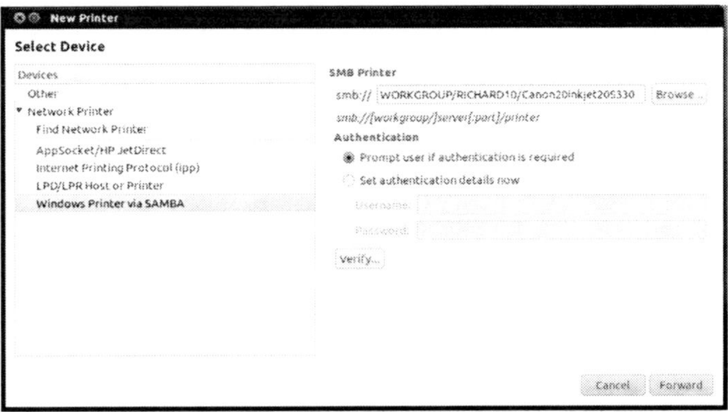

Figure 16-19: Remote Windows printer connection configuration

You then continue with install screens for the printer model, driver, and name. Once installed, you can then access the printer properties just as you would any printer (see Figure 16-20).

To access an SMB shared remote printer, you need to install Samba and have the Server Message Block services enabled using the **smbd** and **nmbd** daemons. The Samba service will be enabled by default. You can use the **service** command to restart, stop, and start the services. Printer sharing must be enabled on the Windows network.

```
sudo service smbd restart
sudo service nmbd restart
```

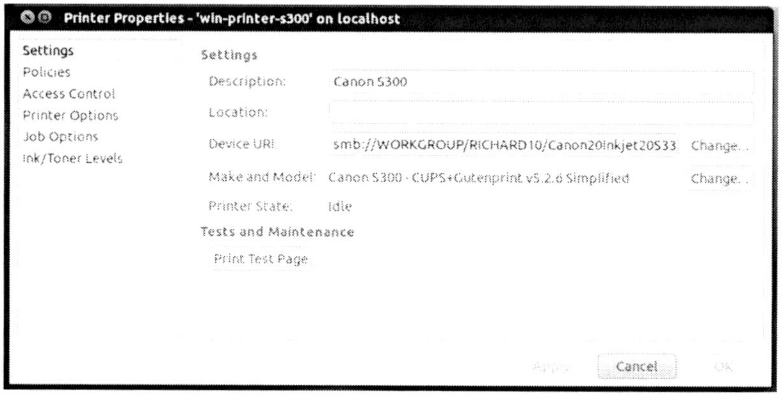

Figure 16-20: Remote Windows printer Settings

Ubuntu Printers remotely accessed from Windows

On an older Windows system, like Windows XP, you can use the Add Printer Wizard to locate a shared printer on a Linux system. Locate the Ubuntu system, click on it, and the shared printers on the Ubuntu system will be listed.

On Windows 7, you first open Control Panels, then select Devices and Printers, click the "Add a printer" item at the top. In the Add Printer dialog click the "Add a network, wireless, or Bluetooth printer" link. Your connected network printers are detected and listed. Choose the one connected to your Ubuntu system. Provide a printer name you want to use for that printer on your system.

Note: If a password prompt prevents you from accessing a Windows printer on Windows 7, you may have to uninstall the "Windows Live Sign In Assistant" on your Windows 7 system.

Table Listing

Figure Listing

Index

B

C

W

w_scan, 209
  channels.conf, 209
w32codecs, 198
wallpaper
  KDE, 335
weather, 115
  indicator-weather, 306
Web, 241
Web browser
  Chromium, 249
  ELinks, 250
  Epiphany, 248
  Firefox, 241
  Konqueror, 248
  Lynx, 250
  ReKonq, 246
Web Browser, 241
webcam, 192
Welcome, 54
wget, 257
windows, 316
  KDE, 349
  sliders, 293
  switching, 295
  tabs (KDE), 350
  tiles, 295
  tiles (KDE), 350
  Unity, 293
Windows
  file systems, 437
  fonts, 131
  printers (Samba), 500
  shares-admin, 445
  system-config-samba, 441
  user-level access, 441, 446
  Windows compatibility layer, 130
  Wine, 130
  Wubi, 81
Windows compatibility layer
  Wine, 130

Wine, 130
  Adobe Digital Editons, 176
wired
  configuration, 468
  Network (System Settings), 103
  network connections, 99
wired configuration
  IPv6, 469
wireless
  airplane mode, 103
  laptop, 98
  Network (System Settings), 103
  network connections, 100
  WPA security, 101
wireless configuration, 470
wireless router, 476
wireless security, 470
wordprocessing
  AbiWord, 172
  Calligra Words, 172
  LibreOffice Writer, 170
workspaces, 297
Wubi, 81
wvdial, 477

X

X Window System
  Displays, 121
  RandR, 121
  vendor drivers, 121
x264, 197
Xine, 203, 205
Xpdf, 175
Xsensors, 416
Xubuntu, 35
Xvid, 212
xvidcore, 197

Z

Zsync, 49

CPSIA information can be obtained at www.ICGtesting.com
Printed in the USA
BVOW07s0520050614

355437BV00023B/116/P